THE INTERNATIONAL LESSON ANNUAL

1985–86
September–August

A Comprehensive Commentary on
the International Sunday School Lessons
Uniform Series

Edited by
HORACE R. WEAVER

Lesson Analysis by
WILLIAM WILLIMON

ABINGDON PRESS
Nashville

THE INTERNATIONAL LESSON ANNUAL—1985–86

Copyright © 1985 by Abingdon Press

ISBN 0-687-19149-1

Library of Congress ISSN 0074-6770

Lines on page 36, "Outwitted," by Edwin Markham, reprinted with permission of the Markham Archives.

Lines on page 92 reprinted from *Collected Verse of Edgar A. Guest,* by Edgar A. Guest, © 1934, with permission of Contemporary Books, Inc., Chicago.

Lessons based on International Sunday School Lessons; the International Lessons for Christian Teaching copyright © 1982 by the Committee on the Uniform Series, and used by permission.

Scripture quotations in this publication unless otherwise noted are from the Revised Standard Version of the Bible, copyrighted 1946, 1952, © 1971, 1973 by the Division of Christian Education of the National Council of the Churches of Christ in the U.S.A., and are used by permission.

Scripture quotations noted Barclay are from the Daily Study Bible, published by The Westminster Press.

Scripture quotations noted Goodspeed are from The Complete Bible: An American Translation by J. M. Powis Smith and Edgar J. Goodspeed. Copyright 1939 by the University of Chicago.

Scripture quotations noted Living Bible are taken from *The Living Bible,* copyright © 1971 by Tyndale House Publishers, Wheaton, IL. Used by permission.

Scripture quotations noted Moffatt are from The Bible: A New Translation by James Moffatt. Copyright 1935 by Harper & Row, Publishers, Inc.

Scripture quotations noted NEB are from The New English Bible. © the Delegates of the Oxford University Press and the Syndics of the Cambridge University Press 1961, 1970. Reprinted by permission.

Scripture quotations noted Phillips are from The New Testament in Modern English, copyright © J. B. Phillips 1958, 1960, 1972.

Scripture quotations noted TEV are from the Good News Bible, Today's English Version. Copyright © American Bible Society 1966, 1971, 1976.

MANUFACTURED BY THE PARTHENON PRESS AT
NASHVILLE, TENNESSEE, UNITED STATES OF AMERICA

Editor's Preface

We appreciate the broad interdenominational use of *The International Lesson Annual*. We would like to share with the teachers of the annual how the scriptures and emphases are selected. We start with a committee of about ten persons, selected from the Committee on Uniform Series, representing various denominations and the three ages levels (children, youth, and adults). Membership of CUS is open to persons from various denominations proposing to use this series and to such general resource persons as those denominations may recommend. So this is an ecumenical work in the educational ministry of the church. The committee, representing some thirty denominations, is convinced that Bible study is basic for faith of all persons—children, youth, and adults.

With this year's study we conclude the last (sixth year) study of the 1980–86 cycle. We have attempted to "cover all portions of the Bible fruitful for group study in churches using these lessons."

The objective of the Uniform Lesson is "to help growing persons increasingly (1) to know the content of the Bible; (2) to understand the message of the Bible in light of their own experiences and relationships; and (3) to be aware of God through his self-disclosure, especially his redeeming love as revealed in Jesus Christ, that they may respond in faith and love—to the end that they may know who they are and what their human situation means, grow as children of God rooted in the Christian community, live in the Spirit of God in every relationship, fulfill their common discipleship in the world, and abide in the Christian hope."

I would call attention to the teachers of these lessons the verbs in this objective: *know, understand, be aware, respond, grow, live, fulfill, abide.*

As a member of the Committee on Uniform Series that participated in the development of the past several cycles, I express deep appreciation for the interdenominational fellowship whose goals we have sought to fulfill in the International Lesson Annual. The continued use of this book helps inspire us to greater depth of dedication.

A word about the structure of each of the fifty-three lessons, each of which has five sections: The first section, "The Main Question," raises the basic question with which each lesson is concerned. The second section, "As You Read the Scripture," exegetically explores the scriptural passages being studied. The third section prints the passage from both the King James and Revised Standard versions. The fourth section, "Helping Adults Become Involved," offers a step-by-step teaching plan. Topics under this latter heading deal with Preparing to Teach, Introducing the Main Question, Developing the Lesson, Helping Class Members Act, and Planning for Next Sunday.

In addition to these five helpful teacher sections are special articles dealing with All Saints' Day, Thanksgiving, the Incarnation, the Trinity, grace, and apocalyptic literature.

The writers of this thirty-first edition continue the high level of distinction and dedication begun by their predecessors. Interdenominational in character, the list of contributors includes Harrell Beck, Howard Colson, Lynne Deming, Bond Fleming, Herbert Lambert, Wilbur Lamm, Robert

Luccock, Pat McGeachy, Robert Rogers, Roy Ryan, Mack Stokes, Harlan Waite, Donald Welch, William Willimon, and Michael Winters.

I am very grateful to Irene Hooper for her stenographic skills, assistance in maintaining schedules, dedication to orderly and helpful correspondence with our many writers, writing of the table of contents, pagination, and her helpful suggestions.

HORACE R. WEAVER, *Editor*

Contents

THIRD QUARTER

The Christian Hope (March 2–April 13)

The Person and Work of the Holy Spirit

UNIT I: THE HOLY SPIRIT ACTIVE IN JESUS (APRIL 20–MAY 4)

UNIT II: THE HOLY SPIRIT ACTIVE IN THE CHURCH (MAY 11–25)

The Letters of Paul—Part II

UNIT I: THE PERSON OF CHRIST

Horace R. Weaver*

TWO LESSONS   **SEPTEMBER 1–8**

This study is the second half of twenty-six sessions on the letters attributed to the apostle Paul. (The first half was treated during September–November 1984). The unifying theme for these thirteen sessions is the church as the Body of Christ. This theme is traced in Paul's doctrinal teachings on the person of Christ Jesus and on the church, through specific internal problems and leadership issues the early church faced. The purpose of this study is to help Christians understand themselves as part of the Body of Christ and how they interact with one another.

There are four units in this quarter. Unit I, "The Person of Christ" (two sessions), introduces Christ as the fullness of God and the one after whom Christians are to pattern their lives for growth. Unit II, "The Church: The Body of Christ" (three sessions) presents the church as the Body of Christ according to God's plan for the church's life in the world. Unit III, "Internal Problems in the Body of Christ" (four sessions), considers practical problems of the first-century church. The personal and pastoral admonitions of a mature church leader (Paul) to leaders in the emerging churches are the topics of unit IV, "Integrity in the Body of Christ" (four sessions).

Unit I, "The Person of Christ," contains two sessions. "Christ, the Fullness of God," September 1, one person suggested to me, puts "all of God that could be put into a human life, Jesus." "Christ, Our Guide to Maturity," September 8, states and explains Paul's goal of maturing into Christlikeness. These lessons clearly show the absolute uniqueness of Jesus of Nazareth as the incarnation of God.

Contributors for the first quarter:

Robert E. Luccock, retired professor, Boston University, Boston, Massachusetts.

Pat McGeachy, associate pastor, Downtown Presbyterian Church, Nashville, Tennessee.

Harlan R. Waite, United Methodist minister engaged in special ministry of Bible education in local churches in southern California.

Donald J. Welch, president, Scarritt College, Nashville, Tennessee.

William H. Willimon, Minister to the University, Duke University, Durham, North Carolina.

---

*Horace R. Weaver, Ph.D. in biblical literature, retired editor of adult publications, Curriculum Resources Committee, Board of Discipleship, The United Methodist Church, Nashville, Tennessee.

Christ, the Fullness of God

Background Scripture: Colossians 1–2

The Main Question—William H. Willimon

Close your eyes for a moment and think about God. What image comes to your mind? Some vague, cosmic force? An old man with a white beard?

The claim of the Christian faith is that one cannot think about God without thinking about Jesus Christ. Christians say that you will see God only by steadily fixing your attention on Jesus, this Jewish carpenter who lived briefly and died violently nearly two thousand years ago.

The great, even shocking claim of the Christian faith is that at a particular time in history, in an out-of-the-way corner of the world, in a cow stable, among a poor Jewish family, the great Creator of this whole dazzling universe, the Master of all creation, became a man.

When we look at Christ, we are looking at God.

Where do you feel closest to God? Some people say they feel close to God when they are in the world of nature. Others say they feel close to God when they are in the presence of other people or when they are using their minds while discussing some great idea or when they watch some great artist at work.

Human beings are born into this world wondering about God. What is God like? Does God care about me? What does God want me to do with my life? What do I have to do to be close to God?

When people—people like the people in your adult class today—ask questions like these, we point them to the Christ, the one in whom "all the fulness of God was pleased to dwell" (Colossians 1:19).

As You Read the Scripture—Robert E. Luccock

Colossians belongs among the great masterpieces of literature that were written in prison. Most scholars date this letter from Paul's final imprisonment in Rome A.D. 60–62. We have no evidence that Paul himself ever visited Colossae, a city on the river Lycus in Phrygia (now Turkey) in Asia Minor. But Paul almost certainly knew the Colossian church well. Four years earlier, during the Apostle's stay at Ephesus, missionaries came to Colossae preaching the gospel. Among them was Paul's beloved servant Epaphras (Colossians 1:7, 4:12). Now, with Paul a prisoner in Rome, that gospel was being seriously undermined at Colossae. So Paul writes this letter in defense of the gospel and against heresy.

Colossians 1:15. "Image of the invisible God, the first-born of all creation," are titles of sovereignty. Christ embodies the sovereign power, purpose, and presence of Almighty God, and through that power, presence, and purpose, "all things were created" (see Hebrews 1:2 and John 1:3).

Verse 16. "All thing were created . . . whether thrones or dominions or principalities or authorities." Paul here affirms that all powers, whether earthly or spiritual, were created in Christ. Nothing is created apart from God's power expressed through Christ, so nothing shall ever have dominion

12

over that power (see Romans 8:38-39). No astrological or spiritual power of any kind can ever transcend the Christ, nor will any be needed to mediate the power or presence of Christ.

Verse 17. Christ is "before all things." Paul is not here speaking of some kind of pre-earthly existence of Jesus. Rather his reference is to the presence and power of God that we recognize in Jesus the *Christ.*

Verse 18. If the church is the body (community) of people whose lives have been made new in Christ, then Christ must be the head. Just as the head (brain, mind, spirit) gives the animating force and direction to the human body, so the spirit of Christ energizes and directs the body of the church. In his spirit the church lives and moves and has its being (see Paul's sermon in Athens, Acts 17:22-28). Christ is the "beginning," that is, the moving power which gives life to the church. A church that is faithful will order its life according to the mind of Christ. He is the "first-born from the dead." Here, of course, Paul reminds us of the resurrection, the *living* Christ who must be preeminent in everything.

Verses 19-20. The point one must not miss here is that in Christ God expressed *all* of the divine love, power, and purpose. God did not distribute such fullness partially among many spirits. God's purpose is to *reconcile,* to overcome the barriers and alienation which people have lifted against such love. This peace of reconciliation God gave through the cross of Christ.

Chapter 2:8-10. We have no way of knowing precisely what "philosophy and empty deceit" might have been making a prey of the Colossians. Paul's reference to the "elemental spirits of the universe" strongly suggests the Gnostic heresy. The Gnostics believed that what God revealed and offered in Christ by itself was not enough. According to this view people had also to deal with the "elemental spirits of the universe," commonly found in the stars and planets. We would receive secret and saving knowledge from such spirits, after the manner of astrology. Paul saw this as an enormous danger to the Body of Christ, like a deadly disease corrupting the people of Christ. So he emphatically declares that the whole *fullness* of God's power dwells in the living Christ. Christ has power over all dominions, angels, spirits, and principalities. In Christ's mind is all the rule and authority the church needs.

Selected Scripture

King James Version	Revised Standard Version
Colossians 1:15-20	*Colossians 1:15-20*
15 Who is the image of the invisible God, the firstborn of every creature:	15 He is the image of the invisible God, the first-born of all creation;
16 For by him were all things created, that are in heaven, and that are in earth, visible and invisible, whether *they be* thrones, or dominions, or principalities, or powers: all things were created by him, and for him:	16 for in him all things were created, in heaven and on earth, visible and invisible, whether thrones or dominions or principalities or authorities—all things were created through him and for him. 17 He is before all things, and in him all things hold together. 18 He is the head of the body, the church; he is the beginning, the first-born from the dead, that in everything he
17 And he is before all things, and by him all things consist.	
18 And he is the head of the body,	

the church: who is the beginning, the firstborn from the dead; that in all *things* he might have the preeminence.

19 For it pleased *the Father* that in him should all fulness dwell;

20 And, having made peace through the blood of his cross, by him to reconcile all things unto himself; by him, *I say,* whether *they be* things in earth, or things in heaven.

might be pre-eminent. 19 For in him all the fulness of God was pleased to dwell, 20 and through him to reconcile to himself all things, whether on earth or in heaven, making peace by the blood of his cross.

Colossians 2:8-10

8 Beware lest any man spoil you through philosophy and vain deceit, after the tradition of men, after the rudiments of the world, and not after Christ.

9 For in him dwelleth all the fulness of the Godhead bodily.

10 And ye are complete in him, which is the head of all principality and power.

Colossians 2:8-10

8 See to it that no one makes a prey of you by philosophy and empty deceit, according to human tradition, according to the elemental spirits of the universe, and not according to Christ. 9 For in him the whole fulness of deity dwells bodily, 10 and you have come to fulness of life in him, who is the head of all rule and authority.

Key Verse: **And he is the head of the body, the church: who is the beginning, the firstborn from the dead; that in all things he might have the preeminence. (Colossians 1:18)**

Key Verse: **He is the head of the body, the church; he is the beginning, the first-born from the dead, that in everything he might be pre-eminent. (Colossians 1:18)**

The Scripture and the Main Question—William H. Willimon

The Image of God

One of the persistent, deadly problems within the religious life is our human tendency to keep our religious thoughts vague, abstract, and ill-defined. Note how religious people sometimes talk. We use speech full of high-sounding words like *spiritual, theological, love, personhood.*

All of this sounds good. Everyone is in favor of truth, love, and personhood. But what do these high-sounding abstractions mean in our everyday lives? What would need to happen in us if we were to make these ideals into reality?

Better to keep religion abstract and vague than to ask such specific questions. It's safer that way. We can thus transform religion into sentimentality or noble thoughts or grand principles and opinions that don't have the slightest impact on our everyday lives.

There are some religions that deal mainly in noble ideas. There are some religions that relegate religion mostly to the realm of the emotions. But Christianity is not one of those religions. Christianity bids us look squarely into the life, teachings, deeds, death, and resurrection of Jesus if we would know the true God. We thus agree with Paul when, in his letter to the church as Colossae, he says, "He is the image of the invisible God" (Colossians 1:15).

The term *image* could apply to a physical likeness. More often in the ancient world it was used in the sense of someone who was a representative of a king or person in authority who exercised the authority of the person who had sent him or her. Thus, the "image" represented the person who had sent the delegate out. Jesus, as the Son of God, represents God to the human race.

This is a sobering thought. This man from Nazareth is the representative of God to the world, the one who carries out God's purposes to the world. When we relate to him, we are relating to God. When we witness his deeds, we are witnessing God's deeds.

In other words, Jesus makes the presence of God concrete, specific, and tangible. God does not choose to be some aloof, invisible, incomprehensible being far off in the sky somewhere. God chooses to be among us in Christ, this "image of the invisible God."

This reminds us all to take care lest our religion get too "spiritual," abstract, vague, and far removed from the realities of human life. We must keep our faith tied to the facts of life—the life and death of this man—if we are to see God as God truly wants to be seen.

We don't know precisely what problems in the church at Colossae prompted this letter, but we can be sure that they arose because someone in the church there had the wrong ideas about God. Someone was trying to make God over into his or her own image. We also understand this. We are forever trying to transform God into someone who thinks, looks, and acts like us.

Paul bids them look again at Christ as the "image of the invisible God." Christ gives specificity to our notions about God, chastens our opinions about the Creator, and tests our values.

Who Is in Charge Here?

Paul calls Christ not only the "image of the invisible God" but also "the first-born of all creation" (1:15). At this time many people in the Greco-Roman world believed in the existence of different varieties of heavenly beings, all with distinct functions and responsibilities. Evidently someone at Colossae was spreading around the same notion about Christ. Christ is simply one of these angelic figures who rules the world.

"No!" says Paul. Christ *is* God. Jesus is not far removed from the Father. It is not easy to understand the precise meaning of the term *firstborn*. One might understand it in temporal terms—Christ is God's first child. But one can also understand it in the sense of "authority." Christ is the first ruler of the whole created order.

This is why Paul has that long list of those ideas and beings which some were arguing had to be worshiped on equal footing with Christ (1:16). Christ is over all things—including the church (1:18).

Paul is simply trying to say that where God is, Christ is, and vice versa. What are the practical implications of this insight for our lives?

How often do we hear someone—perhaps on the occasion of some tragedy or misfortune—say, "Well, this is just God's will"? Insurance policies sometimes label hurricanes, tornadoes, and other natural disasters as "acts of God."

But if what Paul says is true, namely that where God is in charge, Christ is in charge, then ought we not to say, "This is *Christ's* will" or this is an "act of *Christ*"?

That puts it a bit differently, doesn't it? Would you find it possible to look upon the devastation of a tornado, the death of a little child, the ravages of disease and say, "This is the work of Christ?" I doubt that you could.

Christ is the face of God. Our God is not some aloof, uncaring, unknown diety. Our God lived, suffered, and died right here on earth with us in the form of Jesus the Christ. He is the image of God, the firstborn, the one who shares all things with God. Christ is in charge.

Christ, the Head of All

The Christian religion is not some big, empty basket which we can fill with any content we wish or make it mean anything we want it to mean. Christ himself is the content of our faith.

Evidently a number of people were confused at the church in Colossae. Someone had victimized them through what Paul calls "philosophy and empty deceit, . . . tradition" (2:8).

People who do not understand who is in charge are often victims of those who harass other people by filling their heads with false ideas. Need we remind ourselves of tragedies like the Jonestown massacre several years ago to see the tragedy of people led astray by false teachers? From time to time, cults have arisen in Christianity, often taking some aspect of the Christian faith or adding some human opinion to the faith, and then leading people astray.

Paul confronts the false teachers of his day by referring Christians to Christ. He is the test of all our doctrine and practice. "For in him the whole fulness of deity dwells bodily" (2:9).

Someone you know believes in reincarnation (the belief that we go through a number of lifetimes, in different bodily forms). A neighbor of yours says that he has been told in a dream that he should divorce his wife, leave his children, and go "serve the Lord." Someone else says that "the church ought to stick to saving souls and stay out of economic, political, and worldly concerns."

I have listened to each of these notions at some time in my ministry. Perhaps you have heard them too. How do we know what is right? What does God want from us? Sometimes it can be confusing.

Paul says that Christ "is the head of the body, the church" (1:18). Only by referring our questions to him, only by using his words and life to test our beliefs will we be preserved from confusion and be brought to the true knowledge of the true God.

Helping Adults Become Involved—Harlan R. Waite

Preparing to Teach

This week's lesson opens a series of thirteen studies on the letters of Paul. Since it builds on a similar series presented in the fall of 1984, you may find it helpful to review that earlier series.

By way of general preparation, expand your understanding of Paul by further reading. A helpful summary appears in "The Letters of Paul," by S. MacLean Gilmour, an article in *The Interpreter's One-Volume Commentary on the Bible*, edited by Charles M. Laymon (Nashville: Abingdon Press, 1971), pages 1136-43. In *The New Testament: An Introduction* (New York: Harcourt Brace Jovanovich, 1974), Norman Perrin presents a clear outline of "Paul and His Letters" and "Deutero-Pauline Christianity" (pages 89-141).

More specifically, read Colossians. Pay particular attention to the focal passages for today's lesson (Colossians 1:15-20; 2:8-10). Note the ideas that you consider important for you and your class. Then turn to "As You Read the Scripture," noting especially the definitions and explanations of key words and phrases. Finally, read "The Main Question" and "The Scripture and the Main Question" for help in developing your own presentation of the lesson. An additional resource is "The Letter of Paul to the Colossians" by Victor Paul Furnish, in *The Interpreter's One-Volume Commentary on the Bible*, pages 856-64. Ask your minister for help in locating some of these materials.

Your purpose in presenting today's lesson will be threefold: to introduce the series on Paul and his letters, to help your students understand the message of Colossians, and to discover its relevance for twentieth-century Christians.

The following outline may be useful in organizing the lesson:

I. Paul speaks to his churches.
II. Jesus is the living likeness of God.
III. Jesus establishes our value systems.
IV. Jesus is the head of the church.

Introducing the Main Question

How do we know what God is like, and what effect does the deity have on our lives? This twofold question provides the focus for today's lesson. Suggest to your class that in a sense the question seems unanswerable. We often say that God is invisible and infinite. How then can we support the Christian claim that we can know God? Let your class discuss for a few moments how we teach our children. At each stage of their development, we introduce them to realities which they have not experienced or understood. Our approach is to compare the unfamiliar with something familiar, the new with something old. We use comparisons to help them grow in understanding.

So it is in our faith. We can see, hear, know, and experience God to the extent that we see, hear, know, and experience Jesus. Our image of God is shaped by our understanding of Jesus. Indeed, did not Jesus himself use analogy to help us understand the meaning of the kingdom of God? It is "like" a mustard seed, a buried treasure, a living relationship.

Developing the Lesson

I. Paul speaks to his churches.

Recall the series on Paul which the class studied last fall. Review briefly, then introduce the present course. Note that the unifying theme will be the church as the Body of Christ and that the purpose of this study will be to help class members understand themselves as a part of that body, both individually and in their interactions with each other.

Preview briefly the four units, identifying them as "The Person of Christ," "The Church: The Body of Christ," "Internal Problems in the Church," and "Integrity in the Body of Christ." Introduce the main question as suggested by Dr. Willimon and in the section above. Give a short description of the problem faced by the Christians at Colossae, as set forth in the resources noted above (particularly Perrin and *The Interpreter's One-Volume Commentary on the Bible*).

17

II. *Jesus is the living likeness of God.*

Blaise Pascal was a French physicist, mathematician, and philosopher who lived during the seventeenth century. One of the outstanding intellects of all time, he is still recognized as a leading scientist. His greatest discovery, however, was in the realm of faith. On a small piece of paper which he sewed in his clothing and wore next to his heart, he wrote words to this effect: "God is not the God of philosophy; he is the God of Abraham, of Isaac, of Jacob, and of Jesus." Point out to your class that throughout the Bible, human beings found God in people and in personal affairs of life. While other cultures turn to nature and to philosophy for answers to their religious questions, Hebrews and Christians have turned to the world of human relationships—to the events of history—to find God. Biblical faith thus has its roots in fact; at the same time, facts were subjected to interpretation, and the meanings found in the world of facts produced the flowers and fruits of Jewish and Christian faith.

To Christians, of course, Jesus is the great event of all time. In him we "see" God. Share Dr. Willimon's discussion of the main question and his observation regarding "the image of God."

III. *Jesus establishes our value systems.*

Observe that Jesus is the authority for our moral and spiritual values. We reason that if our purpose in life is to do God's will, and if Jesus is the one who reveals God's will to us, then Jesus becomes the central authority for our system of values.

Ask the class to discuss these questions: In what ways do we experience tension between Christian values and the values of our culture? To narrow the question down, what roles do news media, political parties, business affairs, and social groups have in determining our value systems? For example, is the way we spend our money determined more by investment principles, economic factors, and popular styles or by our own purpose in life, our sense of stewardship, our observation of human needs around us?

Review "Who Is in Charge Here?" Pursue the question raised by Dr. Willimon regarding the practical implications of the authority of Christ for our lives.

IV. *Jesus is the head of the church.*

Share with the class Dr. Luccock's interpretation of Colossians 1:15-20, as he presents it in "As You Read the Scripture." The words *image, firstborn, before all things,* and similar expressions indicate sovereignty, priority (rather than antiquity), and preeminence (rather than preexistence). "He is the head of the body, the church" (Colossians 1:18). Refer your class to Paul's metaphor of the church as a body in Romans 12:3-8 and I Corinthians 12:4-27. Perhaps two students who read well could read these passages aloud to the class. Note that in the experience of each of us, the body expresses thoughts, emotions, and intentions. So it is with the body we call the church. How well do we express the intentions of God as we know them through Jesus?

Helping Class Members Act

Ask your students to evaluate the extent to which the class and your local church think of themselves as the Body of Christ. Is there a need to awaken this concept in the minds of your members? How might this be done?

Planning for Next Sunday
Examine the teacher's materials for next Sunday's lesson and preview the theme for your class. Ask your students to read Paul's letter to the Philippians, noting the differences between 3:2–4:9 and the rest of the letter.

LESSON 2   SEPTEMBER 8

Christ, Our Guide to Maturity

Background Scripture: Philippians 3–4

The Main Question—William H. Willimon

A recent commentator on the American church scene called us "a church of stillborn Christians." There is much truth in her statement. In our preaching and teaching we have often been guilty of an overstress upon the first steps of faith and too little emphasis upon the growth and maturation of faith. We are forever urging people to take the first step but fail to tell them what to do next! Being "born again" has been a popular American evangelical concern. But what do we do after we are born? That's the question.

The Bible consistently pictures our relationship with God as a matter of growth and change. Our God is a living God and, as we grow, God grows with us. God's demands upon us also grow, in line with our developing capacities.

But growth can be difficult. It is painful to give up our immature ideas, our false images, our limited notions. Perhaps that's why many of us simply stop growing. We come to a plateau in our religious development.

"When I was a child," Paul writes to the Corinthians, "I thought like a child, I reasoned like a child; when I became a man, I gave up childish ways" (I Corinthians 13). A childish faith is fine—for children. But God wants his children to grow up, to deepen their faith and understanding.

An enthusiastic young man came to tell his pastor that he had been "born again." His was the enthusiasm of the youthful new convert to the faith. His pastor listened to him excitedly tell of his conversion. Then he said, "This is all fine, son. But don't forget that the Lord isn't finished with you yet. No matter how great an experience you have had on Sunday night, there is still another Monday morning with its challenges. The Lord will go with you."

As You Read the Scripture—Robert E. Luccock

When we read Paul's letter to the Philippians, we make two striking discoveries: this is Paul's letter most filled with joy and hope, and it is also concerned with thoughts of death that may soon await the Apostle. Philippians is the letter of paradox and irony: rejoicing and martyrdom.

Philippi was the place to which Paul first came in Europe to establish a Christian church (see Acts 16:9-15, "Come over to Macedonia and help us").

19

Like Colossians, Paul most likely wrote this letter—perhaps his last surviving letter—from his Roman prison. He wrote it to do three things: to send his thanks and love to this church which had supported him more than any other (Philippians 1:3-7, 4:15-16) and for whom he had special affection; to warn them against future dangers (Philippians 3:2-3, 18-19); and to exhort them to copy his own example of suffering for Christ's sake (Philippians 3:17, 4:9).

Philippians 3:13-14. To gain Christ, to know a righteousness that depends on faith, to know the power of his resurrection, to become like him in death, and to attain the resurrection—these are what Paul wants to obtain and make his own (Philippians 3:8-11). This is "mature" faith (Philippians 3:15).

In "forgetting what lies behind," Paul refers to *all* of his past life, especially whatever *successes* he may have achieved. He counts even these as "loss" (Philippians 3:8).

Verses 15-16. "Mature" suggests those with experience and wisdom to know and appreciate the new faith in Christ. And especially to know that *more of the race is yet to be run.* One of the dangers to which the Philippians must have been exposed was from the people who imagined that once they were confessing Christians they "had it made."

Verse 17. This verse sounds arrogant and presumptuous. No. New Christians needed a living role model for how they were to live. The Apostle *demonstrated* the new life in Christ.

Verses 18-19. Paul may have warned here against Christians who believed they were beyond rules and against others who believed that grace was large enough to cover everything. Neither group cared to discipline appetites or carnal instincts.

Verse 20. The Christian's obedience is not to the standards of the surrounding community, but to a commonwealth not of this world.

Verse 21. This body which we now inhabit is subject to change and decay. Paul's hope is for the day when this lowly body will be changed for the glorious body of eternal life (see I Corinthians 15:35-53).

Chapter 4:1. "My joy and crown" refers to the faithfulness of the Philippians, Paul's exceeding joy.

Verses 4-6. Paul can say, "Rejoice" because "the Lord is at hand." The certainty of the Lord's coming gave Paul his undiscourageable joy. Wesley translated "forbearance" as "yieldingness." Others have said "gentleness," "courtesy." It means a refusal to retaliate. "Have no anxiety"—one commentator explains this seeming counsel of perfection: "The way to be anxious about nothing is to be prayerful about everything." The unthankful person cannot pray because he or she has no sense of the goodness of God.

Verse 8. These are things almost universally agreed to be right and proper for all people, the virtues of pagan ethics. Paul exhorts Christians to think on these things, not to disregard them just because they have attained a new life.

Verse 9. This section concludes with a promise: the God of peace will be your safeguard.

Selected Scripture

King James Version

Philippians 3:13-21

13 Brethren, I count not myself to have apprehended: but *this* one thing *I do*, forgetting those things which are behind, and reaching forth unto those things which are before,

14 I press toward the mark for the prize of the high calling of God in Christ Jesus.

15 Let us therefore, as many as be perfect, be thus minded: and if in any thing ye be otherwise minded, God shall reveal even this unto you.

16 Nevertheless, whereto we have already attained, let us walk by the same rule, let us mind the same thing.

17 Brethren, be followers together of me, and mark them which walk so as ye have us for an ensample.

18 (For many walk, of whom I have told you often, and now tell you even weeping, *that they are* the enemies of the cross of Christ:

19 Whose end *is* destruction, whose God *is their* belly, and *whose* glory *is* in their shame, who mind earthly things.)

20 For our conversation is in heaven; from whence also we look for the Saviour, the Lord Jesus Christ:

21 Who shall change our vile body, that it may be fashioned like unto his glorious body, according to the working whereby he is able to subdue all things unto himself.

Philippians 4:1, 4-9

1 Therefore, my brethren dearly beloved and longed for, my joy and crown, so stand fast in the Lord, *my* dearly beloved.

....

4 Rejoice in the Lord alway: *and* again I say, Rejoice.

Revised Standard Version

Philippians 3:13-21

13 Brethren, I do not consider that I have made it my own; but one thing I do, forgetting what lies behind and straining forward to what lies ahead, 14 I press on toward the goal for the prize of the upward call of God in Christ Jesus. 15 Let those of us who are mature be thus minded; and if in anything you are otherwise minded, God will reveal that also to you. 16 Only let us hold true to what we have attained.

17 Brethren, join in imitating me, and mark those who so live as you have an example in us. 18 For many, of whom I have often told you and now tell you even with tears, live as enemies of the cross of Christ. 19 Their end is destruction, their god is the belly, and they glory in their shame, with minds set on earthly things. 20 But our commonwealth is in heaven, and from it we await a Savior, the Lord Jesus Christ, 21 who will change our lowly body to be like his glorious body, by the power which enables him even to subject all things to himself.

Philippians 4:1, 4-9

1 Therefore, my brethren, whom I love and long for, my joy and crown, stand firm thus in the Lord, my beloved.

....

4 Rejoice in the Lord always; again I will say, Rejoice. 5 Let all

21

5 Let your moderation be known unto all men. The Lord *is* at hand.

6 Be careful for nothing; but in every thing by prayer and supplication with thanksgiving let your requests be made known unto God.

7 And the peace of God, which passeth all understanding, shall keep your hearts and minds through Christ Jesus.

8 Finally, brethren, whatsoever things are true, whatsoever things *are* honest, whatsoever things *are* just, whatsoever things *are* pure, whatsoever things *are* lovely, whatsoever things *are* of good report; if *there be* any virtue, and if *there be* any praise, think on these things.

9 Those things, which ye have both learned, and received, and heard, and seen in me, do: and the God of peace shall be with you.

men know your forbearance. The Lord is at hand. 6 Have no anxiety about anything, but in everything by prayer and supplication with thanksgiving let your requests be made known to God. 7 And the peace of God, which passes all understanding, will keep your hearts and your minds in Christ Jesus.

8 Finally, brethren, whatever is true, whatever is honorable, whatever is just, whatever is pure, whatever is lovely, whatever is gracious, if there is any excellence, if there is anything worthy of praise, think about these things. 9 What you have learned and received and heard and seen in me, do; and the God of peace will be with you.

Key Verse: **Be careful for nothing; but in everything by prayer and supplication with thanksgiving let your requests be made known unto God. And the peace of God, which passeth all understanding, shall keep your hearts and minds through Christ Jesus. (Philippians 4:6-7)**

Key Verse: **Have no anxiety about anything, but in everything by prayer and supplication with thanksgiving let your requests be made known to God. And the peace of God, which passes all understanding, will keep your hearts and your minds in Christ Jesus. (Philippians 4:6-7)**

The Scripture and the Main Question—William H. Willimon

Pressing On

In a way it is a bit surprising to hear one so wise and experienced in the faith as Paul admit that he had not yet arrived so far as his relationship to Christ was concerned. In writing to the Philippians, Paul says he still has some growing to do (Philippians 3:13-14). He tells the Philippians that they have some growing to do too.

This is particularly refreshing since religious people so often act as if they have already arrived. We sometimes imply that we know everything and have no growing to do. We project the image of the mature Christian as someone who is fixed, closed, and finished.

Sometimes our professed maturity and sureness may not be as mature as we would like it to appear. Psychologists tell us that the so-called true believer who appears to be rock hard in his or her faith may be in fact engaging in a cover-up of troubling inner questions and insecurities.

Children often have an excessive need to be right because they feel that they are so often wrong. Fanatic believers who are always trying to shout everyone else down may, in reality, be desperately trying to convince *themselves*.

For such people Christianity becomes a hard and fast set of rules, a set of proper opinions which must be adhered to. Doubters must be cast out. No questions. The Christian life becomes a closed club for those who are in the know, those who don't ask questions or change their minds.

How different in this view of faith from that which Paul expresses in Philippians 3–4! Paul says that he himself is pressing on, and he urges the Philippians to do the same.

Alas, we are a nation of people who expect everything instantly, in a moment, with no risk or cost or pain. We want to be changed, done over, made perfect *now*. Who wants to wait for God to make us perfect? Who wants to wait to grow up?

So we reduce Christianity to some simplistic package that you can accomplish quickly and without effort. We thus imply that the Christian life is something petty and inconsequential.

Paul knows better. He knows that, when one is dealing with Christ himself, there are great expectations, great risks, great changes required which may take a great deal of time and effort.

Therefore Paul bids us to join him in pressing on toward "the upward call of God in Christ Jesus" (3:14).

Forward to What Lies Ahead

"But one thing I do," says Paul, "forgetting what lies behind and straining forward to what lies ahead, I press on toward the upward call of God in Christ Jesus" (3:13-14). For Paul, the Christian life is one of progress by slow degrees toward some distant goal.

How do we progress in our faith? Paul suggests that he grows by forgetting and remembering. We grow first by forgetting things we have believed or thought in the past. Childhood images of God are fine for children. But are some of these images adequate for adults?

When I was growing up, we often sang the little song in Sunday school, "Jesus Loves the Little Children." We joyfully sang that Jesus loves all the little children—"red and yellow, black and white, they are precious in his sight." But did we really believe that? We had only white children in our Sunday school. On the playground we were allowed to play with only those children who looked like us. So, in spite of the song, I grew up with the assumption that Jesus loved children who looked like us.

Through many and sometimes painful experiences, I gradually came to question this point of view. During the war in Southeast Asia, I came to question the notion that God was only on our side, that God loved only the Americans and not the North Vietnamese. I came to see the error of our white segregation. In other words, I had to forget what I had assumed to be right in the past.

Likewise, we must strain "forward to what lies ahead" in our faith. We worship a living God, not a dead memory. That "good old-time religion" is fine—for the good old days. But what about today? Has God ceased to speak? Was God concerned only with the daily affairs of the Babylonians, the Israelites, and the Assyrians and not with the political problems of the Americans, the Canadians, and the Russians? No. Our God is a God who, in the words of the angel at the empty tomb, "is going before you." Our God goes on before us into the future and beckons us to go with him.

We make the Christian life sound dull by the way we usually present it. We portray Christianity as mere acceptance of a body of ancient beliefs, assent to some old doctrines, closed-minded adherence to a rigid set of opinions. "You've just got to accept this on faith," we sometimes say.

Paul knows otherwise. He presents the Christian life as high adventure, a constant process of growth and development, of forgetting what is past and pressing on to what lies ahead.

Ask your group: What have you had to put behind you in your beliefs, attitudes, and opinions, and what have you had to struggle to accept in order to become the sort of person God wants you to be? You will probably be surprised by their responses. They know, from firsthand experience, that the Christian life is no safe, snug harbor. The Christian life is high adventure.

Following the Example

In a way, it is a bit of a shock to hear Paul tell the Philippians to "join in imitating me, . . . you have an example in us" (3:17). This sounds like a conceited, pride-filled statement if ever there was one. Imagine standing up before your class next Sunday morning and saying to them, "Now, class, I want all of you to imitate me and to live your lives by my example." It might be your last Sunday teaching that class!

What can Paul mean when he urges the church to "join in imitating me"? Consider the context. Paul has been urging the Philippians to grow up, to mature in their faith, and to give up their childish ways. He tells them that growth is essential for the Christian life.

Paul's own faith journey is a good example of the truth of which he speaks. At one time Paul had looked upon himself as a religious expert, a wise and knowledgeable theologian. This wise man was therefore scandalized by those rabble-rousing Christians with their heretical, revolutionary notions. Paul was determined to be a good, religious man and put an end to these innovators—if he had to kill every one of them to do it.

Then, on the Damascus road, Paul was turned around. He knew not whether to describe what happened to him there as "birth" or "death." It felt like both at the same time. It was the death of his old, limited notions of God's love. It was the birth of a whole new way of looking at the world and looking at himself. Paul was thrown off his horse and set on a new, adventuresome path.

So, when Paul tells the Philippians to imitate him, he is telling them to imitate him in growing up, in putting aside the past, and in reaching out to the future. Sometimes that growth can be painful, as painful as birth itself. But it is essential. Our God is a living God who will not be contained in our little notions, our puny concepts. Like Paul, we must be willing to grow, to change, to let go, and to grasp the new if we are going to be disciples of this Lord.

Helping Adults Become Involved—Harlan R. Waite

Preparing to Teach

Begin by reading Philippians 3:2–4:9. Although only a portion of this will be printed, the entire passage is necessary to provide context for the central emphasis of this lesson. "As You Read the Scripture" provides important explanations which you can share with your class. Additional help is available in "The Letter of Paul to the Philippians" in *The Interpreter's One-Volume Commentary on the Bible*, pages 845-55.

You will also find help for developing the theme in "The Main Question" and "The Scripture and the Main Question."
Consider using this outline:

  I. Examine the scripture.
     A. Paul and the Philippians
     B. Paul's past experience
     C. Paul's appeal
 II. Say good-bye to the past.
     A. Childhood memories
     B. Adolescent certainties
     C. Adult rigidity
III. Press on toward the goal.
     A. The need for goals
     B. Intentionality
     C. The goal of personal development
 IV. Follow Paul's example.
     A. "Join in imitating me"
     B. Discipleship
     C. Christ's example
     D. The integrity of faith

Introducing the Main Question

Members of your class will recall seeing children playing a game called "Freeze." The children move about until the leader calls, "Freeze." At that point, everyone stands still regardless of the position assumed. How odd, even grotesque, some of them look. Some of us play the game of life that way. At some point in our lives, we freeze, becoming victims of what psychologists call arrested development. We hang on to habits, ideas, and relationships that provide emotional satisfaction, comfort, or security. Paul's message serves to unfreeze us.

In recent years we have often heard, "Today is the first day of the rest of my life." Dr. Willimon reminds us that God is not finished with us yet. God expects more of us. Dr. Willimon states the main question this way: What do we do after we are born? Use his discussion of the main question to introduce your lesson.

Developing the Lesson

I. Examine the scripture.

A. Paul and the Philippians

In your background reading you have discovered that Paul had a very warm relationship with the Christians at Philippi. In chapters 1, 2, and 4, we hear him expressing thanks for their support. In Philippians 3:2–4:9, which may be a fragment of another letter, his message is strikingly different. Recalling last week's assignment, ask your students to identify and discuss the differences.

B. Paul's past experience

Paul's past experience is important to note. Ask the class to describe the past which Paul is putting behind him. Note that it is a past of privilege as a Pharisee, of legal and rigid moralism, and of intolerance.

C. Paul's appeal

Paul's appeal suggests that some of the members of the Philippian church may have been holding on to the past. Note the reference in 3:2-3 to the so-called Judaizers, who felt that they must hang on to certain aspects of Judaism even while they embraced the new faith. Paul appeals to them to set their minds on new goals.

II. Say good-bye to the past.

A. Childhood memories

Ask your class to recall people and events which they remember from their childhood and continue to cherish. Some of the strongest emotional ties we have in life are related to early childhood experiences. Discuss the difficulty people face in getting beyond them.

B. Adolescent certainties

Adolescent certainties often hang on to inhibit our growth. Students in the second year of college are often teased about the name of their class, for they are called sophomores—wise fools. Self-assertion is an appropriate mode of behavior for adolescents, who are rightfully attempting to establish themselves as independent individuals. The problem arises when sophomoric attitudes continue into adulthood, a phenomenon we often see among strongly opinionated persons.

C. Adult rigidity

Adult rigidity is an expression of this sophomoric attitude and reveals a failure to grow. Old prejudices survive; traditions become all-important; and the creativity of the Holy Spirit is frustrated as adults are unable to leave the past behind in favor of new understandings and modes of life.

III. Press on toward the goal.

Such was Paul's advice toward people who were not continuing to grow after their new birth in Christ.

A. The need for goals

Ask your class to discuss what is required of us if we would grow spiritually. The facts they mention might include some of the following: acknowledge need; drop pretenses; focus thinking on things "worthy of praise" (Philippians 4:8); allow the creative power of the Holy Spirit to challenge traditions; forget the past, its grudges, opinions, securities, etc.; look to others as examples of growing life; and learn to be forbearing with others who differ from us. Refer the class to Dr. Willimon's discussion of "Forward to What Lies Ahead."

B. Intentionality

Intentionality is an important aspect of our growth. If we are tempted to drift in the direction of improvement, we need to heed Paul's word to "press on" with strong intentionality.

C. The goal of personal development

Note Paul's statement of his goal of personal development in Philippians 4:8. He used a catalogue of virtues which were common in the society of the day and adopted them as entirely appropriate to Christian growth. Certainly, Christians could not be any less true, honorable, just, pure, lovely, gracious than their non-Christian neighbors. Paul accepted these virtues as "worthy of praise" and displays of "excellence." He enjoined the Philippians to "think about these things."

IV. Follow Paul's example.

A. "Join in imitating me"

In inviting the Philippians to "join in imitating me" (3:17), Paul was not trying to make Christians of Philippi into replicas of himself. Rather he was exhorting them to join him in his "pilgrim's progress." Paul claimed no perfection for himself; he simply felt that his direction was right, and he invited the church to be his companions on the way. Share with the class Dr. Willimon's discussion, "Following the Example."

B. *Discipleship*

Discipleship inevitably means learning and growing. To follow Paul would be to follow Jesus himself, in whom Paul had found his new life. Refer the class to II Corinthians 4:5-6, where Paul describes the essence of his own conversion and his commitment to Jesus Christ as Lord.

C. *Christ's example*

Christ's example was important to Paul. Notice in Philippians 2:5-8 how he lifts up the servant motivation of Jesus. Refer your class to Romans 12:9-21, where Paul clearly echoes the Sermon on the Mount. Recall Galatians 3:28, where Paul restates the kind of inclusive love Jesus had when he told the story of the good Samaritan.

D. *The integrity of faith*

The integrity of faith was highly important to Paul. In Philippians 4:9, he enjoins his brothers and sisters at Philippi to *do* what they had learned from him. Action must reveal the depth of one's profession of faith.

Helping Class Members Act

Dr. Willimon presents a question which will bring your students face-to-face with their need for growth: What have you had to put behind you in your beliefs, attitudes, and opinions and what have you had to struggle to accept in order to become the sort of person God wants you to be? Discuss this question as a prelude to personal commitment.

Planning for Next Sunday

Ask your students to read Ephesians 1–2, and select someone to prepare an outline of these chapters. Recruit a volunteer to report on the origin, the use, and the importance of the book in the early church. Raise this question for discussion next week: In what ways and to what extent does our desire for self-sufficiency stand in the way of spiritual growth?

UNIT II: THE CHURCH: THE BODY OF CHRIST
Horace R. Weaver

THREE LESSONS   **SEPTEMBER 15–29**

This unit is taken from what many regard as the most sublime of all the Pauline writings: the letter to the Ephesians. The theme is God's purpose in establishing the universal church of Christ Jesus. This church is drawn from both Jew and Gentile, and as such is composed of persons from many nationalities whose lives have been saved from hate, greed, jealousy, and dishonesty—they have been saved by the grace of God. His love in calling each and all has been acknowledged; as a consequence their responses to God have been expressions of gratitude for what he is and has done for them.

Ephesians may have been written by a disciple of Paul (perhaps Onesimus, the runaway slave) who gathered into one body *(corpus)* the various letters Paul had written to the churches and to individuals. This letter (Ephesians) may be a "circular letter," of which copies may have been made and distributed by Tychicus (6:21-22) to the churches in Asia Minor. The letter has as its theme the claim that Christ Jesus is the head of the church—in fact, is the Body of the church.

The three lessons of this unit deal with the following emphases: "How the Body of Christ Is Formed," September 15, stresses the fact that persons are saved not by doing certain good things, but by accepting what God has done for them, and also the fact that both Gentiles and Jews are a unity in Christ—neither one being favored over the other by God. "How the Body of Christ Grows," September 22, emphasizes the beatific virtues educed by love as both Jew and Gentile mature side-by-side in Christlikeness. "Being Christ's Body in the World," September 29, encourages Christians to put aside the old manner of life and "to be renewed in the spirit of your minds," as was seen in Christ Jesus.

LESSON 3   SEPTEMBER 15

How the Body of Christ Is Formed

Background Scripture: Ephesians 1–2

The Main Question—William H. Willimon

In a seminary preaching class one can learn a lot about the state of American religion. After a few weeks of being subjected to the sermons by student preachers, I could summarize about 90 percent of the sermons I heard as having this simple theme: *three or four things you need to do in order to be a Christian.*

And of course, such preaching has its appeal. We are a nation of practical, high-achieving, hard-working people. We take pride in being self-made, self-sufficient.

"Thanks, but I'd rather do it myself," is a national slogan.

So we come to church seeking practical, specific guidance for life. Studies show that we like sermons that clearly tell us what we are supposed to *do.*

Of course, as Christians, we do expect that our beliefs should lead us to action, and, as the scripture so often says, words of love without coresponding deeds of love are hollow.

But what if, in the deepest matters of our lives, we are recipients rather than achievers? What if our relationship to God is based more on what God has done and is doing for us rather than on what we do for God? What if we are saved, preserved, and loved not because of our deeds but *in spite* of them?

If this is the case, then we are Christians mainly because of God's grace rather than because of our achievements, and the Christian life is a response to something which is offered. What a shock it is to us practical, hard-working, high-achieving, self-sufficient people to hear that, in the end, "by grace you have been saved . . . ; this is not your own doing, it is the gift of God" (Ephesians 2:8).

As You Read the Scripture—Robert E. Luccock

Whether Paul wrote the letter to the Ephesians himself or whether it is the work of a devoted follower of Paul some years after the Apostle's death, as most biblical scholars now believe, is of no consequence to our purpose in this study of how the Body of Christ is formed. Ephesians remains one of the great documents of Christian faith, whoever wrote it. Much of Paul's thinking finds eloquent expression here, and the letter has become almost the charter of the ideal of a world ecumenical church that would include all the followers of Christ. We may be thankful that some time after the apostles themselves had died a treatise like Ephesians was written to reinforce the faith of the Christian churches and to declare their unity in Christ.

Paul spent about three years in Ephesus. The Christians there would have had a special and very personal interest in this letter. It is probable that the letter was written to be circulated widely throughout the Greco-Roman world.

Ephesians 1:3-4. "Every spiritual blessing" refers to the gifts which only *God* has given us, or *could* give us. They are "only to be found in heaven" (translation by William Barclay). But God offers these gifts in the present age to all who will receive them "in Christ." God "chose us"; he destined in the very purpose of creation that believers in Christ would be a "holy" people in the world.

Verses 5-6. God made it the design of the creation that we could become God's sons and daughters, whose obedience it would be to praise "the glory of the generous gift which He freely gave us in the Beloved" (Barclay). See Mark 1:11.

Verses 7-8. "Redemption . . . forgiveness" has a parallel in Colossians 1:14. Paul's thought in the letters which we know to be his, as in Ephesians here, saw the primary consequence of Christ's death to be forgiveness. Such release from sin's power transforms life. We might say it redeems life. It is not a price we pay, or that Christ pays, to God as barter for our forgiveness. Rather it is a declaration of God's grace.

Verses 9-10. "All wisdom and insight" means that in Christ we are given knowledge of God's eternal purpose, as well as sound sense for discerning God's will in day-to-day living. God's plan is to unite "all things" in Christ when the new age begins.

Chapter 2:8-9. "By grace you have been saved." This is one of the towering texts in all of Christian literature. It stands as the central pillar in Paul's thought. Paul always put it in the present tense: "to us who are being saved" (I Corinthians 1:18). The act of faith on our part, "through faith," is a neverending response to the grace given once and for all in Christ's death and resurrection. It is not our own doing, that is, *our* "works," that saves us. It is not even our faith first of all. It is God's "gift" of grace.

Verses 11-13. The writer points out that the Gentiles have until now been separated from Christ, not knowing Israel's saving history. Now they are no longer strangers to the covenants of God's promise.

Verses 14-16. "The dividing wall of hostility" is the separation between Jew and Gentile, symbolized by the partition in the temple beyond which Gentiles could not pass. Now in Christ that wall is down. Jews and Gentiles are now "one body" in Christ, their hostility ended. How different our history would have been if people on both sides had understood that!

Selected Scripture

King James Version	Revised Standard Version

Ephesians 1:3-10

3 Blessed *be* the God and Father of our Lord Jesus Christ, who hath blessed us with all spiritual blessings in heavenly *places* in Christ:

4 According as he hath chosen us in him before the foundation of the world, that we should be holy and without blame before him in love:

5 Having predestinated us unto the adoption of children by Jesus Christ to himself, according to the good pleasure of his will,

6 To the praise of the glory of his grace, wherein he hath made us accepted in the beloved.

7 In whom we have redemption through his blood, the forgiveness of sins, according to the riches of his grace;

8 Wherein he hath abounded toward us in all wisdom and prudence;

9 Having made known unto us the mystery of his will, according to his good pleasure which he hath purposed in himself:

10 That in the dispensation of the fulness of times he might gather together in one all things in Christ, both which are in heaven, and which are on earth; *even* in him.

Ephesians 2:8-16

8 For by grace are ye saved through faith; and that not of yourselves; *it is* the gift of God:

9 Not of works, lest any man should boast.

10 For we are his workmanship, created in Christ Jesus unto good works, which God hath before ordained that we should walk in them.

11 Wherefore remember, that ye *being* in time past Gentiles in the flesh, who are called Uncircumcision by that which is called the Circumcision in the flesh made by hands;

Ephesians 1:3-10

3 Blessed be the God and Father of our Lord Jesus Christ, who has blessed us in Christ with every spiritual blessing in the heavenly places, 4 even as he chose us in him before the foundation of the world, that we should be holy and blameless before him. 5 He destined us in love to be his sons through Jesus Christ, according to the purpose of his will, 6 to the praise of his glorious grace which he freely bestowed on us in the Beloved. 7 In him we have redemption through his blood, the forgiveness of our trespasses, according to the riches of his grace 8 which he lavished upon us. 9 For he has made known to us in all wisdom and insight the mystery of his will, according to his purpose which he set forth in Christ 10 as a plan for the fulness of time, to unite all things in him, things in heaven and things on earth.

Ephesians 2:8-16

8 For by grace you have been saved through faith; and this is not your own doing, it is the gift of God—9 not because of works, lest any man should boast. 10 For we are his workmanship, created in Christ Jesus for good works, which God prepared beforehand, that we should walk in them.

11 Therefore remember that at one time you Gentiles in the flesh, called the uncircumcision by what is called the circumcision, which is made in the flesh by hands—12

12 That at that time ye were without Christ, being aliens from the commonwealth of Israel, and strangers from the covenants of promise, having no hope, and without God in the world:

13 But now in Christ Jesus ye who sometimes were far off are made nigh by the blood of Christ.

14 For he is our peace, who hath made both one, and hath broken down the middle wall of partition *between us;*

15 Having abolished in his flesh the enmity, *even* the law of commandments *contained* in ordinances; for to make in himself of twain one new man, *so* making peace;

16 And that he might reconcile both unto God in one body by the cross, having slain the enmity thereby.

remember that you were at that time separated from Christ, alienated from the commonwealth of Israel, and strangers to the covenants of promise, having no hope and without God in the world. 13 But now in Christ Jesus you who were far off have been brought near in the blood of Christ. 14 For he is our peace, who has made us both one, and has broken down the dividing wall of hostility, 15 by abolishing in his flesh the law of commandments and ordinances, that he might create in himself one new man in place of the two, so making peace, 16 and might reconcile us both to God in one body through the cross, thereby bringing the hostility to an end.

Key Verse: **For by grace are ye saved through faith; and that not of yourselves:** *it is* **the gift of God. (Ephesians 2:8)**

Key Verse: **For by grace you have been saved through faith, and this is not your own doing, it is the gift of God. (Ephesians 2:8)**

The Scripture and the Main Question—William H. Willimon

He Chose Us

"Mommy, I want to do it myself," says the four-year-old learning to tie his shoes, struggling to grow up. In fact, growing up is one long, arduous process of learning to do it for ourselves. Our image of adults is that they are independent, self-sufficient, on their own, doing it all for themselves.

Recently, at a board of trustees meeting at a small college, the dean of students was describing the new policies regarding student behavior at the school. "We intend to stop babying the students," she said. "We are going to stop holding their hands, stop telling them that this or that is bad for them, stop mothering them. We want them to be adults."

Listening to the dean started me to thinking. "What is an adult?" I asked myself. If an adult is a totally self-sufficient, autonomous, detached, isolated person, then I suppose that the college should do its best to make its students into that kind of people.

The trouble is, every adult I know who has that image of himself or herself is in big trouble now. The person who convinced himself, "I can live my life on my own without help from anyone else," the one who brags about being a "self-made man," the woman who claims, "I don't need anyone to lean on, I'm too strong for that"—their lives are often testimony to the sterility, the danger, the immaturity of these claims of independence.

No one is literally a "self-made man"; none of us can claim to be able to make it on our own. We are the beneficiaries of countless gifts, of untold sacrifices by unknown persons whose lives and deeds have made us who we are. The self-made man or woman is a tragic delusion, a myth made of our own limited understanding of how deeply dependent we are upon one another for survival.

What is true of human relationships is true for divine-human relationships as well—we are dependent upon God to do for us what we cannot do for ourselves.

Paul begins his letter to the Ephesians by reminding them why they are where they are. They are Christians not because of their good deeds, their deep feelings, or their astute belief. They are Christians because God has chosen to bless them (1:3). God has chosen them (1:4); God has destined them to be his beloved children (1:5); God has forgiven them their sin (1:7).

Note the difference between this approach to the faith and that which we usually take. How often do we listen to a sermon or to a church school lesson asking, "What must *I* do? What do I need to believe? What choices must I make?"

That approach gets it all backward, according to Paul. First we must talk about what *God* has done before we dare ask and then answer questions about our human response.

"What must I do to be your little boy?" a child might ask his mother. The question shows an ignorance of the way parents behave, a lack of understanding of the way love works.

"Nothing, dear, absolutely nothing" is the mother's reply.

Saved by Grace

Why must we learn and relearn this lesson over and over? We are who we are because of what *God* has done, not because of what we do.

I suppose we must relearn this truth because we human beings enjoy thinking of ourselves as godlike deciders, choosers, and shapers of our destiny. We would rather see our lives as our achievement than as a sum of many gifts.

So perhaps it is only natural for the church to fall into the trap of talking about our relationships to God the same way we talk about our bank accounts. "What must we do to be saved?" people ask. The church often replies: tithe, attend regularly, read your Bible daily, be good to others, do this, do that. In other words, we subtly put ourselves in place of God.

Listen to us as we describe our faith. "Since *I* took Jesus as my personal savior"; "Since *I* gave my life to Christ," we say. This gets it backward, implying that we are related to God by our own choice, our belief, our good work.

Doesn't the Bible say, over and over again, that "he chose us" (1:4)? God chose Israel, "the least of nations." God chose a humble family in Nazareth. God chose those whom the world regards as unworthy to be worthy of his love. The Bible says that we don't take Jesus—*he takes us!* We don't give our lives to Christ—*he takes our lives!* The amazing story of the gospel is not that we chose God but that God, in Jesus Christ, wonder of wonders, chose us. That's why grace is called *"amazing* grace." We are always forgetting that the word *grace* means "gift."

Luther sat in his study and read these words, "For by grace you have been saved through faith . . . not because of works, lest any man should boast" (2:8-9). Those words thundered forth in his brain and shook the whole church. We are saved, not because of what we do or don't do, but because of what God has done.

Created for Good Works

But some may object that all this sounds too easy. If it is true that we are saved by grace, chosen, adopted, blessed by God, not because of what we have done but in spite of what we have done, then why not do anything we please? Why should people take all the trouble to be good if God is going to save them, forgive them, love them anyway?

That question is not explicitly raised in these passages from Ephesians, but it is at least implicit in what Paul says about the love and grace of God.

If the whole story of being a Christian were told in Ephesians 2:8-9, we might well assume that Christians are those who merely hear God's word of grace in Jesus Christ and then simply sit back and enjoy it. But Paul continues from his opening declaration, "By grace you have been saved . . . not because of works." Let me speak of the implications of that gracious fact.

We are saved by God, not for smug, conceited self-righteousness. In fact, God's grace undercuts any cause for self-righteousness or boasting, as Paul says. We are saved "for good works" (2:10).

We don't love the poor, feed the hungry, work for justice, pray, give *in order to* be loved by God. We do these good works *because* we are loved by God.

I think of it through this analogy. A young man is married to a young woman. He thinks to himself, I must work hard to earn her trust; I must be caring, faithful, and kind so that she will love me. But the longer the man is married, the more he learns that true marriage is not that way at all. He realizes that he is yoked to one who has given herself totally to him, without conditions, "for better for worse, for richer, for poorer." He is overwhelmed by her trust of him, deeply humbled that anyone should love him so much, believe in him so deeply.

He finds, to his surprise, that he *is* a caring, faithful, and kind person. Her love has transformed him. His fidelity to her is not some achievement of his, not something which he tries hard to accomplish. His fidelity is simply his grateful, spontaneous response to her love.

Do you see this as a parallel of our relationship to God? We are God's "workmanship" (2:10), people who have been recreated by God's love. We who have been the grateful recipients of his good works become those who *do* good works. Our lives and deeds are but a response, a sort of hymn of thanksgiving, to what God has done to us and for us.

We are able to love because he first loved us. We were once separated from him, strangers (2:12). "But now in Christ Jesus you who once were far off have been brought near" (2:13). So what can we do but live our lives accordingly?

Being a Christian is no easy matter. Much is demanded of us. But these good deeds are not done in order to get somewhere with God. They are done because we have already arrived. We give ourselves to his service, not in order to get God to do something for us, but in order to respond to what God has already done for us.

"For he is our peace" (2:14).

Helping Adults Become Involved—Harlan R. Waite

Preparing to Teach

Begin by reading Ephesians 1-2. Note especially the emphases on God's initiative in choosing us and on bringing diverse elements in the Christian fellowship into unity.

Study "As You Read the Scripture," "The Main Question," and "The Scripture and the Main Question."

Broaden your background by reading "The Letter of Paul to the Ephesians" in *The Interpreter's One-Volume Commentary on the Bible*, pages 834-44. Norman Perrin's *New Testament* (referred to in lesson 1) has a very helfpul discussion of Ephesians on pages 129-33. Locate a copy of Robert Frost's poem, "Mending Wall," and ask someone who reads well to prepare to share it with the class at the conclusion of the session.

Recruit someone to research and report on Ephesians, using the resources noted above. Someone else may be willing to work out an outline of the first two chapters and share it with the class.

Here is a possible outline for this session:

I. The early Christians seek unity.
   A. Authorship and situation
   B. The sense of the scripture
II. God chooses us.
   A. The heritage of faith
   B. A call to mission
   C. Sons and daughters, not beggars
III. We respond to God's call.
   A. Achiever motivations
   B. Self-justification
   C. Acknowledging what God has done
IV. We choose each other.
   A. The dividing wall
   B. The role of love

Introducing the Main Question

Share with the class Dr. Willimon's story about the dean of students' decision to "stop babying the students." Ask class members to think about dependence and independence in their human relationships and in their divine-human relationship. Take note of any verbal responses that are offered.

Developing the Lesson

I. The early Christians seek unity.

A. Authorship and situation

To help the class understand what the letter to the Ephesians says, call for the report on the authorship and situation of the book, as assigned. Then present an outline of the first two chapters.

B. The sense of the scripture

Discuss the sense of the scripture, noting the key ideas mentioned above in "Preparing to Teach." Emphasize the twin themes of God's initiative and the human response.

II. *God chooses us.*

A. *The heritage of faith*

Recall for the class the centuries-old conviction of the people in Israel that God had chosen them. As examples, note that Abraham is pictured not as seeking God but as receiving and responding to God's call. Then read to your class Deuteronomy 7:6-8, a poignant passage in which Moses reminds Israel that God has chosen them simply because he loves them. Early Christians inherited this basic conviction and considered themselves called by God as a new Israel.

B. *A call to mission*

Both Israel and the Christian community understood God's call as a summons to mission. God chose his people not out of favoritism, for he loves all people on earth; he chose them for responsible action in the world on his behalf, obeying his commandments and witnessing to his love.

C. *Sons and daughters, not beggars*

Suggest that there is a significant difference between God's calling us and our seeking God. When we seek God, it is usually to ask him for something for ourselves; whereas, when God seeks us he is asking us to do something for others. Our approach makes us beggars; God's initiative makes us sons and daughters.

In all of this discussion of God's initiative toward us, make use of Dr. Willimon's comments in "He Chose Us" and "Saved by Grace."

III. *We respond to God's call.*

A. *Achiever motivations*

Refer to Dr. Willimon's discussion of our achiever mentality. Is it not almost compulsive with us that we seek credit, or at least self-satisfaction, in what we ourselves have accomplished? Share Dr. Willimon's ideas with the class.

B. *Self-justification*

Self-justification seems to be a universal human failing. Recall for your class the story of the so-called "rich young ruler" in Mark 10:17-22; Matthew 19:16-22; and Luke 18:18-23. Matthew puts the question of the rich man this way: "Teacher, what good deed must I do, to have eternal life?" Is this not a question all of us ask?

C. *Acknowledging what God has done*

Biblical faith turns this around. First of all, we must acknowledge what God has done for us. Share with your class some of the thoughts Dr. Willimon has shared in the section "He Chose Us."

Suggest that there is a temptation to downplay good works in our emphasis on salvation by our faith in God's grace. First John declares, "Little children, let us not love in word or speech but in deed and in truth" (3:18). Even Paul, champion of the doctrine of justification by faith, has declared in Romans 2:6-13, "For he will render to every man according to his works. . . . For it is not the hearers of the law who are righteous before God, but the doers of the law who will be justified." Jesus made the same emphasis in his parable of the last judgment (Matthew 25:31-46). In the minds of both Jesus and Paul, however, good works were not undertaken for the sake of self-justification but rather as an expression of gratitude for God's gifts to us, a response of loving human beings to the love of God.

IV. *We choose each other.*

A. *The dividing wall*

Ephesians 2:14 declares that Jesus "has broken down the dividing wall of hositility." Jesus had earlier declared that the law and the prophets could be summed up in a twofold commandment: love God and love your neighbor. Point out that as the Christian community moved beyond the confines of Judaism to include Gentiles, it experienced a great deal of conflict. Hostilities between Jew and Gentile threatened to stand in the way of loving relationships.

Take a few moments to have the class list factors that divide the church today, such as denominationalism, the distinction between clergy and laity, the tensions between liberals and conservatives, the gap between professionals and volunteers.

B. The role of love

Ask the class to discuss the role of love in resolving these internal tensions. At the end of the discussion share this quatrain by Edwin Markham:

> He drew a circle that shut me out—
> Heretic, rebel, a thing to flout.
> But love and I had the wit to win:
> We drew a circle that took him in!

Helping Class Members Act

Call attention to the social distance which often separates human beings from one another, whether in the church or in the world at large. Ask the class to identify some of the dividing walls that need to be removed. Conclude by having someone read Robert Frost's poem "Mending Wall," a satire on the often expressed view that "good fences make good neighbors." It declares with Ephesians, "Something there is that doesn't love a wall."

Planning for Next Sunday

Preview next Sunday's lesson and raise this question: What personal qualities, talents, and relationships are required for the growth of the church? Ask your students to read Ephesians 4:1-16 as a basis for discussion. Make other assignments as suggested in next week's "Preparing to Teach."

LESSON 4   SEPTEMBER 22

How the Body of Christ Grows

Background Scripture: Ephesians 4:1-16

The Main Question—William H. Willimon

The parents had gone through a nightmare with their youngest son. Unlike their other two children, the boy never seemed to do anything right. He always did poorly in school; he was a perpetual discipline problem. They felt that they had tried everything with him but nothing seemed to work. Finally, they gave up on him. When the youth came home drunk one night, they threw him out of the house.

"You will never amount to anything," his father shouted at him from the doorway. "You are determined to be a bum and a bum is all that you'll ever be."

Now alone, without anyone to support him, the young man got a job as a janitor at an advertisizing agency. Each day he swept the floors and cleaned away the trash in the art department. He became fascinated by the work he saw going on there. He saw the artists making beautiful pictures with a few strokes of their pens. He started sketching faces in his spare time. When he went back to his room each night, he studied art books which he got at the city library.

He timidly asked one of the artists to look at his work. The artist told the boy, "You have real talent. You ought to develop this. Work at it. You could really be something with gifts like yours."

The boy did indeed develop his talent. He eventually went to art school and became a widely admired portrait painter. "And I had it in me all along," he said of his life, "but nobody had ever encouraged me to find it."

"Lead a life worthy of the calling to which you have been called," Paul tells the Ephesians (4:1). That's the great challenge for all of us—to mature into lives which are worthy of the great gifts God has given us, to have as much faith in ourselves as God has in us.

As You Read the Scripture—Robert E. Luccock

Ephesians 4:1-16. Verses 1-6 offer the indicative of what God has done and what gifts God has given to those who are called in the Lord. Verses 11-16 present the imperative of how Christians are to live if they maintain the unity of the Spirit.

Verse 1. The word *therefore* emphasizes that these are not arbitrary imperatives; they are inescapable consequences. *Because* God has done this, *therefore* we are to do thus and so. God has "called" ("destined," Ephesians 1:5) us to have a part in fulfilling the divine design.

Verse 2. The writer now mentions some of the qualities that make for unity. Some translators render the original Greek "humility" rather than "lowliness," and "gentleness" rather than "meekness." Goodspeed's translation reads "bearing with one another lovingly." "In love" (Greek: *agapē*) means loving others "in Christ" to the farthest limit, never revengeful or bitter, but seeking always their highest good.

Verse 3. People embraced by God's Holy Spirit find themselves in unity or harmony, including Jews and Gentiles as they live together. Peace comes as a consequence of that unity. Some have recognized the truth the other way: peace in Christ provides the unity. But one way or the other, we must understand it always as the unity of the Christian fellowship in Christ.

Verses 4-6. The writer expresses his faith in a sevenfold affirmation, beginning with the unity of the church, "one body," and moving to the declaration of "one God." Like Paul in his letter to the Colossians, the writer here leaves no possibility of believing in more than one God or being guided by more than one Spirit or accepting more than one church in Christ. (See also I Corinthians 12:12-13.)

Verse 7. One Spirit gives a variety of gifts.

Verse 11. Compare the gifts listed here with those in I Corinthains 12:28-30. "Prophets" and "apostles" were a unique, once-and-for-all group. "Evangelists" may have been persons who moved from place to place as missionaries, the next generation of apostolic ministry. "Pastors and teachers": very probably these offices were combined in one person. Moffatt renders the verse: "some to shepherd and teach." For these duties above all the gifts were given.

Verse 12. Without the comma after "saints" the sentence gives the true sense of the writer: the gifts are given "in order to fit his people for the work of service" (Goodspeed). The "saints" were the faithful members of the churches.

Verse 13. The reference "to mature manhood" is to the whole church, "until we all attain to the unity." Nowhere in these verses are we to think in any terms other than the building up of the church. This statement of purpose precludes any divisions or contentions between parties in the church.

Verse 14. The metaphor vividly suggests a rudderless ship driven about by variable winds. We must not be like children chasing after every new notion that blows into their minds, undisciplined by the truth in Christ.

Verse 15. The same thought that Paul writes in Philippians 2:5 is found here: Christ is the head of the church. The body grows only when everyone grows into the mind of Christ. And in so doing, the body grows into the unity found in the one mind—hence the at-one-ment with God.

Verse 16. Both Moffatt and Goodspeed find the emphasis on the "functioning of . . . the due activity of each part," enabling the body to grow to wholeness. It echoes I Corinthians 12:14-26.

Selected Scripture

King James Version

Revised Standard Version

Ephesians 4:1-7, 11-16

1 I therefore, the prisoner of the Lord, beseech you that ye walk worthy of the vocation wherewith ye are called,

2 With all lowliness and meekness, with longsuffering, forbearing one another in love;

3 Endeavouring to keep the unity of the Spirit in the bond of peace.

4 *There is* one body, and one Spirit, even as ye are called in one hope of your calling;

5 One Lord, one faith, one baptism,

6 One God and Father of all, who *is* above all, and through all, and in you all.

7 But unto every one of us is given grace according to the measure of the gift of Christ.

. . . .

11 And he gave some, apostles; and some, prophets; and some, evangelists; and some, pastors and teachers;

Ephesians 4:1-7, 11-16

1 I therefore, a prisoner for the Lord, beg you to lead a life worthy of the calling to which you have been called, 2 with all lowliness and meekness, with patience, forbearing one another in love, 3 eager to maintain the unity of the Spirit in the bond of peace. 4 There is one body and one Spirit, just as you were called to the one hope that belongs to your call, 5 one Lord, one faith, one baptism, 6 one God and Father of us all, who is above all and through all and in all. 7 But grace was given to each of us according to the measure of Christ's gift.

. . . .

11 And his gifts were that some should be apostles, some prophets, some evangelists, some pastors and teachers, 12 to equip the saints for

12 For the perfecting of the saints, for the work of the ministry, for the edifying of the body of Christ:

13 Till we all come in the unity of the faith, and of the knowledge of the Son of God, unto a perfect man, unto the measure of the stature of the fulness of Christ:

14 That we *henceforth* be no more children, tossed to and fro, and carried about with every wind of doctrine, by the sleight of men, *and* cunning craftiness, whereby they lie in wait to deceive;

15 But speaking the truth in love, may grow up into him in all things, which is the head, *even* Christ:

16 From whom the whole body fitly joined together and compacted by that which every joint supplieth, according to the effectual working in the measure of every part, maketh increase of the body unto the edifying of itself in love.

the work of ministry for building up the body of Christ, 13 until we all attain to the unity of the faith and of the knowledge of the Son of God, to mature manhood, to the measure of the stature of the fulness to Christ; 14 so that we may no longer be children, tossed to and fro and carried about with every wind of doctrine, by the cunning of men, by their craftiness in deceitful wiles. 15 Rather, speaking the truth in love, we are to grow up in every way into him who is the head, into Christ, 16 from whom the whole body, joined and knit together by every joint with which it is supplied, when each part is working properly, makes bodily growth and upbuilds itself in love.

Key Verse: **But speaking the truth in love, may grow up into him in all things, which is the head, *even* Christ. (Ephesians 4:15)**

Key Verse: **Speaking the truth in love, we are to grow up in every way into him who is the head, into Christ. (Ephesians 4:15)**

The Scripture and the Main Question—William H. Willimon

A Worthy Life

What do people hear when they come to church? What is the message they receive within the message? In your adult class this Sunday, what is the word they will take home with them?

I daresay that many people will leave church with a message that runs something like this. You must now go out and try hard to be good. Get your marriage together, raise perfect children, don't lose your temper, tithe, clean up your mind, improve your racial attitudes. The message in brief—shape up and start acting like somebody.

When a father sits his son down on the side of the bed one evening and urges his boy, "Make something out of yourself," the implication is that the boy isn't worth much as he is. Sometimes all the boy hears is, "I am disappointed in you. You are a failure as a person. Please try to be better."

Our lives thus become what the psychologists call self-fulfilling prophecies. That is, a person who is told that he or she is no good usually ends up acting that way. The prophecies of worthlessness are fulfilled in our worthless behavior.

There is another way for a father to talk to his son. That way is to sit down with the boy and tell him how you love him, how you believe in him more than he may believe in himself, how you have great hope for his life and great trust in his goodness.

That way is the better way. I believe it is the way of today's passages from Ephesians. When Paul tells the Christians at Ephesus to lead a worthy life, it sounds as if he is singing the same old, familiar song we sing so often—shape up and start acting like somebody. Paul's list of behavior in the fourth chapter of Ephesians sounds like a shopping list of all the good things we ought to do in order to become somebody: "meekness," "patience," "forbearing," "unity" (4:2-3). But note that Paul doesn't just say to them, "Lead a worthy life." Rather, he says, "Lead a life *worthy of the calling to which you have been called*" (4:1, italics added).

This statement precedes anything Paul says about the behavior of Christians. It is the foundation of his ethics. Christians are not simply a group of people who are trying hard to act like somebodies, they *are* somebodies because of the gracious call of God in Christ. Their good behavior is the result of their calling rather than the cause of their calling.

So Paul begins his discussion of our behavior by speaking first about God's behavior. Can you hear the difference between this way of looking at people and the way we often look at ourselves? How might the church need to change its teaching and preaching to convey what God has done for us before we talk about what we are to do for God?

The Gifts of God

But we haven't told the whole story if all we tell people is that they have been called by God to be his people. The Bible is clear that God calls us not simply to bless us, yet never to make us smug and complacent. God calls us because God wants to do some good thing for the world through us. We are called for responsibility.

In the Bible, people are not called in order that they may feel comfortable and complacent. People are called to do something. After speaking of the call of God in our baptism (4:4-7), Paul then lists the various responsibilities that arise out of that call. Some are prophets, some evangelists, some teachers, and so forth. Baptism is our ordination into ministry. It is the bestowal of the gift of responsibility.

In the early baptismal rites, the newly baptized person was given a new white robe as a sign of new life and a lighted candle with the words, "Let your light so shine, that people may see your good works and give glory to your Father in Heaven." These signs made clear that people were being called in baptism, not for self-centered salvation, but for salvation which made itself known through service.

It is tragic that the church later came to think of its pastors as the only ministers in the church. We lost sight of the baptismal obligations of all Christians.

But look carefully at our text today. Paul says that God has given the church the gift of various kinds of leadership—apostles, prophets, evangelists, pastors, and teachers (4:11). Why were these gifts given? As an honor for a few really good Christians? So that these "professional" ministers might do all the ministry for the church? No. Paul says these leaders are given "to equip the saints for the work of ministry, for building up the body of Christ" (4:12).

Pastors are to serve the people who serve the world. Leaders are given to the church, not to take over the ministry of the church, but to build up the church for its shared ministry. These pastors and teachers equip the rest of us for ministry; they help us grow up into all that our baptism calls us to be (4:13).

Growing Up in Christ

Do we put enough stress on growth in our faith? Ephesians indicates that we are called and gifted so that we might grow up into all that God wants us to be, "so that we may no longer be children" (4:14).

Unfortunately, sometimes we ask our pastors and teachers to forsake their calling and protect us from growth rather than enable us to grow. We want our teachers to simply assure us that whatever we have always thought was right is right. Don't ask us to stretch our minds or grow in our faith. We want our pastors to tell us what to believe, as a parent speaks to a child, rather than to let us think and act for ourselves. When pastors or teachers cooperate with our attempts to avoid growth, they not only do our spiritual lives a disservice but also forsake what Ephesians 4 says they are called to help us do—"to grow up in every way to him who is the head, into Christ" (4:15).

Helping Adults Become Involved—Harlan R. Waite

Preparing to Teach

Using the Good News Bible (Today's English Version, TEV), read Ephesians 4:1-16. Keep in mind the theme of the lesson, noting how quality of life, talent, and loving spirit contribute to the growth of the church. Consult "As You Read the Scripture," "The Main Question," and "The Scripture and the Main Question" for assistance in developing the theme.

Ask one or more persons to research the roles of different members of the early church: apostles, prophets, evangelists, pastors, and teachers. Articles on each of these may be found in The Interpreter's Dictionary of the Bible, ed. George Arthur Buttrick (Nashville: Abingdon Press, 1962). Ask someone else to be prepared to lead the class in a responsive reading of the Beatitudes in Matthew 5:3-10, using the Good News Bible. Make arrangements for each member of the class to have a copy of the Beatitudes.

Consider using this outline:

I. The letter offers instruction and encouragement.
  A. Qualities of Christian life
  B. Christian maturity
  C. The goal of church growth
II. True growth rests on character.
  A. The foundation of ministry
  B. Essential spiritual qualities
III. Effective ministry depends on the cultivation of talents.
  A. Varied gifts
  B. A shared ministry
IV. Maturity requires upbuilding in love.
  A. A sevenfold affirmation
  B. Receptiveness to truth
  C. A cooperative spirit

41

FIRST QUARTER

Introducing the Main Question

Dr. Willimon deals with the question of how the church grows by telling a story. A young man who had been rejected by his family found someone who believed in him. Personal encouragement released hidden possibilities in the young man, and he became a successful painter.

Similarly, early Christians were often ill-treated. There were those, however, who believed deeply in their hidden potential. They encouraged latent talents and saw them develop into effective tools for the building up of the Body of Christ.

Developing the Lesson

I. The letter offers instruction and encouragement.

A. Qualities of Christian life

The first task in interpreting and applying any passage of scripture is to hear what it says.

In the first place, and perhaps most basically, members of this struggling fellowship were reminded of the qualities of the Christian life which provide the foundation for growth (4:1-6).

B. Christian maturity

Second, they are reminded that every member of the Body of Christ is to be equipped for the work of ministry, cultivating gifts which they will use to build up the church.

C. The goal of church growth

This teaching section warns against immaturity and instability, and points to the ultimate goal of growth in the church. That goal includes the harmonious functioning of the church in the ministry to which God has called it.

II. True growth rests on character.

A. The foundation of ministry

The foundation of ministry consists of personal qualities. Refer the class to the list in 4:1-3—humility, gentleness, patience, forbearance in love, and eagerness in maintaining unity. Ask the class to compare this list with the Beatitudes in Matthew 5:3-10.

B. Essential spiritual qualities

The emergence of such qualities does not just happen. They may lie latent until drawn out by the encouragement and inspiration of other people. Use Dr. Willimon's story of father and son in his discussion of "A Worthy Life." Let the class discuss the question at the end of that section.

III. Effective ministry depends on the cultivation of talents.

A. Varied gifts

Essential as are spiritual qualities, they must be implemented by the cultivation of gifts bestowed upon Christians by God. Recall for the class Dr. Willimon's description of the early baptismal rites in his discussion of "The Gifts of God." Baptized Christians were responsible for making a public witness, and they did so by cultivating and using their various skills. Point out that "the saints" referred to in 4:12 are all the members of the church, not a special group of leaders. Everyone had a role in ministry. Some would be prophets, others apostles, others evangelists or pastors or teachers. If you made the assignments suggested in "Preparing to Teach," call for the reports on these functions performed by church members.

B. A shared ministry

Emphasize the fact that the early Christian church was a shared ministry. Refer to Dr. Willimon's view that the church has left the job of ministry to its

42

professional pastors. But everyone has a contribution to make in this shared ministry. God-given talents have been bestowed upon us as our equipment or tools.

IV. *Christian maturity requires upbuilding in love.*

A. *A sevenfold affirmation*

Commenting on 4:4-6, Dr. Luccock stresses the sevenfold affirmation of unity. Share this with the class. Point out that this affirmation should be in the forefront of our thinking as we learn to work together for the growth of the church.

B. *Receptiveness to truth*

The appeal is made in 4:15 to speak the truth in love. Dr. Willimon challenges us in the paragraphs entitled "Growing Up in Christ." He observes that we often put comfort above spiritual stimulation. Recall the story of Amos, who challenged Israel to "seek good . . . and establish justice" (Amos 5:14-15). He decried the hypocrisy of worship and called for true righteousness (Amos 5:21-24). Tragically, God's people at Bethel did not listen to this man who spoke the truth. They took his message as conspiracy and ran him out of town (Amos 7:10-13).

Tell the story of Maicaiah in I Kings 22. In short, four hundred prophets had approved Jehoshaphat's plan to go to war. Only Maicaiah disapproved. Jehoshaphat paid no attention to him, saying, "I hate him, for he never prophesies good concerning me, but evil" (I Kings 22:8). Many congregations want their leadership to tell them only what they like to hear. Ephesians challenges us at this point; it enjoins church leadership to speak the truth in love.

C. *A cooperative spirit*

If we are to have the unity described in the sevenfold affirmation and if we are to speak in the spirit of love, we need to put away our competitive impulses and learn to cooperate with one another. Such is the message of Ephesians 4:16. A reading of I Corinthians 13 reveals that such a cooperative spirit was not always present in the church. There was indeed discord in the church at Corinth, and we may judge by reading between the lines that some of it was expressed in the boasting of certain parties that their talents were more important than the talents of others. This led Paul to enjoin his Corinthian brothers and sisters to "desire the higher gifts" (I Corinthians 12:31). At that point he writes of love, characterizing it as not jealous, boastful, arrogant, rude, or irritable, but patient, kind, and forbearing. Only in this spirit can a church be built up to true maturity in Christ.

Helping Class Members Act

According to the suggestion made in "Preparing to Teach," call upon the person recruited to lead in a closing commitment, using the Beatitudes (Matthew 5:3-10) as they appear in the *Good News Bible*.

Planning for Next Sunday

Ask your class to read Ephesians 4:17–5:20 and prepare to discuss how the church lives in the world. Pose this question: How do Christians maintain their integrity as they deal with tensions between Christian and unchristian values and life-styles? Make assignments as suggested in next week's "Preparing to Teach."

Being Christ's Body in the World

Background Scripture: Ephesians 4:17–5:20

The Main Question—William H. Willimon

Do you believe that people can change—really change—their lives? Personality traits are deep, persistent, and not easily modified. "You can't teach an old dog new tricks," we say. We have seen people time and again think that they have turned over a new leaf, changed, converted, only to fall back into their old ways. "Our virtues are spontaneous; our vices are habitual," notes Emerson in his *Essays*.

"Put off your old nature," Paul urges the Ephesians. But who is able to do this? Change can be painful. As we are converted, something is gained, but something is also lost and the loss can be painful indeed. "Save me, Lord," prayed one of the saints, "but not yet." He knew.

In the early church, when someone was baptized, that person was led to the baptismal pool; disrobed; and stripped of all jewelry, fancy clothes, or other external signs through which the world honors people. Then the person was plunged under the waters as a sign of both cleansing of former uncleaness and drowning of the old self. Then the new Christian was given a white robe to symbolize putting off the old nature and putting on Christ (4:22-24).

In these dramatic acts the early church attempted to make clear that being a Christian involved a clear break with the old and a bold embrace of the new. Old habits, values, and goals must be washed away so that new life can take their place. How are such conversion and transformation possible? This is part of the concern behind today's passages. These passages affirm that Christians live in the world as changed persons.

As You Read the Scripture—Robert E. Luccock

The last half of Ephesians contains four exhortations. The first, chapter 4:1-16, entreats Christians to attend to church unity. Through unity the Body of Christ grows. The second injunction, Ephesians 4:17–5:20, urges those who follow Christ to do away with pagan ways. When believers put on "the new nature," the Body of Christ lives in the world.

Ephesians 4:17-24. These verses comprise the general appeal to put off the old nature and put on the new.

Verse 17. The word *Gentiles* here means the non-Christian Gentiles. Within the unity of the church this writer no longer sees the distinction between Jew and Gentile Christians (see Galatians 3:28).

Verses 17-19. Compare this description of the immorality of the pagan world with that in Romans 1:21-32. "Futility" says that the heathen pursue "empty things" (Barclay) that profit nothing to the soul or *life* (see Matthew 16:26 and I Corinthians 13:1-3). Such "darkness," "futility," being "alienated from the life of God" come from "ignorance," that is, from not knowing the truth that is in Jesus. This kind of ignorance God overlooks (Acts 17:30). When "light" (Ephesians 5:8-9) dawns, the darkness of ignorance is dispelled. But "hardness of heart" leads to alienation from God, which is sin. The Authorized Version reads "past feeling." The continued allowance of this sin finally makes the heart "callous" so that persons greedily give themselves up to every kind of "licentiousness," especially to immoral sexual behavior. "Given themselves up to" means giving in to vagrant desires of whatever kind take a person's fancy.

Verses 20-24. The metaphor "put off . . . put on" suggests clothing. New clothing demands new character. But character requires constant renewal as in II Corinthians 4:16: "our inner nature is being renewed every day." Paul uses the word *renewed* also in Romans 12:2.

Chapter 4:25–5:2. These verses deal with special entreaties.

Verse 25. "Members one of another" establishes that the admonitions in this passage refer to the Christians' life together in the church.

Verses 26-29. Four pairs of traits contrast Christian and heathen behavior: "Falsehood"—"truth," "sin"—"anger dispelled," "steal"—"honest work," and "evil talk"—"edifying" speech. Anger itself is not sin, although we are to avoid it if possible. But harboring anger gives "opportunity to the devil."

Verse 30. The promise made here repeats that given in Ephesians 1:13. When we first believed in Christ, we received the Holy Spirit as a seal or warranty of our inheritance until the time comes. This verse also reminds us that to violate the belongingness-to-each-other of the church in the ways listed is to grieve the Holy Spirit. The writer of I John 4:20 makes the same connection: love of God and love of one another.

Verses 31-32. These sins must be "put away": bitterness, wrath, anger, slander, malice. "Be kind, . . . tenderhearted, forgiving," walking in love, imitating God—such are the fitting traits for members of the Body of Christ if it is to live.

Chapter 5:2. The writer thinks not of the atonement here. "As Christ loved us and gave himself up for us" testifies instead that the kind of love Christians see in Christ they are to bear to one another.

Selected Scripture

King James Version	Revised Standard Version
Ephesians 4:17-32	*Ephesians 4:17-32*
17 This I say therefore, and testify in the Lord, that ye henceforth walk not as other Gentiles walk, in the vanity of their mind,	17 Now this I affirm and testify in the Lord, that you must no longer live as the Gentiles do, in the futility of their minds; 18 they are darkened in their understanding, alienated from the life of God because of the ignorance that is in them, due to their hardness of heart; 19 they have become callous and have given themselves up to licentiousness, greedy to practice every kind of uncleanness. 20 You did not so learn Christ!—21 assuming that you have heard about him and were taught in him, as the truth is in Jesus. 22 Put off your old nature which belongs to
18 Having the understanding darkened, being alienated from the life of God through the ignorance that is in them, because of the blindness of their heart:	
19 Who being past feeling have given themselves over unto lasciviousness, to work all uncleanness with greediness.	
20 But ye have not so learned Christ;	
21 If so be that ye have heard him,	

and have been taught by him, as the truth is in Jesus:

22 That ye put off concerning the former conversation the old man, which is corrupt according to the deceitful lusts;

23 And be renewed in the spirit of your mind;

24 And that ye put on the new man, which after God is created in righteousness and true holiness.

25 Wherefore putting away lying, speak every man truth with his neighbour: for we are members one of another.

26 Be ye angry, and sin not: let not the sun go down upon your wrath:

27 Neither give place to the devil.

28 Let him that stole steal no more: but rather let him labour, working with *his* hands the thing which is good, that he may have to give to him that needeth.

29 Let no corrupt communication proceed out of your mouth, but that which is good to the use of edifying, that it may minister grace unto the hearers.

30 And grieve not the holy Spirit of God, whereby ye are sealed unto the day of redemption.

31 Let all bitterness, and wrath, and anger, and clamour, and evil speaking, be put away from you, with all malice:

32 And be ye kind one to another, tenderhearted, forgiving one another, even as God for Christ's sake hath forgiven you.

Ephesians 5:1-2

1 Be ye therefore followers of God, as dear children;

2 And walk in love, as Christ also hath loved us, and hath given himself for us an offering and a sacrifice to God for a sweet-smelling savour.

Key Verse: And that ye put on the new man, which after God is created in righteousness and true holiness. (Ephesians 4:24)

your former manner of life and is corrupt through deceitful lusts, 23 and be renewed in the spirit of your minds, 24 and put on the new nature, created after the likeness of God in true righteousness and holiness.

25 Therefore, putting away falsehood, let every one speak the truth with his neighbor, for we are members one of another. 26 Be angry but do not sin; do not let the sun go down on your anger, 27 and give no opportunity to the devil. 28 Let the thief no longer steal, but rather let him labor, doing honest work with his hands, so that he may be able to give to those in need. 29 Let no evil talk come out of your mouths, but only such as is good for edifying, as fits the occasion, that it may impart grace to those who hear, 30 And do not grieve the Holy Spirit of God, in whom you were sealed for the day of redemption. 31 Let all bitterness and wrath and anger and clamor and slander be put away from you, with all malice, 32 and be kind to one another, tenderhearted, forgiving one another, as God in Christ forgave you.

Ephesians 5:1-2

1 Therefore be imitators of God, as beloved children. 2 And walk in love, as Christ loved us and gave himself up for us, a fragrant offering and sacrifice to God.

Key Verse: Put on the new nature, created after the likeness of God in true righteousness and holiness. (Ephesians 4:24)

The Scripture and the Main Question—William H. Willimon

Changing the Old for the New

A few years ago the best-selling book *Passages* documented the changes which adults go through in life. That book revealed adulthood as a time of growth, development, and transition. Previously, many of us thought of an adult as someone who had stopped growing. An adult was someone whose life was fixed, staid, and finished.

We now know, from studies in adult development, that adults go through many significant transitions in their lives.

The teenager is not alone in growing up. Adults in their forties, sixties, even eighties are facing new challenges and crises that can lead to growth. The majority of Americans, for instance, will have two or three different careers during their lives. A mobile society, in which the average American family moves every two to seven years, is a society in constant flux and development. When can it ever be said that any of us has fully "grown up"?

But, of course, when Paul tells the Ephesians to "put off your old nature which belongs to your former manner of life" (4:22), he is not just talking about the natural changes and transitions which we all go through in life. He is talking about the changes which we go through as Christians.

"No longer live as the Gentiles do," he says (4:17). The Ephesians once lived like that. But now they must see themselves as radically changed people in Christ. The word radical comes from the Latin *radix*, meaning "root." A radical is literally someone who is changed from the bottom up, uprooted from his or her old life, and planted somewhere else. Paul is talking about the Christian life in today's passages as a radical change of life—a change from top to bottom.

To be a Christian means to be uprooted, to be set at odds with the surrounding world. "Everybody else is doing it" is no alibi for a Christian because a Christian is clearly called to be different. Take a moment and think about your world—its values, customs, habits, and visions. In what ways does the Christian collide with the way of the world? If Paul were writing to us, telling us to take care not to "live as the Gentiles do," what would he tell us?

"Put off, put away" Paul tells the Ephesians. They still have some growing to do, some changing before they will be fully formed into this faith—and don't we all?

Renewed in the Spirit

Paul has a long list of behavior through which the Ephesians might show that they have indeed changed and put away their old selves (4:25-32). All of these changes are simply the life-style modificiations which are to be expected of those who recognize Jesus as the Lord of their lives.

The Christian faith, whatever it does to us, will not leave us as our same old selves. To be related to this Lord and his church is to risk reformation. This faith is that of Peter opening his eyes to the "clean" amidst what he had previously judged to be "unclean." It is Paul being turned around on the Damascus road, Augustine giving up his profligacy, Francis of Assisi forsaking his riches, Luther nailing his theses, Wesley descending to the level of open-air preaching, and the list goes on.

The changing and renewing by the Spirit goes on in your life and mine. How often have you come to church seeking only to be confirmed in your belief, to be assured that everything in your life was fixed, in place, neatly tied down; only to be thrown into disarray by a discussion in a church school class or by a reading from Scripture or by a sermon? This is the risk of keeping close to a living God whose Spirit is forever working in our lives.

As we said earlier, when the first Christians were baptized, they put on new white robes. Perhaps all this talk about the Ephesians' need to "put off your old nature" is related to baptism. Many scholars think that Ephesians may be a collection of post- or prebaptismal teaching. Whether this is so or not, baptism is a fitting symbol for the kind of life-death, birth, renewal, cleansing which characterize the Christian life all along the way. We may come to these waters singing "Just as I Am," but we will not stay just as we are once the Spirit is loose in our lives. This is a born-again type faith—a faith of change, fresh beginnings, and people who are forever putting away something which is old and less valuable for something far better.

Imitators of God

Being a Christian would be a relatively simple matter if all God expected of us was to believe this or that, feel a certain feeling in our hearts, or come to church regularly. But something more radical is expected of us.

"Be imitators of God," Paul tells the Ephesians. Can he be serious? How is it possible for common folk like us, in all our weakness, frailty, confusion, and humanity to be imitators of God almighty? This is too great a burden for us to bear. We can change, but can we change *this* much? "As beloved children," Paul says (5:1). In other words, Paul does not tell the Ephesians that they should struggle heroically to become who they are not. Rather, he urges them to become who they are, namely, beloved children of God. The changes, the conversion urged upon Christians are not to transform nobodies into somebodies but to enable the somebodies to live like somebodies.

No one ever told us it was easy to be a Christian. Here is a faith that does not suit our natural inclinations, a faith with so bold a vision that we can spend our whole lives growing to it. It is not easy to act like a Christian, to forgive, to watch our language, to care for others. But the difficulty comes in being children of God and, like all young children, trying to imitate our parent in all that we do.

In the Middle Ages, when a boy joined a monastic order he was given a monk's robe to wear. But monks' robes came in only one size, so he was given a robe whose cut was more suited to a grown man rather than to a boy of ten or twelve. The lad looked strange in this oversized garment. The robe was given to the boy in confidence that, given time, he would grow to the robe until one day it would fit. Someone would say, "Yes, that's you. It fits you fine."

So it is with us and the designation "Christian." This is far too much to lay upon our small lives at first. But the church baptizes us in confidence that, given time and the work of the Spirit, we shall grow to it until that day when it can be said of us, "Yes, that's you—*Christian.*"

Helping Adults Become Involved—Harlan R. Waite

Preparing to Teach

This is the last of the three-lesson unit which focused on the nature and functioning of the Body of Christ. Review the last two lessons and prepare to remind your students of the emphases of the series thus far.

Read Ephesians 4:17–5:20, noting the major units of thought. Select those ideas which will help your class understand the church and its relationship to the world. Fill out your understanding by consulting "As You Read the Scripture," "The Main Question," and "The Scripture and the Main Question."

Since a part of this week's lesson will deal with major changes which Christians experience in their spiritual growth, assign one or more of your students to read some reports on the conversion experiences of Paul, Augustine, Francis of Assisi, Martin Luther, and John Wesley.

A possible outline for this lesson is presented here:

I. Christians must be different.
 A. Do not live as Gentiles do.
 B. Put off your old nature.
II. Put on the new nature.
 A. Put the past behind.
 B. Change is painful.
 C. Live as beloved children.
III. Be imitators of God.
 A. Children imitate parents.
 B. Life-style must change.
 C. Walk in love.

Introducing the Main Question

Open your class with the central question: Can adults really change? Is adult conversion a valid experience? How is it possible? Let the answers come first from reports assigned in "Preparing to Teach."

You may wish to add the story of the conversion of the man who wrote *Ben-Hur*. Lew Wallace was an unbeliever. In a conversation about Jesus with a like-minded friend, he remarked that he thought the life of Jesus would make an interesting romance. His friend challenged him to do it, and he set about writing a novel. His research brought him face-to-face with Jesus, and the encounter changed his life. Conclude this introductory portion of your lesson by affirming that adults have in fact changed; therefore, any adult can change. Ephesians insists that they must.

Developing the Lesson

I. Christians must be different.

 A. Do not live as Gentiles do.

This is the theme of the portion of Ephesians which we study this week. Share with the class Dr. Luccock's introductory paragraph, in which he offers a general description of Ephesians 4. Note that its first major theme is "Do not live as the Gentiles do" (4:17).

 B. Put off your old nature.

Explain that since the author was writing to Gentile Christians, he was referring to non-Christian Gentiles; and he goes on to describe their life-style and their character. Gentile Christians must put behind them old ways in which they were brought up. In their place they must install Christian values and patterns of behavior.

II. Put on the new nature.

 A. Put the past behind.

The fact that the author of Ephesians found it necessary to advise putting the past behind is an implicit recognition that such an action is difficult.

Share with the class Dr. Willimon's quote from Emerson: "Our virtues are spontaneous; our vices are habitual."

B. *Change is painful.*

Moreover, change is painful. Observe that this was especially true for the Gentiles who became Christian. For the Jews (with their ethnic covenant with God), there was a certain continuity as the Christian church became a "new Israel"; but for Gentiles there was no such continuity. They found it necessary to make an almost complete break with the past.

C. *Live as beloved children.*

Point out that for the author of Ephesians, this means living as beloved children of God. Indeed, Christians were "born" into a new kind of fellowship and a new life-style. Share Dr. Willimon's description of baptism in "The Main Question" and in the section "Renewed in the Spirit" in "The Scripture and the Main Question. It was indeed a new birth.

Supplement the lesson by recalling for your class John 3:1-8, the famous passage regarding the new birth. Nicodemus was a religious leader who did not understand the full depth of spirituality. When Jesus told him that he must be "born anew," he misunderstood. English translations fail to communicate what was apparent in the original Greek. The word translated "anew" also means "from above." Jesus was really saying that one must be born "from above," not "again." This is John's way of expressing what the other gospels had said: "Except ye . . . become as little children. . . ."

Develop this theme of being children a bit more by pointing out that childhood is not only the consequence of birth but also the first stage of growing into maturity. Share with the class Dr. Willimon's beautiful illustration of the young monk whose robe was too large for him. He was expected to wear it until it fit him!

III. *Be imitators of God.*

A. *Children imitate parents.*

The image of the child persists. Ephesians 5:1 reads, "Therefore be imitators of God, as beloved children." Develop the theme touched upon briefly by Dr. Willimon that all young children try to imitate their parents. Suggest that if the new birth is real, imitating the Divine Parent comes very naturally. Since Jesus is the revealer of God's will, to imitate Jesus is to imitate God.

B. *Life-style must change.*

Leaving the essence of this imitation of God to the last, the writer of Ephesians first suggests that life-style must change. Note in Ephesians 4:25—5:20 how many specific modes of conduct are mentioned. Ask your class members to read the passage and identify them. As they are identified, discuss how each of these may be found in our conduct today, both within and without the church. Is there not much of the old which we yet have to put away?

John Homer Miller tells a story in his *Why We Act That Way* about a young woman who had been confirmed in the church. Someone asked her how she knew that she was really a Christian. Her answer was this: "Now I do not sweep the dirt under the rugs." She validated her inner experience by changing her behavior.

C. *Walk in love.*

Note that the climax of this appeal for a change of life-style comes in Ephesians 5:2. Having enjoined his readers to "be imitators of God, as beloved children," the author states the essence of this imperative: "Walk in love, as Christ loved us and gave himself up for us, a fragrant offering and sacrifice to God."

Helping Class Members Act

To bring this lesson into focus and provide a base for some responsive action, answer the question posed by Dr. Willimon. Consider the values and life-styles of our society and discuss the ways in which they conflict with the Christian way of life. To paraphrase Dr. Willimon, if the author of Ephesians were writing to us, telling us to take care not to "live as the Americans do," what would he tell us?

Planning for Next Sunday

Assign I Corinthians 1:10–4:21 as the basic reading for the next session. Some may be willing to read the entire letter to identify tensions and conflicts not reported in the first four chapters. Recruit reporters and a panel of three students to carry out assignments explained in next week's "Preparing to Teach."

UNIT III: INTERNAL PROBLEMS IN THE BODY OF CHRIST

Horace R. Weaver

FOUR LESSONS   **OCTOBER 6–27**

The theme of this unit, "Internal Problems in the Body of Christ," is taken from Paul's letters to the Corinthians. Corinthian letters are most valuable to Christians because first, they throw light on the character and mind of the apostle Paul, and second, they give living pictures of the practical problems in the early life of the Christian church of the first century.

Paul apparently chose to write to outstanding cities of the Roman Empire to whose countries he would carry his message. These cities included Ephesus, Athens, Antioch, and Corinth. Corinth was located just west of the famous acropolis dedicated to fertility religion (where approximately one thousand "holy women," who were dedicated to Aphrodite, lived); and near the famous arena where Romans held their annual sport contests.

First and Second Corinthians are formed from four of Paul's letters to Christians living in Corinth. In them Paul is concerned with various doubts and suspicions which created conflict among the members of this early church. Paul also writes about several doctrinal and ethical problems that could split their fellowship.

Four sessions relate directly to such concerns as noted above. "A Divided Church," October 6, illustrates the division which came when early Christians boasted as to who their (obvious "superior") minister was when they were converted. "Immorality Weakens the Body of Christ," October 3, almost duplicates the list of sins modern churchpeople must deal with in our fellowship; the position Paul takes is that there are some things Christians cannot do, and some things they must do if they are to be Christlike. "The Church in Conflict with Culture," October 20, may be summarized in the sentence, "Look unto the Rock from which you were hewn." "Who Are

51

True Church Leaders?" October 27, is answered by describing those whose life-style is such that "the life of Jesus may be manifested in our mortal flesh" (II Corinthians 4:11).

LESSON 6   OCTOBER 6

A Divided Church

Background Scripture: I Corinthians 1:10–4:21

The Main Question—William H. Willimon

There is probably much truth to the charge that if the church is ever destroyed, it will fall from forces within rather than forces without. Our internal life is often our most damaging critic in the world's eyes.

Congregations become notorious for their petty squabbles. Denominations split apart over minute details of doctrine. I remember standing in the middle of a small midwestern town while one of its citizens pointed out the various churches to me.

"That one on the corner was the first church. That one a block to the right of it was formed a few years later when some of the folk got mad at something the preacher said. The church to your left was organized by the people who were opposed to the new hymnal back in the 1930s. Outside of town you'll find the last breakaway church which recently organized itself. What they got upset over, I can't remember. Probably they can't either."

What sort of witness does our divisiveness present to the rest of the world? What does it do to *us*?

If it is any consolation, today's lesson reminds us that squabbles and disputes are not new for the church. From the beginning, the church has been plagued by divisions between Christians who see things differently. One reason that the letters of Paul talk so much about the value of Christian unity is that there was so little of it in the first churches!

Recently, we made a typographical error in our church's Sunday bulletin and switched some letters. The error transformed our UNITED METHODIST CHURCH into THE UNTIED METHODIST CHURCH. We smiled, but we also knew there is often more than a kernel of truth in the designation of the churches as "untied."

Think about your church and the divisions there between rich and poor, old and young, educated and uneducated, committed and uncommitted— the possibilities for division are limitless.

What are the possibilities for unity? We will be asking that question in today's lesson.

As You Read the Scripture—Robert E. Luccock

Evidence found within First and Second Corinthians leads to the strong probability that Paul wrote at least four letters to the church at Corinth. I Corinthians 5:9 speaks of an earlier letter about associating with immoral persons. (We may have at least a portion of that letter in II Corinthians

6:14–7:1.) The Corinthians responded to Paul's earlier letter (see I Corinthians 7:1), seeking his counsel on troublesome matters that had arisen since he left Corinth for Ephesus. Messengers must also have brought word of these troubles, whereupon the Apostle dispatched what we now call First Corinthians. (Two other letters were to follow. Of these we shall speak in lesson 9.)

I Corinthians 1:10. Paul is about to speak imperatively to the Corinthians, with stern judgment on some of the things they were doing. He takes great care to appeal, at the very beginning, by the authority of Christ. This is not his own counsel, but admonition from the Lord! "No dissension": the word *dissension* suggests rifts or fissures, the opening up or splitting apart of the unity the church should know in Christ.

Verse 11. "Chloe's people" were possibly slaves of a woman of Corinth. They brought the distressing news of unhappy divisions in the church.

First Corinthians sets forth a number of matters over which the church could well have quarreled: what Christians should do with their freedom (6:12); whether Christians should marry in view of their belief in an early end to the world (7:36-38); how slaves are to behave (7:17-24); food laws (10:27-29); speaking in ecstatic tongues (14:6-12); the resurrection (chapter 15). It may be that some dissension over these matters cut across the "party lines" drawn up around different teachers.

Verse 12. Paul, Apollos, Cephas—around these personalities apparently divisions had gathered. Not surprisingly, one faction rallied around the person and teaching of Paul himself. Apollos was a Hellenistic Jewish Christian from Alexandria. He was no doubt an eloquent teacher, for which the Alexandrian school was noted, and may have visited Corinth following Paul's mission there. Cephas (Simon Peter) may also have visited Corinth. Or his exalted position in the Jerusalem church may have inspired a partisan loyalty. Was there really a "Christ party"? It hardly seems likely. This could be the work of a later editor. Or Paul could be saying to the Christians, "I do not belong to any of these parties. I belong to Christ."

Verse 13. Paul's provocative questions measure the depth of his distress. "Is Christ divided? Was Paul crucified for you?" To put it thus makes it sound like blasphemy. By these questions Paul reminds the Corinthian partisans that their faith is founded in Christ. They cannot appeal to others as the source of their faith.

Verses 14-15. Crispus was the ruler of the Corinthian synagogue (Acts 18:8). Gaius, a Greek, was Paul's host in Corinth (Romans 16:23). One is startled to learn that Paul baptized so few when so many were being converted to the Christian faith. From this we should not infer that Paul deprecated baptism. Preaching and organization were his main concerns. Others followed Paul's work with baptizing. Notice that baptism was "in the name of Christ," that is, the name, the power and authority that is above every name (Ephesians 1:21). If there is *one* baptism (Ephesians 4:5), the church allows no place for factions making rival claims of authority.

Selected Scripture

King James Version	Revised Standard Version
I Corinthians 1:10-15	*I Corinthians 1:10-15*
10 Now I beseech you, brethren, by the name of our Lord Jesus	10 I appeal to you, brethren, by the name of our Lord Jesus Christ,

53

Christ, that ye all speak the same thing, and *that* there be no divisions among you; but *that* ye be perfectly joined together in the same mind and in the same judgement.

11 For it hath been declared unto me of you, my brethren, by them *which are of the house of* Chlō´-ē, that there are contentions among you.

12 Now this I say, that every one of you saith, I am of Paul; and I of Ă-pŏl´-lŏs; and I of Çē´-phăs; and I of Christ.

13 Is Christ divided? was Paul crucified for you? or were ye baptized in the name of Paul?

14 I thank God that I baptized none of you, but Crispus and Gâı´-ŭs;

15 Lest any should say that I had baptized in mine own name.

I Corinthians 3:5-15

5 Who then is Paul, and who *is* Ă-pŏl´-lŏs, but ministers by whom ye believed, even as the Lord gave to every man?

6 I have planted, Ă-pŏl´-lŏs watered; but God gave the increase.

7 So then neither is he that planteth any thing, neither he that watereth; but God that giveth the increase.

8 Now he that planteth and he that watereth are one: and every man shall receive his own reward according to his own labour.

9 For we are labourers together with God: ye are God's husbandry, *ye are* God's building.

10 According to the grace of God which is given unto me, as a wise masterbuilder, I have laid the foundation, and another buildeth thereon. But let every man take heed how he buildeth thereupon.

11 For other foundation can no man lay than that is laid, which is Jesus Christ.

12 Now if any man build upon this foundation gold, silver, precious stones, wood, hay, stubble;

that all of you agree and that there be no dissensions among you, but that you be united in the same mind and the same judgment. 11 For it has been reported to me by Chlo´e's people that there is quarreling among you, my brethren. 12 What I mean is that each one of you says, "I belong to Paul," or "I belong to Apol´los," or "I belong to Cephas," or "I belong to Christ." 13 Is Christ divided? Was Paul crucified for you? Or were you baptized in the name of Paul? 14 I am thankful that I baptized none of you except Crispus and Ga´ius; 15 lest any one should say that you were baptized in my name.

I Corinthians 3:5-15

5 What then is Apol´los? What is Paul? Servants through whom you believed, as the Lord assigned to each. 6 I planted, Apol´los watered, but God gave the growth. 7 So neither he who plants nor he who waters is anything, but only God who gives the growth. 8 He who plants and he who waters are equal, and each shall receive his wages according to his labor. 9 For we are God's fellow workers; you are God's field, God's building.

10 According to the grace of God given to me, like a skilled master builder I laid a foundation, and another man is building upon it. Let each man take care how he builds upon it. 11 For no other foundation can any one lay than that which is laid, which is Jesus Christ. 12 Now if any one builds on the foundation with gold, silver, precious stones, wood, hay, straw—13 each man's work will become manifest; for the

13 Every man's work shall be made manifest: for the day shall declare it, because it shall be revealed by fire; and the fire shall try every man's work of what sort it is.

14 If any man's work abide which he hath built thereupon, he shall receive a reward.

15 If any man's work shall be burned, he shall suffer loss: but he himself shall be saved; yet so as by fire.

Key Verse: For other foundation can no man lay than that is laid, which is Jesus Christ. (I Corinthians 3:11)

Day will disclose it, because it will be revealed with fire, and the fire will test what sort of work each one has done. 14 If the work which any man has built on the foundation survives, he will receive a reward. 15 If any man's work is burned up, he will suffer loss, though he himself will be saved, but only as through fire.

Key Verse: No other foundation can anyone lay than that which is laid, which is Jesus Christ. (I Corinthians 3:11)

The Scripture and Main Question—William H. Willimon

Is Christ Divided?

It is difficult for us to know with precision the sources of Corinthians' problems. Evidently, the Corinthian church had broken up into competing factors, possibly on the basis of which missionary had converted them to the faith (1:10-13). "I belong to Paul," boasted some. "I belong to Apollos" or "I belong to Cephas," said others (1:12).

We can understand some of this. It would be natural for a person to feel a special affection and loyalty to the teacher who first led him or her to Christ. We know from our own experience that pastors often win a fiercely loyal personal group within a church. Whenever a pastor leaves a church, there is a crisis for those members who joined the church during that pastor's time there. They may not relate as easily to the new pastor. All of us relate better to some people than to others. Did these people see themselves joining a pastor or joining a church? Some of these same dynamics must have been at work in Corinth. "I belong to Cephas"; "I belong to Apollos."

It is to Paul's credit that he does not allow himself to be drawn into this personality contest. Surely he must have been tempted to say, "Look here, I have had better training than Apollos," or "Can Cephas claim anything as dramatic as my experience on the Damascus road?"

Paul doesn't approach the Corinthian problem this way, for to do so would only confirm the Corinthians' misunderstanding that the church was some sort of personality cult. He confronts their divisiveness by asking, "Is Christ divided? Was Paul crucified for you? Or were you baptized in the name of Paul?" (1:13).

The Apostle counters their factionalism by reminding them of who called them, saved them, formed them into the church—Christ himself.

Christ is not divided, so neither are the followers of Christ who make up his Body, the church. We belong to Christ, not to some other person. Paul gives thanks that he baptized no one at Corinth lest some misguided person should be giving him, rather than Christ, credit for the faith (1:14-16). To do so would, in Paul's words, empty the cross of its power (1:17).

When I began the pastoral ministry, an older pastor told me, "If you leave a church and everything falls apart, then you have been building the church around yourself, not Christ."

I believe that Paul would agree with that observation.

Some Plant That Others May Harvest

One of the most difficult aspects of being a pastor is that you don't often see clearcut, discernible results of your work. It would be good to know how your words or deeds have affected people's lives. It would be good to see your labors in the church confirmed by increased membership, more dedication, new converts. Unfortunately for our pastoral egos, it does not often work that way.

Anyone who works with people has this same problem. The elementary school teacher labors long and hard to teach young children. He or she may often wonder what impact is being made on their young lives, what will become of these children. But such results may take years—even a lifetime—to see.

So we must be content to share the results with others, to labor in the faith that our efforts are not in vain.

Paul takes delight that he does not deserve all the credit for the Corinthians' faith. He and Apollos were mere servants for God's work (3:5). "I planted," says Paul, "Apollos watered, but God gave the growth" (3:6).

Many in your class can probably confirm this process in the growth of their own faith—we are indebted to many servants of God for helping us come to where we are today—children's church school teachers of long ago, pastors, scout leaders, coaches, countless individuals who sowed seeds of faith in our lives.

Perhaps our problem is that we all want to be *harvesters* rather than planters. We want to reap tangible results for our labors, take credit for the fruit that ripens.

Paul is willing to sow so that others can reap. Such a willingness takes patience and humility, yes. But it also takes faith that we do not labor in vain. The fruit is God's to give. We serve, whether we get to enjoy the fruit or not.

The last church I served enjoyed phenomenal growth while I was there—one hundred and fifty members out of a small community. Many gave me credit for the growth. But I knew better. A dedicated, retired pastor had labored long and hard to prepare the soil, plant, and water so that I might come along and reap. As Paul says, God gave the growth.

The simple acknowledgment that the growth and survival of the church are not the achievements of men and women but are gifts from God might go a long way toward the eradication of some of the personality conflicts and factionalism in the church. "For we are God's fellow workers" (3:9).

The Sure Foundation

Paul then switches images from that of a farmer sowing a field to a builder constructing a house. The foundation of this house which we build is Christ (3:11). "Let each man take care how he builds upon it," warns Paul (3:10). This is a rich symbol for us to use in thinking about the church.

How do we build our churches? On the popularity and appeal of a preacher? Upon the common opinions and prejudices of the members? By simply grouping together people from the same race, same socio-economic situation?

If this is how we build, then it's little wonder that churches fall to pieces—popularity is a fragile commodity. Opinions change, and people who have nothing better to unite them than the color of their skin or the level of their income have too little to keep them together through the tough challenges of life.

So we should build upon a sure foundation.

Helping Adults Become Involved—Harlan R. Waite

Preparing to Teach

The divisions in the church at Corinth as described in I Corinthians 1:10–4:21 have a contemporary ring. As you read, try to relate the problems Paul found at Corinth to the subtle and not-so-subtle divisions within our church today. If you are able to read the entire book, you will find additional points of division. Some of these will be discussed in the next three lessons.

For background, consult "As You Read the Scripture," "The Main Question," and "The Scripture and the Main Question." Refer to the first lesson of this quarter for references to studies that offer a very clear analysis of Paul's letters to the Corinthians.

Ask some of your students to share the leadership of this lesson. Ask for reports on Paul, Apollos, Cephas, and Corinth. Materials for these reports may be found in *The Interpreter's Dictionary of the Bible*.

Select a panel of three persons to help you introduce the main question. Suggest that these three meet together to plan how they will deal with the question as stated below.

Consider this proposal of an outline for your guidance in organizing the lesson:

   I. Paul deals with tensions between Christians.
     A. The Corinthian correspondence
     B. The enthusiasts
     C. Paul's nonpartisan strategy
  II. Divisiveness is found in churches today.
     A. An old and recurring problem
     B. Evidences
     C. Effect
 III. We seek solutions to divisiveness.
     A. Unproductive methods
     B. Productive approaches

Introducing the Main Question

This week's lesson focuses around this question: How can we identify and deal with divisions within the church? Open your session with the panel discussion. At the conclusion of the presentation, continue by looking at divisions in the church at Corinth and using Paul's letter as a mirror to reflect divisions which may be in our churches today.

Developing the Lesson

I. Paul deals with tension between Christians.

A. The Corinthian correspondence

Observe that most of the subject matter of Paul's letters to the church at Corinth deals with conflict. Various forms of conflict will be discussed in the next few weeks. Today's lesson focuses on factionalism which grew out of personal loyalties to different Christian leaders. Paul, "speaking the truth in love" (Ephesians 4:15), attacked the problems directly. He singled out the quarreling groups as being the followers of Cephas (Peter), Apollos, and himself. Without mincing words, he declared such petty loyalties as unworthy of Christians.

B. The enthusiasts

Explain to the class that Apollos and Cephas were simply representative of a larger group of preachers who had won the hearts of the Corinthians. Without naming them, Paul was referring to what we call the "enthusiasts" (enthusiasm is literally "in-God-ism"). That he had them in mind is evident from his use of certain phrases, of which the following are a few examples: "preach . . . with eloquent wisdom" (1:17), "cleverness of the clever" (1:19), "lofty words" (2:1), "peddlers of God's word" (II Corinthians 2:17), "to practice cunning or to tamper with God's word" (II Corinthians 4:2), and "these superlative apostles" (II Corinthians). These phrases, many of them set as contrast to the way Paul worked, describe the "enthusiasts," who considered themselves spiritually above Paul and the other Christians.

C. Paul's nonpartisan strategy

Direct the attention of the class to I Corinthians 3:5-11. Note Paul's nonpartisan strategy.

II. Divisiveness is found in churches today.

A. An old and recurring problem

In his comments on "The Main Question," Dr. Willimon has cited some instances of divisiveness in churches of the twentieth century. Share with the class the typographical error which described his church as "The Untied Methodist Church." Sometimes an inadvertent error calls attention to a real fault.

B. Evidences

Ask the class to list evidences of division in your church, or churches with which they are acquainted. The personal loyalties to present or past ministers, rival grouping around certain lay leaders, claiming priority for one program over against another, petty reactions to peculiar behavior, the age gap—these and many others may well be mentioned as frustrating the Christian ideal of unity. List them on the chalkboard.

C. Effect

Observe that differences are not necessarily divisive. Since our focus, however, in this lesson is on divisive differences, continue the class discussion by asking what effect the divisive spirit has on church life. In "The Main Question," Dr. Willimon asks, "What sort of witness does our divisiveness present to the rest of the world? What does it do to us?" Let the class speak to both points. Close this discussion by evaluating Dr. Willimon's statement at the beginning of "The Main Question": "If the church is ever destroyed, it will fall from forces within rather than forces without."

III. We seek solutions to our divisiveness.

A. Unproductive methods

Point out that among the many solutions we undertake, some are productive; others are unproductive. In his discussion of "The Sure Foundation," Dr. Willimon suggests some superficial approaches to holding the church together. One is the appeal of a strong preacher, who through his popularity can win the loyalty of a congregation. Another is playing upon the common opinions and prejudices that may prevail in the parish.

Beyond these, racial and socio-economic groupings have been used to preserve harmony. Share with the class Dr. Willimon's response to these approaches.

B. *Productive approaches*

Turning to productive approaches, let the class discuss how Paul approached the problem of divisiveness in his own church. Among the answers you may find the following: (1) Paul made no attempt to hide discord but brought it out into the open, (2) he put factional loyalties in their proper perspective by emphasizing the overriding loyalty of Christians to Christ, (3) he made a conscious effort to downplay personal ego as a unifying force, (4) he shared the credit with his colleages in ministry, (5) he accepted the servant role in imitation of Christ and urged his people to do the same, and (6) he gave God the credit for the harvest of which human beings had been planters and waterers.

Helping Class Members Act

Refer the class to the last two paragraphs in Dr. Willimon's discussion of "The Main Question." Put the problem as he had stated it, using his question as the first step toward action. Add this final question: What are we going to do about it? Let the class decide on one or two actions which may be taken to eliminate divisions in your congregation.

Planning for Next Sunday

Announce the theme for next Sunday and request that your students read I Corinthians 5–6. Ask them to think about the central question as defined in "The Main Question" and "Preparing to Teach" for next week.

LESSON 7   OCTOBER 13

Immorality Weakens the Body of Christ

Background Scripture: I Corinthians 5–6

The Main Question—William H. Willimon

"It is actually reported that there is immorality among you," Paul writes the Corinthians (5:1).

What's this? Sin in the *church?* How can that be? Well, we were not born yesterday. We know the church. Few of us active church members bear delusions about the purity and perfection of the church. But it is a bit disturbing to learn that the first Christians were infected with church members whose immoral life-styles were "of a kind that is not found even among pagans" (5:1). Even from the first, the church was threatened by immoral practices which weakened the body.

We live in a rather permissive, live-and-let-live age. Many think it old-fashioned to be concerned about people's personal behavior. What we do in the privacy of our own bedrooms is our business and no one else's. Who cares as long as no one gets hurt?

We have lost confidence in our values. Old standards of right and wrong don't seem as clear as they once did. Our world is so new and unusual that we must invent our rules as we go. We are on our own. Old values can't be trusted, so we say.

Besides, we Christians don't want to appear a bunch of prudes, killjoys. The teenager's excuse, "Everyone else is doing it," has become a slogan of our society. "Everyone" cheats on income tax, experiments with drugs, drinks and drives, takes marriage vows loosely, disobeys stop signs, and on and on.

Often our goal as contemporary Christians is to blend in to the surrounding society lest we appear prudish, out of step, and backward. This is the "real" world; one must adjust to the status quo rather than resist it. Nothing is really "good" or "bad"—it all depends on the particular situation and how I feel about it at the moment.

These and other contemporary ethical notions are challenged in today's lesson.

As You Read the Scripture—Robert E. Luccock

In Paul's time Corinth may have had a population of 600,000, comparable to Boston or Washington today. It was a great commercial center, second only to Athens, at the east-west crossroads of the Mediterranean world. A thousand priestesses attached themselves to the temple of Aphrodite; they plied their trade as prostitutes in the city. Degeneracy of every imaginable form flourished in Corinth; an ancient proverb had it that "not for every man is the voyage to Corinth." "To live like a Corinthian" was slang for debauchery.

Is it any wonder that Paul's letter deals explicitly with the immorality which the Corinthian Christians saw all around them? Chapters 5 through 7 deal with matters of sex and property, of marriage and celibacy. Chapter 6:9-10 speaks of the moral standards of the kingdom of God and the requirement of chastity among church members.

Verses 9-10. Paul lists nine vices of the degenerate life, loosely tolerated in that fleshpot, but unacceptable for persons hoping to enter the kingdom of God. Among them notice the gross sins of felonious behavior—thieving and robbery; the sins of disposition—greed and mockery; the sins of sensual indulgence—drunkenness, adultery, and homosexual practice. Homosexuality was common everywhere in the Greco-Roman world, and accepted nearly everywhere, especially the use of young boys by men for erotic purposes. Paul will not permit any of it as behavior becoming to Christians.

Verse 11. Apparently some Corinthian Christians had once practiced these vices. Now that they have been washed (see Romans 6:3-6 on baptism) and brought close to Christ and are at peace with what Christ wants them to be, such sins no longer have power over them.

Verses 12-13. The libertines in Corinth would argue that they are no longer under the law; Christ has set them free. They may have heard Paul say this (see Galatians 5:1). But Paul answers to higher criteria: Are all things *helpful?* Do some things make us *slaves,* either to passion or gluttony? Even though the resurrected body will be different from this present body (I Corinthians 15:35-38), Paul still says that immoral indulgence of this body is a sin against the Lord; what we do in our bodies now affects the state of our souls both now and hereafter.

Verse 14. Paul here anchors his whole argument against immorality in the conviction that God who raised Jesus from the dead will also raise those whose bodies are joined with the Lord. This gives to Paul's exhortation a force far greater than a moralistic diatribe. His imperatives have life-and-death consequences eternally.

Verse 16. The quotation comes from Genesis 4:24 where "the two" are man and wife, not a parallel to joining bodies in prostitution.

Verse 18. "Every other sin . . . is outside the body." Paul's own words contradict that assertion (Romans 1:29-31; see also Jesus in Matthew 5:28). Paul wants the Corinthians to understand that immorality against one's own body is no less sinful than offense against another person.

Verses 19-20. These verses declare that the body is a temple of the Holy Spirit. We are joined in body to the Lord. Our bodies are "members of Christ." Therefore when a man joins his body to a prostitute it is not only his body or the body of the prostitute which he defiles; it is Christ's body as well. It is as though he took Christ to the brothel. What could be more profane than that! To illicit sexual indulgence is joined the sin of blasphemy. If what we do with our bodies is not compatible with Christ, it is immoral.

Selected Scripture

King James Version

Revised Standard Version

I Corinthians 6:9-20

9 Know ye not that the unrighteous shall not inherit the kingdom of God? Be not deceived: neither fornicators, nor idolaters, nor adulterers, nor effeminate, nor abusers of themselves with mankind,

10 Nor thieves, nor covetous, nor drunkards, nor revilers, nor extortioners, shall inherit the kingdom of God.

11 And such were some of you: but ye are washed, but ye are sanctified, but ye are justified in the name of the Lord Jesus, and by the Spirit of our God.

12 All things are lawful unto me, but all things are not expedient: all things are lawful for me, but I will not be brought under the power of any.

13 Meats for the belly, and the belly for meats: but God shall destroy both it and them. Now the body *is* not for fornication, but for the Lord; and the Lord for the body.

14 And God hath both raised up the Lord, and will also raise up us by his own power.

I Corinthians 6:9-20

9 Do you not know that the unrighteous will not inherit the kingdom of God? Do not be deceived; neither the immoral, nor idolaters, nor adulterers, nor sexual perverts, 10 nor thieves, nor the greedy, nor drunkards, nor revilers, nor robbers will inherit the kingdom of God. 11 And such were some of you. But you were washed, you were sanctified, you were justified in the name of the Lord Jesus Christ and in the Spirit of our God.

12 "All things are lawful for me," but not all things are helpful. "All things are lawful for me," but I will not be enslaved by anything. 13 "Food is meant for the stomach and the stomach for food"—and God will destroy both one and the other. The body is not meant for immorality, but for the Lord, and the Lord for the body. 14 And God raised the Lord and will also raise us up by his power. 15 Do you not know that your bodies are members of Christ?

15 Know ye not that your bodies are the members of Christ? shall I then take the members of Christ, and make *them* the members of an harlot? God forbid.

16 What? know ye not that he which is joined to an harlot is one body? for two, saith he, shall be one flesh.

17 But he that is joined unto the Lord is one spirit.

18 Flee fornication. Every sin that a man doeth is without the body; but he that committeth fornication sinneth against his own body.

19 What? know ye not that your body is the temple of the Holy Ghost *which is* in you, which ye have of God, and ye are not your own?

20 For ye are bought with a price: therefore glorify God in your body, and in your spirit, which are God's.

Shall I therefore take the members of Christ and make them members of a prostitute? Never! 16 Do you not know that he who joins himself to a prostitute becomes one body with her? For, as it is written, "The two shall become one flesh." 17 But he who is united to the Lord becomes one spirit with him. 18 Shun immorality. Every other sin which a man commits is outside the body; but the immoral man sins against his own body. 19 Do you not know that your body is a temple of the Holy Spirit within you, which you have from God? You are not your own; 20 you were brought with a price. So glorify God in your body.

Key Verse: But ye are washed, but ye are sanctified, but ye are justified in the name of the Lord Jesus, and by the Spirit of our God. (I Corinthians 6:11)

Key Verse: You were washed, you were sanctified, you were justified in the name of the Lord Jesus Christ and in the Spirit of our God. (I Corinthians 6:11)

The Scripture and Main Question—William H. Willimon

You Were Washed

"The unrighteous will not inherit the kingdom of God," says Paul (6:9). The kingdom is such that it demands a complete change of life. This is not a kingdom without boundaries in which anything goes and any behavior is accepted. A kingdom without boundaries is no kingdom at all.

To say that we are saved by God's grace—accepted just as we are—does not mean that we are *left* just as we are. People who enter this faith are people who are willing to form their lives accordingly.

First, Paul lists the behavior that he regards as immoral (6:9-10). His list fairly well covers the waterfront—idolatry (misguided religion), adultery (betrayal of trust), homosexuality (forsaking of nature), thievery (taking advantage of others), and drunkenness (abuse of self) are among the sins he lists. It's all there—our material, sexual, religious immorality.

Paul might have said to the Corinthians, "Don't do these things because God will punish people who do things like this." That response is implied in these verses, but it is not at the heart of the matter.

Rather, Paul argues that though the Corinthians were once people who acted this way (6:11), they can no longer live like this without appearing absurdly out of step with who they now are.

Once they were nobodies: forlorn, lost, pagans without hope or purpose.

That past life is the source of the Corinthians' continued immorality. But now, something has radically changed who the Corinthians are.

"You were washed, you were sanctified, you were justified in the name of the Lord Jesus Christ and in the Spirit of our God" (6:11). Here Paul returns to the image of baptism. Even as water washes us clean, even as water refreshes us, even as we are conceived and born in water—so baptism signifies that as we become Christians and join the church, we are cleansed from our former values and attachments; we are refreshed and strengthened to live a new life distinct from the old; we are born again as new persons.

All Paul is urging the Corinthians to do is to become who they are. Baptism has made them new people—now they are to act like it. Now they must either adjust their actions in accordance with their new lives or appear oddly out of step with the way things are.

In baptism the Corinthians have been transferred to a new kingdom. They are now citizens of a different country. They speak a different language. Occasionally their former accents will crop up in their speech, even as their immorality appears now. But that does not change their new citizenship. It is now too late for their old habits and attitudes. They are changed people—so they might as well wake up and start living like changed people.

The scandal of immorality among Christians is that such behavior violates who we are. The basis of morality among Christians is that it is our simple, grateful human response to who God has made us in Christ.

All Things Are Lawful

It is sad that we often think of Christian morality in a restrictive way: don't do this, don't do that. We thus remind the world of H. L. Mencken's definition of a Puritan as someone who is horrified by the possibility that somewhere someone is having a good time!

Paul has a more expansive view of Christian morality. "All things are lawful for me," he declares (6:12). *All* things? As Christians we are free from petty rules and regulations, overscrupulosity, and the harried, desperate attempt to try to be good little boys and girls in order that God might accept us.

Christians are those who declare that, in Jesus Christ, God *has* accepted us. We are therefore free to live without fear and timidity.

The poor, pitiful person who is always fearful of saying the wrong thing or of making a mistake or of offending someone is hardly the person who is able to risk the bold acts that this faith demands—all things are lawful.

"But not all things are helpful," says Paul (6:12), thus countering what might otherwise degenerate into a licentious, self-centered ethic or no ethic at all. This is the great qualification upon a Christian's great freedom. If a Christian were accepted and set free to simply follow the dictates of his or her own conscience or to look out for the interests of number one, then morality would be a rather simple matter—I am free to do whatever makes me feel good. But this is all the "morality" many contemporary people have.

God's Temple

"Do you not know that your body is a temple of the Holy Spirit?" Paul asks (6:19). Christian morality is not a matter of simply obeying this rule or that one. It is a matter of honoring what is holy. When we abuse our bodies or use them in immoral ways, we are desecrating something wonderful and holy which God has created.

Paul urges morality on the basis of who we are. Our immorality is shocking, not simply because it is the failure to obey the rules, but because it is a disregard for what is holy. Sexual immorality is unholy, not because Christians are prudes who think that sex is evil, but because Christians are those who honor the body as a work of God. We are not free to abuse our bodies because we are not free to desecrate anything which God has wondrously created. This is an exaltation of human sexuality rather than a denigration of it.

"You are not your own," says Paul (6:19). We are free, but not free to live only for ourselves in selfish, self-centered ways. We were "bought with a price" (6:20). We are owned by another.

"Do your *own* thing," counsels contemporary ethical wisdom. "If it makes you feel good, do it."

Christians do things differently.

Helping Adults Become Involved—Harlan R. Waite

Preparing to Teach

If, as we suggested last week, I Corinthians is a mirror in which we see ourselves, we look again this week to see reflections of immorality in our own church. Hold up the looking glass by reading I Corinthians 5–6 and note the problems Paul confronts: incest (5:1-13), litigation (6:1-11), and "the enthusiasts" (6:12-20; see last week's lesson).

The focus of this week's lesson is 6:9-20. Study "As You Read the Scripture" for background. Plan the development of your lesson with the help of "The Main Question" and "The Scripture and the Main Question." The article on I Corinthians in *The Interpreter's One-Volume Commentary on the Bible* will provide additional help. See also references to general reading materials in our previous lessons.

Here is a possible outline for this week's lesson:

I. Paul confronts Corinthian immorality.
  A. Failures in loyalty and behavior
  B. Unchristian conduct
  C. Libertinism
II. Christian morality roots in who we are.
  A. The old view: legalism
  B. The new view: personal response
  C. Morality and identity
III. Morality is more than obeying rules.
  A. Honoring God's creation
  B. Witnessing as the Body of Christ and expressing love for the world
  C. Boundaries of God's kingdom

Introducing the Main Question

Observe that, as in Paul's day, Christian values stand in striking contrast to the values accepted in the world around us. Today's discussion will center around the nature of Christian morality and the need for church members, living in a secular culture, to maintain their Christian integrity. What effect does the immorality of society have upon the church?

Andrew Mutch tells the story in "Growing Sins" of an old bridge in the Scottish highlands which spanned a rocky cleft. It was a massive structure, built of stone and mortar. Year after year people crossed that bridge, feeling perfectly safe; but there came a time when it was pronounced hazardous and was closed to traffic. The damage had been done by a tiny birch seed that had been carried there by the wind and deposited in a small opening above the keystone. There it took root, grew into a sapling, and finally became a tree whose roots penetrated the masonry and forced it apart. This story is a parable of how moral values which are basically alien to the Christian life find their way into the church and destroy its integrity.

Developing the Lesson

I. Paul confronts Corinthian immorality.

A. Failures in loyalty and behavior

Recall last week's discussion, noting the failure of the Corinthians to place their loyalty in the right person. Suggest that Paul (in this week's lesson) turns to another kind of failure, that of unseemly behavior.

B. Unchristian conduct

If your students have read I Corinthians 5 and 6, ask them to identify the major themes. If not, give them a general outline of the two chapters as indicated above in "Preparing to Teach." It is important to note that immorality for Paul is not simply sexual; for he places litigation by Christians in pagan courts in his list of immoral actions. Ask the class to define immorality, and lead them to the realization that anything conceived by Jesus as threatening human well-being, anything that is counter to the will of God, is immoral. Acknowledge that Christianity has a radical ("root") sense of morality. Note what Dr. Luccock calls the "nine vices of the degenerate life" in verses 9 to 10.

C. Libertinism

The remaining verses of chapter 6 have to do with the "libertines." Refer to Dr. Luccock's discussion of 6:12-13 and the last paragraph of Dr. Willimon's discussion entitled "All Things Are Lawful."

II. Christian morality roots in who we are.

A. The old view: legalism

The old view, in which Paul himself had been brought up, was a legalistic one. Morality consisted in obeying the rules set forth by the religious community, based on the Torah (the Pentateuch or the Law). They accomplished a very important purpose of putting God in the center of everyday life. Suggest that the problem lay in the fact that rules were obeyed for their own sake, not for deeper reasons. Paul explains this to the Christians at Rome when he writes, "Israel who pursued the righteousness which is based on law did not succeed in fulfilling that law. Why? Because they did not pursue it through faith, but as if it were based on works" (Romans 9:31-32a).

B. The new view: personal response

Christians brought to the community of faith a new understanding of morality. They observed the law not as a rigid code to which they were legally bound to conform but rather as a guide to their grateful response to God's gracious action on their behalf. In place of a static, legalistic concept, they offered a dynamic, personal view of morality.

C. Morality and identity

Refer the class to Dr. Willimon's claim that Paul sought not so much to punish as to correct behavior. He pleaded for conduct which was appropriate to the identity of Christians. (See Dr. Willimon's discussion of "You Were Washed" and his discussion of "God's Temple.")

Ask the class to describe the identity of the early Christians. Your students will undoubtedly mention their individual identity as children of God, expressed through their baptism. They may also be interested in defining identity collectively, for the early Christians thought of themselves as the Body of Christ. In any event, as Dr. Willimon so often points out, morality is an expression of who we are; and this means that our conduct must be appropriate to children of God and members of the Body of Christ.

III. Morality is more than obeying rules.

A. Honoring God's creation

Share Dr. Willimon's comments on "God's Temple," in which he stresses that in all we do, we must honor God's creation. Since our bodies are created to be a dwelling place of God, they should be used in ways that fittingly express him.

B. Witnessing as the Body of Christ and expressing love for the world

Point out that, as the Body of Christ, we are called to witness to him; and what we do with our bodies expresses our inner commitment. In expressing God's love for the world through our actions, we are obligated by our commitment to act in ways that are helpful to others, not simply gratifying to ourselves.

C. Boundaries of God's Kingdom

Finally, refer to the thought expressed in "You Were Washed," which insists that the kingdom of God, of which Christians are citizens, has boundaries. Discuss these thoughts with the class.

Helping Class Members Act

W. N. Smith observed in "Seven Deadly Sins," "Someone has said that the seven deadly sins of society are these: policies [politics] without principles, wealth without work, pleasure without conscience, knowledge without character, commerce and industry without morality, science without humanity, worship without sacrifice." Ask your class to list ways in which this description fits our world. Perhaps letters could be written to government, business, educational, and religious agencies, expressing the concern raised by Dr. Smith.

Planning for Next Sunday

Observe that there is inevitable tension between God's will and human conduct. Announce next Sunday's theme and ask your class members to read I Corinthians 8:1–11:1. Note the assignments suggested in next Sunday's "Preparing to Teach" and recruit volunteers to accept responsibility for them.

The Church in Conflict with Culture

Background Scripture: I Corinthians 8:1–11:1

The Main Question—William H. Willimon

In Will Campbell's memorable autobiography, he describes an argument he had with a friend. "You know, Preacher Will," his friend said, "that church of yours is just like an Easter chicken my little girl once had."

Campbell's friend described the "Easter chicken"—a little chick dyed purple. The chick was put in the pen with the other chicks, but they would have nothing to do with this strange, purple creature. They pecked it and chased it away from the food. The little purple chick stayed by itself, different, alone.

But then, as the "Easter chicken" grew older, it began to lose its purple plumage. The new feathers were not purple. They were red. The growing chick began to look and act more like the other chickens. It began to fight for itself, peck the others when they pecked it and, in general, became one more chicken. The once scorned and persecuted "Easter chicken" was just another Rhode Island Red.

Campbell got the point of his friend's parable about the church as an acculturated, accommodated "Easter chicken."

"But the Easter chicken does lay eggs, doesn't she?" he asked.

"Sure," his friend replied. "But *all* chickens lay eggs. Who needs an Easter chicken for that?" The Boy Scouts help youth. The Red Cross offers relief. The YMCA, the Rotary Club, the PTA.

Is the church simply one more useful, helpful human organization? Or is the church distinctly different?

As You Read the Scripture—Robert E. Luccock

The Corinthians had asked Paul about the matter of eating food that had been offered to idols in pagan religious ritual. In addressing this question Paul faces the larger issue of how a Christian is to live in a pagan society.

Paul concedes that in itself eating such food should not offend the Christian. Christians know that pagan gods do not exist, and eating food offered to these nonexistent gods should have no effect on the one who eats. But not everyone knows this. Eating consecrated food can be offensive to some and injurious to others who might be weak enough in their faith to believe that some properties of the pagan god could be imbibed with the food. Followers of Christ are not to abuse their freedom in any way that causes another to stumble. Christians acknowledge "the priority of love over liberty" and a call to "renunciation of rights for the sake of others."

I Corinthians 10:6-14, 31. Paul reminds his hearers that what happened to the Israelites in the wilderness is a warning to Corinth in the present time. He recalls five episodes.

Verse 6. (See Numbers 11:4-34.) Let the Corinthians not suffer God's retribution as did the Israelites for once again "desiring the well-fed life of Egypt."

Verse 7. (See Exodus 32:4, 6.) The episode of the golden calf stands as caution against setting up "idols made by human hands." To follow the practice of pagans was difficult to resist, especially under wilderness privation.

Verse 8. (See Numbers 25:1-9.) Idolatry and sexual immorality often went hand in hand, as they did with the Baal of Peor in the Numbers account, and as they did for the Corinthian Christians. (Paul came up one thousand casualties short of Numbers!)

Verse 9. (See Numbers 21:5-6.) The Israelites lost their faith in God's promise and leading. In their impatience they "put the Lord to the test" by questioning God's motives and indeed God's power. The question must have baffled the Christians in Corinth: Why should we be under such discipline while the pagans enjoy so much, especially since Christ has set us free?

Verse 10. (See Numbers 16:41-49.) Because "the congregation . . . of Israel murmured against Moses," they were afflicted with a mighty plague.

The Corinthians were to understand this grim recital as a warning that even the people of the covenant could suffer God's punishment and wrath. So could the Christians of the *new* covenant. Only in this one place does Paul use the Greek word for *destroyer*. Perhaps Ephesians 6:11-12 comes close to Paul's meaning, "the wiles of the devil."

Verse 11. The Corinthians, Paul reminds them, are living in "the end of the ages." All the more urgent that the fate of so many Israelites of the Exodus not come upon them.

Verses 12-13. Such words are intended to encourage the Christians of Corinth in their struggle with temptation.

Verse 31. Paul enunciates in this statement a most important principle for making moral choices. Neither the act nor the behavior in itself is primary; to reduce the moral life to a set of prohibitions is to fall back into legalism, from which the Christian faith has set people free. Although certain things are always morally wrong—fornication, idolatry, for example—the moral criterion must always be whether what is considered can be done to the glory of God. Paul applies this principle to the whole conflict between the church and culture.

Selected Scripture

King James Version

I Corinthians 10:6-14, 31

6 Now these things were our examples, to the intent we should not lust after evil things, as they also lusted.

7 Neither be ye idolaters, as *were* some of them; as it is written. The people sat down to eat and drink, and rose up to play.

8 Neither let us commit fornication, as some of them committed, and fell in one day three and twenty thousand.

Revised Standard Version

I Corinthians 10:6-14, 31

6 Now these things are warnings for us, not to desire evil as they did. 7 Do not be idolaters as some of them were; as it is written, "The people sat down to eat and drink and rose up to dance." 8 We must not indulge in immorality as some of them did, and twenty-three thousand fell in a single day. 9 We must not put the Lord to the test, as some of them did and were destroyed by serpents; 10 nor grumble, as some

9 Neither let us tempt Christ, as some of them also tempted, and were destroyed of serpents.

10 Neither murmur ye, as some of them also murmured, and were destroyed of the destroyer.

11 Now all these things happened unto them for ensamples: and they are written for our admonition, upon whom the ends of the world are come.

12 Wherefore let him that thinketh he standeth take heed lest he fall.

13 There hath no temptation taken you but such as is common to man: but God *is* faithful, who will not suffer you to be tempted above that ye are able; but will with the temptation also make a way to escape, that ye may be able to bear *it*.

14 Wherefore, my dearly beloved, flee from idolatry.

....

31 Whether therefore ye eat, or drink, or whatsoever ye do, do all to the glory of God.

I Corinthians 11:1
1 Be ye followers of me, even as I also *am* of Christ.

Key Verse: **Whether therefore ye eat, or drink, or whatsoever ye do, do all to the glory of God. (I Corinthians 10:31)**

of them did and were destroyed by the Destroyer. 11 Now these things happened to them as a warning, but they were written down for our instruction, upon whom the end of the ages has come. 12 Therefore let any one who thinks that he stands take heed lest he fall. 13 No temptation has overtaken you that is not common to man. God is faithful, and he will not let you be tempted beyond your strength, but with the temptation will also provide the way of escape, that you may be able to endure it.

14 Therefore, my beloved, shun the worship of idols.

....

31 So, whether you eat or drink, or whatever you do, do all to the glory of God.

I Corinthians 11:1
1 Be imitators of me, as I am of Christ.

Key Verse: **Whatever you eat or drink, or whatever you do, do all to the glory of God. (I Corinthians 10:31)**

The Scripture and the Main Question—William H. Willimon

In recent years there has been much talk about the need for the church to serve the world. Certainly, as Christ's disciples, we are called to reach out to the needs of others. Thus the church is often urged to get out of its cozy sanctuaries and into the world.

But as I read church history, the problem is not how to get the church out into the world but how to keep the world from subverting the church. Time and again in our history, the church has had its message co-opted by the world, its vision distorted by worldly concerns, its goals scaled down to the world's standards of justice.

"Everybody else is doing it," once the teenager's plea, has become out motto as we adapt ourselves to the status quo. And so the church has become victim of what the theologian Jürgen Moltmann calls "chameleon

69

theology"—victim of every passing fad, champion of only the most popular causes, espouser of merely conventional wisdom.

Paul's words to the church at Corinth remind us that this cultural accommodation is not new. In a number of areas—sexual morality, dietary customs, treatment of the poor—the Corinthians assumed that it was enough for them to do as everyone else was doing. Paul challenges their easy alliance with the world and warns them of its consequences.

Even as today's scripture lesson urges us to look back in our past to the Corinthian church for guidance, Paul urges the Corinthians to look back into their past and profit from the mistakes of the ancestors in their temptations.

"Our fathers were all under the cloud, and all passed through the sea," Paul reminds them (10:1). Israel was saved from Egyptian slavery and passed through the sea to freedom.

"Nevertheless with most of them God was not pleased; for they were overthrown in the wilderness" (10:5). Perhaps the Israelites assumed that, because God had chosen them for liberation, they had it made. They were free to act as they pleased. But their time in the wilderness showed the sad results of this line of reasoning. They were led astray into idolatry. They adopted the false gods of their neighbors and were destroyed. So Paul warns, "Therefore let any one who thinks that he stands take heed lest he fall" (10:12).

Perhaps some Christians in Corinth assumed that, because they had been baptized and liberated, they need not worry about the seductive life of the world. They can eat, drink, love, and act as they wish. They are the Chosen People, what have they to fear?

Paul reminds the Corinthians that it was this same smug attitude that spelled trouble for their ancestors in the faith. They had too much confidence in the strength of their faith and too little regard for the seductive power of the world.

Jesus told a parable about some good seed that was sown in some bad soil. The seed was fine. But the soil, choked with weeds, stunted the growth of the seed and the young plants died. So it is with this faith. "Now these things happened to them as a warning" (10:11).

Do All to the Glory of God

The particular issue that gave rise to Paul's warning to the Corinthians was the question of whether or not Christians could eat meat that had been offered to idols. This was probably meat which came from livestock that had been sacrificed in pagan temple ceremonies in Corinth.

In one sense, because idols were nothing, the consumption of meat offered to an idol was of little consequence to Christians (10:19). But in another sense, this matter of food offered to idols is a major concern. Paul seems to counsel the Corinthians to avoid eating such food—lest their consumption cause someone who is less sure of his or her faith to be led astray (10:25).

But, "if one of the unbelievers invites you to dinner," the Christian may go and eat provided that the Christian eats "with thankfulness" (10:30). What difference would that make?

To eat "with thankfulness" would mean to eat in recognition that this food is a gift from God. Whenever we say thanks in a table blessing before a meal, we are recognizing that we are dependent upon these gifts of God. In so doing, our eating and drinking become an act of worship. What we do with our food, drink, money, customs, nation, family, or business is no small matter for the Christian. These good gifts of God, when used and abused for our own selfish ends, become as idols to us. We forget that they are divine gifts and begin to think of them as human achievements. That is where the trouble begins.

How often has the church been tempted to look upon things the same way that the world looks at things! We build big, expensive churches—to the glory of God or to our own glory? We put property rights above human rights. We speak of ourselves as "self-made" men and women and forget the gifts that God has given us. We think of ourselves as Chosen People—chosen for privilege but not for responsibility. We put job, money, nation, customs, popularity, comfort—anything—before God. This is idolatry, no matter what we call it.

Our sin is always a matter of worshiping a false god (10:7). Pride is self-idolatry. Greed is thing-idolatry. We do what we do for ourselves and our security, comfort, and vanity rather than for the glory of God. Thus we are no better than pagans.

As Paul tells the Corinthians, the sin isn't in the gift itself—the food, money, nation, job, family. The sin is in our idolatrous abuse of the gift. So Paul advises, "Whether you eat or drink, or whatever you do, do all to the glory of God" (10:31).

Christians will find that in comparison to much of the world, they have peculiar opinions about money, race, war, politics, careers, and other people because they look at all matters in a different way than the world looks at things.

They are different because they bow down to a different God.

A Warning

The temptations of the world are so subtle. We forsake our faith so easily. "Come on, everybody else is doing it," people say. "Look, you have to adjust yourself to the real world," someone advises. "What difference does it make as long as nobody gets hurt?" another asks. The distinctions between the church and the world are so easily blurred, and we so easily fall prey to false gods.

What fascinates me about these passages from First Corinthians is that at a time when the church was fighting for its very life, it fought not by reducing its stance to a position so innocuous and generalized that any person could affirm it but by making careful, clear distinctions between itself and the world.

I think there is a warning here for us.

Helping Adults Become Involved—Harlan R. Waite

Preparing to Teach

Read I Corinthians 8:1–11:1. Give careful attention to "As You Read the Scripture," noting especially the allusions to the books of Numbers and Exodus which occur in I Corinthians 10:6-10. Assign each of these Old Testament passages to one of your students, and ask them to tell about them in class.

Familiarize yourself with Dr. Willimon's "The Main Question" and "The Scripture and the Main Question."

FIRST QUARTER

One further assignment may be made in preparation for section three of the lesson (see below). Ask someone to read I Maccabees 1:1–2:64 and Daniel 3 and 6. These stories of the three young men in the fiery furnace and of Daniel in the lions' den were written at the time of the resistance movement led by the Jewish Maccabees, ca. 167 B.C. All of these passages will contribute greatly to the lesson's theme that the church cannot allow itself to be shaped by the pagan world around it.

As a possible outline for this lesson, consider the following:

    I. Paul calls for faithfulness to the gospel.
       A. The problem of food
       B. Defense against "enthusiasts"
       C. Warning against unchristian conduct
   II. The church often accepts the world's standards.
       A. The world moves into the church.
       B. "I have a controversy."
       C. The church looks at life as the world does.
  III. Do all for the glory of God.
       A. A lesson from the past
       B. False worship
       C. The Maccabees and Daniel; the fundamental principle

Introducing the Main Question

Dr. Willimon expresses the central concern of this lesson in the last paragraph of "The Main Question." He tells the story of "an acculturated, accommodated Easter chicken." Use this story and the question it introduces as the opening for your lesson.

Developing the Lesson

I. Paul calls for faithfulness to the gospel.

A. The problem of food

He observed that many members of his church had taken on the designation "Christian" only to go on living as their non-Christian neighbors. The first problem he tackles is the failure of Christians to be considerate of their Christian neighbors. This lack of consideration showed itself in the attitude toward food (see 8:1-13; 10:23-30). Paul's central thought is that, although traditional scruples about food are no longer binding on Christians, it is selfish and unkind to use this freedom in a way that is offensive to someone who may retain the old scruples.

B. Defense against "enthusiasts"

Point out that a second major theme is Paul's defense against the "enthusiasts." More will be said of them in next week's lesson.

C. Warning against unchristian conduct

Observe that the central emphasis of this week's lesson will be on chapter 10 and note that Paul links the bad behavior of his congregations to the improper conduct of the people of Israel during their period of wandering in the desert. Read verses 6-10, one at a time. As each verse is read, call on the report (assigned in advance) regarding the Old Testament passage as identified by Dr. Luccock. Then complete your survey of the background scriptures by noting that Paul expands on his theme of idolatry (10:14-22), challenges smug complacency (10:11-13), and recapitulates the essential consideration for Christians: Do all for the glory of God. . . . Be imitators of me, as I am of Christ" (10:31–11:1).

II. *The church often accepts worldly standards.*

A. *The world moves into the church.*

Quote Dr. Willimon's statement to the effect that it is harder to get the world out of the church than it is to get the church into the world.

B. *"I have a controversy."*

Refer the class to Hosea 4:1-2, a passage which would have been well known to Paul. The first statement may come as a surprise to many: "The Lord has a controversy with the inhabitants of the land." In Hosea's day, the religious leaders were in conflict with the world because they felt that the world behaved in ways unacceptable to God. Although many Christians are uncomfortable with controversy, conflict with the world is inevitable if the church is to stand in the tradition of Hosea, Daniel, the Maccabees, Jesus, and Paul. Ask the class to discuss to what extent the church enters into controversy with the world.

C. *The church looks at life as the world does.*

Dr. Willimon observes in several places that the church looks at life and approaches its problems as the rest of the world does. He cites our interest in good buildings, property rights, self-sufficiency, and privilege, noting that they are forms of idolatry. Raise this question for discussion: On the basis of our biblical tradition, how would Christians and non-Christians differ regarding money, race, war, politics, and careers?

III. *Do all to the glory of God.*

A. *A lesson from the past*

Not simply in matters of food, but in *whatever* we do, we must seek the advantage of all as we imitate Christ. Share Dr. Willimon's discussion of this as found in his comments in "Do All to the Glory of God." Observe that our profession of faith does not go very deep when it is not validated by a life shaped by God rather than by the world.

Here is an opportunity for two other references to biblical teaching. The first is from the Ten Commandments: "You shall not take the name of the Lord your God in vain" (Exodus 20:7; Deuteronomy 5:11). Is it not vanity to call ourselves God's children and take his name upon us when we do not behave as he wants us to?

B. *False worship*

The second reference is to the famous temple address in Jeremiah 7:1-11. The prophet Jeremiah points out that it does no good to honor the temple if at the same time one dishonors the requirement of justice in society. Pious men and women would recite the formula, "This is the temple of the Lord, the temple of the Lord, the temple of the Lord" (Jeremiah 7:4). Listen to Jeremiah's response: "Behold, you trust in deceptive words to no avail. Will you steal, murder, commit adultery, swear falsely, . . . and go after other gods . . . only to go on doing all these abominations? Has this house, which is called by my name, become a den of robbers in your eyes?" In Paul's day, although the situation was different, the experience was essentially the same. Christians were boasting that they were "born again" but were actually living according to the mores of the world around them.

C. *The Maccabees and Daniel; the fundamental principle*

At this point, call for the reports on the Maccabees and Daniel, pointing out that they serve as a model for all Christians who would refuse to water down their faith under pressure from the world about them. Paul states the fundamental principle in his letter to the Romans: "Do not be conformed to this world but be transformed by the renewal of your mind, that you may prove what is the will of God, what is good and acceptable and perfect" (Romans 12:2).

Helping Class Members Act

Lead the class in evaluating the attitudes and conduct of the church, both at large and in your local parish. In what ways is the church different from other organizations which operate service programs and attempt to be morally uplifting in the community? Ask your minister to meet with the class for a discussion of this issue and to preach a sermon as a way of sharing the class's concern with the church.

Planning for Next Sunday

Share with the class the central question for next week's discussion: What are the characteristics of true leadership in the church? Ask your students to read II Corinthians 3, 4, and 11 and Titus 1:5-9, noting that these are portions of two different letters (see the first section of next Sunday's "Developing the Lesson").

All Saints' Day
DONALD J. WELCH

On a campus where I was teaching a few years ago posters appeared on bulletin boards advertising a party on November 1. A campus Christian group was sponsoring a "Day-After-Halloween Party." This serves as a good example of the way many Christians today regard All Saints' Day.

Most of us Protestants have difficulty with the label *saints*. In our minds, a saint is pictured as a statue in some cathedral where he or she is venerated and candles are lit. We forget that the apostle Paul often referred to any believer in Christ as a saint. Early in Christian history, the term came to be applied to those believers who died and entered Paradise.

Soon a question arose. How do we know that a person is actually in Paradise? The answer was easy in regard to some. Surely the eleven apostles were thus rewarded for their service and sacrifice. Surely so were those early Christians who died while confessing or defending the faith. Stephen would be such a confessor and martyr. As to others, the medieval and modern church developed elaborate proofs. If prayers to a deceased believer were answered consistently or miracles were performed in his or her name, that was proof of sainthood. Since thousands of claims were made by followers or loved ones, it became necessary for the church to develop a more elaborate mechanism—*canonization*—for recognition.

When a saint was canonized, a day was set aside on the calendar on which the life and deeds of the saint could be remembered. Soon the calendar literally was filled with saints' days. If a person were named for a saint—Patrick, for instance—that saint's day, March 17, became his or her special day or feast day.

What does all of this have to do with a special festival called All Saints' Day? In the early centuries, the church leaders recognized that there was no

74

way to commemorate officially every true believer who had died and gone to Paradise. The Eastern Church very early set aside the first Sunday after Pentecost (Trinity Sunday) for the remembrance of all saints. In the seventh century, Pope Boniface IV designated May 13 for the same purpose. In the ninth century, Pope Gregory IV moved the day of the feast to November 1 so that the many pilgrims coming to Rome could be accommodated and fed more easily after the harvest. (See Francis X. Weiser, *Handbook of Christian Feasts and Customs.* New York: Harcourt, Brace, 1958.)

During the Reformation, the observance of All Saints' Day might have been cast aside along with other "popish" practices except for the historical coincidence that Martin Luther nailed his ninety-five theses on the door of the cathedral at Wittenberg on the eve of All Saints' Day, thus making the day a special one for all who followed Luther.

For English-speaking Protestants, a popular celebration incorporated the beginning of the pagan Celtic new year, which fell near the first of November, into the observance of All Hallows Day, the English name for All Saints' Day. Humankind's imagination and powers to speculate about the world beyond the grave began to mix saints, demons, witches, ghosts, and goblins into one sacred/secular brew.

In the United States, the day has been little observed outside of the Roman Catholic, Orthodox, and more liturgical Protestant churches. It is overshadowed by Reformation Sunday, Halloween, stewardship campaigns, and football games. In some churches, however, it is a time for calling the roll of all of the members of the parish who have died during the year; thus becoming a church Memorial Day.

What have we lost by minimizing or neglecting All Saints' Day? At first glance, the loss may appear to be minimal. Pragmatic as we are, shouldn't we concentrate more on the lives of present-day Christians than on the deaths of ancient martyrs? Perhaps we should, but in so doing we lose at least three important perspectives.

First, we tend to forget that we are the inheritors of a faith that has been bought with a price. We enjoy the fruits of the labors of all of those who preceded us. In a nation that enjoys religious freedom, we forget that in past days Christians were put to death for confessing Jesus Christ as Lord. Had they not been willing to sacrifice their lives in times past, we would not be able to live our lives in religious freedom.

There are places in the world today where persons are imprisoned and killed for exercising the Christian faith. Totalitarians of various political persuasions recognize that those who boldly proclaim Christ, who came as the truth that sets all persons free, are a threat to any regime that denies human rights.

In setting one day aside to commemorate all saints and martyrs, we recognize that we are bought with a price. The day may come in our own lives when we will be called to be faithful even unto death. All Saints' Day helps us understand ourselves as Christians with a history of courage and faithfulness.

Second, it is good to remind ourselves that we who are living saints (believers in Jesus Christ) are not separated from those saints who have died. We are surrounded by "so great a cloud of witnesses" (Hebrews 12:1), and Sunday after Sunday we rise to boldly proclaim in the Apostles' Creed that we believe in "the communion of saints."

Superstition and fake spiritualism often rob us of a persistent biblical affirmation that there is not an impenetrable wall between the living and the dead. Those who died before us are present yet, and the recognition of their presence provides strength and courage for the living of these days.

This knowledge helps us understand that death is a part of life. It assists us accept our own death as inevitable; yet the remembrance of the saints who have passed this way before removes the fear of our own death.

Third, we live in an age that cries out for heroes. Where are the national and world leaders we need so much? We also stand in need of great heroes of the faith. A roll call of the saints and their deeds should inspire any of us to press harder and climb higher in our pilgrimage of faith. This list is not limited to those saints who have been recognized or canonized. There is someone in the memory of each of us whose life and example have influenced us and made us better persons. On this November 1, let us add the name of that person to the roster of all the saints. Let us give thanks to God for that life and in joyful praise join with the hosts of others in the communion of the saints. Alleluia!

LESSON 9   OCTOBER 27

Who Are True Church Leaders?

Background Scripture: II Corinthians 3, 4, 11; Titus 1:5-9

The Main Question—William H. Willimon

Who are the leaders you most admire? Do you think of Roosevelt, Kennedy, Truman? These men made great contributions in the area of politics and statesmanship. They were powerful people in their day and they did much to change the course of history because they knew how to use power and used it well.

But perhaps when you hear the word *leader* you think of a different sort of person. Perhaps you don't think of politicians at all. Rather you may think of people who, though they did not wield political power, did much to change the world simply by the force of personality. People like Mother Teresa, Martin Luther King, John Wesley, and Gandhi come to mind. These people remind us that leadership is not simply a matter of how many votes one receives in an election or how powerful the armies at one's disposal.

From the beginning the church had certain peculiar notions about leadership. The church has leaders—but not as the world conceives of leadership. To his disciples Jesus said, "It shall not be so [as it is among worldly leaders] among you" (Mark 10:43, Luke 22:26, Matthew 20:26).

How are Christian leaders different? In numerous places in the Scriptures, it is made clear that Christian leaders lead not through coercion, intimidation, or the politics of power which so often characterize the style of worldly leaders. Christian leaders are different.

Leaders in the church are urged to lead not by "domineering over those in your charge," says Peter, "but being examples to the flock" (I Peter 5:3). At an early date, Christian leaders are designated by the Greek term *diakonia*

76

(from which we get our word *deacon*), which means literally "waiter," "butler," "servant."

Obviously, in calling its leaders "servants," the church intended to say something very different about who are leaders and about how they lead. This is the main concern of Paul's thought on Christian leadership which we shall focus upon today.

As You Read the Scripture—Robert E. Luccock

Some time after Paul sent I Corinthians he must have learned that things had gone from bad to worse in the church there. Persistent divisions sundered the congregation; false prophets "disguis[ed] themselves as apostles of Christ." Out of extreme disappointment, pain, and much anger Paul wrote what has come to be known as the "severe letter." We believe II Corinthians 10–13 may be part of that letter. To read those four chapters is to be impressed at once with their severe tone of reprimand and warning.

After sending such a letter Paul could find no peace until he knew how the church had received it, because he loved the Corinthian church so much. In Macedonia, Paul met Titus who bore him good news. All was well again in Corinth (II Corinthians 7:8-9). Rejoicing, Paul sent off a letter of thanksgiving and reconciliation. This is what we now have as II Corinthians 1–9—the most personal of all Paul's letters.

In II Corinthians 4, Paul describes what the apostolic ministry is like. *Apostle* is a Greek word meaning "one who is sent forth."

II Corinthians 4. Paul is "one sent forth by Jesus Christ." This chapter tells how one will act who has been sent forth by the Christ.

Verse 1. Despite the sufferings listed in II Corinthians 11:23-33, Paul does "not lose heart," because the task is his "by the mercy of God." *We* refers first to Paul, but to all other apostles as well.

Verse 2. "Shameful, hidden things" would be an accurate translation. The Apostle will not act in a devious way, not tell half-truths, not withhold any truth in order to manipulate people. Paul says in effect, "My entire ministry is an open book for everyone to see, even as God sees it all."

Verses 3-4. Paul has spoken (II Corinthians 3:13-15) of the veil that is over the minds (hearts) of those who will not see or hear the salvation God has offered in Christ. The god of this world (the devil, the evil one, the ruler of this present age) has blinded such veiled persons. They are "perishing." Paul uses the image of light (Genesis 1:3—"Let there be light") to identify the gospel with the Creator. This image is familiar in John's writings (John 8:12, 12:46, I John 1:5-7). The "light of the gospel" enables us to see the glory of the risen and exalted Christ.

Verse 5. Apostolic authority (the authority of Christian leadership) is not in the apostles (or in the persons who represent Christ), but in the Christ in whose name the apostles come. Apostles are the servants of the ones to whom they have been sent, "for Jesus' sake."

Verse 6. Light has shone for the apostles in order that they can give the light of the knowledge of God to others.

Verses 7-12. Paul's statements here about ministry do two things: they encourage those who may suffer for their faith; they also confound the Corinthians who were so self-assertive, seeking partisan advantage. God has disclosed his power not through the strong and triumphant but through frail, weak, unpromising human beings. (Note Isaiah's suffering servant,

Isaiah 53:2-3.) Jesus was himself despised and rejected by the powerful. His life must be manifested now in those who fulfill his role of suffering and death. (See especially I Corinthians 1:26-29.) The Corinthians are to remember that not many of them are wise or powerful by worldly standards. Yet God chose them that through them God might let the light of Christ shine. Here is our finest model of Christian ministry, whether by laypersons or ordained.

Selected Scripture

King James Version	Revised Standard Version

II Corinthians 4:1-12

1 Therefore seeing we have this ministry, as we have received mercy, we faint not;

2 But have renounced the hidden things of dishonesty, not walking in craftiness, nor handling the word of God deceitfully; but by manifestation of the truth commending ourselves to every man's conscience in the sight of God.

3 But if our gospel be hid, it is hid to them that are lost:

4 In whom the god of this world hath blinded the minds of them which believe not, lest the light of the glorious gospel of Christ, who is the image of God, should shine unto them.

5 For we preach not ourselves, but Christ Jesus the Lord; and ourselves your servants for Jesus' sake.

6 For God, who commanded the light to shine out of darkness, hath shined in our hearts, to *give* the light of the knowledge of the glory of God in the face of Jesus Christ.

7 But we have this treasure in earthen vessels, that the excellency of the power may be of God, and not of us.

8 *We are* troubled on every side, yet not distressed; *we are* perplexed, but not in despair;

9 persecuted, but not forsaken; cast down, but not destroyed;

10 Always bearing about in the body the dying of the Lord Jesus, that the life also of Jesus might be made manifest in our body.

II Corinthians 4:1-12

1 Therefore, having this ministry by the mercy of God, we do not lose heart. 2 We have renounced disgraceful, underhanded ways; we refuse to practice cunning or to tamper with God's word, but by the open statement of the truth we would commend ourselves to every man's conscience in the sight of God. 3 And even if our gospel is veiled, it is veiled only to those who are perishing. 4 In their case the god of this world has blinded the minds of the unbelievers, to keep them from seeing the light of the gospel of the glory of Christ, who is the likeness of God. 5 For what we preach is not ourselves, but Jesus Christ as Lord, with ourselves as your servants for Jesus' sake. 6 For it is the God who said, "Let light shine out of darkness," who has shone in our hearts to give the light of the knowledge of the glory of God in the face of Christ.

7 But we have this treasure in earthen vessels, to show that the transcendent power belongs to God and not to us. 8 We are afflicted in every way, but not crushed; perplexed, but not driven to despair; 9 persecuted, but not forsaken; struck down, but not destroyed; 10 always carrying in the body the death of Jesus, so that the life of Jesus may also be manifested in our bodies. 11 For while we live we are always being given up to death for

11 For we which live are always delivered unto death for Jesus' sake, that the life also of Jesus might be made manifest in our mortal flesh.

12 So then death worketh in us, but life in you.

Jesus' sake, so that the life of Jesus may be manifested in our mortal flesh. 12 So death is at work in us, but life in you.

Key Verse: **For we preach not ourselves, but Christ Jesus the Lord; and ourselves your servants for Jesus' sake. (II Corinthians 4:5)**

Key Verse: **For what we preach is not ourselves, but Jesus Christ as Lord, with ourselves as your servants. (II Corinthians 4:5)**

The Scripture and Main Question—William H. Willimon

We Have This Ministry

First we must confront a basic misunderstanding which many people have about the nature of the church and its leadership. When asked the question, "Who is a minister?" most of us would respond by describing someone who is paid by the church to lead a congregation. Ministers are people who work for the church on a full-time basis. The laity are all those other Christians who work elsewhere to support the full-time ministry of the minister.

This view of church leadership makes it sound as if a congregation has one minister who is supported by a group of laypeople. But this view is not true to the New Testament picture of church leadership.

When Paul writes to the church at Corinth and says, "having this ministry by the mercy of God" (II Corinthians 4:1), he is not simply talking to a group of professional, full-time, seminary-trained pastors. He is addressing the leaders of the whole church, including those whom we often think of as "laity."

Elsewhere Paul makes it clear that "ministry" includes all baptized Christians. Ministry or service is not limited to those who are paid to do it. It includes everyone who has a share in Christ's liberating work in the world. Sometimes those whom we regard as laity have better opportunities to perform ministry to the world than those whom we regard as clergy.

I think that we might do better to make a distinction between "ministers"—that is, all of us who are baptized to Christ's service—and "pastors"—that is, all those whom the church calls for the specialized ministry of teaching, preaching, and upbuilding the church. The role of these pastors is to equip the ministers for their ministry. Pastors are those who "equip the saints" (Ephesians 4:12) for their ministry in the world.

Unfortunately, due to our fuzzy understanding of ministry, we often thought of pastors who take away the ministers' responsibility for serving the world in Christ's name. We do not have to perform their God-given ministry. We have pastors to enable and support the laity in their own distinctive ministries.

This is much the same as Paul says to the Corinthians when he claims that "what we preach is not ourselves, but Jesus Christ as Lord, with ourselves as your servants for Jesus' sake" (4:5).

With Ourselves as Your Servants

In the church, the role of the laity is not simply to give of their money, prayers, talents, and time to support the pastors in their ministry. The role of the laity is to receive the support of the pastors so that the laity can perform their service.

How unfortunate that sometimes people say, "That is Reverend Jones's church" or "The Reverend Dr. Smith is head of that congregation." This confirms the erroneous impression that the church exists to care for and to support the clergy rather than that the clergy exists to care for and to support the church (people).

So a preacher stands up in the pulpit and says, "I want to thank all of you for coming out on a bad morning like this one," as if the people are there to flatter and please the pastor rather than to worship God. Or, when a pastor moves from one church to the next, some people stop attending the church because their favorite pastor has left—as if the purpose of their church membership were to admire and support the pastor rather than to be equipped for their ministry.

Paul was constantly bothered by the "personality cult" approach to forming the church. In both of his letters to the church at Corinth, he opens with an attack upon those leaders who have formed the congregation around their personality rather than around the truth of the gospel. Paul does not care whether the people like him personally. He cares that they hear the gospel and are brought to faith in Christ, not faith in Paul.

So Paul says to the Corinthains, "For what we preach is not ourselves, but Jesus Christ as Lord" (4:5).

Sometimes pastors' personalities get in the way of the gospel. We find ourselves attracted to a person rather than attracted to the truth of Christ. Paul's words should remind us that this is an aberration of true Christian proclamation.

A Christian, whether that Christian be a pastor or any other type of Christian minister, is someone who bears a "treasure in earthen vessels" (4:7). That is, he or she is a typical, frail, limited human being who bears witness to the glorious, unlimited, liberating power of the truth which is Jesus Christ.

Paul's analogy of a treasure in an earthenware jar says two things to me. First, it reminds us that we are to always be more attentive to the truth which a person bears than to the personality of that person. Many laypeople can testify to the truth that a pastor whom they may have not liked personally, a pastor with whom they may have had many disagreements, was the very person who aided their Christian growth and insight. The truth transcended the earthen vessel.

Second, Paul's analogy says something to those leaders in the church who are struggling to be witnesses in spite of their human limitations. The earthen vessel may be inadequate. Fortunately, the truth we bear witness to is adequate. You as a church school teacher may often feel that someone better educated, better trained, with more time to devote to lesson preparation would make a better teacher for your adult class. Perhaps. But you are the person whom God has called and the church has chosen to teach this class, so you must do the best you can to bear witness to the truth as you teach. Thereby you show, as did Paul in his ministry, that "the transcendent power belongs to God and not to us" (4:7).

Any church leader, no matter how well endowed with natural gifts or spiritual insights, will have times when he or she feels "afflicted, perplexed, persecuted, struck down" (4:8-9). Paul, perhaps the greatest and most well endowed of early church leaders, felt this way from time to time and so do we. Leadership in the church is not an easy matter. We are working with people, with all their foibles and frailties, and we are working with the gospel in all its complexity and demands. So we need not expect leadership to be easy.

But just as Jesus was struck down but triumphed, so do we. The world may look at us and see only weakness and frailty. But we know that in our weakness, in our humanity, we bear witness to the poor of God. This keeps us going; "we do not lose heart" (4:1).

That the Life of Jesus Might Be Manifested

In the world, leadership is often a matter of who can grab the most power and who can use that power in the most efficient, ruthless manner. The people whom we call "leaders" are often those who have learned the skills of dominance, intimidation, and coercion.

But distinctively Christian leadership, as Paul makes clear, bases itself on the model of Christ. Jesus manifested strength in his weakness. He thereby showed how powerless is that which we regard as powerful and how powerful are those persons whom we regard as weak. He was the one who led others by serving others.

Did you see the movie *Gandhi*? Gandhi was not a Christian, but his style of leadership certainly reflected Christian principles. If you saw the movie, perhaps you recall the scene where the little half-naked man enters the British viceroy's office. The viceroy is the man of power, with the whole might of the British Empire to back him up in whatever he does. Earlier, he laughed at the thought of this little man being a threat to the old order.

"What can a man do who doesn't even own a pair of shoes?" he had scornfully asked.

The viceroy found out what the little man could do. That little man organized thousands of other little men and women who marched, filled the jails, and conducted their peaceful, noncooperative movement until they brought the mighty British Empire to its knees, and India won its independence.

The viceroy was forced to concede the powerlessness of leadership which cuts itself off from the will of the people. Gandhi proved that truth and goodness will always bring down those structures which the world erects to prop up its falsehood and inequalities.

Christian leadership need not resort to cunning, deceit, or coercion. It derives its force from another source. Its model for success is a young man hung on a cross whose death led us to freedom.

Helping Adults Become Involved—Harlan R. Waite

Preparing to Teach

The background scripture for this week's lesson is II Corinthians 3, 4, and 11; and Titus 1:5-9. Note especially the presence of preachers and teachers whose message and method were in conflict with those of Paul. Secure help from Dr. Luccock's "As You Read the Scripture" and Dr. Willimon's "The Main Question" and "The Scripture and the Main Question." If you have been able to locate a copy of *The New Testament* by Norman Perrin (see lesson 1 in this series), read his description of "II Corinthians" on pages 104-5. Observe that he identifies six letters, fragments of which are combined to constitute what we know as II Corinthians. Perrin also has a

good description of the "enthusiasts" (pages 51, 55, 95-96, 100, and 103).
The following outline is offered as a guide to your organization of the letter:

    I. Paul defends his apostleship.
      A. Paul's contacts with Corinth
      B. Paul's commission, his rivals, and the enthusiasts
    II. True leadership is Christlike.
      A. The model of Christ
      B. The character of church leaders
    III. All Christians are ministers.
      A. Shared leadership
      B. Roles of informal leaders
      C. Sheep and disciples

Introducing the Main Question

Robert E. Lee has become an honored American, admired by both North and South. Charles F. Wishart reflects on his character in a short article entitled "Robert E. Lee's High Moment" in *Treasury of the Christian Faith*. Lee's courage and wisdom in war paved the way for a fine offer from a commercial institution which would have paid him a large salary. Instead, he responded to the challenge of a small, struggling college, accepting a small salary to serve as its president. There he began to rebuild the physical, moral, and spiritual life of the South. His life reflected the character of Paul, who knew great adversity, accepted suffering, performed as a servant, and left a great spiritual legacy after him. Use his story to introduce the main question: What are the characteristics of true leadership in the church?

Developing the Lesson

I. Paul defends his apostleship.
  A. Paul's contacts with Corinth
Recall for the class that Paul was in constant communication with his churches in person and by letter. Review the Corinthian correspondence as described in Norman Perrin's article (see "Preparing to Teach" above), noting that Paul made many efforts to ease the conflict and defend his ministry.
  B. Paul's commission, his rivals, and the enthusiasts
Note that the passages we are dealing with today follow a statement in II Corinthians 2:17, where Paul speaks of his commissioning by God. This sets the stage for his defense against his rivals. Although he does not name them, the fact that he deals with Moses and the law in chapter 3 seems to indicate that some of the rivals were so-called "Judaizers," Jewish preachers who still insisted that in order to become a Christian, one must first be circumcised. Chapter 4 may refer to the same persons. In chapter 11, however, we seem to have a picture of the "enthusiasts." Recall that we have met them before in this series, having heard Paul refer sarcastically to their "eloquent wisdom" (I Corinthians 1:17), their arrogance (I Corinthians 4:19), and their libertine life-style (I Corinthians 6:12-20; 10:23). He sarcastically calls them "peddlers of God's word" (II Corinthians 2:17) and "superlative apostles" (II Corinthians 11:5, 12:11), toward whom he feels not at all inferior. Major features of this religious enthusiasm included ecstatic speech, divinations, miracles, and false claims to apostleship.

II. True leadership in the church is Christlike.

A. *The model of Christ*

Share with the class Dr. Willimon's comments and refer to his use of Gandhi as an illustration. Point out that Paul had pictured Jesus as a servant in Philippians 2, following the theme of the stories in Mark 10:35-45, Matthew 20:20-28, and Luke 22:24-27. Refer to these in developing the servant theme.

Observe that the acceptance of the cross by Jesus, who persevered to the end in his ministry, provides the model for Paul's spirit as he expresses it in II Corinthians 4:7-10. This is a crucial passage and should be underscored.

B. *The character of church leaders*

Titus 1:5-9 offers another view of the nature of Christian leadership. Although it comes from a time later than Paul and applies to the qualifications of ordained ministers, it sets up standards of character that are appropriate for everyone. Read this to the class as a summary of this portion of your lesson.

III. All Christians are ministers.

A. *Shared leadership*

As has been pointed out earlier in this series, we tend to leave the leadership of our churches to ordained clergy or elected lay officers who are given the responsibility to conduct the life of the church. This kind of organization smacks more of a business corporation than of a Christian community. Emphasize that although such "stated" leaders as we have just mentioned have perfectly legitimate functions to fulfill, informal leadership provided by the membership at large is indispensable to the health of the church.

B. *Roles of informal leaders*

Draw the class into a discussion of what roles church members may take as they engage in informal leadership. Suggest that in recent years, with our increasing emphasis on participation in small groups, many ways of exercising leadership have been identified. They include proposing new ideas, raising questions, requesting clarification, and challenging assumptions. Have the class list activities that can involve church members in leadership roles (caucuses, conferences with stated leaders, conversation with others regarding important issues, ad hoc committees, letters to the governing board, and so on).

C. *Sheep and disciples*

Close the discussion by observing that the metaphor of pastor and sheep in the Old Testament is not used by Paul. He sees the church members not as sheep following a protecting shepherd, but as apostles, persons "sent forth" to witness. That is the model for any church member today.

Helping Class Members Act

Discuss with your class members the possibility of scheduling a seminar on informal leadership in the church. Share your ideas with the church at large through a lay speaker in a worship service or other meeting. Encourage the nominating committee to approach annual assignment of responsibility in terms of a *distributed or shared leadership* program.

Planning for Next Sunday

Inform the class that next week's study, "Confronting False Teachers," will be a follow-up of Paul's dealings with such persons. Ask them to read I

Timothy 1 and 4 and Titus 2:1-5. Make the assignments suggested in next Sunday's "Preparing to Teach." Raise some of the questions posed in other sections of that lesson.

UNIT IV: INTEGRITY IN THE BODY OF CHRIST
Horace R. Weaver

FOUR LESSONS   **NOVEMBER 3-24**

Unit IV, "Integrity in the Body of Christ" is based on passages of Scripture drawn from the Pastoral Letters (I and II Timothy and Titus). The major passages are from I and II Timothy, whose author was very likely a disciple of the apostle Paul. The writer apparently was a pastor, or perhaps a "superintendent" or bishop who held responsibilities for pastors in various churches.

These Pastoral Letters were and are very significant in the life of the church, for they show great concern for pastors to study diligently and thoughtfully over matters of faith and orders. All doctrines are significant for life, and should therefore not be treated as though it "really doesn't matter what one believes, as long as one is sincere." False prophets have notoriously been sincere; the problem is they were wrong! Diligence in study and thoughtful concern over not only the traditions inherited but also the claims to new insights and theologies are required. These new claims may be right, but they need to be tested for validity, not for the sincerity of the believers.

So this unit considers the personal and pastoral admonitions of an administrative elder to leaders in the new and emerging churches. The four sessions are bound together under the theme "Integrity in the Body of Christ." "Confronting False Teachers," November 3, affirms the goodness of God's world (as against heretical teachings that the world is evil), and denies the need for ascetic living. "Keeping Life's Priorities Straight," November 10, states a Christian's hierarchy of values should be "righteousness, godliness, faith, love, steadfastness, gentleness." "Things Worth Remembering," November 17, suggests we honor our spiritual mentors and holydays (holidays). "One in Christ Jesus," November 24, is based on the magnificent personal letter from Paul to his spiritual son Philemon, stating that the slave Onesimus is also his son; therefore, his spiritual sons are brothers in Christ and should be treated as such by one another.

Confronting False Teachers

Background Scripture: I Timothy 1, 4; Titus 2:1-5

The Main Question—William H. Willimon

"It doesn't really matter what you believe as long as you are sincere." How many times have you heard that? The assumption behind that phrase is that our beliefs are simply a relative matter of difference in opinion, opinions that really don't make much difference in the long run. Our beliefs are merely a "head trip" of abstract, intellectual ideas which have little to do with how we live.

But the notion that "it doesn't really matter what you believe as long as you are sincere" can be easily disproved by looking at history. Down through the ages, sincere people have done horrible things due to their false beliefs, all the while sincerely believing that they were right.

The Nazis were sincere in their racist notion that the Jews were evil. White segregationists sincerely believed that black people were inferior. The depth of their sincerety did not make them right! Their beliefs were lies. Lies can be countered only by an appeal to the truth, by argument, testimony, and demonstration of error.

Sometimes we say, "It doesn't really matter what you believe as long as you are sincere," because it's easier that way. This mushy sentimentalism preserves us from having to search for answers, to debate, to use our minds and think!

For the Christian, truth is not determined by majority vote, nor is it a matter of many sincere people sincerely believing in something. Truth has its source in God and God's will for our lives. Something dear is at stake in what we believe, so we must search for the truth, difficult though that task may be.

As You Read the Scripture—Robert E. Luccock

If the Pastoral Letters (I and II Timothy and Titus) had not accomplished the purpose for which they were written, there might have been no Christian church after the second century. That gives these letters a historical importance in the New Testament second only to the first three gospels with their account of the life, death, and resurrection of Jesus. The letters to Timothy are the work of a pastor (whether a bishop we cannot tell from the letters themselves), advising and encouraging other pastors under his care in resisting false teaching and avoiding querulous disputes in their congregations. These letters were written against the heresies that in the second century threatened to sweep over and drown the church in speculations, vain discussions, asceticism, and commerce with the demonic world. The writer, deeply indebted to Paul for the faith which the Apostle transmitted to him and doubtless for some of the materials in the letters, wrote under Paul's name to give his words commanding authority.

I Timothy 4:1-5. "In later times" is a way of saying, "We are living in the last days." "Giving heed to deceitful spirits and doctrines of demons" is a sign that the end of the age approaches. Some heretical sects taught Christians not to marry and to refrain from certain foods. The writer of this letter rejects the heresy that flesh is evil and only spirit is good. All God's creation is good (Genesis 1:4). Food and marriage are both good if they are thankfully received and consecrated by "the word of God and prayer." *Whatever can be consecrated to God is permitted and encouraged.* We might say, "Whatever can be offered for God's use . . ."

Verses 6-10. The good minister will carry out the instructions contained in this letter. Notice the emphasis of this writer: the "words of faith," as distinct from faith as a "trusting relationship" found in earlier Pauline letters, and "good doctrine" (I Timothy 1:10—"sound doctrine") as the teachings had once been delivered to the churches by the true apostles. It has been said that in those early years "the church was an island in a sea of paganism." This letter underscores the critical importance for ministers to teach and preach the true faith to congregations; otherwise they are at the mercy of a mishmash of alien philosophy rendering the faith unrecognizable.

Verses 7-8. "Godless and silly myths" refers to all the farfetched and unreliable corruptions of the true gospel story that then circulated among heretics.

Verses 11-16. These verses summarize the minister's responsibilities. Apparently some people held the ministers in contempt because they were younger than the earlier apostles. The only way to silence that criticism is by show of character. Quite certainly the writer plans to come on a supervisory visit. When he comes the ministers are to be faithfully carrying out their pastoral tasks. (Notice the analogy to Mark 13:34, "each with his work" to do.) The chief tasks of the ministers were to be "public reading of scripture," preaching, and teaching of sound doctrine. The minister would have read the Old Testament Scriptures, writings of the apostles, hymns, and devotional writings.

Verse 14. "Gift" in this case means not the gifts of the Spirit of which Paul earlier wrote (Galatians 5:22), but rather the office which the minister holds by virtue of "the laying on of hands," one of the early references to formal ordination and a structured "order" of ministries.

Selected Scripture

King James Version	Revised Standard Version

I Timothy 4

1 Now the Spirit speaketh expressly, that in the latter times some shall depart from the faith, giving heed to seducing spirits, and doctrines of devils;

2 Speaking lies in hypocrisy; having their conscience seared with a hot iron;

3 Forbidding to marry, *and commanding* to abstain from meats, which God hath created to be received with thanksgiving of them which believe and know the truth.

1 Timothy 4

1 Now the Spirit expressly says that in later times some will depart from the faith by giving heed to deceitful spirits and doctrines of demons, 2 through the pretensions of liars whose consciences are seared, 3 who forbid marriage and enjoin abstinence from foods which God created to be received with thanksgiving by those who believe and know the truth. 4 For everything created by God is good, and nothing is to be rejected if it is

4 For every creature of God *is* good, and nothing to be refused, if it be received with thanksgiving:

5 For it is sanctified by the word of God and prayer.

6 If thou put the brethren in remembrance of these things, thou shalt be a good minister of Jesus Christ, nourished up in the words of faith and of good doctrine, whereunto thou hast attained.

7 But refuse profane and old wives' fables, and exercise thyself *rather* than godliness.

8 For bodily exercise profiteth little: but godliness is profitable unto all things, having promise of the life that now is, and of that which is to come.

9 This *is* a faithful saying and worthy of all acceptation.

10 For therefore we both labour and suffer reproach, because we trust in the living God, who is the Saviour of all men, specially of those that believe.

11 These things command and teach.

12 Let no man despise thy youth; but be thou an example of the believers, in word, in conversation, in charity, in spirit, in faith, in purity.

13 Till I come, give attendance to reading, to exhortation, to doctrine.

14 Neglect not the gift that is in thee, which was given thee by prophecy, with the laying on of the hands of the presbytery.

15 Meditate upon these things; give thyself wholly to them; that thy profiting may appear to all.

16 Take heed unto thyself, and unto the doctrine; continue in them: for in doing this thou shalt both save thyself, and them that hear thee.

received with thanksgiving; 5 for then it is consecrated by the word of God and prayer.

6 If you put these instructions before the brethren, you will be a good minister of Christ Jesus, nourished on the words of the faith and of the good doctrine which you have followed. 7 Have nothing to do with godless and silly myths. Train yourself in godliness; 8 for while bodily training is of some value, godliness is of value in every way, as it holds promise for the present life and also for the life to come. 9 The saying is sure and worthy of full acceptance. 10 For to this end we toil and strive, because we have our hope set on the living God, who is the Savior of all men, especially of those who believe.

11 Command and teach these things. 12 Let no one despise your youth, but set the believers an example in speech and conduct, in love, in faith, in purity. 13 Till I come, attend to the public reading of scripture, to preaching, to teaching. 14 Do not neglect the gift you have, which was given you by prophetic utterance when the council of elders laid their hands upon you. 15 Practice these duties, devote yourself to them, so that all may see your progress. 16 Take heed to yourself and to your teaching; hold to that, for by so doing you will save both yourself and your hearers.

Key Verse: **Take heed unto thyself, and unto the doctrine; continue in them: for in doing this thou shalt both save thyself, and them that hear thee. (I Timothy 4:16)**

Key Verse: **Take heed to yourself and to your teaching; hold to that, for by so doing you will save both yourself and your hearers. (I Timothy 4:16)**

FIRST QUARTER

The Scripture and the Main Question—William H. Willimon

Some Will Depart

It is comforting to learn from today's lesson that doctrinal controversy has occurred in the church from its earliest days. This insight is comforting because debates over correct belief have characterized the church in our own day—fundamentalists battle with liberals over the nature of the Bible, advocates of "right to life" argue with those who believe that abortion is a matter of freedom of choice, and the list of debates over beliefs goes on.

To many people, disagreement among Christians is a shocking sign of the unfaithfulness of the church. If we were really acting like Christians, they say, then we could agree on everything. But people only argue over things that are significant, and we only become angered when something important to us is threatened.

In a sense, pity the church that has nothing significant enough to argue about! Every time the church debates a point of belief, we are asserting that what we believe *does* make a difference. Our actions are based upon our beliefs. Our basic values determine the sort of people we are. So what we believe is worth debating.

Down through the history of the church, the church would have been better off if some courageous Christian had confronted false teachers. Before the Civil War in America, a number of so-called theologians made learned arguments alleging that the Bible taught that black people are inherently inferior and therefore fit objects for enslavement. Before the First World War, numerous American church leaders argued that Germany was an evil nation and it was our Christian duty to make war with the kaiser. Later, when people learned that our role in that war was, in great part, due to the urgings of rich American munitions producers, many became bitter that their church leaders had led them astray.

More recently, we think of the church leaders in pre-war Nazi Germany who tried to make peace between the Christian faith and Nazism. What is good for Germany is good for Christ, they argued. They thus helped twist the cross of Christ into the swastika.

Wouldn't the church have been better off to remind itself, in Paul's words to Timothy, that "some will depart from the faith by giving heed to deceitful spirits and doctrines of demons" (4:1)?

Teach These Things

What we believe is a serious matter. In the name of religion, people have committed some of the worst atrocities in history. The church has a duty to confront falsehood in whatever form it takes, particularly when that falsehood is found in the church.

A woman came into my office awhile back. She was visibly worried and upset. She had not slept in two days. Through her tears she told me that a friend of hers at work had told her that she must hold a certain belief "or you and your family will be damned to hell." Her friend then quoted certain obscure passages of Scripture to back up her claim of the essentialness of this belief for salvation.

"She knows the Bible so much better than I do," the woman said. "I didn't know how to disagree with her, even though I believe that she couldn't be right. It has me worried sick."

I then explained to her that this was a most obscure, debatable doctrine

88

which had been rejected in a church council many centuries ago. It was mentioned in only two places in the Bible and, even there, no one can be sure what is actually meant. In no way could this doctrine be considered an essential Christian belief.

The woman was greatly relieved. This experience made her determined to learn more about the Bible and her own church's beliefs—which isn't a bad idea for any of us.

What do you believe? Does it make any difference in your life? Of course it makes a difference, in all sorts of conscious and unconscious ways. So we should examine our beliefs. Presumably, one of the reasons that adults participate in your church school class is that they wish to examine their beliefs, to gain skills in discerning truth from falsehood, and to receive help from their church in deciding what they believe.

Evidently this was part of Paul's purpose in writing to Timothy. Paul sought to help this young Christian leader to examine doctrine. In this case, someone had been teaching that celibacy and dietary restrictions were divinely ordained (4:3). Paul rejects this asceticism on the basis of the Christian belief that "everything created by God is good, and nothing is to be rejected if it is received with thanksgiving" (4:4). He uses a basic Christian belief to test this new, superficial notion.

One can imagine how many good, sincere Christians might have been thrown into confusion by this false teaching about marriage and food. Paul has contempt for those who would put such unwarranted obstacles in the path of believers. A duty of a Christian leader, in Paul's view, is to help struggling Christians in the task of theological discernment.

Do Not Neglect the Gift

But how do we know truth from falsehood? To many people, religion is such a vague, debatable subject that they despair of finding any sure guides for judgment. They fall back upon the old "it doesn't matter what you believe as long as you are sincere" attitude. To them, everything is relative—you have your beliefs and I have mine. Religion is a private affair, so who can say what is right and what is wrong?

The Christian faith is not as relative and vague as we sometimes imagine. God has not left us alone in a mire of diverse and unsolvable opinions. God has given us certain gifts of discernment.

Our God-given reason is one such gift. We can use our reason to determine truth just as Paul reasons with Timothy that, if God created everything, how can something which God created be called unclean?

The Bible is another gift. "Attend to the public reading of scripture," Paul advises Timothy, "to preaching, to teaching" (4:13). Every time the Bible confronts us in the reading and preaching on Sunday morning or in study in class we are gaining a valuable (indeed, the most valuable) gift for Christian discernment.

In the case of dietary abstenance, Paul knows that Genesis says that everything God created is "good"—including food and human sexuality ("male and female he created"). So how can this belief withstand the test of Scripture?

"Do not neglect the gift you have," Paul tells Timothy. God has given us many gifts to guide us along our Christian pilgrimage. Therefore we should develop these gifts. "Take heed to yourself and to your teaching; . . . for by so doing you will save both yourself and your hearers" (4:16).

FIRST QUARTER

Helping Adults Become Involved—Harlan R. Waite

Preparing to Teach

Read the background scriptures for this week's lesson—I Timothy 1 and 4 and Titus 2:1-5—making notes of the key ideas. Consult Dr. Luccock's "As You Read the Scripture," and Dr. Willimon's "The Main Question" and "The Scripture and the Main Question."

Consider the following as a possible outline:

I. A Christian leader exhorts his colleagues.
    A. The importance of the Pastorals
    B. Belief at a time of testing
II. Beliefs do make a difference.
III. False teachers exploit the faithful.
    A. A caution about judging
    B. Examples of contemporary false teaching
IV. Sometimes we misdirect our fire.
    A. Our attacks on religious leaders
    B. Confrontation by good example

In preparation for the third section of this lesson, assign the following scripture passages to members of your class, requesting them to report on the main ideas when called upon during this session: (1) Matthew 6:2, 5, 16; (2) Matthew 11:7-10, 14; Isaiah 42:1-4; Luke 4:16-19; (3) Luke 18:9-14; Matthew 23:23-24; Matthew 5:7; (4) Jeremiah 8:8-11, 15, 18-22; (5) Luke 12:13-34; Mark 10:17-25; and (6) I Kings 21:1-20.

Introducing the Main Question

This lesson centers on this theme: What difference does belief make in our lives? Read aloud Dr. Willimon's "The Main Question" as the opening of your session.

Developing the Lesson

I. A Christian leader exhorts his colleagues.
A. The importance of the Pastorals
The leader's advice is as pertinent to us as to early Christians. Share with the class Dr. Luccock's comments on the importance of the Pastoral Epistles.
B. Belief at a time of testing
Focus on I Timothy 4 by noting, first of all, that many claims compete for our attention and acceptance. Reminiscent of the time of the Maccabees, when pagan ideas did in fact lead some of the Jews to abandon their faith, the passage calls Christians to "good doctrine" and "godliness."
II. Beliefs do make a difference.
Dr. Willimon notes this in "The Main Question." Ask the class to identify how our convictions lead us to do what we do in the fields of health, personal careers, family life, politics, social problems, and the church. To illustrate, some people have stopped smoking because they have *strong beliefs* about its effect on health; and by the same token, others continue to smoke because they *believe* smoking is harmless. Bring the discussion to the central point by asking the class to identify *Christian* beliefs that really make a difference in the lives of church members.

90

III. False teachers exploit the faithful.

   A. A caution about judging

Identifying false teachers may be risky, since it is so easy to take a self-righteous, holier-than-thou attitude toward people who have different religious convictions. At the same time, we can make certain distinctions in the spirit of love. At this point, share with the class Dr. Willimon's comments on the false teachers who have misled America and Germany.

   B. Examples of contemporary false teaching

Share the comments in the next six paragraphs and call on the appropriate scripture report as assigned in "Preparing to Teach" to help your class identify false teaching.

   1. Call attention to television programs which build on the personality of a colorful preacher. Note that ego cults develop around these personalities, even as they do in local churches where people attend worship services because they "like the preacher." Call for the report on Matthew 6:2, 5, and 16.

   2. Suggest that worship services are sometimes more entertaining than challenging. Is our church leadership catering to comfort, or is it calling people to a vital witness? Call for the report on Matthew 11:7-10, 14; Isaiah 42:1-4; and Luke 4:16-19.

   3. Some church leaders emphasize individual religious experience and play down social concern. Call for the report on Luke 18:9-14; Matthew 23:23-24; and Matthew 5:7.

   4. Consider the "peace of mind" ministries of the church. Call for the report on Jeremiah 8:8-11, 15, 18-22. Note that some have found peace of mind by escaping from the world, refusing to face up to its turmoil and its burdens. Others have found the kind of peace of mind which is symbolized by the hub of a wheel, which turns quietly and without agitation while bearing the load of the entire vehicle.

   5. Some of the more sensational televised evangelists preach a gospel of money, declaring that salvation means prosperity. How easily they forget the cross and the image of the servant who suffers (see Isaiah 53). Call for the report on Luke 12:13-34 and Mark 10:17-25.

   6. A very common emphasis from our pulpits is an appeal for patriotism. It is often easily assumed that a critic of one's nation is not patriotic, as "love it or leave it" bumper stickers frequently proclaim. Note that the great prophets of the Bible spoke out against falsehood and evil precisely because of their concern for their country. Recall how King David was challenged by Nathan (II Samuel 11:1–12:7*a*), Jeroboam by Amos (Amos 7:7-16), and Ahaz by Isaiah (Isaiah 7:3–8:8). Call for the report on I Kings 21:1-20, the story of Elijah's confrontation with Ahab. Underscore his emphasis that the survival of a nation, to say nothing of its prosperity, depends on justice for all (cf. our Pledge of Allegiance).

IV. Sometimes we misdirect our fire.

   A. Our attacks on religious leaders

Point out that we are so often inclined to criticize leaders of our own congregation that we fail to tackle the larger issues. We let petty differences of opinion divide us (I Corinthians 1:11; 3:3). We don't like the minister's sermon style or delivery (see II Corinthians 10:10); and we compare him with the last minister, whom we liked better. As the passage from Titus indicates, the real issues are matters of character and relationship, only secondarily are the concerns about skill. Read aloud Titus 2:1-5 and ask your class to discuss how criteria such as these would make a difference in interpersonal relationships.

B. *Confrontation by good example*

Observe that, like the prophets, we need to stand together as a church and deal with the moral problems around us (see Matthew 23:23-24).

If you can find Edgar Guest's poem entitled "Sermons We See," read it as the closing statement. It begins,

> I'd rather see a sermon than hear one any day,
> I'd rather one should walk with me than merely show the way,

The sermon ends this way,

> For I may misunderstand you and the high advice you give,
> But there's no misunderstanding how you act and how you live.

Helping Class Members Act

Look for ways of encouraging dialogue between persons of differing opinions. Discuss how your class can act as an agent of reconciliation.

Planning for Next Sunday

Ask your class members to read I Timothy 6:6-21. Note that the main concern of this lesson is how we keep our priorities straight. Ask each person to make a list of personal and church activities, projects, and/or goals, and to come prepared to share them. Note that the class will be asked to rank them in order of priority.

LESSON 11   NOVEMBER 10

Keeping Life's Priorities Straight

Background Scripture: I Timothy 6:6-21

The Main Question—William H. Willimon

Here is a young person at the beginning of her life. She has, as we say, "the world at her feet." She sets a course for her life, determines her goals, decides on the sort of person she hopes to be in twenty or thirty more years of life.

But something happens along the way. She compromises, makes adjustments, succumbs to this or that temptation, takes a path other than the one she intended, and that makes all the difference. She ends up being not at all the person she intended to be. What happened?

So Jesus told a story about seeds falling upon different types of soil. Some seed fell upon good ground, grew and developed, and brought forth good fruit. Other seed fell on rocky ground where the soil was shallow. It grew quickly but, when the hot sun scorched the earth, the young plants had no roots and they died. Yet still other seed fell upon the ground which was choked with weeds. The weeds crowded out the young plants, competed with them for moisture and nutrients, and eventually overcame the plants and they died.

What do you make of this parable? In what ways does it illustrate the human problem of keeping our lives pointed in the right direction, keeping our priorities straight, and developing the sort of roots that will enable us to bear good fruit?

"Aim at righteousness," Paul tells Timothy. Aiming ourselves and keeping ourselves in the right direction are the concerns of today's lesson.

As You Read the Scripture—Robert E. Luccock

I Timothy 6:6-19. The closing verses of this letter to Timothy address two concerns: godliness with a "contented spirit" (Moffatt translation), and a challenge to the pastor to "keep your commission free from stain" (Moffatt).

Verses 6-8. The author of the letter says here that godliness (religion) brings with it great gain, but only to those with "contented spirit." Those who expect that "religion is a paying concern" (Moffatt) are "depraved in mind." The Christian will be content with the minimum indispensables. Earlier Paul had written to the Philippians that he had learned to be content in whatever state he was (see Philippians 4:11-12). Jesus so spoke in the Sermon on the Mount (Matthew 6:25-33.)

Verses 9-10. The proverb here quoted (verse 10) is clear: it is not money itself that is the root of all evil, but the "love of money." Money may represent many senseless attractions and hurtful desires; loving these things plunges a person into "ruin and destruction." We cannot but think again of Jesus' words about loving God and mammon (Matthew 6:24), and the parable of the rich fool told by Luke (Luke 12:16-21). Loving money seduces a person from "the faith."

Verses 11-16. "Paul" begins his final challenge to Timothy by addressing him as "man of God." Nowhere else in the New Testament is anyone so spoken of. The purpose of the title is to impress Timothy and all "Timothys" that they are especially designated by God for their office. All Christians are to be obedient to these obligations, but particularly the pastors.

In the list of virtues, "righteousness" means in this place right behavior, and "faith" stands for obedience to the teachings. In the earlier letters of Paul, "righteousness" and "faith" mean a faithful and trusting relationship with God. This does not reflect a basic contradiction in the understanding of faith. It points rather to a different need in a later time. When Paul wrote to the Romans and Corinthians, he was addressing converted Greeks about the nature of the Christian faith. The Pastoral Letters address ministers who must secure the Christian teaching against erosion into heresy.

"Take hold of the eternal life" infers that Timothy had already entered such life when he made his confession. Was this at his baptism? (See Romans 6:1-5.) The earliest Christian confession was "Jesus is Lord." By the time of this letter there may have been an expanded creed. The reference to Jesus' confession before Pilate may have been to such a creedal statement, "suffered under Pontius Pilate." Or it may have been a reminder of the crucifixion, to raise for Timothy the prospect that he too might have to be a martyr for the faith.

Verse 14. Keeping the commission ("commandment") meant unstained faithfulness to the Pauline Christian teaching.

Verses 15-16. This stirring doxology sounds like a liturgical exclamation adapted from the public worship of that time. It echoes the very words as well as the tone of the liturgical parts of the book of Revelation. "Our Lord" will come in God's good time. No suggestion is made here that they should expect it soon.

Verses 17-19. These verses are an anticlimax following such a paean of praise. Yet they contain important imperatives for the pastor. They put the Christian readers in mind of Jesus' words about "treasure in heaven" (Matthew 6:19-20).

Selected Scripture

King James Version	Revised Standard Version

I Timothy 6:6-19

I Timothy 6:6-19

6 But godliness with contentment is great gain.

7 For we brought nothing into *this* world, *and it is* certain we can carry nothing out.

8 And having food and raiment let us be therewith content.

9 But they that will be rich fall into temptation and a snare, and *into* many foolish and hurtful lusts, which drown men in destruction and perdition.

10 For the love of money is the root of all evil: which while some coveted after, they have erred from the faith, and pierced themselves through with many sorrows.

11 But thou, O man of God, flee these things; and follow after righteousness, godliness, faith, love, patience, meekness.

12 Fight the good fight of faith, lay hold on eternal life, whereunto thou art also called, and hast professed a good profession before many witnesses.

13 I give thee charge in the sight of God, who quickeneth all things, and *before* Christ Jesus, who before Pontius Pilate witnessed a good confession;

14 That thou keep *this* commandment without spot, unrebukeable, until the appearing of our Lord Jesus Christ:

15 Which in his times he shall shew, *who is* the blessed and only

6 There is great gain in godliness with contentment; 7 for we brought nothing into the world, and we cannot take anything out of the world; 8 but if we have food and clothing, with these we shall be content. 9 But those who desire to be rich fall into temptation, into a snare, into many senseless and hurtful desires that plunge men into ruin and destruction. 10 For the love of money is the root of all evils; it is through this craving that some have wandered away from the faith and pierced their hearts with many pangs.

11 But as for you, man of God, shun all this; aim at righteousness, godliness, faith, love, steadfastness, gentleness. 12 Fight the good fight of the faith; take hold of the eternal life to which you were called when you made the good confession in the presence of many witnesses. 13 In the presence of God who gives life to all things, and of Christ Jesus who in his testimony before Pontius Pilate made the good confession, 14 I charge you to keep the commandment unstained and free from reproach until the appearing of our Lord Jesus Christ; 15 and this will be made manifest at the proper time by the blessed and only Sovereign, the King of kings and Lord of lords, 16 who alone has immortality and

Potentate, the King of kings, and Lord of lords;

16 Who only hath immortality, dwelling in the light which no man can approach unto; whom no man hath seen, nor can see: to whom *be* honour and power everlasting. Amen.

17 Charge them that are rich in this world, that they be not high-minded, nor trust in uncertain riches, but in the living God, who giveth us richly all things to enjoy;

18 That they do good, that they be rich in good works, ready to distribute, willing to communicate;

19 Laying up in store for themselves a good foundation against the time to come, that they may lay hold on eternal life.

Key Verse: **Follow after righteousness, godliness, faith, love, patience, meekness. (I Timothy 6:11)**

dwells in unapproachable light, whom no man has ever seen or can see. To him be honor and eternal dominion. Amen.

17 As for the rich in this world, charge them not to be haughty, nor to set their hopes on uncertain riches but on God who richly furnishes us with everything to enjoy. 18 They are to do good, to be rich in good deeds, liberal and generous, 19 thus laying up for themselves a good foundation for the future, so that they may take hold of the life which is life indeed.

Key Verse: **Aim at righteousness, godliness, faith, love, steadfastness, gentleness. (I Timothy 6:11)**

The Scripture and the Main Question—William H. Willimon

We Shall Be Content

What do you think is the major reason that people become sidetracked in their life's pilgrimage? What factors lead us astray? For some, the pursuit of pleasure seems to be the trap. Pleasure is such a momentary, short-lived phenomenon that its pursuit can be a neverending, desperate wandering from one "high" to the next while our lives become ever more shallow, ever more unpleasurable.

Others go after popularity, prestige, perpetual youth, power. The way of life is narrow and full of opportunities for failure.

"In the middle of life's journey," writes Dante in the opening lines of his *Inferno*, "I came to a dark wood where the straight way was lost." That is a real image, isn't it? This is the much discussed "midlife crisis," the time in life where our visions become blurred and the once sure path we set out upon in our youth meanders and we wake up one day and don't know where we are. But of course, we can lose our way at any stage in life, not just in midlife.

A score of factors may lead us astray. But, in the Bible, it is fair to say that the "desire to be rich" (6:9) heads the list of life-diverting temptations. Our desire for popularity, prestige, perpetual youth, power, or a host of other idols is usually expressed through our lust for money. Money is how we hope to buy the things we so earnestly desire. Money is the great social divider, the primary way we are taught to give significance to our lives.

So, in talking to the young Timothy, a young man at the beginning of his career, the wiser, older Paul notes that "the love of money is the root of all evils; it is through this craving that some have wandered away from the faith" (6:10).

Paul clearly appreciated the alluring, seductive, idolatrous properties of money. Like the story Jesus told of the rich fool, money deludes us into thinking that if we can just accumulate more things, build bigger barns, and buy a larger life insurance policy, we will insulate ourselves from the ravages of death, sickness, dependency, aging, and all the other facts of life that cause us anxiety.

Money is "the root of all evils" in the sense that it is the source of so much of our envy, overwork, compulsiveness, marital stress, and family breakdown. A friend of mine who is the pastor of an affluent congregation stated that the greatest social ill in his congregation was "work." As an outgrowth of people's greed, their careers had become the major source of stress, heartache, and destruction in his church.

Note that Paul doesn't simply say that money alone is "the root of all evils." The "*love* of money is the root of all evils" (6:10). As Augustine said, sin is falling in love with something other than God. Money is the great idol whose worship distracts and disfigures our lives.

We have all seen the truth of Paul's observation that "those who desire to be rich fall into temptation" (6:9). I have long said that one of the most important things for a young couple to decide on the eve of their marriage is how much money they need in order to live. If they don't, their marriage easly becomes the harried, frantic treadmill of accumulating which brings so many marriages to grief. I tell them what the major cause of marital breakdown among American couples is—disagreements about money.

If a couple's only goal in marriage is to accumulate as many possessions as possible, then that is all they will ever get out of marriage.

So I agree with Paul that it is important to sort out our "wants" from our true "needs," our "desires" from our "necessities." "If we have food and clothing, with these we shall be content," says Paul (6:8).

"It's getting harder and harder to make a living," a friend of mine said recently. But is that really true, particularly in our part of the world? Does he mean that it is difficult to obtain food and clothing? No. He means that it is harder and harder to obtain the two cars, the swimming pool, the video players, the four telephones—the list gets longer and longer when we look for contentment in our possessions, when we know not what would make us content.

Aim at Righteousness

What is our aim in life? Where are we heading? These are questions we must ask, not only when we are young like Timothy, but throughout our lives. "Fight the good fight," urges Paul (6:12).

In a way, the Christian life does feel like a kind of warfare. We are constantly facing difficult choices, hard questions, and it makes all the difference how we decide. The very word *decide* means, in its Latin derivation, "to cut off." Every time we decide (or fail to decide), we cut ourselves off from one path in favor of another.

Consider the plight of a young family and its questions. What does it mean to form family life today around the Christian vision? Sometimes it feels like a kind of warfare—we shall spend our money this way, we shall send our children to these schools, we shall use our free time to this advantage, and so on. In these choices we give shape and substance to our lives.

Wouldn't it be easier if we could separate "economic" from "spiritual" issues? Wouldn't it all be simple if we could neatly divide our lives into monetary or religious or recreational or political segments that could be kept separate from one another?

Unfortunately, that is just what many of us attempt to do. But Paul's words to Timothy remind us that life doesn't work that way. How we spend our time *is* a spiritual issue. What we do with our money *is* a religious question. A look at our checkbook stubs or our church pledge card would probably tell more about the state of our religious life than looking at us while we are seated in church would.

In our decisions as Christians about politics, economics, recreation, ethics, career, pleasure, we are setting the course for our lives. We are either strengthening or weakening our orientation toward Christ. In these ways we are laying "a good foundation for the future" (6:19).

Take Hold of the Life

The Christian life doesn't just happen. We don't become Christian by drinking the right water or by happening to live in a certain neighborhood. We become Christian by the gradual, lifelong, sometimes perilous process of learning to "take hold of the life which is life indeed" (6:19). We keep on this narrow way by keeping our eyes focused upon the light.

It is so easy to lose this way. "Certainly I believe that church is important," a man said to me the other day. "But I have to provide for my family, don't I? They are my neighbor too. Right? I'm only working seven days a week for them. I'll try to take time out for church later, when I finally get my business going. There will be time then. I'm all for going to church and taking my family to church, but a man does have to keep things in perspective, doesn't he?"

Jesus told a story. One man built his house on the sand, another built on more solid ground. The rains came down and—well, you know the story.

Helping Adults Become Involved—Harlan R. Waite

Preparing to Teach

Read I Timothy 6:6-21 and select the key ideas you wish to use for your lesson. Consult Dr. Luccock's "As You Read the Scripture" and Dr. Willimon's "The Main Question" and "The Scripture and the Main Question." Since Dr. Willimon makes use of the parable of the sower and its explanation, read Mark 4:1-20. Other New Testament references dealing with wealth are: Matthew 6:19-21; Mark 10: 17-25, 12:41-44; Luke 12:13-21, 19:1-9; James 2:1-7.

The following outline may prove helpful as a guide:

      I. To seek for gain is to experience loss.
         A. The hedonistic paradox
         B. Jesus and riches
         C. The subversive side of the coin
     II. Aim at righteousness.
         A. Intentionality
         B. The need for direction
         C. Making choices
    III. Accept the role of a steward.
         A. Contentment
         B. The spiritual side of the coin
         C. A giving heart

FIRST QUARTER

Introducing the Main Question

Open by reading Mark 4:1-9. Explain that this parable was originally used by Jesus as a word of encouragement to his disciples. In essence, he was saying that their labors would bear fruit; for much of the truth they shared would fall on fertile soil, even though some of it would fall elsewhere. Observe that as the early church grew and adapted some of Jesus' stories to its changing situation, early Christians saw how people in their communities, both inside and outside the church, responded to Christian preaching. For some it went in one ear and out the other; others took it momentarily, only to lose it in the midst of their cares and anxieties; still others received it with enthusiasm, only to abandon their new faith under the pressure of old conditions or non-Christian neighbors. For the most part, however, early Christians listened, took it seriously, and bore fruit. Now read Mark 4:10-20. Next, tell Dr. Willimon's story of the young lady for whom the future held much promise, but who compromised and finally lost her faith.

Developing the Lesson

I. To seek for gain is to experience loss.

A. The hedonistic paradox

Some four hundred years before Jesus, a Greek philosopher by the name of Aristippus advanced the doctrine that pleasure or happiness is the highest good and the chief aim of human life. This philosophy, called hedonism, has been widely accepted by human beings everywhere.

B. Jesus and riches

Even philosophers have stated that there is a "hedonistic paradox." People who seek pleasure do not always find it. Jesus said, "For whoever would save his life will lose it; and whoever loses his life for my sake and the gospel's will save it" (Mark 8:35; see also the passages suggested in "Preparing to Teach").

C. The subversive side of the coin

Although money in and of itself is not evil, there is a subversive side of the coin. It is "the love of money" (I Timothy 6:10). Point out that the Greek connotes avarice, miserliness, and covetousness. These attitudes are destructive of personality and of human relationships, two values which stand high on the list of Christian priorities. Share with the class Dr. Willimon's discussion to this effect.

By way of illustration, share with the class Ralph Korngold's story in *Two Friends of Man* of an Englishman who described Wall Street in one of his letters. "I am writing in Wall Street, where the money-changers congregate, and where affluence and beggary are seen side by side. . . . It is rightly named *Wall* Street—for those who habitually occupy it in quest of riches at the expense of mankind, are *walled* in from the sympathies of human nature, and their hearts are fleshless and hard as the paving stones on which they tread or the granite and marble buildings which they have erected and dedicated to their idle gain."

II. Aim at righteousness.

A. Intentionality

In the midst of this kind of a world, Timothy was given this advice: "Shun all this, *aim at righteousness*, godliness, faith, steadfastness, gentleness" (I Timothy 6:11). Share with the class Dr. Willimon's "Take Hold of Life," in which he says, "The Christian life doesn't just happen." The life of righteousness needs to be intentional.

B. *The need for direction*

The life of righteousness involves goal setting and aggressive action: "Fight the good fight" (I Timothy 6:12).

C. *Making choices*

Refer the class to Dr. Willimon's section entitled "Aim at Righteousness." Emphasize his statement that Christian leadership—yes, all Christian living—demands decision; and our choices should rest on a foundation of Christian values. Point out that choice is a function of freedom from the dictates of tradition, from pressures from self-appointed authorities, even from so-called practical necessity. The opportunity for choice opens up creative possibilities for us to express love in the daily decisions out of which our conduct flows.

III. *Accept the role of a steward.*

A. *Contentment*

This means making good use of what one has, not seeking to acquire something more. Share with the class the story of a United States senator who tried to throw his weight around during World War II, when sugar was rationed. Coming through a cafeteria line, he demanded more sugar than was allowed to any one individual. The attendant behind the counter simply retorted, "Stir what you have." She had somewhat the same view of the author of our letter as he enjoins "contentment." In his commentary on verses 6-8, Dr. Luccock recalls Paul's feeling when he wrote to the Philippians (4:11-12): "I have learned, in whatever state I am, to be *content*" (italics added). The Greek word expresses a feeling of self-sufficiency—not the arrogant assertion that one can do it alone, but rather the humble willingness to accept a given situation and deal with it creatively.

B. *The spiritual side of the coin*

There is a spiritual as well as a subversive side of the coin. Dr. Willimon declares that how we spend our time and money is an indicator of our spiritual maturity. Suggest that Christians necessarily acquire and use money as a means of exchange. Our challenge is to see the meaning in money, the possible creative uses to which it may be put, the way in which it can be invested in humane enterprises to enhance life.

C. *A giving heart*

Jonathan Swift once said, "The fool is the one who keeps his money in his heart instead of his head." This is the spirit of a family who suddenly became rich when oil came through on the two city lots they owned. They used the money to build a large house in a rural area. Feeling that this money was a gift of God, the family opened their home to retreats and other meetings. All that they had was dedicated to God and used for the benefit of others as well as themselves.

Helping Class Members Act

As assigned last week, ask your students to share their lists of personal and church activities, projects, and/or goals. List them on the chalkboard and ask the class to rank them in order of priority, defending their ranking on the basis of Christian values.

Planning for Next Sunday

Ask the members of your class to read II Timothy, noting the major emphases. Suggest that the discussion next week will center around how we use the gift of memory to assist us in our growth as Christians.

Things Worth Remembering

Background Scripture: II Timothy

The Main Question—William H. Willimon

I think that one of the best things about the church is the way it brings different generations together. Sometimes the church is criticized for being too homogeneous, too full of people who look exactly alike.

But of all the human gatherings of which I am a part, the church puts me in close contact with more different kinds of people than any other society. I glanced over the list of leaders for our congregation and noted that we have officers who range in age from fourteen to eighty. I look out on a Sunday morning congregation where toddlers are embraced by octogenarians and youth adopt grandparents and people are role models for others whom they might not have even known had they not been in church. The church is an intergenerational gathering if ever there were one.

The intergenerational quality of the church is more important today than ever. In American society people tend to be segregated by age. Our peer group becomes our most important group. Suburban neighborhoods tend to attract families with people from one age group. So we have "retirement communities" for people in that age bracket, and "young adult apartments."

Our scripture today is the moving testimony of a veteran Christian missionary to a younger colleague, Timothy. Paul speaks to him as "my son." He shares with Timothy the wisdom gleaned from years of toil for the sake of the gospel.

Think back upon your own life. Who were your mentors, those older adults who helped you find direction and meaning in your life, those more experienced persons who pointed you toward things worth remembering?

Where would you be today without their encouragement and guidance? Or, on the other hand, in what ways are you sharing your experiences and insights with those who are coming after you so that they might be better Christians?

As You Read the Scripture—Robert E. Luccock

Chapters 1 and 3 of II Timothy set forth what qualities of life and what gifts are given for the practice of ministry, what faithful ministers must anticipate, and what resources they may draw upon. (While these were written expressly for ordained ministers, all church people "who serve in Christ's name" are to think of themselves in these terms.)

II Timothy 1:1. This letter comes with the authority of an "apostle"; the writer declares in whose warrant he speaks: "the will of God." Just as in a worship service today things are done "in the name of the Father, and of the Son, and of the Holy Spirit," so here the final authority is not Paul but God's promise of life in Christ.

Verse 2. "My beloved child" identifies Timothy as a protégé in the faith, or a pupil, of "Paul" who writes the letter—a superior officer writing to a younger minister under his charge.

Verses 3-4. Paul nearly always began his letters with a thanksgiving. This thanksgiving is notably personal. "Your tears" may refer to a particular anguish of ministry which the two men shared. Or it may be a recollection of tears in general over the agony and the ecstasy of ministry. If "Paul" is now in prison in Rome, his longing "to see you" is understandably poignant, perhaps never to happen.

Verse 5. Timothy stands in a three-generation succession of unbroken Christian faith. He must not forget the importance of such continuing family training.

Verse 6. Along with the family nurture is the "gift of God" bestowed through the laying on of "Paul's" hands. "Rekindle" means to "stir up" or "stir into flame" (NEB). A banked fire will not do; it must repeatedly be stirred to "white heat" (Barclay).

Verse 7. The spirit of ministry will have power; it will express love and demonstrate self-control. We might render the latter "sober good sense" or "control in the face of panic or passion." The import of these five verses is that one needs both home (family) and church (training) together for the genesis and maintenance of the spirit of ministry.

Chapter 3:10. More than mere watching, "observed" translates "follow," or "by the side of," connoting a participant more than a spectator. Phillips translates the verse "You, Timothy, have known intimately both what I have taught and how I have lived." Equipment for the work of ministry comes through knowing *and* doing.

Notice the four qualities singled out as the marks of ministry: faith, patience, love, steadfastness.

Verse 11. We read in Acts 13–14 the account of Paul's persecutions in the region of Timothy's home in Asia, bringing Paul's history, even geographically, close to Timothy.

Verse 12. "All who live a godly life" must expect persecution (see Matthew 10:16-25). One commentator sums it up: "The credentials of the true Christian are his/her scars." The godly will be "brought safely through" persecution. Not so the seducers and impostors who degenerate into deceiving others *and themselves!*

Verses 16-17. The Scripture (the Old Testament, almost certainly the letters of Paul, perhaps the Gospels) serves these purposes: teaching, reproof, correction, training in right conduct. Timothy should find it worth remembering "from whom [he] learned [the faith]." He should recall also that the "man of God" is equipped by training not just to save himself but to do the good works of Jesus Christ.

Selected Scripture

King James Version	Revised Standard Version
II Timothy 1:1-7	*II Timothy 1:1-7*
1 Paul, an apostle of Jesus Christ by the will of God, according to the promise of life which is in Christ Jesus,	1 Paul, an apostle of Christ Jesus by the will of God according to the promise of the life which is in Christ Jesus,
2 To Timothy, *my* dearly beloved son: Grace, mercy, *and* peace, from God the Father and Christ Jesus our Lord.	2 To Timothy, my beloved child: Grace, mercy, and peace from God the Father and Christ Jesus our Lord.

3 I thank God, whom I serve from *my* forefathers with pure conscience, that without ceasing I have remembrance of thee in my prayers night and day;

4 Greatly desiring to see thee, being mindful of the tears, that I may be filled with joy;

5 When I call to remembrance the unfeigned faith that is in thee, which dwelt first in thy grandmother Lō'-ĭs, and thy mother Eû-nī'-cē; and I am persuaded that in thee also.

6 Wherefore I put thee in remembrance that thou stir up the gift of God, which is in thee by the putting on of my hands.

7 For God hath not given us the spirit of fear; but of power, and of love, and of a sound mind.

II Timothy 3:10-17

10 But thou hast fully known my doctrine, manner of life, purpose, faith, longsuffering, charity, patience,

11 Persecutions, afflictions, which came unto me at An'-tĭ-ŏ<u>ch</u>, at Ī-cō'nĭ-ŭm, at Lystra; what persecutions I endured: but out of *them* all the Lord delivered me.

12 Yea, and all that will live godly in Christ Jesus shall suffer persecution.

13 But evil men and seducers shall wax worse and worse, deceiving, and being deceived.

14 But continue thou in the things which thou hast learned and hast been assured of, knowing of whom thou hast learned *them;*

15 And that from a child thou hast known the holy scriptures, which are able to make thee wise unto salvation through faith which is in Christ Jesus.

16 All scripture *is* given by inspiration of God, and *is* profitable for doctrine, for reproof, for correction, for instruction in righteousness:

3 I thank God whom I serve with a clear conscience, as did my fathers, when I remember you constantly in my prayers. 4 As I remember your tears, I long night and day to see you, that I may be filled with joy. 5 I am reminded of your sincere faith, a faith that dwelt first in your grandmother Lo´is and your mother Eunice and now, I am sure, dwells in you. 6 Hence I remind you to rekindle the gift of God that is within you through the laying on of my hands; 7 for God did not give us a spirit of timidity but a spirit of power and love and self-control.

II Timothy 3:10-17

10 Now you have observed my teaching, my conduct, my aim in life, my faith, my patience, my love, my steadfastness, 11 my persecutions, my sufferings, what befell me at Antioch, at Ico'nium, and at Lystra, what persecutions I endured; yet from them all the Lord rescued me. 12 Indeed all who desire to live a godly life in Christ Jesus will be persecuted, 13 while evil men and impostors will go on from bad to worse, deceivers and deceived. 14 But as for you, continue in what you have learned and have firmly believed, knowing from whom you learned it 15 and how from childhood you have been acquainted with the sacred writings which are able to instruct you for salvation through faith in Christ Jesus. 16 All scripture is inspired by God and profitable for teaching, for reproof, for correction, and for training in righteousness, 17 that the man of God may be complete, equipped for every good work.

17 That the man of God may be perfect, throughly furnished unto all good works.

Key Verse: Wherefore I put thee in remembrance that thou stir up the gift of God, which is in thee by the putting on of my hands. (II Timothy 1:6)

Key Verse: I remind you to rekindle the gift of God that is within you through the laying on of my hands. (II Timothy 1:6)

The Scripture and the Main Question—William H. Willimon

The Gift That Is Within You

Paul begins his letters to his young friend Timothy with the admonition to "rekindle the gift of God that is within you" (1:6).

Paul, wise counselor that he was, knew the best way to bring out the best in his friend. Rather than see Timothy as a young man who was ignorant and foolish, a mere boy in need of advice and correction, Paul begins by accentuating the gifts that Timothy has. He reminds Timothy of what he has rather than what he lacks.

When a parent sits a child down one evening and talks with him or her, urging the youth to "make something out of yourself," the parent is implying that the child isn't worth much as he or she is. A better way is for the parent to sit down with the child and say that the child has great talents, worthwhile gifts, and promising abilities, and offer the hope that the child will use them well. That is the approach of Paul in his words to Timothy.

Unfortunately, in our dealings with our children and youth, we accentuate the negative rather than the positive. We lecture them, nag them, scold them. Our words thus become what psychologists call self-fulfilling prophecy. That is, if people are constantly told that they are worthless, they will eventually start acting that way. A child who is told "you are irresponsible," will eventually believe that and act irresponsibly. What do we expect? The child is only fulfilling our evaluation of him.

Youth can learn from the experience of their elders. But the problem is often that their elders do not know how to share their experiences with youth in such a way that the youth do not resent or resist their elders' advice.

The older adult who says, "Boy, when I was your age I never spoke like that to my father!" is sure to elicit a most negative reaction from a child.

A better way might be to say, "I used to get angry with my father too. I couldn't understand why he set up so many rules for me. I didn't always see that he was doing it because he loved me and wanted to spare me some pain in life. I don't blame you for questioning some of my rules. But I hope that you'll try to understand that I have these rules for you because I love you."

I once knew an older man whose gift was the ability to discover talent in young people and to help them use their talents. He had few advantages in his own life. Because his family had been poor, he had little formal education. But his experiences of poverty made him all the more determined to help others develop their gifts to the fullest.

One day he fell into a conversation with a young man who made a delivery at his home. He found that the young man wanted to be an artist. "Unfortunately, I will be a delivery man for the rest of my life because I don't have the funds to go out on my own."

He took up the young man's cause and made it his own. He spoke to some of his friends, got the young man a scholarship to a nearby school of art, and today that young man is painting beautiful pictures rather than delivering packages.

Would that we all had the gift of helping others discover and develop their God-given abilities!

You Have Observed My Life

"Now you have observed my teaching, my conduct, my aim in life, my faith, my patience, my love, my steadfastness, my persecutions," Paul says to Timothy (3:10-11). Paul sees himself as an example to his younger colleague.

It is a fearful thing to be an example for a younger person. One of the troublesome things about being a parent is that your children are always looking at your behavior and learning from their observations. Sometimes we parents complain that our children don't do what we tell them to do. Alas, too often they are learning all too well by observing us.

"Daddy, why did you not stop for that red light?" they ask. "Mommy, you're not sick, why did you tell Mrs. Jones that you were not at church school because you were ill?" The question is not *if* the young will learn by our example but rather *what* example are we giving them?

Paul clearly sees himself as an example to Timothy. But it is interesting to note that he sees himself as an example, not simply of success and achievement, but as an example of suffering, failure, and struggle. "All who desire to live a godly life in Christ Jesus will be persecuted," Paul assures Timothy (3:12).

I think we do the young a great injustice if we only share with them our victories and our joys but never our failures and our sadness. In looking back over our lives, sometimes we only remember the good days, not the bad. In some ways it is good that the human brain seems to filter out the bad and preserve the good.

But we must not make life appear to be easier than it really is, especially when we are being examples to the young. One of the good things about reading history or biography is that such reading reminds us that every life, even the very greatest of lives (perhaps we should say *especially* the very greatest of lives), has its dark days. When we hide these aspects of life from the young, we give them a false impression of reality and set them up for great disappointment when their lives do not work that way.

In talking with a young man who had gone through a painful divorce, I asked, "Was there anything your parents did or did not do in bringing you up that contributed to your difficulties in marriage?"

He replied, "No, not really. My parents had a wonderful marriage. I can't blame my marital failures on them."

Then, in a more reflective mood, he said, "I suppose if my parents did anything 'wrong' for me, it would be that they made marriage look too easy. I just assumed that everyone who got married was automatically happy. They should not have shielded me from their marriage, good marriage though it was."

In talking about Christian discipleship, Paul does not pull any punches with Timothy. He tells him that it will be rough. It has been rough for Paul; it will be rough for Timothy.

We learn not only from others' paths to happiness, but we learn also from their journeys through pain. Many older adults can testify to the young that the bad or difficult times of life, while we would not have wished them upon ourselves, can contribute to the good of life.

Sometimes the young, in their lack of experience, expect life to be all good times, perpetual good health, with no disappointments or failures. This is not life; especially, it is not the Christian life. As Paul says, the Christian life is a tough challenge, and there are many people who would willingly lead us astray (3:12-13).

That the Man of God May Be Complete

Finally, Paul urges Timothy to be attentive to Scripture, just as we are being attentive to Scripture in our adult church school class today.

Many of us, like Timothy, have "from childhood . . . been acquainted with the sacred writings" (3:15). But we know that it is not enough to simply be exposed to the Bible as a child. New adult demands require new biblical understandings so we must continue to confront the Bible at each stage in life.

In a way, our study of Scripture is the ultimate intergenerational way to grow. In the Scripture, we learn from our elders in the faith. We listen to their stories and grow in our own faith stories. A person who doesn't know the Bible is limited only to his or her own experience—which can be a very limited view indeed.

So we keep studying the Scriptures. We keep before us the things worth remembering so that we might be taught, reproved, corrected, and trained in righteousness (3:16), so that we, in our own age and in our own place, might be "complete, equipped for every good work" (3:17).

Helping Adults Become Involved—Harlan R. Waite

Preparing to Teach

Although only a portion of this week's background scripture is printed, read all of II Timothy. Augment your understanding by reading Dr. Luccock's "As You Read the Scripture" and Dr. Willimon's "The Main Question" and "The Scripture and the Main Question."

Here is a possible outline for your guidance:

    I. Fulfill your ministry.
       A. A call to witness
       B. The nature and audience of the Pastoral Letters
   II. Rekindle the gift of God within you.
       A. Continuing immaturity
       B. The fear of change
       C. The need to grow
 III. The sacred writings instruct us.
       A. The inspiration of the Scriptures
       B. The power of the Scriptures
       C. The lessons from the elders

Introducing the Main Question

Share with the class the affirmation that memory is a precious gift of God. It keeps us in touch with time-honored values which need to be preserved, even if modified and updated. It also quickens our awareness that we, like our forebears, can meet the challenges of life in creative ways.

Ask the class to discuss the memories that have become sacred to our country. At Thanksgiving, class members will recall and celebrate the memory of pilgrims. List several other great moments of our national life to illustrate the importance of memory. Acknowledge, incidentally, that some of our memories are negative: "Remember the *Maine*"; "Remember Pearl Harbor." Emphasize that the Christian gospel of love offers us correctives at this point.

Bitter memories have found their way even into the Scriptures (see Psalm 137:7-9). However, memories have focused chiefly on great positive experiences that provide models for the attitudes and behavior of successive generations. For example, the Exodus version of the Ten Commandments holds the sabbath day in remembrance because it celebrates God's creation of the world (Exodus 20:8-9). The version of the Ten Commandments in Deuteronomy calls for the observation of the sabbath day as a day of remembrance of the Exodus (Deuteronomy 5:15). Share with the class Psalm 77:11-20, another memory of the great event of deliverance.

Some memories are designed to give warnings. Refer the class to Luke 17:32-33—"Remember Lot's wife. Whoever seeks to gain his life will lose it, but whoever loses his life will preserve it." For the story of Lot's wife, see Genesis 19:24-26.

Of course, the early Christians remembered Jesus and shared his memory with others. Later generations of Christians remembered not only Jesus but also the apostles. The writer of the Pastoral Letters (I and II Timothy and Titus) remembered Paul and the impact he made on their lives.

Developing the Lesson

I. Fulfill your ministry.

   A. A call to witness

This exhortation is a call to witness by word and example. The great examples to follow are Jesus (2:8) and Paul (3:10).

   B. The nature and audience of the Pastoral Letters

Share the notation by Dr. Luccock that the Pastorals, cast in the form of letters from Paul to Timothy and Titus, were really manifestos written about A.D. 125 and directed to all church members to help them fulfill their ministry as Christian witnesses.

II. Rekindle the gift of God within you.

   A. Continuing immaturity

Ask the class to discuss why the word *rekindle* is used. Had the early Christians, like so many of us, lost their fire, their enthusiasm, their aggressiveness? It was not uncommon in those days, nor is it today, that Christians "settled in" and inadvertently frustrated their growth. A counselor of adults once remarked at the end of an unsuccessful day, "Of all the curable illnesses that afflict mankind, the hardest to cure, and the one most likely to leave its victim a chronic invalid, is adolescence." How many of us have ceased to grow as Christians? To what extent do we still view the Bible in terms of the lessons we were taught as children?

   B. The fear of change

Sometimes it is simply fear of change that inhibits growth. When John Wesley organized his class meetings, several of his followers objected that they had had no such meetings in the past. Why did they have them now? Wesley responded by saying that they should have had them earlier. They were designed to prevent Christians from losing their vitality. He insisted

106

that Methodists should be open to instruction, so that every day they could be wiser than they were before.

C. *The need to grow*

The need to grow was expressed very forcibly in a letter to the congregation of the City Temple in London. Dorothy Sayers wrote that we learn the technical terms involved in our vocations, but we shy away from learning the theological language that is at the heart of our faith. We are as much the poorer in our Christian understanding as the electrician who knows nothing about ohms, amperes, and volts.

III. *The sacred writings instruct us.*

A. *The inspiration of the Scriptures*

Dr. Willimon calls the study of Scripture "the ultimate intergenerational way to go." Share some of his ideas, then turn to the theme of the inspiration of Scripture (see II Timothy 3:16). There are two levels from which to view this matter. On the level of factual human experience, the Bible started in experience; experience was reflected upon and yielded certain meanings; meanings were shared in what has been termed *oral tradition*; oral tradition was put in written form; writings came to be highly valued; and some centuries later, that which started as meaningful experience came to be sacred writing, or Scripture.

On the theological level, the people who first told what had happened to them felt that God was a part of their experience. It was people sensitive to God who selected the oral traditions and, later, the writings to form what would later become our Bible. Thus the Bible is inspired in the sense that God was a part of the process, from experience to canonization.

It is significant to note that by A.D. 125 Paul was being quoted (II Timothy 2:11 equals Romans 6:8) or alluded to (II Timothy 2:12 alludes to Romans 8:17). By A.D. 140, II Peter counts Paul among the Scriptures (II Peter 3:16).

B. *The power of the Scriptures*

The Scriptures have proved their power through the centuries. Let the class recall instances where certain movements in history have had their roots in the Bible (the Reformation, the Declaration of Independence, for example). Henry VIII of England forbade the reading of Scripture in English. He recognized the power that was inherent in the Word and considered it a threat to this reign.

C. *The lessons from the elders*

Even as we learn from our elders today, we learn from our elders of long ago. The Bible extends our circle of conversation to include wise and devoted people of ages past who still have a word for us.

Helping Class Members Act

Let the class discuss how it might promote the use of the Bible in your church. Call on denominational leaders, neighboring pastors, teachers in nearby colleges, or your own local minister to conduct a survey of the Bible, laying out its historical settings, its message, and its meaning for today.

Planning for Next Sunday

Announce next week's theme and ask your students to read Philemon; Galatians 3:23-29; and I Corinthians 12:12-13. Look over the suggestions for developing the lesson and recruit several students to report on the various supplemental scripture passages which are suggested.

Thanksgiving

PAT McGEACHY

Most of the holidays that we celebrate in our churches are literally *holy days*. That is, they are days set apart by the church to remember one of the great acts of God or an event in Jesus' life or an important doctrine. Many of them, like Christmas and Easter, began as Christian festivals and collected to themselves pagan and secular customs (trees and rabbits and the like) from the countries into which Christianity was introduced. But *Thanksgiving*, at least in the United States and Canada, began as a political holiday and has since become a part of our traditional church calendars.

Or did it? It depends on where you start. The first nationwide day of Thanksgiving in the United States was proclaimed by George Washington, and the custom was revived by President Abraham Lincoln. He probably would never have done this had it not been for the persistence of an editor, Sarah Josepha Hale, who had campaigned for many years for such a celebration. Ever since then, our presidents have formally announced such a day each year, usually on a Thursday in November. (In 1941 Congress established the fourth Thursday as a legal holiday.)

But of course, as every school child knows, the custom goes back much further than Lincoln. A thanksgiving was called by Governor William Bradford in the new Plymouth colony after the 1621 corn harvest promised new hope to the freezing, starving Puritans. It was a three-day feast. Then, in 1623, the governor called for a special Day of Thanksgiving with prayers as well as celebration. Men, women, and children, including both native Americans and colonists, took part in the preparations and the feasting. The custom spread throughout the colonies, and from time to time thanksgiving was proclaimed in the young American nation in various states.

Thanksgiving is a natural act, as spontaneous as applause. When something really good happens, we instinctively cry, "Thank God!" just as some folk denounce the deity when they are unhappy. It is all the more remarkable, then, that Lincoln called for national gratitude during the height of the Civil War, calling for "a day of thanksgiving and praise to our beneficent Father." It is a measure of the man that our country finally was given a national day of gratitude when its grief was heaviest.

Perhaps in this respect, Lincoln's instincts were hearkening back to a tradition even older than the country he was serving. We had long before been admonished (Ephesians 5:20) to express our gratitude in good times as well as bad, "always and for everything giving thanks in the name of our Lord Jesus Christ to God the Father." I Thessalonians 5:18 says, "Give thanks in all circumstances; for this is the will of God in Christ Jesus for you." This is *not* natural and spontaneous. My father-in-law, a respected pediatrician, used to become very upset with some of the mothers of his patients who would order their children to say, "Thank you," to the doctor after a painful visit (involving a shot of some sort). "That's too much to expect of the child," he would say. "*You* know that this is a good thing, but the child doesn't understand it." It takes a Job to say in time of calamity, "Blessed be the name of the Lord" (Job 1:21).

But Job's example is a good one, and Lincoln's instincts were right. So was Governor Bradford: nearly half of his people had perished in the harsh winter prior to that first good harvest. How shall we deal with calamity and misfortune? What do we do in a world like ours, riddled with problems from starvation to terrorism? How dare we be thankful when so many are homeless, unemployed, and without hope? Well, it will not help the troubled folk of the world for us to spend our time in bemoaning and wringing our hands. Let us rather count our blessings, draw on such powers as we possess, and, thanking God for our gifts, use them in the service of those in need.

At the heart of our understanding of Thanksgiving lies our practice of Holy Communion or the Lord's Supper. Sometimes this sacrament is called the *Eucharist*. Most Christians will remember that this Greek word means "thanksgiving." Indeed, if you travel in Greece today, you will hear people saying "thank you" to one another using just that word, *eucharistó*. The word comes from an even older word meaning "grace" or "favor," the gifts of God. (The words *charismatic* and *charity* come from the same root.) Communion is called Eucharist because of the great prayer of thanksgiving that is offered, thanking God for the gracious gift of Christ's body and blood, as well as for the gifts of bread and wine. Here we are "celebrating" a tragedy: rejoicing over a broken body and shed blood. And here we come to some understanding of how, in the midst of tragedy, we can be full of thanksgiving.

On the night when his best friends let him down, Jesus, Paul tells us (I Corinthians 11:24), took bread and *"when he had given thanks,* he broke it" (italics added). Thus the roots of our thankgiving really go even behind the New Testament to the feast of the Passover, and the seder prayer:

> Praised art Thou, O Lord our God,
> King of the universe,
> Creator of the fruit of the earth.

Our Hebrew ancestors thus gave thanks on their dark night of deliverance, and so should we, even in our hour of need, turn to God in gratitude. It is a commandment from of old:

> Enter his gates with thanksgiving,
> and his courts with praise!
> Give thanks to him, bless his name! (Psalm 100:4)

It is a song from harvests centuries older than that on the Plymouth shore:

> Let all the people praise thee!
> The earth has yielded its increase. (Psalm 67:5-6)

Indeed it goes back to the dawn of recorded history, to the strange story of the calamity that wiped out the world and the thanksgiving of its only survivor and his family: "Then Noah built an altar to the Lord" (Genesis 8:20). In good times and bad we are to show our gratitude to the One who has promised: "While the earth remains, seedtime and harvest, cold and heat, summer and winter, day and night, shall not cease" (Genesis 8:22).

It is good for us to give thanks as a nation each year, whether times be perilous or prosperous. And it is good for us as individuals to develop good habits of showing our gratitude, not because God needs to hear us, but because we need to learn to live victoriously. In winter, let us thank God for the north wind that drives our roots deep, and in spring for the sweet new grain with its bread for the world. From the surgeon's knife to the year's report card, let us rediscover the ancient reality that the truth sets us free, and give thanks to God in all things. On this one point, at least, Church and State seem to be agreed, and we have a holiday called by the secular authorities and blessed by our spiritual leaders. Perhaps here both halves of our split selves, one foot in this world and one in heaven, may walk together.

LESSON 13 NOVEMBER 24

One in Christ Jesus

Background Scripture: Philemon; Galatians 3:23-29;
I Corinthians 12:12-13

The Main Question—William H. Willimon

Dear Paul:

Thank you for your letter. I am pleased to hear that you are well.

Frankly, your letter came as somewhat of a shock to me. You know the grief Onesimus has caused me. I paid good money for him. You know that the law protects my property rights, and Onesimus is my property. When he ran away from my house, taking with him some of my goods, it caused us great distress. I was therefore shocked that he should have found you and that you should have befriended him.

But, I can assure you, the greatest shock of all was to read your request that I receive Onesimus back into our household "as a beloved brother." Really, Paul, could you expect me to go against all reason, to go against my anger and bad memories, to go against our law itself and just let bygones be bygones so far as Onesimus is concerned?

Even though your letter was written in your usual beautiful style, it caused me great anger when I read it.

That is, it angered me when I *first* read it. Upon second reading your words began to work on me. As you say, we have been through a lot, you and I. You helped found this little church at my house and I shall always be grateful for your leading my family and friends to Christ.

I also began to realize that I have no right to receive the grace of Christ who accepted me, sinful though I am, as his child unless I am also willing to accept Onesimus. I was a slave, in a manner of speaking. I was in bondage to my old ways, my pagan beliefs, and Christ has freed me. So why should I hold the past against Onesimus?

Good friend Paul, you have done it to me again! You have turned my world upside down and shown me the truth! Go ahead, send Onesimus back to me, and I shall receive him as my brother. I shall do it, as you say, not because you command me but for the sake of love.

Isn't it strange? What strange things the love of Christ does to us! A year ago I would have killed Onesimus if I could have laid my hands upon him. Now, I shall indeed receive him. I shall forgive. I shall do even more than you ask.

Apphia and Archippus send their love.

Philemon

110

As You Read the Scripture—Robert E. Luccock

Being Paul's most personal letter, Philemon reveals a great deal about the Apostle's character at work. In this letter the Apostle practices what he has preached. In Galatians 3:23-29 and II Corinthians 12:12-13, Paul declared that all Christians who are baptized into Christ become members of one body. Whether Jew or Greek, slave or free, man or woman—*all are one in Christ.* That is the general principle. In the letter to Philemon we have a specific instance where Paul and Philemon are called to practice this principle. Paul asks Philemon (or Archippus, if Onesimus belonged to him) to receive the runaway slave back as a brother in Christ—still a slave, but now recognized as a beloved brother in the Lord.

Verses 1-2. Comparing these verses with Colossians 4:7-17, one strongly suspects that Paul wrote Colossians and Philemon at about the same time. A wide consensus of scholars holds that "the church in your house" meant Philemon's house, most likely in Colossae. Whether Paul's prison was in Rome or Ephesus we do not know, although tradition tends to favor Rome. If that is true, he wrote the letter during the last two or three years of his life.

Verses 4-7. A thanksgiving is offered according to Paul's usual letter-writing pattern.

Verse 8. The Jerusalem Council had conferred on Paul great authority over the churches in the Greek-Gentile world. As an apostle so endowed, he could have insisted on whatever he deemed best concerning the runaway slave, even demanding of Philemon that the slave be given to him.

Verse 9. Instead he "appeals to" Philemon on behalf of Onesimus, not by coercive authority, but "for love's sake." Paul puts the case so that Philemon's goodness might be "of your own free will" (verse 14).

An "ambassador" represents one who is the head of a community, state, or kingdom. Christ is the head of the church, Paul his ambassador. (See II Corinthians 5:20 and Ephesians 6:20.)

Verse 10. Onesimus apparently became a protégé of the Apostle. Maybe he turned to Paul for help or offered his help to Paul in prison. Probably the slave became a believer under Paul and so thinks of him as his "father in the faith." For what does Paul now appeal? Does it not appear, considering everything said in the letter, that he is asking Philemon to release Onesimus to him, so that the slave may become "useful" for the gospel in Paul's company?

Verse 16. Paul now asks that Onesimus be treated as more than a slave, in fact, *as a brother!* He does not even hint that he be set free. Paul does not question the institution of slavery. No one did. Emancipation of slaves lay far ahead in time. What Paul asks is in itself profoundly radical: that the slave be treated as a brother, and that he be received as Philemon might receive Paul.

Verse 20. Paul may have written these words with a knowing smile—to remind Philemon of the spiritual debt between them. How could Philemon miss Paul's graciously veiled desire to have Onesimus as his own? We don't know whether Philemon acceded to Paul's wish. But would the letter be included in the New Testament if he had not? In fact, a most plausible hypothesis has it that this slave was the Onesimus who became bishop of Ephesus in later years, and that it was he who initiated the publication of the Pauline letters. So began the formation of the New Testament. In any case, such a demonstration as this letter gives as to how all social, racial, and sexual barriers can be—must be—transcended in the church makes this letter one of the most precious possessions in Christian literature.

Selected Scripture

King James Version

Revised Standard Version

Philemon 1-3, 8-20

1 Paul, a prisoner of Jesus Christ, and Timothy *our* brother, unto Phí-lē´-mon our dearly beloved, and fellow-labourer,

2 And to *our* beloved Apphia, and Är-chĭp´-pŭs our fellow-soldier, and to the church in thy house:

3 Grace to you, and peace, from God our Father and the Lord Jesus Christ.

. . . .

8 Wherefore, though I might be much bold in Christ to enjoin thee that which is convenient,

9 Yet for love's sake I rather beseech *thee*, being such an one as Paul the aged, and now also a prisoner of Jesus Christ.

10 I beseech thee for my son Ō-nĕs´-ĭ-mŭs, whom I have begotten in my bonds:

11 Which in time past was to thee unprofitable, but now profitable to thee and to me:

12 Whom I have sent again: thou therefore receive him, that is, mine own bowels:

13 Whom I would have retained with me, that in thy stead he might have ministered unto me in the bonds of the gospel:

14 But without thy mind would I do nothing; that thy benefit should not be as it were of necessity, but willingly.

15 For perhaps he therefore departed for a season, that thou shouldest receive him for ever;

16 Not now as a servant, but above a servant, a brother beloved, specially to me, but how much more unto thee, both in the flesh, and in the Lord?

Philemon 1-3, 8-20

1 Paul, a prisoner for Christ Jesus, and Timothy our brother.

To Phile´mon our beloved fellow worker 2 and Ap´phia our sister and Archip´pus our fellow soldier, and the church in your house:

3 Grace to you and peace from God our Father and the Lord Jesus Christ.

. . . .

8 Accordingly, though I am bold enough in Christ to command you to do what is required, 9 yet for love's sake I prefer to appeal to you—I, Paul, an ambassador and now a prisoner also for Christ Jesus—10 I appeal to you for my child, Ones´imus, whose father I have become in my imprisonment. 11 (Formerly he was useless to you, but now he is indeed useful to you and to me.) 12 I am sending him back to you, sending my very heart. 13 I would have been glad to keep him with me, in order that he might serve me on your behalf during my imprisonment for the gospel; 14 but I preferred to do nothing without your consent in order that your goodness might not be by compulsion but of your own free will.

15 Perhaps this is why he was parted from you for a while, that you might have him back for ever, 16 no longer as a slave but more than a slave, as a beloved brother, especially to me but how much more to you, both in the flesh and in the Lord. 17 So if you consider me your

17 If thou count me therefore a partner, receive him as myself.

18 If he hath wronged thee, or oweth *thee* aught, put that on mine account;

19 I Paul have written *it* with mine own hand, I will repay *it:* albeit I do not say to thee how thou owest unto me even thine own self besides.

20 Yea, brother, let me have joy of thee in the Lord: refresh my bowels in the Lord.

partner, receive him as you would receive me. 18 If he has wronged you at all, or owes you anything, charge that to my account. 19 I, Paul, write this with my own hand, I will repay it—to say nothing of your owing me even your own self. 20 Yes, brother, I want some benefit from you in the Lord. Refresh my heart in Christ.

Key Verse: **For by one Spirit are we all baptized into one body, whether we be bond or free; and have been all made to drink into one Spirit. (I Corinthians 12:13)**

Key Verse: **By one Spirit we were all baptized into one body—Jews or Gentiles, slaves or free—and all were made to drink of one Spirit. (I Corinthians 12:13)**

The Scripture and the Main Question—William H. Willimon

One in Christ Jesus

We believe the hymn was sung at the baptism of early Christians. As the first rays of Easter light dawned, as the new Christian arose from the baptismal waters, the congregation may have stood and sung, "For in Christ Jesus you are all sons of God, through faith. For as many of you as were baptized into Christ have put on Christ. There is neither Jew nor Greek, there is neither slave nor free, there is neither male or female; for you are all one in Christ Jesus" (Galatians 3:26-28).

In the world we live in are certain distinctions: male, female, rich, poor, uneducated, educated. We divide the world through these lines of distinction. But in baptism, all the old, worldly distinctions get washed away. Rising up through the baptismal waters, "there is neither slave nor free, there is neither male or female."

One can imagine how radical these words sounded in the ancient world where slavery was an accepted custom, women were often regarded as a little more than their husband's property, and Jews and Greeks regarded one another as untouchable and subhuman. From the beginning the church countered these distinctions and called people to unity in Christ.

Elsewhere, Paul switches from the symbol of a living body to make his point about unity in Christ. First Church Corinth was a bitterly divided congregation. Disputes over matters like speaking in tongues, the Lord's Supper, and baptism had divided the Corinthians into a dozen bickering factors. The Corinthians were not divided due to distinctions of sex or race but rather over questions of theology and church practice. Religion, which should be a source of unity, had become a source of bitter controversy—as it still is the source of some of our most bloody disagreements today.

"For just as the body is one and has many members," Paul says, "and all the members of the body, though many, are one body, so it is with Christ. For by one Spirit we were all baptized into one body—Jews or Greeks, slaves or free—and all were made to drink of one Spirit" (I Corinthians 12:12-13). Once again baptism, which begins the Christian life, is seen as the

113

beginning of the end of the worldly distinctions by which we live before we become Christians. A body which is divided is a dying body. A church which divides up people on the basis of their race or class is a dying church.

Paul strikes this note of oneness in Christ again and again in his writings, but nowhere more beautifully than in his touching letter to Philemon, the subject of today's lesson.

Our Beloved Fellow Worker

Today's lesson takes us back to the first days of the church, days when the church met in the homes of some of its more affluent members. Philemon was an early Christian who opened his home to his fellow Christians for worship. He was undoubtedly a dedicated Christian, possibly a man who had braved persecution and social ostracism because of his faith. But, in Paul's mind, Philemon still has some growing to do as a Christian.

"I appeal to you for my child, Onesimus," Paul writes Philemon (verse 10). Onesimus is a runaway slave who stole from his master but has since been converted to Christianity. Paul seeks reconciliation between Onesimus and his master, Philemon.

How strange is the gospel, strange because of the changes it effects in our lives. Onesimus is a slave, a person without rights, the property of another man, a thief. But Christ has turned his life around. Now, Paul dares to call him his own son, "my very heart" (verse 12). One wonders about the changes in Onesimus' life due to his conversion, in his own view of himself and his value as a child of God.

The gospel also works in strange, wonderful ways in how we look at other people. Prior to his conversion, Paul would probably not have befriended a former slave. The Romans had strict laws regarding the treatment of slaves. A person who protected and befriended a runaway slave might face severe penalties. Paul has not only converted Onesimus to the faith but has made the slave a fellow worker in spreading the gospel.

Now Paul approaches Philemon, "our beloved fellow worker" (verse 2), in hopes of averting Philemon's punishment of his runaway slave. Paul entreats Philemon to "receive him as you would receive me" (verse 17). What is the basis of this appeal?

Paul says that he could command Philemon to receive Onesimus (verse 8), "yet for love's sake I prefer to appeal to you" (verse 9) He wants Philemon to do this out of love and not out of simple obedience to Paul's wishes (verse 14). He bases his request not on some appeal to humanitarian good will, but rather on Philemon's faith. Because Philemon is a Christian, he is bound to receive Onesimus as a brother "both in the flesh and in the Lord" (verse 16).

Our relationship to Christ thus changes our relationship to other people. We cannot pray "Our Father" without coming to see all of God's children as our brothers and sisters. We cannot draw distinctions between those we would love and those whom we would not love after we see how God's love in Christ embraces everyone.

Wouldn't it be a lot easier to be a Christian if we were not constantly called to change and grow in our attitudes—particularly our attitudes toward other people? Poor Philemon! Before he became a Christian, it was enough for him to divide the world between free and slave. But now, he can separate people, discriminate against others, judge other people by the color of their skin or by their sex or race or nationality only by going against the very faith he holds.

How strange is this good news which makes relatives out of strangers!

For Love's Sake

I was sitting in a discussion group with a group of laypeople in a church in a southern town. I said, "Paul says that when we become Christian, we 'die to our old selves and are born again into new people.' Have you had experiences in your own life which bear witness to this idea?"

One by one, each person told how he or she had been called upon to "die" in order to be "reborn." Interestingly, nearly all mentioned their attitudes about the racial issue. As one woman said, "I used to think that I couldn't live in a world—unlike the Old South—where black people were treated equally. But I was wrong. God helped me see the error of my ways and led me to a totally new point of view."

I daresay that woman would feel a close kinship with Philemon. Unfortunately, we are not told in the Bible how Philemon responded to Paul's appeal for Onesimus. Whatever he did, surely Philemon knew that he had come face-to-face with the demands of the gospel.

Time and again we must learn the truth of Paul's claim that we are all "one in Christ."

Awhile back, my church's denomination was attacked in an article in a popular national magazine. Our church was accused of sending mission funds into countries that were controlled by Communist governments. The article implied that such relief work was un-American and subversive.

We had much discussion in our congregation about the article. A number of people were deeply disturbed that the church might be sending money to people who were hostile to our government and our way of life.

"Feed 'em today, fight 'em tomorrow," said one angry man. "We have no business being friends in any way with these godless, Communistic atheists."

Someone else spoke up. She had traveled widely in many parts of the world, including mainland China. She told the group of attending a worship service in Peking, of the unity she had experienced with Chinese Christians in that service.

"These are our brothers and sisters," she said. "You can't simply dispose of them by calling them 'godless atheists.'"

The discussion began to turn. We talked about what it must be like being a Christian in a country where the government is hostile to the church. We decided that these were the countries where the church should be the most active in helping support our brothers and sisters in Christ to stand firm in their faith.

"Feed 'em today, fight 'em tomorrow" is not a New Testament expression. Nor is the notion that God cares only for those of us who live in the United States, nor is the idea that our way of life and our form of government are the only Christian possibilities.

Philemon would probably tell us that the belief of "one in Christ Jesus" turns that sort of thinking upside down.

Helping Adults Become Involved—Harlan R. Waite

Preparing to Teach

Read the scriptures assigned for today in this order—Philemon; Galatians 3:23-29; and I Corinthians 12:12-13. Note the sequence: an appeal to accept a former slave as a brother, the assertion that the distinction between slave and free is meaningless in Christ, and the affirmation that we experience unity as members of the Body of Christ.

115

FIRST QUARTER

Read Paul's letter to Philemon in the Phillips translation to capture more accurately his warm personal style. As you read, note the humane attitude, the sense of humor, and Paul's sense of irony. There is a play on words not apparent in the English, but obvious in the original Greek: the name Onesimus means "useful." Paul plays on this theme in verse 11; and in verse 20, the word "benefit" is the same root word as the name of the slave.

Dr. Luccock's "As You Read the Scripture" will provide important background for your understanding of the letter. As you develop the ideas for presentation, consult Dr. Willimon's "The Main Question" and "The Scripture and the Main Question."

The following outline may be a possible organization for your lesson:

I. Philemon gets a new brother.
   A. A "father" and two sons
   B. A promise of usefulness
   C. An appeal to love
   D. Paul's most personal letter
II. The church struggles with old prejudices.
   A. Jew and Greek
   B. Slave and free
   C. Male and female
III. Christ turns our values upside down.
   A. A revolutionary gospel
   B. Change in a Christian life
IV. We need one another.

Introducing the Main Question

Point out that today's lesson centers around these questions: How does our Christian faith affect our human divisiveness? To what extent and in what ways are we willing and able to implement the gospel of love and reconciliation in our everyday life?

Dr. Willimon has taken a look into the heart of Philemon to see what struggle may have been going on in his life. Read to your class his imaginary letter from Philemon to Paul, in answer to the letter we are studying today.

Developing the Lesson

I. Philemon gets a new brother.

A. A "father" and two sons

Since Paul calls himself "father" to Onesimus in verse 10, he lays the foundation for asking his "son" Philemon to accept Onesimus as a brother (verse 16). Suggest that there may have been a twinkle in Paul's eye as he wrote verses 9 and 10. The Greek word translated "ambassador" in the Revised Standard Version is more properly translated "old man" (as indeed it is in the Phillips translation, in the King James Version, in Moffatt's translation, and in The Living Bible). Is it possible that "an old man" who is unmarried could have a child? Yet Paul claims that he has become a father (in prison!). He surely must have been enjoying this figure of speech.

B. A promise of usefulness

Paul's sense of humor appears again as he plays on the name Onesimus in verses 11 and 20 (see "Preparing to Teach"). There is also a bit of fun in his mock formality and the touch of irony in verses 18-19.

Note, also, how much at home Paul feels with Philemon. In verse 22, he says, "Prepare a guest room for me."

C. *An appeal to love*

Finally, notice the manner in which he puts forth his request. He might well have exercised his authority as a spiritual leader. However, Paul appeals to Philemon's Christian spirit in the confidence that Philemon will indeed do even more than he asks. Thus it becomes a matter of genuine love on the part of Philemon, not a yielding to the pressure of authority.

D. *Paul's most personal letter*

Summarize by sharing Dr. Luccock's introductory paragraphs, noting that this is Paul's most personal letter. The warmth, sense of humor, play on words, and touch of irony reveal Paul as a sensitive human being.

II. *The church struggles with old prejudices.*

It is apparent that in the early church harmony did not come naturally (see Acts 6:1; 15:1-11; I Corinthians 1:10-13; and Galatians 2). Read Galatians 3:23-29 aloud, and observe that the mention of points of tension shows what good reason Paul had to be concerned about Philemon's acceptance of Onesimus.

A. *Jew and Greek*

Ask the class to identify religious tensions we experience today which correspond to the conflict between Jew and Greek in Paul's day (for example, divisions between denominations; conservatives versus liberals; Protestants versus Catholics; Christians versus Jews and Moslems).

B. *Slave and free*

Pursue the matter of divisive prejudices by noting that social class distinctions and prejudices are the modern counterpart of the division between slave and free. Identify the people in our society who feel trapped by economic or cultural conditions (the poor, the powerless, the disenfranchised). By contrast, identify the "free"—people who are powerful and wealthy enough to manipulate political, economic, and social affairs.

C. *Male and female*

Finally, let the class discuss the matter of equality between male and female. Acknowledge that Paul did indeed place certain limits on the participation of women in the church. At the same time, he recruited women, supported many of their rights, and commended them for the leadership they exercised in the Christian congregations. While Paul was not entirely free from conventional prejudices of his time, he sowed the seed for the emergence of women in roles of leadership; and we may build on his assertion that "there is neither male nor female."

III. *Christ turns our values upside down.*

A. *A revolutionary gospel*

The Christian gospel, outwardly a simple call to the good life, has proved to be a revolutionary gospel. Refer your class to Acts 17:1-15, which tells a typical story of trouble which erupted almost everywhere Paul preached. Observe the cry of the authorities of Thessalonica: "These men who have turned the world upside down have come here also" (Acts 17:6).

B. *Change in a Christian life*

Noting that the gospel demands change in a Christian's life, share with the class Dr. Willimon's story of the difference of opinion over the use of missionary funds. Let your class evaluate the different views expressed. Note in conclusion that in Christ, narrow loyalties give way to larger ones.

Children of the law move beyond their truly great heritage to become children of faith; supporters of cultural institutions and conventions rise above them to become citizens of the kingdom of God. Let the class identify ways in which we may respond to a world that is becoming steadily smaller by letting our hearts grow considerably larger.

IV. We need one another.

A. H. Boutwell tells of a trip which Anne and Charles Lindberg described in their book *North to the Orient.* At an isolated community where they stopped, they found that the only two clergymen were not on speaking terms. Boutwell concludes by alluding to I Corinthians 12:21—"when the eye says to the hand, 'I have no need of thee,' the whole body is discredited." Read I Corinthians 12:14-25 aloud.

Helping Class Members Act

Have the class identify root causes of tension among members of your church. Recruit a panel of three or four persons to study selected issues and offer to present them before women's groups, men's fellowships, the governing body of the church, and/or the congregation.

Planning for Next Sunday

Look ahead to next week's "Preparing to Teach." Inform your class of the theme. Ask your students to read the background scripture and come prepared to discuss the main question.

SECOND QUARTER
Advent: To You a Savior

Horace R. Weaver

FOUR LESSONS   DECEMBER 1–22

The next four lessons focus on the coming of Jesus as a baby in Bethlehem and the meaning of this event for Christians today. Jesus is presented as the fulfillment of God's promise to the Jewish people for a Messiah, which has ultimate significance for all people of all time.

During the reign of Caesar Augustus (27 B.C.–A.D. 14), Emperor of Rome, Herod the Great died (4 B.C.). Herod was succeeded by his son Archelaus, who in turn was succeeded by procurators. Luke connects Caesar and Jesus in an interesting way: Caesar sent out an edict of registration which caused Jesus to be born in the "city of David." At Jesus' birth a choir of angels sang, "Glory to God in the highest, and on earth peace" (Luke 2:14). During Caesar's reign he established the Pax Romana (peace of Rome), and the Roman Senate ordered the erection and consecration of a new altar to Pax Augusta in the Campus Martius. For his efforts toward peace he was hailed as both savior and god—indeed "savior of the whole world." His birthday was hailed as "the good news through him for the world" (Priene inscription 40-42). Luke carefully and subtly makes Jesus (not Augustus!) the one through whom the Lord God and heaven will bring peace on earth. Luke is the only writer of the Synoptic Gospels who calls Jesus Savior—could that have been anything other than intent? Who is Savior: Augustus or Jesus the Messiah? Can a decree by the Roman Senate bear more significance than a decree from God via angels? "Glory to God in the Highest!"

The first of two courses in this quarter deals with "Advent: To You a Savior." (The second course, of two units, is "Jesus Teaches About the Christian Life.") There are four lessons based on advent scriptures: "The Announcement," December 1, explains God's creative actions for the coming of Jesus to and through Mary; "The Birth of Jesus," December 8, describes Joseph's preparations for the coming of Jesus as well as Jesus' birth; "Good News of Great Joy," December 15, expresses the joy of the shepherds' experience of the good news; then "Star in the East," December 22, reviews the lovely story of the (Babylonian?) magi (astrologers) who are led by their pseudoscientific studies to the manger scene.

Contributors for the second quarter:

Bond Fleming, retired United Methodist minister of the North Georgia Conference, now residing in Oxford, Georgia.

Roy H. Ryan, Section on Christian Education, Board of Discipleship, The United Methodist Church, Nashville, Tennessee.

William H. Willimon.

R. Michael Winters, associate pastor in Christian education and Outreach, First Presbyterian Church, Gallatin, Tennessee.

The Announcement

Background Scripture: Isaiah 9:1-7; Luke 1:26-56

The Main Question—William H. Willimon

It is an odd way to begin the story of a Messiah. The very name Messiah means "God's anointed one." The Messiah was the long-awaited deliverer of Israel.

What's so odd is the way the story of this Messiah begins. His advent is announced, not to the powerful and the mighty, the vain and the glorious, but to a lowly, unmarried, peasant woman named Mary.

Right here, right at the first, we learn some significant things about this new Messiah by the very way his birth is announced.

Today is the Second Sunday of Advent. *Advent* means "arrival" or "coming." We are preparing ourselves, in these four Sundays of Advent, for the arrival of the Christ.

When Jesus was born in Bethlehem, lots of people missed the announcement because they were looking in the wrong place for the wrong kind of Messiah. Could that happen to us?

The pages of modern history are strewn with the names of a host of false messiahs and their hapless followers—Adolf Hitler, Jim Jones, Josef Stalin, to mention a few.

What does the way Jesus' birth was announced tell us about who this Messiah will be?

As You Read the Scripture—Bond Fleming

Luke and Matthew are the biblical sources for information about the virgin birth of Jesus. We are indebted to Luke for the fullest account of the birth. Luke alone tells the story of the annunciation, or the announcement. There was no news conference called. There was simply a "one-on-one" visitation by Gabriel, God's messenger, to Mary in the little town of Nazareth. The announcement was one of world-shaking, or world-redeeming, importance. But only Mary heard it.

Isaiah 9:2-7. For centuries the Jewish people had hoped for the coming of the Messiah, visioned by the prophets. Look at the vision of hope proclaimed in Isaiah 9:2-7, especially verses 6 and 7. No doubt every Jewish maiden hoped that she might be the one of whom the Messiah would be born. Gabriel told Mary that she was to be the favored one, the mother of "the Son of God."

The name of Joseph, who was "of the house of David," is mentioned in Luke 1:27, before the name of the virgin is given. The virgin birth is mentioned also in Matthew. In Matthew 1:18-21, Mary's pregnancy poses a moral problem for Joseph. In Luke 1:34, the announcement involves a biological problem for Mary. She has no husband to father the child. She is assured that the child will be conceived by the power of God. Her son, the Son of God, will be great and of his kingdom there will be no end.

The doctrine of the virgin birth developed in answer to an early heresy

120

called Docetism. The doctrine is not found in the letters of Paul or in the Gospel of Mark. Heretical Docetists denied the humanity of Jesus; it was only an appearance; he had not actually suffered or died. But the faith of the early church was that God had entered into human life in Jesus Christ for the salvation of mankind. For the early church Christ was both human and divine. He was conceived by a human mother, a virgin, in terms of the promise in Isaiah 7:14. In answer to Mary's asking how, the angel said (verse 35), "The Holy Spirit will come upon you, and the power of the Most High will overshadow you." The child was to be named Jesus (Jesuah or Joshua, which means "the Lord saves"). He was to be "like his brethren in every respect" (Hebrews 2:17).

People in those days often sought signs as proof of God's presence. Zechariah, in Luke 1:18, asks for a sign concerning the promise of a son. Although Mary did not ask for one, a sign or proof is given to her. Note the reference, in verse 36, to her kinswoman Elizabeth, who in her old age had conceived a child and was now in her sixth month.

Luke 1:28-30. Mary is greeted by the angel Gabriel as "O favored one," and, to relieve Mary's anxiety, Gabriel tells her that she has found "favor with God." For Mary the favor of God surely did not mean ease and pleasure and prosperity. During her lifetime Mary experienced great sorrow and heartache as the mother of Jesus. Since then she has been blessed among women. The favor of God, for Mary, is found in her song of praise, the Magnificat, Luke 1:46-55.

There are several stages in Mary's visit from the angel Gabriel. When the revelation came to Mary, she was filled with wonder and awe. But then Mary came to realize, in verse 37, that "with God nothing will be impossible." Such a faith as Mary's leads people to respond to adventuresome challenges with courage. The commitment of Mary, in verse 38, was complete; as the handmaid of the Lord, she pledged to Gabriel, "Let it be to me according to your word."

Selected Scripture

King James Version

Luke 1:26-38

26 And in the sixth month the angel Gabriel was sent from God unto a city of Galilee, named Nazareth,

27 To a virgin espoused to a man whose name was Joseph, of the house of David; and the virgin's name *was* Mary.

28 And the angel came in unto her, and said, Hail, *thou that art* highly favoured, the Lord *is* with thee: blessed *art* thou among women.

29 And when she saw *him,* she was troubled at his saying, and cast in her mind what manner of salutation this should be.

Revised Standard Version

Luke 1:26-38

26 In the sixth month the angel Gabriel was sent from God to a city of Galilee named Nazareth, 27 to a virgin betrothed to a man whose name was Joseph, of the house of David; and the virgin's name was Mary. 28 And he came to her and said, "Hail, O favored one, the Lord is with you!" 29 But she was greatly troubled at the saying, and considered in her mind what sort of greeting this might be. 30 And the angel said to her, "Do not be afraid, Mary, for you have found favor with God. 31 And behold, you will conceive in your womb and bear a

30 And the angel said unto her, Fear not, Mary: for thou hast found favour with God.

31 And, behold, thou shalt conceive in thy womb, and bring forth a son, and shalt call his name JESUS.

32 He shall be great, and shall be called the Son of the Highest: and the Lord God shall give unto him the throne of his father David:

33 And he shall reign over the house of Jacob for ever; and of his kingdom there shall be no end.

34 Then said Mary unto the angel, How shall this be, seeing I know not a man?

35 And the angel answered and said unto her, The Holy Ghost shall come upon thee, and the power of the Highest shall overshadow thee: therefore also that holy thing which shall be born of thee shall be called the Son of God.

36 And, behold, thy cousin Elisabeth, she hath also conceived a son in her old age: and this is the sixth month with her, who was called barren.

37 For with God nothing shall be impossible.

38 And Mary said, Behold the handmaid of the Lord; be it unto me according to thy word. And the angel departed from her.

Key Verse: **He shall be great, and shall be called the Son of the Highest. (Luke 1:32)**

son, and you shall call his name Jesus.

32 He will be great, and will be called
the Son of the Most High;
and the Lord God will give to
him the throne of his father
David,

33 and he will reign over the house
of Jacob for ever;
and of his kingdom there will be
no end."

34 And Mary said to the angel,
"How shall this be, since I
have no husband?"

35 And the angel said to her,
"The Holy Spirit will come upon
you,
and the power of the Most High
will overshadow you;
therefore the child to be born
will be called holy,
the Son of God.

36 And behold, your kinswoman Elizabeth in her old age has also conceived a son; and this is the sixth month with her who was called barren. 37 For with God nothing will be impossible." 38 And Mary said, "Behold, I am the handmaid of the Lord; let it be to me according to your word." And the angel departed from her.

Key Verse: **He will be great, and will be called the Son of the Most High. (Luke 1:32)**

The Scripture and the Main Question—William H. Willimon

The People Who Walked in Darkness

The people who walked in darkness
have seen a great light;
those who dwelt in a land of deep darkness,
on them has light shined. (Isaiah 9:2)

With these beautiful words, Isaiah announces deliverance to the troubled Chosen People.

Time and again in the story of Israel, the Lord is depicted as the one who saves his people in their times of trouble. Noah is saved from the devastating flood. Jacob is preserved in Egypt. When the oppressed people were in slavery, the Lord heard their cries and led them to freedom through the work of Moses. When they were starving in the wilderness, the Lord gave his people manna and water from the rock. This is a God who hears and delivers.

Isaiah tells of the birth of a child who shall be called, "Wonderful Counselor, Mighty God, Everlasting Father, Prince of Peace" (9:6). Whether or not Isaiah was thinking of the Messiah, Christians took these words and applied them to Jesus of Nazareth, who was their Counselor, Father, Prince of Peace.

And the Virgin's Name Was Mary

When we have a good piece of news, it is natural for us to want to share that news with those people who are closest to us. We carefully decide which close friends to share it with first so they can join us in our celebration.

Luke says that when the time was right for God's anointed one to be born, the news was carefully announced to certain privileged people. It is important for us to note who those chosen few were.

They are not the people one might have expected. The birth of the Messiah was not announced to the biblical scholars; in fact, they seemed to have missed the whole thing! It was not announced to the high priest in the temple or to the politicians in the statehouse. None of these high and mighty ones got the news.

The news comes first "to a virgin betrothed to a man whose name was Joseph, of the house of David; and the virgin's name was Mary" (Luke 1:27).

It might not shock us that Mary was the first to get the news. After all, she was the mother-to-be of the child.

But to an early hearer of this story, living in second-century Palestine, it might seem a strange story indeed. In that part of the world, in that day, women were considered to be second-class citizens at best. Women were on the bottom of society, the virtual property of their husbands. Not only are we told that Mary was a woman, but she was an unmarried woman.

A woman's only hope then was for a good marriage. As an unmarried woman, this Mary could have had no property or status. Also, as an unmarried pregnant woman—well, you can imagine her difficult situation.

And yet it was to this person that the angel Gabriel first told the news—along with aging Zechariah and Elizabeth, who were thought to be lowly for other reasons.

Even in today's society, where advances have been made in social justice, women and the aging are often relegated to second-class status. These two groups are often on the poverty level. They are not traditionally thought to be among the powerful and influential. So we are able to sense some of the surprise and shock of this story of deliverance.

To this unmarried woman, Gabriel says, "Hail, O favored one, the Lord is with you" (1:28).

Hail, O Favored One!

Evidently, from the way the story of the annunciation reads, Mary was frightened by the arrival of Gabriel. And why not? It is always a frightening thing to find oneself face-to-face with the purposes of God and to find out that you are chosen to be part of those purposes.

Perhaps Mary felt like her old kinswoman Sarah, who was also told that she was to bear a child into the world. Sarah laughed because it seemed impossible for a woman her age to be giving birth to a child. Mary did not laugh, but she was certainly frightened by the prospect of it all.

After all, Mary was in a rather frightening position.

A few years ago, my church youth group did (or undid) the story of the nativity in a Christmas pageant which they wrote and directed themselves. Which part of the story fascinated these teenagers the most? They spent a major part of the drama dealing with Mary's annunciation and Joseph's response. They depicted Mary nervously, hesitatingly telling Joseph that she was pregnant. Then we saw Joseph fuming and ranting about the stage until the angel came to him too, telling him that he should not be angry.

The congregation squirmed in their seats throughout this segment. It was embarrassing to witness all this, especially embarrassing to witness it in church!

And yet, let's face it, Mary was in a rather embarrassing situation. Like Sarah before her, she felt herself out of place in the way the world judges right and wrong. She felt that she was the wrong person, the wrong time, the wrong place. But unlike Sarah, Mary responded, not with a laugh but with "Behold, I am the handmaid of the Lord; let it be to me according to your word" (1:38).

Handmaid of the Lord

In her response, Mary becomes a model for discipleship. In fact, Mary was often called the first disciple since she is the first in the story of Jesus to respond affirmatively to the call of God and to place her life at God's disposal.

"I am the handmaid of the Lord," she says. She is God's assistant, a co-worker with God in bringing about the deliverance of the people who sit in darkness.

Do you know any Marys in your church—people who are approached by God for some surprising, difficult, unexpected work of deliverance and who say yes?

He retired from a prominent position with a major oil company. Now he looked forward to a quiet retirement with long days on the golf course and nothing to concern himself with except how to lower his golf score.

But one day his minister approached him with a problem. It seems that their church, located in a decaying neighborhood downtown, was being inundated with requests for aid from people who were down on their luck. The pastor found it impossible to do her work and help all these people too. She came to him, asking him to use his expertise in business, in management and organization, to help the church assist these unfortunate folk.

He thought of all the reasons that he was not the right person for the job, all of the reasons why he ought to turn her down. But something in him told him that this was something which the Lord really wanted him to do.

So he gave it a try. In a month he had a large program under way, staffed by twenty volunteers, distributing cash, food, and clothing to needy families and individuals. Because he knew people all over town, he knew just the right person to call on for the donation of a blanket or food or a hot meal. He also knew how to get good legal advice, how to negotiate with creditors and landlords. He became a servant of the Lord.

In a way, he was like Mary, who, going about minding her own business, was met by an angel who told her that God wanted her to manage some of his business. Mary said yes and thereby pointed out to us the way to discipleship.

When God's messengers come into our lives, asking us to be God's assistant, will we be able to respond as Mary did? Will we be able to see God working out salvation for the world through us?

Let us pray that we might.

Helping Adults Become Involved—Roy H. Ryan

Preparing to Teach

Today we begin a course of four lessons for Advent. These four sessions deal with "Advent: To You a Savior."

As you prepare to teach this lesson, it will be important to look at the unit as a whole. Read the biblical material, Dr. Willimon's "The Main Question," Dr. Fleming's comments in "As You Read the Scripture," and Dr. Willimon's "The Scripture and the Main Question." This will give you an overview of the unit and a good feel for what is coming during this high season of Advent.

Your aim in this lesson will be to help persons prepare for the coming of Christ anew in their lives and to challenge them to live with hope and expectation.

It is wise to begin your preparation several days before you are to teach. Study the scripture with a good commentary—such as *The Interpreter's Bible*—if you have one available. Make notes for ideas and illustrations that you might be able to use in your presentation. The following outline may help you organize your plan for teaching.

> Introduction: The importance of expectancy for the coming of Christ.
> I. Mary is visited by the angel.
> A. Found favor with God
> B. To be the mother of the Messiah
> II. Mary is troubled by announcement.
> A. She is not married.
> B. She is assured it is God's doing.
> III. Nothing is impossible with God.
> A. Mary is reassured.
> B. Mary is obedient.
> IV. We live with hope and expectation.
> A. What happens when God comes to us?
> B. Hope for better days

Introducing the Main Question

What is the true meaning of Christmas? How many times have you heard that question? Probably every year since you can remember. But is this not an appropriate question for Christians to ask?

It is easy to do the usual preparation for Christmas. We can buy the tree and decorate it. We can buy gifts for family and friends and mark that off the list! We will probably enjoy the parties and other social and religious activities. But how do we prepare for the coming of Christ? Are we ready to open our lives to the renewing and transforming power of his coming?

The announcement to Mary was quite a shock. She was to be the mother of the Messiah. How does the announcement of Jesus' birth affect you? Our world? What is the significance of this strange and wonderful event?

These are some of the questions and issues you will want to address as you begin this Advent unit.

Developing the Lesson

Read the two background scripture assignments from Isaiah 9:1-7 and Luke 1:26-56. The Isaiah passage sets the context in which the people of Israel viewed the coming of the Messiah. This would have influenced Mary's reaction to this special announcement.

The passage in Luke known as the Magnificat (1:46-55) is one of the cherished passages of the Bible. It is a crucial part of the Christmas story. Luke's account of the announcement and birth of Jesus are the most popular readings for this season.

I. *Mary is visited by the angel.*

A. *Found favor with God*

Blessed indeed! What greater blessing for a Jewish woman than to be chosen to be the mother of the Messiah! Mary was overwhelmed with the thought.

B. *To be the mother of the Messiah*

How can this be? What Mary failed to see and what we often miss in our limited view is that nothing is impossible with God. A humble young woman is chosen to be the mother of the sovereign Lord. He shall be great. The kingdom he will establish will have no end. Is it any wonder that she was "troubled at the saying" (verse 29)?

II. *Mary is troubled by the announcement.*

A. *She is not married.*

What shame is this which is to come upon her! To give birth out of wedlock would seem to be the opposite of "being blessed." The question "How shall this be, since I have no husband?" (verse 34) is at the heart of the doctrine of the virgin birth, a doctrine that has been troubling and sometimes divisive among Christians of various traditions and denominations.

B. *She is assured it is God's doing.*

That is some consolation! God does not always choose conventional ways to enter history. "The Word became flesh" (John 1:14) certainly goes against conventional wisdom. God's self-disclosure may come in strange and unpredictable ways.

III. *Nothing is impossible with God.*

A. *Mary is reassured.*

When the messenger explains what is happening to her and why, she accepts this as God's doing. When strange and wonderful things happen in our lives, we can also be reassured when we believe that God is working in our lives.

B. *Mary is obedient.*

She says in response to the messenger's explanation, "Behold, I am the handmaid of the Lord; let it be to me according to your word." One of the most beautiful characteristics of a faithful Christian disciple is his or her obedience to the Lord. As we shall discover in later lessons this quarter, to be a true disciple calls us to obedience.

IV. *We live with hope and expectation.*

A. *What happens when God comes to us?*

We are sometimes surprised and perplexed, but we are not left hopeless. As those who believe in a God who came to us in Jesus of Nazareth and who still comes to us, we live on the edge of expectation. The message of Christmas is a message of hope. God has not forgotten us.

B. *Hope for better days*

The people of Israel had just about given up hope for a savior (Messiah). The announcement to Mary breaks through that despair and sheds the light of hope again upon God's people. Those who could recognize that Light, those who found in Mary's child a reason to go on in that time and in our own time, can live toward the uncertain future with hope.

Helping Class Members Act

You may want to challenge class members to approach this Advent season with an openness and expectation that will allow a new thing to happen in their lives.

Many persons are depressed during the Christmas holidays. What can we do to give hope and encouragement to those who are down? Think of some concrete ways that we can show others that we live by hope and with expectancy.

Planning for Next Sunday

Ask members of your class to read and reflect on the scripture passages for next Sunday (Isaiah 11:1-9; Micah 5:2; Matthew 1:18-25; Luke 2:1-7).

You might ask one or two persons to be prepared to give a brief personal statement (witness) on "What the Birth of Jesus Means to Me."

LESSON 2   DECEMBER 8

The Birth of Jesus

Background Scripture: Isaiah 11:1-9; Micah 5:2; Matthew 1:18-25; Luke 2:1-7

The Main Question—William H. Willimon

Holding my child in my arms for the first time, I looked into his little face and wondered what this boy might become. Where will he go, what will he do? How high will he climb in his life; how low will he sink?

Any parent looking into the face of any newborn child must wonder the same thing. As an adult, we know how life can be. Life has its joys, yes. But it can also have its sadness, and the sadness can be devastating.

What did Mary feel as she looked into the face of her newborn son? Surely Mary knew enough to know that, if this child were God's Messiah indeed, she had good reason to fear what the future might hold for him.

SECOND QUARTER

In the Italian Renaissance, Raphael painted a picture of Mary with her baby. It has become known as *The Madonna of the Chair*, because Mary is sitting in a chair. It is a picture of a mother tenderly holding her baby. But if you look closer, look into Mary's eyes, you will see that Raphael has painted a rather worried, foreboding look on Mary's face. She draws her son away from us, holding him back with her strong arm. She knows.

In the biblical accounts of first months of Jesus' life, we also get a hint of the dark, sinister forces which swirl around his life, the forces with which he must do battle later. We are given a glimpse of what the future will hold for this Savior of the world and for his followers.

As You Read the Scripture—Bond Fleming

The birth of Jesus marks the dividing point in history in the Western world. Even those who refuse to accept Jesus as Lord acknowledge him as they date their letters, their deeds, and their wills. The printed scripture, only fifteen verses from Matthew and Luke, tells of this significant birth.

The two accounts are quite different. Matthew does not tell of any journey from Nazareth to Bethlehem, but in Matthew 2:5-6, Bethlehem is emphasized as the place where Micah had prophesied that the Messiah would be born. Matthew's Gopel is supposed to have been written to and for the Jews. Matthew makes frequent references to experiences in the life of Jesus which are in fulfillment of promises in the Jewish Scriptures. In 1:22-23, Matthew interprets the virgin birth as the fulfilling of "what the Lord had spoken by the prophet" found in Isaiah 7:14.

Luke 2:1-7. The account in Luke does mention the journey from Nazareth to Bethlehem. It was in Nazareth that Gabriel came to visit Mary. Supposedly both Mary and Joseph lived in the Galilean village. But Joseph's forebears, descendants of David, were from Bethlehem of Judah. From Nazareth to Bethlehem is about eighty-five miles. Luke dates the birth by telling of the required trip to Bethlehem for the purpose of enrollment for taxation.

Verse 5. Mary is referred to as Joseph's "betrothed"; in Matthew 1:18 Mary is spoken of as being "betrothed" to Joseph, but in Matthew 1:20 Joseph is told to "take Mary your wife." A Jewish betrothal became marriage when the groom took the bride to his home; to break a betrothal was like a divorce in that the man had to give the bride a writ of divorce. And a bride whose betrothed fiancé died was considered a widow.

Both gospels mention Joseph and Mary and Bethlehem, and both tell of her firstborn son. Luke tells of the manger scene, which is not found in Matthew's account. The innkeeper, whose rooms were filled, did not know of the celebrated birth that was to take place.

Matthew 1:18-21. Matthew describes Joseph as a just man; he was sympathetic and understanding and open toward God. That is the condition on which the Lord could speak to Joseph and assure him about Mary and tell him to name the child Jesus. Jesus was considered to be Joseph's son; see Luke 4:22. What a father Joseph must have been! Because he was such a good man, Joseph made it easy and natural for Jesus to speak of God as Father in intimate and loving relations.

Luke calls attention to a decree from Caesar Augustus, emperor of the vast Roman Empire, which extended from the island of Britain eastward across the Mediterranean on into Asia. Surely it seemed, as in Luke 2:1, that "all the world" was involved. Luke is concerned with an event, the birth of Jesus, that took place in a stable in a conquered province far from the imperial palace in Rome. There is strong contrast between the long-forgotten impact of the imperial decree of Caesar and the lasting influence of the lowly birth of Jesus.

It is appropriate that the birth of Jesus (a name that means "the Lord saves" or "God's salvation") should take place in Bethlehem, a name that means "the house of bread." The town is located in a fertile plain surrounded by less fertile areas. Bread is mentioned many times in the life and teachings of Jesus; for example, in one of the temptations, in the feeding of the multitudes, and in the prayer Jesus taught the disciples. And Jesus described himself as the bread of life.

Selected Scripture

King James Version	Revised Standard Version

Matthew 1:18-25

18 Now the birth of Jesus Christ was on this wise: When as his mother Mary was espoused to Joseph, before they came together, she was found with child of the Holy Ghost.

19 Then Joseph her husband, being a just *man,* and not willing to make her a public example, was minded to put her away privily.

20 But while he thought on these things, behold, the angel of the Lord appeared unto him in a dream, saying, Joseph, thou son of David, fear not to take unto thee Mary thy wife: for that which is conceived in her is of the Holy Ghost.

21 And she shall bring forth a son, and thou shalt call his name JESUS: for he shall save his people from their sins.

22 Now all this was done, that it might be fulfilled which was spoken of the Lord by the prophet, saying,

23 Behold, a virgin shall be with child, and shall bring forth a son, and they shall call his name Emmanuel, which being interpreted is, God with us.

24 Then Joseph being raised from sleep did as the angel of the Lord had bidden him, and took unto him his wife:

25 And knew her not till she had brought forth her firstborn son: and he called his name JESUS.

Matthew 1:18-25

18 Now the birth of Jesus Christ took place in this way. When his mother Mary had been betrothed to Joseph, before they came together she was found to be with child of the Holy Spirit; 19 and her husband Joseph, being a just man and unwilling to put her to shame, resolved to divorce her quietly. 20 But as he considered this, behold, an angel of the Lord appeared to him in a dream, saying, "Joseph, son of David, do not fear to take Mary your wife, for that which is conceived in her is of the Holy Spirit; 21 she will bear a son, and you shall call his name Jesus, for he will save his people from their sins." 22 All this took place to fulfil what the Lord had spoken by the prophet:

23 "Behold, a virgin shall conceive
    and bear a son,
    and his name shall be called
        Emman´-u-el"
(which means, God with us). 24 When Joseph woke from sleep, he did as the angel of the Lord commanded him; he took his wife, 25 but knew her not until she had borne a son; and he called his name Jesus.

Luke 2:1-7

1 And it came to pass in those days, that there went out a decree from Caesar Augustus, that all the world should be taxed.

2 (*And* this taxing was first made when Cȳ-rē´-nĭ-ŭs was governor of Syria.)

3 And all went to be taxed, every one into his own city.

4 And Joseph also went up from Galilee, out of the city of Nazareth, into Judaea, unto the city of David, which is called Bethlehem; (because he was of the house and lineage of David:)

5 To be taxed with Mary his espoused wife, being great with child.

6 And so it was, that, while they were there, the days were accomplished that she should be delivered.

7 And she brought forth her firstborn son, and wrapped him in swaddling clothes and laid him in a manger; because there was no room for them in the inn.

Key Verse: Thou shalt call his name JESUS: for he shall save his people from their sins. (Matthew 1:21)

Luke 2:1-7

1 In those days a decree went out from Caesar Augustus that all the world should be enrolled. 2 This was the first enrollment, when Quirin´i-us was governor of Syria. 3 And all went to be enrolled, each to his own city. 4 And Joseph also went up from Galilee, from the city of Nazareth, to Judea, to the city of David, which is called Bethlehem, because he was of the house and lineage of David, 5 to be enrolled with Mary, his betrothed, who was with child. 6 And while they were there, the time came for her to be delivered. 7 And she gave birth to her first-born son and wrapped him in swaddling cloths, and laid him in a manger, because there was no place for them in the inn.

Key Verse: You shall call his name Jesus, for he will save his people from their sins. (Matthew 1:21)

The Scripture and the Main Question—William H. Willimon

The Birth of Jesus Christ

"Now the birth of Jesus Christ took place in this way," says Matthew (1:18a).

Matthew records the events which happened in the first days of Jesus' life on earth. Yet, as with any gospel, Matthew's interest is more than the mere recording of events, newspaper style. He wants to show us the *meaning* of those events for the life and message of Jesus.

Whereas Luke centered his attention on Mary and her response to the annunciation of Jesus' birth, Matthew turns his eyes toward Joseph. Poor Joseph the carpenter was in a rather perplexing situation. His fiancée was pregnant. Because he was "a just man," he "resolved to divorce her quietly" (1:19).

The birth of Jesus, far from causing unrestrained joy in the first people to hear of it, causes confusion, fear, and perplexity. You and I are so accustomed to seeing this story played out in church Christmas pageants that we may sometimes miss the bite of the story.

Matthew assures us that the arrival of Jesus threw everyone into confusion. Mary is fearful. Joseph is confused and surprised. The birth of God's Messiah turns everyone and everything upside down. Old truths are swept aside. The old order is shaken.

That is the way it's going to be with this Christ, Matthew seems to say—everything will be turned upside down. There will be good news for some, bad news for others. You can't count on the old orderliness of things. Be willing to be surprised, to be shocked by this Messiah.

For He Will Save His People

"And you shall call his name Jesus, for he will save his people from their sin" (Matthew 1:21).

Luke, like Matthew, is concerned with the meaning of Jesus' birth for his later ministry. When we read Luke's opening to the second chapter, we are given a glimpse of who Jesus is. Unlike Matthew, who begins the story of Jesus with a genealogy telling us who Jesus' ancestors were (1:1-17), Luke begins the story of Jesus this way: "In those days a decree went out from Caesar Augustus that all the world should be enrolled. This was the first enrollment, when Quirinius was governor of Syria" (2:1-2).

Why all this ancient history? Who cares who was governor of Syria back then? In a way, that's exactly the point Luke wants to make.

Luke wants us to see the irony behind Jesus' birth. No one today, except for a few classical scholars, thinks much about Caesar, much less Quirinius. For the most part, these men, so mighty and important in their own day, have faded into the minor backwaters of history.

At one time a decree from Caesar could make the whole world tremble. Today (even in the day when Luke wrote these words) Caesar has long since passed from the scene. He has turned to dust; his monuments are in ruins.

While empires have waxed and waned, emperors both good and bad have strutted their brief moment on the stage of history and exited, the advent of this Jewish carpenter's son from Nazareth signaled the end of history as it had been.

This poor baby and his parents couldn't even find room in the inn. But look how he changed the world! Already, when Luke wrote this, Caesar's empire was becoming a shambles. The Prince of peace, the little, poor, insignificant baby, had turned the world upside down.

You won't read this history on the front page of your morning paper, Luke seems to say. Your morning paper is only concerned with what the world thinks is newsworthy—wars and rumors of wars, politicians and their machinations, economics. Luke is letting us in on the news, the real news, the good news. We are able to read between the headlines, to see the amazing work which God is working among us, a work to which the world is blind.

Where do you think the anointed one of God might be born today? If God chose the poor and the oppressed as the bearers of his only son then, whom might he choose today? Might we miss his advent today because we, like the people of the first century, are looking in the wrong places for his advent?

The opening act of the story of Jesus' birth is concluded with a rather bitter irony. The world was waiting for a savior. The scholars were searching the Scriptures. Caesar's army was on alert. The people were gathered in their places of worship. Expectancy was mounting. And then, God slipped into the world unnoticed because they were looking in the wrong places for the wrong sort of savior.

131

"And she gave birth to her first-born son and wrapped him in swaddling cloths, and laid him in a manger, because there was no place for them in the inn" (2:7).

No Place for Them

Time and again, God's advent among us surprises us. We wait for God to enter our lives. We make preparations. We study, we look, we expect. Then God comes, and we are dismayed to find that we missed the whole thing.

Well, it was Advent at the Northside Church in Greenville, South Carolina. Expectancy was growing as we awaited the advent of the Messiah. Word had it that he would appear among us again on the evening of December 24, late, just at midnight.

You can imagine the excitement around the church. To know that our hoped-for Savior, the one we had told the stories about, the one whom we had praised for hundreds of Sundays, was at last about to appear among us—you could cut the excitement with a knife.

At last we decided to go ahead and renovate the fellowship hall. We put a new coat of paint on the Sunday school rooms so everything would be just so for his arrival.

People got their Christmas buying out of the way early so they would be ready, so that nothing would keep them from the festivities when the Messiah arrived.

We gathered in the church early on the evening of December 24. The organist and choir put the last touches on a glorious anthem for the occasion. A trumpeter had been hired from the nearby university. New candles were placed on the altar. Everyone was in his or her place. The church was packed. People whom we hadn't seen in years were there!

Then came 11:00 P.M.; then the clock struck twelve midnight. Still, no arrival, no advent. Twelve-thirty came and went. Then 1:00 A.M. By this time the children had fallen asleep. We sang another hymn and waited for an hour or so. Then, sadly, everyone quietly filed out and went home to open Christmas gifts.

When the cars had all left the parking lot at the church and the candles were snuffed out and all was dark, a lone figure could be seen making his way past the front door of the church, heading past the building, past this nice neighborhood of well-kept, warm homes, moving toward a poorer part of town, bending into the December wind, going to visit those whom he loved, his own people who knew him, because there was no room for him at the inn, again.

Helping Adults Become Involved—Roy H. Ryan

Preparing to Teach

Read the four scripture passages suggested for this lesson. The Old Testament passages of Isaiah 11:1-9 and Micah 5:2 will help you understand the prophetic expectation of the coming Messiah. The prophets had long foretold the coming of one who would save Israel, who would reestablish the kingdom and would usher in a new age. The Micah passage suggests the birthplace of the promised one, Bethlehem.

The Matthew and Luke references are the main sources for the birth narrative. We will probably hear these familiar passages several times during this season of the Savior's birth. Read Dr. Fleming's and Dr. Willimon's comments on those key passages.

The aim of this lesson is to help persons better understand the birth of Jesus and the nature and purpose of his coming.

Gather the resources you will need, and begin to make notes and organize your thoughts into a workable outline. The following outline is one way to organize your presentation.

> Introduction: The birth of Jesus introduces a
> new order and a new age.
> I. Who is Jesus?
>   A. Mary and Joseph's son
>   B. A special child
>   C. Son of God
> II. The unusual birth
>   A. Matthew's account
>   B. Luke's account
> III. Where do we find Jesus today?
>   A. Among people like Joseph and Mary
>   B. In places like Jerusalem and Bethlehem
>   C. The Christ for all seasons

Introducing the Main Question

How do we respond to the question, Who is Jesus? Our response to that question tends to shape our lives and values in a way that is too profound to fully comprehend. Is Jesus just another famous person, one among many who dot the ages and pages of world history? Dr. Fleming suggests that even those who do not accept Jesus as Savior and Lord can hardly escape his profound influence upon the history of the world.

Where did Jesus come from? There is a great deal of mystery here. Luke and Matthew state that he was a virgin's child, the child of God, more than human flesh. How do we deal with this story in the light of our scientific, skeptical age?

Why did he come? What was God's purpose in his birth, life, death, and resurrection?

Dr. Willimon has given us these questions as the main concern of this lesson. The way you respond to these questions will be crucial to your understanding of the Christian message and the meaning of Jesus' birth.

Developing the Lesson

Be ready to give a brief account of the Isaiah and Micah passages as a background for their understanding of the Messiah.

Pay special attention to the two different accounts of Jesus' birth in Matthew and Luke. In the exegesis, Dr. Fleming points out some of the differences in the two birth narratives. Dr. Willimon devotes a good deal of attention to the same issue in "The Scripture and the Main Question." You may want to help members of the class look at these two stories in some kind of comparative way.

I. Who is Jesus?

This has always been a central question for would-be followers of Jesus. The birth stories help us understand who he was.

133

SECOND QUARTER

A. Mary and Joseph's son

Jesus was considered to be Joseph's son, even though both narratives claim that he was conceived by the Holy Spirit. Matthew traces his genealogy through Joseph back to David and Abraham (Matthew 1:1-16), but in verse 16 he demurs somewhat by saying, "Joseph, the husband of Mary, of whom Jesus was born." Jesus is known as "Joseph's son" (Luke 4:22) by his neighbors and friends.

B. A special child

Mary and Joseph certainly knew this. The shepherds experienced it. The wise men traveled a great distance to see this special child.

C. Son of God

The earliest creeds of the church attest to his unique sonship. The Gospel of John refers to him as "his [God's] only Son" (John 3:16). Christians have held him to be God's son in a special sense, not in the way that we are children of God, but in a different and substantive way. Matthew and Luke both want their readers and hearers to know that Jesus is the son of God, i.e., the Messiah (Christ).

II. The unusual birth

A. Matthew's account

Matthew seems to be aimed more at those who have a Jewish (Hebrew) background. He therefore relates Jesus to David and Abraham in the genealogy in chapter 1. Out of those roots come the new ruler, the Messiah who will usher in the new age.

B. Luke's account

This is probably the more popular of the two accounts. The story is more poetic. Read especially Dr. Willimon's account of Luke's special approach under the heading "For He Will Save His People." The key in Luke's story seems to be summarized by Dr. Willimon in his statement, "The advent of this Jewish carpenter's son from Nazareth signaled the end of history as it had been."

III. Where do we find Jesus today?

Where do we see evidence of Jesus' presence? Where do we need to look to find him? Dr. Willimon says that Luke seems to say that the world missed the advent of Jesus because the world was "looking in the wrong places for the wrong sort of savior." This may still be our problem.

A. Among people like Joseph and Mary

A carpenter and a housewife. Common folk, not royalty. That is not to say that Jesus is not to be found among the wealthy, the "well-bred," the "uncommon" folk. His humble beginning set the tone for his life and ministry. He challenged those who had wealth and position with the demands of a God who calls for servanthood and stewardship.

B. In places like Jerusalem and Bethlehem

He is found "where cross the crowded ways of life" and in places like a lonely shepherd's watch on a rocky hillside. And in our time, where? In all the places of the earth where people are hungry, ill-clothed, and oppressed. Jesus stands among us—all of us—in his risen power.

C. The Christ for all seasons

Make no mistake, the Christmas story does not end with the last present unwrapped and the tree planted or burned or thrown out or stored away. This child, this amazing child, this man, this Savior lives on in all seasons, in all ages, for all sorts of people, for all times.

Helping Class Members Act

Discuss with class members ways they can help make the birth of Jesus real by the way they celebrate Christmas this year.

Where do you see evidence of Jesus in your community? How can you identify with him in the hurts, the injustices, the hunger of people all around you?

Planning for Next Sunday

Ask persons to read Luke 2:8-20 and to think about the question, Why is Jesus' birth "good news of great joy"?

LESSON 3   DECEMBER 15

Good News of Great Joy

Background Scripture: Luke 2:8-20

The Main Question—William H. Willimon

I suppose if we take our cue from the Christmas angels, we should be beside ourselves with joy as we come a week closer to Christmas. We should be running about to tell someone the good news of the birth of Christ.

The word *angel* comes from a Greek word that means "messenger." Our word *evangelism* comes from a similar root. It means "good messsages" or "good news." An evangelist is someone who tells the good news of Jesus Christ to others.

Today "evangelism" often means an attempt to get inactive church members to attend church more often or an effort to visit in our neighborhood in order to attract more families like ours into the church. Church growth strategists sometimes speak of the need for churches to practice "homogeneous growth." The idea is that churches grown by attracting people who closely resemble the people they already have as members. Spread the gospel, but only among people like us.

When Jesus was born, says Matthew, visitors came to the manger from those segments of society who were on the outside—the poor and the lowly.

Someone has just been to the doctor for a test. The lump that has been growing on the back of the neck looks suspicious. Is it malignant? There is the anxious waiting, the unknowning. Then, at last, the results come back. Praise God! The test is negative. No problem, no problem at all.

Whom will she tell the good news to first? Who will be the privileged one? Watch carefully, for the one she selects to tell first will be that person who means the most to her, her closest friend and confidant.

When Jesus was born, the angel told the good news to "shepherds out in the field" (Luke 2:8). Let us ponder the significance of that as we study today's lesson.

135

SECOND QUARTER

As You Read the Scripture—Bond Fleming

The story told in the printed scripture, Luke 2:8-20, is perhaps the most familiar of all Christmas stories. It is so familiar that we may fail to find its deep meaning.

Luke 2:8-9. The region where the shepherds were was near Bethlehem, David's city. They were startled from the routineness of keeping watch over their flock by the appearance of the angel and the glory of the Lord as it shone around them. Maybe they had been talking about a sheep that was sick or the price of wool or the fate of Israel in contrast to her glory under King David. Their anxiety and fear over this surprising visitation were overcome by the message of the angel, and their hearts were thrilled by the good news of great joy.

Verses 10-11. The good news was for the shepherds and for all the people and especially to all Israel; yet Luke may have intended here to lift up the universalism of the gospel. The good news of great joy was that there was to be born in the city of David, the greatest of the kings of Israel, "a Savior, who is Christ the Lord." Nowhere else in the Gospels is the term *Savior* applied to Jesus. (Note Isaiah 43:3 and 45:15. Note also Luke 1:47, and Acts 5:31 and 13:23.)

Verse 12. The promise of the angel was to be confirmed by a sign. Zechariah wanted a sign concerning the promised birth of a son (Luke 1:18-22), and the angel Gabriel gave Mary a sign (Luke 1:36-37) to convince her that "with God nothing will be impossible." Small wonder that a sign was given to these shepherds, because the news, unless God were in it, would be overwhelming and unbelievable. Consider it: a Savior was born in a stable, and they would find the babe lying in a manger. The enternal God passed over the high and the mighty to begin with the meek and the lowly. This has something to say concerning respect for place and position, and the inability to see the possibilities in the small and the simple.

Verses 13-14. The news was so good that a multitude of the heavenly host joined the angel in praising God. This reminds one of the response of Jesus to the Pharisees who asked him to rebuke his disciples for their rejoicing on the journey to Jerusalem. Jesus answered (Luke 19:40), "I tell you, if these were silent, the very stones would cry out." The heavenly host had the right priority: first, glory to God, and then peace on earth. We are not able to have peace—on earth or in our lives—unless we see thing in terms of God's will for all humankind.

Verses 15-19. The shepherds went to Bethlehem to see for themselves. They found Mary and Joseph and the babe, as it had been told them. They shared their experience with those in the stable—their experience of God and their inspired vision of peace and good will. Their hearers wondered at what they said. But Mary remembered, as mothers usually do. She pondered what she had heard. What she heard gave added meaning to her earlier experience with Gabriel.

Verse 20. The shepherds returned to their duties with the sheep. Their lives were different. No doubt even the sheep could tell a difference. The shepherds were more joyous and confident. They continued to glorify and praise God "for all they had heard and seen." Great experiences, such as the one that came to these shepherds, or the one that happened to Moses in Exodus 3:1-7, still come.

Selected Scripture

King James Version

Luke 2:8-20

8 And there were in the same country shepherds abiding in the field, keeping watch over their flock by night.

9 And, lo, the angel of the Lord came upon them, and the glory of the Lord shone round about them: and they were sore afraid.

10 And the angel said unto them, Fear not: for, behold, I bring you good tidings of great joy, which shall be to all people.

11 For unto you is born this day in the city of David a Saviour, which is Christ the Lord.

12 And this *shall be* a sign unto you; Ye shall find the babe wrapped in swaddling clothes, lying in a manger.

13 And suddenly there was with the angel a multitude of the heavenly host praising God, and saying,

14 Glory to God in the highest and on earth peace, good will toward men.

15 And it came to pass, as the angels were gone away from them into heaven, the shepherds said one to another, Let us now go even unto Bethlehem, and see this thing which is come to pass, which the Lord hath made known unto us.

16 And they came with haste, and found Mary, and Joseph, and the babe lying in a manger.

17 And when they had seen *it*, they made known abroad the saying which was told them concerning this child.

18 And all they that heard *it* wondered at those things which were told them by the shepherds.

19 But Mary kept all these things, and pondered *them* in her heart.

20 And the shepherds, returned, glorifying and praising God for all

Revised Standard Version

Luke 2:8-20

8 And in that region there were shepherds out in the field, keeping watch over their flock by night. 9 And an angel of the Lord appeared to them, and the glory of the Lord shone around them, and they were filled with fear. 10 And the angel said to them, "Be not afraid; for behold, I bring you good news of a great joy which will come to all the people; 11 for to you is born this day in the city of David a Savior, who is Christ the Lord. 12 And this will be a sign for you: you will find a babe wrapped in swaddling cloths and lying in a manger." 13 And suddenly there was with the angel a multitude of the heavenly host praising God and saying,

14 "Glory to God in the highest, and on earth peace among men with whom he is pleased!"

15 When the angels went away from them into heaven, the shepherds said to one another, "Let us go over to Bethlehem and see this thing that has happened, which the Lord has made known to us." 16 And they went with haste, and found Mary and Joseph, and the babe lying in a manger. 17 And when they saw it they made known the saying which had been told them concerning this child; 18 and all who heard it wondered at what the shepherds told them. 19 But Mary kept all these things, pondering them in her heart. 20 And the shepherds returned, glorifying and praising God for all they had heard and seen, as it had been told them.

the things that they had heard and
seen, as it was told unto them.

Key Verse: I bring you good
tidings of great joy, which shall be
to all people. (Luke 2:10)

Key Verse: I bring you good news
of a great joy which will come to all
the people. (Luke 2:10)

The Scripture and the Main Question—William H. Willimon

Shepherds out in the Field

In last week's lesson we noted how curiously the birth of Jesus is reported
by Luke. Caesar Augustus ("divine") requires all the world to be taxed. Yet
moving in silently, in the form of a baby, is the Son of God. The Caesars, so
powerful in the world's eyes, will be defeated by this little baby before the
story is over.

Now Luke turns our attention away from the manger toward the fields
outside Bethlehem. There, keeping watch over their flocks, are shepherds.
Shepherds formed the lowest order of Near Eastern society. Their work was
regarded as menial and demeaning. Yet, it was to these poor, lowly people
that God's angel came to give the good news.

Had not Mary sung, when she was told that she was to give birth to Jesus:

> He has put down the mighty from their thrones,
> and exalted those of low degree;
> he has filled the hungry with good things,
> and the rich he has sent empty away. (Luke 1:52-53)

Mary sings of a Messiah who comes to save the poor and the oppressed, to
liberate the downtrodden. That Messiah's appearance is confirmed by the
angel's words to the shepherds.

How interesting that the angelic messengers did not go to the priests at
prayer in the temple, did not first proclaim the birth to the governmental
authorities. The angels fill the sky over the heads of poor shepherds,
enabling these poor people to be the first to go to the manger "and see this
thing which has happened, which the Lord has made known to us" (2:15).

No wonder that singing is such an important part of our Christmas
celebration. In the opening chapters of Luke's Gospel, everyone does seem
to be singing—Mary, Zechariah, the angels. There are moments in life when
prose just will not do, when only poetry can express our deepest feelings.
There are times when we need music in order to adequately express our joy.

The birth of Jesus is recorded by Luke as an occasion of that kind. It is as if
the whole world is breaking into song. Little wonder that when you and I
think of the miracle of Christmas, we find that we must do so through
Christmas carols and poetry.

For to You Is Born a Savior

The shepherds go to Bethlehem. There they find the babe, just as the
angels told them. The child is "wrapped in swaddling cloths and lying in a
manger" (2:12).

The poor shepherds thus see the babe who is, like them, poor and lowly.
What could be more weak and needy than a newborn infant? How striking
for God to take this form to enter the world!

Here is a preview of the sort of ministry that Jesus will undertake when he becomes an adult. He will save, not by lording over people or by using force and power. That is the world's way. Rather, he will yoke himself in solidarity with those he comes to save. He will become one of them, stand beside them, suffer as they will suffer, and die as they must die.

Other religions speak of salvation by the gods they worship. But only Christianity makes this bold affirmation of a God who loves so much that he dares to become a human being; not only that, but dares to become an infant human being, a poor infant human being. This is the miracle of the Incarnation that separates Christianity from the rest of the world's great faiths.

The Danish philosopher Søren Kierkegaard tells the parable of the king who wished to tell his subjects how much he loved them and cared for them. How could he tell them? A royal decree? No. That was too cold, too aloof. "What does a king really know about us?" they would ask.

He could go among them in his royal robes with his soldiers and impressive entourage, but that would be too grand. They would all bow down before him, not out of love but out of fear. That was not what he wanted.

So he decided to come among them dressed in rags, as some of them dressed. He would live where they lived and thereby would show them the way to a more abundant life. His love would be demonstrated by his presence as one of them.

Ironically, the people's reaction, when the king in rags revealed who he really was, was anything but admiration.

"This man can't be our king," they shouted. "Kings are high and lifted up, not like us. Kings are all powerful, not lowly. We will not have this poor man for our king!"

Therein is both the beauty and the tragedy of the story of Jesus, the God who comes among us in the flesh, a little, lowly one coming to other lowly ones.

The Shepherds Returned, Glorifying God

Of course, the shepherds who adorn our Christmas cards and yearly church school Christmas pageants do not really resemble the poor shepherds of Luke's story. They are, like most things in our commercial Christmas celebrations, idealized images of what we wish shepherds looked like. Real shepherds, like the real sheep they were watching over, probably had a scruffy, unkempt appearance.

We romanticize and idealize the nativity. Yet Luke seems to go to great lengths to convince us that there was little romantic about it. There is little romance in a cow stable!

No, this is all real life, as real as today's headlines. It is a story about poverty, about the embarrassment of Joseph, the fear of Mary, the cruelty of Herod. This isn't some once-a-year fantasy trip into nowhere. Here is a story for where you and I make our homes.

The shepherds, these poor, lowly people, come to the manger. They see that the one who comes has come for them, for the wretched of the earth. They praise God for what he is doing for them, then they returned, glorifying God for what they had seen (Luke 2:20).

There is the challenge for us today. The struggle for us is to come to the manger and worship, here in church this Sunday. Then we are to rise and return home, back to the Monday morning realities of life, the struggle to make a living, to find meaning in life. Can we take the vision of the child-savior with us?

It would be wonderful to remain in the warm glow of the manger, to stay in perpetual adoration before the infant Christ. But no, we must go back home, back to the fields or the office or the classroom. There is where the battle must be fought; there is where Christ's message and mission rise or fall.

"And the shepherds returned, glorifying and praising God for all they had heard and seen, as it had been told them" (Luke 2:20).

Helping Adults Become Involved—Roy H. Ryan

Preparing to Teach

We are one week closer to Christmas. The excitement is building. The joyful news is being proclaimed in word, in music, and in deed. The spirit of Christ is once again finding its rightful place in the lives of people.

Your spiritual preparation for teaching is just as important as your intellectual preparation. These lessons of Advent/Christmas are of such great significance that we approach our teaching task with "fear and trembling."

Read and reread the Luke passage, 2:8-20. Give it a chance to penetrate your very being. Perhaps you would like to commit it to memory or to paraphrase it (put it in your own words) so you can tell it or read it with the proper emphasis and with deep personal meaning.

The aim of this lesson is to help us understand how God works through messengers to share the wonderful good news of Jesus and to stimulate us to share the good news with all people.

Perhaps the following outline will help you give form and sequence to this wonderful story:

Introduction: The good news is for all people.
I. The shepherds hear the good news.
  A. The good news is for all people.
  B. A savior is born.
II. God gives signs.
  A. A baby in a manger
  B. A song of peace
III. The shepherds see for themselves.
  A. They go with haste.
  B. They go away to tell others.
  C. They go rejoicing.

Introducing the Main Question

When you have good news to tell, who is the first to hear? Most of us enjoy telling good news. We probably choose those whom we love most to be the first to hear and share our good news.

The very first to hear about the coming of Jesus were two older adults (Zechariah and Elizabeth) and a young, unmarried woman, Mary.

At the Savior's birth, lowly shepherds were the first to hear. Dr. Willimon suggests that shepherds were on the lowest rung of the socio-economic ladder of that time and place.

Why would God choose such lowly people to be "the first to know"? We can never really answer that question. We only know what the gospel writer makes plain—God's good news is not for the high and mighty only. It is for all people, including those who are deemed "most likely not to succeed."

The question is whether we believe that the Christmas message of joy, hope, and peace is for all people. If we do believe that, what are we to do about it?

Developing the Lesson

Retell the story in Luke 2:8-20. Put it in your own words. Highlight the main points of the story as you understand it.

The shepherds play an important role in this unfolding drama. It might be helpful if you could acquaint yourself with information about shepherds of that era—who they were and what their lives were like.

Remember the aim of the lesson: to help us understand how God uses messengers to tell us the good news and to stimulate us to share that good news with all people.

I. The shepherds hear the good news.

The first to hear the earth-shattering news of the birth of Jesus are the people who live close to the earth, people of no great significance, lowly shepherds.

A. The good news is for all people.

We should be glad for that. We are included! God does not intentionally leave out anyone. Jesus Christ came to save the whole creation. Ultimately it would not be good news if it were for only a select few. The angel messenger proclaims good tidings, joyful tidings, not just to the shepherds but "to all the people." This gospel we proclaim is a univeral message of God's love for all people, all tribes, all nations—every person!

B. A savior is born.

This baby of Bethlehem, the city of David, is not just the deliverer of Israel. He is not just a provincial king. He comes to set us all free. He is "King of kings and Lord of lords" (Revelation 19:16), and to his reign there will be no end. The Savior comes to seek and to save that which is lost. He comes to bring reconciliation between God and all persons. We call him Savior.

II. God gives signs.

God is always leaving evidence of his presence in the world. God is never without witnesses. "Day to day pours forth speech and night to night declares knowledge" (Psalm 19:2). We need to sensitize our ears and eyes to discern the signs of God's presence in our midst. Jesus said, "Whoever has ears to hear, let him hear."

A. A baby in a manger

The baby is a sign to the shepherds. This is not exactly what most faithful Jews were looking for as a sign of the Messiah's coming. It is probably not where modern people would look for a king, a savior, or even a leader to be born. We still have our Lincolns and log cabins in this world, but they are few and far between. It is nevertheless a sign, a sign of the humanity of Jesus, a sign of servanthood that his life would portray. It is a sign for us to look carefully to where God is revealing love, justice, and righteousness in our time.

B. A song of peace

The message fills the air. How we need to hear and believe that word from God in our time! Jesus Christ brings the hope for peace and the possibility of peace, not just the absence of hostility but active good will. The human race stands on the brink of self-destruction. How can our hearts and minds be freed from the clutter of arms production and tough talk so that we can still hear the song of peace? Discuss this with our class.

III. The shepherds see for themselves.

A. They go with haste.

Once they got the message, they went into action. This was too big to miss. How do we respond to the clear call of God when we are challenged to see God—wherever that revelation may occur? "He who hesitates is lost." The shepherds did not hesitate to go to the stable to see this baby who would change the world.

B. They go away to tell others.

How could they resist sharing what they had seen? When God has become real in our lives, how can we avoid telling others what wonderful things have happened to us? We can then appreciate Jesus' later words of commission to "go . . . and make disciples of all nations, baptizing . . . teaching."

C. They go rejoicing.

They have found new hope. They cannot contain their joy. It overflows into rejoicing. Joy is an inevitable product in the life of anyone who has experienced the new life in Christ.

Helping Class Members Act

Where are the signs of God's presence (self-disclosure) in our day? Class members might be asked to reflect on this in the coming week and be ready to discuss it next Sunday (or whenever you meet). Help them to look in places and among people where they will be going about their routine activities. They will see, and hopefully participate, in deeds of kindness and in acts of love. They will seek justice and resist evil.

Help them look beyond the personal and the interpersonal relationships for signs of God's presence. What about between nations? Where are the signs of peace with justice?

Planning for Next Sunday

Read Matthew 2. Be ready to discuss the "signs of God's presence" suggested above.

The Incarnation

MICHAEL WINTERS

Every year when we remember and celebrate the story of the birth of Jesus, we are given again an occasion to think about its meaning. *Incarnation* is the theological concept which explains the meaning of God's becoming a human being in Jesus. The word *incarnation* is from the Latin *in* and *caro* (flesh). The first chapter of John's Gospel declares, "the Word become flesh and dwelt among us" (John 1:14).

Whenever we think about the Incarnation we must think about its meaning for us in our lives and our ministry in the church. This is especially important if we model our ministry after God's care for us.

There are three words in our language that help us understand the dynamics of caring. The first is *apathy*. Apathy is the inability or failure to care. *Apathy* is a word that we use in the church at times to describe the reason for our lagging ministries.

The second word is *sympathy*. *Sympathy* is the word that we use most often to describe the way we usually care for people. Whenever someone dies in our church we express sympathy to the grieving family. We genuinely share their sorrow.

The third word describing the dynamics of caring is *empathy*. This is a word that we do not use as often in our churches. Empathy describes a way of caring for others that goes beyond sorrow. It is a way of caring in which we assume the other's burden and misfortune. Their burdens become ours. *Empathy* is the word which best describes God's caring for us expressed in the Incarnation of Jesus Christ.

God "empathized" with our human condition through Jesus of Nazareth. God experienced birth, a childhood, education, adolescence, work, parental dissatisfaction, anger, ideals, frustration, suffering, and death. These are human experiences that we all have, and God has had them too. What better way could God express caring than by fully identifying with us in our human predicament?

So the Incarnation of God in Jesus provides us a model of ministry. It is the model of empathy. As God has identified with our human condition, walking among us, suffering with and for us—even to death—so our ministry should assume these incarnate proportions.

So far, expressed here, the Incarnation of God in Jesus was a way of demonstrating for all humanity God's own intimate knowledge of the human condition. There is another side to the meaning of the Incarnation in John's Gospel.

John's theology of the Incarnation can be seen most clearly when it is compared to the other gospel accounts. In Matthew and Luke there is much detail surrounding the birth of Jesus. John's expression of the Incarnation stands in contrast. While Matthew and Luke are clear that Jesus was not just an ordinary human being, they are also clear that Jesus was, in fact, made of the stuff of life and experienced all the stuff of life that was most common and ordinary. They seem to be emphasizing Jesus' humanity.

John's tendency is to emphasize the divinity of Jesus. When John tells his story of Jesus, he is at the same time telling us about God. In John, the Incarnation is the opportunity for all of humanity to discover that God is creator, life, and light (John 1:3, 4). Over and over again through out his gospel, John tells his readers who Jesus is: "*I am* the light of the world" (John 8:12); "*I am* the way, and the truth, and the life" (John 14:6); "*I am* the bread of life" (John 6:35, italics added). John uses a formula that every Jew would immediately identify as that which belongs most intimately to God. John records Jesus calling himself by the divine name, "I Am": "Truly, truly, I say to you, before Abraham was, *I am*" (John 8:58, italics added). Every Jew would understand. Many would want to take stones to throw at him, for this would be blasphemy.

The "I Am" formula is first found in Exodus 3:14. This is the story of God speaking to Moses from the burning bush. You remember that it is here where God told Moses to go speak to the Pharaoh of Egypt to demand the release of the Jewish slaves. But Moses was reluctant to be the Jewish advocate. God said to Moses, "Say this to the people of Israel, 'I AM has sent me to you'" (Exodus 3:14). No two words can summarize the Incarnation better than *I am*.

The Incarnation in John's view, then, enables us to comprehend who God is. God is the very heart of life itself. God is bread and light and truth. God is. God is "I AM." When the Incarnation is understood in these terms, then the church's ministry is the protection of the sanctity of all life.

There is one final element of the Incarnation yet to explore here. Any effective public speaker will say that the task of public speaking is to take some abstract idea and make it concrete. There are many ways to say this. Some people call this "fleshing it out"—in other words, illustrating the idea so everyone can understand it. Nowhere is this more true than in the sermon event. The purpose of the sermon is to take the word of God and make it fresh and new and alive. The preacher's model for preaching is based, in part, on the incarnate reality of God expressed by John, "And the Word became flesh and dwelt among us" (John 1:14).

If you can think of God as the Word or the abstract, *un*knowable idea and Jesus as the flesh, concrete, knowable idea, then you have understood the meaning of the Word's becoming flesh and dwelling among us. The Incarnation is the way the church talks about God becoming known to us through Jesus of Nazareth.

When the Incarnation is understood as God's way of informing creation about the nature and being of God, then our ministry becomes sharing what we have discovered about God. In Jesus Christ we have discovered that God is merciful, compassionate, humble, meek, forgiving, kind, and most of all, loving. The Incarnation of God calls the church to minister through the proclamation of the good news of Jesus Christ.

The Incarnation discloses the important nature of God's caring. It is *empathy*. It reveals that God is the very essence of life. And the Incarnation informs us of the character of God's nature, which may be summed up in the word *love*.

LESSON 4   DECEMBER 22

Star in the East

Background Scripture: Matthew 2

The Main Question—William H. Willimon

This week we Christians will celebrate the birth of Christ. This is one of the great high and holy weeks of the year for us. For this week, boundaries between the various Christian groups and denominations will come down and we will join hands with all Christians all around the world and worship our Lord and Savior at his birth.

But what about those people who are not Christians? Well, we know that birthdays are family affairs. Birthdays are times when we call in our most intimate friends and family and celebrate. So we will not invite those who are outside our faith. This is a party for the insiders, those of us who are Christians.

Whether you look at the tragedy in Lebanon, the chaos in Northern Ireland, the tensions in the Middle East or right in your own neighborhood, you can see that religion is often the great dividing factor among people. Protestant and Catholic, Jew and Gentile, Christian and Moslem, we divide our world on the basis of our religious beliefs.

But what if there comes a Messiah whose goal is not to separate the world into the insiders and outsiders, the saved and the damned, the enlightened and the ignorant; rather, whose mission is to call everyone—all nations and peoples—to God? Who should celebrate the birth of one who breaks down the barriers we erect between people and calls everyone to a kingdom that knows no boundaries?

As You Read the Scripture—Bond Fleming

Matthew 2:1-6. Matthew gives the place of Jesus' birth and the approximate time. There is strong contrast in the mention of Bethlehem and Herod. Bethlehem was the birthplace of David, the greatest of Israel's kings; Micah had prophesied that Bethlehem would be the birthplace of "a ruler who will govern my people Israel" (Matthew 2:6; see Micah 5:2).

Herod, on the other hand, was much feared and hated. He ruled c. 40–4 B.C. He was not Herod the Great to the Jews, but Herod the Edomite Slave. Joseph Klausner's book *Jesus of Nazareth* tells of Herod's persecution of the Jews and of their hatred of Herod. Note the number of times Herod's name is mentioned in Matthew chapter 2. It was in character for this jealous and selfish king to slaughter the male babies (descendants of David) in and around Bethlehem; he slew any and all rivals for the throne.

The contrast between Herod and Jesus is even greater: palace or stable; power or weakness; cruelty or compassion. But the meek inherited the earth, and Herod is remembered only by contrast.

The story of the wise men is a fitting tribute for the birth of the king. We cannot be sure just where they were from, nor where they saw the star in the East. The point is not one of place and astronomy but one of vision and loyalty. They came to bring their gifts and to worship him.

The wise men came to Jerusalem and inquired concerning the one whose birth had inspired the star. Herod and all Jerusalem were troubled, and rightly so. Apparently they had not seen the star. They were not sensitive to the possibilities; the wise men were.

The religious leaders sought the Scriptures and found Micah's prophecy about Bethlehem. The town is not so little today, although Phillips Brooks's hymn will make it so always; his poem tells the beautiful story of Christmas. The name Bethlehem means "house of bread." It was an appropriate place for the birth of one who is the bread of life. How appropriate, too, and accurate, is the descriptive picture in Phillips Brooks's poem, "The hopes and fears of all the years are met in thee. . . ."

Verses 7-8. Herod was cunning and cruel. He had put members of his own family to death because they were potential rivals to his throne. He met with the wise men in secret, to ask that they let him know where the newborn king was. Herod would surely not have worshiped him but murdered him. It would have been more in keeping with Herod's character if he had sent a murderer acting as guide with the wise men.

Verses 9-11. It is supposed that the visit was later than the visit by the shepherds, who were near Bethlehem. Chronology is not as important as

145

meaning and influence. The star led them to the place where Mary and the child were. The wise men rejoiced with great gladness and worshiped him and paid homage to him with their appropriate gifts.

Verse 12. In those days people received messages in dreams. Consider the examples of messages in dreams to Joseph in Matthew 1:20 and 2:13. The wise men might not have discerned Herod's spirit earlier, but they were warned about him in a dream. They went back home another way.

Herod was foiled in his scheme. He became so enraged that he slaughtered all male offspring of David under two years of age in the region. Joseph fled to Egypt with Mary and the child. After Herod's death, his son Archelaus ruled in Judea. He was also a cruel king. Joseph came back, but forsook Judea and went to live in Nazareth in Galilee (see Matthew 2:19-23).

Selected Scripture

King James Version

Revised Standard Version

Matthew 2:1-12

1 Now when Jesus was born in Bethlehem of Judaea in the days of Herod the king, behold, there came wise men from the east to Jerusalem,

2 Saying, Where is he that is born King of the Jews? for we have seen his star in the east, and are come to worship him.

3 When Herod the king had heard *these things,* he was troubled, and all Jerusalem with him.

4 And when he had gathered all the chief priests and scribes of the people together, he demanded of them where Christ should be born.

5 And they said unto him, In Bethlehem of Judaea: for thus it is written by the prophet,

6 And thou Bethlehem, *in* the land of Juda, art not the least among the princes of Juda: for out of thee shall come a Governor, that shall rule my people Israel.

7 Then Herod, when he had privily called the wise men, inquired of them diligently what time the star appeared.

8 And he sent them to Bethelhem, and said, Go and search diligently for the young child; and when ye

Matthew 2:1-12

1 Now when Jesus was born in Bethlehem of Judea in the days of Herod the king, behold, wise men from the East came to Jerusalem, saying, 2 "Where is he who has been born king of the Jews? For we have seen his star in the East, and have come to worship him." 3 When Herod the king heard this, he was troubled, and all Jerusalem with him; 4 and assembling all the chief priests and scribes of the people, he inquired of them where the Christ was to be born. 5 They told him, "In Bethlehem of Judea; for so it is written by the prophet:

6 'And you, O Bethlehem, in the land of Judah,
are by no means least among the rulers of Judah;
for from you shall come a ruler who will govern my people Israel.'"

7 Then Herod summoned the wise men secretly and ascertained from them what time the star appeared; 8 and he sent them to Bethlehem, saying, "Go and search diligently for the child, and when you have found him bring me word,

146

have found *him,* bring me word again, that I may come and worship him also.

9 When they had heard the king, they departed; and, lo, the star, which they saw in the east, went before them, till it came and stood over where the young child was.

10 When they saw the star, they rejoiced with exceeding great joy.

11 And when they were come into the house, they saw the young child with Mary his mother, and fell down, and worshipped him: and when they had opened their treasures, they presented unto him gifts; gold, and frankincense, and myrrh.

12 And being warned of God in a dream that they should not return to Herod, they departed into their own country another way.

that I too may come and worship him." 9 When they had heard the king they went their way; and lo, the star which they had seen in the East went before them, till it came to rest over the place where the child was. 10 When they saw the star, they rejoiced exceedingly with great joy; 11 and going into the house they saw the child with Mary his mother, and they fell down and worshiped him. Then, opening their treasures, they offered him gifts, gold and frankincense and myrrh. 12 And being warned in a dream not to return to Herod, they departed to their own country by another way.

Key Verse: **When they saw the star, they rejoiced with exceeding great joy. (Matthew 2:10)**

Key Verse: **When they saw the star, they rejoiced exceedingly with great joy. (Matthew 2:10)**

The Scripture and the Main Question—William H. Willimon

When Jesus Was Born in Bethlehem

You have probably seen those sumptuous paintings or plaster manger scene figures of the three "kings" who followed the star from the East and came to worship the infant Christ. They are usually depicted as three men, though the Bible does not tell us how many there were. They are often depicted as older, oriental men. One of them is usually a black man. Tradition has given them names. But Matthew, the only gospel which tells of these strange visitors from afar, mentions none of these details about them. (Their names and kingdoms are discussed in noncanonical gospels.)

In order to understand the significance of these visitors, we must free ourselves from much that we've always thought about them. It is significant that Matthew places their visit at the beginning of his gospel. Luke begins his story of Jesus with a biographical account of the manger birth, whereas Matthew begins his story, after the opening genealogy, perhaps one or two years after Jesus' birth. (That's why Herod decided to kill not only newborn babies but all those two years of age and under.) While our Christmas pageants and popular lore usually associate the three "kings" with the nativity, we must not just tack them on to Luke's story. The visitors have great significance for Matthew in showing who the Christ is and what he will mean for the world.

Matthew does not say that the visitors from the East were kings, nor is the translation of the Greek word *magi* as "wise men" (RSV and King James translations) very helpful. They are called *magi,* the Greek word for magicians and astrologers. We, of course, get our word *magic* from this root. The magi may have been considered to be "wise men" in the pagan lands from whence they came, but to the Jews who first heard this story, they were sorcerers, idolaters, and often charlatans of the sort which the Scriptures clearly condemned.

Paul had some choice words for another magus in Acts 13:6-12, calling him a "son of the devil." The Moffatt translation of *magi* as "magicians" is much more accurate. These visitors were not so much the traditional "we three kings of Orient are" of our Christmas carols, but rather, to the Jewish reader in the first century, were average, gentile, pagan magicians and astrologers. They were outsiders of a low order, dabblers in pagan myths, watchers of the stars. These outsiders had a religion and a race which made them repugnant to Bible-believing people who were awaiting the Messiah.

We Have Seen His Star in the East

The point of Matthew's tale is that these strange visitors—the outsiders—were the first persons to come worship the Messiah of Israel. "To worship" means to ascribe worth to something (from the Old English *weorthscipe*), to submit totally to another's authority. The magi are thus the first to see the worth and to worship the child.

These gentile star-gazers come to the manger, bow down, and worship; relinquishing their gold, frankincense, and myrrh to the new king. Perhaps these gifts were the "tricks" of their trade, the elements used in their alchemy. Or perhaps they were merely costly elements, symbolizing that the magi gave the child everything of value they had.

The magi's star-gazing tells them that something important, cosmic, and far-reaching is happening in the world. But it cannot tell them exactly where it is to happen. That secret is locked in the Scriptures which only the Chosen People have. Therefore they must come to the priests and scribes for exact information (2:1-6).

Therein lies the tragic paradox of Matthew's story. The Chosen People (let us read this "church") have the Scriptures. Yet, tragically, they are unable to see that which the Scriptures plainly foretell. They are tools of King Herod the fox.

The coming of the Gentiles to the mountain of Zion is a frequent Old Testament theme, voiced often by Matthew's favorite prophet, Isaiah (Isaiah 2:2-3). This pilgrimage of the nations to Zion was expected to begin the reign of the Messiah. According to Matthew, it began with the coming of visitors from the East. The prophecy is fulfilled. The pilgrimage of the Gentiles begins, not to Mount Zion, but to Bethlehem and its messianic Lord.

With Matthew's fondness for relating Old Testament scripture to events in Christ's life, it is strange that he did not mention Numbers 24:17, which speaks of a star arising out of Jacob, or Isaiah 60:3, which says, "Nations shall come to your light, and kings to the brightness of your rising." Even if he didn't quote these passages, they do speak to the joyful event told in this story.

Yet there is sadness behind the joy because the Chosen do not see the advent of their long-awaited Savior. Perhaps these "insiders" are blinded by their "old-time religion," their pride, their indifference; and so the doors of the kingdom are swung open for the "outsiders." You may recall a number of Matthew's parables where this same point is made (cf. Matthew 8:10-11; 12:42, 22:1-10).

It's all enough to make one ask, Who are the outsiders and insiders in our own day? What aspects of our lives, as insiders, may keep us from recognizing the advent of our Savior this Christmas even as we so hectically prepare for his arrival?

The world hungers for a Savior this Christmas as never before. We are the ones to whom the secret of the ages has been given. To us has been given the good news that God has acted to redeem our world. What are we doing with that good news?

They Departed Another Way

A few years ago we were privileged to host a church leader from a new country in Africa. He told us of the persecutions the church had suffered during a recent revolution in his country, about the struggles they had had with a new, Marxist-oriented government.

We marveled at the fortitude and enthusiasm of these new Christians. He told us that the church was growing at the rate of 20 percent a year in his country.

The irony hit us. Here we are in a supposedly "Christian" country, yet our denomination is losing members at the rate of about 3 percent a year. Once we sent missionaries to the "dark continent" in order to convert these "outsiders."

The day may come, even in our own lifetime, when Africa may be sending missionaries to us!

The child who is born in the stable at Bethlehem brings good news to the world, the whole world. He will be the light to the nations, the Savior of all peoples. Let us celebrate his advent among us with joy, let us ring the bells and sing his praises to the four corners of the world, "for we have seen his star in the East, and have come to worship him" (2:2).

Then we can go back to the four corners of the world another way—the way of love and grace for all people.

Helping Adults Become Involved—Roy H. Ryan

Preparing to Teach

This Sunday nearest Christmas will be a special day of celebration in our church. The mood of joy and celebration should also carry over into our class. It will be an appropriate time to conclude the unit "Advent: To You a Savior."

Read the biblical material and the comments by Dr. Fleming and Dr. Willimon, along with your regular denominational class resource on the International Lessons. All of these sources will assist you as you prepare to teach.

The aim of this lesson is to enable us to experience the advent of Jesus Christ, to discern the place(s) of his coming, and to welcome him as Savior and Lord.

To help achieve this aim, the following outline is suggested. You may wish to use this outline as a starting point for organizing your presentation.

Introduction: What a gracious gift of God that we are enabled to see the advent of God's son and to welcome him as Lord and King!

I. Wise men come to see Jesus.
   A. Who are these "wise men"?
   B. What brought them in search of the child?
II. Search diligently for the child.
   A. Herod attempts to trick them.
   B. The magi find Jesus.
III. The wise men depart another way.
   A. These "outsiders" worship Jesus.
   B. They heed God's warning.
   C. They would never be the same again.

Introducing the Main Question

Dr. Willimon writes about the curiosity that, in their wait for the Messiah, in their poring over the Scriptures, many of Jesus' own people failed to see the advent of their Messiah. But unbelievers, strange foreigners like the magi were able to see. Why? Why, indeed! This is the main question for us.

As the church (the people of God), do we still miss his coming? Are we always able to "discern the signs of the times"? Do we become so fascinated with the study of the Scriptures that we miss their most obvious meaning? Do we look for Jesus in the wrong places?

Are we more like the "scribes" and other religious leaders Herod called together to interpret the Scriptures, or like the wise men who followed the star, who looked for a vision—and found it in a lonely stable in Bethlehem?

Is there something of the Scrooge in each of us that blinds us to the meaning and joy of Christmas? If so, how can we so attune our lives to the spirit of Christ that we are able to find him in all of his manifestations of love, justice, and righteousness?

Developing the Lesson

Read or ask some member of the class to read Matthew 2:1-12. Summarize the story told in these verses.

You may wish to give an introduction about the wise men. Dr. Willimon's comments in "The Scripture and Main Question" may provide you with some new insights. Are these men really kings of the Orient as we have learned to sing about, or were they really star-gazers and astrologers?

This is a beautiful story. Try to capture something of its beauty through the reading and the telling.

I. Wise men come to see Jesus.

A. Who are these "wise men"?

Are they really kings from the Orient or are they astrologers? Dr. Fleming suggests that the story of the wise men is a fitting tribute for the birth of Jesus. He goes on to say, "We cannot be sure just where they were from, nor where they saw the star in the East. The point is not one of *place and astronomy but one of vision and loyalty*" (italics added).

As suggested above, Dr. Willimon calls them "strange visitors." Who do you think they were? What is the meaning of this story?

B. What brought them in search of the child?

They evidently observed the stars very closely. Each new star or conjunction of planets or a change in the glow of a star set their heads spinning. They interpreted these as signs of great happenings.

They report to Herod that they have "seen his ['king of the Jews'] star in the East." Their only purpose in coming seems to have been to bow down and worship. They did not come to "get" but to "give." They brought their gifts as a token of their worship.

II. Search diligently for the child.

A. Herod attempts to trick them.

He wants them to report on the child's whereabouts as soon as they find him. They are to "search diligently" and then let Herod know. Herod makes it sound as if he also wants to worship this newborn king. The wise men, not being very wise about Herod, did not realize at the time what Herod really had in mind.

B. The magi find Jesus.

They follow his star and it leads them to "the house" (Matthew's word) where Jesus was. They offer their gifts. Their gifts were certainly fit for a king.

They went with rejoicing. Their experience was not unlike that of the shepherds. To be a part of this earth-shaking drama was enough to excite and cause rejoicing.

Like the shepherds and the magi of long ago, those who truly seek Jesus will surely find him!

III. The wise men depart another way.

A. These "outsiders" worship Jesus.

Many of the "insiders" never accepted Jesus as Savior and Lord. Jesus talked later in his ministry about having sheep which were not of his fold. This story helps us again see the universal nature of Jesus Christ and his mission. Who are some "outsiders" in our world today who may come closer to truly worshiping and serving Jesus than those of us who are "insiders"?

B. They heed God's warning.

They go home another way. God communicates in a variety of ways, perhaps even including dreams. They do not let Herod know where Jesus is.

C. They would never be the same again.

No person coming into the presence of Jesus of Nazareth can ever be the same again. The New Testament and church history are replete with stories to attest to that fact. Jesus Christ has a transforming effect on all who are touched by his presence.

Helping Class Members Act

Help class members reflect on the following propositions:
1. What does it mean for us to bring our gifts to Christ?
2. How do we discern the will of God? What of dreams? Visions? Prayers?

Planning for Next Sunday

Alert the class members to the new course, "Jesus Teaches About the Christian Life." The theme of unit 1 is "Principles of Christian Living"; the title of the first lesson is "Doing God's Will." Ask members to read Mark 4:26-32, Matthew 22:34-40, and Luke 18:9-14 for the next lesson.

Jesus Teaches About the Christian Life

UNIT I: PRINCIPLES OF CHRISTIAN LIVING

Horace R. Weaver

FOUR LESSONS   **DECEMBER 29–JANUARY 19**

The four previous lessons dealt with "Advent: To You a Savior." The theme of the next nine lessons is "Jesus Teaches About the Christian Life." Jesus' announcement of the kingdom of God is the heart of the gospel. It is both promise and challenge. The promise is that people will be empowered individually and collectively to do God's will. The challenge is for all who hear to live in loving relation to God and to one another, reaching out in service to those in need.

Unit I, "Principles of Christian Living," consists of four lessons: "Doing God's Will," December 29, is based on two foci: loving God and loving your neighbor as yourself; "Persons Are Important," January 5, emphasizes the primacy of persons above all institutions; "The Inwardness of Morality," January 12, declares ethical law and moral action to be matters of attitude, disposition, and thought; "Ways Christians Serve," January 19, must include service to "the least of these" if our actions are to reflect kinship with Christ and God.

LESSON 5   **DECEMBER 29**

Doing God's Will

Background Scripture: Mark 4:26-32; Matthew 22:34-40; Luke 18:9-14

The Main Question—William H. Willimon

Many people in our day think of Jesus and his teachings as a purely individual, personal matter. "Religion is a private affair," they say. Religion is something that you practice in private, something for the inner recesses of your own heart, not something for public display.

They will tell you that religion is a matter of feeling or mainly a matter of thinking the right thoughts. Of course, the value of looking at things this way is that it keeps religion safely sealed off from most of the important matters in life. It keeps religion in our hearts or in our heads and out of our daily lives, out of the tug and pull of life's most pressing problems.

There may be some religions of which it can be said that they are "a private affair." But Christianity is not one of those religions. Jesus came preaching not only a philosophy of life but a way of life. He came not only speaking of certain values and ideals but also inviting people to be part of a

152

kingdom. That kingdom was a public, visible, corporate matter. It required not only a change of mind but also a change of life.

"The kingdom of God is at hand," cried Jesus.

To be a citizen of a certain country is to imply that we speak the language of that kingdom, obey its laws and customs, and derive our identity from its identity. What is this new kingdom to which Jesus calls us and what are the demands of citizenship?

As You Read the Scripture—Bond Fleming

The key verse is Mark 1:15: "The time is fulfilled, and the kingdom of God is at hand; repent, and believe in the gospel." Mark is the earliest of the Gospels, and this key verse is supposedly the first statement from Jesus. It remains the central message of Christianity. John had preached "a baptism of repentance for the forgiveness of sins" (Mark 1:4). Jesus preached repentance too, but added a new note of believing in the good news, whereas John's message had a note of fear and doom.

Mark 4:26-29. The parable of the self-growing seed helps to describe the "kingdom of God." Neither Matthew nor Luke uses this parable; it may be because of the implication of a phrase in verse 27, "he knows not how," that could not be implied of God. In Mark it comes soon after the parable of the sower and the seeds.

Jesus is trying to assure his hearers of the kingdom's coming, once the seed is sown. When the farmer plants the seed, he has complete confidence that the seed will germinate and grow, although he does not know how. Nature is dependable. Likewise, have confidence in the coming of the kingdom; we may not know how it comes, but God who is the harvester does know and is the guarantor of the harvest. The teachings of Jesus center on the coming of God's kingdom.

Matthew 22:34-40. Jesus was asked a question about the great commandment by a lawyer who was trying to test him. In his answer Jesus gives a summary of the law by using two scripture verses, Deuteronomy 6:5 and Leviticus 19:18. Love God first and completely, and let that love inspire and sustain love of your neighbor. There were so many laws that rabbis and prophets described the essence of religion in shorter focus. Note the requirements in Micah 6:8, or consider the golden rule in Matthew 7:12.

Our view of God is exceedingly important in our lives; it determines how we live. Different views of God inspire and cause different life-styles. Jesus commands that we love God, a God of creative and self-giving love, with all that we have and are. When we love a God like this, we will love our neighbors as we love ourselves. We ought to love (have good will and intentions toward) ourselves as children of God. But God comes first and inspires the proper love of self and of others.

Luke 18:9-14. The parable of the Pharisee and the tax collector illustrates the commandments to love God and to love our neighbor. Jesus certainly did not mean that all Pharisees and all tax collectors were like these. These were used as examples. The story has its setting in the temple in Jerusalem.

We get to know these men by their prayers and their self-revealing attitudes. This Pharisee was so righteous by accepted tests that he was haughtily self-righteous. He held himself aloof from others because he felt himself better than they were. He did not pray so much as he bragged to God about bad things he did not do and about ritualistic things that he did do. He represents the type of good citizen who would be welcomed into clubs and churches. He felt no lack; he saw no need; he had earned and expected God's approval. It was hardly possible for God to exalt him above his own self-exaltation.

The tax collector was by himself too, but from a sense of unworthiness. He sought God and prayed for mercy and forgiveness. He felt lowly enough to be lifted, and he was. He repented and believed in the gospel, and the kingdom of God came for him. He was more justified before God than the ritualistic Pharisee was.

Selected Scripture

King James Version

Revised Standard Version

Mark 4:26-29

26 And he said, So is the kingdom of God, as if a man should cast seed into the ground;

27 And should sleep, and rise night and day, and the seed should spring and grow up, he knoweth not how.

28 For the earth bringeth forth fruit of herself; first the blade, then the ear, after that the full corn in the ear.

29 But when the fruit is brought forth, immediately he putteth in the sickle, because the harvest is come.

Matthew 22:34-40

34 But when the Pharisees had heard that he had put the Sadducees to silence, they were gathered together.

35 Then one of them, *which was* a lawyer, asked *him a question,* tempting him, and saying,

36 Master, which *is* the great commandment in the law?

37 Jesus said unto him, Thou shalt love the Lord thy God with all thy heart, and with all thy soul, and with all thy mind.

38 This is the first and great commandment.

39 And the second *is* like unto it, Thou shalt love thy neighbour as thyself.

40 On these two commandments hang all the law and the prophets.

Mark 4:26-29

26 And he said, 'The kingdom of God is as if a man should scatter seed upon the ground, 27 and should sleep and rise night and day, and the seed should sprout and grow, he knows not how. 28 The earth produces of itself, first the blade, then the ear, then the full grain in the ear. 29 But when the grain is ripe, at once he puts in the sickle, because the harvest has come."

Matthew 22:34-40

34 But when the Pharisees heard that he had silenced the Sad'ducees, they came together. 35 And one of them, a lawyer, asked him a question, to test him. 36 "Teacher, which is the great commandment in the Law?" 37 And he said to him, "You shall love the Lord your God with all your heart, and with all your soul, and with all your mind. 38 This is the great and first commandment. 39 And a second is like it, You shall love your neighbor as yourself. 40 On these two commandments depend all the law and the prophets."

Luke 18:9-14

9 And he spake this parable unto certain which trusted in themselves that they were righteous, and despised others:

10 Two men went up into the temple to pray; the one a Pharisee, and the other a publican.

11 The Pharisee stood and prayed thus with himself, God, I thank thee, that I am not as other men *are,* extortioners, unjust, adulterers, or even as this publican.

12 I fast twice in the week, I give tithes of all that I possess.

13 And the publican, standing afar off, would not lift up so much as *his* eyes unto heaven, but smote upon his breast, saying, God be merciful to me a sinner.

14 I tell you, this man went down to his house justified *rather* than the other; for every one that exalteth himself shall be abased; and he that humbleth himself shall be exalted.

Key Verse: **The time is fulfilled, and the kingdom of God is at hand: repent ye, and believe the gospel. (Mark 1:15)**

Luke 18:9-14

9 He also told this parable to some who trusted in themselves that they were righteous and despised others: 10 "Two men went up into the temple to pray, one a Pharisee and the other a tax collector. 11 The Pharisee stood and prayed thus with himself, 'God, I thank thee that I am not like other men, extortioners, unjust, adulterers, or even like this tax collector. 12 I fast twice a week, I give tithes of all that I get.' 13 But the tax collector, standing far off, would not even lift up his eyes to heaven, but beat his breast, saying, 'God, be merciful to me a sinner!' 14 I tell you, this man went down to his house justified rather than the other; for every one who exalts himself will be humbled, but he who humbles himself will be exalted."

Key Verse: **The time is fulfilled, and the kingdom of God is at hand; repent, and believe in the gospel. (Mark 1:15)**

The Scripture and the Main Question—William H. Willimon

The Kingdom of God

In a church where I once served, one of the women who was a long-time church leader often commented, "God must have really wanted a church here because that's the only reason I can think of why we have a church here today."

She then recalled the days when the church was being formed. There was little money to build a church. Members held barbecue dinners to buy the land, then they held garage sales to help buy a building. People could remember a day when the church treasurer would report a total of forty-five cents in the church coffers!

What amazed people, in looking back on the past struggles of that congregation for existence, was how in the world they survived. There was a real sense in that church that, though we must struggle and dedicate ourselves to the task of building, only GOD can build and sustain a church.

We often forget that truth. Often those of us who are most anxious for the church to survive and prosper are the ones most likely to forget that GOD, not we, gives growth to the church.

How often have you heard that favorite sermon illustration about the statue of Christ that was damaged in World War II? You know, the one about the statue of Christ that had its hands blown off during a bombing raid? After the war, they put a sign under the statue reading, "Christ has no hands but our hands."

It's a memorable illustration, and true, but only true up to a point. Christ has not had his hands blown off. The Bible says that God is busy in our world, busy in ways that we don't often appreciate or see. The challenge is to be involved with God, not to be involved in place of God.

One can imagine the church to which the parable of the seed growing secretly (Mark 4:26-29) was first addressed. Undoubtedly, they were a small, persecuted little band of believers who were fighting for their very lives as God's people. Would the church be exterminated after the first generation? Jesus had preached about the advent of a new kingdom. But now, fifty or so years after the death and resurrection of Jesus, where was the kingdom?

To these struggling, despondent believers, the parable of the seed must have given encouragement. The sower plants the seed and then goes to bed to sleep. The sower does not work the seed up out of the ground—only God can do that.

Mysteriously, while we are sleeping, the seed germinates. One day we go out to the garden and are surprised to find little green shoots peeping up out of the earth. They mature. We can water, fertilize, and till the garden, but we can't make it happen. The harvest comes as a gift of God.

Perhaps that's why I have never been a good gardener. Patience is not one of my virtues. I want to see the harvest now or at least by tomorrow. I get tired of waiting. A few years ago, I had a garden which was not very successful. When I asked a veteran gardener what he thought was wrong, he told me, "I think you have worked it too much."

I was surprised that it was actually possible to work too hard in a garden. "Yes," he said, "you have tilled the earth too deep and too often, thus damaging the root system and weakening the plants. You should have been more patient."

Patience is a difficult virtue to cultivate. It takes time for your children to grow up and for you to see how they turn out. It takes patience to wait and see how the business you begin turns out, whether it prospers or not. A teacher must be patient with young learners until they get the point of the material which she or he is trying to teach them.

The kingdom of God takes patience too. We don't build that kingdom. We may sow the seed and till the ground, but others may harvest. It is not always for us to see the fruits of our labors.

Years ago I went, somewhat reluctantly, to speak at a youth meeting in an obscure part of our state. I remember it well because it was a dark, rainy night, and I wanted to be anywhere but there. When I got there, there were only about a dozen or so teenagers gathered. I don't really remember what I said. All I wanted to do was to say my speech and leave.

Recently, when I was speaking on a college campus, a young woman came up to me, introduced herself, and told me that she was preparing for work in an overseas mission of the church. She wanted to be a nurse and to provide health care to people in developing countries in the name of Christ.

"You had a big part in my decision," she said. "Even though you didn't know it, the night that you came to speak to the youth rally, what you said really touched me. That night I decided to give my life to something important which God wanted me to do. That's why I'm here."

"The seed should sprout and grow, he knows not how" (Mark 4:27b).

The Great and First Commandment

Yet to say that the growth of the kingdom finally belongs to God is not to say that we should do nothing. As citizens of this kingdom, we must obey our sovereign. We may not have as our responsibility the building of the kingdom, but we do have the responsibility to signal and sight the presence of that kingdom in our daily lives.

To speak of the work of Jesus as the formation of a kingdom implies that the work of Jesus has boundaries, identifiable limits, and characteristics. The kingdom is open to all, but it requires commitment.

We live in a permissive age where an "anything goes" philosophy pervades everything. "It doesn't really matter what you believe as long as you are sincere," many people say.

Matthew reminds us that Jesus had definite, identifiable standards for his followers. They came to Jesus one day and asked, "Teacher, which is the great commandment in the law?"

Let us listen carefully for Jesus' response. He did not say, "Don't worry about laws and standards. Do you own thing. If it feels good, do it. Don't worry about right and wrong, do what makes you happy."

Our local radio station has a program in which listeners can call in to a person who is identified as a "therapist." You tell her your problem, and she gives you advice. Time and again her advice can be summed up as, "Look after yourself, do what makes you happy, and don't worry about anybody else."

They asked Jesus what they ought to do with life and he replied, "You shall love the Lord your God with all your heart, and with all your soul, and with all your mind" (Matthew 22:37). In other words, love God with everything you have.

The second commandment builds upon the first. If God is lord of our life, if we give over everything that we have to God, then we also give ourselves totally to those whom God loves. "You shall love your neighbor as yourself" (22:39).

How different is the shape of this kingdom than the competing kingdoms which bid for our allegiance today! Today we are told, by myriad self-help psychologies and philosophies, that we find meaning in life by loving ourselves more and more, by giving ourselves totally to ourselves without a thought for God or other people.

Jesus obviously counseled another path to the abundant life.

He Who Humbles Himself Will Be Exalted

Elsewhere Jesus tells a parable about two men who go up to the temple to pray. One is a despised tax collector, the other a pious Pharisee (Luke 18:9-14).

The shock is how the story ends. The bad man, not the good man, comes back from the temple "justified" by God. "For every one who exalts himself will be humbled, but he who humbles himself will be exalted" (18:14).

What a topsy-turvy kingdom this is! Good people end up on the outside, bad people end up justified. Those whom we regard as on top end up on the bottom. We find our lives by losing them; we save ourselves by giving ourselves—what sort of kingdom is this?

That is the question, the eternal question which confronts us all.

SECOND QUARTER
Helping Adults Become Involved—Roy H. Ryan

Preparing to Teach

This lesson begins a new unit entitled, "Principles of Christian Living." Study this lesson with that theme in mind.

"The kingdom of God" and "the kingdom of heaven" were two common phrases on the lips of Jesus. If you have a concordance, it would be good to look up the New Testament passages that include one of these phrases.

The idea of the kingdom ("reign") of God is such a key idea in the teaching of Jesus that it deserves our careful and prayerful study.

Read all three of the background scripture passages suggested for this lesson. As you study, ask the questions, What does this passage *say*?; What did Jesus *mean* by this? and What does it mean to me (us) today?

This simple method of Bible study can help you get on the inside of these passages and discover some meanings that you may have missed before.

The aim of this lesson is to help us understand the nature of the kingdom of God and how we are to participate in God's reign.

The following outline is suggested:

> Introduction: If we are to understand who Jesus was and what his mission was, we must give attention to the central note in his preaching—the kingdom of God (God's reign).
> I. The announcement of the kingdom
>   A. A central theme in Jesus' preaching
>   B. A dream coming true
> II. The nature of God's reign
>   A. God's will and way established
>   B. The kingdom "within"
>   C. The kingdom coming
> III. Living in the kingdom
>   A. A kingdom of love
>   B. A kingdom of righteousness
>   C. A kingdom of justice
> IV. The kingdom as God's gift

Introducing the Main Question

Do we believe and live as if this babe in Bethlehem, whom we call Lord and Savior, is really the Lord of all and has come to establish that reign among us?

If we really believe that Jesus Christ is Lord, it will affect every dimension of our lives and relationships. If the God whom Jesus came to reveal claims our loyalty, if his will truly has sway in our lives, it will be reflected in the way we think, act, and relate to all of his creation. When this happens, we then experience the kingdom which Jesus proclaimed.

What are some of the understandings of the kingdom held by members of your group? Is it a place? Is it a certain people? Discuss.

Developing the Lesson

Read Mark 1:15 to begin your lesson. Then read one or more of the suggested passages in Mark, Matthew, and Luke to start your lesson on "the reign of God."

Emphasize the centrality of "the kingdom of God" in Jesus' preaching and teaching. Dr. Willimon suggests that it may be one of the most neglected aspects of our faith. If that is true, it makes your task in teaching all the more significant!

I. The announcement of the kingdom

A. A central theme in Jesus' preaching

As noted earlier, the announcement of the coming kingdom and the call to "prepare" for it and "accept" it was central in the preaching and teaching of Jesus. Mark 1:15 sets the tone for this emphasis. There was no question in the mind of Jesus that God would ultimately establish his rule over all creation.

B. A dream coming true

This coming kingdom is a dream coming true for all those who have longed for and waited for God's rule. The prophets had foretold a day in which God's justice and righteousness would prevail. Jesus' invitation to all was "to repent and accept" this kingdom that God was bringing into reality. What a dream come true if all of humanity could learn to live in love, peace, and justice!

II. The nature of God's reign

A. God's will and way established

This kingdom will be one in which God's will and way will prevail. It will be experienced by all those who through humble faith and repentance accept this gift (Luke 18:9-14). Isaiah 9:7 describes in part the nature of this coming kingdom as envisioned by the prophets and confirmed by Jesus.

B. The kingdom "within"

The kingdom is within when God's will and way become our will and way. It can never be fully known and realized by an individual, but we can have a foretaste of glory divine when we surrender our lives to God's will.

C. The kingdom coming

It is always "coming" and never fully realized; it is the "not yet" that keeps calling us toward love, righteousness, and justice. God is "giving" us the kingdom as we are able to receive it, as we are prepared to accept it.

III. Living in the kingdom

A. A kingdom of love

Those who love God and neighbor, says Jesus, are already experiencing God's reign. In I John, we are told that "whoever loves is of God." If God is love, those who love are under God's reign.

B. A kingdom of righteousness

Such a goal is stressed by Jesus. "Doing right"; doing the loving deed; and ministering to the hungry, the prisoner, the sick (Matthew 25) are what citizenship in the kingdom is all about.

C. A kingdom of justice

Justice is the theme of the promised kingdom in the Old Testament (see especially the book of Amos) and is fulfilled in the life and teaching of Jesus. The *just* do indeed live by faith!

IV. The kingdom as God's gift

Those who live by faith and have experienced the grace (the unmerited favor of God) of God know that it is indeed "the Father's good pleasure to give us the kingdom." We do not "build" the kingdom; we receive it, we experience it, and we live in it.

Helping Class Members Act

Where do we see God's will being done in our world? If we believe that God's reign will be evidenced by love, justice, and righteousness, then as Christians we will want to be identified with such acts in our world.

Help class members see that one way to live their Christian discipleship in the world is to identify themselves with the causes and movements that seek to bring love and justice.

Planning for Next Sunday

Ask persons to read the scripture and to make notes for the upcoming lesson, "Persons Are Important."

LESSON 6   JANUARY 5

Persons Are Important

Background Scripture: Matthew 10:28-31; Mark 2:23–3:6

The Main Question—William H. Willimon

We Americans tend to be impressed by size. We are the land of the colossial Statue of Liberty, the Empire State Building, the World Trade Center, the USS *Enterprise,* the state of Texas, and the Astrodome.

Bigger is better.

Every town, it seems to me, no matter how small, seems to be able to boast the biggest something—the biggest water tower, the widest main street, the largest hamburger sales—something which makes the town notable. The implication, of course, is that bigger is better and the worth of things is measured only by their size. Little means insignificant and unimportant. Big means valuable and worthwhile.

Perhaps that is why life in modern America often feels terribly impersonal and lonely. We eat at fast-food restaurants where we shuffle through like cattle at a feed trough to receive our preprocessed, assembly-line food. We are known not by name but by social security number.

Do you think that the individual is as important today as he or she once was? Try straightening out your electric bill when you are corresponding with a computer somewhere (as I had the misfortune of doing the other day) and see how important you feel.

"I am a human being. Do not fold, spindle, or mutilate me!" said a placard carried by a student in a university protest demonstration in the 1960s.

Is bigger always better?

As You Read the Scripture—Bond Fleming

The passage from Matthew (10:28-31) is part of a longer section in which Jesus counsels his followers to be courageous even in the face of persecution. Indeed, those who fail to put and keep loyalty to Jesus first are not worthy of him! The promise of finding life is for those who are willing to lose their lives for Christ's sake. Cowardice kills the soul. Proclaim the gospel boldly, as from the housetops.

Matthew 10:28-31. Two main ideas are included here. The first emphasis is upon the power of God. Satan or people can harm or kill the body, but not the soul. God can assign both body and soul to hell. We ought so to fear this powerful God that we will not have to fear any person.

The second emphasis is upon this powerful God's concern for each human being. Two times in these four verses the hearers are told not to fear. God's concern is personal, and his concern is constant.

Mark 2:23-28. Here are two brief stories. Both episodes take place on the sabbath. The sabbath was a holy day, and hundreds of restrictive rules had been developed to make sure that it was kept holy. The stories illustrate Jesus' teaching about the exceeding worth of persons; persons are worth more than traditions—even the sacred traditions concerning the sabbath.

The criticism for plucking the grain was religious, not economic. In Deuteronomy 23:25, such plucking of grain was permitted. But nothing was said then about the sabbath. The restrictive rules about the sabbath were devised later. Jesus defended the disciples with an argument from the greater to the lesser. Surely, Jesus implied, what David did, as told in I Samuel 21:1-6, was worse than what the disciples had done.

Then, in Mark 2:27, Jesus proclaimed the heretical teaching concerning the sabbath and man. The final test of any system is what it does to or for persons. This does not make people the measure of all things, but it does mean that all things are measured by their impact upon persons.

Chapter 3-6. The worth of persons and the emphasis on human rights are even more evident. This event took place on the sabbath also; in this case Jesus is the offender. He heals the withered hand of a man whose name and station are not given; he was just a person in need. Jesus could meet that need, and did, even on the sabbath. The Pharisees were more concerned with the traditions regarding the sabbath than with the man. Jesus was more concerned with the human being; to meet his need was more important than to observe the restrictive tradition.

This story is told also in Matthew 12:9-14 and in Luke 6:6-11. Neither of them mentions Jesus' anger, but anger was appropriate. Mark explains the anger; it was because of their inhumanity and their bigotry. All three accounts of the healing tell of the blinding anger of the Pharisees. They were so angry at Jesus that they would not, or could not, appreciate the good deed that was done. The Pharisees surely had no love for the Herodians, far from it. But they would join with them in an effort to maintain the status quo and to get rid of Jesus.

Jesus got into more trouble because of his teaching about the value of persons than for his teaching about the love of God. As a matter of fact, Jesus joined the two. Persons are of great worth and importance because they are children of the eternal God of love.

Selected Scripture

King James Version	Revised Standard Version

Matthew 10:28-31

28 And fear not them which kill the body, but are not able to kill the soul: but rather fear him which is able to destroy both soul and body in hell.

29 Are not two sparrows sold for a farthing? and one of them shall not fall on the ground without your Father.

30 But the very hairs of your head are all numbered.

31 Fear ye not therefore, ye are of more value than many sparrows.

Matthew 10:28-31

28 And do not fear those who kill the body but cannot kill the soul; rather fear him who can destroy both soul and body in hell. 29 Are not two sparrows sold for a penny? And not one of them will fall to the ground without your Father's will. 30 But even the hairs of your head are all numbered. 31 Fear not, therefore; you are of more value than many sparrows.

Mark 2:23-28

23 And it came to pass, that he went through the corn fields on the sabbath day; and his disciples began, as they went, to pluck the ears of corn.

24 And the Pharisees said unto him, Behold, why do they on the sabbath day that which is not lawful?

25 And he said unto them, Have ye never read what David did, when he had need, and was an hungered, he, and they that were with him?

26 How he went into the house of God in the days of Ă-bī'-ă-thär the high priest, and did eat the shewbread, which is not lawful to eat but for the priests, and gave also to them which were with him?

27 And he said unto them, The sabbath was made for man, and not man for the sabbath:

28 Therefore the Son of man is Lord also of the sabbath.

Mark 2:23-28

23 One sabbath he was going through the grainfields; and as they made their way his disciples began to pluck heads of grain. 24 And the Pharisees said to him, "Look, why are they doing what is not lawful on the sabbath?" 25 And he said to them, "Have you never read what David did, when he was in need and was hungry, he and those who were with him: 26 how he entered the house of God, when Abi'athar was high priest, and ate the bread of the Presence, which it is not lawful for any but the priests to eat, and also gave it to those who were with him?" 27 And he said to them, "The sabbath was made for man, not man for the sabbath; 28 so the Son of man is lord even of the sabbath."

Mark 3:1-6

1 And he entered again into the synagogue; and there was a man there which had a withered hand.

2 And they watched him, whether he would heal him on the sabbath day; that they might accuse him.

3 And he said unto the man which had the withered hand, Stand forth.

Mark 3:1-6

1 Again he entered the synagogue, and a man was there who had a withered hand. 2 And they watched him, to see whether he would heal him on the sabbath, so that they might accuse him. 3 And he said to the man who had the withered hand, "Come here." 4 And

4 And he said unto them, Is it lawful to do good on the sabbath days, or to do evil? to save life, or to kill? But they held their peace.

5 And when he had looked round about on them with anger, being grieved for the hardness of their hearts, he saith unto the man, Stretch forth thine hand. And he stretched it out: and his hand was restored whole as the other.

6 And the Pharisees went forth, and straightway took counsel with the Hĕ-rō´-dĭ-ăns against him, how they might destroy him.

he said to them, "Is it lawful on the sabbath to do good or to do harm, to save life or to kill?" But they were silent. 5 And he looked around at them with anger, grieved at their hardness of heart, and said to the man, "Stretch out your hand." He stretched it out, and his hand was restored. 6 The Pharisees went out, and immediately held counsel with the Hero´-di-ans against him, how to destroy him.

Key Verse: **Fear ye not therefore, ye are of more value than many sparrows. (Matthew 10:31)**

Key Verse: **Fear not, therefore; you are of more value than many sparrows. (Matthew 10:31)**

The Scripture and the Main Question—William H. Willimon

You Are of More Value

"But even the hairs on your head are all numbered," says Jesus (Matthew 10:30). God knows the very number of hairs on our head! No sparrow falls to the ground except by the knowledge of God.

I think it is fair to say that it would be rather astounding to teach people of the first century. In that time, in that part of the world, human life must have seemed cheap. Life was, in the words of English philosopher Thomas Hobbes, "solitary, poor, nasty, brutish, and short."

Yet Jesus could assert that every person was valued. If God values the sparrows which fill the air, how much more must God value you!

In our own day we face new challenges to the dignity and welfare of the individual human being. The debate over abortion is, in great part, an argument over the comparative worth of individuals. Is the individual mother's right to decide more important than the individual fetus's right to survive? We have learned what a complex question this is. We have also learned what an emotional question it is—and well it should be, for we are arguing over the very worth of life itself.

The advent of the computer has been a mixed blessing. In one sense, the computer could help to individualize and personalize life. By being able to store and to retrieve large amounts of data, we can tailor education to suit the needs of the individual learner. We can diagnose illnesses quicker and more effectively than before.

But we can use the computer to invade people's privacy too. A computerized world could reduce us all to the level of faceless, nameless numbers.

It isn't the computer which is the culprit. As usual, the problem is in the people. Will we use this new tool to enrich human life or to impoverish it? The choice is up to us.

There is evidence that we are witnessing a sort of backlash against the notion that bigger is better. In the past century we have seen businesses expand to the size of multinational corporations. The national government has quadrupled in size, along with the national budget. Small towns have exploded into great cities and vast suburbs. Shall all this expansion be for the better or for the worse?

Many people today are becoming disenchanted with bigness. They tire of working in giant corporations and choose instead to work in small businesses where they can know the people with whom they work and people can know them.

"Small is beautiful" is the slogan of a movement which seeks to institute a simpler, less complicated life-style. Many young people, having grown up in a large city or suburb, choose to make their new homes in small towns or in rural areas, feeling that a simpler, natural way of life is more wholesome and humane.

In the past decade, there has been a dramatic rediscovery of the virtues of the small membership church. For so long, the standard for measuring an effective church was the large, downtown, multistaff church with a thousand or more members. These were the churches with the large choirs, impressive organs, three or four paid professional staff people, and sprawling buildings.

Small churches were often made to feel backward and inadequate. The Sunday school literature would instruct the children's class to break up into small groups of three or four when only three or four children might be in attendance that day in the entire Sunday school. The music was written for four-part harmony when the little choir had only a tenor and two sopranos. The small church got the distinct impression that it was second rate.

Fortunately, there have been a host of books (such as *Small Churches Are Beautiful* and *The Small Church: Valid, Vital, and Victorious*) that have discovered the distinct identity and the unique gifts of small-membership churches. There are lots of things a small church cannot do, but there are many things, many very important things, that small churches may do better than large churches.

In a small-membership church, people are treated as individuals. When people are absent, they are missed. Everyone is needed. The level of participation and giving is usually always higher in a small church than in a large church. In fact, some even argue that the church, with its strong emphasis on individuals and upon the worth of every person, ought to limit congregations to a maximum of four or five hundred persons.

In an impersonal world, the local church, whatever size it is, must learn ways of stressing the value of persons as individuals. People are tired of being treated as faceless, nameless numbers. They long for human groupings that treat them like family, that take the time and the trouble to know them and their needs. No church can survive in the future if it does not take every person seriously.

Take a moment and think about your church. In what ways does your congregation stress the worth of every person? How might your congregation improve this aspect of its ministry?

"Fear not," Jesus told his followers. "You are of more value than many sparrows" (Matthew 10:31).

Lord of the Sabbath

They were walking through the grainfields one sabbath. Jesus and his followers picked some of the grain and ate it. His critics attacked him for this, accusing Jesus of breaking the sabbath.

To their criticism, Jesus recalled how David had eaten the bread off the altar in the tabernacle when he and his men were hungry (Mark 2:25-26). Then he tells them, "The sabbath was made for man, not man for the sabbath; so the Son of man is lord even of the sabbath" (2:27-28).

Once again we see Jesus as the Lord who puts people over principles sometimes. How tragic that the sabbath laws, which were a unique way of humanizing life in ancient Israel, had become an end in themselves, a source of dehumanizing!

The sabbath was a time of rest for animals and people. Unlike the rest of the world, Israel believed that its God desired rest and renewal for all living things. Even in times of great national need, the sabbath was kept as a time of rest and restoration. It was a great gift, particularly for the poor who, without the sabbath, would have probably had no rest from their labors.

But here the sabbath seems to have become an end in itself. Jesus says that human need sometimes takes precedent over religious regulations.

"We can't have a day care center in our church because the noise of the children might disturb people who come here to pray. It's not reverent to have so much noise in church."

"If our church supports this home for unwed mothers, these wayward women are going to think that it's fine for them to go out and sin again, and then where will we be?"

"Is it true that the church youth group went out on Sunday and worked on the homes of the elderly? I don't think that's proper activity for a Sunday afternoon."

To Do Good or to Harm, to Save or to Kill

One of the saddest, most accusatory episodes in the Gospels occurs in Mark 3:1-6. A poor, afflicted man is brought to Jesus for healing. "And they watched him, to see whether he would heal him on the sabbath, so that they might accuse him" (3:2).

How tragic that the religious leaders of his day do not see the man and his plight! They see only the religious regulation and its demands.

Fortunately, when Jesus looks at the man, when he looks at you and me, he sees individuals. He sees our individual needs and ministers to us as individuals, in spite of what propriety and tradition may demand.

We can all take comfort in that.

Helping Adults Become Involved—Roy H. Ryan

Preparing to Teach

Last week the lesson introduced the idea of the kingdom (reign) of God as the living out of love, justice, and righteousness. As you prepare for this lesson, you will begin to see the connection. In God's kingdom every person is of worth. Persons are more important even than rules and regulations.

The Reverend Jesse Jackson has challenged and inspired thousands of black youth by having them say over and over, "I'm somebody."

Parents who always put their children down will mark them for life with a negative image of themselves. Parents who build their children up with the right amount of praise can help them grow up knowing they are of worth.

One of the greatest contributions we can make in the church is to preach and teach this eternal truth, that every person is of worth in God' sight.

Read the scripture passages for this lesson and begin to make notes early in the week.

The aim of this lesson is to help persons understand and appreciate their importance, their worth, no matter what their status in life or how little and insignificant they may feel in the presence of bigness and the impersonal world in which they live.

A possible outline for your presentation follows.

> Introduction. In God's kingdom, every person is important. God does not create anyone or anything insignificant!
> I. Do not fear people.
>   A. Early Christians faced persecution.
>   B. God is the ultimate power.
> II. God cares for all his creation.
> III. Persons are worth more than rules and regulations.
>   A. The sabbath is for persons.
>   B. The test of any system is what it does to people.
> IV. The Pharisees missed the point.

Introducing the Main Question

Dr. Willimon wonders whether, in a vast, faceless, nameless wilderness where people count for little and people feel lost and worthless, there is a word from the Christian faith.

Do you agree with this assessment of the heart of this lesson? If so, what is your response?

Ask the class to discuss the answer. What, indeed, does the Christian faith have to say to those who feel they are unimportant?

What are some ways the church through the good news can assure persons they are of worth? Who are some of the people in your community who probably feel their lives are worthless? What can the church do to help them find new hope and meaning for their lives?

Rehearse with the class how the Scriptures deal with this issue.

Developing the Lesson

The lesson from Matthew admonishes the followers of Jesus, "Do not fear those who kill the body but cannot kill the soul" (Matthew 10:28a). The theme of "do not be afraid" runs through the teachings of Jesus. The early Christians must have gained great comfort from this teaching. What are the implications for us?

Jesus let his disciples pluck grain on the sabbath. He also healed a man with a withered hand on the sabbath. Both were in violation of "the [unwritten, i.e., the oral] law." Are persons of more value than laws and traditions? This is still a critical issue for many people.

I. Do not fear people.

A. Early Christians faced persecution.

This word from the Master must have given them courage. Misplaced fear can immobilize us. We are to "fear" only God. This "fear" of God is not the same as "to be afraid," rather, it is more like "stand in awe of" God. Whatever obstacles stand in our way of being good witnesses to our faith, whatever fears keep us from victorious living, have no place in the Christian life.

B. *God is the ultimate power.*

"If God be for us, who can be against us?" Jesus reminds his hearers that God takes account of a sparrow that falls. How much more significant are we who are made in the image of God! Dr. Willimon reminds us that, in a world of bigness, "God cares about us." That is a great affirmation to live by.

II. *God cares for all his creation.*

The marvelous story of creation in Genesis 1 tells us that "God saw everything that he had made, and behold, it was very good" (Genesis 1:31a). There is such a balance in nature, in the created order, that nothing can be called insignificant, certainly not persons who have been given dominion (responsibility) over the other creatures (Genesis 1:26).

III. *Persons are worth more than rules and regulations.*

A. *The sabbath is for persons.*

It's not the other way around! It is amazing how many sincere Christians have been enslaved by "keeping the rules" instead of being liberated by the "grace of God that sets us free." The Jewish people had become burdened by hundreds of rules and regulations about sabbath observance. Jesus sought to correct the rules and set the record straight.

B. *The test of any system is what it does to people.*

That is true of religion, politics, economics, you name it! Rabbi Abraham Heschel, and outstanding leader in the Jewish community, has said, "The test of a people is how it behaves toward the old [people]." He said this in relation to how older persons are treated in this country. It holds true for any system. It would seem obvious, however, that those systems that oppress, that keep people in submission to the state (or church), that do not practice justice and mercy, cannot be pleasing to God.

IV. *The Pharisees missed the point.*

They were so hung up on "keeping the law" that they were willing to let people go hungry or remain sick rather than break the rules.

Helping Class Members Act

This lesson may spark some interesting discussion. Be prepared to deal with the moral dilemma that many people face in regard to "keeping rules" and when (if ever) bending or breaking the rules is justified.

In 1968, when the General Conference of The United Methodist Church passed a resolution on "The Rule of Law and the Right of Dissent," many church members were troubled. Is it ever right to break a law, even if it seems to us to be an unjust law?

Think of ways you can help your class members appropriate this important lesson in their lives.

Planning for Next Sunday

Ask class members to read Mark 7:1-23 and Matthew 5:21-30 and be ready to discuss the "inwardness of morality" and how we determine our authority for what is right and wrong.

The Inwardness of Morality

Background Scripture: Mark 7:1-23; Matthew 5:21-30

The Main Question—William H. Willimon

H. L. Mencken once defined a Puritan as "a person who is terrified by the thought that somewhere someone is having a good time." For many this is the stereotype of religious people. Religious people are those who are caught in a miserable tangle of oppressive rules, regulations, and ordinances through which they labor to live a holy life.

Don't do this; don't do that. This is how many people picture us Christians. My own mother remembers how people used to regard activity on Sunday. In their attempt to "keep the sabbath holy," her parents forbade her and her brothers and sisters to play in the front yard. Play in the backyard was permissible. They could read, but they could not read novels of any kind. One can imagine how many children grew up wondering what on earth was the point of Christian views about Sunday.

It is easy to pervert some valuable religious idea into a maze of petty, inconsequential rules that trivialize our faith. We thus miss the whole point. The trivialization was often the crux of the matter in Jesus' frequent controversies with the Pharisees.

In the 1950s, when terrible North Sea storms ravaged Holland and threatened that country's dikes, a little Dutch village was in danger of flooding. Because it was Sunday, many of the villagers felt that it would be improper to work on the dikes. They were strict sabbatarians who had scruples about any work on Sunday.

The young pastor at the village church attempted to rally the reluctant villagers by appealing to the conflict Jesus had with the Pharisees. He quoted Jesus' saying that "the sabbath was made for man." He recalled how Jesus and his disciples broke sabbath laws when they were hungry.

One old man replied, "Now I see that what I always feared is true—our Lord was a liberal!"

As You Read the Scripture—Bond Fleming

Mark 7:1-2. The passages from Mark 7 involve a controversy concerning the outwardness of tradition in contrast to the inwardness of morality. Verses 1 and 2 provide the occasion for the controversy. The Pharisees had been watching Jesus and apparently had called for some assistance from Jerusalem. This investigating committee was trying to spy on Jesus, not to follow him. Their spirit was negative; they favored the status quo; they refused to see any good in what Jesus said or did.

Verses 3-15. The main criticism was that some of the disciples ate without washing their hands. Verses 3 and 4 are a parenthetical explanation of traditions in Judaism for the non-Jewish readers; such explanations appear repeatedly in Mark, which was written for the Romans. The opponents of Jesus pose the question in verse 5: Why don't they live like we do?

Jesus responded, but for a moment ignored the carping criticism. In verses 6-12, Jesus lifts the discussion to the main issue, that is, the traditions of the elders; one of the traditions is the ceremonial washing of hands. In verse 14, Jesus directs his words to their question, at least obliquely. In verse 15, there is the statement of a fundamental principle concerning defilement. Defilement is not caused by something that goes into a person from the outside, as from eating with unwashed hands, but is caused by something that comes out of a person from within. There is here an emphasis upon the inwardness of morality. It takes purity of heart, not ceremonial conformity, to see God.

Verses 17-23. Verse 15 must have been part of a parable, because in verse 17 when Jesus is alone with the disciples, they ask him to explain the parable. The explanation is related to food. Food enters the stomach, not the heart, and is later evacuated. The parenthetical statement in verse 19, about declaring all foods clean, relates directly to the question of eating with unwashed hands.

One of the most profound teachings of Jesus concerns his emphasis upon the inwardness of morality and religion. This emphasis is stated twice in Mark 7:20, 23. In verses 21 and 22 Jesus explains and even lists the things that come from "within, out of the heart," that defile a person.

Matthew 5:21-22. Matthew 5 is a part of the Sermon on the Mount. Verses 21 and 22 give the first of six instances in which the new law surpasses the old. Note the phrase, "But I say unto you." Jesus did not cite references; he spoke with the authority of truth.

Jesus goes far beyond actual murder. Murder is forbidden in both lists of the Commandments, Exodus 20: 13 and Deuteronomy 5:17. Where does murder begin? It begins in the heart, with anger. The seriousness of this judgment against anger is evident in the verses that follow; reconciliation with a brother is preliminary to the effective offering of gifts at the altar, Matthew 5:23-24.

Apparently the criticism of the sins of anger, verse 22, lists them in ascending order. As anger grows, we begin to hurl insults and then call each other names. Finally we come to blows, injury, and murder. Our law courts do not take action until there is violence involving civil disturbance. But Jesus is concerned with the inner feelings and motives. Judgment against anger is severe. He would have us root out even the beginnings of anger that may end in violence and murder.

The key verse, from Psalm 51:10, is a penitential prayer that recognizes the inwardness of morality; it is a plea that God will cleanse our hearts and put within us "a new and right spirit."

Selected Scripture

King James Version	Revised Standard Version
Mark 7:1-5, 14-23	*Mark 7:1-5, 14-23*
1 Then came together unto him the Pharisees, and certain of the scribes, which came from Jerusalem.	1 Now when the Pharisees gathered together to him, with some of the scribes, who had come from Jerusalem, 2 they saw that some of
2 And when they saw some of his disciples eat bread with defiled, that is to say, with unwashen, hands, they found fault.	his disciples ate with hands defiled, that is, unwashed. 3 (For the Pharisees, and all the Jews, do not eat

3 For the Pharisees, and all the Jews, except they wash *their* hands oft, eat not, holding the tradition of the elders.

4 And *when they come* from the market, except they wash, they eat not. And many other things there be, which they have received to hold, *as* the washing of cups, and pots, brasen vessels, and of tables.

5 Then the Pharisees and scribes asked him, Why walk not thy disciples according to the tradition of the elders, but eat bread with unwashen hands?

....

unless they wash their hands, observing the tradition of the elders; 4 and when they come from the market place, they do not eat unless they purify themselves; and there are many other traditions which they observe, the washing of cups and pots and vessels of bronze.) 5 And the Pharisees and the scribes asked him, 'Why do your disciples not live according to the tradition of the elders, but eat with hands defiled?"

....

14 And when he had called all the people *unto him,* he said unto them, Hearken unto me every one *of you,* and understand:

15 There is nothing from without a man, that entering into him can defile him: but the things which come out of him, those are they that defile the man.

16 If any man have ears to hear, let him hear.

17 And when he was entered into the house from the people, his disciples asked him concerning the parable.

18 And he saith unto them, Are ye so without understanding also? Do ye not perceive, that whatsoever thing from without entereth into the man, *it* cannot defile him;

19 Because it entereth not into his heart, but into the belly, and goeth out into the draught, purging all meats?

20 And he said, That which cometh out of the man, that defileth the man.

21 For from within, out of the heart of men, proceed evil thoughts, adulteries, fornications, murders,

22 Thefts, covetousness, wickedness, deceit, lasciviousness, an evil eye, blasphemy, pride, foolishness:

23 All these evil things come from within, and defile the man.

14 And he called the people to him again, and said to them, "Hear me, all of you, and understand: 15 there is nothing outside a man which by going into him can defile him; but the things which come out of a man are what defile him." 17 And when he had entered the house, and left the people, his disciples asked him about the parable. 18 And he said to them, "Then are you also without understanding? Do you not see that whatever goes into a man from outside cannot defile him, 19 since it enters, not his heart but his stomach, and so passes on?" (Thus he declared all foods clean.) 20 And he said, "What comes out of a man is what defiles a man. 21 For from within, out of the heart of man, come evil thoughts, fornication, theft, murder, adultery, 22 coveting, wickedness, deceit, licentiousness, envy, slander, pride, foolishness. 23 All these evil things come from within, and they defile a man."

Matthew 5:21-22

21 Ye have heard that it was said by them of old time, Thou shalt not kill; and whosoever shall kill shall be in danger of the judgment:

22 But I say unto you, That whosoever is angry with his brother without a cause shall be in danger of the judgment: and whosoever shall say to his brother, Rā´-că, shall be in danger of the council: but whosoever shall say, Thou fool, shall be in danger of hell fire.

Key Verse: **Create in me a clean heart, O God; and renew a right spirit within me. (Psalm 51:10)**

Matthew 5:21-22

21 "You have heard that it was said to the men of old, 'You shall not kill; and whoever kills shall be liable to judgment.' 22 But I say to you that very one who is angry with his brother shall be liable to judgment; whoever insults his brother shall be liable to the council, and whoever says, 'You fool!' shall be liable to the hell of fire.

Key Verse: **Create in me a clean heart, O God, and put a new and right spirit within me. (Psalm 51:10)**

The Scripture and the Main Question—William H. Willimon

With Hands Defiled

For the Jew, every meal is a religious occasion. The Jew makes no distinction between religious and nonreligious meals. Every meal is a sign of God's gifts of food and our dependence on these gifts. We get our practice of saying a blessing [i.e., thanking and praising God] before eating from the Jews. When we say a prayer before we eat, we thereby claim the dinner table as a holy place.

This view of the table typifies the Jewish belief that religion should permeate every facet of life. No distinction is made between sacred and secular. Our God is Lord of all. The genius of the Jewish religion is the insight that even something so commonplace and mundane as the sharing of food and drink can be an occasion for communion with God.

The Pharisees are much maligned in most of the gospel writings. Today's scripture is no exception. But the glory of the pharisaical approach to religion was the belief that all of life stood under God's love and care. How one ate, drank, bathed, treated one's children, cared for one's livestock—all were important issues of religious morality.

In our own day when many attempt to make a neat separation between what they call "religion" and "politics" or try to segment their lives into areas that are "secular" and "sacred," we should have a new admiration for the Pharisees of old who urged continuous examination of every aspect of our lives in order to be sure that our lives properly reflect God's claim upon all life. The Pharisees were only trying to make religion relevant to everyday life.

Therefore, one does not come from the push and shove of the marketplace and sit down at the table to enjoy God's gifts without proper respect and preparation for this holy meal. Purification is required lest one defile the table (Mark 7:3-4). In other words, when we read of the Pharisees and their dietary and purification requirements, we are reading about sincere, religious people who are only trying to relate their religious beliefs to everyday life.

The Tradition of the Elders

But Mark's stories of the Pharisees suggest that something is greatly amiss in their piety. Somehow the religious practices which should be leading people closer to God have become a tiresome, meaningless burden that hinders their relationship with God.

At various points, the Pharisees are depicted as those who challenge Jesus. How ironic that these religious authorities and devoted practitioners of the faith are among Jesus' chief critics! Somehow they have gotten sidetracked.

They ask Jesus, "Why do your disciples not live according to the tradition of the elders, but eat with hands defiled?" (Mark 7:5).

This verse should be dearly loved by every eight-year-old lad who has resisted his mother's attempts to get him to wash his hands before dinner!

But, of course, the objection to unwashed hands is not a matter of hygiene. It is a matter of religious practice. Jesus and his disciples have broken with the "tradition of the elders."

In responding to his critics, Jesus charges that they "have a fine way of rejecting the commandment of God, in order to keep your tradition!" (7:9). In Jesus' view, the Pharisees have allowed nonessential, human "tradition[s] of men" (7:8) to crowd out the essential commands of God.

And isn't this the way it often is for us? We are forever allowing some human standard of righteousness to be blown all out of proportion until it overshadows basic belief.

If you had asked me when I was a young boy, "Who is a Christian?" I'm sure that I would have replied, "A Christian is someone who doesn't smoke, never curses, refuses to drink alcohol, and always puts fifty cents in the collection plate."

A limited view of Christianity this may be, but it was the impression I received from the church of that day. Not smoking, not using profanity, not drinking may all be worthwhile habits for the Christian to cultivate. But who would argue that they have anything to do with the heart of our faith? To be honest about it, most of these moral precepts reflect later cultural standards of approved behavior rather than fundamental biblical concerns.

A friend of mine who is a missionary tells me that this is one of the greatest challenges on the mission field: to sort out the fundamental, biblical vision of the Christian faith from the mere cultural accretions, the "tradition[s] of men" that have accumulated over the years. Missionaries want to be sure that they are proclaiming the gospel—not some culturally conditioned form of the gospel which is only our society's tradition.

Hear . . . and Understand

Time and again Jesus comes into conflict with these who uphold their traditions at the expense of receiving God's view of revelation.

It's not simply a matter of loyalty to the "good old-fashioned religion"; it's also a matter of what we believe to be the purpose of religion.

For Jesus' critics, religion was mostly a matter of externals—keep this dietary law, follow this regulation, wash that dish. One value of such religion is that it aids us in building ourselves up and in neatly separating ourselves from other people whom we deem to be less holy than we are.

Thus we can observe who smokes, who drinks, or who attends church regularly and then make neat distinctions between the holy and the unholy, the saved and the damned. And you can be sure on which side we will place ourselves!

It was this sort of smug self-righteousness that seemed to anger Jesus. He well understood that the Pharisees' problem was not their inability to follow the externals of religion. Their problem was internal—in the smug, haughty attitude by which they used religion to build themselves up and to put others down.

For the common person of Jesus' day, the Pharisees' complicated ritualistic details were virtually impossible to follow. In their poverty, most of the common people had enough to do just to get enough food to live without worrying about the cleansing of the dish.

Jesus thus defends the lowly. As usual, he sides with the poor and oppressed against the aloof, smug religious establishment. The things within a person's heart are the ultimate defilement (7:14-20). From within comes our perverted need to turn even religion into a means to cut ourselves off from those who should be our neighbors, to inflate our pride while we put others down.

So Jesus implies that we ought to expend more energy worrying about the internals than the externals. The essential, basic matters such as how we look upon our brothers and sisters, how we judge and condemn one another, how we pervert the blessings of religion into burdens to lay upon someone elses' back so we can stand a little taller—these should be our concerns.

Jesus helps us to hear the true music of faith above the clamor of our petty little rules and dead traditions. He helps us to understand that we are our own worst enemies in matters of religious faith. If we want to know the source of our deceit, envy, pride, and foolishness (7:22), we need only look within ourselves.

Helping Adults Become Involved—Roy H. Ryan

Preparing to Teach
Read the scripture passages, Matthew 5:21-30 and Mark 7:1-23, with a commentary such as *The Interpreter's Bible* to help you better understand the background and meaning of these passages. Dr. Fleming's comments found in "As You Read the Scripture" and Dr. Willimon's "The Scripture and the Main Question" will also help broaden your grasp of the meaning of the biblical material.

This lesson is closely related to last week's lesson, which dealt with the relationship of persons to rules and regulations. This lesson helps us look beyond the outward keeping of rules and traditions to the inwardness of our motives and thoughts. We are here offered a key insight into the Christian understanding of life.

The aim of this lesson is to help us understand that the nature of true religion is not determined by following "the tradition of men" but by the thoughts, attitudes, and motives within us that compel our actions. Rituals and traditions have their place in the Christian way of life, but they must never replace God's commandments to love him and to love and serve the neighbor.

Organize your presentation carefully and allow for discussion on this crucial matter. The following outline may help:

Introduction. The heart of Christianity is located in our motives, thoughts, and attitudes, not in outward traditions and rituals.

I. With hands defiled
    A. Jewish understanding of religion
    B. The Pharisees—sticklers for minutiae

II. The tradition of the elders
    A. Jesus criticized
    B. Human standards—short

III. To hear and understand
    A. When "traditions" get in the way
    B. Looking on the "inside," not the "outside"

Introducing the Main Question

What is the essence of Christianity? Is it to be found in following certain prescribed rituals and traditions? Is it merely what we verbally profess to believe? Is it refraining from bad habits? Is it found inside or outside the person?

You may wish to engage members of the class in describing in simple terms what they consider to be the essence (the essential nature) of Christianity. That seems to be what this lesson is all about.

Why not use the two illustrations in Dr. Willimon's "The Main Question" as a way of getting into the lesson? First, mention his own mother's experience of growing up in a strict family. Second, recount the rather sad but humorous account of a young pastor's efforts to help his parishioners prepare for the floods which threatened their hometown in Holland in the 1950s.

Developing the Lesson

The passage in Mark describes a classic confrontation between Jesus and the Pharisees. They see his disciples eating without washing their hands. That goes against their (oral) tradition of "washing before eating." It is not just a matter of hygiene—it is a religious issue. Jesus cuts to the heart of the issue by telling them that it is not what goes in a person that defiles the person but what comes from within our thought-life (Mark 7:15).

Matthew 5:21-30 is a part of the Sermon on the Mount. In this passage, Jesus says that true religion can be measured not simply by keeping the commandments outwardly but by being cleansed inside so that what we do is motivated by love of God and neighbor.

I. With hands defiled

    A. The Jewish understanding of religion

The Jews did not neatly separate religious and secular life as we are prone to do. Therefore, their religious rules, rituals, and traditions guided their every act.

    B. The Pharisees—sticklers for minutiae

The Pharisees were the strictest of the religious leaders. They sought to dot very *i* and cross every *t*. They gave Jesus a lot of trouble because he was too much of a "free spirit" to fit into their legalistic mold. He allowed his disciples to break "the rules," like not washing their hands before plucking and eating grain on the sabbath!

II. The tradition of the elders
A. Jesus criticized

Jesus seemed to be under constant criticism by those who saw him as a threat to their traditions. He was seen as a radical by those who were dedicated to preserving the status quo. It is difficult for us to think of Jesus as a radical, but when we really examine his teachings we may discover what the old man in Dr. Willimon's story discovered, "Our Lord was a liberal!" He certainly was liberal compared to his main critics, the Pharisees.

B. Human standards—short

We fall short of God's will and God's way. We tend to let too many of our own human values and traditions get into our religious life and water it down to a common denominator of the culture's values. A good example is the social and cultural "norms" regarding race before the 1960s and the strong leadership of Dr. Martin Luther King and others. Many "Christians" were following human standards (too many of us still do) on questions of racial justice and equity rather than God's will.

III. To hear and understand
A. When "traditions" get in the way

Jesus calls us to turn back to the essence of Christianity, to love God and neighbor and let all our attitudes, motives, and actions come from that center of value.

B. Looking on the "inside," not the "outside"

The measure of our Christian discipleship is not how well we keep the traditions of persons, but how well we live from the inside out by the help of God's grace and forgiveness.

Helping Class Members Act

What changes would be called for in our lives if we lived truly from the "inside out" rather than simply following the traditions of our elders on the prevailing values of our culture?

What actions and attitudes would we need to change in order to show God's love rather than what is expected by people around us?

Planning for Next Sunday

The lesson next week is focused on "Ways Christians Serve." Ask class members to read Matthew 25:31-46 and be prepared to discuss its implications for our daily lives.

LESSON 8   JANUARY 19

Ways Christians Serve

Background Scripture: Matthew 25:31-46

The Main Question—William H. Willimon

"You never know what good you might be doing," we sometimes say. True. The teacher who prays for patience to endure another hour with an unruly class of children, the church which tries to collect clothing for the city's poor, the church school class which adopts a needy family at Christmas. You never know.

Of course, the reverse is also true. You never know what harm you might be doing. The unkind word, the thoughtless gesture, the hasty decisions all may cause pain or heartache in someone else's life. Wouldn't life be much easier for us to live if we could predict the consequencies of our actions before we act?

Unfortunately, there are no guarantees because we do not have a crystal ball to tell us a certain action will yield the right results and hoped-for consequences.

The other day a woman at my church went to answer a knock at the door. She found a man standing there with a beautiful flowering plant.

"Lady," he said, "this is for you. You probably don't remember me, but we met five years ago."

She honestly could not recall ever having seen the man before.

"Five years ago I stood with you at the corner bus stop on a cold, gray March morning. I was down on my luck. I had lost my job as an accountant; I was ready to give up. But you stood there and smiled at me. I don't remember exactly what you said to me, but I know that you gave me hope. You were excited because you had just planted an azalea bush, I remember that."

"An azalea bush?" she asked.

"Yes, and you got me to thinking. I had always loved plants. Well, here is a plant from my nursery. My flower business is going great. I wanted you to know how much you helped somebody."

And she said, "Lord, when did I see thee . . . ?"

As You Read the Scripture—Bond Fleming

The scripture, Matthew 25:31-46, is a parable concerning the last judgment. It expresses clearly the noblest ethical emphases of Old Testament and of Jesus. We are held accountable to God both for what we do and for what we fail or neglect to do.

Religion involves more than ethical concern for others; it involves faith and trust in God and loyalty to him. But genuine religion produces the fruit of concern for others. For example, note the emphases in James 1:27 or 2:14-16, and consider our respect for the *good* Samaritan in Luke 10:30-37. (Jesus does not use this word in describing the Samaritan.) James Henry Leigh Hunt's poem "Abou Ben Adhem" combines the two, love of fellowmen and love of God.

Matthew 25:31-32. "Son of man" occurs in the parable only in verse 31; "king" is used in verses 34 and 40. The reference is to Jesus as the glorified Son of man or the King Messiah; the angelic hosts surround the throne, and all nations are gathered to be judged. (The judgment of all nations, many of which had not yet heard of the King Messiah, might be judgment by common humanity; all of the world religions include some form of the golden rule.)

The division into two groups, sheep and goats, was simple for the shepherd, because in Palestine the sheep were usually white and the goats black. The shepherd could tell them apart even at dusk. The point in the division represents the definiteness of judgment by the King Messiah.

Verse 34. The *commendation* in this verse should be compared to the *condemnation* in verse 41. There is a note of joy and welcome in one, and a note of curse in the other—"Depart." The blessed are to "inherit the kingdom prepared for you from the foundation of the world." There was a place "prepared" for the others also. There is in the universe a fundamental difference between good and evil, and the difference is eternal.

Verses 35-36, 42-43. These passages too should be noted in contrast. The lists are the same, except that in one the needs were met, while in the other they were not met. In meeting these needs, more common to the poor and the outcasts than to the middle class or well-to-do, we are serving Christ. And in refusing to meet these needs, or in failing to do so, we are failing to serve Christ. It is burdensome and upsetting to be concerned about others.

The most striking thing about this parable of judgment is the element of surprise, both by the chosen and by the condemned. The actions that are commended are simple acts of service which many people do every day without being self-consciously aware of doing praiseworthy deeds. These are ways in which Christians serve. Likewise, the neglected actions are left undone by those who procrastinate or by those who are callously indifferent to the needy and less fortunate. The personality of Jesus was so far extended as to include humankind. Whoever helped anyone in need was helping Jesus, and whoever failed to lend a helping hand to anyone in need spurned Jesus.

Verses 37-39. In these verses and in verse 44, the lists are reviewed again. Both the commended and the condemned are so surprised that they are unbelieving; they want evidence. The answer of the king to both groups is found in verses 40 and 45. Note how similar, yet how different the answers are. The answer in verse 40 is the key verse because it is positive—life-affirming. The teaching appears to be about the future, but it also concerns our present life.

Selected Scripture

King James Version

Matthew 25:31-46

31 When the Son of man shall come in his glory, and all the holy angels with him, then shall he sit upon the throne of his glory:

32 And before him shall be gathered all nations: and he shall separate them one from another, as a shepherd divideth *his* sheep from the goats:

33 And he shall set the sheep on his right hand, but the goats on the left.

34 Then shall the King say unto them on his right hand, Come, ye blessed of my Father, inherit the kingdom prepared for you from the foundation of the world:

Revised Standard Version

Matthew 25:31-46

31 "When the Son of man comes in his glory, and all the angels with him, then he will sit on his glorious throne. 32 Before him will be gathered all the nations, and he will separate them one from another as a shepherd separates the sheep from the goats, 33 and he will place the sheep at his right hand, but the goats at the left. 34 Then the King will say to those at his right hand, 'Come, O blessed of my Father, inherit the kingdom prepared for you from the foundation of the world; 35 for I was hungry and you gave me food, I was thirsty and you gave me drink, I was a stranger and you welcomed

35 For I was an hungered, and ye gave me meat: I was thirsty, and ye gave me drink: I was a stranger, and ye took me in:

36 Naked, and ye clothed me: I was sick, and ye visited me: I was in prison, and ye came unto me.

37 Then shall the righteous answer him, saying, Lord, when saw we thee an hungered, and fed *thee?* or thirsty, and gave *thee* drink?

38 When saw we thee a stranger, and took *thee* in? or naked, and clothed *thee?*

39 Or when saw we thee sick, or in prison, and came unto thee?

40 And the King shall answer and say unto them, Verily I say unto you, Inasmuch as ye have done *it* unto one of the least of these my brethren, ye have done *it* unto me.

41 Then shall he say also unto them on the left hand, Depart from me, ye cursed, into everlasting fire, prepared for the devil and his angels:

42 For I was an hungered, and ye gave me no meat: I was thirsty, and ye gave me no drink:

43 I was a stranger, and ye took me not in: naked, and ye clothed me not: sick, and in prison, and ye visited me not.

44 Then shall they also answer him, saying, Lord, when saw we thee an hungered, or athirst, or a stranger, or naked, or sick, or in prison, and did not minister unto thee?

45 Then shall he answer them, saying, Verily I say unto you, Inasmuch as ye did *it* not to one of the least of these, ye did *it* not to me.

46 And these shall go away into everlasting punishment: but the righteous into life eternal.

me, 36 I was naked and you clothed me, I was sick and you visited me, I was in prison and you came to me.' 37 Then the righteous will answer him, 'Lord, when did we see thee hungry and feed thee, or thirsty and give thee drink? 38 And when did we see thee a stranger and welcome thee, or naked and clothe thee? 39 And when did we see thee sick or in prison and visit thee?' 40 And the King will answer them, 'Truly, I say to you, as you did it to one of the least of these my brethren, you did it to me.' 41 Then he will say to those at his left hand, 'Depart from me, you cursed, into the eternal fire prepared for the devil and his angels; 42 for I was hungry and you gave me no food, I was thirsty and you gave me no drink, 43 I was a stranger and you did not welcome me, naked and you did not clothe me, sick and in prison and you did not visit me.' 44 Then they also will answer, 'Lord, when did we see thee hungry or thirsty or a stranger or naked or sick or in prison, and did not minister to thee?' 45 Then he will answer them, 'Truly, I say to you, as you did it not to one of the least of these, you did it not to me.' 46 And they will go away into eternal punishment, but the righteous into eternal life."

Key Verse: **Inasmuch as ye have done** *it* **unto one of the least of these my brethren, ye have done** *it* **unto me. (Matthew 25:40)**

Key Verse: **As you did it to one of the least of these my brethren, you did it to me. (Matthew 25:40)**

The Scripture and the Main Question—William H. Willimon

Life is full of surprises. Just when you think you have everything all figured out—boom—there comes some new insight, some unexpected revelation. I suppose if we are going to stay Christians, we had better count on being surprised again and again.

One of the constant surprises is that God does not look at things the way we do. "My ways are not your ways, my thoughts are not your thoughts," Isaiah hears the voice of God say. What is right to us is not always right to God. What we call goodness sometimes appears very different in God's eyes. Here is a man whom we call the most outstanding citizen of the community. But God might look upon this man as a money-grabbing, power-hungry, ruthless operator because of the way he has achieved his status and earned his living.

Jesus was forever reminding people that God sees things and judges people differently from the way we do. Here is a woman who gives only a tiny coin at church next to a man who builds a church educational building—but the rich man is called a miser while the woman's mite is praised. Or here is a man we might call an outcast, an infidel, because he is a Samaritan. But Jesus calls him a true neighbor. Why? Because God judges people in different ways than we judge people.

Jesus told another story about the judgment of God, the story which is the focus of today's lesson—the story of the great judgment, Matthew 25:31-46. In this memorable story, there are surprises for everyone, the good and the bad. There are surprises, not because God is capricious and unpredictable, but simply because God looks at things differently from the way we look at things.

He Will Separate Them

For many people, perhaps many of the people in your class, the very idea of judgment is disturbing. To some, the idea that a God of love will judge people, damning some while blessing others, is repugnant to what they have experienced of God.

For other people, the notion of some final day when all the nations shall be gathered before the throne of God to be judged (25:31-32) is an archaic notion with little relevance for today. It is an ancient idea which can be disposed of with no loss to the Christian faith.

And yet, some people take the idea of a last judgment quite literally. Their idea of God encompasses a god who must some day clearly point out who is good and who is bad. The evil ones must be punished. The good ones must be rewarded.

In a way, all of these people could profit from an encounter with today's story of the great judgment.

First, is the notion of judgment so incomprehensible? If, as we believe, God is love, how can God be loving without being just? And how can God be just if there is no judgment? If good is not finally distinguished from bad, if those who have received nothing but oppression in life are never lifted up, and if things are never set right, then how can it be said that God is good?

The Christian faith affirms that the will of God will ultimately triumph, that good shall prevail over evil. God's love is not aloof and passive. It is active, engaging, risking love. Things shall be set right. The idea of some final, great judgment is an attempt to picture this divine work in setting things right.

But why doesn't God simply leave things as they are? Why doesn't God just let us be? Because if God simply "let us be," God would not be love. God loves us by helping us to be all that we can be—by prodding, calling, judging, encouraging, disciplining us forward. God's love would not be love if it did otherwise. Consider the parents of a young child. The growing child may say, "Why are Mother and Daddy always giving me rules to follow? Why were they so cruel as to spank me when I disobeyed them and ran into the street? They must be bad parents."

No, they judge their child and teach their child to judge for himself because they love the little boy. Their judgment is a function of their love. If they did not have rules, did not help the child discern right from wrong, if they just "let him be," they would be cruel parents indeed.

In the end, Jesus says, the Son of man shall gather all the nations together, not just the holy nations, *all* the nations; and he shall judge, separating "the sheep at his right hand, but the goats at the left" (25:33).

Perhaps we can believe that there is judgment; after all, we experience enough judgment in everyday life. When we look back upon our lives, when we look at our children, when we read the Bible—we are judged in so many ways, why do we doubt that God shall and does judge us?

Lord, When Did We See Thee?

But here is where the real trouble starts. For how shall we be judged? On what basis? And who shall be the judge?

Every day we judge other people. "That man ought to hang for what he did," we say. "She is an evil person who is up to no good," we charge. Our courts of law judge people. Fortunately, our justice system's standards of judgment are more fair than the standards by which we personally judge others. But even the most noble standards of judgment, administered in the most impartial way, fall far short of the judgments of God, so the scripture says.

Reread the story of the great judgment. Where is your face in this story? To be honest, I always see my face among the sheep. In other words, I am sure that God's judgments are exactly like my own judgments. God looks at things in the same way as I do.

But isn't the point of the story that, when God judges us, God does not judge the way we do? Ask yourself, What is the dominant emotional tone of this story of the great judgment? Surprise. The surprise is that, in the end, God judges us and our actions in ways that shock and surprise us.

The delightful thing about this story is that both the sheep and the goats, both the doers of good works and those who did not do good works, are surprised. "Lord, when did we see thee?" they both ask (25:37-45). Those who welcomed the stranger, clothed the naked, and fed the hungry are surprised that in so doing they aided the Lord himself. The good are as surprised by their goodness as the evil are surprised by their badness.

What does this mean? That God is a capricious, mysterious, unpredictable God? No. It simply means that God looks at things differently from the way we do. In the end, when our lives are examined by the divine judge, there shall be surprises, good news and bad news, for us all.

Our hope in the end is not in the good that we do or avoid doing, for sometimes we don't really know the good or the ill we are causing. In the end, our hope is in the love and mercy of God. The purpose of a Christian funeral, therefore, at the end of a person's life, is not to speculate prematurely on how God shall judge this life. Rather, in death we are to proclaim the same hope that held us in life—the love and mercy of God.

For finally, we Christians do have hope. It is not hope based on the goodness of our lives, but hope based upon the goodness of God. Do we fear the judgment? No, because we know who the judge shall be. We already know the name, the life, and the love of the One who sits on the throne.

It was he who said, on another occasion, "Father, forgive them, they know not what they do."

Helping Adults Become Involved—Roy H. Ryan

Preparing to Teach

This may prove to be a disturbing lesson for many. The idea of a God who judges our actions is foreign to many modern Christians. We have tended to talk more about God as loving and forgiving in the contemporary church. You will want to be prepared to help class members understand the nature of God as loving and just, a God who calls us to faith and action, to work for love and justice in the world.

The Interpreter's Bible, volume 7, will provide a helpful interpretation of Matthew 25:31-46. You may also wish to check other sources to help in understanding this key passage in the Bible.

The aim of this lesson is to help Christians understand that there is a fundamental difference between good and evil built into the very order of things. This lesson should help us understand judgment in the context of love and discipline.

Make notes as you read and study. Try to imagine the responses you can expect from class members. Organize your presentation in such a way as to address the concerns and questions of class members.

The following outline is one way to organize your presentation.

> Introduction. A God of love and justice requires love and justice of those who "are created in his image."
> I. Judgment is sure.
>   A. The Son of man is judge.
>   B. Judgment is based on doing.
> II. Life is full of surprises.
>   A. The "righteous" are surprised.
>   B. The "unrighteous" are also surprised.
> III. We are called to do the will of God.
>   A. "You did it to one of the least of these."
>   B. "You did it to me."

Introducing the Main Question

Our lives are under the judgment of God. This passage depicts, in graphic terms, a "last" judgment. On closer examination of this passage, one will see that the "judgment" is really upon our everyday acts, the way we treat others, the way we respond to human need. Jesus describes this judgment scene as a time when "all the nations" will be judged. Does this mean corporate judgment? If so, how does our nation stack up? If he really means that each individual is judged, how do I stack up?

Most of the members of your class will probably see this in personal and individualistic terms. You may seek to deal with both dimensions. What does God require of nations? What does God require of individuals?

There may be disagreements as to how and when judgment comes, but the Christian faith affirms that God is loving and just and that we, who are made in his image, will ultimately be held accountable. If we believe in the ultimate triumph of good over evil, judgment is sure.

Developing the Lesson

This picture of the great judgment presents a troubling scene. Some are judged righteous, some unrighteous. Some are rewarded. Some are punished.

How does this fit with your understanding of God as loving and forgiving? How does it fit with a God of justice and righteousness? Is there contradiction here?

Dr. Willimon suggests that "God loves us . . . by prodding, calling, judging, encouraging, disciplining us forward." He goes on to compare God's love and judgment with a caring parent who, because he or she loves the child, disciplines (judges) him or her. Is this a helpful analogy or does it break down? Would a loving parent ever give up and curse a child into "the eternal fire"? (Matthew 25:41).

I. Judgment is sure.

A. The Son of man is judge.

He is the only one capable of judging us. He "knows our frame"; he has been a part of our humanity. He knows how we are tempted, yet he lived without sin. If anyone can judge us fairly, it is Jesus Christ.

B. Judgment is based on doing.

Some Christians are turned off by this passage because they want to emphasize that we are saved by our right belief. This picture of judgment comes down on the side of action. Your actions speak louder than words (what you say you believe).

II. Life is full of surprises.

A. The "righteous" are surprised.

They were not fully aware that their acts of love and justice were to be counted. They lived for others, sought the welfare of others, loved their neighbors because they had the love of God within. We never know what good we may be doing in "little" acts of mercy.

B. The "unrighteous" are also surprised.

They did not know that they were being judged by what they failed to do. They did not realize that in the presence of human need the failure to act responsibly is sin. "Lord, when did we see thee hungry?"

III. We are called to do the will of God.

A. "You did it to one of the least of these."

When we engage in acts of love and justice "to the least of these," we do them to Christ. God cares about people. When people are oppressed, hungry, sick; when they are treated unjustly, it breaks his heart. When people act to feed the hungry, clothe the naked, and minister to the sick, they are ministering as to the Lord himself. Jesus Christ so identified himself with suffering humanity that any act of kindness to those who are down and out is an act of kindness to Jesus Christ.

B. "You did it to me."
The promise comes ringing down across time and space. When, Lord? When you do anything for anyone who is suffering, anyone oppressed, you are doing something for me. You will indeed be blessed.

Helping Class Members Act
Ask class members to identify the hungry, the naked, the sick in their community. What are they doing to minister to them?
How are prisoners treated in the jails and prisons in your community? What is being done in the name of Jesus to show love and compassion?

Planning for Next Sunday
Ask two or three members of the class to investigate some areas of need in your community that your class might be able to help meet. Assign the scripture lessons, Matthew 18:21-35 and John 8:2-11, for study.

UNIT II. DIRECTIONS FOR DISCIPLES
Horace R. Weaver

FIVE LESSONS　　　　　　**JANUARY 26–FEBRUARY 23**

Unit II, "Directions for Disciples," consists of five sessions focusing on the practical disciplines of Christian living which find outward expressions of obedience to the will of God in daily living. The five sessions are as follow: "Be Forgiving," January 26, for as we are merciful to our debtors, so God will measure his mercy toward us; "Who Is My Neighbor?" on February 2, the answer to which determines whether or not we are saved (have eternal life); "Share Your Possessions," February 9, is the reverse of hoarding and coveting; "Called to Make Peace," February 16, requires an ability to differentiate between the things that make for peace and those that make for conflict and war; "Bear Your Cross" February 23, attempts to help disciples learn that greatness comes through humility and service, not through high positions.

LESSON 9　　　　　　**JANUARY 26**

Be Forgiving

Background Scripture: Matthew 18:21-35; John 8:2-11

The Main Question—William H. Willimon

It was in the early 1960s, in the midst of the civil rights movement. Tensions were running high in the little southern town. The formerly all-white high school was being integrated. Violence had been threatened. It was a dangerous situation.

A young pastor in town decided to try to minister to the situation. He called on people to work with the local school authorites to help make a smooth and peaceful transition. He preached on racial justice and offered his church as a center for interracial dialogue groups.

It would have been good if people in town had welcomed the young pastor's efforts. It would have been good if the town had responded to his challenge to live the faith in this situation.

Unfortunately, that did not happen. His own parishioners threatened to ask him to move if he continued. Attendance and giving at his church dropped by over half. His children were derided and threatened at school. Parents forbade their children to ask the pastor's children to play after school. Mysteriously, his wife was fired from her job. Matters came to a sad conclusion when, one night as he was returning home from a meeting, the pastor's car was forced off the highway by another car. He was seriously injured, so seriously that he felt he should resign from his pastorate due to his poor health.

Now this might have been the end of the story—a typical story of another person who fell victim to human cruelty, evil, and injustice.

But the story did not end there. Ten years later, he was serving as pastor of a smaller church in another state. A search committee from his old church appeared one day and asked him to consider returning to them as their pastor.

All the old memories came rushing back into his mind, the old hurt, the old bitterness. How could he possibly forgive them? Why would they think he could forgive them?

As You Read the Scripture—Bond Fleming

Matthew 18:21-35. This is a parable of the limits of forgiveness. The rabbis taught that three pardons were enough. In Luke 17:4, Jesus tells his disciples that they should forgive a penitent seven times. But in Matthew, Jesus proposes limitless forgiveness.

Verses 21-22. The discussion between Peter and Jesus is a prelude to the parable of the unforgiving servant, which is found only in Matthew. Peter asks Jesus if seven times is enough to forgive. Jesus answers and urges that we forgive seventy times seven times. We should live forgivingly.

But what if the offender does not repent? We cannot make him repent, but we can offer forgiveness, and so free ourselves of the poisonous spirit of revenge.

Verses 23-27. This parable illustrates the principle of forgiveness emphasized in the Lord's Prayer; see Matthew 6:12, 14-15; Mark 11:25. God freely forgives even sinners and outcasts; it is a high privilege to be forgiving because we have been forgiven. It was and is a fact of life that persons cannot accept forgiveness unless and until they forgive others.

The idea of a king, as in verse 23, was often used in parables; here the king is a symbol for God. There were many servants, as implied in verse 31, but only two are main characters in the parable.

The amounts of the debts are used for comparison. The first servant, in verse 24, owed the king ten thousand talents or about ten million dollars. When he could not pay, the king, in verse 25, threatened to enslave him and his family and sell all that the servant had, to apply on the loan. In verses 26-27, the servant pleads for time and promises to pay back everything. It was impossible! The king had such compassion that he forgave the servant and closed the account.

Verses 28-34. The forgiven servant has an unforgiving spirit. A fellow servant, perhaps of lesser ability, owed the first servant a hundred denarii, or about twenty dollars. This was about one six-hundred-thousandth part of what had been owed the king, which had been forgiven.

The poor servant made the same plea for patience and offered the same promise—to pay the debt in full—but to no avail. The forgiven servant would not forgive or even be patient with his debtor. He had the second servant thrown in prison until the debt was paid.

The unforgiving servant's failure to forgive or to show compassion angered the other servants. The man was not worthy of the king's forgiveness. They informed the king of what had taken place. The king was angry too. He called the unforgiving servant back and decried his failure to be forgiving, as he had been forgiven. The account was reopened, and the debtor was imprisoned until the debt should be paid in full.

Verse 35. The message of the parable is so clear and so compelling that the conclusion is evident. Jesus warns that God, the forgiving heavenly Father, will in effect imprison with anger and frustration all those who do not forgive from their hearts.

John 8:2-11, which is a part of the background scripture, tells the story of the attempt by the scribes and Pharisees to trap Jesus. But they themselves were caught. In the example of the woman caught in adultery, Jesus exposed the hypocrisy of unforgiving persons.

Selected Scripture

King James Version

Matthew 18:21-35

21 Then came Peter to him, and said, Lord, how oft shall my brother sin against me, and I forgive him? till seven times?

22 Jesus saith unto him, I say not unto thee, Until seven times: but, Until seventy times seven.

23 Therefore is the kingdom of heaven likened unto a certain king, which would take account of his servants.

24 And when he had begun to reckon, one was brought unto him, which owed him ten thousand talents.

25 But forasmuch as he had not to pay, his lord commanded him to be sold, and his wife, and children, and all that he had, and payment to be made.

26 The servant therefore fell down, and worshipped him, saying,

Revised Standard Version

Matthew 18:21-35

21 Then Peter came up and said to him, "Lord, how often shall my brother sin against me, and I forgive him? As many as seven times?" 22 Jesus said to him, "I do not say to you seven times, but seventy times seven.

23 "Therefore the kingdom of heaven may be compared to a king who wished to settle accounts with his servants. 24 When he began the reckoning, one was brought to him who owed him ten thousand talents; 25 and as he could not pay, his lord ordered him to be sold, with his wife and children and all that he had, and payment to be made. 26 So the servant fell on his knees, imploring him, 'Lord, have patience with me, and I will pay you everything.' 27 And out of pity for him the lord of that servant released him and for-

Lord, have patience with me, and I will pay thee all.

27 Then the lord of that servant was moved with compassion, and loosed him, and forgave him the debt.

28 But the same servant went out, and found one of his fellow-servants, which owed him an hundred pence: and he laid hands on him, and took *him* by the throat, saying, Pay me that thou owest.

29 And his fellow-servant fell down at his feet, and besought him, saying, Have patience with me, and I will pay thee all.

30 And he would not: but went and cast him into prison, till he should pay the debt.

31 So when his fellow-servants saw what was done, they were very sorry, and came and told unto their lord all that was done.

32 Then his lord, after that he had called him, said unto him, O thou wicked servant, I forgave thee all that debt, because thou desiredst me:

33 Shouldest not thou also have had compassion on thy fellow-servant, even as I had pity on thee?

34 And his lord was wroth, and delivered him to the tormentors, till he should pay all that was due unto him.

35 So likewise shall my heavenly Father do also unto you, if ye from your hearts forgive not every one his brother their trespasses.

gave him the debt. 28 But that same servant, as he went out, came upon one of his fellow servants who owed him a hundred denarii; and seizing him by the throat he said, 'Pay what you owe.' 29 So his fellow servant fell down and besought him, 'Have patience with me, and I will pay you.' 30 He refused and went and put him in prison till he should pay the debt. 31 When his fellow servants saw what had taken place, they were greatly distressed, and they went and reported to their lord all that had taken place. 32 Then his lord summoned him and said to him, 'You wicked servant! I forgave you all that debt because you besought me; 33 and should not you have had mercy on your fellow servant, as I had mercy on you?' 34 And in anger his lord delivered him to the jailers, till he should pay all his debt. 35 So also my heavenly Father will do to every one of you, if you do not forgive your brother from your heart."

Key Verse: **Judge not, and ye shall not be judged: condemn not, and ye shall not be condemned: forgive, and ye shall be forgiven. (Luke 6:37)**

Key Verse: **Judge not, and you will not be judged; condemn not, and you will not be condemned; forgive, and you will be forgiven. (Luke 6:37)**

The Scripture and the Main Question—William H. Willimon

"Forgive and forget," we sometimes say. But few things in life are more difficult. When someone has wronged us, wronged us deeply, part of our humanity is taken away. Violence has been done to us. When people are hurt by other people, it is natural and understandable that these people should react in anger, fear, and hostility.

Sometimes that anger turns inward. We nurture it, feed it, keep it close to our hearts, lying in wait for a time when we can get even, settle the score. Often such anger eats away at our lives, destroying us from within. Thus the offense that has been done becomes even greater. The wound is not healed. Rather, it festers until it poisons our whole life. Such is often the case with unforgiven wrong.

I have known people who, because of some hurt they suffered at the hands of some pastor or layperson, withdrew from their church, shut themselves off from others, closed up their anger within themselves, and declared that they would never set foot in that church again as long as they lived. Whom did they punish? Undoubtedly, their church suffered somewhat because of their absence. But they suffered more.

Wouldn't their lives have been better if they could have found the strength to "forgive and forget"?

But we need to look at this matter of forgiveness a bit closer. Recently, a group of veteran civil rights activists gathered. They had been involved with the "Freedom Riders" in the 1960s. They sought to change segregationist laws regulating interstate transportation. A group of armed men had entered a bus and had brutally beaten the riders with ax handles and baseball bats. Local law officers stood by and watched the beating without stopping the violence until the Freedom Riders were beaten senseless. All of the men still bear scars of that experience. One of the men, a college professor, has never walked since that day.

One of the Riders, looking back upon the horror, said, "This brings back many painful memories. I can forgive. I have forgiven, but I have not forgotten."

I Forgave You

"Forgive and forget" may not only be an unrealistic demand, it may not be part of the unique Christian vision of forgiveness. Consider the parable Jesus told about the unforgiving servant (Matthew 18:23-35).

When we pray in the Lord's Prayer, "forgive us our trespasses as we forgive those who trespass against us," are we simply saying, "forgive and forget"? Is forgiveness, from a Christian perspective, simply a matter of putting certain painful memories out of our minds?

Let us examine the story Jesus told to answer Peter's question about forgiveness. Peter begins the dialogue by asking, "Lord, how often shall my brother sin against me, and I forgive him?" (18:21). Jesus answers, as he often does, by telling a parable. A king forgives a servant a very large debt. Then the servant turns around and throws one of his debtors into jail because he cannot pay a very small debt. The king is furious. And why not? "I forgave you all that debt because you besought me; and should you not have had mercy on your fellow servant, as I had mercy on you?" (18:32-33).

The parable is an answer to Peter's question. It also uncovers the peculiar, distinctive nature of Christian forgiveness. Christians forgive because of, as a result of, in response to their forgiveness by God. Thus, Christian forgiveness is not a simple matter of "forgive and forget." It is not some noble, heroic act by an amazingly gracious person. We forgive as God in Christ has forgiven us.

Like the servant in the story, we owed the king so much—our lives, our families, our salvation. Even when we hung his beloved Son on a cross, even when we rejected him, he forgave us. Is forgiveness of our brothers and

187

sisters and their small misdeeds too much to expect of those who have been forgiven so much?

Sometimes we can't forget the wrongs that others do to us. Hurt, pain, insult, envy, cruelty are not easy to forget. But we don't need to forget in order to forgive. We did all this and worse to God's Son and yet he forgave us. "I had mercy on you," he reminds us (18:33).

Christian forgiveness is thus based on who Christians are, on what has happened to them in Jesus Christ. So, in one sense, Christians are called upon not to "forget and to forgive," but rather, to "remember and forgive." Remember what God has done for you—now go and do the same for others.

Sometimes it is hard to forgive because we do not remember. We forget all the times we have thoughtlessly wronged others. We forget how much it has meant for someone to offer us forgiveness for our misdeeds. We forget the story of our forgiveness in Christ. Remember—and forgive.

How Many Times?

"How often shall I forgive my brother?" Peter wants to know. Seven times? That certainly ought to be reasonable, more than reasonable. It is hard enough to forgive someone once, much less seven times!

We are like Peter. We want to know what are the minimal requirements for righteousness. What is reasonable to expect of disciples? Tithe? Give some of our income excess to the poor? Attend church at least once a week? Volunteer to drive the youth groups to the mountains next week? That ought to do it. That ought to be enough. Surely God wouldn't expect more of us than that.

In response to this how-little-can-I-do-and-still-get-by-as-a-disciple question, Jesus tells the story of the forgiving king to remind us all of how great a debt has been forgiven us. This reminder renders all our questions rather irrelevant. How small of us to expect some little, petty, minimal standard of righteousness when we have been so extravagantly, graciously forgiven. The very question shows that we have not fully grasped the greatness of God's love toward us.

Jesus responds to Peter, "I do not say to you seven times, but seventy times seven" (18:22 [some manuscripts read "seventy-seven"]). In other words, forgiveness is beyond calculation. We are to forgive others without limit, an infinite number of times for an infinitely terrible set of wrongs against us.

Even as God's love and forgiveness of us have no limits, so we are to love and forgive others. In our lives, in the way we forgive others, our calling is to mirror some of the divine graciousness in the way we treat other people.

Such forgiveness would be impossible if it were based simply on human good will—for you know how shallow and short-lived is most of our good will.

Forgiveness is based not on good will but upon God's forgiveness of us. Jesus says, in effect, "Your debts against God are forgiven, your sins agaist your Creator are blotted out—now you, go and do likewise."

Helping Adults Become Involved—Roy H. Ryan

Preparing to Teach

"Forgive and forget." How often have we heard that statement? How difficult it is to do!

This lesson is about forgiveness. Forgiveness is relevant to our lives. We all need to learn how to receive and give forgiveness in our human relations. As

Christians, we have experienced God's bountiful forgiveness and are thus enabled to forgive others. Sounds easy!

Read the scripture passages. Use a concordance to look up other passages dealing with forgiveness. Be as well versed in the Scripture as you can be before you teach this lesson.

The aim of this lesson is to help persons understand and experience the forgiveness of God as the basis for offering forgiveness in our interpersonal relationships.

Develop an outline for your presentation that makes sense to you. The outline below is one way to organize the material.

> Introduction. We are called to be forgiving people, not because it is easy, not because it makes us look good, but because God in Christ has forgiven us.
>   I. How often must I forgive?
>   A. Why forgive?
>   B. How many times?
>   II. Forgive and forget.
>   A. Is it possible to forget?
>   B. Remember and forgive.
>   III. There is a basis for forgiveness.
>   A. "Forgive us our trespasses."
>   B. Who keeps score?

Introducing the Main Question

Ask members of the group who are willing to share an experience in which they have been forgiven. How did it feel?

Also give an opportunity to any member of the group who can share an experience of forgiving someone else. How did it feel?

You may wish to tell Dr. Willimon's story about the young pastor who was terribly mistreated because of his stand for civil rights in the 1960s. Ask your group the questions posed at the end of the story. How could he possibly forgive them? Why would they think he could forgive them?

Why is forgiveness hard for some people to give? To receive? Perhaps one reason some people find it difficult to forgive others is that they do not know how to accept God's forgiveness and thus continue to live under the burden of guilt.

Developing the Lesson

The teaching of Jesus and his action recorded in John 8:2-11 stand as a good illustration of the forgiving love of God. A woman taken in adultery is brought to Jesus. Her accusers no doubt think that Jesus will take sides with them and condemn her to be stoned to death. Instead, Jesus stoops down and writes on the ground (or dust on the limestone pavement of the temple area). The accusers continued to ask for his judgment. He then makes a very interesting observation. "Let him who is without sin among you be the first to throw a stone" (John 8:7). That stopped them dead in their tracks! We are all sinners standing in need of God's forgiveness.

The Matthew passage, 18:21-35, deals with the limits of forgiveness. The Pharisees taught: forgive three times. The disciples must have thought that to forgive "seven times" would be more than generous (Matthew 18:21). Peter and the others must have been knocked back on their heels when Jesus said, "seventy times seven," which probably means unlimited forgiveness.

SECOND QUARTER

Most of us could probably handle seven, but not "seventy times seven," or even "seventy-seven" as some manuscripts state.

I. How often must I forgive?

A. Why forgive?

Jesus knew that to hold a grudge, to be unforgiving, is a sure way to illness and despair. It is like a cancer that gradually eats away at the body and spirit. To carry the burden of guilt of unforgiven sins or to be unforgiving in one's relationships is bound to lead to illness.

B. How many times?

What are the limits? What can be excluded? Do I have to keep on forgiving? Peter obviously thought that seven time would be generous. Jesus in essence said that was not generous enough! Is this humanly possible? Probably not. This kind of loving, forgiving spirit comes only from God. We are able to forgive because we have been forgiven. "Lord, we are able."

II. Forgive and forget.

A. Is it possible to forget?

Probably not. We cannot erase those experiences of hurt or deception by others. Read Dr. Willimon's comments on this question. But we cannot afford to harbor anger or a grudge. It will eat away at our health and happiness. When we have forgiven someone who has wronged us, we need to set about the task of blocking it out of our minds so that we are no longer burdened by the memory.

B. Remember and forgive.

Dr. Willimon suggests this is the way for Christians to live. I like that! Let us remember that we are forgiven by God, and out of this remembering we have the grace and strength to forgive others.

III. There is a basis for forgiveness.

A. "Forgive us our trespasses."

"Forgive us our trespasses as we forgive those who trespass against us." So goes the prayer of our Lord. It seems to suggest that unless we are forgiving, we cannot be forgiven. The story in Matthew 18:21-35 of the rich landowner forgiving a servant a large debt but the servant not forgiving his employee a small debt illustrates the point.

B. Who keeps score?

Seven times seems to be enough, says Peter. Not so, says Jesus. In human relationships we cannot afford to keep score. God's love and forgiveness are so boundless that scores are not necessary. Whoever keeps score will tend to want "to even the score" rather than be forgiving (see Matthew 5:23-24).

Helping Class Members Act

At the end of the class session, you might ask members of the class to take two or three minutes of silence to think about the application of this lesson to their lives. Perhaps some of them are holding grudges and would like to be freed from that burden. Others may have wronged someone and need to go to that person and ask forgiveness. Give them enought time to think about what actions they should take. Pray for them to have the grace and strength to set things right so far as it is possible.

Planning for Next Sunday

The next lesson is an interesting one. Ask members to read Luke 10:25-37. Ask them to be ready to discuss what it means "to love your neighbor as yourself."

Who Is My Neighbor?

Background Scripture: Luke 10:25-37

The Main Question—William H. Willimon

When I went to college, someone gave me some advice—don't argue over religion or politics. It wasn't bad advice. In those interminable dormitory "bull sessions," religion and politics are favorite topics because one can argue about these subjects forever without coming to many easy or clear conclusions.

Recently, in talking with a group of laypersons about the sort of preaching they enjoyed, I noted that many of them said, "I like a sermon which helps me to think about things in a new way." In other words, a sermon is mostly an intellectual exercise, and attempt by the preacher to make us think.

That way we can listen to a sermon as if we were listening to an academic lecture. We can then agree or disagree before going home to eat lunch. Of course, we don't intend to do anything. We just think about religion rather than live it.

Sometimes people participate in an adult church school class in this same detached, aloof, intellectualized way. We gather on Sunday, hear about and then politely discuss some interesting religious ideas, and that is all there is to it. We can keep religion safely detached from our everyday lives and thus what we do at church on Sunday will not have the slightest meaning for what we do the rest of the week.

And so a man asks Jesus, "Teacher, what shall I do to inherit eternal life?" (Luke 10:25). What a question! The greatest minds of every age have pondered that one. The learned lawyer will be able to have an endless conversation with Jesus, think a few long thoughts, shake hands, and go home after a little intellectual game.

But Jesus, as he so often does, turns the question back toward the young lawyer's life, away from abstract ideas. He tells him a story that points right at his life: "A man was going down from Jerusalem to Jericho, and he fell among robbers."

As You Read the Scripture—Bond Fleming

Luke 10:25-28. Jesus was often put to the test by lawyers or scribes, and by Pharisees. The question asked here seems genuine: How can I be saved? It is the same question the ruler asks in Luke 18:18. In answer to the ruler Jesus recites a list of rules or laws, but goes on to challenge the ruler to sacrificial dedication.

The discussion with the lawyer in Luke 10 is more involved. Similar discussions are found in Matthew 22:34-40 and in Mark 12:28-31. The conclusion, in all three instances, involves a summarizing of the many, many (613) commandments into only two: love God first and completely, and love your neighbor as yourself. The key verse, Luke 10:27, is fundamental both in Judaism and in Christianity, although the word *mind* does not appear in Deuteronomy 6:4-5.

191

In Matthew and Mark, Jesus gives the summary, but in Luke the questioning lawyer gives it, from Deuteronomy 6:4-5 and Leviticus 19:18. This suggests that the summary was familiar to the Jews and Judaism; it was not original with Jesus. At any rate, Jesus commends the lawyer for his answer, in Luke 10:28, and challenges him by saying, "Do this, and you will live."

Verse 29. It is hard to say whether the lawyer was continuing to test Jesus or actually beginning to search for an answer. In any case, he was trying to justify himself. He showed love for himself; and his question enabled Jesus to show him what was involved in loving one's neighbor—an indirect answer to the question, "Who is my neighbor?"

Verses 30-35. This is one of the most familiar and most challenging of the parables of Jesus. It was a parable, although surely incidents of robbery and beatings might have occurred on this steep and winding road. The emphasis is not on the poor man who was robbed and left half-dead. It is on the Samaritan. (Jesus did not use the term *good* in speaking of him; we have added that term, because we think he was "good.")

The priest and the Levite were criticized by implication, because religious leaders would be expected to surpass others in their concern to help those in need. [Two hundred chief priests lived in Jerusalem; two thousand "ordinary" priests, such as Zechariah, lived outside Jerusalem as did the 7,600 Levites.] Perhaps it was their time off, and they were going down to Jericho or up to Jerusalem. But both of them failed to show love or concern.

To have the Samaritan as the hero of the story was to add insult to injury. Why, or how, would a Samaritan be traveling alone in Jewish territory? We should not try to find answers to all the questions we can raise about parables. He may have been a businessman with connections in Jerusalem. Apparently he was welcome and trusted at the inn.

The important thing is that the Samaritan, despised by the Jews, was the one who had compassion on the wounded person. The wounded man was not a despised Jew to the Samaritan; he was a person, a human being in need. Note the time-consuming, tender, loving care he showed in spite of the risk of serious danger to himself. This was followed by gracious and sacrificial concern at the inn. He gave the innkeeper about two days' pay and offered to repay other expenses when he came back.

Verses 36-37. The use of the word *neighbor* in verse 36 is not the same as it was in verse 29. But the lawyer had the answer to his question. Who is my neighbor? My neighbor is anyone who needs me, and anyone whom I can help. To help our neighbor is an expression of love for God.

Selected Scripture

King James Version	Revised Standard Version
Luke 10:25-37	*Luke 10:25-37*
25 And, behold, a certain lawyer stood up, and tempted him, saying, Master, what shall I do to inherit eternal life?	25 And behold a lawyer stood up to put him to the test, saying, "Teacher, what shall I do to inherit eternal life?" 26 He said to him, "What is written in the law? How do you read?" 27 And he answered, "You shall love the Lord your God with all your heart, and with all your
26 He said unto him, What is written in the law? how readest thou?	
27 And he answering said, Thou shalt love the Lord thy God with all	

thy heart, and with all thy soul, and with all thy strength, and with all thy mind; and thy neighbour as thyself.

28 And he said unto him, Thou hast answered right: this do, and thou shalt live.

29 But he, willing to justify himself, said unto Jesus, And who is my neighbour?

30 And Jesus answering said, A certain *man* went down from Jerusalem to Jericho, and fell among thieves, which stripped him of his raiment, and wounded *him,* and departed, leaving *him* half dead.

31 And by chance there came down a certain priest that way: and when he saw him, he passed by on the other side.

32 And likewise a Levite, when he was at the place, came and looked on *him,* and passed by on the other side.

33 But a certain Samaritan, as he journeyed, came where he was: and when he saw him, he had compassion *on him,*

34 And went to *him,* and bound up his wounds, pouring in oil and wine, and set him on his own beast, and brought him to an inn, and took care of him.

35 And on the morrow when he departed, he took out two pence, and gave *them* to the host, and said unto him, Take care of him; and whatsoever thou spendest more, when I come again, I will repay thee.

36 Which now of these three, thinkest thou, was neighbour unto him that fell among the thieves?

37 And he said, He that shewed mercy on him. Then said Jesus unto him, Go, and do thou likewise.

soul, and with all your strength, and with all your mind; and your neighbor as yourself." 28 And he said to him, "You have answered right; do this, and you will live."

29 But he, desiring to justify himself, said to Jesus, "And who is my neighbor?" 30 Jesus replied, "A man was going down from Jerusalem to Jericho, and he fell among robbers, who stripped him and beat him, and departed, leaving him half dead. 31 Now by chance a priest was going down that road; and when he saw him he passed by on the other side. 32 So likewise a Levite, when he came to the place and saw him, passed by on the other side. 33 But a Samaritan, as he journeyed, came to where he was; and when he saw him, he had compassion, 34 and went to him and bound up his wounds, pouring on oil and wine; then he set him on his own beast and brought him to an inn, and took care of him. 35 And the next day he took out two denarii and gave them to the innkeeper, saying, 'Take care of him; and whatever more you spend, I will repay you when I come back.' 36 Which of these three, do you think, proved neighbor to the man who fell among the robbers?" 37 He said, "The one who showed mercy on him." And Jesus said to him, "Go and do likewise."

Key Verse: **Thou shalt love the Lord thy God with all thy heart, and with all thy soul, and with all thy strength, and with all thy mind; and thy neighbour as thyself. (Luke 10:27)**

Key Verse: **You shall love the Lord your God with all your heart, and with all your soul, and with all your strength, and with all your mind; and your neighbor as yourself. (Luke 10:27)**

The Scripture and the Main Question—William H. Willimon

To Inherit Eternal Life

"What shall I do to inherit eternal life?" the lawyer asks Jesus. In a way, this is the foundational religious question. It may be the question behind all our other questions, the question which may have brought many to your class this Sunday morning.

What must I do to be fulfilled? What do I have to do to have meaning in my life? How can I feel close to God? These are questions adults often ask. Behind them is the question which begins the dialogue in today's scripture from Luke 10.

In the New Testament, "eternal life" meant more than some world we hope to go to after we die. "Eternal life" included our relationship with God after death, but it was seen as a relationship we can begin now. Whenever we are rightly related to God and God's purposes for our lives, we are living "eternal life"—that is, we are in *covenant* with God. In fact, any hope for life with God after death was based upon our relationship with God now, in this life.

So the lawyer was asking, "What must I do to have a full, meaningful life with God?" Perhaps he expected Jesus to enter into some high flown religious discussion with him, a theological discussion using abstract words and ideas. Jesus does ask him what the Scripture says (Luke 10:26), and the young lawyer shows that he knows his Bible by heart.

But as he quotes the familiar words of Deuteronomy 6:5 and Leviticus 19:18 to Jesus, the inquisitive lawyer perhaps senses that his dialogue with Jesus is taking an unexpected turn.

"You shall love the Lord your God with all your heart, and with all your soul, and with all your strength, and with all your mind" he says (10:27). Fine enough. The prime activity of any faith is love of God. But how to love God? By going to church, yes. By studying the Bible, yes. By using all the gifts God has given us—heart, soul, strength, and mind—to love God.

But it was the phrase, "and your neighbor as yourself" that proved to be discomfiting. My neighbor? So Jesus does not want to talk about things up in the sky somewhere. He wants to talk about our lives right now, here on earth, about neighbors.

I knew a "religious" man when I was growing up. The whole community regarded him as the prime example of what a Christian ought to be. He taught a church school class, led a men's Bible study group, tithed, studied Scripture. But I learned from first-hand experience that he was a ruthless businessman. He often fired his employees for small infractions of company policy. He supported a racist organization and was unfaithful to his wife.

No doubt he assumed that he was pursuing "eternal life" through his various religious observances and superior knowledge of the Scriptures.

From Jesus' reply to the searching lawyer, we are unable to assume that we can love God without loving our neighbor. Our love of neighbor testifies to our love of God.

Here was an earnest man who wanted to have a talk about God. Jesus turns the conversation into a talk about neighbors. What does that tell us about the religion of Jesus?

Who Is My Neighbor?

Still the questions keep coming from the lawyer.

"Love my neighbor? Fine, but who is my neighbor anyway?" he asks.

This was no simple question for people in Jesus' day. Surely Jesus would not say that gentile unbelievers are neighbors. How can people be our neighbors when they don't worship our God? Surely the soldier in the Roman occupation force is not our neighbor. Who, then, is our neighbor?

To be honest, "Who is my neighbor?" is no simple question for our day, either. The lines we draw across the world exclude other races, other nations, other religions from our neighborliness. We don't intend to be neighbors to folk who will not be neighbors to us.

So in response to our narrow definitions of neighbors, Jesus tells a little story, one of his most beloved and familiar stories.

A man was going down from Jerusalem to Jericho and fell among robbers who stripped him and left him for dead. A priest and a Levite came by but passed the dying man on the other side of the road. But then, down the road came a Communist—I mean a Samaritan. Or was he a Buddhist? Or was he a citizen of Peking?

At any rate, he was a man who was different from us—another race, another nationality, another religion. Everything was "wrong" about this Samaritan, everything except what he did.

"And when he saw him, he had compassion, and went to him and bound up his wounds, . . . and brought him to an inn, and took care of him" (10:33-34).

As a Samaritan, he might not have known all the biblical reasons for showing good will toward the injured man. The priest and the Levite knew the Bible. The difference was that the Samaritan acted compassionately. What is more, he not only moved to help the man, but he stayed with him and used his own money to make sure that the man was cared for until he made a complete recovery.

Now, who was the neighbor? Not people who *know* the answers to the questions, but people who *act* upon the answers!

Go and Do Likewise

There was once a family in our town who had fallen upon hard times. The father lost his job, became discouraged, began to drink heavily, and eventually deserted his wife and children. The mother had little education and few skills so she found it virtually impossible to get a job. Besides, she had three young children to care for at home. Money ran out. They had no food or money for fuel oil for winter.

In desperation, the mother came to a nearby church for help. The pastor at the church could only spare her a few minutes of time, but he gave her twenty dollars, telling her that this was the maximum amount that he was allowed to give her. The woman went home, spent the twenty dollars on a week's worth of groceries and, by the end of the week, was desperate again.

The pastor happened to mention the poor family's plight to a parishioner who became interested. She visited the woman, made a list of her clothing needs, and presented the case to her church school class the next Sunday. Class members offered to invite the children into their homes so the mother could get job training. The class decided to have a garage sale to raise money for fuel oil. One of the class members hired the woman at her store until she could finish her training for a better job.

Now, I ask you, which Christian proved to be the neighbor to the family in need?

SECOND QUARTER

Helping Adults Become Involved—Roy H. Ryan

Preparing to Teach

This may be one of the most difficult lessons to teach in this entire unit! Why? Because we have dealt with this idea so many times that it may get boring. Surely there are new thoughts and new insights to be gained as we once again talk about "love your neighbor."

Read the scripture lesson in Luke 10:25-37. I would suggest you also read I John (the entire epistle is only five chapters). Note especially I John 4:19-21. Though the term *brother* is used in I John, it could easily be replaced by *neighbor*.

The aim of this lesson is to help adults know that "keeping the commandments" involves more than intellectual assent (belief) to a creedal statement. It involves active good will expressed in deeds of love. This lesson again reminds us that we must do more than talk a good game as Christians; we must act lovingly and responsibly.

As you read the Scripture, use a commentary such as *The Interpreter's Bible* and make notes as you read. Think of illustrations from everyday life you can use to make your presentation come alive. Read and use Dr. Willimon's and Dr. Fleming's comments.

The following outline can serve as a starter for organizing the lesson.

> Introduction: The question "Who is my neighbor?" is one we continually need to ask. And we need to be responsive when the answer comes to us through this parable of the (good) Samaritan.
> I. What shall I do to inherit eternal life?
>   A. A crucial question
>   B. A continuing question
> II. Who is my neighbor?
>   A. "A certain man"
>   B. Who was the neighbor?
> III. Go and do likewise.
>   A. Love as active good will
>   B. Can anyone love the neighbor?

Introducing the Main Question

Dr. W. A. Smart, a revered professor at Emory University many years ago, once told this story. He said he was in a part of Altanta some distance from his home and saw smoke rising from a fire. He thought it was in the direction of his home. He headed toward home and the closer he got, the more sure he was that it was his house on fire! As he came to his neighborhood, he was more convinced that it was his house. But, he said, "As I turned down my street I was somewhat relieved to see that it was not my house, but my neighbor's house on fire!" He told the story to deal with the main question of this lesson, "Is it possible to love my neighbor as myself?"

From a human point of view, it is not possible. But by God's grace it is possible to live in a relationship of active good will toward the neighbor near and far.

Developing the Lesson

This lesson involves one of the most critical questions human beings can ask: "What must I do to inherit eternal life?" Because of the way Jesus

196

responded to that question, it also deals with another crucial question, "Who is my neighbor?" These questions are closely connected in this lesson. We will be looking at both.

Jesus responded to the lawyer's question by telling a story. The story of the man who was beaten and left by the roadside and finally helped by a Samaritan illustrates vividly what it means to be a neighbor. This story probably shocked and surprised those who heard it. The hero is a Samaritan! Dr. Fleming reminds us in his exegesis of the passage that we have added the word *good* and that Jesus simply called him a Samaritan. Jesus was not generous with the use of the word *good*. He had reminded his disciples that "no one is good but God" (Mark 10:18).

I. *What shall I do to inherit eternal life?*

A. *A crucial question*

This question is one that has been in the heart and on the lips of religious people for centuries. There seems to be within us a desire to live. In fact, a theologian, Paul Tillich, has suggested that the ultimate fear for human beings is the fear of "non-being," This religious quest, this desire for continuing "existence," this concern for "eternal life" is deep-seated. The lawyer was asking our question for us.

B. *A continuing question*

The question haunts us in our religious pilgrimage. The Christian faith supplies the best possible answer in this quest. "God so loved the world . . . that [we might] have eternal life" (John 3:16). We have the answer in Jesus Christ, and by his grace we can love God and neighbor. In him we have abundant, eternal life. This is indeed good news!

II. *Who is my neighbor?*

A. *"A certain man"*

So begins this pointed story. "Just anyone"—a man with no name, no race, it did not matter. He was hurt; he needed help; the Samartian provided the help needed. What more could be asked of anyone? My neighbor is anyone who needs help.

B. *Who was the neighbor?*

The one who helped. It did not matter that he was a "half-breed," a lowly (in the eyes of Jesus' Jewish contemporaries) Samaritan. He came to the aid of one he did not know. If we pass by in the face of human need, as the priest and Levite did, how can we say the love of God is within us?

III. *Go and do likewise.*

A. *Love as active good will*

Love, in the Christian sense, is not a romantic or sentimental emotion. It is active good will. "Talk is cheap." Love is sometimes hard and demanding. The followers of Jesus need to ask in every situation, What is the loving thing to do? The loving act may sometimes go against tradition—but it is God in action. God is love.

B. *Can anyone love the neighbor?*

The story told by Dr. Smart about his neighbor's house on fire aptly illustrates the difficulty of following that commandment. But, when Jesus Christ becomes Lord of our lives, it is possible for our motives, attitudes, and actions to reflect the love of God. John Wesley called this "perfection," to be so captured by the Spirit of Christ that we can live our lives from the motive of love.

Helping Class Members Act

Who are some of the people in your community who have been robbed, hurt, and left by the roadside? Are they children who have been abused, the unemployed, the poor, the people with handicapping conditions, the elderly who are afraid to venture outside their homes or apartments after dark? Look around. Identify who your "neighbors" are and begin to plan for ways to show your love.

Planning for Next Sunday

The next lesson will deal with Christian stewardship. Jesus had a lot to say about the way we use our possessions. Ask members to study Matthew 6:19-21; Luke 12:13-21, 27-34.

LESSON 11   FEBRUARY 9

Share Your Possessions

Background Scripture: Matthew 6:19-21; Luke 12:13-21, 27-34

The Main Question—William H. Willimon

"Money, money, money makes the world go around," sings a character in a popular Broadway musical. When one thinks of all the anxiety, grief, stress, and physical harm that come as a direct result of our frantic pursuit for possessions, one must agree that it does indeed seem as if money is the most important thing in the world.

Arguments about money are the primary cause of marital stress among couples. Daily our newspapers tell of people who kill other people for the smallest sums of cash—to say nothing of those of us who are literally murdering ourselves in our harried ratrace of achievement and accumulation.

Just because we are Christian doesn't mean that we are immune from these tensions about money. One of my parishioners stayed home one Sunday because he was ill. As he switched his television channels looking for a worship service, a television evangelist was making a tearful appeal for funds to build a hospital where Jesus would reveal the cure for cancer—if viewers would send in twenty dollars per month. Another evangelist needed funds to keep his new television station solvent. Money, money, money.

The tough aspect of money and material possessions is that we need a certain amount of them in order to live. Our possessions enrich our lives in countless ways. But, as we have noted, our possessions can also make us miserable.

What makes the difference? That is the question behind today's scripture concerning possessions.

Two brothers are in a heated argument about money. They come to Jesus, asking the master to settle their feud. He responds by telling them a story about a rich man who thought that his full barns could save him.

As You Read the Scripture—Bond Fleming

Luke 12:13-15. The favor which the man asked Jesus to do involved not an ethical problem but a legal one, one to be handled by the lawyers and judges. Jesus did not deny that there was a problem, but he was not a judge or a divider; he was a preacher of the gospel, the good news of God's kingdom. Preachers today are sometimes asked to side with one member of a family against another. It undermines the spiritual influence of the preacher to take sides in family squabbles.

Did Jesus know more about the questioner than the question implies? One can't be sure. But Jesus took the occasion to give a warning against covetousness, a sin which is seldom confessed. A person who covets cannot be a true seeker after God. Earlier in the chapter, verses 4 and 5, Jesus stressed that one should fear only God. A part of the warning against covetousness in verse 15 is the conclusion that "a man's life does not consist in the abundance of his possessions," even if they include the world.

Verses 16-21. The twofold warning about coveting and possessions inspires the parable of the rich fool. The man was guilty of coveting and of equating the good life with possessions. His life was devoted to accumulating things. His big problem was where to store the increase. He does not express any concern for the less fortunate. He builds greater barns so that he can keep all he has for himself.

The word *I* appears many times in the farmer's monologue; this is a word that does not appear in the Lord's Prayer, Luke 11:2-4. He was thinking within himself, talking to himself; and planning for himself. He says nothing of retirement, but he does plan to take it easy, to eat, drink, and be merry. Could a man who was so self-centered actually be merry?

Verses 20-21. The man achieved the goal of selfish satisfaction, but only for a day. Materialistic security offers no security against the uncertainties of life. He might have died happy, but he died and left all that he had accumulated. In his calculations he failed to consider his neighbors. Perhaps more important, he forgot about the shortness of time and the reality of God. In verse 21 Jesus sets forth the obvious moral. This is akin to the moral in the devotional reading about the rich man and Lazarus.

Verses 27-31. This passage is in contrast to the anxious and eager concerns for gaining and possessing things. Jesus does not recommend laziness or indolence; he urges us to be free of covetousness and to have faith. Consider the lilies which do the work of neither men nor women. God has concern for even the lowest forms of life. Have faith. The Father knows that we need things to eat and to drink. We are to seek God's kingdom first, before we seek material things, and as an antidote to our anxieties about them.

Verses 32-34. In verse 31 we are told to "seek his kingdom," but in verse 32 we are told it is the "Father's good pleasure to give you the kingdom." When we seek it, it is given to us. How can we make this happen? By using our possessions wisely, by sharing them with those less fortunate and thus trading our earthly treasures for treasures in heaven. Thieves steal our purses. Moths destroy expensive rugs and tapestries. Giving to the poor was a recognized way of buying treasures in heaven. This emphasis on what we treasure is found also in the background scripture, Matthew 6:19-21.

Selected Scripture

King James Version	Revised Standard Version

Luke 12:13-21, 27-34

13 And one of the company said unto him, Master, speak to my brother, that he divide the inheritance with me.

14 And he said unto him, Man, who made me a judge or a divider over you?

15 And he said unto them, Take heed, and beware of covetousness: for a man's life consisteth not in the abundance of the things which he possesseth.

16 And he spake a parable unto them, saying, The ground of a certain rich man brought forth plentifully:

17 And he thought within himself, saying, What shall I do, because I have no room where to bestow my fruits?

18 And he said, This will I do: I will pull down my barns, and build greater; and there will I bestow all my fruits and my goods.

19 And I will say to my soul, Soul, thou hast much goods laid up for many years; take thine ease, eat, drink, *and* be merry.

20 But God said unto him, *Thou* fool, this night thy soul shall be required of thee: then whose shall those things be, which thou has provided?

21 So *is* he that layeth up treasure for himself, and is not rich toward God.

. . . .

27 Consider the lilies how they grow: they toil not, they spin not; and yet I say unto you, that Solomon in all his glory was not arrayed like one of these.

28 If then God so clothe the grass, which is to-day in the field, and to-morrow is cast into the oven; how much more *will he clothe* you, O ye of little faith?

Luke 12:13-21, 27-34

13 One of the multitude said to him, "Teacher, bid my brother divide the inheritance with me."

14 But he said to him, "Man, who made me a judge or divider over you?" 15 And he said to them, "Take heed, and beware of all covetousness; for a man's life does not consist in the abundance of his possessions." 16 And he told them a parable, saying, "The land of a rich man brought forth plentifully; 17 and he thought to himself, 'What shall I do, for I have nowhere to store my crops?' 18 And he said, 'I will do this: I will pull down my barns, and build larger ones; and there I will store all my grain and my goods. 19 And I will say to my soul, Soul, you have ample goods laid up for many years; take your ease, eat, drink, be merry.' 20 But God said to him, 'Fool! This night your soul is required of you; and the things you have prepared, whose will they be?' 21 So is he who lays up treasure for himself, and is not rich toward God."

. . . .

27 Consider the lilies, how they grow; they neither toil nor spin; yet I tell you, even Solomon in all his glory was not arrayed like one of these. 28 But if God so clothes the grass which is alive in the field today and tomorrow is thrown into the oven, how much more will he clothe you, O men of little faith! 29 And do not seek what you are to eat and

29 And seek not ye what ye shall eat, or what ye shall drink, neither be ye of doubtful mind.

30 For all these things do the nations of the world seek after: and your Father knoweth that ye have need of these things.

31 But rather seek ye the kingdom of God; and all these things shall be added unto you.

32 Fear not, little flock; for it is your Father's good pleasure to give you the kingdom.

33 Sell that ye have, and give alms; provide yourselves bags which wax not old, a treasure in the heavens that faileth not, where no thief approacheth, neither moth corrupteth.

34 For where your treasure is, there will your heart be also.

Key Verse: **Take heed, and beware of covetousness: for a man's life consisteth not in the abundance of the things which he possesseth. (Luke 12:15)**

what you are to drink, nor be of anxious mind. 30 For all the nations of the world seek these things; and your Father knows that you need them. 31 Instead, seek his kingdom, and these things shall be yours as well.

32 "Fear not, little flock, for it is your Father's good pleasure to give you the kingdom. 33 Sell your possessions, and give alms; provide yourselves with purses that do not grow old, with a treasure in the heavens that does not fail, where no thief approaches and no moth destroys. 34 For where your treasure is, there will your heart be also.

Key Verse: **Take heed, and beware of all covetousness; for a man's life does not consist in the abundance of his possessions. (Luke 12:15)**

The Scripture and the Main Question—William H. Willimon

Take Heed and Beware

If you were to chart human life, noting the predominant concerns at each stage in life's pilgrimage, concern about material possessions would mark each step along the way.

The little child begs for a dime for candy, holds his breath, clenches his teeth, and screams if Mommy doesn't hand it over.

The teenager, in a desperate attempt to be accepted as one of the crowd, buys special shoes and clothes which are "in" at the moment. Quality is not the goal in these purchases. The main thing is to buy things that will ensure popularity. At an early age, we come to associate possessions as the way to win friends and to achieve a sense of personal well-being.

The college student, while sometimes deriding his parents' preoccupation with house, car, job, and prestige, longs for the best car, the best stereo in the dorm. She "burns the midnight oil," in hopes of getting the grades to get the job. It's not a desire for knowledge that motivates her. It is a desire for a job that shall yield a sufficient income up to her expectations.

The middle-age couple who neglect their children in order to fulfill every possible material desire for their children; the older couple who are filled with anxiety over the future of a lifetime of accumulation. Is this life?

A man comes to Jesus and asks him to settle an inheritance dispute. But Jesus doesn't get involved in the brothers' squabble over the money. Instead, he uses this as an occasion to warn everyone, "Take heed, and beware of all covetousness, for man's life does not consist in the abundance of his possessions" (Luke 12:15).

Take heed lest today's vain desires become tomorrow's necessities. Take heed lest the worthless things in life crowd out the worthwhile things in life. That's often the way it is with money.

Here we have two brothers who have become alienated from each other over an inheritance. Have you ever known that to happen in a family? A lawyer friend of mine declares, "The best thing a parent can do for his or her children is to spend all the money while he or she is alive and leave nothing so that the family will not be destroyed later in a dispute over the will."

How sad to see a family rent asunder over possessions! How sad to see a life corrupted or destroyed in pursuit of the abundance of something which, while important, cannot alone lead to an abundant life!

So Is He Who Lays Up Treasure

Here is a man whom we might call the epitome of success "the American way." He has built his business up from nothing into a thriving, prosperous venture. He sits on the boards of two corporations and serves as a trustee at a major university. We would call him a model citizen.

But God, so Jesus implies in his parable of Luke 12:16-21, might call this fine, prosperous person a fool—a man who thought he had so much but in reality had nothing.

All his financial achievements, his full barns, his stocks and bonds, his insured bank accounts—what good do they do him as the angel of death taps him on the shoulder and he breathes his last?

This man who in the eyes of the world appears so wise is in reality very foolish. He foolishly thought that his wealth could shield him from death. "So is he who lays up treasure for himself, and is not rich toward God" (12:21).

We put our money in an IRA to insure against problems when we grow old. We install a burglar alarm system to protect our possessions. We build bigger houses, bigger warehouses, bigger savings accounts. We pass things along to our heirs so they can build even bigger barns, bigger savings accounts.

But when we are tapped upon the shoulder, what then? "And the things you have prepared, whose will they be?" (12:20).

Where Your Treasure Is

Consider the lilies, says Jesus. See their beauty, their luxuriance, yet what have they done to earn their beauty? Their glory comes as a gift from God. "Fear not," Jesus says (12:32).

But this is easier said than done. Anxiety over our material things is a major source of emotional and physical health problems. Sometimes our anxiety is related to fears about providing for the basic necessities of life. Often it is related to fears over obtaining things that are in no way necessary for our survival.

Recently, Americans were asked by public opinion researchers, "Are you happier today than you were ten years ago?" A vast majority of those asked responded no. This is interesting since, even with inflation and unemployment, Americans' buying power in the 1980s had taken a sizeable jump over that in the 1970s.

Why don't we feel happier and more financially prosperous?

The reason, say psychologists, is what is called the "adaptation level phenomenon." This means that our levels of expectation in life adapt to our levels of achievement.

Simply stated, the more we have, the more we want. Our incomes may have risen. But our income never rises as fast as our expectations.

No wonder that as we attempt to "lay up treasure" for ourselves, we are doomed to perpetual unhappiness. We can never get as much as we want. We may get what we need, but what we want is another matter.

If God gives the lilies of the field what they need, these fragile plants which are "alive in the field today and tomorrow [are] thrown into the oven" how much more will God supply our needs? (12:28). But our wants—not our needs—are our big problem.

There are those who try to present the Christian faith as unconcerned with material things. Nothing could be further from the truth. Christianity is concerned with keeping our possessions in their place, so to speak.

While Jesus may have had no possessions of his own, he knew the power our material things can exercise over us. "For where your treasure is, there will your heart be also" (12:34). A person's checkbook stubs can tell us as much as anything else about his or her heart.

In a recent stewardship emphasis at our church, one of our members said, "I wish the church could spend more time about the real business of Jesus Christ and not waste so much time talking about money."

What is the real business of Jesus Christ? What if we talked about money as much as Jesus talked about it? Jesus had no delusions about human nature. He knew—our hearts tend to be wherever our money is.

When we would like to keep our religion "spiritual"—divorced from daily anxieties and fears, abstract and irrelevant—Jesus says, "Let's talk about money."

Helping Adults Become Involved—Roy H. Ryan

Preparing to Teach

Money is difficult for some people to talk about. It is usually a sensitive issue in the church. Some think the leaders of the church talk too much about money. Consider Jesus. He talked about "money" and "possessions" a great deal. Why? Because he recognized the human tendency of building our lives around "things." He saw the futility of that kind of life and wanted to warn his followers about the folly of putting our trust in things that decay instead of in eternal values.

Read the scripture lessons from Matthew and Luke. Read Dr. Fleming's and Dr. Willimon's helpful comments. You may also wish to read and study other materials related to stewardship issues.

The aim of the lesson is to help adults understand the proper place of material possessions in our lives and how to use those possessions rather than be possessed by them.

The following outline may be helpful to you as you prepare your presentation.

> Introduction. Why did Jesus talk so much about material possessions? Could it be that he recognized the folly and disappointment that come to those who trust in "things" rather than in God?

SECOND QUARTER

I. Beware of covetousness.
  A. A person's life is not measured by possessions.
  B. Take your ease—pay the consequences.
II. O men of little faith!
  A. Look at the lilies.
  B. Do not be anxious.
III. Where is your treasure?
  A. Beware of storing up treasures.
  B. Seek God's kingdom and his righteousness.

Introducing the Main Question

What if you were given a million dollars, tax free, to do with as you wished? What would you do? This might be a good question to use with your class as a discussion starter. It should elicit some interesting responses.

How many of us have said at one time or another, "If I only had a million dollars, I would ———"? What would we do? Are we sure? How would it change our lives? What would we do differently? How would we treat other people? What kinds of causes would we support?

Each of us probably knows at least one person who would be called "wealthy." What is the person like? Some are generous. Some are miserly. Some change when they get a little wealth. Some seem to be just regular people. Maybe the trick is the kind of person, not the amount of wealth.

This lesson is about stewardship. It is also about getting our loyalties and values straight.

Developing the Lesson

The story in Luke 12:13-21 is an interesting one. Someone wants Jesus to settle a dispute over an inheritance. Jesus does not want to become involved in taking sides. Instead, he tells a story. A rich farmer had such an abundant harvest that he decided to tear down his barns and build bigger ones and then sit back and take it easy. The emphasis in the story is on the selfishness of the farmer. He seemed to have no regard for anyone else. "*I* will say to *myself*—*I* will take it easy." As in all things, God has the last word. No matter how much we stash away, no matter how big our bank account, death is the great equalizer. *We have no ultimate security except in God.*

How well do we use what we have? Regardless of how much we have of this world's goods, our destiny is in the hands of God.

I. Beware of covetousness.

A. A person's life is not measured by possessions.

It is a natural inclination in most of us to get things, to surround ourselves with material possessions. If only I had a better house, a better salary, a better car, how much better life would be! Perhaps. But there is no guarantee. Jesus said, "A man's life does not consist in the abundance of his possessions" (12:15).

B. Take your ease—pay the consequences.

Jesus had some pretty harsh things to say about the rich who did not show concern for their less fortunate neighbors (Dives and Lazarus, Luke 16:19-31). The prophet Amos also spoke harsh words against those who had wealth and who treated the poor without regard to justice (Amos 6:4-7).

II. O men of little faith!
   A. Look at the lilies.
   How utterly beautiful lilies are, yet they do not "toil and spin." Look at the ravens; they don't plant crops but God feeds them. This does not mean that we are to sit and do nothing. Rather, Jesus seems to be saying that we should not exhaust our energies accumulating "things."
   B. Do not be anxious.
   Do not be overly concerned about what you are to eat and drink. Do not let the pursuit of material possessions become an obsession. We want to earn our daily bread, and perhaps a little dessert now and then, but we refuse to let our lives be consumed by a passion for things that do not ultimately satisfy.
III. Where is your treasure?
   A. Beware of storing up treasures.
   Concentrate on investing in eternal things, not in earthly things. Value the spiritual gifts of love, patience, kindness. Think on these things. Live by these values.
   B. Seek God's kingdom and his righteousness.
   Other things will fall in place.

Helping Class Members Act

Ask class members to go over their check stubs (or cancelled checks) for the past month and see what it says about their values and life-style. Most of us probably spend most of our income for food, shelter, clothing, and transportation. But many of us also have money to spare. How much of what we make do we spend for others who are in need? How much to promote God's work through his church? How much to causes of love and justice in the community?

If our heart will be where our treasure is, what do our check stubs reveal about our loyalties and values?

Planning for Next Sunday

The topic for the next lesson is "Called to Make Peace." The background scripture is Matthew 5:9, 38-48 and Luke 6:27-36. Ask the class members to read and study these passages along with their church school material. Give them a hint about the next lesson and ask them to be prepared to discuss what it means to be "called to make peace" in today's world.

LESSON 12   FEBRUARY 16

Called to Make Peace

Background Scripture: Matthew 5:9, 38-48; Luke 6:27-36

The Main Question—William H. Willimon

One of the hazards of being in church often, of reading and studying the Bible daily, is that it all begins to make sense. The unfamiliar, strange words of Scripture become familiar and commonplace. The demands of Jesus, which once might have impressed us as being odd and severe, gradually become expected, predictable.

So as we read the Bible we start saying to ourselves, "Fine thing, the Bible. Says what it ought to say. Says what I think."

Thus the words of Jesus which may have struck their original hearers as a shock and a scandal have a very different effect on us. That is, the effect is different until we come to passages such as our scripture for today's lesson. These tough words speak of making peace, turning the other cheek, and loving our enemies.

Is there anything more demanding, more shocking, more at odds with our way of doing things than words such as these?

Now even the most complacent of minds realizes, in reading biblical words like these, that he or she has come to a head-on collision with our way of looking at things. Here is God's way of looking at things.

"Blessed are the peacemakers," says Jesus in his Beatitudes, "for they shall be called sons of God" (Matthew 5:9).

Blessed? In this world, those who try to make peace are looked upon as impractical idealists. They get stepped on, taken advantage of, abused. They get hit on the right cheek and then on the left. How can they be called "blessed"?

Peacemakers can only be seen as "blessed" when we view them in a totally different way—God's way of viewing people.

As You Read the Scripture—Bond Fleming

Matthew 5:9. This is the key verse for the lesson. Peace means more than the mere absence of strife. It is a positive condition of well-being. A peacemaker is one who believes in the possibility of peace, who seeks it, and who is willing to sacrifice to make it a fact. It is much easier to fan the flames of strife than to build relationships of reconciliation.

Verses 38-42. This passage is concerned with the principle of retaliation. Here is one of the many instances in which Jesus criticizes and goes beyond the traditions of the Jews and the explicit teachings of the Old Testament. See Exodus 21:23-25, Leviticus 24:19-20, or Deuteronomy 19:21 for expressions of the principle of retaliation. By the time of Jesus, retaliation was sometimes escaped by offering monetary equivalents.

Jesus' teaching regarding revenge is revolutionary. It is so revolutionary that we often explain it away as being figurative language. Some reject the teaching as nonsense. But Jesus meant it; he set forth the teaching as the way to break the poisonous cycle of revenge and as the way to make peace. The fact that some person wrongs me does not give me a right to do wrong. We cannot reveal the mind of Christ or the will of God through the spirit of revenge.

Jesus commands us to refrain from striking those who strike us, but not because of cowardice. We are to overcome evil with moral strength and creative good will. To give the cloak to the person who sued for the coat represented real suffering, because the cloak was a bed covering at night, not just the outer garment by day. The Roman soldier could compel the conquered Jew to carry his pack for one mile, by law. Do that, and then offer to carry it a second mile! Verse 42 relates to the usually expected generosity of the religious person.

Verses 43-47. There is no specific teaching in the Old Testament that says one should hate one's enemy. The hating of enemies must have been a practice in Jesus' time. In Leviticus 19:15-18 there is counsel to love one's neighbor; neighbor is used in the sense of a fellow-Israelite. Jesus set forth a new law of love, a command to love our enemies.

Jesus teaches love of enemies not in the sense of liking everybody, but in the sense of acceptance and creative good will. We are to "pray for those who persecute" us. We are to treat our enemies and our persecutors as God treats those who are evil or unjust. He does not withhold sunshine or rain from them. Nor should we withhold our objective good will and our love. Verses 46 and 47 contain challenging illustrations. His followers surely wanted to be better and do better than the despised tax collector or the Gentile. They loved those who loved them and welcomed their brethren. Then we must love those who do not love us, our enemies; and we must be friendly to sinners. Thus we may make for peace, and so be children of our Father in heaven. In verse 48 is the call to be perfect—in love—as our heavenly Father is perfect.

Luke 6:27-35. This passage comes from the sermon on the plain (Luke 6:17-49) which is similar to, yet has differences from, the Sermon on the Mount in Matthew 5–7.

Verse 31 gives a simple statement of the golden rule. Some form of the golden rule is found in the major world religions; religions are closer together in ethics than in theology.

Selected Scripture

King James Version	Revised Standard Version

Matthew 5:9, 38-48

9 Blessed *are* the peacemakers: for they shall be called the children of God.

....

38 Ye have heard that it hath been said, An eye for an eye, and a tooth for a tooth:

39 But I say unto you, That ye resist not evil: but whosoever shall smite thee on thy right cheek, turn to him the other also.

40 And if any man will sue thee at the law, and take away thy coat, let him have *thy* cloak also.

41 And whosoever shall compel thee to go a mile, go with him twain.

42 Give to him that asketh thee, and from him that would borrow of thee turn not thou away.

43 Ye have heard that it hath been said, Thou shalt love thy neighbour, and hate thine enemy.

Matthew 5:9, 38-48

9 "Blessed are the peacemakers, for they shall be called sons of God.

....

38 "You have heard that it was said, 'An eye for an eye and a tooth for a tooth.' 39 But I say to you, Do not resist one who is evil. But if any one strikes you on the right cheek, turn to him the other also; 40 and if any one would sue you and take your coat, let him have your cloak as well; 41 and if any one forces you to go one mile, go with him two miles. 42 Give to him who begs from you, and do not refuse him who would borrow from you.

43 "You have heard that it was said, 'You shall love your neighbor and hate your enemy.' 44 But I say

44 But I say unto you, Love your enemies, bless them that curse you, do good to them that hate you, and pray for them which despitefully use you, and persecute you;

45 That ye may be the children of your Father which is in heaven: for he maketh his sun to rise on the evil and on the good, and sendeth rain on the just and on the unjust.

46 For if ye love them which love you, what reward have ye? do not even the publicans the same?

47 And if ye salute your brethren only, what do ye more *than others?* do not even the publicans so?

48 Be ye therefore perfect, even as your Father which is in heaven is perfect.

Luke 6:31, 34-36
31 And as ye would that men should do to you, do ye also to them likewise.

. . . .

34 And if ye lend *to them* of whom ye hope to receive, what thank have ye? for sinners also lend to sinners, to receive as much again.

35 But love ye your enemies, and do good, and lend, hoping for nothing again; and your reward shall be great, and ye shall be the children of the Highest: for he is kind unto the unthankful and *to* the evil.

36 Be ye therefore merciful, as your Father also is merciful.

Key Verse: **Blessed** *are* **the peacemakers: for they shall be called the children of God. (Matthew 5:9)**

to you, Love your enemies and pray for those who persecute you, 45 so that you may be sons of your Father who is in heaven; for he makes his sun rise on the evil and on the good, and sends rain on the just and on the unjust. 46 For if you love those who love you, what reward have you? Do not even the tax collectors do the same? 47 And if you salute only your brethren, what more are you doing than others? Do not even the Gentiles do the same? 48 You, therefore, must be perfect, as your heavenly Father is perfect."

Luke 6:31, 34-36
31 And as you wish that men would do to you, do so to them.

. . . .

34 And if you lend to those from whom you hope to receive, what credit is that to you? Even sinners lend to sinners, to receive as much again. 35 But love your enemies, and do good, and lend, expecting nothing in return; and your reward will be great, and you will be sons of the Most High; for he is kind to the ungrateful and the selfish. 36 Be merciful, even as your Father is merciful.

Key Verse: **Blessed are the peacemakers, for they shall be called sons of God. (Matthew 5:9)**

The Scripture and the Main Question—William H. Willimon

You Have Heard It Said

Down the street from me there is a church that has erected a small sign out front. Each week the church put a different slogan on its sign. One week it read, "Six days of work and only one day of worship make one weak."

I suppose that if someone who knew little about the Christian faith looked at that billboard, he or she might conclude that cute slogans compose the message of Christianity. That person would assume that the teachings of Jesus are mainly simple moralisms, little guides for better behavior, catchy slogans for bumper stickers. Christianity is only a collection of conventional wisdom.

But today's scripture reminds us that the teachings of Jesus are considerably more demanding than mere conventional wisdom. "You have heard it said," Jesus begins his teaching (Matthew 5:38). In other words, traditional wisdom says, conventional morality teaches, 99 percent of all American believe . . .

We have heard it said, "God helps those who help themselves." (I was a grown man before I learned that this teaching, so frequently heard while I was young, is not in the Bible!) Or we have heard it said, "You had better look out for Number One." We have often heard, "Never give a sucker an even break." These little aphorisms make up the stock of conventional, popular, traditional wisdom.

"But I say to you," says Jesus (Matthew 5:39). Here Jesus puts himself at odds with conventional wisdom. He turns the tables on the older teaching. He thus shows that he comes to break down the traditional barriers, to challenge conventional notions of right and wrong.

Traditional morality has a stock of ready answers for our moral dilemmas: "An eye for an eye and a tooth for a tooth" (5:38). "You shall love your neighbor and hate your enemy" (5:43). Jesus makes shocking demands: "If any one strikes you on the right cheek, turn to him the other also." "Do not resist one who is evil." "Love your enemies" (5:39, 44).

I can think of few things more difficult than love of enemies. How would it be possible to survive in life, run a business, raise our children, and make our car payments if we lived like that? In this world, people who turn the other cheek, do not resist evil, and love their enemies are looked upon as hopelessly naïve dreamers.

But, of course, Jesus is talking about a kingdom other than that of the world, a kingdom where a different Lord reigns, where different visions of right and wrong dominate. Conventional wisdom defines wisdom as getting by, not rocking the boat, playing the game, and thus getting ahead. But here, in these teachings of Jesus, we are face-to-face with a very different way of looking at things—God's way.

Do you think the church does a good job of holding up this peculiar, countercultural vision for our people? Or does the church simply proclaim what is practical? Has the church been content to simply talk about what works rather than what is right?

A few years ago a man in my church asked me to come by and talk with him. I could tell he was deeply agitated from the moment I entered his home. He told me that a supervisor at work was making his life miserable. Evidently, the supervisor was attempting to force him out of the job and was doing this by ridiculing, harassing, and belittling him on the job.

"I can't take it any longer," he said. "I hate him so much for what he has done to me. I'm afraid that one day I may fly into a rage and kill him. What can I do?"

"Have you thought about praying to God to give you strength in this situation?" I asked. "That might help. Each day, before you go to work, why not pray? As Jesus said, we are to love our enemies."

He looked rather confused. "I never heard us pray for any enemies in church before."

That told me something. Sunday after Sunday he had come to church where he had been led to pray for the sick, personal needs, world problems, but not for enemies. The church had failed to help him make contact with the radically different nature of Christian discipleship.

"For if you love those who love you, . . . do not even the Gentiles do the same?" Jesus asks (5:46-47).

Love Your Enemies

"And as you wish that men would do to you, do so to them," counsels Jesus (Luke 6:31). This is the "golden rule."

But how is it humanly possible for people like us in a world like this to "love your enemies, and do good, and lend expecting nothing in return" (6:35)?

Behavior like this seems impossible, incomprehensible. It can only be explained as the peculiar response by people to the peculiar way they have been loved by God. We can love like this because we have been loved.

The key idea is that God is kind to the ungrateful and the selfish. We can be kind to others, even to our enemies, because we know how kind God has been to us. "Be merciful, even as your Father is merciful" (6:36).

In other words, as Christians, our ethics arises out of our gratitude for what God has done for us through Jesus Christ. Our ethics is not some heroic effort by us to be good. It is our natural response to God who has been so good to us.

Be Merciful

A preacher related a story of a young seminarian in Chicago. The young man graduated from seminary but could not find a church that would hire him immediately, so he took a job as a city bus driver while he awaited a parish position.

One day as he was driving his bus, three young men boarded. They arrogantly walked past the coin box. When he asked them to pay, they sneered at him and took their seats in the rear of the bus. He decided not to challenge them.

The next day the same three men got on at the same bus stop. Again they boarded the bus and refused to pay. This time he drove the bus until he saw a policeman. He stopped the bus and asked the policemen to throw the three men off the bus. Then he drove on.

The day after that, the three men got on his bus, dragged him out of his seat, and beat him severely. His nose was broken, two of his teeth were knocked out, and he had to spend three days in the hospital.

Meanwhile the police arrested the three young men and charged them with assault. He was asked to come to their trial and testify. By this time he was thoroughly discouraged. He had gone to seminary hoping to serve Christ. But what had it gotten him? He had failed as a Christian minister, failed even as a bus driver. He watched as the judge sentenced the young men to a month in jail. At that moment he rose to his feet and said, "Judge, I want to serve the sentence for them."

"You can't do that," said the judge. "These people nearly killed you. Why should you want to help them? No one has ever taken anyone else's punishment."

"Oh, yes, he did," replied the young man. And he told the whole courtroom the story of that one who was merciful.

Helping Adults Become Involved—Roy H. Ryan

Preparing to Teach

In a world torn by wars, terrorism, and revolutions all over the globe, this word of Jesus is especially relevant to our generation. What a challenge Jesus has given his followers, "Love your enemies" (Matthew 5:44), and what a reward for those who are "peacemakers, for they shall be called sons of God" (Matthew 5:9).

Read and study the passages in Matthew and Luke. Use *The Interpreter's Bible* or some other commentary to help you understand and interpret these important passages. Dr. Fleming gives some helpful insights in the section "As You Read the Scriptures" as does Dr. Willimon in "The Main Question" and "The Scripture and the Main Question."

Another way to prepare might be to watch your newspaper this week and cut out those articles that deal with efforts to make peace. Some would be on the international scene while others might be local. Be ready to share some of these stories with your class.

The aim of this lesson is to help adults better understand the nature of peacemaking, the radical nature of Jesus' teaching, and to be ready to take the consequences of taking his teaching seriously.

The following outline is one way of organizing the lesson for your presentation.

> Introduction. Jesus calls us to a radical way of life when he says we are to love our enemies. But he says that those who make peace will be blessed. Who said it is easy to be a Christian!
> I. Traditional wisdom about human relationships
>   A. "You have heard it said"
>   B. From a human point of view
> II. Called to be peacemakers
>   A. The peacemakers of God
>   B. Starting with love
> III. The "golden rule"—radical love
>   A. "Do unto others . . ."
>   B. The price of radical love

Introducing the Main Question

Do these words of Jesus about loving your enemies and being peacemakers sound too idealistic? Look again. What are the alternatives? Surely we do not wish to be troublemakers. Do we really get anywhere by hating other persons, even our enemies? Hate destroys the hater. Love is the positive value in creation that builds toward health and happiness. To hate is to shatter the image of God within us and to make us less than human.

How is it possible to love those who might "do us in"? How can we be peacemakers in a world torn into so many struggling factions? Certainly our own strength will not suffice. To be able to love and to be a peacemaker come as a gift of God's grace to those who seek and are open to the gift.

Developing the Lesson

What is peace? Dr. Fleming suggests that it "means more than the mere absence of strife. It is a positive condition of well-being." He goes on to define a peacemaker as "one who believes in the possibility of peace, who seeks it, and who is willing to sacrifice to make it a fact."

Dr. Willimon says that "those who try to make peace are looked upon as impractical idealists. They get stepped on, taken advantage of, abused." Even if that happens, Jesus says they will be "blessed."

And what about the golden rule? Is that old-fashioned? The modern version, according to a lot of people, is, "Do it to the other fellow before he has time to do it to you!" What do you think?

As for "loving your enemies," how can that be? Is not that idea a contradiction of terms? Jesus must have thought it possible. Do you think it is possible?

I. Traditional wisdom about human relationships

A. "You have heard it said"

This phrase is used by Jesus many times to point out the difference between his teaching and the traditions of his own religious heritage. This did not sit well with the Pharisees and other religious leaders of his day. It was certainly seen as radical. Who is this person who dares to go counter to the teaching of the elders? As we look at Jesus' teaching today, we do feel it is superior to some of the Old Testament teachings. Who of us would accept the notion of "an eye for an eye and a tooth for a tooth"? One issue that you may wish to discuss at this point is whether capital punishment fits more nearly the old way of thinking or Jesus' way.

B. From a human point of view

Is it possible to love our enemies? From a human viewpoint, probably not. But with God all things are possible. The transforming love of Jesus Christ enables us to be and do what God calls us to be and do as disciples.

II. Called to be peacemakers

A. The peacemakers of God

They are blessed because they attempt to bring things into harmony with God's purposes. God's will is for peace; therefore, those who work for peace are doing God's work. Peacemakers are often caught in the middle. They may indeed get trampled on, but *ultimately* they will receive the blessing of God.

B. Starting with love

Only when God is working in and through us do we have the capacity to love completely. If we love all people, we will be dedicated to bringing and keeping peace.

III. The "golden rule"—radical love

A. "Do unto others . . ."

That could really revolutionize human relationships. J. C. Penney, the great businessman who built the company that bears his name, sought to build his life and his business on that rule. It seems to work when it is really tried.

B. The price of radical love

We may "get slapped on the other cheek" and be forced to go "the second mile," but Jesus said "love your enemies" and thus show forth the love of God in your life. The Christian disciple learns that he or she is vulnerable but not a coward!

Helping Class Members Act

Where are the places of unrest and discord in your community? How might you be involved as a "go-between" to bring peace, to build trust, and to facilitate communication?

How do we operate in our own homes and families? Do we seek to work things out, seek reconciliation where there are differences, settle quarrels? Peacemaking in the home may be the true test of our Christian discipleship.

How do we operate on the world scene? What can we do to help bring about peace with justice in our world? "A better world begins with me."

Planning for Next Sunday

Ask class members to read the scripture lessons in Mark 8:34-35; 9:33-37; and 10:35-45 and be ready to discuss what it means to bear one's cross.

LESSON 13   FEBRUARY 23

Bear Your Cross

Background Scripture: Mark 8:34-35; 9:33-37; 10:35-45

The Main Question—William H. Willimon

"Something good is going to happen to you," proclaimed the television evangelist. Earlier in a sermon, he had gleefully announced that "Christianity is the best deal a person ever had."

That day, before his sermon, he had interviewed a man who was introduced as a "new Christian."

"John, tell us what happened when God came into your life," he said.

John told how his once failing business had been turned into a great financial success. He was now the president of a multimillion dollar corporation. He had a beautiful home on a Florida island. His marriage was happier. His children were better behaved. His health was perfect and "I have a smile on my face twenty-four hours a day." All of this came, he said, when "God came into my life."

Undoubtedly, good things can indeed happen to us when we follow Jesus. The improved lives of countless people are testimony to how God can help us.

But what is the main point of Christian discipleship? Ought we to proclaim the gospel so that we imply "Come to Jesus and all your problems will be solved and everything will be made right in your life"?

Is that the message of Christ?

Let's be honest. We are selfish. We want all our aches and pains to be cured. We want a life which is immune from heartache, pain, and struggle. We're looking for rewards from our religion, not responsibilities; a cushion, not a cross.

The trouble is, the one we follow walked up a narrow way, a way which led through suffering, rejection, and death, a way up a hill called "place of the skull."

Ought we to expect faith in him to shield us from the same cross?

As You Read the Scripture—Bond Fleming

Mark 8:34-35. Jesus was glad when Peter had acknowledged him as the Christ. "They are beginning to understand," Jesus thought. But in verse 32 it is obvious that the disciples did not understand or accept Jesus' role as the suffering servant. Their failure to comprehend inspired Jesus to declare, in verse 34, "If any man would come after me, let him deny himself and take up his cross and follow me."

There are two difficult words in verse 34, *deny* and *cross*. These words were important in Jesus' life and teaching, although they may be offensive to would-be followers. This self-chosen way of Jesus—of self-denial and cross-bearing—was God's will for Jesus, and thus also for Jesus' followers. Only if they are willing to lose sight of their lives, for Christ's sake and the gospel's, is there a chance to save their lives. Mark's earliest readers lived in a time of persecution and martyrdom; they understood.

Chapter 9:33-35. Capernaum was the home base for Jesus. He had returned home from a teaching mission with the disciples. On this trip Jesus had told the disciples (verse 31) that he would be persecuted and killed. They did not understand the teaching and were afraid to ask him. Anyway, they were busy discussing which of them was the greatest. The contrast between Jesus' teaching and their discussion intensified their embarrassment when Jesus asked, "What were you discussing?" They could not bring themselves to tell him; but Jesus knew.

Verses 36-37. These verses serve to illustrate the emphasis in verse 35. The point is, it takes childlike humility to enter the kingdom of heaven. To receive a little child in the name of Christ requires a spirit of humility that precludes feelings of greatness. Such humility opens the door to greatness in the kingdom.

Chapter 10:35-40. Here is another instance in which the disciples, from the inner group, fail to understand the message of Jesus. James and John, of all people, ask a special favor of Jesus—to have the chief places in his kingdom. It seemed so out of character for James and John to make such a request that Matthew, in chapter 20:20, has their mother make the request. The reply of Jesus seems to be an answer to James and John, not to their mother.

They asked their favor out of ignorance and ambition. They said they could drink his cup and undergo his baptism. They did not know that it was a cup of suffering and a baptism of disaster and death. It is probable, though, that both these apostles died as martyrs before Mark's Gospel was written.

In verse 40 Jesus seems to accept the position in the coming kingdom which they attributed to him. However, he is unable to grant their request for the chief places. They are to be filled by right, not by favor. There are some who read foreordination or predestination in Jesus' answer. Others think that God prepared the conditions to be met for the places but did not designate who would sit in them.

Verses 41-45. As might be expected, the other ten were upset and angry. Jesus had to start again. He called them together and told them that the Gentiles enjoy lordship and exercise of authority. In verse 43 Jesus said, "whoever would be great among you must be your servant." This statement transforms the traditional notion of greatness. Greatness is measured not in terms of the number of our servants, but in terms of the quality and extent of our service.

Selected Scripture

King James Version	Revised Standard Version

Mark 9:33-37

33 And he came to Că-pĕr'-nă-ŭm: and being in the house he asked them, What was it that ye disputed among yourselves by the way?

34 But they held their peace: for by the way they had disputed among themselves, who *should be* the greatest.

35 And he sat down, and called the twelve, and saith unto them, If any man desire to be first, *the same* shall be last of all, and servant of all.

36 And he took a child, and set him in the midst of them: and when he had taken him in his arms, he said unto them,

37 Whosoever shall receive one of such children in my name, receiveth me: and whosoever shall receive me, receiveth not me, but him that sent me.

Mark 9:33-37

33 And they came to Caper'na-um; and when he was in the house he asked them, "What were you discussing on the way?" 34 But they were silent; for on the way they had discussed with one another who was the greatest. 35 And he sat down and called the twelve; and he said to them, "If any one would be first, he must be last of all and servant of all." 36 And he took a child, and put him in the midst of them; and taking him in his arms, he said to them, 37 "Whoever receives one such child in my name receives me; and whoever receives me, receives not me but him who sent me."

Mark 10:35-45

35 And James and John, the sons of Zebedee, come unto him, saying, Master, we would that thou shouldest do for us whatsoever we shall desire.

36 And he said unto them, What would ye that I should do for you?

37 They said unto him, Grant unto us that we may sit, one on thy right hand, and the other on thy left hand, in thy glory.

38 But Jesus said unto them, Ye know not what ye ask: can ye drink of the cup that I drink of? and be baptized with the baptism that I am baptized with?

39 And they said unto him, We can. And Jesus said unto them, Ye shall indeed drink of the cup that I drink of; and with the baptism that I am baptized withal shall ye be baptized:

40 But to sit on my right hand and on my left hand is not mine to give;

Mark 10:35-45

35 And James and John, the sons of Zeb'edee, came forward to him, and said to him, "Teacher, we want you to do for us whatever we ask of you." 36 And he said to them, "What do you want me to do for you?" 37 And they said to him, "Grant us to sit, one at your right hand and one at your left, in your glory." 38 But Jesus said to them, "You do not know what you are asking. Are you able to drink the cup that I drink, or to be baptized with the baptism with which I am baptized?" 39 And they said to him, "We are able." And Jesus said to them, "The cup that I drink you will drink; and with the baptism with which I am baptized, you will be baptized; 40 but to sit at my right hand or at my left is not mine to grant, but it is for those for whom it has been prepared." 41 And when the ten heard it, they began to be indignant at James and

but *it shall be given to them* for whom it is prepared.

41 And when the ten heard *it,* they began to be much displeased with James and John.

42 But Jesus called them *to him,* and saith unto them, Ye know that they which are accounted to rule over the Gentiles exercise lordship over them; and their great ones exercise authority upon them.

43 But so shall it not be among you: but whosoever will be great among you, shall be your minister:

44 And whosoever of you will be the chiefest, shall be servant of all.

45 For even the Son of man came not to be ministered unto, but to minister, and to give his life a ransom for many.

Key Verse: **Whosoever will come after me, let him deny himself, and take up his cross, and follow me. (Mark 8:34)**

John. 42 And Jesus called them to him and said to them, "You know that those who are supposed to rule over the Gentiles lord it over them, and their great men exercise authority over them. 43 But it shall not be so among you; but whoever would be great among you must be your servant, 44 and whoever would be first among you must be slave of all. 45 For the Son of man also came not to be served but to serve, and to give his life as a ransom for many."

Key Verse: **If any man would come after me, let him deny himself and take up his cross and follow me. (Mark 8:34)**

The Scripture and the Main Question—William H. Willimon

Who Will Be the Greatest?

He was a dedicated, hard-working employee. He had given thirty years of his adult life to the company. But the company changed management, and the new management changed many of the old company policies. Things were very different now.

He noted that many questionable practices were becoming commonplace. To his surprise, he found that company inventories were sometimes falsified. Cheaper, inferior parts were sometimes substituted for regulation parts in their product.

He found all this to be deeply troubling. After discussing the matter with his wife, praying about it with his pastor, and thinking about what he should do, he decided to confront the new company president and tell him that he thought what was happening was wrong.

"Look, what are you? Some kind of saint? This is the world, man, the real world. Everybody's doing this. We're only trying to keep up," was his boss's reaction.

For his efforts at honesty, for this attempt to be courageous, speak up, and do what is right, this man was unceremoniously fired. This caused great economic hardship for his family. Today he is forced to work two low-paying jobs just to make ends met. I wish I could say that his life is easier or that he is happier because of his determination to do what is right, but that is not how the story goes.

I am reminded of something Martin Luther once said. "A man becomes a theologian, not by reading, speculating, and comprehending but by dying and being damned for the sake of the Gospel."

Luther was speaking of the hard, sometimes perilous, often dangerous path which one takes as a follower of Jesus Christ. It is that path which we reflect upon in today's lesson.

Jesus and his disciples are on the road. When they get to where they are going Jesus asks them, in effect, "What was all the fuss about back there on the road?"

And the disciples are silent. They are silent because they are ashamed. They have been discussing who should be greatest in the kingdom. Who shall sit on the cabinet when we get Jesus elected as Messiah? Who shall receive the greatest glory? The greatest rewards? After all, isn't that what discipleship is all about?

No, says Jesus. "If any one would be first, he must be last of all and servant of all" (Mark 9:35). Here is an odd kingdom, a kingdom not of crowns, kings, pomp and circumstance, but of the poor, the children, the little ones, the least and the last. He puts a child in the midst of them as an illustration of what he is talking about, for who is more helpless, more weak, more vulnerable than a child (9:36-37)?

Are You Able to Drink the Cup?

James and John want Jesus to do something spectacular for them: "Grant us to sit, one at your right hand and one at your left, in your glory," they say (10:37). Is this too much to ask? They have left everything and followed Jesus! Jesus asks them, "Are you able to drink the cup that I drink, or to be baptized with the baptism with which I am baptized?" (10:38). You know what he means by the "cup" and the "baptism"? He is talking about his cross. Once again, the content of discipleship is determined by the cross.

"If any man would come after me, let him deny himself and take up his cross and follow me," he says (8:34).

What does it mean to take up the cross? Jesus does not necessarily mean that we are to bear some condition that befalls us in life, such as a physical or emotional infirmity. These circumstances may cause us pain, but they are not necessarily the "cross" of which he speaks here.

Rather, the "cross" is something that we willingly take up as a result of being disciples of Christ. Jesus could have refused to take up his cross. He could have chosen to be successful by the world's standards of success. He could have raised an army, waged war against the Roman occupational forces. He could have become a miracle worker, a great lecturer in Hillel's school of theology, used his powers to achieve glory and prestige.

But he willingly chose another way. He chose to be obedient to God's will for his life. He chose to drink the cup of death. He chose to be thrust under the waters of suffering and death on the cross. Thereby he pointed the way for us.

We Christians are always in danger of getting the wrong idea about the Christian faith. It is so easy to assume that the point of being a Christian is to accept Christ so that everything will work out for the best for us. But to accept Christ also means to accept the cross.

Jesus notes that the Gentiles lord over one another, worship power and glory. "But it shall not be so among you; but whoever would be great among you must be your servant, and whoever would be first among you must be slave of all" (10:43-44).

217

Jesus himself is the example of this sort of leadership. He "came not to be served but to serve, to give his life as a ransom for many" (10:45).

What does this say to us about leadership in the church? The first Christian leaders were called *deacons,* a word which is derived directly from the Greek word meaning "butler" or "waiter." A deacon is someone who waits upon, who serves others. All Christian work is service, not privilege or prestige. In the church, everyone is a minister, that is, everyone is a servant of others.

Alas, not long after Jesus spoke these words, by the fourth century, the church had made peace with the world. Christian leaders started emulating worldly leaders. Bishops started wearing fine robes, stoles, expensive jeweled rings so that a Christian leader looked like a governmental leader. In the light of today's scripture lesson, this would be degeneration rather than progress in Christian leadership.

The Way of the Cross

"Take up thy cross," the Savior said,
"If thou wouldst my disciple be;
Deny thyself, the world forsake,
And humbly follow after me."

These are the words of a familiar hymn which we often sing. They are, as today's scripture suggests, the very heart of the gospel. A church where I once served has three steel crosses which stand over a modern sanctuary. They call to mind the basic symbol of our faith.

Do you think the cross remains the central image of the Christian faith? Or have other, less biblical symbols taken the place of the cross? Alas, I fear that for many the symbol of the Christian faith is a large, expensive, dominating building with an impressive sign out front. Or the symbol of the faith is a richly furnished sanctuary with an expensive pipe organ, well-dressed parishioners, finely attired clergy, or an expensive, well-equipped gymnasium for the youth of the church, or, well, the new symbols go on. Do these symbols say to the world that the church now exists to be served rather than to serve?

The cross is not optional equipment for disciples. The person who really attempts to live this faith doesn't have to go looking for a cross to bear; it will come. And when it comes, the decision will be, as it was for our Lord himself, whether to take up or to avoid the cross.

She had grown up in the small southern town. All of her family were there. She had never wanted to live anywhere else. Now, she was married and was raising her children in the town of her birth. Everything in the town was what she knew, what she loved.

But then there came that day in the early 1960s when the local high school decided to integrate its classes. Nearly all the white people in town were dead set against the idea. Even some of the local pastors criticized the desegregation plan. When one pastor spoke in favor of the plan, he was quickly silenced by irate parishioners, who threatened to fire him if he spoke again.

She had been a Christian all her life. What should she do? She prayed about it. She agonized over the possible response of her family and friends, and the repercussions any actions on her part might have for her family.

Then she decided that this was the right thing to do, the only thing she could do and still call herself a disciple of Jesus Christ. She spoke out at a public meeting on the subject of school integration. She invited a number of black parents to her home to meet some of her friends so that they could get to know one another better and talk about ways to accomplish the integration in a peaceful manner.

What do you think happened to this Christian who took up the cross? Finish the story with your class members and see what they think happens to those who decide to follow Jesus.

Helping Adults Become Involved—Roy H. Ryan

Preparing to Teach

This lesson concludes the unit "Directions for Disciples." You may wish to review briefly the lessons in this unit beginning with January 26 on forgiveness. We have been dealing with the heart of what it means to be Christian. The lesson for this Sunday, "Bear Your Cross," is the culmination of what discipleship is all about.

Read the scripture, Mark 8:34-35; 9:33-37; and 10:35-45, with a commentary in hand. Make notes as you study. Ask three questions of the text: (1) What does it say? (2) What does it mean? (3) What does it mean to me (us)?

Read also Dr. Fleming's and Dr. Willimon's comments on these passages. Both of them have given some helpful insights into the meaning of these important passages.

The aim of this lesson is to help us see and grasp the true meaning of discipleship-servanthood, symbolized most profoundly by the cross.

Look at the following outline as you prepare. You may wish to use this outline as you organize your presentation.

Introduction: Mark 8:34, "If any man would come after me, let him deny himself and take up his cross and follow me," may be the most descriptive statement in the Bible regarding the nature of discipleship. Another statement of Jesus also gets to the heart of what it means to be his follower, "Whoever would be great among you must be your servant" (Mark 10:43).
   I. Whoever would be great ("first")
      A. On being a servant
      B. On being like a child
   II. Are you able?
      A. To follow Jesus
      B. To die on a cross
   III. The way of the cross
      A. Deny yourself.
      B. Take up your cross.

Introducing the Main Question

What are some modern symbols of Christian discipleship? Read Dr. Willimon's comments in the section "The Main Question." You may wish to read this section to your students as a way of introducing the main question. Which is the most prevalent symbol of Christianity today, success or servanthood? They do not have to be mutually exclusive—but they often are. Does following Jesus guarantee success and happiness? What do you think?

You may wish to engage the class members in a discusson of what it means in our day "to take up your cross" and "to be a servant or minister to all."

Developing the Lesson

James and John, two of Jesus' disciples, ask a favor of Jesus. They wonder if they might be his closest advisers and share in his rule when the kingdom of God comes. This starts his discourse on suffering and servanthood (Mark 10:35-45). James and John misunderstood the nature of the kingdom Jesus came to establish. It would not be like earthly kingdoms where people "lord it over" one another and where power would be the measure of success. Rather, in this kingdom the greatest would be "servant of all" and the leader would be humble and open like a little child (Mark 9:36-37).

If Jesus did not come to be served but to serve, can his disciples expect to do any less? (Mark 10:45). This way of servanthood was difficult for those early disciples to understand. It is still difficult for us to understand and accept.

I. *Whoever would be great ("first")*

A. *On being a servant*

If we really had a choice, most of us would rather have servants than be a servant! Right? Jesus stooped down to wash his disciples' feet. This act of lowly servanthood probably symbolizes the nature of true discipleship as much as any image we have in the Bible. Some professions and occupations lend themselves to serving more than others. We sometimes refer to "helping professions" or "service occupations." But if our occupation or profession does not call us to serve others, how do we go about living our servanthood as Christians?

B. *On being like a child*

Christians are not called to be childish but child*like*. There is a vast difference! Jesus probably meant that his followers are to have those qualities of a child, such as trust, innocence ("be as wise as serpents and innocent as doves," Matthew 10:16), openness, and vulnerability.

II. *Are you able?*

A. *To follow Jesus*

Following Jesus requires a willingness to go all the way to the cross. Many of us have sung, " 'Are ye able," said the Master, 'to be crucified with me?' " The reply was, " 'Yea,' the sturdy dreamers answered, 'to the death we follow thee.' " But are we really able to follow him when the going gets tough? The true test of our discipleship is found not in the easy times when all is going well, but in the hard times when the world is caving in on us.

B. *To die on a cross*

Death on a cross may be more than we are asked to do as followers of Jesus. Maybe we do have to die, die to the old self, to our self-centeredness, to the easy way out, to always playing it safe. If we are to become new persons in Christ, it will be necessary for us to do some dying. But the good news of the gospel is that resurrection is victorious over death!

III. *The way of the cross*

A. *Deny yourself.*

"Take up [your] cross and follow me" (Mark 8:34), Jesus said. That means that we can no longer live for selfish purposes but must be willing to be loving, self-giving, and oriented toward the needs of our neighbors.

B. *Take up your cross.*

This is a voluntary commitment, not something God or someone else places upon us. Jesus wants us to turn our backs willingly on all that is selfish and narrow and to live toward the future in an attitude and style of serving others.

Helping Class Members Act

Review the main points of the five lessons in this unit. You may want to list those five lesson topics on the board as a reminder of what you have been studying. Involve the class members in recalling some of the things that have been helpful to them, things that will make a difference in their lives.

Some members of the class might be willing to share new insights that have come or resolutions they have made to live differently as a result of these lessons.

Conclude with a prayer for all the class members that they may be faithful in their Christian discipleship.

Planning for Next Sunday

Ask class members to look ahead to the next new unit: "The Christian Hope." The first lesson is "A Living, Confident Hope." The scripture to be used is I Peter 1–2:10. Ask the class to study the material and to make notes for next Sunday's lesson.

THIRD QUARTER
The Christian Hope

Horace R. Weaver

SEVEN LESSONS   MARCH 2–APRIL 13

This course of seven lessons explores the theme "The Christian Hope." The scriptures chosen for this study are taken from the general letters of the New Testament and include three selections from I and II Peter, three from the Johannine letters, and one from the letter of Jude.

The first letter of Peter seems to have been dictated by Peter to Sylvanus (5:12), who was a missionary companion of Paul (II Corinthians 1:19; I Thessalonians 1:1). It was written in Rome shortly after the persecutions of Nero in A.D. 64, so it includes the problem of suffering and persecution for their faith in Jesus Christ.

The second letter of Peter was written much later, about A.D. 125–135. It shows dependence on Jude (perhaps the brother of Jesus) and refers to all the letters of Paul (3:15). So we see the concerns of the early church, such as false teachers. The first letter of John also deals with heretical views of Gnostic teachers, such as those who teach that God did not become man in Jesus (4:2; see also II John 7). Jude was also written to warn Christians of false teachers. Though the content of their teachings is barely touched, their immoral life and methods are clearly described (verses 4, 7, 11, 16, 19).

The theme ("The Christian Hope") is beautifully developed as follows: "A Living, Confident Hope," March 2; "A Hope Worth Suffering For," March 9; "A Hope Worth Waiting For," March 16; "A Hope Leading to Action," March 23, Palm Sunday; "A Hope Focused on Jesus," March 30, Easter; "A Hope Built on Truth," April 6; and "A Hope Worth Guarding," April 13.

Contributors for the third quarter:

Robert G. Rogers, associate professor of Bible and religion and director of the Honors Program at Hampden-Sydney College, Hampden-Sydney, Virginia.

Mack B. Stokes, bishop of The United Methodist Church and professor of theology and dean of doctoral studies at Oral Roberts University, Oklahoma City, Oklahoma.

William H. Willimon.

R. Michael Winters.

A Living, Confident Hope

Background Scripture: I Peter 1:1–2:10

The Main Question—William H. Willimon

"Hope springs eternal" says the poet. Sometimes it seems as if hope is a scarce commodity in contemporary life. After all, if you read your morning paper—the accounts of human evil, suffering, and pain, the grim stories of war and injustice, the pictures of accidents, natural disasters, and calamities—one could easily be tempted to give up hope. To be hopeful in the face of all these causes for hopelessness would seem an act of sheer stupidity.

Little wonder, then, that many in our age have given up hope. The pessimists have more credibility than the optimists—for those who predict the triumph of the dark side of things are more often right than those who expect the best. Suicides, growing problems with drug and alcohol addiction, are evidence that hope is in short supply these days.

Wherein is our hope? Is hope to be based simply upon a cheerful disposition, a Pollyanna-type naïveté which simplistically looks upon the good things of life and ignores the bad?

Recently I talked with a woman who suffered from severe depression. Her depression had made her unable to hold a job or to fulfill her family obligations. Finally she had to be institutionalized because of her problem. I talked with her at the hospital, and we discussed her struggle.

"I don't know anything good to live for anymore," she said. "The whole world seems like it is in dismal shape. Who knows what may come tomorrow? Everything is out of control, hopeless."

What would you say to this person? What word of encouragement and hope?

That word is the concern of today's lesson.

As You Read the Scripture—Mike Winters

According to tradition, Peter is the author of this letter, though there is some internal evidence that might indicate otherwise. The letter is sent to Jews of the Diaspora, who had been exiled and scattered into Asia Minor at several points in their nation's history. Peter thought of the church as the true Israel.

The occasion of the writing is to exhort Gentiles as well as Jewish Christians to have faith and hope in the face of certain persecution. To the Jews of the Diaspora, salvation meant a life free of persecution.

I Peter 1:3-9. In the accepted form of Greek letters written at the time of this one, greetings were followed by words of thanks. The thanksgiving in this letter is an elaborate testimony to God, the giver of hope.

Verse 3. The resurrection of Jesus Christ was the seal of the potency of life. God, the giver of life, used the resurrection to show that life in Christ was a force stronger than death. Christ, who died and was raised from the dead, is the living hope.

223

Verse 4. The inheritance is life—not just existence, but *real* life—that cannot be destroyed or diminished in any way.

Verses 5 and 9. Here is an allusion to the doctrine of justification by grace through faith. Faith is the means to this life. The question of when this life will be revealed was a critical one for those facing the persecutions of the day.

Verses 6-7. Paul would say, I am saved by faith in Jesus Christ, not by works. James would argue, "Faith by itself, if it has no works, is dead" (James 2:17). Does faith make demands of us or does faith imply faithful action, the works of faithfulness? Peter weaves them together. For those who are willing to do what faith requires, this time of persecution may lead to a strengthening of faith.

Verse 8. Faith provides insight into the mystery of Christ that cannot be seen with mortal eyes.

Verses 10-12. The grace and hope that come through faith and provide insight into the mystery of life in Christ are a matter of prophetic inquiry and angelic interest. Neither prophet nor angel could fully see what the church knows in faith.

Verses 13-21. Peter appeals to the Diaspora to be holy through their certain persecutions. They are encouraged not to compromise their faith.

Verse 13. "Gird up your minds" is a mixed metaphor. Girding loins was the practice of pulling the outer garment up between one's legs to free the legs for running. Similarly, in the face of persecution, Christians' minds must be set and ready, quick and agile. The appeal to sobriety calls the Diaspora to calmness and readiness—steadiness. It may be that this appeal to sobriety was an exhortation to moderate a giddy expectation that the "last time" was at hand and that Christ would come and deliver them. The appeal is to alertness and readiness of mind and a steady faith in the face of present danger.

Verses 14-16. These verses are reminders of Paul's appeal, "Do not be conformed to this world but be transformed by the renewal of your mind" (Romans 12:2). Holiness is the identifying characteristic of God (Leviticus 11:44-45). It is more than a list of ethical do's and don'ts. Holiness is the very strength and stability of faith, a needful quality for those under persecution who are tempted to compromise.

Verse 17. People of faith, "conduct yourselves with fear [or reverence] throughout the time of your exile."

Verses 18-19. The ransom of exiles held captive is the blood of Christ, which is more precious than silver or gold. It is a pure and worthy sacrifice. Its purity alone can atone for all sins of all people.

Verses 20-21. As the Jews of the Diaspora were destined (1:2), so is Christ. Christ too is a part of God's plan, destined from before the foundation of the world. Christ is the object of our hope.

Verses 22-25. The key phrase is "love one another." This is the purpose of the imperishable church.

Chapter 2:1-10. Here are the building plan and the structure of the church.

Verse 10. Compare Hosea 2:23 and the expression of God's hope that his disobedient people can again be God's people.

Selected Scripture

King James Version

I Peter 1:3-9, 13-21

3 Blessed *be* the God and Father of our Lord Jesus Christ, which according to his abundant mercy hath begotten us again unto a lively hope by the resurrection of Jesus Christ from the dead,

4 To an inheritance incorruptible, and undefiled, and that fadeth not away, reserved in heaven for you,

5 Who are kept by the power of God through faith unto salvation ready to be revealed in the last time.

6 Wherein ye greatly rejoice, though now for a season, if need be, ye are in heaviness through manifold temptations:

7 That the trial of your faith, being much more precious than of gold that perisheth, though it be tried with fire, might be found unto praise and honour and glory at the appearing of Jesus Christ:

8 Whom having not seen, ye love; in whom, though now ye see *him* not, yet believing, ye rejoice with joy unspeakable and full of glory:

9 Receiving the end of your faith, even the salvation of your souls.

....

13 Wherefore gird up the loins of your mind, be sober, and hope to the end for the grace that is to be brought unto you at the revelation of Jesus Christ;

14 As obedient children, not fashioning yourselves according to the former lusts in your ignorance:

15 But as he which hath called you is holy, so be ye holy in all manner of conversation;

16 Because it is written, Be ye holy; for I am holy.

17 And if ye call on the Father, who without respect of persons judgeth according to every man's work, pass the time of your sojourning *here* in fear:

Revised Standard Version

I Peter 1:3-9, 13-21

3 Blessed be the God and Father of our Lord Jesus Christ! By his great mercy we have been born anew to a living hope through the resurrection of Jesus Christ from the dead, 4 and to an inheritance which is imperishable, undefiled, and unfading, kept in heaven for you, 5 who by God's power are guarded through faith for a salvation ready to be revealed in the last time. 6 In this you rejoice though now for a little while you may have to suffer various trials, 7 so that the genuineness of your faith, more precious than gold which though perishable is tested by fire, may redound to praise and glory and honor at the revelation of Jesus Christ. 8 Without having seen him you love him; though you do not now see him you believe in him and rejoice with unutterable and exalted joy, 9 As the outcome of your faith you obtain the salvation of your souls.

....

13 Therefore gird up your minds, be sober, set your hope fully upon the grace that is coming to you at the revelation of Jesus Christ. 14 As obedient children, do not be conformed to the passions of your former ignorance, 15 but as he who called you is holy, be holy yourselves in all your conduct; 16 since it is written, "You shall be holy, for I am holy." 17 And if you invoke as Father him who judges each one impartially according to his deeds, conduct yourselves with fear throughout the time of your exile. 18 You know that you were ransomed from the futile ways inherited from your fathers, not with

18 Forasmuch as ye know that ye were not redeemed with corruptible things, *as* silver and gold, from your vain conversation *received* by tradition from your fathers;

19 But with the precious blood of Christ, as of a lamb without blemish and without spot:

20 Who verily was foreordained before the foundation of the world, but was manifest in these last times for you,

21 Who by him do believe in God, that raised him up from the dead, and gave him glory; that your faith and hope might be in God.

perishable things such as silver or gold, 19 but with the previous blood of Christ, like that of a lamb without blemish or spot. 20 He was destined before the foundation of the world but was made manifest at the end of the times for your sake. 21 Through him you have confidence in God, who raised him from the dead and gave him glory, so that your faith and hope are in God.

Key Verse: Blessed *be* the God and Father of our Lord Jesus Christ, which according to his abundant mercy hath begotten us again unto a lively hope by the resurrection of Jesus Christ from the dead. (I Peter 1:3)

Key Verse: Blessed be the God and Father of our Lord Jesus Christ! By his great mercy we have been born anew to a living hope through the resurrection of Jesus Christ from the dead. (I Peter 1:3)

The Scripture and the Main Question—William H. Willimon

Tested by Fire

Scholars believe that the first letter of Peter was written sometime during the latter half of the first century to a group of Christians somewhere in Asia Minor. While anything we say about the original audience comes by way of conjecture, we can assume that they were mainly gentile converts to Christianity (1:14, 4:3), who were now undergoing "various trials" (1:6).

Their trials may have been government persecution. In A.D. 64, the emperor Nero launched a bloody persecution of the church in hopes of putting an end to this troublesome Christian movement. Perhaps the Christians who first heard this epistle had been on the receiving end of this terror.

Thank God that most of us have never known what it means to be persecuted or tortured for our faith. We live in a land which has, thus far, encouraged freedom of expression in religion.

But let us not forget that there are Christians in many parts of the world today who do know firsthand what it means to be "tested by fire" (1:7). New totalitarian regimes do not look kindly upon those who refuse to give ultimate allegiance to earthly kingdoms. They may try to mask their cruelty under the guise of "law and order" or "patriotism" or "the good of the people," but it is, by whatever name the Neroes of this world call it, persecution.

While in no way comparing the little insults and injuries which we North American Christians may suffer because of our beliefs, there are those even in our neighborhood who could relate to the concerns of this first letter of Peter.

Christians who go against the grain of popular sentiments, who question their government's values or the standards of conventional morality, may find that they are subjected to social ostracism, public scorn, or economic punishment.

A young pastor dared to question the priorities of a government which made severe cuts in health and human services programs while making large increases in military spending. Her church was in a town where many worked for a military contractor. Two months after she preached her sermon about the need to turn "swords into plowshares," she was forced out of her pastorate.

Life itself offers people the possibility "to suffer various trials" (1:6). A friend is stricken with incurable cancer, someone dear to you dies, you are laid off from your job—while these trials may not come to you because of your Christian faith, they often provide severe tests of our faith.

Many people, in suffering life's trials, lose their faith. They become bitter, angry, and despairing of the goodness of life. Their faith is "tested by fire," and it burns away. Wherein is our hope?

In This You Rejoice

All this thought about the trials which often beset Christians because of their faith and in spite of their faith makes doubly surprising the opening tone of First Peter.

"Blessed be the God and Father of our Lord Jesus Christ!" says the writer (1:3). "In this you rejoice, though now for a little while you may have to suffer various trials" (1:6).

How is it possible to urge these poor, persecuted, forlorn Christians to rejoice? "In this you rejoice," says the writer. In what can they rejoice?

One must be careful when attempting to console those who are suffering some great difficulty. Perhaps you have had the sad experience, when you were going through a time of grief, of having someone trying to console you with superficial words of cheap consolation.

"You just have to accept this as God's will," the person might say. "Things will work out for the best."

Is that the attitude of First Peter? Is the writer's call to "rejoice with unutterable and exalted joy" (1:9) a petty encouragement to put on a happy face, think positively, and hope that it will all work out?

No. The writer urges these Christians to hope, even in the midst of their persecutions, because they are among those who "have been born anew to a living hope through the resurrection of Jesus Christ (1:3).

They are those who know something the world and its rulers, in their blindness, cannot know. Even though they were not among those who first witnessed the resurrection (1:8), they believe in the truth of the resurrection—that God has triumphed in Jesus Christ, that death has no more dominion, that love has conquered hate, and that goodness is victorious over evil.

Even though "for a little while you may have to suffer various trials" (1:6), they know who has won the battle. That knowledge is now the source of their rejoicing even in the midst of their trials.

"Set your hope fully upon the grace that is coming to you at the revelation of Jesus Christ" (1:13), says the writer. Here is a sure hope based not upon some simpleminded view that everything will turn out all right or that the suffering of the present time is only an illusion or that all that is required is for these hurting people to smile and think positively. This hope is based on the work of Jesus Christ. As surely as Christ overcame death, danced out of the tomb on Easter, "disarmed the principalities and powers" (as Paul says in Colossians), so we shall eventually be victorious in him.

"Through him you have confidence in God, who raised him from the dead and gave him glory, so that your faith and hope are in God" (1:21).

No wonder that we, who so often put our hope and faith in ourselves, our abilities, or the goodness of other people, often find ourselves in hopeless situations.

Confidence in God

In a time of trial, we often seek consolation from a variety of sources. Sometimes we take drugs or use alcohol in an attempt to numb our frayed nerves. Or we spend hours in conversation with ourselves, weighing all the possibilities, chewing our fingernails, pacing the floor, wondering what will happen next. We live in an age of anxiety, an age not too unlike the unstable time when the first letter of Peter may have been written.

It is a time of false messiahs and competing philosophies, all promising to give us peace and hope. What we need is not some temporary, quick therapy or self-help technique. We need to know that some power, some force greater and better than our own, is in charge. Only that can sustain us when the going gets really rough.

In response to our questions about the future, to our gnawing anxieties, the Christian faith points toward the empty tomb and proclaims a risen Lord who holds us and our future in the palm of his hand.

Our faith and our hope are in God.

Helping Adults Become Involved—Robert G. Rogers

Preparing to Teach

As you begin this series, "The Christian Hope," you should take time to preview all seven lessons. Notice how the individual topics fit together. While thinking about the next seven Sunday lessons, try to imagine (and perhaps jot down on paper) various ways the topic for each might apply to specific circumstances of persons or events in your own congregation and hometown. This process will help you relate the focus of each lesson to needs and concerns of class members.

Your specific aim in this first lesson is to show how it is possible for the modern Christian to have hope in the midst of the difficulties of the present world. To accomplish this, you will examine the faith of the first-century Christians who also faced uncertain times.

Read over the assigned lesson carefully, paying special attention to the scripture assigned. You might also read the headlines of the newspaper to note current problems in the world. A chalkboard or a large writing pad in the classroom would be useful.

Introducing the Main Question

Dr. Willimon has clearly identified the main question: What word of encouragement and hope can be offered to a broken and hurt world? He suggests two types of problems: (1) global problems, such as war and natural disasters, and (2) personal problems, such as drug or alcohol addiction. You will probably want to address both with the class.

You might simply read aloud some of the headlines from a current paper to illustrate the range of problems. Another approach would be to ask members of the class to share their knowledge of problems in the community or the world. These could be written on the chalkboard or pad as a reminder during the rest of the lesson. One word of caution is needed. This portion of the class should not become a hand-wringing session. Your goal is to acknowledge that there is much trouble in the world, but you do not want your class to be overwhelmed by it. Remember, the joy of a vibrant Christian faith helps persons cope with problems in life!

Developing the Lesson

Having noted with the class the many problems in the world, you now want to turn to specific ways in which the Christian gospel helps us face times of trouble and despair.

You might divide the lesson into three sections:

> I. God identifies with our suffering.
> II. The Son of God triumphs over the world.
> III. Hope is present in the Christian community.

I. God identifies with our suffering.

The assigned scripture describes a God of mercy and compassion. He does not create the world and then ignore it. Rather, he continues to be concerned about his creation. Even in the midst of persecutions, whether in New Testament times or in the present day, the God of Christian faith is aware of the pain suffered by the human community. As Dr. Willimon notes, being a Christian does not mean that one thereby avoids pain or trouble. (In fact, he suggests that one's faith commitment may lead one to get into trouble!)

At this point some members of the class may be willing to share their own perceptions regarding the presence of God in times of trouble. You could also think together about problems of religious persecution down through the centuries. What type of faith kept (or keeps) persons aware of the love of God in the midst of such trials?

Conclude this section of the lesson by noting that initially God identifies with human suffering in the most tangible fashion: by sending his Son to suffer and die on the cross.

II. The Son of God triumphs over the world.

A major theme of the assigned scripture is the resurrection of Jesus Christ. As the crucifixion was the sign that God identified wholly with human suffering, so the resurrection is his answer to the worst that "the world" can do. Sin and suffering and death do not finally prevail. Discuss with your class the meaning of the resurrection by noting the words recorded in Dr. Willimon's section "The Scripture and the Main Question." In the life, death, and especially resurrection of Jesus Christ, how is God triumphant? How do love and goodness triumph over hate and evil?

It might also be useful to read together I Peter 1:8-9. How does resurrection faith depend on things unseen? Is it necessary to see something to believe it is true? Notice how faith in God's promises provides a pathway to salvation.

You could point out that even belief in the resurrection does not prevent our having to face problems. However, it does provide us with God's assurance of eternal life. When viewed from that perspective, our current problems become less significant. Still, as Christians, we are called forthrightly to live in the world and to alleviate suffering wherever we can.

Close this portion of the lesson by giving a brief summary which will also serve as introduction to the concluding section. It might be as follows: God identifies with human suffering and sends his Son to live and die for the human community. Through the death and resurrection of Jesus, God has defeated the final enemies—sin and death. By belief in God's saving action, we too are invited to share in Christ's victory. It is primarily in the Christian fellowship that we receive support and encouragement to take on the problems of life here on earth.

III. Hope is present in the Christian community.

You might continue by suggesting that Christian hope is founded on an awareness of God's love as exemplified by the gift of his Son. Remind the class of I John 4:19: "We love, because he first loved us." This verse illustrates what Christian life should be in each congregation.

How can we best witness to hope for ourselves and for the whole world? Is not such Christian hope rooted in the love and acceptance we experience in the life of the church? Does not the quality of life in our church give us strength to face difficulties in the world? Discuss some of these questions with the class, noting that the fellowship of the church should be flexible enough to support us both in facing the bad times and in celebrating in times of joy. What are some practical ways this can be done?

Examine with the class the concluding verses for today's reading (I Peter 2:9-10). Point out that our hope as Christians must not be hidden behind the walls of our churches. Rather, being persons of faith, "God's own people," involves an obligation to share our conviction. We are called to be ambassadors of hope to our community, nation, and world.

Helping Class Members Act

Suggest that class members learn by heart I Peter 1:21-22. These verses summarize nicely the intention of today's lesson. Ask members to think of ways they can work within the various groups of the church to create the atmosphere of love which supports such hope as the verses record. Write suggestions on the chalkboard. Is your church providing the necessary support for members as they deal with difficulties?

Planning for Next Sunday

The next lesson examines whether having a commitment of faith and hope might entail suffering. In preparation, ask the class to read I Peter 2:11–5:14. They might also read the account of Jesus' prayer in the garden of Gethsemane (Mark 14:32-42).

A Hope Worth Suffering For

Background Scripture: I Peter 2:11–5:14

The Main Question—William H. Willimon

He was a born salesman. Since his childhood, he had been able to sell anyone anything. It seemed natural for him to make a career out of sales. He went to school and studied business. Then after college, he studied for his license in real estate. At last he joined a prestigious real estate firm in his hometown.

Things went well for him. He quickly demonstrated his gift as a salesman. In a couple of years, he was top house salesman in the company. Soon he was promoted to sales manager with a dozen salespersons working under him.

Then came the day one of his salespersons told him about a dilemma he faced. It seems that a black family was inquiring about a house the firm had for sale in an all-white neighborhood.

"What should I do?" the salesman asked. "You know how those people feel about this race issue. If we show that family this house and they buy it, we will never get another listing in this town."

The sales manager pondered the situation, thought about it, prayed about it. The next day, he called his salesman and told him that "the only right thing to do is to treat this family like any other. We must show them the house, and if they want to buy it, we'll sell it to them. This is the only right thing to do; the only Christian thing to do."

I wish this person's right actions had yielded pleasant consequences for him. I wish his righteousness had been rewarded.

Actually, his boss hit the ceiling when he heard what he had done. The boss called him on the carpet and when he defended his action, the boss unceremoniously fired him. He not only fired him, but he spread the word around to other real state companies in the area that this man was "a troublemaker, an oddball who can't be trusted."

He has yet to find another position in real estate sales.

As You Read the Scripture—Mike Winters

The remainder of this first letter of Peter defines the structure of institutions and behavior of Christians during the then-present siege of persecution. Finally, the letter ends by looking to its beginning, offering hope and encouragement in the face of the "fiery ordeal."

I Peter 2:11-12. The Jews of the Diaspora are reminded again that they are exiles. They are aliens in a foreign land. They are citizens of a holy nation of another time and another place. In the history of the Jews was the constant, prophetic plea that during their wanderings among the nations they should not compromise their faith and heritage for the sake of an easier passage to the promised land. They were to maintain their distinctiveness as God's covenant people and not be led astray by foreign ways and foreign gods (Deuteronomy 7).

THIRD QUARTER

Chapter 2:13–3:12. It was a customary practice of the time to detail patterns of behavior in the various relationships of the home and larger society. These were called "house rules." Here are house rules for Christians in persecution (compare the house rules of Ephesians 5:21–6:9). The rules are to be followed with a consciousness of the witness for Christ which our behavior offers.

Chapter 2:13-17. Questions arise here: How does a Christian submit to an unjust and violent regime? How can one live freely in an oppressive political regime?

Verses 18-20. Servants are exhorted to submit, even to unjust masters. There is apparent reward for those who suffer unjustly.

Verses 21-25. Christ in his innocent suffering provides the example for all those who suffer. (Isaiah 53:5-12 is a prophetic song of the servant's vicarious suffering.)

Chapter 3:1-7. Given the context of the times in which this text was written, when a wife was considered the property of her husband, these lines are no real surprise. But it is surprising to find a hint of a new equal status between man and woman as "joint heirs of the grace of life." This would have been a radical notion to Peter's readers.

Verses 8-12. Compare this to Colossians 3:12-17, where Paul calls the saints to put on love. Love is the cement that binds all people together.

Verses 13-17. It is true more often than we like to think that those who are zealous for what is right are persecuted.

Verse 14. See Matthew 10:28 which says, "Do not fear those who kill the body but cannot kill the soul."

Verse 15. The defense is a rational, thought-out, simple statement of faith.

Verse 16. A clear conscience? The guilty deserve what they have coming to them, but the holy who are persecuted shame their persecutors by the high level of their moral and spiritual lives.

Verses 18-22. The righteous Christ died for the unrighteous.

Chapter 4:1-6. Christ has wrought a radical change in the lives of those who believe, which should result in a whole new life-style decidedly different from the Gentiles' reckless and riotous living. Christians are urged to love one another with hospitality, generosity, service. Their love will sustain them in the time of persecution.

Verses 12-19. A relationship with Christ does not exempt the Christian from persecution and suffering. Instead, suffering may be made more likely because of our attempt to follow Christ.

Verse 13. Sharing Christ's suffering is the very same ministry of the church today. The church is the Body of Christ and should show forth the same compassion and love for the world which Christ Jesus himself demonstrated.

Verse 14. See Matthew 5:11-12, which allows for those who suffer for Christ to "rejoice and be glad."

Verses 15-16. Suffering because of sin is one thing. Suffering because of righteousness is quite another.

Verse 17. For Peter, the last times were at hand.

Verse 18. Here is a harsh reminder that none of us deserves salvation, not even the righteous.

Verse 19. Suffering Christians must do what is right and trust the rest to God.

Chapter 5:1-5. Here are house rules for the church: tend the flock; be examples to the flock; be subject to the elders; clothe yourselves with humility.

Verses 6-11. Peter's final exhortations are: humility, sobriety, and endurance.

Selected Scripture

King James Version

Revised Standard Version

I Peter 3:13-17

13 And who *is* he that will harm you, if ye be followers of that which is good?

14 But and if ye suffer for righteousness' sake, happy *are ye:* and be not afraid of their terror, neither be troubled;

15 But sanctify the Lord God in your hearts: and *be* ready always to *give* an answer to every man that asketh you a reason of the hope that is in you with meekness and fear:

16 Having a good conscience; that, whereas they speak evil of you, as of evildoers, they may be ashamed that falsely accuse your good conversation in Christ.

17 For *it is* better, if the will of God be so, that ye suffer for well-doing than for evil-doing.

I Peter 4:12-19

12 Beloved, think it not strange concerning the fiery trial which is to try you, as though some strange thing happened unto you:

13 But rejoice, inasmuch as ye are partakers of Christ's sufferings; that, when his glory shall be revealed, ye may be glad also with exceeding joy.

14 If ye be reproached for the name of Christ, happy *are ye;* for the spirit of glory and of God resteth upon you: on their part he is evil spoken of, but on your part he is glorified.

15 But let none of you suffer as a murderer, or *as* a thief, or *as* an evildoer, or as a busybody in other men's matters.

I Peter 3:13-17

13 Now who is there to harm you if you are zealous for what is right? 14 But even if you do suffer for righteousness' sake, you will be blessed. Have no fear of them, nor be troubled, 15 but in your hearts reverence Christ as Lord. Always be prepared to make a defense to any one who calls you to account for the hope that is in you, yet do it with gentleness and reverence; 16 and keep your conscience clear, so that, when you are abused, those who revile your good behavior in Christ may be put to shame. 17 For it is better to suffer for doing right, if that should be God's will, than for doing wrong.

I Peter 4:12-19

12 Beloved, do not be surprised at the fiery ordeal which comes upon you to prove you, as though something strange were happening to you. 13 But rejoice in so far as you share Christ's sufferings, that you may also rejoice and be glad when his glory is revealed. 14 If you are reproached for the name of Christ, you are blessed, because the spirit of glory and of God rests upon you. 15 But let none of you suffer as a murderer, or a thief, or a wrongdoer, or a mischiefmaker; 16 yet if one suffers as a Christian, let him not be ashamed, but under that name let him glorify God. 17 For the time has come for judgment to begin with the household of God;

16 Yet if *any man suffer* as a Christian, let him not be ashamed; but let him glorify God on this behalf.

17 For the time *is come* that judgment must begin at the house of God; and if *it* first *begin* at us, what shall the end *be* of them that obey not the gospel of God?

18 And if the righteous scarcely be saved, where shall the ungodly and the sinner appear?

19 Wherefore let them that suffer according to the will of God commit the keeping of their souls *to him* in well-doing, as unto a faithful Creator.

Key Verse: **But rejoice, inasmuch as ye are partakers of Christ's sufferings; that, when his glory shall be revealed, ye may be glad also with exceeding joy. (I Peter 4:13)**

and if it begins with us, what will be the end of those who do not obey the gospel of God? 18 And
"If the righteous man is scarcely saved, where will the impious and sinner appear?"

19 Therefore let those who suffer according to God's will do right and entrust their souls to a faithful Creator.

Key Verse: **Rejoice in so far as you share Christ's sufferings, that you may also rejoice and be glad when his glory is revealed. (I Peter 4:13)**

The Scripture and the Main Question—William H. Willimon

Suffering for Righteousness' Sake

"Now who is there to harm you if you are zealous for what is right?" asks the writer of the first letter of Peter.

Who is there to harm you? Plenty of people do not value the work of those who are "zealous for what is right." People love darkness better than light, says the Bible.

Consider the plight of those early Christians to whom this first letter of Peter was addressed. We do not know the precise circumstances of their situation, but we do know that they were being persecuted for their beliefs. Evidently they were being persecuted by the governing authorities, because there is a discussion of the Christian relationship to the governing authorities earlier (2:13-17).

These are no superficial words of comfort. The "fiery ordeal" was no small matter. Imagine having to see your loved ones put to death—perhaps by fire—for their faith, as these first Christians undoubtedly did.

Need we review the long line of historic and contemporary Christian martyrs to be reminded of the world's typical reaction to those who are "zealous for what is right"? We receive our prophets by stoning them. We label them as dangerous subversives, threats to law and order, revolutionaries, and troublemakers.

"The church has grown on the blood of its martyrs" is an old saying. We are Christians today; we hold this faith and sit in comfortable churches only because many thousands have paid for this faith by their blood.

These people were called before governmental and religious authorities and were unafraid to boldly "account for the hope" that was within them

(3:15). Whom do you think about when you hear the word *martyr?* Which servant of righteousness do you admire when you look back upon the history of the church? Stephen? Peter? Paul? Wycliffe? Huss? Martin Luther King? These were the people who believed the truth of today's scripture passages: "It is better to suffer for doing right, if that should be God's will, than for doing wrong" (3:17).

Do Not Be Surprised

Unfortunately, few of us think about suffering for our faith. Most of us live in a land with a great degree of religious tolerance. In popular American Christianity, the faith is often presented as the solution to all of our problems, the source of perpetual happiness, and a good thing for nice people.

Are you depressed? Is your business failing? Do you have marital problems? Do your children misbehave? Come to Jesus and solve your problems, cure your aches and pains, be happy.

Alas, this is the message we often preach.

But today's passages from First Peter remind us that the gospel is often the beginning of problems, problems which we would have gladly avoided if we had been left to ourselves. The people who first followed Jesus paid dearly for their discipleship. It wasn't an easy road that he called them to walk. Our Lord himself perished on a cross. Why should we expect it to be so different for us?

So, the writer says, "Beloved, do not be surprised at the fiery ordeal which comes upon you to prove you, as though something strange were happening to you. But rejoice in so far as you share Christ's sufferings" (4:12-13).

Often when we encounter suffering or difficulty in life, we ask ourselves, "Why did this happen to me?" or "What did I do to deserve this?" as if any suffering in life is unfair, unwarranted, unexpected.

Today's scripture suggests that suffering may be the mark of a Christian. Rather than being the unmaking of a Christian, suffering forms us into the sort of people who, in our sufferings, resemble Christ. The cross is still the mark of discipleship.

In fact, if our faith has never caused us any suffering, we may need to question our faithfulness.

A few years ago, my church was the host of a Christian family from Korea. The husband was a Presbyterian pastor of a fairly large congregation in a large Korean city. He was well-educated, handsome, and a leader within the church there. But trouble started when he began critizing the repressive policies of his government.

"Stick to saving souls and stay out of politics," advised some of his friends. Some leaders in his church accused him of being unpatriotic. His family became the subject of government surveillance and harassment. Eventually, he was hounded out of his native land. He now sought refuge in a foreign country.

Listening to his testimony made me wonder. Have we American Christians grown so self-satisfied and complacent, so timid and lethargic that we are in danger of forfeiting our claim of faithfulness to the gospel? Does our lack of persecution arise because everything in our society is already good or because we have made an easy peace with the dominant values of that society and don't want to rock the boat?

"It is a great privilege to suffer for the sake of Christ," said our Korean friend. "This puts us at the very heart of his gospel. It reminds us of how Christ suffered for us. What I am going through is the typical way our faith has grown and endured through the ages."

His testimony is one with that of today's scripture: "If one suffers as a Christian, let him not be ashamed, but under that name let him glorify God. For the time has come for judgment to begin with the household of God" (4:16-17).

A Faithful Creator

It's enough to make a person ask how those early Christians could endure pain, persecution, even death itself and still speak of rejoicing in the midst of their suffering (4:13).

Rejoice? How can one rejoice when one is on the receiving end of social disapproval, ostracism, governmental persecution, economic injustice? It doesn't feel like a time for rejoicing. It feels more like a time for tears and the self-pitying, soul-searching, "What did I do wrong?"

Curiously, when these early Christians encountered persecution, their "fiery ordeal," they could ask, in effect, "What did I do *right*?" How did my meager witness, my little actions and words, win me a place alongside Christ in his suffering? Not everyone gets the opportunity to suffer for and with Christ, even as he suffered for us. What did I do to be worthy of this honor?

Of course, this is a very different way of viewing social disapproval, ostracism, governmental persecution, economic injustice, and the other sources of suffering a faithful Christian might face.

It is the point of view engendered by a faith which knows the truth and is willing to pay the cost for witnessing to that truth. It is a hope that is based upon something more substantial than the approval or disapproval of other people, a hope that is able to rejoice, even in suffering, because it believes the truth of the word.

"Therefore let those who suffer according to God's will do right and entrust their souls to a faithful Creator" (4:19).

Helping Adults Become Involved—Robert G. Rogers

Preparing to Teach

In this second lesson in the series on Christian hope, you should try to help class members see that the hope that Christian faith provides should enable us to live confidently even in the face of adversity or suffering. Before class, try to think of persons of faith who have lived difficult lives, those whose example you can commend to the class. One thinks immediately of Albert Schweitzer or Martin Luther King or other well-known figures. You might also find less-heralded examples in a church periodical or magazine. How do humans learn to live heroically? What role does their faith play in giving them strength?

In addition to reading over the assigned lesson, you should study the account of Jesus' suffering in the garden of Gethsemane (Mark 14:32-42). What role did faith play in his willingness to accept the suffering of the cross?

Introducing the Main Question

What does it "cost" to follow one's Christian convictions? The story told by Dr. Willimon is a powerful example of personal suffering stemming from doing the right thing and making the Christian choice. The life of religious conviction is not lived in a safe, remote castle; rather, it is spent in the world, living with the harsh realities of decision making. Hard choices bring consequences which we might like to avoid if we could. So it was with Jesus in Gethsemane!

Help members of the class see for themselves the implications of today's lesson. Are there pressures on Christians in your town such as those faced by the sales manager in the story? Are Christians tempted to go along with the prevailing values (even if they are wrong) so as not to "rock the boat"? How do we determine what our priorities should be as followers of Christ? Perhaps members of your class would be willing to share some of the difficult decisions they face as Christians. You might have an example of your own to begin the discussion.

Developing the Lesson

Acknowledge the variety of difficult, even painful, decisions Christians face, and use this to serve as background for the remainder of the lesson. Specifically, you might deal with the topic in three ways:

I. Difficult decisions and suffering
II. Suffering as act of piety
III. Confident Christian living

I. Difficult decisions and suffering

It would be helpful to discuss with the class the relationship that exists between decision making and suffering. That is, how we decide to act may well result in personal pain or suffering. Refer to the example of the salesman in "The Main Question." What forms might such suffering take: social? financial? physical? One's personal "stand" might lead to social ostracism (being shunned by friends and associates) or financial ruin or perhaps emotional or physical disability. What is the "cost"? How do we personally feel about such risks? These and other questions might help the class struggle with the pros and cons of personal decisions within their own individual situations.

Remember, each person finally has to decide for himself or herself what action to take as based on Christian conscience. There will be honest differences of opinion among the members of your class. Your role is to aid them in thinking about the issue, not to tell them what specific choice to make. Of course, it would be appropriate to emphasize the potential danger of a "watered-down gospel" if Christians become too comfortable and complacent, unwilling to take risks for the sake of Christ.

II. Suffering as act of piety

Assuming that class members are now thinking about Christian risk taking, try to help them see that accepting the suffering that results from a moral choice is, in fact, an act of Christian piety (or worship). Initially, you might refer to the example of Jesus' suffering in Gethsemane. Briefly retell the story to refresh class members' memories. Note that even Jesus did not wish to suffer pain if it were not necessary. Yet he asserted God's will for him; this assertion was an act of piety, a sign of his love for God. Use the story of Jesus as a model for class members to consider. Not all Christians are called to be crucified, but do we individually have our "Gethsemanes"?

Do we offer our struggle and our suffering to God as a statement of our Christian faith?

Next, turn to the example of Christian martyrs down through the ages. Not all Christians will be placed in such dire situations as the martyrs, but it is good to reflect on their examples and derive courage from their acts of devotion to the cause of the gospel. To facilitate discussion, you might remind the class of the first Christian martyr, Stephen (Acts 7:54-60). Or perhaps you would prefer to mention some contemporary martyrs if you have had an opportunity to think about this before class time. Try to avoid presenting the martyrs as superhumans. They were not! In most instances they were ordinary Christians who made difficult choices.

III. Confident Christian living

In the last portion of the class, you should first emphasize God's eternal love as response to the suffering endured by faithful Christians. Beyond the problems, anxieties, and, yes—suffering of this world is a God who cares about us. He is One to whom our pain and suffering are not the final answer. Just as the agony of Gethsemane and the suffering on the cross were not the final chapter in the life of Jesus, so the resurrection of Jesus provides for Christians the foundation of hope for eternal life beyond our present sufferings. We too can affirm that our suffering is only temporary in the light of eternity.

You should also mention the role of the local congregation in providing the support and encouragement necessary for confident Christian living. Not all Christians will make the same decision or be willing to take risks to the same degree. Yet, can we find ways to support one another in exploring and making the hard moral choices? Do we love and affirm one another as people of God even if not all persons in the congregation choose the same path? Try to involve the class in discussion of these and related questions. Probably no issue tests the quality of church fellowship any more criticially than our ability to support another's moral decision when it differs from one we would make. Yet, even Jesus urged the disciples (and us?) to make free decisions about what to believe and how to act.

Helping Class Members Act

I Peter 3:14-15 would be helpful verses to commit to memory as they are a good summary of today's lesson. Suggest that class members think about specific ways for your church to support every person in his or her Christian decision making. How can we be accountable to one another without being judgmental?

Planning for Next Sunday

Suggest that the class read the entire second letter of Peter as background for the lesson on Christian hope and waiting. Psalm 23 might also be helpful scripture as they think about the topic. Ask them to think about their feelings when waiting for someone or something to come. This is especially good to do during Lent.

A Hope Worth Waiting For

Background Scripture: II Peter

The Main Question—William H. Willimon

Much of our life is spent waiting for somebody or something.

I write these notes while sitting in an airport waiting room filled with folk who are waiting for the belated arrival of Flight #329. Looking about the room, it is obvious that many have had enough of this waiting. A tired little child is beginning to fuss and stamp his feet. His beleaguered mother is growing cross and irritable with him. A businesswoman across from me is lighting up her third cigarette; the man beside her stares dejectedly at the ceiling. When will our flight finally come?

It is not easy to wait. I am an impatient person who wants everything when I want it, *now*. I suppose that I share this impatience with many other Americans. We are a land of fast cars, instant oatmeal, microwave cooking, and minute steaks. We hate to wait. We pride ourselves on our push-button efficiency and the speed with which we can travel from one place to the next.

When I was a student in the 1960s, *Time* magazine called us the "New Generation." We wanted peace, justice, harmony, equality, affluence *now* and we were angry when we did not get it on demand.

How far away is the ancient world of the second letter of Peter from the world of this airport waiting room! How quaint seems that world of emperors and ancient customs when I compare it with this jet-age world where I make my home!

Or is it?

These first Christians knew what it meant to wait, to wait and wait and still not see their hopes fulfilled. Their initial excitement over Christ's resurrection had cooled. Now they waited for final deliverance. They waited and hoped.

And so do we.

As You Read the Scripture—Mike Winters

II Peter. The question of authorship of II Peter is not a recent one. The earliest church writers in the second and third centuries disputed Peter's authorship.

The letter is addressed to those who have believed. Whether addressed to specific people or a specific church is not clear. Perhaps some of the readers were recipients of I Peter, as suggested by II Peter 3:1.

The author's purpose is to condemn the teaching which rejected the Second Coming of Christ. Second Peter links the moral fabric of society to the correct teachings of the faith. False prophets and false teachers will be judged accordingly.

Verses 3-11. Reliance on the great promises of God is the source of life. Failure to rely brings corruption to our lives. Second Peter calls the readers to supplement their faith with love and virtue. This is essential for all who would be effective and fruitful in the faith.

239

Verses 12-21. These verses may be condensed to say that II Peter has something very important to say. Here the message of II Peter is validated.

Chapter 2:1-10a. False prophets have always deluded the people with false teachings. False prophets always dilute the strong words that are too hard to accept. They in fact lie, and their lie is often the easy way—the way the weak and unwary would go. Read Jeremiah's bout with the false prophet Hananiah in Jeremiah. The false prophets are always destroyed in the end (Jeremiah 28:17).

Verses 10b-22. Here is a stark and vivid picture of the tyranny of these false p˙ ᴐphets. They are hedonistic, lawless, and irreverent. See Jude 8, which says, "these men in their dreamings defile the flesh, reject authority, and revile the glorious one."

Chapter 3:1-2. First Peter is certainly the intended reference to another letter. (I Peter 1:10-12 are "the predictions of the holy prophets.")

Verses 3-4. The day of the Lord's coming is in question here. Evidently, scoffers ridiculed the notion of Christ's coming. The delay of the Second Coming (*parousia*, in the Greek) was a critical problem for the early church. The church had to begin to deal with the apparent delay of his return. The *parousia* is the time when Christ will come in power and glory for the purpose of judging the world. The *parousia* would mark the end of the present age. The expectation of the members of the early church was that Christ would return *in their lifetime*. As time went by and the first Christians ("the fathers") died, they had to rethink their expectation and give an answer to the scoffers who began to chide them. II Peter 3:8 counsels wisely, "With the Lord one day is as a thousand years."

Verses 5-6. The author is convinced of the power of God to create and the power of God to destroy (as evidenced in the allusion to the great flood).

Verse 7. God will once again destroy the ungodly.

Verse 8. The scoffers chide the believer because of the delay of the *parousia*, but here the believer is given the fact of God's eternal rule. The *parousia* may be delayed, but in God's plan it is still close at hand.

Verse 9. The reason for the *parousia's* delay is God's patience with sinners. God waits, hoping that all should repent before the end.

Verse 10. The day of the Lord will come when least expected.

Verses 11-13. The kingdom of God, the new heaven and new earth, await those who endure till the day of the Lord.

Verses 14-18. Knowing of and waiting for God's kingdom, the faithful are exhorted toward holiness with patience. The delay of the *parousia* only means the repentance and inclusion of more in God's new kingdom.

Selected Scripture

King James Version

Revised Standard Version

II Peter 3:1-13

1 This second epistle, beloved, I now write unto you; in *both* which I stir up your pure minds by way of remembrance:

2 That ye may be mindful of the words which were spoken before by the holy prophets, and of the com-

II Peter 3:1-13

1 This is now the second letter that I have written to you, beloved, and in both of them I have aroused your sincere mind by way of reminder; 2 that you should remember the predictions of the holy prophets and the commandment of

mandment of us the apostles of the Lord and Saviour:

3 Knowing this first, that there shall come in the last days scoffers, walking after their own lusts,

4 And saying, Where is the promise of his coming? for since the fathers fell asleep, all things continue as *they were* from the beginning of the creation.

5 For this they willingly are ignorant of, that by the word of God the heavens were of old, and the earth standing out of the water and in the water:

6 Whereby the world that then was, being overflowed with water, perished:

7 But the heavens and the earth, which are now, by the same word are kept in store, reserved unto fire against the day of judgment and perdition of ungodly men.

8 But, beloved, be not ignorant of this one thing, that one day *is* with the Lord as a thousand years, and a thousand years as one day.

9 The Lord is not slack concerning his promise, as some men count slackness; but is longsuffering to us-ward, not willing that any should perish, but that all should come to repentance.

10 But the day of the Lord will come as a thief in the night; in the which the heavens shall pass away with a great noise, and the elements shall melt with fervent heat, the earth also and the works that are therein shall be burned up.

11 *Seeing* then *that* all these things shall be dissolved, what manner of *persons* ought ye to be in *all* holy conversation and godliness,

12 Looking for and hasting unto the coming of the day of God, wherein the heavens being on fire shall be dissolved, and the elements shall melt with fervent heat?

13 Nevertheless we, according to his promise, look for new heavens

the Lord and Savior through your apostles. 3 First of all you must understand this, that scoffers will come in the last days with scoffing, following their own passions 4 and saying, "Where is the promise of his coming? For ever since the fathers fell asleep, all things have continued as they were from the beginning of creation." 5 They deliberately ignore this fact, that by the word of God heavens existed long ago, and an earth formed out of water and by means of water, 6 through which the world that then existed was deluged with water and perished. 7 But by the same word the heavens and earth that now exist have been stored up for fire, being kept until the day of judgment and destruction of ungodly men.

8 But do not ignore this one fact, beloved, that with the Lord one day is as a thousand years, and a thousand years as one day. 9 The Lord is not slow about his promise as some count slowness, but is forbearing toward you, not wishing that any should perish, but that all should reach repentance. 10 But the day of the Lord will come like a thief, and then the heavens will pass away with a loud noise, and the elements will be dissolved with fire, and the earth and the works that are upon it will be burned up.

11 Since all these things are thus to be dissolved, what sort of persons ought you to be in lives of holiness and godliness, 12 waiting for and hastening the coming of the day of God, because of which the heavens will be kindled and dissolved, and the elements will melt with fire! 13 But according to his promise we wait for new heavens and a new earth in which righteousness dwells.

and a new earth, wherein dwelleth righteousness.

Key Verse: The Lord is not slack concerning his promise, as some men count slackness; but is long-suffering to us-ward, not willing that any should perish, but that all should come to repentance. (II Peter 3:9)

Key Verse: The Lord is not slow about his promise as some count slowness, but is forbearing toward you, not wishing that any should perish, but that all should reach repentance. (II Peter 3:9)

The Scripture and the Main Question—William H. Willimon

Since You Wait

The second letter of Peter may have been the last book of the New Testament. Scholars believe that it was written nearly one hundred years after the earthly ministry of Jesus; written to a waiting church.

Put yourself in the situation of these ancient Christians. For nearly a hundred years the church had been waiting for the promised return of Christ. Christ had come and gone. Now they awaited Christ's Second Coming. Now their main concern was when that coming would occur. It had been a long, slow wait.

To these disappointed, despairing, disillusioned, short-of-hope Christians, this letter attempted to bring comfort and encouragement.

Can you feel how hard it must have been for the early Christians to wait? Christ had come, died, and risen. The New Age had dawned. But what had changed? In this long one hundred years of waiting, a couple of generations of Christians had lived and died in the faith, in the hope that Christ would come soon. In one hundred years of waiting they were still a small, struggling, unheralded, persecuted band of believers clinging to a hope which the pagan world thought to be ridiculous. Year after year with no return, no end, no deliverance, no sign of when Christ would finally come.

Can you feel how hard it must have been for them to wait? I think we can. Now nearly two thousand years have come and gone and Christ still has not returned. The world looks at the church which proclaims the redemption of the world—and yet why doesn't the world look more redeemed?

How pitifully little the world has changed in these two thousand years. There are wars and rumors of wars. Evil still parades about in the guise of oppressive regimes, petty dictators, and military might. There are still poverty, hunger, sickness, suffering. Who doesn't get discouraged and disillusioned while waiting for two thousand years for all this to end?

For us, and for those ancient Christians, waiting is one of the most difficult tasks.

"I could believe in your Redeemer," said Friedrich Nietzsche to the Christians of his day, "if only the world looked more redeemed."

Do you remember the play by Samuel Beckett entitled *Waiting for Godot?* Two characters sit on a park bench and talk and wait for a man called Godot, a man who never comes. They wait, kill time, and talk, but Godot nevers shows. Some say this is a kind of parable about Christians waiting for God. We wait, cool our heels, talk, kill time, but God does not come. Wherein is our hope in this long time of waiting?

The Lord Is Not Slow

What was the word to these earliest of Christians waiters? "But do not ignore this one fact, beloved, that with the Lord one day is as a thousand years, and a thousand years as one day. The Lord is not slow about his promise as some count slowness, but is forbearing toward you, not wishing that any should perish, but that all should reach repentance" (II Peter 3:8-9).

Delay is not proof that the Lord is not coming, for God is eternal and does not measure time as we do. We measure the passages of hours and days by our limited human perspective. We grow impatient because we are only able to see as far as our own span of time.

Any of us who have young children know that their experience of time is conditioned by their brief life. "How much farther do we have to go, Mommy?" they ask before the car had hardly had time to leave the garage on a trip.

"You will go to the birthday party in one hour," we tell them. That hour seems like an eternity to a five-year-old who waits for the big event. Do you remember, when you were a child, that someone told you she was thirty-five years old? You thought, "Will I ever be *that* old?" Now thirty-five doesn't seem old at all! It all depends on your perspective.

The writer of the second letter of Peter reminds the waiting Christians that it all depends on your perspective. Seen from our perspective, the promised completion of God's work which was begun in Christ seems to be taking forever. But remember that "with the Lord one day is as a thousand years." Like little children, we grow impatient, lose heart, and give up hope because of our limited vision.

Besides, there is more at stake in our failure to keep heart during our wait than simply our limited human perspective on time. The delay of Christ's promised return is partly due not to the Lord's unfaithfulness but to his faithfulness. God is said to be "forbearing toward you, not wishing that any should perish" (II Peter 3:9). If only a few were to be saved and reached with the good news of the gospel, then things might as well be ended now. But this is not the way God wants it to work. Others must also be brought to the light, others must be reached with the good news, others must be invited into the kingdom. So there is still time, still time to wait—and to work.

We have a terrible expression in our speech—"killing time." For most of us, that is exactly what our times of waiting are—killing time. We simply cool our heels, twiddle our thumbs, take a nap, and do nothing. But the writer implies that our times of waiting can be times of importance for us. As the writer says, this time to wait is an important time of witness, activism, and outreach for the church. God has graciously given us this time so "that all should reach repentance" (3:9).

Think back in your own life when time to wait has been redeemed as important time for you—not simply time to kill time. The doctor told you that you would have a two-month recuperation period from your operation. You wondered to yourself what in the world you would do with that much time on your hands. But, to your surprise, your time of recuperation was a time of restoration, recovery, and renewal—not just in body but also in spirit. I still remember my recuperation from a serious illness. For the first (and, alas, last) time in my life I had time to simply sit, look out on the activity of the birds in the yard, and do nothing. Of course, I wasn't really "doing nothing." Rather, I was doing something I had never had time to do before—enjoy the world of nature.

So many of our times of waiting are experiences of "killing time" because we see these intervals in our lives not as an opportunity but as a curse. So, the writer of Second Peter says, "Use this time to the fullest. Be about the work God has given you to do. Redeem this time of waiting by making it a time of witness so that others might be brought to the same faith which you now have."

Time to Wait

The church is now in the Christian season of Lent—the forty-day period before Easter. During these forty days, the church has traditionally stressed the need for proper preparation of ourselves so that we will be ready for the full significance of the Easter miracle when it comes in a few weeks.

Alas, we modern Americans hate to wait for anything. We want it all now, at the snap of a finger, with the push of a button. We want salvation, maturity, happiness, joy now and we don't want to wait for them at all. We are like impatient children who are spoiled by having indulgent parents who jump at every beck and call.

But life isn't like that, is it? Most of the things that are worthwhile in life require waiting. A good marriage, the birth of a child, growing up, the end of school, good friends—the most important things in life take time. We are often disappointed by the superficiality of it all.

As Christians we are waiting for something deep, abiding, and eternal—the salvation of the world, the completion of that divine work which was begun in the stable at Bethlehem, the making of a new heaven and earth. You don't get that sort of revolution in a moment—it takes time.

But we want things on our terms, on our own time, not in God's good time. We expect everything to be made over and finished in a moment, in the snap of a finger. Patience is still an essential virtue for God's people. But it is a virtue in which we need constant training.

You might take a moment to ask your class what it might do to use this forty-day Lenten time of waiting to good advantage, so that it is more than simply killing time. Many churches find that Lent is a good time to visit inactive members or to put forth a special emphasis on attracting new members. When they do this, they find that the end of the Lenten season, Easter Day, is a time of true renewal and new birth for them because of the preparation and work they have put in during the days before Easter.

Lent is also a good time for a renewal of our personal devotional life. Some congregations sponsor daily Bible-reading programs or publish special Lenten devotional materials for individuals and families to use each day during this season. Waiting time need not be wasted time.

And so we wait, as the Christians waited in a time so long ago for a return of their Savior. We too wait for that time of final redemption and consummation. We also wait throughout our lives for the arrival of big and little events. Life is waiting. As we have said, that wait can be hard, long, frustrating, and depressing.

But this waiting time can also be a time of rediscovery, renewal, restoration, and witness. What makes the difference? It seems to depend on how you look at it. Our hope is not in some minor event, not in some temporary plan for human betterment. Our hope is in the work of the Lord, and that work takes time—God's own good time. So we wait in hope, knowing that, in all our days, God is still at work, even as God has been at work in all the ages past.

We wait according to his promise to make all things new, even us! We are the ones who "wait for new heavens and a new earth in which righteousness dwells" (3:13).

Helping Adults Become Involved—Robert G. Rogers

Preparing to Teach

As you begin preparing for class, remember the special significance of waiting during the Lenten period. As you read II Peter, look for elements of Christian hope present even during the time of the church's waiting for the Lord. Your aim should be to help the class learn to find meaning in waiting so that each day becomes a time of preparation for the coming that God has promised.

As you asked the class at the end of last week's session, so you too should analyze how you react to waiting. Think about how different people respond to waiting. (Dr. Willimon suggests a few ways in "The Main Question.") How is Lent a special time of waiting? Does our knowing what is to come affect our time of waiting?

A chalkboard or large writing pad should also be available for recording different views on the meaning of waiting.

Introducing the Main Question

Begin class by reading aloud the first line of Dr. Willimon's "The Main Question." "Much of our life is spent waiting for somebody or something." All of us can identify with his statement. And, if we are truthful about it, we usually regard waiting time as wasted. We want to get on with our personal business, but someone or something delays us. Our response is often one of frustration, even anger. How dare someone interfere with our time!

Probably everyone in the class has feelings like those just described. Yet waiting is a fundamental dimension of the Christian faith. We are in the midst of Lent, waiting for God's drama of salvation to be reenacted. We wait for the kingdom of God, for the time of true love and fellowship among all peoples. Like the early Christians described in II Peter, we wait for Jesus to come again! How can we turn a time of waiting into a time of preparation? Ask the class to think about ways to foster patience and hope during the period of waiting.

Developing the Lesson

If class members have ideas about ways to make a waiting period more meaningful, record these on the chalkboard or writing pad. If not, move into the lesson and divide it into the following portions:

I. We respond to a delay.
II. Important things take time.
III. Use waiting time creatively.

I. We respond to a delay.

Spend a few moments finding out class views on the Second Coming and its delay. Do they believe their Christian faith is diminished somewhat because Jesus has not come again? Do you feel the same anxieties on the question as did the early Christians described in II Peter? There may well be different points of view in your class, and you should be careful that no one member is made to feel that his or her view is unimportant. Perhaps some members will speak of the coming kingdom of God while others prefer to use the more traditional idea of the Second Coming of Jesus. It is quite possible that, in terms of Christian hope, both views affirm much the same idea: the belief that God is at work in the world, bringing salvation to those who respond in faith.

Remind the class that even though Jesus has not come again, nor has the kingdom come in its fullest sense; nevertheless, there is good reason for Christian hope. The God who moves history toward his ultimate purposes is the same God who created and sustains the universe and everything within it. A "delay" does not mean that nothing is happening in the meantime! Ask members to share ways they believe God is acting within history today.

II. Important things take time.

In this portion note the distinction between God's time and human time. Whereas we want things to happen right away, that is not the way most important events occur, even within the human sphere. It takes time for a love relationship to bloom and mature into a lasting bond. It requires years for the full promise of a child to come to fruition in young manhood or womanhood. Point out these models as good examples from a human perspective of the way God's plan for the world is unfolding. Things worth waiting for take time. It is our problem, not God's, that we are so anxious to have things happen right now.

You need to acknowledge that the process of movement toward God's kingdom seems painfully slow at times and even difficult to discern. Yet, our Christian hope rests in God's promises to redeem. A good passage to summarize for your class at this time is Romans 8:18-25. Paul, too, acknowledged the frustration involved in waiting. Yet, with him, does not our faith also rest on the sure knowledge that God, in his time, is saving us? Notice particularly two sentences in Romans: "Now hope that is seen is not hope. For who hopes for what he sees?" Have the class ponder for a moment the meaning of those verses. How can we bolster others' faith at those moments when we seek proof on our own terms and do not find it? How can we open our lives to seeing new and unexpected ways in which God is at work? Discuss.

III. Use waiting time creatively.

Now you want to move the class toward a consideration of how to use our present time in the best way. In brief, while waiting for God's final plan to be completed, what should Christians be doing? Remind the class of Dr. Willimon's highlighted expression: "killing time." Point out that this is the worst possible response, for it says that the present time we have (really a gift from God) is useless! Yet if as Christians we believe that God is Lord over all history, how can even the present age be of no value? Does not every moment of life have meaning if we attempt to use it well?

The key word for Christians to consider while waiting is *preparation.* Have the class share for a few moments various implications of the word. In faith, we are preparing for life beyond the grave; by our actions we are helping prepare the way for God's coming kingdom on earth. The present takes on added meaning when viewed from the perspective of God's future. Remind your people of the parable of the rich fool (Luke 12:16-21). Jesus tells us that the present is to be used not to acquire riches for ourselves, but to be rich toward God. In attempting to be "rich toward God," are we not using the time of delay as an opportunity for preparation?

Helping Class Members Act

Have the class memorize II Peter 3:9. This will remind them that sharing the good news with others is a way to consciously use time well.

Suggest that class members keep a personal time log for several days to determine their use of time. This might remind them that present time is a gift from God to be used creatively.

Planning for Next Sunday

The next class session is Palm Sunday, and the topic links Christian hope with action. Ask the class to read the assigned scripture: I John 1–3. Suggest that they also read Mark 11:1-10, the story of Jesus' entry into Jerusalem.

Class participants should reflect on the meaning of Palm Sunday as a deed that publicly identifies Jesus as the Messiah.

LESSON 4   MARCH 23

A Hope Leading to Action

Background Scripture: I John 1–3

The Main Question—William H. Willimon

"Who tells you who you are?" asked the preacher for the day. His was a stirring question. Who gives us our identity?

Many speak of an "identity crisis" among people in today's world. People do not know who they are. They are a conflicting mass of costumes, masks, quick-change postures, and different names and roles, a patchwork quilt of personality. "Who am I?" they ask.

The teenager's quest for identity has become stretched out over many decades in a person's life. Men and women in middle age go through the midlife crisis, in which they change roles, switch personalities, uproot themselves, and move on to some other life-style. Who are we?

Who tells us who we are? A host of philosophies, pop-psychologies, clubs, organizations, cults, and religions compete for our allegiance. All propose, in some way or another, to tell us who we are. You are a consumer, a spender of money, a covetor of all the gadgets, possessions, and things that make up the "good life." You are mostly a sexual being, lusting and lusted after. You are mostly a brain, a thinking, reasoning, detached bundle of nerve cells. You are . . .

And the answers go on and on, all proposing to solve our identity crisis, tell us who we are and what we ought to be doing.

So much of the New Testament, when you think about it, is concerned with questions of identity. To these first Christians, it was crucially important to be careful that you answer to the right name, adopted the right values, and kept your eyes fixed on the right goals.

Who tells you who you are? Today's scripture has a definite answer to that crucial question. "See what love the Father has given us, that we should be called children of God; and so we are" (I John 3:1).

As You Read the Scripture—Mike Winters

II John 1–3. First John is a pastoral letter written in the same style as the Gospel of John. First John is written to encourage the faithful in their spiritual walk (chapters 2 and 3). First John also sought to correct the Gnostic/Docetic heresy, which denied the humanity of Jesus (chapter 4).

A word about the Gnostic heresy: Gnostics were either libertines or ascetics. They devalued the human body and set it over against the soul. Therefore, it did not matter if one sinned in the body or did not sin in the body. It simply did not affect the condition of the soul.

Chapter 1:1-4. The introduction asks the reader to reach back to the cosmic beginning. Compare this look back to the beginning in 1:1 with Genesis 1:1 and John 1:1. Interestingly enough, at this point in the church's history, the divinity of Jesus was not in question. It was his *humanity* that had to be defended. Here I John declares that the evidence of the humanity of Jesus of Nazareth is verified by eyewitnesses.

Verse 3. The knowledge of God through Jesus Christ is the basis for the fellowship of the church as well as the basis for life. John says, "In him was life."

Verses 5-10. In these verses are five conditional phrases which dramatically contrast life in darkness with life in light. John 1:4-5 similarly underscore the potency of light. In darkness we are deceived, but in light the truth is made known.

Verses 8-9. Everyone has sinned. Compare Romans 3:23. Admitting sin is the first step to righteous living.

Chapter 2:1. The goal of Christian living, stated negatively, is to live without sinning. Stated positively, the purpose of life in Jesus Christ is to dive headlong into obedience to God. And if in rash, impetuous obedience one should sin, Christ will intercede.

Verse 2. The power of the atonement is sufficient not only to atone for the sins of those who believe, but also for the whole world.

Verses 3-4. Gnostics were preoccupied with "knowledge." In what does true knowledge of God consist? "Obedience" is the answer given here. Genuine knowledge of God changes the way we live our lives.

Verses 5-6. Obedience to God is summed up in the command to love. The model for obedience is Jesus Christ.

Verses 7-11. The new commandment is an old commandment: "love." Those who do not love walk in darkness. This is a stern warning to Gnostics who connect light with good and darkness with evil.

Verses 12-14. This message is to everyone: little children, fathers, young men.

Verses 15-17. Deuteronomy 6:5, James 2:8, and John 15:12 summarize the "royal law" to love God and to love one another.

Verses 18-27. The false teachers who have come among them are Christ's opponents (Antichrist). These would-be deceivers are self-deceived.

Verses 28-29. Having been warned about the deceivers, I John exhorts his readers to abide in Christ. Apart from him they can do nothing. Only as they are grafted into Christ through faith can they do Christ's will, and thus only then can they be ready for the *parousia*. John 15:1-11 speaks of this grafting and suggests that those who are grafted in Christ bear the fruit of love.

Chapter 3:1. Jesus was not received well by his own townspeople (John 1:11). The children of God should expect no better.

Verses 2-3. The church is already the Body of Christ. When Christ appears, it will be obvious who we are. Colossians 3:4 says. "When Christ who is our life appears, then you also will appear with him in glory."

Verses 4-10. The children of God live righteously as Christ did. This is how God's people are known.

Verses 11-18. The message is love. The command is love. Obedience is love for one another—costly, sacrificial love.

Verses 19-24. The work of God is faith in Jesus Christ, whom God has sent (see John 6:28-29).

Selected Scripture

King James Version

I John 2:1-6

1 My little children, these things write I unto you, that ye sin not. And if any man sin, we have an advocate with the Father, Jesus Christ the righteous:

2 And he is the propitiation for our sins: and not for ours only, but also for *the sins of* the whole world.

3 And hereby we do know that we know him, if we keep his commandments.

4 He that saith, I know him, and keepeth not his commandments, is a liar, and the truth is not in him.

5 But whoso keepeth his word, in him verily is the love of God perfected: hereby know we that we are in him.

6 He that saith he abideth in him ought himself also so to walk, even as he walked.

I John 2:28-29

28 And now, little children, abide in him; that, when he shall appear, we may have confidence, and not be ashamed before him at his coming.

29 If ye know that he is righteous, ye know that every one that doeth righteousness is born of him.

Revised Standard Version

I John 2:1-6

1 My little children, I am writing this to you so that you may not sin; but if any one does sin, we have an advocate with the Father, Jesus Christ the righteous; 2 and he is the expiation for our sins, and not for ours only but also for the sins of the whole world. 3 And by this we may be sure that we know him, if we keep his commandments. 4 He who says "I know him" but disobeys his commandments is a liar, and the truth is not in him; 5 but whoever keeps his word, in him truly love for God is perfected. By this we may be sure that we are in him: 6 he who says he abides in him ought to walk in the same way in which he walked.

I John 2:28-29

28 And now, little children, abide in him, so that when he appears we may have confidence and not shrink from him in shame at his coming. 29 If you know that he is righteous, you may be sure that every one who does right is born of him.

I John 3:1-3

1 Behold, what manner of love the Father hath bestowed upon us, that we should be called the sons of God: therefore the world knoweth us not, because it knew him not.

2 Beloved, now are we the sons of God, and it doth not yet appear what we shall be: but we know that, when he shall appear, we shall be like him; for we shall see him as he is.

3 And every man that hath this hope in him purifieth himself, even as he is pure.

Key Verse: **Abide in him; that, when he shall appear, we may have confidence, and not be ashamed before him at his coming. (I John 2:28)**

I John 3:1-3

1 See what love the Father has given us, that we should be called children of God; and so we are. The reason why the world does not know us is that it did not know him.

2 Beloved, we are God's children now; it does not yet appear what we shall be, but we know that when he appears we shall be like him, for we shall see him as he is. 3 And every one who thus hopes in him purifies himself as he is pure.

Key Verse: **Abide in him, so that when he appears we may have confidence and not shrink from him in shame at his coming. (I John 2:28)**

The Scripture and the Main Question—William H. Willimon

If Anyone Does Sin

Most scholars believe that I John was written toward the close of the first century. This means that it was written to a congregation or congregations within the early church during a time when the church was becoming an established institution.

Many early Christians, as we know from earlier lessons in this unit, expected Christ to return very soon. But that did not happen. Now, in I John, Christians are coming to terms with the fact that the church will not be a short-lived phenomenon. The church will be here for a while. How then should the church conduct itself while it waits in hope?

This is the context for the concerns of today's scripture. Evidently, many early Christians had thought that when a person becomes a Christian, that person is no longer capable of sin. Baptism washes away the person's tendency toward sin and makes the person pure and sinless.

Unfortunately that pure, spotless, sinless condition was not the way it worked out. Even after baptism, even after a sincere effort to commit one's life totally to Christ, people still fell into sin. What then?

The church could have gone in a number of different directions. Some probably advocated excommunicating the offender, throwing him or her out of the church for good. We know from early church documents that this was sometimes done. After all, aren't Christians supposed to live sinless lives?

There was another way, and it seems to be the way which is advocated in today's lesson from I John. "If we say we have no sin, we deceive ourselves" (1:8). Remember, these words are being written to *Christians*. Right at the beginning of this treatise, the author admits that Christians are capable of sin.

The writer then states that these words are being written "that you may not sin" (2:1). Lest someone think that just by obeying the admonitions of this letter, he or she will keep pure and spotless, free from any possibility of sin, the writer is quick to add, "But if any one does sin, we have an advocate with the Father, Jesus Christ the righteous" (2:1).

Sin among Christians is a fact. You may not want it to be that way; there may be perfectly good reasons why it should not be that way; but it is.

"Christians aren't perfect, just forgiven" says a bumper sticker I saw the other day. I am not big on bumper stickers, but I think that is a good one. At least it is one which is in line with our scripture today.

Sometimes people criticize the church by saying that they wouldn't join the church because "the church is full of hypocrites." Well, the church is full of sinners, and some of our sins are part of the sin of hypocrisy. But these people outside the church make the mistake of assuming that this is somehow a criticism of the church, as if we are embarrassed by our collection of sinners.

The church does not claim to be a collection of the pure and the sinless. We claim to be a collection of sinners who are forgiven and reconciled to God. The church is full of sinners, forgiven sinners who are filled with the hope of living better lives.

A family once left the church I was serving because a person in the congregation had "insulted us over the telephone one night." Now I do not condone rudeness, unkindness, and insults in people's conversations. But, people being what they are, this sometimes happens. So what do we do?

Evidently the family was surprised that someone, especially someone who is a Christian, would allow himself to talk like this. I was not too surprised. I knew that this person had been under a great deal of pressure at work lately. That didn't excuse his rudeness—but it did help me to be a bit more understanding toward his behavior.

The thing that disturbed me was that the family was unable to understand or to forgive this person. They were angry and hurt and left the church. I wish that they could have seen this episode as an opportunity to practice what the church is always preaching—not that we are perfect people, but that we are people who always stand in need of forgiveness. "We have an advocate with the Father, Jesus Christ the righteous; and he is the expiation for our sins, and not for ours only but also for the sins of the whole world" (2:1-2).

Children of God

Christian hope has a special quality. It is not based upon our belief that we are, down deep, basically good people who always do good things. It is not based upon who we are. Rather, it is based upon what God has done in Jesus Christ.

Even when we sin, we are still able to have hope and confidence because of something we know about ourselves—we are loved. First John says it so beautifully: "See what love the Father has given us, that we should be called children of God; and so we are" (3:1).

Who tells us who we are?

The Bible tells us who we are. "Jesus loves me, this I know, for the Bible tells me so," we sing as children. We have hope, not in ourselves, but in the power of God's love to overcome our sin, our rebellion, our weaknesses. The writer says that we are "called children of God." We have this relationship with God, not on the basis of our natural endowments or human nature, but because God has called us to be his children. This is who we are. Our identity is a gift of God's love, not our personal achievement.

I suppose that it is true to say that both Christians and non-Christians sin. We all act in ignorance of God's will or in outright rebellion against God's will.

And yet there is a difference between the Christian and the non-Christian. That difference is that a Christian knows who he or she is—a cherished, beloved child of God. And that knowledge makes all the difference.

Like little children we are able to come to our heavenly Father and confess our sins, ask forgiveness, and reach out for love. We are not homeless orphans or nobodies. By the gracious call of God we are somebodies. Our relationship with God is dependent not upon our goodness but upon the goodness of God.

Abide in Him

Christian good works flow from a Christian's identity. As Luther said, you only get apples from an apple tree. You can't pick apples from a thorn bush! Our being precedes our doing.

Sometimes people say, "Well, we may be members of different denominations, but we are all working to go to the same place."

But this statement misunderstands the truth in today's lesson. Christians are not those who are working hard to get somewhere or to make the grade with God; we are those *who have arrived!* We are not nobodies earnestly trying to become somebodies. We are royalty, God's own beloved children.

We don't have to spend our lives trying to prove our love for God because in Jesus God had proved his love for us. This makes all the difference.

So our good deeds are done *because* we are God's children, *not* in order to be God's children. We are simply trying to live in accordance with who we are.

"Everyone who thus hopes in him purifies himself as he is pure" (3:3). We are surprised to find that, day by day, in our attempt to live the Christian life, to simply be whom we are called to be, we become as we have been called—beloved children of God.

We are those who are given a hope and, because of that hope, live lives which are determined by it. It is a hope which does not let us go, even in—especially in—our sin.

As we move through Holy Week this week and move with our Lord toward the cross, let us think upon this and take heart. Even when we betrayed him, he did not cease calling us his children. And so we are.

Helping Adults Become Involved—Robert G. Rogers

Preparing to Teach

The scripture for this week is I John 1–3, but you may wish to read the entire letter. Since this is Palm Sunday, review the story of Jesus' triumphal entry (Mark 11:1-10), which you assigned as suggested reading to the class.

Keep in mind your aim for this lesson: to focus on Christian identity (who we are as a people) and its meaning for our actions in the world. In your preparation try to think of ways in which the identity of Jesus became known—first to his followers, then to the larger world. In what ways do others know us as followers of Jesus Christ?

Remember also that the "arrival" on Palm Sunday is a reminder that God is acting in the world even now—before the end of time. How did Jesus' entry into Jerusalem serve as a vital witness to God's work? How does that act centuries ago continue to offer us hope today?

Introducing the Main Question

Perhaps the thoughtful Christian encounters no more difficult issue than definition of self. By what values do we guide our lives? What are the sources of those values? Do we allow commercial advertising to shape our notion of womanhood? manhood? successful living? Do we conform to what others want us to be? Do labels such as Democrat or Republican or Independent define us?

Are our self-identity and style of living subtly shaped by numerous outside influences? Members of your class will be able to relate to this question. We are constantly bombarded by hidden and not-so-hidden messages telling us how to look and act. How should we, as Christians, respond to these attempts at persuasion? By what values and distinguishing characteristics should Christians be defined? How might the life of Jesus serve as a model to help in our process of self-identity?

Today's lesson focuses on the question, Who tells you who you are? In seeking answers we struggle with the meaning of Christian faith. And the values we affirm—if truly Christlike—are a visible sign to the world of God's love.

Developing the Lesson

Commence by asking the class to identify dominant values that contemporary culture is emphasizing. Read Dr. Willimon's suggestions in "The Main Question." You might suggest others, such as consumerism or the cult of youth. Write the different suggestions on a chalkboard or writing pad so they are visible throughout the class session.

Develop the lesson in three sections:

I. Turning toward Jerusalem
II. Defining who we are
III. Affirming hope through deeds

I. Turning toward Jerusalem

In this section ponder how the major decisions Jesus made in his life told others who he was. Instead of remaining safely in Galilee, he chose willingly to obey the will of God. As Luke 9:51 records: "When the days drew near for him to be received up, he set his face to go to Jerusalem." It was a costly decision, one that demanded his life. Yet it clearly identified for all time who Jesus was!

Encourage the class to think about what dominant values the life of Jesus presented to the world. Specifically, what did (and does) the "Jerusalem decision"—as reflected in Palm Sunday—represent? To begin the discussion, you might suggest that Jesus exemplifies compassion and self-giving. Write class ideas on the board or pad opposite the values of contemporary culture written earlier. The immediate contrast between the two sets of values should be obvious. Jesus was concerned about the needs of others, whereas many contemporary values tend to be of a "me first" mentality.

In his life Jesus acted in accord with the demands of *agape*. This Greek work defines a type of love that is selfless, putting the welfare of another before one's own needs or desires.

II. *Defining who we are*

After letting the class members contemplate for a while the life of Jesus, you will want them to begin consideration of their own lives as Christians. For us in the twentieth century, the example of Jesus is only the beginning point of self-examination. We too have our "Jerusalem decisions" to make. Perhaps they do not have the same devastating consequences as that one made by Jesus, but the major decisions in our lives do matter. By the options we select, we proclaim the values in which we believe. Are we willing to leave the safety of our own little "Galilee" and turn toward "Jerusalem," whatever that may mean for us personally?

Class members may wish to share some of the difficult personal decisions they are facing or have faced. As teacher, you might also be prepared to share an example from your own life. (Be sure that it involves an issue concerning the welfare of other persons rather than one that is oriented toward self.) Acknowledge that such decisions usually involve some personal "cost," even pain. After some moments of sharing have occurred, it might be helfpul to ask how the church fellowship can best support individuals as they face their own "Jerusalem decisions."

Continuing class conversation, you could raise the question: How can we begin to move from a world-centered definition of who we are toward a Christ-centered one? What are the values that we want to hold as Christians? How might these values shape and direct our decisions in life?

III. *Affirming hope through deeds*

In the final portion of the lesson, you are trying to help class members understand that Christian decision making not only helps define who we are; such decisions are necessary precisely because we seek to be followers of Jesus. In the deeds that follow from the decisions that we make, our discipleship is proclaimed. As Dr. Willimon suggests, "Christian good works flow from a Christian's identity." Remind the class that we are enabled to do the right thing not because we are inherently good. Rather, because God first loved us we have the capacity to act. We have experienced his *agape* (love), and this assurance gives us the ability to share that love with others. Indeed, is not the quality of our discipleship diminished if we shy away from those decisions that lead to the sharing of *agape*?

Conclude the lesson by employing again the theme of Christian hope. Our hope is grounded in the conviction that God loves us. We know this especially in the life of Jesus Christ. This knowledge gives us courage to make the difficult choices in life. "By this we know love, that he laid down his life for us; and we ought to lay down our lives for the brethren" (I John 3:16).

Helping Class Members Act

Ask the class to memorize I John 3:18 as a good summary of today's lesson. Pose an issue for them to think about during the coming week. What are specific ways that we/I can support other Christians in their decision making and, in turn, be supported by them in ours/mine?

Planning for Next Sunday

This coming week is Holy Week, a period which is both the most solemn and most joyous occasion in the Christian year. As the class reads I John 4–5, ask them to reflect on the meaning of our "new life in Christ."

You might also suggest that they read the Easter morning account from their favorite gospel. How does the Christian life depend on our participation in his dying and his rising?

———————

A Hope Focused on Jesus

Background Scripture: I John 4–5

———————

The Main Question—William H. Willimon

Thor Hall has noted that many psychiatrists with whom he has been acquainted have a low opinion of churches and religion in general. This is not to say that all psychiatrists are down on religion, but it does seem that many are.

I remember meeting a woman who was a director of a treatment center for alcoholics. Upon meeting me and hearing that I was a pastor she asked, "Are you one of those fundamentalist preachers? I've got no use for them."

I replied that I had never thought of myself as a fundamentalist and doubt that anyone else would think of me that way. Why did she ask?

"Well, I think they are the cause of so many problems which I find in addicted people. We have our patients do a biography on themselves when they come here for treatment. About two-thirds of them always begin, 'I was raised in a good Christian home.'"

She was angry that their so-called good Christian homes had down the seeds of fear, self-doubt, and guilt which proved to be fertile ground for the disease of alcoholism.

"What image of God did they receive in those 'good Christian homes'?" I asked. They received a picture of God as an angry, aloof, judging deity who punishes and strikes down.

In preparing for this lesson, I called a friend of mine who is a psychiatrist and asked him if he felt that our negative images of God and religion could contribute to mental disorders.

"Without a doubt," was his reply. "Psychotic, emotionally sick people whom I have treated often believe in a god who seems to be a strict, unyielding being to whom miserable humanity relates with guilt, fear, and trepidation."

Afraid of God? On this Easter Day, as we travel to the empty tomb and reflect upon the miracle that has taken place among us in the resurrection, what sort of God do we meet? Is this a God of fear or hope who greets us in the resurrection of Christ?

As You Read the Scripture—Mike Winters

I John 4–5. In these two chapters *confess* (4:2), *know* (4:13) and *believe* (5:1) seem to form the foundation of the writer's thought. They are words which undergird Christian theology and the Christian's relationship to God through Jesus Christ.

Chapter 4:1-6. In this day of acceptable diversity in the church, what is the test by which the limits of diversity are judged? The limits of diversity in the first- and second-century church were clear to the writer. Anyone who did not "confess" the full humanity of Jesus Christ was a false spirit. The Gnostic thought denied the incarnation of God in full human form.

The spirit of the Antichrist is the spirit of the false prophet. The spirit of truth is God's Spirit and is of God. It is the Spirit given to those in whom God abides (3:24, 4:13).

Verses 7-12. Whoever is of God holds the key to truth and error (4:6). The test to discern who is of God is summarized in our love for one another. Our love for one another is the Christian's response to God's love for us through Jesus Christ.

Verse 13. God's Spirit is love (4:7). We who abide in God have been given the Spirit of love (4:12).

Verses 14-15. The early Christian creedal affirmation was "Jesus is Lord." This focused on Christ's resurrection and present reigning. The writer affirms Jesus as Savior, which focuses on Christ's death on the cross and the atonement.

Verse 15. Those in whom God abides are without sin (3:9), love one another (4:12), abide in God and have God's own Spirit (4:13), and confess Jesus, Son of God (4:15).

Verse 16. The sense of the words translated "know" and "believe" does not fully convey the personal drama of coming to know and believe or the continuing effect of knowing and believing. John 6:69 uses these two words to describe this process of knowing and believing, as is also intended here.

Verse 17. Love is perfected as we become more and more like the one whom we follow. We have confidence in the face of judgment.

Verse 18. Those who know and believe and in whom God abides (and who abide in God) do not fear God's judgment.

Verses 19-21. Our love for God and one another is our first appropriate and meaningful response to God's love for us. God has initiated this relationship of love. Ours is a responding, answering love.

Chapter 5:1. In believing that Jesus is the Christ we become children of God. This believing must be understood in the context of "knowing" (4:13) and "confessing" (4:2).

Verses 2-3. Jesus said, "My yoke is easy, and my burden is light" (Matthew 11:30). Whoever is of God is yoked to this twofold commandment to love.

Verses 4-5. In John 16:33, Jesus comforts his disciples saying, "In the world you have tribulation; but be of good cheer. I have overcome the world." Those who believe share in a victory which overcomes the world.

Verses 6-8. The water alludes to Jesus' baptism. The blood alludes to Jesus' death on the cross. The Spirit is the Spirit of truth (4:2).

Verses 9-10. The credibility of a testimony is increased when there are collaborating witnesses.

Verses 11-12. God and God's Spirit collaborate, confirming for the believer the testimony which we have received, the mystery of life in Jesus.

Verses 13-21. We are confident that we *have* eternal life. We are confident that our prayers are heard and answered. We may be confident also of the veracity of I John's teaching regarding the proper understanding of God in Jesus Christ.

Verses 18-20. In summary: I John refutes Gnosticism, listing what in fact can really be known: "one born of God does not sin"; "the whole world is in the power of the evil one"; "the Son of God has come and has given us understanding."

Selected Scripture

King James Version	Revised Standard Version

I John 4:13-17

13 Hereby know we that we dwell in him, and he in us, because he hath given us of his Spirit.

14 And we have seen and do testify that the Father sent the Son *to be* the Saviour of the world.

15 Whosoever shall confess that Jesus is the Son of God, God dwelleth in him, and he in God.

16 And we have known and believed the love that God hath to us. God is love; and he that dwelleth in love dwelleth in God, and God in him.

17 Herein is our love made perfect, that we may have boldness in the day of judgment: because as he is, so are we in this world.

I John 5:1-12

1 Whoever believeth that Jesus is the Christ is born of God: and every one that loveth him that begat loveth him also that is begotten of him.

2 By this we know that we love the children of God, when we love God, and keep his commandments.

3 For this is the love of God, that we keep his commandments: and his commandments are not grievous.

4 For whatsoever is born of God overcometh the world: and this is the victory that overcometh the world, *even* our faith.

5 Who is he that overcometh the world, but he that believeth that Jesus is the Son of God?

6 This is he that came by water and blood, *even* Jesus Christ; not by water only, but by water and blood. And it is the Spirit that beareth witness, because the Spirit is truth.

I John 4:13-17

13 By this we know that we abide in him and he in us, because he has given us of his own Spirit. 14 And we have seen and testify that the Father has sent his Son as the Savior of the world. 15 Whoever confesses that Jesus is the Son of God, God abides in him, and he in God. 16 So we know and believe the love God has for us. God is love, and he who abides in love abides in God, and God abides in him. 17 In this is love perfected with us, that we may have confidence for the day of judgment, because as he is so are we in this world.

I John 5:1-12

1 Every one who believes that Jesus is the Christ is a child of God, and every one who loves the parent loves the child. 2 By this we know that we love the children of God, when we love God and obey his commandments. 3 For this is the love of God, that we keep his commandments. And his commandments are not burdensome. 4 For whatever is born of God overcomes the world; and this is the victory that overcomes the world, our faith. 5 Who is it that overcomes the world but he who believes that Jesus is the Son of God?

6 This is he who came by water and blood, Jesus Christ, not with the water only but with the water and the blood. 7 And the Spirit is the witness, because the Spirit is the truth. 8 There are three witnesses,

7 For there are three that bear record in heaven, the Father, the Word, and the Holy Ghost: and these three are one.

8 And there are three that bear witness in earth, the Spirit, and the water, and the blood: and these three agree in one.

9 If we receive the witness of men, the witness of God is greater: for this is the witness of God which he hath testified of his Son.

10 He that believeth on the Son of God hath the witness in himself: he that believeth not God hath made him a liar; because he believeth not the record that God gave of his Son.

11 And this is the record, that God hath given to us eternal life, and this life is in his Son.

12 He that hath the Son hath life; *and* he that hath not the Son of God hath not life.

the Spirit, the water, and the blood; and these three agree. 9 If we receive the testimony of men, the testimony of God is greater; for this is the testimony of God that he has borne witness to his Son. 10 He who believes in the Son of God has the testimony in himself. He who does not believe God has made him a liar, because he has not believed in the testimony that God has borne to his Son. 11 And this is the testimony that God gave us eternal life, and this life is in his Son. 12 He who has the Son has life; he who has not the Son of God has not life.

Key Verse: **This is the record, that God has given to us eternal life, and this life is in his Son. (I John 5:11)**

Key Verse: **This is the testimony, that God gave us eternal life, and this life is in his Son. (I John 5:11)**

The Scripture and the Main Question—William H. Willimon

The Savior of the World

A number of years ago, in a sermon, noted preacher Edmund Steimle pointed out that the disciples reacted to the news of Jesus' resurrection with a curious emotion—*fear.*

Look over the gospel accounts of that first Easter morning and the days immediately afterward and you will find that fear filled the disciples. We might expect that they would feel happy or excited or triumphant.

But is their response so surprising? Think of many of the accounts of divine-human encounters in the Old Testament: Moses before the burning bush, Isaiah in the temple. These are stories of people face-to-face with God Almighty. And they are depicted as people who are scared to death.

And why not? It can be a fearful thing to fall into the hands of a living God. If we can relegate God to the dusty pages of ancient history, if we can convince ourselves that God is some mysterious, aloof, distant being who never touches us or our lives, then we have little to fear. But to come to a tomb on a Sunday morning expecting to find a dead, decaying body only to be surprised that Jesus is risen, is set loose in the world, is alive and going on before us—well, we must admit that this is a bit disarming, even frightening.

Time and again we try to tame God, to domesticate God into a being who is more manageable for us, less theatening, less demanding. But Easter reminds us that our God will not stay tied down. Our God is risen, alive, at work.

And this realization can be as frightening to us as it was to Christ's first disciples. Our Savior comes to meet us as a God who is alive and well. But whether that meeting be one of fear or of joy depends on who this Savior is, doesn't it? It depends on what he looks like, what he wants from us, what he does to us and for us.

"God is love," says today's scripture (I John 4:16). We are being met by a God who is love embodied and personified, and that makes all the difference to our fears.

That We May Have Confidence

Many of us have our fears about God implanted in us from childhood. How many children have lain awake at night in terror because someone gave them a fiery vision of demons and devils and told them that this was what religion is all about? Sometimes a misguided parent tells children that God will punish them when they steal cookies from the cookie jar. These visions have their effect upon us.

What is the response of today's scripture lesson to this sort of religion? First, the epistle says, "Whoever confesses that Jesus is the Son of God, God abides in him, and he in God. So we know and believe the love God has for us" (4:15-16).

Those who know Jesus know God. In the life, death, and teachings of this man from Nazareth we have seen as much of God as we ever hope to see. Jesus shows us what God is like.

Sometimes we say, when some tragedy happens, "Well, this is just God's will." We may say it in an attempt to comfort a grieving friend. But what does this say about God? I have seen people who were embittered against God for life because, when some horrible event happened in their life, someone said, "This is God's will," and they believed it. If God did this horrible thing, then who could possibly love God? they thought.

And yet, if the Christian faith is true, Jesus is one with God. Could we say, when something terrible happens, that it is *Jesus'* will? I doubt that we could because terrible events do not square with the Savior who healed, loved, accepted, invited, and expressed compassion.

Jesus gives content to our image of God. If our image of God cannot square with the revelation of God which we have received in Christ, then we may need to adjust our image of God. When we look at the words, life, and service of Jesus, we know the truth of the words *God is love.*

Knowledge of the nature of God as love gives us confidence (4:17). Our confidence is based upon our knowledge of what God is like. If God is love and we abide in God, then we are confident that nothing can separate us from that love, that we need not have fear because God's love is stronger than any other power in our life. This is the very ground of our hope.

I remember talking with a social worker who impressed upon me the power of our early childhood relationships with our parents. She told me that if a child experienced confusion, disorientation, and hostility from its parents in the early years of his or her life, then that child seemed to be invariably headed for trouble in adulthood. Abusive parents produce children who will in turn often abuse *their* children. Prisons are full of people who have carried the scars of childhood into their sad, disordered, criminal adult lives.

Christians are those who have experienced acceptance and love from their parent, God. This makes a difference in how we relate to the world.

Because we have been loved, we are able to show love. We love from the security and confidence of knowing that God will never let us go, that God keeps reaching out to us in love, even when we are most unlovable.

Therefore today's scripture now moves from statements about our relationship with God to the implications of that relationship in our dealings with other people.

"Every one who believes that Jesus is the Christ is a child of God, and every one who loves the parent loves the child" (I John 5:1). We cannot pray the Lord's Prayer, "Our Father, who art in heaven . . ." without coming to see all men and women as our brothers and sisters. We cannot love the parent without loving those whom the parent loves. Here is the basis for Christian ethics.

Our relationships with other people are based upon our relationship with God. Our goal is to treat other people as God has treated us and as God treats other people.

In other words, we are seeing on a divine-human scale what many of us experience on a human scale. If someone has a good parental relationship, that person is able to relate favorably with others. That person has learned that the world is a trustworthy, good place and lives accordingly. Our relationship with God determines the shape of our relationships with others.

The Son has Life

"He who has the Son has life; he who has not the Son of God has not life" (5:12).

Imagine what your life would be like if you did not know Christ. What would you think about the world? What would be your fears? You might be convinced that this world is an utterly hostile place, an alien and uncaring environment in which to live.

Christians are able to live with a sure confidence, a confidence based not upon themselves or upon some Pollyanna-like simple-minded optimism. Rather, it is a confidence based upon what we have experienced of God's love.

In this life there is much to fear. We live under the shadow of the mushroom cloud; there are wars and rumors of wars, ecological disasters, shortages of important commodities, overpopulation, and other pressing and frightening problems.

But we have confidence even in the face of these problems because "He who is in you is greater than he who is in the world" (4:4). Fortunately for our fears, "We are of God" (4:6).

On this Easter, what are your fears? What are the seemingly insurmountable problems that cause you anxiety?

Now ask yourself, What difference does it make to my fears that Jesus Christ is risen from the dead, that he is alive and in the world, and that he loves me?

Helping Adults Become Involved—Robert G. Rogers

Preparing to Teach

You will be teaching this lesson on Easter Day, the most significant day in the Christian calendar. Therefore, your primary aim will be to emphasize the meaning of God's love as manifested in the resurrection. How are our lives different because of this event? Does our knowledge of God's love influence how we treat other persons? Think of these and related questions as you read the assigned scripture and prepare your lesson.

In addition to reading I John 4–5, read at least one gospel account of the resurrection story. If you have time, read all four accounts (Matthew 28; Mark 16; Luke 24; John 20–21). How is Christian hope expressed in each of the four? How do the women and the disciples react to the news of God's marvelous act of salvation? Notice especially the mixture of fear and awe. How would you have reacted if you had visited the empty tomb on that first Easter morning?

Introducing the Main Question

In Dr. Willimon's "The Main Question," he reminds us of the way many people think of God. They are afraid! To some, the word *God* conveys an image of a stern, all-powerful being who is to be feared because he judges and condemns. Unfortunately, this image is all too often reinforced in our churches.

The initial reaction of the women and the disciples to the empty tomb was also a sense of fear. What had happened? Where had Jesus gone? What had God done? To a large extent, their fear (and indeed ours) is based on uncertainty, a sense of dread about those things humans cannot control or fully understand. And even in the twentieth century we do not fully comprehend the mystery of Jesus' resurrection.

In the process of introducing the topic, ask class members to think about their own perceptions of God. It would be helpful to jot down some of their ideas on a chalkboard or writing pad. Likely their ideas of God have grown and matured during their adult years, but most will remember childhood images they had. What caused these ideas about God to change?

Developing the Lesson

In presenting the lesson you want to show ways in which God's love (not his wrath) is evident in our lives. In the process, it is important to emphasize that our fear of death is overcome by the resurrection; this promise of eternal life is the greatest proof of God's love for us.

Divide the lesson into the following sections:

I. Distinguishing between fear and awe
II. The resurrection as proof of God's love
III. The power of love to conquer fear

I. Distinguishing between fear and awe

Consider for a moment the development of human relationships. If we are afraid of another person, how does that limit the quality of the relationship we can have with him or her? By contrast, if we regard another with respect, not fear, do new possibilities of communication and friendship open up? In brief, you want the class to see how crippled our human relationships become when fear dominates our responses.

Now turn again to the divine-human relationship. Ask the class members to think a bit more about their own faith development. Acknowledge that not all Christians have childhood memories of a fearful God, but many do. Yet most Christians would agree that a mature faith cannot rest on fear. Through what process did class members learn not to fear the Creator but to regard him with respect and awe? Many of us can remember particular events or persons who helped our relationship with God to develop. At this point, some members may be willing to share briefly a key person or event that was especially helpful in shaping their view of God.

II. The resurrection as proof of God's love

As the Creator, God deserves the respect and awe with which we regard him. Indeed, such a recognition is essential to an appropriate understanding of the relationship between the Creator and those whom he created. But the Christian gospel goes beyond even this in describing the divine-human covenant. We are called not to fear God, but to revere him; this reverence is a response of love to the divine love freely offered. On Easter morning, we examine this most conspicuous example of God's love for us and all humanity.

Devote some time to a consideration of the first Easter morning. Remind the class of the initial response to the empty tomb: fear and dread. Yet the first witnesses to the resurrection soon learned that God has raised Jesus from the dead! Their fear was turned to joy and thankfulness. The crucifixion had seemingly been a triumph for sin and death. Now the resurrection provided hope based on God's act in behalf of humanity. The resurrection of Jesus is ultimate "proof" of God's love.

Now turn to the present Easter Day. How do class members view the meaning of the empty tomb? How do they view God as a result of the resurrection? Can they identify with the various emotions of the first Christians? Would they, like doubting Thomas, have asked for "proof" of the resurrection? These and similar questions would be useful to raise to aid your class in identifying with the meaning of Easter.

III. The power of love to conquer fear

The author of I John writes: "There is no fear in love, but perfect love casts out fear" (I John 4:18a). In this concluding portion of the lesson, emphasize that belief in Jesus' resurrection enables us to live confidently, freed from the fear of death. Begin by turning again to the first Easter. Point out how the disciples and other witnesses grew steadily more bold in their Christian faith (as based on the resurrection) to the stage where the risen Lord could entrust the spread of the gospel to their care. Indeed, the "perfect love" of God cast out their initial fear.

Now ask the class to consider how the faith of those first Christians can be an example to us today. Can we too regard the empty tomb (the resurrection) as the proof that proclaims God's perfect love? Does such belief help us to overcome our fear, not only of God, but of death? Are we therefore emboldened to go forth and witness to the good news?

Read aloud I John 4:19: "We love, because he first loved us." Suggest that the resurrection is precisely that form of God's love that gives us the strength to go forth and love others in his name. You might ask members to think particularly of what it means when life triumphs over death and love over fear.

Helping Class Members Act

Suggest that the class memorize I John 4:10-11 as a means of remembering today's lesson. Ask them to think in the days and weeks after Easter of specific ways they individually and the church corporately can be agents of love in a world torn by fears and doubts. In this way they are "living proof" that God in Christ lives and moves within the human community.

Planning for Next Sunday

Next Sunday's lesson will emphasize how Christian hope is built on truth. In preparation, your class should read II John and III John. These brief letters provide excellent summaries of the relationship of Christian truth and living in the world. Ask your people to contemplate how truth and right living are related in their own lives.

LESSON 6   APRIL 6

A Hope Built on Truth

Background Scripture: II John and III John

The Main Question—William H. Willimon

"You shall know the truth and the truth will make you free," said the large roman letters which were engraved over the door of our high school.

As a youth, I didn't know that those words were from scripture—I suppose at the time I thought they were a slogan the principal made up!

Of course, the pursuit of truth is a worthy task for educators. "What is truth?" Pilate asked as he tried Jesus. Our whole lives are spent wrestling with that weighty question. What is true, what is worthy and worthwhile, what endures?

But we live in a permissive, broad-minded, tolerant, pluralistic age when anything goes. Truth is a relative commodity in our time—or so we seem to believe. Truth is relative to background, ethnic heritage, point of view, life-style. My truth may not be your truth. There are two sides to every question. We all see things differently. And so it goes. One person's truth is another's falsehood.

But is that true?

Is everything so relative? Is there anything which is either true or false—your point of view has little to do with it?

"The truth shall make you free" the words say. Free from what? From anxiety over the uncertainty of life? Free to face the facts and know what is real in life and what is false? Free to hope, not on the basis of some self-created fantasy, but on the basis of what is true? This is the freedom we all seek—freedom which only comes through a knowledge of the truth.

Is such certainty possible in this age of relativity? Can we be sure that our hope, particularly in these days following Easter, is based upon what is *true*?

These are the questions, the big, challenging, demanding questions we shall be exploring in today's lesson.

As You Read the Scripture—Mike Winters

II John and III John. These letters are written by an elder. The term *elder* in Judaism is both a reference to an older person and may also connote any office of leadership (unrelated to age). In Christianity, the office of elder implied religious responsibilities.

Second John is written "to the elect lady and her children." This is likely a personification of the church. Third John is a letter to an individual, Gaius. Gaius is a friend of the writer who has, perhaps, opened his home to certain messengers of the truth. In the unidentified church of which Gaius is a part, a certain Diotrephes has challenged the elder's (writer's) authority, shunning the messengers of truth.

Second John repeats the theme in First John and the warning against the Antichrist deceiver. Readers are reminded of Christ's true humanity and of his command to love.

II John 1:2. The truth is the "coming of Jesus Christ in the flesh" (verse 7).

Verse 3. "Grace, mercy, and peace" as benefits from God and from Jesus Christ are related to, and perhaps flow from, truth and love.

Verse 4. The elder's joy is that there are at least *some* who are following the truth. If all were following, there would have been no need for this letter. "Following the truth" is an idiomatic phrase. Literally, they are those who "walk in the truth."

Verse 5-7. The new commandment is the summary of the old law which became, with Jesus, the foundation of Christian living (John 13:34, I John 2:7). Followers of truth are those who follow the commandment of love.

There is a natural connection between truth and love for the writer. Love has the power to draw together the widest diversity. Together the faith community can stand fast against heresy—in this case, the Gnostic heresy.

Verse 8. The reward is eternal life for those who confess the coming of Jesus Christ in the flesh (I John 4:2, Matthew 5:12).

Verse 9. The Gnostics denied that God came among us *in the flesh* in Jesus Christ. "Going ahead" with this heresy would have disastrous consequences. It could lead to Christianity without Christ.

Verse 10-11. Do not welcome—shun those messengers who do not acknowledge the coming of Jesus Christ in the flesh. Or become identified with the cause of the Antichrist.

III John 1. The writer who speaks so often of the command to love expresses love for Gaius in the opening of this letter.

Verse 2. The prayer that all may go well with Gaius is an indication that all is not well. In today's hypertensive society, we know the relationship between health and stress. Perhaps the condition in the church placed Gaius in a stressful, unhealthy condition.

Verse 3. Here and in II John 4 the writer rejoices in the truth. The "brethren" were messengers of truth who had been shunned by Diotrephes (III John 9), but welcomed by Gaius (III John 5-6).

Verse 4. "My children" indicates a very close relationship between the elder and those who follow (walk) in the truth.

Verses 5-8. Here are acknowledgment and encouragement for Gaius and others who have done right. The elder's concern for strangers in the faith hinges on the truth (II John 10-11). While the author warns them to shun false teachers, he urges warm reception of the faithful.

Verses 9-11. Diotrephes has challenged the elder's authority. He has done so at his own risk for he has heard the truth. There is no excuse for his error. His pride is his undoing.

Selected Scripture

King James Version

II John 1-11

1 The elder unto the elect lady and her children, whom I love in the truth; and not I only, but also all they that have known the truth;

2 For the truth's sake, which dwelleth in us, and shall be with us for ever.

3 Grace be with you, mercy, *and* peace, from God the Father, and from the Lord Jesus Christ, the Son of the Father, in truth and love.

4 I rejoiced greatly that I found of thy children walking in truth, as we have received a commandment from the Father.

5 And now I beseech thee, lady, not as though I wrote a new commandment unto thee, but that which we had from the beginning, that we love one another.

6 And this is love, that we walk after his commandments. This is the commandment, That, as ye have heard from the beginning, ye should walk in it.

7 For many deceivers are entered into the world, who confess not that Jesus Christ is come in the flesh. This is a deceiver and an ăn´-tĭ-chrīst.

8 Look to yourselves, that we lose not those things which we have wrought, but that we receive a full reward.

9 Whosoever transgresseth, and abideth not in the doctrine of Christ, hath not God. He that abideth in the doctrine of Christ, he hath both the Father and the Son.

10 If there come any unto you, and bring not this doctrine, receive him not into *your* house, neither bid him God speed:

11 For he that biddeth him God speed is partaker of his evil deeds.

Revised Standard Version

II John 1-11

1 The elder to the elect lady and her children, whom I love in the truth, and not only I but also all who know the truth, 2 because of the truth which abides in us and will be with us for ever:

3 Grace, mercy, and peace will be with us, from God the Father and from Jesus Christ the Father's Son, in truth and love.

4 I rejoiced greatly to find some of your children following the truth, just as we have been commanded by the Father. 5 And now I beg you, lady, not as though I were writing you a new commandment, but the one we have had from the beginning, that we love one another. 6 And this is love, that we follow his commandments; this is the commandment, as you have heard from the beginning, that you follow love. 7 For many deceivers have gone out into the world, men who will not acknowledge the coming of Jesus Christ in the flesh; such a one is the deceiver and the antichrist. 8 Look to yourselves, that you may not lose what you have worked for, but may win a full reward. 9 Any one who goes ahead and does not abide in the doctrine of Christ does not have God; he who abides in the doctrine had both the Father and the Son. 10 If any one comes to you and does not bring this doctrine, do not receive him into the house or give him any greeting; 11 for he who greets him shares his wicked work.

III John 2-4

2 Beloved, I wish above all things that thou mayest prosper and be in health, even as thy soul prospereth.

3 For I rejoiced greatly, when the brethren came and testified of the truth that is in thee, even as thou walkest in the truth.

4 I have no greater joy than to hear that my children walk in truth.

Key Verse: **I have no greater joy than to hear that my children walk in truth. (III John 4)**

III John 2-4

2 Beloved, I pray that all may go well with you and that you may be in health; I know that it is well with your soul. 3 For I greatly rejoiced when some of the brethren arrived and testified to the truth of your life, as indeed you do follow the truth. 4 No greater joy can I have than this, to hear that my children follow the truth.

Key Verse: **No greater joy can I have than this, to hear that my children follow the truth. (III John 4)**

The Scripture and the Main Question—William H. Willimon

The Truth Which Abides in Us

Read over today's scripture from the little-known letters of II and III John, and you will realize that the letters are from a time which is different from our own. The word *truth* keeps popping up in today's lesson. These early Christians are addressed as those "who know the truth," those of whom the writer says "I love in the truth" (II John 1).

I say that this time was different from the time of today's church because I suspect that only a few of us trouble ourselves greatly over "the truth" today. Open-mindedness is the supreme virtue today. In a multiracial, multiethnic, multilingual society, we have learned the values of tolerance and pluralism. History has chronicled the tragic results of intolerance, bigotry, and prejudice. So "live and let live" is our motto. You have your opinion, I have mine, and what difference does it all make anyway?

We therefore can't afford to get too agitated over questions of truth—we don't want to be accused of being closed-minded, narrow, or judgmental toward the sincerely held opinions of others.

Not so for these early Christians. Evidently, they believed that there was something important at stake in what they believed. People's vision of the truth determines who they are and what they do. Therefore, the church must be attentive to what people regard as true.

We all know that what a person believes makes a difference in how that person lives. If you believe that the truth of this world is dog-eat-dog competitiveness, rivalry, and struggle, then you are justified in trying to look out only for yourself and in doing everyone else in.

If you believe that the truth is that no one is in charge in the world, that life is without purpose or direction, that the universe is merely spinning wildly about without any point to it all, then live for today, grab what happiness you can, and don't ask for much out of life.

Tragically, hundreds of thousands of modern people hold one of these opinions about the truth. The results of such belief and its attendant behavior are all around us.

To some, it may seem as if the church gets unduly worked up over matters of belief and doctrine. We have had some bitter, tragic, even pointless battles over doctrines in the past. But at least give the church credit for knowing that it *does* matter what we believe, that truth cannot be determined by majority vote, that truth is real, and it is worth fighting for.

So II John says flatly that anyone who "does not abide in the doctrine of Christ does not have God" (verse 9).

Deceivers in the World

A few years ago a person asked to talk to me about a problem. She told me that she had spent two days in utter misery and had had two sleepless, horrible nights because someone had told her that if she and her family did not believe some obscure doctrine, they would be damned to hell forever. I talked with her about the doctrine and explained that it had cropped up from time to time in the church but had long ago been condemned as a heresy because it was deemed to be unbiblical. She seemed relieved.

This conversation reminded me that even now matters of doctrine are a worthy concern for the church. There are still people— in the words of today's scripture, "many deceivers"—who roam abroad in the world (verse 7). Need we be reminded of the horrors of the Jonestown massacre in which an insane but smooth-talking messiah led hundreds of innocent people to their death?

Many Christian parents have watched with dismay as their children have forsaken their families and their churches and joined cults. There are so many false prophets roaming about in the world, all too willing to prey upon some helpless and confused person. Therefore, matters of truth and doctrine are still serious considerations for the church.

"Jesus Christ died to take away your sins, not your brains" said a clever advertisement in a local newspaper. The church that bought that advertisement wanted to tell the world that the truth of Jesus Christ is not threatened by questions, searching, probing, and discussion. Here is a truth that can stand the tests of inquiry because it is *the* truth.

So when you think about it, the church is a community of the truth. In the church people discuss, think, argue, debate, read, search so that their understanding of the truth, the truth as in Jesus Christ, might be deepened. One reason that you are participating in an adult church school class is that you are a searcher for the truth. We are followers of the truth. But because that truth strikes the world as something very different from its false truth, we must keep exploring that truth, nurturing it in our lives, replenishing it, refurbishing it for ourselves. As the third letter of John says, "No greater joy can I have than this, to hear that my children follow the truth" (verse 4).

A number of years ago, a young woman in our church left her family and joined a popular cult. I had spent a number of hours trying to counsel her. She had grown up in a poor home situation, had experimented with drugs, and had lived a chaotic, disordered life during her teenage years. The church had tried to relate to her, but it had failed.

I watched her leaving with a great sense of sadness. I was sad that, in spite of our earnest efforts, we were unable to ground her in the truth, *the* truth which is embodied in Jesus Christ. She was crying out for something to tie her life to, something that would endure, something that would give her hope and security.

I'll tell you what I would like. I would like for the church to be a place where the truth is so boldly and confidently proclaimed, where we are so ready to reach out with a firm love to people who are troubled and wandering, that people will be able to see the truth, believe the truth, and will be made free.

Look to Yourselves

Of course, today's scripture reminds us that cults, false messiahs with their false doctrines, and doctrinal controversy are nothing new for the church. We cannot know the precise arguments and debates which gave rise to the writing of these letters of II and III John, but we can assume from what we have here that it was a time of bitter struggle in the church concerning what is true and what is false. Here is a church that knew, in its confrontation with the world, that the truth is worth fighting for and fighting over, that the lures and false hopes of the world must be confronted with something more substantial than mere open-mindedness and mushy tolerance.

A clue to the problem is given in verse 7 of II John. "For many deceivers have gone out into the world, men who will not acknowledge the coming of Jesus Christ in the flesh." What is going on here?

Many scholars believe that this is a sign of an early confrontation with one of the oldest heresies in the church—*Docetism.* Docetism was more a tendency than a full-blown doctrine. The Docetists held that Christ did not really come in the flesh. He only appeared to be incarnate, in the body, in the flesh. He only seemed to be a man. The word *Docetism* comes from the Greek word *dokeo* which means "I seem." In other words, to the Docetists, Christ only seemed to be human. He was really pure God.

The Docetists claimed that they were honoring Christ, showing him respect, through this belief. They were scandalized by the notion that God could lower himself to become a person, in the flesh. If God really did become a human being, if God were born of a woman, if he suffered, died, and was buried; then God would not really be God, they reasoned. God for the Docetist is aloof, omnipotent, untouched by humanity. God is above all that.

The writer of II John strongly condemns this notion. The writer knows that Docetism is a life-or-death matter for the Christian religion. The Docetist, while appearing to respect Jesus by putting him on some kind of pedestal, is really making Jesus irrelevant by removing him from everyday human needs and everyday human life. If Jesus were not really a human being, if he were just some sort of demigod walking around who only appeared to be a man, then he is irrelevant to us. How could such a creature really understand what it means for us to live in the world, to be tempted, to suffer, to be rejected?

Second John knows the truth—Jesus did not simply *appear* to be a man; he was in every way like us. The glory of God is that God loved us so much that God came among us, lived where we live, suffered what we sometimes suffer so that God might show us the way to glory. This is the truth, the truth upon which all Christian hope is based. Destroy that truth, and you have destroyed our hope.

In our times of suffering, disappointment, grief, hopelessness, and darkness we can take heart and have hope because Jesus Christ really did come "in the flesh." He is there, not as some unknowing, unknowable, aloof diety, but as our brother, our friend, our companion. Only a God who dares to come to us "in the flesh" can help.

Knowing the seriousness of the issues at stake here helps to explain some of the harsh language within this short letter of II John. Because Docetism is a fundamental challenge to the very heart of our hope, the writer says, "If any one comes to you and does not bring this doctrine, do not receive him into the house or give him any greeting; for he who greets him shares his wicked work" (II John 10-11).

Alas, we must admit that sometimes the church has fought over petty, inconsequential matters rather than truly fundamental, important matters. What is really basic and important? we may ask. The only way to answer that question is through constant study and discussion, deep grounding in the Bible and its teachings, such as you are attempting to do in your adult class.

When we look at Jesus Christ, his words and his life, we see not simply *a* truth, but *the* truth. For us Christians, the truth is a person; it is personal. Christ is the source of our life, the ground of our hope. Therefore we do well to know this truth, defend it, and constantly reflect upon its meaning for our lives. For when we are freed by this truth, we are free indeed.

Helping Adults Become Involved—Robert G. Rogers

Preparing to Teach

This week you will be teaching about yet another facet of Christian hope: assurance that is based on knowledge of the truth. Your aim is to help students define what is central to Christian truth. On what can one stake his or her faith? A secondary consideration is to show that knowing the truth should not lead to self-righteousness.

Read II John and III John carefully. As part of your preparation, make a list for yourself of the doctrines or beliefs you affirm as the essential core of Christian truth. You might also think about a good working definition of *tolerance*. How can one affirm Christian truth as one believes it and still give credence to another person's sincerely held conviction? What do you consider the limits of tolerance to be? Are there some Christian beliefs that are not debatable? These and similar questions would be helpful to think through as you prepare for class.

Introducing the Main Question

We live in an age where truth is sometimes difficult to find. Various leaders in society are evasive when asked direct questions. Truth is often hidden beneath a façade of distortions and lies. The phrase, "That statement is no longer operative!" has become a favorite of many political figures. What they really mean is that they did not tell the truth the first time.

Christians live in this kind of world. Members of your class have all had to deal with the frustration of not knowing who or what to believe. The class might spend a few moments simply sharing perceptions of distortions and half-truths (or half-lies!) present in our current society. How should we deal with this kind of world? Are there standards of measurement by which Christians can evaluate the world?

As people of faith, Christians affirm that the Scriptures reveal God's ultimate truth. How can our common study of God's word enlighten us? What is the role of thinking in the Christian faith? Is our faith endangered when we use human reasoning to think about the meaning of God's truth?

Developing the Lesson

In "The Scripture and the Main Question," Dr. Willimon accurately notes the dilemma faced by contemporary Christians. In a society that values a variety of opinions and open-mindedness, proclaiming and living by the truth make a difficult task. Yet that is precisely what this lesson is designed to address in three basic sections:

I. Discerning Christian truth
II. Practicing Christian humility
III. Sharing the truth of Christianity

I. Discerning Christian truth

Perhaps you ought to commence this section by asking the class members to discuss what they consider to be the central core of Christian teaching. Mark on the chalkboard the general beliefs—for example, Jesus as the Son of God. (Remind the class of Dr. Willimon's discussion of Docetism.) You should avoid listing too many, but do include any essential beliefs that might not have been mentioned by class members.

Point out that these basic beliefs have been held as true by Christians for centuries. However, do not discourage the class from thinking about the various authentic ways of interpreting some Christian beliefs. Call attention to the newspaper advertising mentioned by Dr. Willimon: "Jesus Christ died to take away your sins, not your brains." The human mind is one of God's greatest gifts, and it should be used in the service of Christian truth. To affirm that Christian hope is based on belief in God's promises does not mean that we cease to think.

You might emphasize that being a Christian "seeker of truth" involves discussion, study, and prayer. It is a process which at times is solitary but usually is appropriately done within the fellowship of the church. Suggest that within the bonds of *agape* in the church, Christians ought to nourish one another but be prepared also to admonish each other in the light of God's truth.

II. Practicing Christian humility

As Christians, we believe that we know God's ultimate truth. But we need to remember that it is God's truth, not ours! It is sometimes a fine line between knowing God's truth and being boastful about one's knowledge. Perhaps the class would like to spend some time discussing how truth and humility fit together in the Christian life.

As mortals, we need to remember that our understanding of God and his ways is limited by our own sin and imperfection. Such limitation is obviously placed on us, not on God. Ask the class to think about how we can affirm the ultimate truth of God's revelation in Christ and yet be somewhat less certain that we understand it perfectly. Remind them that even Paul did not claim to know God's truth completely and fully. "For now we see in a mirror dimly, but then face to face. Now I know in part; then I shall understand fully, even as I have been fully understood" (I Corinthians 13:12).

Because we are considerably less than perfect, we need to recognize that our current beliefs should not be "set in concrete." God may have further truth to impart to us—individually and collectively. As we mature in our faith, our understanding of his truth undoubtedly deepens and perhaps even changes somewhat. Help the class members recognize that ultimately the knowledge that we are perfectly loved by God is the most basic of Christian truths. Within this framework of divine love, there is room for some sincere differences of opinion on this doctrine or that one.

III. *Sharing the truth of Christianity*
Is it enough simply to know God's truth and be humble about such knowledge? Are we not called to do something more? Direct the class to consider again the events surrounding the first Easter. In Matthew's account, the disciples encounter the risen Lord. Those who had doubted the resurrection now know the truth. However, that is not sufficient. They are commanded to go forth and preach this truth to all peoples (Matthew 28:16-20).

The scripture assigned for today also affirms this commandment to share the truth. In III John 8 we are told that it is a privilege to support those who travel forth to preach God's word so "that we may be fellow workers in the truth."

Conclude this section by quoting II John 1-2. How does God's truth "abide" in us? Do we proclaim his truth to others by the quality of life we lead? If we love one another and love God's creation, are we living examples of God's truth? In expressing such love to others, do we offer our deepest expression of Christian hope—faith in God's future? What specific forms might such acts of love take to be authentic witnesses to the truth of God?

Helping Class Members Act
Ask class members to think further about the relationship between specific beliefs and Christian disciplship. For example, how should our belief in the Incarnation (God's becoming man in Jesus Christ) influence the way we treat our fellow human beings? Did God become man because all human life is precious? How should this truth influence the form our Christian witness takes?

Planning for Next Sunday
Ask the class to read the letter of Jude. It describes the problems caused by divisions and strife in the church. They might think of ways the church is divided today. How can we work to heal the divisions? How does hope based on God's truth give us strength to do this task?

LESSON 7   APRIL 13

A Hope Worth Guarding

Background Scripture: Jude

The Main Question—William H. Willimon

My church is next door to a synagogue. We share parking lots. The lot is full on both Friday and Sunday. It works out very well.

The rabbi at the synagogue and I get together for coffee occasionally. One day, the rabbi was complaining about some of the pressures his people are under in our town—remarks made by other people, stereotypical and prejudicial remarks about Jews which people in our town sometimes make. He told me that it was not easy living in a society where they are a minority faith.

"We are forever having to tell our young" he said, "you are special; you are a Jew. That means that you live by a different set of standards than other people. You have a different story, a different point of view, a different claim upon your life."

Listening to the rabbi reminded me of a conversation which I had heard not a week before in a young couples' church school class in my church. The class was discussing the difficulties of raising Christians in today's world. They talked about the problem of sex and violence on television, the dilemma of living in a neighborhood where only a few of the families are involved in church.

I told the rabbi, "You may not believe this, but I have heard people talking just like you, right here in my own church. We also are having to tell our children—that's fine for everybody else, but not for you. You are special, you are a Christian, that makes you different. You have a different set of values, different standards that make you special."

In past lessons in this unit we have focused upon the special nature of Christian hope. Now, using the little-read letter of Jude, we shall finally speak about the need to guard this hope, nurture it in our young, and protect it in the church.

As You Read the Scripture—Mike Winters

Jude. This fiery letter climaxes with two of the most beautiful verses in all of Scripture (Jude 24-25). Yet the full content of the letter is a fierce denunciation of heresy and immorality. The principle object of the writer's scorn is that perversion of God's good grace that results in immorality.

The authorship of this letter is uncertain. There seem to be several "Judes" who are listed among the possible candidates. Most debate centers around Jude the brother of Christ. He is the one to whom tradition has attributed authorship. The arguments both for and against are convincing.

It is likely that Jude 4-16 was borrowed by II Peter 2:1-22.

Verses 1-2. "Jude, a *slave* of Jesus Christ" would be a better translation. It describes the writer's complete loyalty to Christ. The concept of "slave" conveys better the truth that the Christian's loyalty is not grounded in himself or herself. Nor is the Christian loyal merely by choice. Rather, God has *bound* the Christian with the bonds of grace.

Likewise, "those who are called" conveys the theological principle that God has exercised the initiative in "calling." Our faith and our service are impossible unless God's grace goes before us. In this sense "the called" are "kept for Jesus Christ." Faithfulness begins outside us with God. It is maintained by God also (compare Jeremiah's call in Jeremiah 1:4). God is the source of our faith and our ability to persevere in faith.

Verse 3. "Beloved" has a dual meaning. It is God's endearing name for those who are called. It is also the endearing name of Christians for one another. But it is not *just* an endearing name. It describes complete devotion and loyalty of one for another.

"Our common salvation" is accessible to all who avail themselves of God's grace.

"Contend for the faith" is a good summary of Jude's message and his purpose in writing. The "saints" (all who believe in Jesus Christ) are exhorted to rebuff doctrinal misrepresentations.

Verse 4. "Ungodly persons" had infiltrated the ranks of Christian faith. They could be identified by their licentiousness. They justified their immorality by saying that the grace of God had freed them from the law. Traditionally, they have been called antinomians, literally, "opponents of the law." Their aim was to bring the "beloved" into a bondage other than bondage to "our only Master [God] and Lord, Jesus Christ." (Galatians 2:4 speaks of "false brethren . . . who slipped in to spy out our freedom . . . in Christ Jesus, that they might bring us into bondage").

Verses 5-7. The Jews of the Exodus were not permitted to enter the land of promise because of their rebellion (Numbers 14.26-35).

Jude's sources for the fall of the angels are principally noncanonical. Sodom and Gomorrah were destroyed because of their immorality (Genesis 19).

Verse 8. Having given examples of God's judgment for "ungodly people," Jude points out that there are present-day ungodly people who continue in their erring ways.

Verse 9. "Michael contending with the devil" alludes to another noncanonical source called the "Ascension of Moses."

Verse 10. These ungodly persons err in that they follow their irrational animal instincts without restraint.

Verses 11-13. The way of Cain alludes to his murder of Abel, his brother (Genesis 4:8-16). Balaam's error refers to Numbers 22-24. See Numbers 16:1-34 for reference to Korah's rebellion.

Verses 14-15. Jude quotes Enoch, another noncanonical source.

Verses 17-18. The Antichrist will come in the last hour (I John 2:18).

Verse 19. Divisions occur where there is no love.

Verses 20-21. The "beloved" are grounded in God expressed in an early trinitarian formula.

Verses 22-23. There is urgency of Christian duty to reclaim those who are in error.

Verses 24-25. Not only does God work faith and service in the believer, God also works righteousness in the believer.

Selected Scripture

King James Version	Revised Standard Version

Jude 1-4, 17-25

1 Jude, the servant of Jesus Christ, and brother of James, to them that are sanctified by God the Father, and preserved in Jesus Christ, *and* called:

2 Mercy unto you, and peace and love, be multiplied.

3 Beloved, when I gave all diligence to write unto you of the common salvation, it was needful for me to write unto you, and exhort *you* that ye should earnestly contend for the faith which was once delivered unto the saints.

Judge 1-4, 17-25

1 Jude, a servant of Jesus Christ and brother of James,

To those who are called, beloved in God the Father and kept for Jesus Christ:

2 May mercy, peace, and love be multiplied to you.

3 Beloved, being very eager to write to you of our common salvation, I found it necessary to write appealing to you to contend for the faith which was once for all delivered to the saints. 4 For admission has been secretly gained by some

4 For there are certain men crept in unawares, who were before of old ordained to this condemnation, ungodly men, turning the grace of our God into lasciviousness, and denying the only Lord God, and our Lord Jesus Christ.

....

17 But, beloved, remember ye the words which were spoken before of the apostles of our Lord Jesus Christ;

18 How that they told you there should be mockers in the last time, who should walk after their own ungodly lusts.

19 These be they who separate themselves, sensual, having not the Spirit.

20 But ye, beloved, building up yourselves on your most holy faith, praying in the Holy Ghost,

21 Keep yourselves in the love of God, looking for the mercy of our Lord Jesus Christ unto eternal life.

22 And of some have compassion, making a difference;

23 And others save with fear, pulling *them* out of the fire; hating even the garment spotted by the flesh.

24 Now unto him that is able to keep you from falling, and to present *you* faultless before the presence of his glory with exceeding joy,

25 To the only wise God our Saviour, *be* glory and majesty, dominion and power, both now and ever. Amen.

Key Verse: **Now unto him that is able to keep you from falling, and to present *you* faultless before the presence of his glory with exceeding joy, to the only wise God our Saviour, *be* glory and majesty, dominion and power, both now and ever. Amen. (Jude 24-25)**

who long ago were designated for this condemnation, ungodly persons who pervert the grace of our God into licentiousness and deny our only Master and Lord, Jesus Christ.

....

17 But you must remember, beloved, the predictions of the apostles of our Lord Jesus Christ; 18 they said to you, "In the last time there will be scoffers, following their own ungodly passions." 19 It is these who set up divisions, worldly people, devoid of the Spirit. 20 But you, beloved, build yourselves up on your most holy faith; pray in the Holy Spirit; 21 keep yourselves in the love of God; wait for the mercy of our Lord Jesus Christ unto eternal life. 22 And convince some, who doubt; 23 save some, by snatching them out of the fire; on some have mercy with fear, hating even the garment spotted by the flesh.

24 Now to him who is able to keep you from falling and to present you without blemish before the presence of his glory with rejoicing, 25 to the only God, our Savior through Jesus Christ our Lord, be glory, majesty, dominion, and authority, before all time and now and for ever. Amen.

Key Verse: **Now to him who is able to keep you from falling and to present you without blemish before the presence of his glory with rejoicing, to the only God, our Savior through Jesus Christ our Lord, be glory, majesty, dominion, and authority, before all time and now and for ever. Amen. (Jude 24-25)**

The Scripture and the Main Question—William H. Willimon

Contend for the Faith

One of the difficulties of reading the Epistles, or for that matter nearly any segment of Scripture, is to reconstruct the original situation to which these holy words were first addressed. It is safe to assume that the original writers did not write their words with us in mind. They wrote to speak to some pressing need of the church in their time and place. We read their words as scripture today because we are convinced that what they said has enduring significance for the church of every age.

But we will not fully realize that enduring significance if we do not understand something of the original context. Then we are better able to apply the message to our situation.

To whom was the letter of Jude addressed? We do not know from where it was sent or to whom. But even a casual reading of the letter tells us some very definite things about *why* it was written.

The author begins, "I found it necessary to write appealing to you to contend for the faith which was once for all delivered to the saints" (verse 3). Evidently we are in the midst of a battle. But unlike some of the other battles in the early church, this battle is not with pagans or with oppressive governmental rulers; this battle is with other Christians. Unnamed persons have, in the writer's words, perverted the "grace of our God into licentiousness and deny our only Master and Lord, Jesus Christ" (verse 4).

Unfortunately, we are given little hint as to the content of their teaching. We are only told that they are immoral, covetous, and reject authority. They are dismissed as "worldly people, devoid of the Spirit" (verse 19). Because they lack love (verse 12), they have created serious and deadly divisions in the church (verse 19).

Lacking information on the precise content of the teaching of these false teachers, we do better to focus simply on the problem of false teaching in the church. We treated the problem of false teaching somewhat in last week's lesson.

In urging these early Christians to "contend for the faith," the writer reminds them that they should not be unduly surprised that they have false prophets to contend with. The apostles predicted that the church would be beset by such doctrinal arguments (verses 17-18).

Sometimes as we look back into the history of the church, we are a bit embarrassed by the ferocity and animosity of our past doctrinal disputes. Time and again, Christians have shed the blood of fellow Christians in various "religious" wars. It still goes on today.

In our own time, some estimate that there may be as many as seven hundred different denominations of Christians in the United States alone. Each one of these groups undoubtedly believes that its doctrine is pure and worth defending from the errors of other groups.

The sad sight of bickering, feuding, divided Christians may lead many of us to simply throw up our hands and say, "Enough already!" Who cares? What difference does it make what you believe? Go ahead and think and let think. You have your point of view, I have mine, and what difference does it make?

I remember serving a church where, in a town of four or five thousand persons, there were six different churches. Each congregation assumed that it had a corner on the truth and that the others were in total error.

Therefore, cooperation among the various congregations was impossible. Each little congregation struggled alone, fighting for its life by fighting with its fellow churches.

There is little to defend in our divisiveness and our bitter disputes among ourselves. Such bickering has been a poor witness to the rest of the world. And yet . . .

Keep Yourselves in the Love of God

In our reaction against absurd and harmful doctrinal divisions and disputes, let us not delude ourselves into thinking that what we believe makes no difference. The problem is not solved simply by declaring that all beliefs are equally valid and that the Christian faith is a relativized, amorphous mass of conflicting beliefs that don't make much difference anyway.

As we have discussed in previous lessons in this unit, what we believe *does* make a difference, a big difference.

If you want a ten-dollar word for the heresy that inflicts many Christians in our age, that word is *ultralatitudinarianism.* That's a mouthful, isn't it? It simply means that we have pushed tolerance to the extreme. Unwilling to go through the demanding task of argument, debate, study, prayer, and listening to one another, we have lazily decided to accept everyone's opinion as equally valid and to condemn nothing. Doctrinal latitude can be a good thing. But we have allowed such latitude as to make a mockery of the faith itself.

A generation ago, the world might have looked at Christians and been shocked by their bickering over theology. Today, the world might look at us and simply be bored because we don't seem to have anything important enough to fight for.

Certainly, sometimes our doctrinal debates have been bloody and harsh. But we at least recognize that we usually fight only for what is important. The ferocity of our debate is often an indication of the seriousness of the subject.

The trick, I suppose, is to be able to sort out the essentials from the nonessentials, so far as our beliefs are concerned. Too often we have shed blood over the nonessentials, only to let the essentials drift away in a swamp of relativity.

What beliefs would you stand up and fight for? How much latitude should we allow in what a person can believe and still call that person a Christian?

These are some of the concerns of today's scripture. Are they still concerns for today's church?

Of course, while we are sorting out and while we are debating and even fighting, let's be sure that we are doing it in a way that is appropriate for Christians.

Some years ago, someone put out a little book called *How to Fight Like Christians in the Church.* What? Can Christians fight in church? The author's contention was that sometimes controversy, debate, and argument are essential in the church. The test is whether we argue, fight, and debate like Christians or like pagans!

It is one thing to challenge someone else's point of view on some important beliefs; it is another thing to tell that person, in effect, "You are an evil, bad, terrible person for holding an opinion like that."

To be honest, parts of today's scripture sink to that level of name-calling and vicious personal accusation. In the heat of an argument, we sometimes say things we shouldn't.

But the author says, "Keep yourselves in the love of God" (verse 21). That's good advice, particularly in the midst of church controversy and debate. We should constantly remind ourselves that we are debating with fellow Christians who believe that we have been both loved and cherished by God. Whether or not we are beloved human beings is not a matter of debate. We are debating the implications of that love for us. So we should carry out our argumentation like Christians, keeping ourselves "in the love of God."

Build Yourselves Up

Today's scripture doesn't tell us what we are to fight for in our doctrines and beliefs. It tells us only that it is important to fight for the truth.

So you gather with your class on Sunday morning. You study, question, debate. Sometimes your arguments may be fierce because you are discussing important matters. Just remember that it is all done in love, all done so that we may be better disciples.

In so doing, the ancient path to truth reappears today; our hope is nurtured and guarded; and we persevere in the faith.

Helping Adults Become Involved—Robert G. Rogers

Preparing to Teach

This is the last lesson in the series on Christian hope. As part of your preparation, think back over the last six lessons. Are there any remaining issues that need further attention? If so, you might devote a portion of class time to review and clarification.

The basic aim of this lesson is to study how to retain the treasure of Christian truth, which is God's gift to us. What are our obligations to ourselves and to others in the community when we have heard the good news? What are the Christian truths worth fighting for? Think of these questions as you study and prepare for Sunday.

Read the letter of Jude closely. Notice that it has many Old Testament references. You might spend some time reviewing the stories in their original biblical settings just in case class members have questions. Use a concordance or biblical commentary to aid in finding the right Old Testament books.

Introducing the Main Question

No longer can we assume that we live in a Christian society (if indeed we ever could make such a claim!). Rather, we live in a world where thoughtful Christians have to make choices that may run counter to the prevailing values of society. In standing for certain principles, Christians may well be called on to defend their understanding of Christian truth. Are we threatened by such a prospect? Would we just as soon let our Christian convictions be "low profile" (in contemporary jargon) so as not to offend anyone by raising any unpleasant issues? How far should we bend to accommodate other points of view?

The above-mentioned issues are not easy to resolve. The place to take a stand is not always readily apparent. Yet, as Christians, we must affirm what we believe and why it is important to us. Not only does our personal integrity demand that we witness to the truth, but others look to us as models.

Children in the congregation, would-be converts, the world at large all judge the sincerity of our faith by our willingness to defend its truths.

Developing the Lesson

Perhaps your class members will want to spend some time discussing what it means for the Christian community to serve as the model to the world. Can they think of specific moral issues which the Christian faith quite clearly addresses? If so, jot these down on the chalkboard or writing pad.

In developing the lesson, emphasize that Christian hope is not to be guarded by hiding it away in a safe place. Instead, it is to be defended out in the marketplace where people live and make decisions. Divide the lesson into three sections:

I. Contending for the faith
II. Learning to set limits
III. Risking controversy

I. Contending for the faith

Explore with your class this question: How can we stand up for our Christian beliefs without being un-Christlike? There is a delicate balance between being right and being self-righteous. Our ultimate goal in defending Christian truth is not to put forth a view for our own benefit (although we should know where we stand and why!). Our primary task as witnesses for Christ is to present our faith to others in the most winsome fashion possible.

Emphasize that the possibility of faith comes as a gift from God; it is not something that we have earned. If we have benefited because of a gift from God, should this not affect the manner in which we share our faith with others? The parading of one's ego is not a Christian virtue; quiet humility is!

Ask the class to discuss ways they believe to be most effective in sharing one's Christian faith with others. (You might jot these down on the board.) Also ask if there are any negative ways of presentation which should be avoided because they tend to discourage others from hearing the good news.

II. Learning to set limits

In our pluralistic society, where many different religious opinions are held, a certain degree of tolerance is not only desirable, but necessary for the common good. Certainly no thoughtful Christian would want to impose views on others. We need to have respect for another person's sincerely held religious convictions. This principle would seem to hold true whether it is applied to those within the church fellowship or those without.

Before proceeding further, find out if the above-mentioned principle represents a generally acceptable view of religious tolerance. At what points would class members modify this? Work with the class in defining the limits to a rather general tolerance. Is Dr. Willimon correct when he claims that Christians "have lazily decided to accept everyone's opinion as equally valid and to condemn nothing"? Admittedly, within the fellowship of the church, we are sometimes reluctant to be too candid because we have to continue living with one another. When should we speak out—even if it means offending someone? If we know that another's view on an important issue is decidedly non-Christian or perhaps anti-Christian, dare we *not speak out*?

III. Risking controversy

Assuming the class believes in the importance of standing up for the faith and setting some limits to the diversity of Christian opinions, suggest the final step in guarding Christian hope. As people of faith, we must be willing to risk controversy. Both within our churches and in the larger community, speaking for Christian truth will necessarily be controversial at times. If the faith we profess is always polite and acceptable, never in any way offensive, then it is some type of cultural religion, but it is not Christianity!

How willing are members of your class to take an unpopular stand? What examples might our Christian tradition offer to such persons? You could, of course, point out the various models in the New Testament: Jesus, Paul, and Peter. Or you might remind them of the prophetic ministry of Old Testament figures such as Amos, Isaiah, Jeremiah, and Ruth.

Finally, remind the class that there has always been controversy in the church. Indeed, the church can be most alive when there are lively debates and vigorous differences of opinion on significant issues. Ask your people to define significant issues in your church (or even in your hometown). Help them to distinguish between "significant" and "trivial" and between "Christian debate" and "petty bickering." Dr. Willimon suggests a good operating principle for dealing with controversy in the church. Remember that all persons are beloved of God; that is not at issue. What is worth debating are "the implications of that love for us."

Helping Class Members Act

Suggest that each member think about the relationship between Christian debate on a significant issue and the effectiveness of the church's witness to the world. Is the quality of our faith judged by our willingness to face the difficult questions? Jude 20-21 are good verses to consider when meditating on the central issues of Christian faith.

Planning for Next Sunday

Assign Luke 1:5-56 and 2:21-40 to read for next Sunday. Since the next lesson begins a unit on the Holy Spirit, the birth of Jesus as found in Luke is very appropriate. Ask members to think about how hope (the subject for the series just ended) is logically linked to the birth of the Christ child.

The Person and Work of the Holy Spirit

UNIT I: THE HOLY SPIRIT ACTIVE IN JESUS

Horace R. Weaver

THREE LESSONS   **APRIL 20–MAY 4**

The purpose of the course entitled "The Person and Work of the Holy Spirit" is to gain a clearer picture of the role of the Holy Spirit in Jesus' life and in the life of the Christian community. Emphasis is placed both on the dynamic power released by the Spirit and on the way persons relate to God and others when they are living by the Spirit.

The first unit of this course is entitled "The Holy Spirit Active in Jesus." Consisting of three lessons, the unit deals with the role of the Spirit in Jesus' birth ("The Holy Spirit and Jesus' Birth," April 20), calling ("The Holy Spirit and Jesus' Calling," April 27), and ministry ("The Holy Spirit in Jesus' Ministry," May 4). Texts chosen for study come from the gospels of Luke and Matthew. (Neither Mark nor John includes the infancy narratives.)

Development of the Doctrine of the Trinity
BISHOP MACK B. STOKES

The doctrine of the Trinity is the distinctively Christian doctrine of God. This doctrine is not a philosophical idea. It is not and cannot be a human discovery. God has graciously revealed himself in the Bible as Father, Son, and Holy Spirit.

Like other great doctrines, the doctrine of the Trinity is not developed in detail in the Bible. Nevertheless, it is definitely affirmed. We find it in the baptismal formula (Matthew 28:19). It is expressed in the intimate relationships between the Father and the Son in John's Gospel, 1:1-18; 3:35; 5:19-24; 10:15, 18; 12:45; 13:3; 14:8-11. Cf. I John 1:3; 2:22; Matthew 11:27; Luke 10:22; Ephesians 3:5. Paul referred again and again to God the Father and our Lord Jesus Christ (I Corinthians 1:3, 4, 24; 8:6; II Corinthians 1:2-3; Galatians 1:1-5; Ephesians 1:3; 4:5-6; 6:23; Philippians 1:2; Colossians 1:2-3, 15-16; I Thessalonians 1:1-3; 5:9; II Thessalonians 1:2).

As to the Holy Spirit, his deity is affirmed, explicitly or implicitly, throughout the New Testament. (See Matthew 28:19; John 14:16-17, 26; 15:26; 16:7-13, Acts 2; Romans 8; I Corinthians 12–14; Ephesians 2:18; Jude 20-21). The Holy Spirit acted in the birth, life, and death of Jesus. He empowered the apostles and others at Pentecost. He brought nurture, comfort, assurance, special gifts, and countless other blessings to believers in the earliest churches. Even though the word *Trinity* does not occur in the New Testament, the fact that God made himself known as Father, Son, and Holy Spirit is clearly revealed. Therefore it was natural to expect Paul to end one of his letters with the trinitarian benediction (II Corinthians 13:14). And the great creedal statements affirm the Trinity without elaborating upon it extensively.

The primary question which arises in the context of this article is: How did this doctrine develop?

As we might suppose, there have been various theories attempting to explain the origin of the doctrine of the Trinity. For example, some people have said that the mind of human beings is so constituted that sooner or later it had to come out with a trinitarian conception of God. One reason given for this is that there is supposedly something sacred about the number three.

Still others have insisted that this doctrine grew out of the influence of non-Christian trinitarian ideas upon the mind of the church, for there are trinities in other religions. In addition, some have sought to explain the Trinity by the practical demands of human life. We are told, for example, that human beings need a deity who is both Lord of the universe and of life and who graciously makes himself available. So the Trinity was devised by human beings because of their need for ultimate spiritual security.

It is obvious that these theories are not based on any careful study of the Bible. From the standpoint of the biblical revelation, threeness is nothing; other trinities are irrelevant and make no appeal; and humankind's practical needs are incidental to the primary facts of Christian experience.

Moreover, all such efforts to explain the development of the doctrine of the Trinity are alike in being oblivious to the supernatural, redemptive, prearranged plan of God to redeem the world and inaugurate his kingdom. The only adequate explanation of the development of the doctrine of the Trinity is that God himself has taken the initiative to make himself known as Father, Son, and Holy Spirit.

But we need to ask more particularly now what were the major stages in the development of the doctrine of the Trinity in the history of Christianity? Nearly all Christians agree that there is only one God. Tritheism (the idea that there are three gods) has been ruled out, even though there have been some recurring tendencies to speak of God as a kind of "society-in-unity." The Bible makes it clear that there is only one God. On the other hand, Christians have been careful to avoid the idea that this one God expresses himself merely in three different ways so that there is no ultimate Trinity. This idea has been known as modalism, and refers to the notion that God manifests himself in three distinctive or successive modes.

In the doctrine of the Trinity, we are confronted with a profound mystery. No amount of thought has been able to present a fully clear or adequate statement concerning it. Perhaps John Wesley summarized this as well as anyone when he said, "I believe this *fact*. . . , That God is Three and One. But the *manner how* I do not comprehend; and I do not believe it. Now in this, in the *manner*, lies the mystery; and so it may be; I have no concern with it: It is no object of my faith: I believe just so much as God has revealed, and no more. But this, the *manner*, He has not revealed; therefore I believe nothing about it" (*The Works of John Wesley*, Zondervan edition, volume 6, page 204).

Let us return now to the question: How did this doctrine actually develop? The most important stage in the unfolding of the Christian doctrine of the Trinity concerned the processes involved in recognizing Jesus Christ as fully God. In the early days of Christianity, some had said that Jesus became divine when God adopted him as his Son on the occasion of his baptism. This theory is known as adoptionism. Another view was sponsored by Arius of Alexandria (A.D. 280?–336). He developed the idea that Jesus Christ was less than God and more than man. Arius's views were repudiated by the church, and he was declared a heretic.

It was primarily under the leadership of Athanasius (A.D. 298?–373), who was also from Alexandria, that the main direction of the emphasis on Jesus Christ as truly divine as well as truly human came to its most decisive expression. Therefore the church began to think clearly in terms of God the Father and God the Son.

What about God the Holy Spirit? The Spirit of God is referred to again and again in the Old Testament. While there is no clearly developed doctrine of the Holy Spirit in the Old Testament; nevertheless, the recurring emphasis on the Spirit of God as involved profoundly in the affairs of this world—and especially in the lives of people—prepared the way for the later development in Christian thought on the Holy Spirit.

The event that, more than any other event, led the way to emphasizing the Holy Spirit as divine was Pentecost. What the Christians experienced there as well as in subsequent experiences led them to affirm that the Holy Spirit was indeed God himself at work in their lives. And the continuing experience of the power of the Holy Spirit in the lives of Christians in the early communities of prayer and faith led them to affirm the great reality of God the Holy Spirit. In this way we see that the doctrine of God as the Trinity, Father, Son, and Holy Spirit, grew out of the distinctively Christian encounters of God with his people. This in turn led to the later developments of the doctrine of the Trinity in theological forms and in creedal statements. It also led to the Christian understanding that the Holy Spirit is especially at work in the church.

Since it is a primary mission of the Holy Spirit to magnify Jesus Christ as Lord and to bring the people together into a community that bears the name of Jesus Christ, the work of the Holy Spirit is especially important in the life of the church, which is the Body of Christ. The Holy Spirit, then, has been understood to be at work in the worship services of our churches, in the sacraments of baptism and the Lord's Supper, in the call of God to the ministry, and in the life of prayer in the community of faith. In addition, the Holy Spirit is known as the One who empowers the people of God for mission. He empowers them for world evangelization and for service in the causes for justice, peace, and human well-being.

LESSON 8   APRIL 20

The Holy Spirit and Jesus' Birth

Background Scripture: Luke 1:5-56; 2:21-40

The Main Question—William H. Willimon

"I have the Holy Spirit," he said. He spoke as if he had achieved some great status—as if he were saying, "I now have a college diploma."

He then went on to describe all the good things that had happened to him since he had the Spirit—his marriage was happier, his business was prospering, he was content and at peace. It was obvious. Just by looking at him, you could tell that something important had happened to him. Was it the Spirit?

What does it mean to "have the Holy Spirit"?

From listening to my friend talk about having the Spirit, one might assume that the Holy Spirit is something you earn for being a very good Christian, a great achievement. Some have it and some don't, it appears. Can this be true? Is the Holy Spirit optional equipment for a Christian, the possession of a few? Or does the Spirit belong to the very nature of the Christian life?

Another problem in trying to understand what it means to say that one has the Holy Spirit is that, by its very nature, the Spirit seems to be something which is free-floating, beyond definition, vague, and amorphous. At a football game we say, "The fans' cheering shows that they have school spirit." Or we speak of a "spirited horse." Christians are urged to follow the "promptings of the Spirit." Is there any way to determine the precise meaning of what we are referring to when we speak of the Holy Spirit?

Paul urges one of his churches to "test the spirit." Evidently not every spirit is truly the *Holy* Spirit. But how do we know? What will be our criteria for testing, our standards of judgment when we test the spirits?

Many of us think of the Holy Spirit as some vague, faraway, ethereal phenomenon with little relevance to our everyday lives. This unit and its accompanying scripture will lead us to give meaning to our views of the Holy Spirit and to explore the work of that Spirit in our lives.

What does it mean to be filled with the Holy Spirit? That is the concern of today's lesson and the others that follow.

As You Read the Scripture—Mike Winters

Luke 1:5-56; 2:21-40. The Gospel according to Luke is an orderly account of the life of Jesus written to a man named Theophilus. Luke blends the divine and the human natures of Jesus. He uses the components of prophecy and mystery to emphasize Jesus' divinity. He uses the daily drama of human life set against the backdrop of the region of Galilee, the road to Jerusalem, and Jerusalem to emphasize Jesus' humanity.

In the first two chapters, Luke conveys the very ordinary circumstances of the birth of Jesus to Jewish peasants. And yet, the conception and birth of Jesus were adorned, according to Luke, with the fulfillment of prophecy and mystery. Something very special happened in the birth of a child.

Chapter 1:5-25. These are the circumstances of the conception of John, the son of old and barren Elizabeth and disbelieving Zechariah, the priest, who needed a sign.

Verses 14-17. These verses announce the special calling and destiny of John the Baptist.

Verse 15. This verse alludes to Numbers 6:1-4. There the special conditions of the Nazirite (a person set apart to serve the Lord) are set forth. Luke mentions only the condition related to wine and strong drink. John shall be drunk not with wine, but with the Holy Spirit. (See note on 1:35 below.)

Verse 16. This verse alludes to Malachi 4:5-6, which prophesies Elijah's return to prepare the people for the "great and terrible day of the Lord." John the Baptist is the one who will fulfill this purpose.

Verses 26-38. The angel Gabriel announces to Mary, a virgin betrothed to Joseph of the house of David, the conception of a son to be called Jesus.

Verse 35. The child to be conceived will be holy, conceived by the power of the Holy Spirit.

The Holy Spirit and "the power of the Most High" are one and the same. The Holy Spirit is the productive energy of God working through people; events; and political, religious, and social structures to fulfill God's purpose. Now God's Spirit will work through Mary.

The child conceived in Mary will be "the Son of God."

Verse 38. Mary acknowledges her role as a means through which God would work out this purpose. Unlike Zechariah, who needed a sign (verse

18), Mary responded in hope and faith and willingness to let the Holy Spirit work through her.

Verses 39-56. Mary visits Elizabeth.

Verses 41-42. The Holy Spirit filled Elizabeth and she perceived Mary's special role in God's plan: to be the Messiah's mother.

Verses 46-55. This is the "Magnificat." *Magnificat* is the first word of this hymn in the Latin translation. Compare it with Hannah's prayer in I Samuel 2:1-10. In both cases, God is praised as the one who turns things topsy-turvy. The mighty are dethroned The humble are exalted. The hungry are filled with good things while the rich are sent away empty. Mary's song is revolutionary in tone and content.

Chapter 2:21-40. The background for these verses is the established Jewish ritul of circumcision and the purification of Joseph and Mary. Leviticus 12:2-4 is the Old Testament background for this practice.

Verses 25-27. The Holy Spirit worked through Simeon in the recognition of the Christ child. The Spirit had revealed to Simeon that he would not die until he had seen the anointed one. For this he had waited and longed.

Verses 29-32. Simeon's prophetic oracle reveals the universality of the prupose of the Messiah.

Verse 30. Isaiah 52:10 says, "All the ends of the earth shall see the salvation of our God." The probable meaning is in the fuller context of the universal nature of Jesus' mission. But here Luke whispers a view of atonement that does not focus entirely on the cross. God has come among us in the person of Jesus Christ. The Incarnation is, itself, redemptive. Christ assumed our flesh, and in doing so, healed it. When Simeon had seen the infant Jesus, he had seen God's salvation.

Verses 36-38. The eighty-four year-old widow Anna appears (of the Holy Spirit) at precisely the right moment to thank God for the infant redeemer.

Selected Scripture

King James Version

Luke 1:35-42

35 And the angel answered and said unto her, The Holy Ghost shall come upon thee, and the power of the Highest shall overshadow thee: therefore also that holy thing which shall be born of thee shall be called the Son of God.

36 And, behold, thy cousin Elisabeth, she hath also conceived a son in her old age: and this is the sixth month with her, who was called barren.

37 For with God nothing shall be impossible.

38 And Mary said, Behold the handmaid of the Lord; be it unto me according to thy word. And the angel departed from her.

Revised Standard Version

Luke 1:35-42

35 And the angel said to her, "The Holy Spirit will come upon you, and the power of the Most High will overshadow you; therefore the child to be born will be called holy, the Son of God.

36 And behold, your kinswoman Elizabeth in her old age has also conceived a son; and this is the sixth month with her who was called barren. 37 For with God nothing will be impossible." 38 And Mary said, "Behold, I am the handmaid of the Lord; let it be to me according to your word." And the angel departed from her.

39 And Mary arose in those days, and went into the hill country with haste, into a city of Juda;

40 And entered into the house of Zăch-ă-rī'-ăs, and saluted Elisabeth.

41 And it came to pass, that, when Elisabeth heard the salutation of Mary, the babe leaped in her womb; and Elisabeth was filled with the Holy Ghost:

42 And she spake out with a loud voice, and said, Blessed *art* thou among women, and blessed *is* the fruit of thy womb.

Luke 2:25-32

25 And, behold, there was a man in Jerusalem, whose name *was* Simeon; and the same man *was* just and devout, waiting for the consolation of Israel: and the Holy Ghost was upon him.

26 And it was revealed unto him by the Holy Ghost, that he should not see death, before he had seen the Lord's Christ.

27 And he came by the Spirit into the temple: and when the parents brought in the child Jesus, to do for him after the custom of the law,

28 Then took he him up in his arms, and blessed God, and said,

29 Lord, now lettest thou thy servant depart in peace, according to thy word:

30 For mine eyes have seen thy salvation,

31 Which thou hast prepared before the face of all people;

32 A light to lighten the Gentiles, and the glory of thy people Israel.

Key Verse: The angel answered and said unto her, The Holy Ghost shall come upon thee, and the power of the Highest shall overshadow thee: therefore also that holy thing which shall be born of thee shall be called the Son of God. (Luke 1:35)

39 In those days Mary arose and went with haste into the hill country, to a city of Judah, 40 and she entered the house of Zechari´ah and greeted Elizabeth. 41 And when Elizabeth heard the greeting of Mary, the babe leaped in her womb; and Elizabeth was filled with the Holy Spirit 42 and she exclaimed with a loud cry, "Blessed are you among women, and blessed is the fruit of your womb!

Luke 2:25-32

25 Now there was a man in Jerusalem, whose name was Simeon, and this man was righteous and devout, looking for the consolation of Israel, and the Holy Spirit was upon him. 26 And it had been revealed to him by the Holy Spirit that he should not see death before he had seen the Lord's Christ. 27 And inspired by the Spirit he came into the temple; and when the parents brought in the child Jesus, to do for him according to the custom of the law, 28 he took him up in his arms and blessed God and said,

29 "Lord, now lettest thou thy
    servant depart in peace,
    according to thy word;
30 for mine eyes have seen thy
    salvation
31 which thou hast prepared in the
    presence of all peoples,
32 a light for revelation to the
    Gentiles, and for glory to thy
    people Israel."

Key Verse:
**The angel said to her,
"The Holy Spirit will come upon
    you,
and the power of the Most High
    will overshadow you;
therefore the child to be born will
    be called holy,
the son of God." (Luke 1:35)**

The Scripture and the Main Question—William H. Willimon

The Holy Spirit Will Come upon You

There she was—minding her own business, doing the ordinary things any young Jewish peasant girl might be doing on any ordinary day. There was nothing about her which is worthy of particular note. We are told little about her family, her education, her natural abilities. In fact, there was probably little to tell. In Mary's day, women were relegated to the lowest levels of Near Eastern society. They were without power or security, dependent upon their husbands or families for survival. This was Mary.

Do you see the surprise in having Luke begin his account of the coming of Christ by focusing his lens upon Mary? Luke says that the story of Jesus—Lord of Lords, King of Kings, Prince of Peace, Son of God, Messiah—begins with a lowly peasant girl named Mary.

Perhaps we are told so little about her because there was little to tell. Or perhaps Luke is trying to impress us with the fact that Mary's importance in the story of Christ was due not to her family background, her intelligence, her superior education, her prestige in society, or any of the other criteria by which we often judge people. Mary is significant; she is the very beginning of the Jesus story *because of something which God does for her, something God gives her.*

There she is, minding her own business, going about her life, when the angel Gabriel visits her (Luke 1:26-56). Gabriel addresses her, "Hail, O favored one, the Lord is with you!" (1:28).

Mary wonders what this greeting means. It means that, in Gabriel's words, "The Holy Spirit will come upon you, and the power of the Most High will overshadow you; therefore the child to be born will be called holy" (1:35).

Mary is being encountered by the Holy Spirit, empowered for some special work which the Lord has for her to do.

Her story parallels those of other people in the Bible. One is reminded, for instance, of Moses' sister Miriam, who was empowered to aid in the liberation of the children of Israel from slavery. Mary reminds one also of another rather unlikely candidate for motherhood, old Sarah, wife of Abraham. The Lord came to Sarah, even in her advanced age, and told her that she was to bear a child who would be part of God's salvation (Genesis 17).

We might well wonder how this young woman, so unequipped by our standards of what a person needs to do something important, could handle so important a task as being the mother of our Savior.

As the angel tells Mary, "With God nothing will be impossible" (1:37).

Inspired by the Spirit

The point of this passage is that the Lord gives Mary the gifts she needs to do what she is called to do. The old saying, "God never puts upon us more than God gives us strength to bear" is at least true in this case. Mary has the empowerment of the Spirit in order to fulfill her role as "the handmaid of the Lord" (1:37).

Elizabeth, Mary's kinswoman, is also visited by the Spirit (1:39-44). Elizabeth likewise has an important role to play in God's purposes.

What can we learn from these opening chapters of Luke's Gospel? For one thing, we learn that the visit by the Spirit seems to precede some important task that God wants people to do. The Spirit calls us to do something for God, then gives us what we need to do that task.

By implication, this means that we receive the Spirit, the Holy Spirit, not simply to make us feel better or as some sort of privileged personal possession, but *because God has something important for us to do.*

To be "filled with the Spirit" means to be called and equipped to do God's bidding. Thus Mary refers to herself as the servant of God. When we say that someone is "enthusiastic," we mean literally that one is filled with spirit. Mary was filled with the Spirit, and her response was enthusiastic to say the least.

She sings, "My soul magnifies the Lord, and my spirit rejoices in God my Savior, for he has regarded the low estate of his handmaiden" (1:46-48).

Throughout Luke's Gospel, the Spirit is depicted as a holy force that roams about calling people to do God's will and then empowering them to respond to God's call. What was true for them is also true for us today—the Holy Spirit calls us and empowers us to be disciples. The followers of Jesus are those who are *inspired* (literally, "in spirited") for God's work.

She had spent forty hard years working as a teacher in inner-city schools. It was tough and demanding work, so she eagerly anticipated her retirement when she would at last have time to enjoy a well-deserved rest. Finally, that long-awaited day came and she retired at age sixty-five.

Because she was now at home for most of the day, Lila Mae noticed things she had not seen before. Her neighborhood was looking run-down and blighted. Many young adults roamed the streets all day, out of work, getting into trouble. Senior citizens like her had nowhere to go during the day and were fearful to go out of their homes due to the high crime rate in the neighborhood.

"Something ought to be done," Lila Mae said to herself. But who was there to do it? Someone younger than she ought to do it—someone with more talent, more energy, more ability. She looked around, trying a number of social agencies and service groups, but no one was willing or able to help.

"If they will not help, I'll just do it myself," Lila Mae said. And she did. She lobbied constantly at the city council until she was given one of the abandoned houses on her street to use as a community center. She walked miles around town appealing for building materials and equipment. She engaged some of the young men and women to help her work on renovating the house. Then she asked them to run an after-school program for the neighborhood children—a study hall, tutoring, boxing, crafts, art.

Her little house is now known as the Southside Community Center. The neighborhood is a better place in which to live. A number of people have a better outlook toward themselves and their world because of the work of Lila Mae.

Now how do you explain a phenomenon like that? A miracle? That's what many in town call the Southside Community Center. But that makes it sound as if it all just popped up out of nowhere. "Inspiring," is what many people say when they hear Lila Mae's story. It might be more accurate to say that this story is *inspired,* that is, filled with the Spirit. For how can things like this—an older woman turning a whole world upside down—happen unless it is through the prompting and guidance and equipment of the Holy Spirit?

Inspired indeed!

By the Holy Spirit

And so, on the basis for our scripture today, we can say that the work of the Spirit is not as vague and ill-defined as we might think. The Spirit is present whenever people are hearing the call of God and responding to that call in their lives—Mary, Elizabeth, Simeon, or you or me.

What is the Spirit saying to you today? Listen, listen to the promptings of the Spirit in your own life—you are never too young or too old or too uneducated or too poor to hear that voice. It calls your name above all the other voices that tug at you. Listen. And then be bold enough, faithful enough to rise and act upon what you hear.

Rise. Say yes. The Spirit will give you what you need to do its bidding.

Helping Adults Become Involved—Robert G. Rogers

Preparing to Teach

This lesson begins a course on the Holy Spirit. You should browse generally through the six lessons: three centered on Jesus and the Spirit; three emphasizing Christian life and the Spirit. As you commence your preparation, think about your own understanding of the Holy Spirit as found both in the New Testament and in the contemporary life of the church.

The specific aim of this lesson is to demonstrate that the birth of Jesus is a sign of God's Holy Spirit working in the world. Although the assigned lesson uses only Luke's version of the birth, you will also want to read Matthew 1:1–2:23 since most Christians combine the two accounts in their own thinking about Jesus' birth. Note that even though the specific details are different in each, both Luke and Matthew affirm God's active involvement in the world through the person of the Holy Spirit.

Introducing the Main Question

In "The Main Question," Dr. Willimon poses the central question: What does it mean to be filled with the Holy Spirit? Ask your class members to contemplate briefly how they would go about answering this question. Perhaps they can cite the various ways in which they believe the Spirit operates in the world. In all likelihood, their suggestions can be summarized in one general principle: the Holy Spirit is an agent empowering the people of God. Is it not the case that being "touched" by God's Spirit strengthens persons of faith to perform the work of God? We, like Mary, are empowered to be God's witnesses in the world.

The Holy Spirit plays no favorites. One's social or economic status in life is not important. What is essential is our willingness to be God's instrument. It was so with Mary, the mother of Jesus, who willingly accepted her role in God's plan of salvation. So it may be with us today if we allow God to work through us for the greater good of humanity. Discuss for a few moments what such openness to God demands.

Developing the Lesson

Since the class members are now thinking about the potential of the Holy Spirit in their lives, help further the process by developing three areas in the lesson:

I. Defining the Holy Spirit scripturally
II. Being open to the call of the Holy Spirit
III. Living under the guidance of the Holy Spirit

I. Defining the Holy Spirit scripturally

Carefully work through Luke's birth narratives with your class. Ask members to analyze with you the effect the Holy Spirit had on the following persons: Zechariah, Elizabeth, Mary, and Simeon. What did the guidance of the Spirit enable each of them to do or be? How was each empowered to move beyond what he or she had been prior to the coming of the Holy Spirit?

Notice how the Spirit brings deep spiritual insight to each of the persons in the story. Also call attention to the fact that the Spirit brings to each the strength necessary for a unique task. In each instance the ultimate purpose assigned to each Spirit-filled person is the same: to witness to the glory of God. However, each witnessed in a manner best suited to himself or herself. Mary bore the Christ child; Elizabeth bore John the Baptist, who was in turn a witness to Jesus; Zechariah and Simeon were inspired to proclaim the meaning of the two births.

Conclude this portion by asking the class to cite other biblical examples of Spirit-filled persons. (You might suggest some—for example, Ezekiel 36:26-28; Isaiah 61:1-2; Paul.) What qualities in each of them did the Holy Spirit develop and use?

II. Being open to the call of the Holy Spirit

The class has considered biblical examples of the work of the Holy Spirit. Now your task is to focus on ways we Christians can be open to the Spirit's work in our lives today. Perhaps it would be helpful initially to reiterate that God's Spirit works through us as we are, with all our imperfections and shortcomings. To be instruments for God's work, we do not have to be perfect; rather, we should rely on the Spirit to equip us for the task assigned.

Perhaps your class members, like many Christians, become overwhelmed by the things they cannot do rather than encouraged by those they can. How does the Holy Spirit help overcome these fears of failure? Is it not a sign—a symbol of our Christian faith—that God is with us in the choices and actions we are called to make? Ask the class to consider again the situation of Mary. Suppose she had said, "No, God, I cannot." Instead, the Spirit emboldened that young woman of humble circumstances to accept the nurturing process for the Savior of the world! Accepting the direction of the Holy Spirit moves us from a "cannot" to a "can" vision of life.

Emphasize the patience of Elizabeth and Zechariah in waiting many years for God's fulfillment. Yet, the Holy Spirit entered their lives, so the period of waiting was worthwhile. Close this portion by noting that it does not matter whether one is very old, quite young, or somewhere in between. The Holy Spirit can work in the life of any person who is open to the will of God.

III. Living under the guidance of the Holy Spirit

Dr. Willimon tells of Lila Mae, who saw a task that needed to be done and did it; he correctly notes that the story is inspired, clear evidence of the Spirit' working through a devoted person. Encourage your class to analyze the story together. What characteristics in Lila Mae led her to make this commitment? What about Mary? Elizabeth? The phrase "living courageously" seems to describe all three women. They trusted in the Lord to provide them the strength and guidance necessary to complete the mission they accepted. Perhaps you might suggest that in both the biblical and the modern stories, the work of God in the Holy Spirit is twofold: (1) providing vision to see the opportunity for service; and (2) sustaining those who accept the opportunity.

Rabbi Hillel was a famous teacher who lived in the time of Jesus. One of the rabbi's favorite expressions was: "If not me, who? If not now, when?" Does not this attitude toward life describe rather well the person who conscientiously seeks to do the will of God in all circumstances? It would appear that living under the guidance of the Holy Spirit involves openness, courage, and trust. What other characteristics would the class add?

Helping Class Members Act

Suggest that class members think during the coming week about ways they feel God's Spirit has acted in their lives. This process might also give each member opportunity for personal reflection regarding how to seek the Spirit's guidance during various situations. Are there specific characteristics each member wishes to cultivate so as to be more available to the working of the Spirit?

Planning for Next Sunday

Next week, the lesson will entail considering the call of Jesus to his public ministry. As preparation, read Luke 3:15-22 and 4:1-30. Notice especially how being called by the Holy Spirit influences the direction one's life takes. Also notice that evil, as represented by the temptations of Satan, cannot win when confronted by the power of the Spirit.

LESSON 9 APRIL 27

The Holy Spirit and Jesus' Calling

Background Scripture: Luke 3:15-22; 4:1-30

The Main Question—William H. Willimon

At a workshop I attended, the leader asked a group of us to draw a graph that would depict our relationship to God in the course of our lives. The line begins at birth, travels up and down through the years, and ends at our present age.

You can imagine how most of our graphs looked. Most depicted ups and downs. Some began at a low point and moved steadily upward. But the majority of us depicted our lives in their relationship to God as a series of peaks and valleys.

The psychologist Abraham Maslow first spoke of "peak experiences" in people's lives—moments when everything comes together for us, when we see clearly what we ought to do and make major changes of direction in our lives.

If you were depicting a graph of your life, what would it look like? When were the moments when, as if standing on some high mountain peak, you looked out, surveyed your whole life, and set your course on the basis of that view?

We once thought of adulthood as a rather staid, fixed time in life. From recent studies in adult development, such as those reported in books such as *Passages* or *Seasons of a Man's Life*, we know that certain "marker events" characterize adulthood.

In today's lesson, as we continue our exploration of the Holy Spirit, we view some "marker events" in the life of Jesus himself and see some of our own "peak experiences" and "marker events" reflected there.

As You Read the Scripture—Mike Winters

Luke 3:15-22, 4:1-30. John the Baptist has begun his special ministry of preparing the people for the coming of the Lord (1:17, 3:4). He proclaimed the ethics for life in the days of waiting for the Lord (3:10-14).

Chapter 3:15-16. John responds to the people's inquiry into what seemed to them to be his messianic behavior. He denies that he is the Messiah. The level of expectation is already high. But he does not dash their hope. He gives them reason to raise the level of their expectation even higher.

John's baptism with water, a symbol of initiation and cleansing, cannot be compared with the Messiah's baptism with the Holy Spirit and fire, which is real rather than symbolic and really purifies. Acts 1:5 says, "John baptized wih water, but before many days you shall be baptized with the Holy Spirit." John's view of himself and his role in the messianic plan of God is a humble one. He points away from himself and toward the one who is coming.

Verse 17. Winnowing is a means of separating seed husks from grain by pitching the grain and husks into the wind. The wind carries away the lighter husks, while the grain falls back to the floor. This is an image used to demonstrate that the unrighteous will be separated from the righteous.

Verse 21. Jesus was baptized by John. Mark 1:9-11 is a more detailed account of Jesus' baptism.

Luke records many instances of Jesus' prayer life: 5:16; 6:12; 9:18; 9:28-29; 1:21-22; 11:1; 22:41; 23:34, 46.

"The heaven was opened" is a Semitic way of expressing divine involvement, in this case, in Jesus' baptism.

Verse 22. The energy, power, and faithfulness of God's Spirit came in the symbolic form of a dove.

Chapter 4:1-30. The Holy Spirit lead Jesus into the wilderness where he was tested and proved. In the power of the Spirit, he returns to his home, to his own synagogue in Nazareth, where he addresses the people. He defines his messianic purpose, based on Isaiah 61:1-2.

Verse 1. The expression "full of the Holy Spirit" became a way of speaking about the readiness of the church to perform faithfully. Here it is Jesus who is ready—empowered.

Verses 2-13. Much can be said about this wilderness experience. In the final analysis, however, it was a grueling experience that shaped character and defined purpose.

Verse 14. Jesus came from this wilderness experience with his messianic credentials intact. Jesus continued in the power of the Spirit which came upon him at his baptism.

Verse 15. Jesus had been teaching in the synagogue in Capernaum. Now he goes home and preaches his first sermon at his home synagogue.

Verses 16-17. Jesus was committed to the worship of God and the study of his faith. He was in the Nazareth synagogue *because it was his custom.*

Verses 18-19. This text is from Isaiah 61:1-2a. Isaiah's message was one of encouragement to the Jews in Babylonian exile. Jesus uses this text to describe his ministry, which will be one of providing encouragement and hope to those "exiled" by poverty, imprisonment, disease, and oppression—exiled by sin. In some ways this was an announcement of the Levitical jubilee. Leviticus 25:10-12 begins, "You shall hallow the fiftieth year, and proclaim liberty throughout the land to all its inhabitants." In these words, Jesus lays out the dimensions of his messianic mission. The Spirit by which Jesus is anointed is the one which descended on him at his baptism and filled him all the days of his life.

Verses 20-30. The people's feelings about Jesus began with wonder but quickly changed. They asked him why he did not perform miracles in his own town as he had elsewhere. He responded by reminding them of some stories of Elijah and Elisha in which the prophets were sent to help and heal foreigners rather than Israelites. This suggested that the Gentiles were favored by God, and the people were angered to the point of wanting to kill him.

Selected Scripture

King James Version	Revised Standard Version
Luke 3:15-17, 21-22	*Luke 3:15-17, 21-22*
15 And as the people were in expectation, and all men mused in their hearts of John, whether he were the Christ, or not;	15 As the people were in expectation, and all men questioned in their hearts concerning John, whether perhaps he were the Christ, 16 John answered them all, "I baptize you with water; but he who is mightier than I is coming, the thong of whose sandals I am not worthy to untie; he will baptize you with the Holy Spirit and with fire. 17 His winnowing fork is in his hand, to clear his threshing floor, and to gather the wheat into his granary, but the chaff he will burn with unquenchable fire."
16 John answered, saying unto *them* all, I indeed baptize you with water; but one mightier than I cometh, the latchet of whose shoes I am not worthy to unloose: he shall baptize you with the Holy Ghost and with fire:	
17 Whose fan *is* in his hand, and he will thoroughly purge his floor, and will gather the wheat into his garner; but the chaff he will burn with fire unquenchable.	
21 Now when all the people were baptized, it came to pass, that Jesus also being baptized, and praying, the heaven was opened,	21 Now when all the people were baptized, and when Jesus also had been baptized and was praying, the heaven was opened, 22 and the Holy spirit descended upon him in bodily form, as a dove, and a voice came from heaven, "Thou art my beloved Son; with thee I am well pleased."
22 And the Holy Ghost descended in a bodily shape like a dove upon him, and a voice came from heaven, which said, Thou art my beloved Son; in thee I am well pleased.	

Luke 4:16-19

16 And he came to Nazareth, where he had been brought up: and, as his custom was, he went into the synagogue on the sabbath day, and stood up for to read.

17 And there was delivered unto him the book of the prophet Ē-śấ-ăs. And when he had opened the book, he found the place where it was written,

18 The Spirit of the Lord is upon me, because he hath anointed me to preach the gospel to the poor; he hath sent me to heal the brokenhearted, to preach deliverance to the captives, and recovering of sight to the blind, to set at liberty them that are bruised,

19 To preach the acceptable year of the Lord.

Key Verse: **The Spirit of the Lord is upon me, because he hath anointed me to preach the gospel to the poor; he hath sent me to heal the brokenhearted, to preach deliverance to the captives, and recovering of sight to the blind, to set at liberty them that are bruised, To preach the acceptable year of the Lord. (Luke 4:18-19)**

Luke 4:16-19

16 And he came to Nazareth, where he had been brought up; and he went to the synagogue, as his custom was, on the sabbath day. And he stood up to read; 17 and there was given to him the book of the prophet Isaiah. He opened the book and found the place where it was written,

18 "The Spirit of the Lord is upon me,
because he has anointed me to preach good news to the poor.
He has sent me to proclaim release to the captives
and recovering of sight to the blind,
to set at liberty those who are oppressed,
19 to proclaim the acceptable year of the Lord."

Key Verse:
The Spirit of the Lord is upon me, because he has anointed me to preach good news to the poor. He has sent me to proclaim release to the captives and recovering of sight to the blind, to set at liberty those who are oppressed, to proclaim the acceptable year of the Lord. (Luke 4:18-19)

The Scripture and the Main Question—William H. Willimon

The Holy Spirit Descended upon Him

How did your life's work begin? It is always interesting to go back to the beginning of it all, to see how you first took the path which led you to where you are today. What event or circumstance would you point to? A college classroom? a story told by your grandmother? an experience at camp one summer? a sermon you heard in church on a Sunday morning? Where did you begin your life's journey?

In today's scripture we focus upon two episodes from the beginning of Jesus' journey—his baptism and his first sermon at his hometown synagogue.

John the Baptist is baptizing people in the River Jordan as a sign "of repentance for the forgiveness of sins" (Luke 3:3). In his sermon, John predicts the arrival of the Christ, the anointed one who "will baptize you with the Holy Spirit and with fire" (3:16). This Christ will be a mighty one who shall judge Israel, winnowing out the unrepentant and unrighteous (3:17).

To John's surprise, Jesus appears on the banks of the Jordan seeking baptism. John agrees to baptize him, and, as he was doing so, something unusual happened—the Holy Spirit descended upon Jesus (3:21-22). A voice is heard from heaven saying, "Thou art my beloved Son; with thee I am well pleased" (3:22).

Now Jesus begins his ministry. The story picks up tempo, the work begins, and Jesus begins his teaching, preaching, and healing. His baptism is the inauguration of his work.

Luke depicts Jesus' baptism as a time when the Spirit descends upon Jesus telling him who he is. God's favor rests upon him and empowers him. Like the laying on of hands during an ordination, this is Jesus' ordination as the Messiah. The Spirit is laid upon him so that he may begin his saving work.

Think back upon the inauguration day or days when your work began. How did you know that you should be a carpenter, a housekeeper, a mother, a father, a nurse, or whatever it is that God has called you to do?

Was there some John the Baptist who looked at you and said, "You are somebody special. This is who you are and what you should be"?

I remember an American History course I took when I was a freshman in college. I had never particularly liked history. But I worked hard and, when the first exams were returned by the instructor, I was surprised to find that I had made an *A*. The instructor asked me to visit him in his office. "What does he want with me?" I wondered.

"You know, you really have a gift for writing. The content of your exam was good, but the way you expressed that content was the most impressive thing about your work. Have you ever thought of writing as a profession?" he asked.

Well, I did not become a full-time writer, but writing did become an important part of my ministry in the church. If you were to ask me, "How did you become a writer?" I would have to refer to that day long ago when that professor looked at me, saw something about me that I had never seen for myself, and told me what I ought to do with these gifts.

That day at the Jordan, John looked at Jesus and saw someone "who is mightier than I" (3:16). The Holy Spirit descended, telling Jesus who Jesus was. But John also saw who Jesus was. Perhaps the Holy Spirit worked through John to reveal this insight. Note how Matthew (3:17) differs from Luke. In Luke only Jesus heard and spoke. In Matthew it was a proclamation to everybody.

A man in my church told me that he thought of himself as someone who had a "ministry of discovery." I asked him what he meant, and he told me that he tried to discover young talent and point it in the right direction. He could recount a number of promising young artists, teachers, managers, and others whom he had taken an interest in, had given encouragement and information they needed to discover their own vocations, and had urged on their way.

I would call that a work of the Spirit—calling and equipping people for what God wants them to do.

In the Power of the Spirit

"And Jesus returned in the power of the Spirit into Galilee. . . . And he came to Nazareth, where he had been brought up; and he went to the synagogue, as his custom was" (4:14, 16).

The Spirit leads Jesus, after his baptism, to return to his hometown synagogue. You probably know the story. Things went well for him there at first, but when he began to interpret the scripture, his words hit a bit too close to home and the trouble started.

Jesus reads from his favorite prophet, Isaiah:

> The Spirit of the Lord is upon me,
> because he has anointed me to preach good news to the poor.
> He has sent me to proclaim release to the captive. (Luke 4:18)

The Spirit is upon him. Why? The Spirit is upon Jesus in order that he might be empowered and equipped to do some work that God wants to be done. Jesus says in this passage that the Spirit is upon him "to preach," "to proclaim," "to set at liberty" (4:18-19).

I think this is important to note. So often in our own day, we think of the Spirit as a comforter, a good friend, something that makes us feel better, a private and personal possession that is given for our betterment.

But this view does not harmonize with the one that is portrayed in today's lesson. Jesus is given the Spirit in order to do something with it. The Spirit is essential equipment for his vocation.

In our baptism, as in Jesus' baptism, we are given the Holy Spirit so that we might be equipped to do God's will. Our baptism is our ordination as priests in this kingdom, the inauguration day of our ministry.

In the early church, newly baptized persons were given a candle so that their light might shine to the world in which they are to proclaim the good news. They were given a new white robe to symbolize their fresh, new identity in Christ. These baptismal gifts were tangible ways of symbolizing the gift of the Spirit for their ministry.

What is *your* ministry? What gifts have you received from God in your baptism? How has the Spirit equipped you? These are pressing, lifelong questions for any Christian to ponder.

Elsewhere, Scripture often speaks of the comfort of the Spirit or the gifts of the Spirit. We will speak about those aspects of the Spirit in later lessons. But today's scripture speaks of the calling and empowering work of the Spirit, the *prodding* of the Spirit. The Spirit prods and pushes us out into ministry, even as Jesus sensed the Spirit was pushing him out to proclaim the good news.

Most of us have felt the comforting and sustaining work of the Spirit in our lives. Have we also felt the prodding work of the Spirit? I suspect that we have.

Fill in the blanks in your life: The Spirit of the Lord is upon me to _____.

He Has Anointed Me

Well, there you are, sitting in church, minding your own business. You have come to church this morning in hopes of hearing some beautiful music by the choir, an engaging sermon. You have come looking for a little peace and comfort.

But the sermon hits you in a way which you had not expected. The preacher is talking about the needs of the poor, the poor right here in your own town. The church is sponsoring a new after-school project for some of the town's poor children. You have some gifts and some background that make you suited for this job. You think of those kids and the work that could be done with them. You can almost hear a voice speaking, speaking to you, calling your name.

At the end of the service, on the way out of church, you say, "Pastor, put me down as a volunteer for that new program with children. I think I can help."

Now there was a sermon that was literally *inspiring*. You, even you, have demonstrated again that the Spirit still calls people, still empowers people. The Spirit of the Lord is upon you.

Helping Adults Become Involved—Robert G. Rogers

Preparing to Teach

The baptism of Jesus marks the beginning of his public ministry. As Luke records it for us, there are two ways in which the Holy Spirit is involved; at baptism itself, as a sign of God's approval; as a guide and comforter during the time of temptation. You might wish to read the baptism stories recorded in the other gospels (Matthew 3:13–4:11, Mark 1:9-13, John 1:29-34) as background.

The specific aim in this lesson is to show how one's calling or vocation in life is influenced by the Holy Spirit. The biblical model for this is, of course, the life of Jesus, but the principle should be applied to the lives of contemporary Christians. Think of ways (perhaps in your life) that God's Holy Spirit has initiated a divine commission to perform a task. You might talk informally with your minister, asking how he or she felt called by the Spirit to enter Christian ministry.

Introducing the Main Question

Dr. Willimon sets the right tone for the lesson. Christians should always be open to new, perhaps unexpected, possibilities for service. Today's scripture focuses on Jesus as a model for service. However, all of us, in whatever situation in life we find ourselves, have a God-given commission if we but accept it. One does not have to be an ordained minister to receive a call. Indeed, most of the church's ministry is performed by nonordained persons who have nevertheless accepted God's call for their own unique contribution to his work.

Point out to the class that Jesus actually "accepted" his vocational call from God as an adult. Indeed, we know very little about Jesus' childhood and adolescence. Undoubtedly those years were formative ones, but the most important decisions of his life were in his adult period. Are we, as adults, open to the Spirit's leading us into new directions? Or do we assume that all the decisions have been made? Do we believe that a "peak experience" (as defined by Dr. Willimon) at this stage in our lives can cause dramatic change in life direction?

Developing the Lesson

Often Christians do not think of their life's work as a calling. How often does someone say, "Oh, I'm *just* a housewife" or "I'm *just* a local businessman"? The tone in the voice suggests that she or he does not see that job as being of much value. Your task in developing the lesson is to help class members see that every worthwhile life's work has the potential of being a sacred calling from God, guided by his Holy Spirit.

Divide the lesson as follows:

I. Defining our life's calling
II. Our role in being God's instrument
III. The Holy Spirit's role in empowering us

I. Defining our life's calling

Refer to the life of Jesus. Our knowledge of his childhood is sketchy, but we can safely assume that he grew up in Nazareth as a normal boy. Ask the class to imagine some of the experiences and persons that influenced Jesus to commit his life to full-time ministry. Was it a neighbor or a rabbi or some of his relatives or his parents who helped Jesus to define and shape his calling to serve God?

Now ask class members to consider their own lives. What persons influenced their decisions in life? All of us can remember several significant persons or events (perhaps "peak experiences") that were the determining factors in our important life decisions. Often, as we look back on our lives, clear patterns emerge that we did not see when living through those earlier times. As Christians, we affirm that God sends his Holy Spirit to guide and comfort us. Can any members of the class look back on their lives and see the work of the Spirit in the life patterns they have identified? Perhaps some of the older members in particular would be willing to share personal insights from their vantage point of many years.

II. Our role in being God's instrument

As you commence this section, note the connection between being called and serving. Based on the model of Jesus' life, Christians have always viewed their mission as twofold: proclaiming the good news about Jesus and serving in the world as representatives of Jesus. Both are essential to Christian discipleship.

Remind the class of Dr. Willimon's parishioner who had a "ministry of discovery." As his Christian vocation, he helped young people find a life's work that would be useful to society and personally satisfying. Although that man was not an ordained minister, was he not serving as God's instrument (or agent) in the world? Imagine that you were one of the persons that parishioner helped. Would you not view his intervention in your life as one led by the Holy Spirit? Refer to the baptism of Jesus. Was John the Baptist led to his life's work by God's Spirit? Did John, in turn, serve as God's instrument when he baptized Jesus?

Now explore the contemporary meaning for your class. Ask members to think of one specific instance in which they have had opportunity to be a "minister" for God. Perhaps it was a time when the helping individual was in the right place to serve an immediate need. How do we account for our being there at the right moment? Was God directing us through his Spirit to help a fellow human being? Do we approach our daily tasks with an openness and flexibility that will allow the Spirit to use us when the need arises?

III. The Holy Spirit's role in empowering us

On what power can we depend if we are open to God's calling us to perform his work? Begin to answer this with your class by turning to the description of Jesus' temptation in the wilderness. The devil, as the incarnation of evil, tried to sway Jesus from his life's work. Notice what form the temptations took: the need for food, the quest for power, the desire to be like God. (Have we been tempted by similar appeals?) Jesus withstood them all because, as the story relates, he "was led by the Spirit for forty days in the wilderness, tempted by the devil" (Luke 4:1-2).

If Jesus received the guidance of the Holy Spirit, cannot we also expect such a gift from God? The wilderness experience was a lonely, soul-searching time; yet, even there the Holy Spirit was present, giving encouragement and strength in the battle against evil. If God gives us the opportunity to minister, does he not also strengthen us against temptations that would lure us from our calling?

Helping Class Members Act

Use the self-analysis of Christian life suggested by Dr. Willimon. Ask class members to "fill in the blanks" in the following statement (a verse used both by Isaiah and Jesus): "The Spirit of the Lord is upon me to _____." Perhaps they can display their answers at home so that they may see them daily as a reminder.

Planning for Next Sunday

Assign the following biblical passages: Luke 11:5-13 and Matthew 12:22-32. When reading, class members should note how evil is defeated when the Holy Spirit is "let loose" to work in and through our lives. However, the Spirit does not do our work for us. We too are very involved in the battle between good and evil.

LESSON 10   MAY 4

The Holy Spirit in Jesus' Ministry

Background Scripture: Matthew 12:22-32; Luke 11:5-13

The Main Question—William H. Willimon

I have just returned from my daily visit to the hospital. After so many years of pastoral visits to the places of the sick and the dying, one might think that I would be hardened to all this suffering by now, that a visit to the hospital would affect me no more than a visit to the grocery store.

But it doesn't work that way. Every time I come into firsthand contact with sickness and hurting at the hospital, it takes something out of me. I feel it for the rest of the day.

We have made great progress in our world. We have learned to harness so many of the forces of nature, we have conquered so many diseases, eliminated so many sources of human pain. But we have not eliminated pain. The human condition is still one of frequent hurt, suffering, sickness, and death. We haven't overcome that.

And yet, if one simply focuses upon the suffering and the dying, one really hasn't told the whole story. For a hospital, or life itself, is more than simply the scene of human bondage to the forces of death and decay. We also live in a world where good battles with evil—and sometimes triumphs. People are not only suffering in our community hospital, they are also getting better, being cured, conquering.

It is so tempting to look only at the darkness and to forget about the light.

Pessimism invariably sounds more profound, more astute, more courageous than optimism. But you have not told the whole story of our world until you also speak of a power let loose in the world, a power that works for good.

The main question of today's lesson? What is that power and how can our lives be part of its work?

As You Read the Scripture—Mike Winters

Matthew 12:22-32 and Luke 11:5-13. The Holy Spirit is the source of Jesus' power. But to speak of this source as though it were something outside of Jesus, influencing him, would be incorrect. The source of Jesus' power—the Holy Spirit—is in fact the very core of who Jesus is. Systematic theology may separate and categorize the work of God, the Father, Son, and Holy Spirit; but the essential unity of the Trinity remains. The Holy Spirit empowering and working within Jesus is, at the same time, Jesus' own power and his own work.

Matthew 12:22-32. In the verses preceding these, Jesus and his disciples had fed themselves from the grain field on a sabbath. Later, on the sabbath, Jesus healed a man who had a withered hand. The Pharisees accused Jesus of breaking the fourth commandment. (Exodus 20:8-11 begins, "Remember the sabbath day, to keep it holy.")

Verses 22-24. The demoniac in this story is blind and dumb. Compare Matthew 9:32-34, where Jesus cast out a demon and was accused of being in the power of demons himself.

Verse 23. The Son of David is a messianic title. The people are asking how Jesus can be healing people. One answer would be that Jesus is the Messiah.

Verse 24. The Pharisees have another answer: evil magic. Beelzebul is Baalzebub, the god of Ekron (II Kings 1:2), of the Philistines. The Jews called Beelzebul Beelzebub, the "lord of flies." Their indictment against Jesus is that his source of power is demonic.

Verses 25-26. In first-century thought a cosmic war was raging between the forces of good and evil. Satan's kingdom was composed of demons and demon-possessed people. If the Pharisees' claim is true, and Jesus is a demon, then, Jesus argues, there is civil war in Satan's kingdom.

Verse 27. "Your sons" are the disciples of the Pharisees. Their work of casting out demons is seen as good. Yet when Jesus does the same thing, they condemn him. The Pharisees are inconsistent.

Verse 28. The Spirit of the Lord has anointed Jesus to "proclaim . . . recovering of sight to the blind, to set at liberty those who are oppressed" (Luke 4:18). God's kingdom has come in Jesus Christ. The work of Jesus in the power of the Holy Spirit is the work of establishing God's kingdom.

Verse 29. The forces of evil can work only if they are allowed first to overpower the force of good.

Verse 30-32. The only unpardonable sin is to openly accuse the good work of God as being evil. The Holy Spirit, which is the energy of God's work in the world and Jesus Christ, cannot be evil.

Luke 11:5-13. The disciples have asked Jesus to teach them how to pray. Here are sayings on prayer, preceded by the Lord's Prayer (an instructional prayer).

Verses 5-8. The point of this story is summed up in the word *persevere*.

Compare Luke 18:1, where the meaning is also persevere, "pray and not lose heart." *Importune* is a verb meaning to persistently ask.
Verses 9-10. Asking, seeking, and knocking are descriptive of the dynamics of persistent prayer. Matthew 21:22 says," Whatever you ask in prayer, you will receive, if you have faith." James 1:5-8 also underscores the value of faithful prayer.
Verses 11-12. The point here is trust. Children trust their parents to give them the good things for which they ask.
Verse 13. God can be trusted to give us the good things for which we ask. So these sayings teach those who pray to be persistent. They provide encouragement for those who pray persistently. The Holy Spirit is given as a result of prayer. See Luke 3:21-22 and Acts 8:15-17, where the Holy Spirit came upon the occasions of prayer.

Selected Scripture

King James Version

Matthew 12:22-28

22 Then was brought unto him one possessed with a devil, blind, and dumb: and he healed him, insomuch that the blind and dumb both spake and saw.

23 And all the people were amazed, and said, Is not this the son of David?

24 But when the Pharisees heard *it,* they said, This *fellow* doth not cast out devils, but by Bē-ĕl'-zĕ-bŭb the prince of the devils.

25 And Jesus knew their thoughts, and said unto them, Every kingdom divided against itself is brought to desolation; and every city or house divided against itself shall not stand:

26 And if Satan cast out Satan, he is divided against himself; how shall then his kingdom stand?

27 And if I by Bē-ĕl'-zĕ-bŭb cast out devils, by whom do your children cast *them* out? therefore they shall be your judges.

28 But if I cast out devils by the Spirit of God, then the kingdom of God is come unto you.

Luke 11:5-13

5 And he said unto them, Which of you shall have a friend, and shall go unto him at midnight, and say

Revised Standard Version

Matthew 12:22-28

22 Then a blind and dumb demoniac was brought to him, and he healed him, so that the dumb man spoke and saw. 23 And all the people were amazed, and said, "Can this be the Son of David?" 24 But when the Pharisees heard it they said, "It is only by Be-el'zebul, the prince of demons, that this man casts out demons." 25 Knowing their thoughts, he said to them, "Every kingdom divided against itself is laid waste, and no city or house divided against itself will stand; 26 and if Satan casts out Satan, he is divided against himself; how then will his kingdom stand? 27 And if I cast out demons by Be-el'zebul, by whom do your sons cast them out? Therefore they shall be your judges. 28 But if it is by the Spirit of God that I cast out demons, then the kingdom of God has come upon you.

Luke 11:5-13

5 And he said to them, "Which of you who has a friend will go to him at midnight and say, 'Friend,

unto him, Friend, lend me three loaves;

6 For a friend of mine in his journey is come to me, and I have nothing to set before him?

7 And he from within shall answer and say, Trouble me not: the door is now shut, and my children are with me in bed; I cannot rise and give thee.

8 I say unto you, Though he will not rise and give him, because he is his friend, yet because of his importunity he will rise and give him as many as he needeth.

9 And I say unto you, Ask, and it shall be given you; seek, and ye shall find; knock, and it shall be opened unto you.

10 For every one that asketh receiveth; and he that seeketh findeth; and to him that knocketh it shall be opened.

11 If a son shall ask bread of any of you that is a father, will he give him a stone? or if *he ask* a fish, will he for a fish give him a serpent?

12 Or if he shall ask an egg, will he offer him a scorpion?

13 If ye then, being evil, know how to give good gifts unto your children: how much more shall *your* heavenly Father give the Holy Spirit to them that ask him?

lend me three loaves; 6 for a friend of mine has arrived on a journey, and I have nothing to set before him'; 7 and he will answer from within, 'Do not bother me; the door is now shut, and my children are with me in bed; I cannot get up and give you anything'? 8 I tell you, though he will not get up and give him anything because he is his friend, yet because of his importunity he will rise and give him whatever he needs. 9 And I tell you, Ask, and it will be given you; seek, and you will find; knock, and it will be opened to you. 10 For every one who asks receives, and he who seeks finds, and to him who knocks it will be opened. 11 What father among you, if his son ask for a fish, will instead of a fish give him a serpent; 12 or if he asks for an egg, will give him a scorpion? 13 If you then, who are evil, know how to give good gifts to your children, how much more will the heavenly Father give the Holy Spirit to those who ask him!"

Key Verse: **If ye then, being evil, know how to give good gifts unto your children: how much more shall your heavenly Father give the Holy Spirit to them that ask him? (Luke 11:13)**

Key Verse: **If you then, who are evil, know how to give good gifts to your children, how much more will the heavenly Father give the Holy Spirit to those who ask him! (Luke 11:13)**

The Scripture and the Main Question—William H. Willimon

He Healed

The scene is repeated often in Jesus' ministry. Someone who is afflicted with a tragic handicap comes to Jesus seeking healing. This time it is a man who is deaf and blind (Matthew 12:22-28). Jesus heals him.

But a controversy arises over the meaning of this act of compassion. Jesus' critics accuse him of being an agent of "the prince of demons" (12:24).

What is the meaning of Jesus' miracles? Some say that Jesus restored sight to the blind, healed the deaf, and lifted up the cripple because such acts proved that he was the Son of God. He did these acts as proofs of who he really was. Who could fail to believe that Jesus was the Son of God when he performed such mighty deeds?

Of course, the Gospels say that almost *everyone* could look at Jesus' miracles and still fail to believe that they were sufficient evidence that he was the Son of God. If Jesus had intended that his miracles be proof of his divinity, they were rather poor proof.

Jesus must have had another purpose in mind. Or perhaps his miraculous works were simply a spontaneous outpouring of who he was.

Obviously, from today's text, we can see that many looked at the work of Jesus and came to the wrong conclusion. They charged that he cast out demons in the name of the prince of demons. Sickness, they said, is a sign of the presence of evil. So if the sickness is conquered, it must be conquered by some evil force.

Sometimes when people encounter tragic illness or accident, they say, "This must be God's will." Does Jesus support that belief?

In today's lesson, the man's blindness and deafness are ascribed (by both Jesus and his critics) to the work of "the prince of demons" (12:24).

In the story, Jesus clearly says that he banishes this man's affliction, not by the force of evil, but rather by confronting these evil events with the force of good. He says that it is "by the Spirit of God that I cast out demons" (12:28).

Blindness, deafness, accidents, and other tragedies that inflict human life with pain are not the agents of God—they are evidence of the work of evil. But, "by the Spirit of God," these tragedies may be overcome.

Jesus' miracles thus become testimony to the power and compassion of God. God is not on the side of pain, sickness, and death. Rather, the power of God does battle with these evil forces.

When Jesus confronted the blind man, he didn't say to the poor fellow, "Rejoice. God must have a reason for doing this to you. This must be accepted as God's will." Jesus rebuked the evil and restored the man to health. He thus reveals something deep and important about the nature of God—and the nature of our suffering.

So when we encounter the pain and tragedy of life, let us not step back and say coldly, "This is God's will." Rather, when we see medical science conquering diseases, when we see laws passed which make for a safer environment, when we see dedicated people giving their lives in order to conquer demonic forces, let us then say, "*This* is God's will, a sign of God's continuing work for the triumph of good in our world."

The Kingdom Has Come upon You

What message does Jesus himself draw out of this miraculous healing of the blind and deaf man? Jesus says to the wondering crowd, "If it is by the Spirit of God that I cast out demons, then the kingdom of God has come upon you" (12:28).

This miracle is a sign of the long-awaited kingdom of God. God is present in these works of love and power.

How can one tell that the Spirit of God is at work? We can only point to good winning over evil, the suffering being given hope and comfort, and say that these are signs of the near presence of God's kingdom.

Think for a moment about your community. Let your mind's eye wander over faces and places within your town. Now ask yourself where God's Spirit is at work in your town today. What events can you point to and say you see signs of the truth that the kingdom has come upon us?

When diseases are being healed, when political corruption is being ferreted out and banished, when the poor are being given a vision of hope—these are signs of God's work.

Of course, today's scripture reminds us that it all depends upon how you look at it. Many looked at the good work of Jesus and suspected that evil was at play there. Only a few had the eyes to see a sign of the kingdom.

So it is today. Some look at the triumph of good over evil and see nothing but signs of human progress, evidence of human heroism, luck, fate, government achievements, or whatever we call it. But to the eyes of faith, to those who have seen and expected to see the kingdom breaking out in the work of the Spirit, all of this is seen as God's good work among us.

Of course, to be honest we must admit that this is a story about Jesus rather than about us. Jesus had the power to heal people; Jesus was able to utilize the Spirit as a force for human betterment. Jesus healed. But what about *us*?

The Gift of the Spirit

The discussion was about prayer. "Lord, teach us to pray," his disciples asked him (Luke 11:1). So he taught them the Lord's Prayer (11:2-4). Then he continued by telling them a story about prayer. A man is surprised by a visit from one of his friends late at night. Unfortunately he has nothing to give the visitor to eat, so he goes to his neighbor to borrow some bread. But his neighbor, who has already been in bed for a long time, tells him to get lost. But the man keeps beating on the door until the neighbor finally gets up, goes to the cupboard, and gets the bread. "And I tell you," says Jesus. "Ask and it will be given you; seek, and you will find; knock, and it will be opened to you" (11:9).

The persistence of the man was finally rewarded. In prayer, Jesus seems to be saying, it is important to keep at it. Be persistent, not because until you batter down God's door God will not answer you, but because until you open the door of your heart, you can't really hear God.

In this parable Jesus is teaching, as he often did, through hyperbole and overstatement. This parable is one of contrast, not comparison! He is not saying that God is like that lazy, unwilling neighbor who refused to open up until the door was nearly battered in; rather, he says that, "If you then, who are evil, know how to give good gifts to your children, how much more will the heavenly Father give the Holy Spirit to those who ask him!" (11:13).

God is more generous, more gracious about bestowing gifts than we are; therefore, we are justified in expecting God to give divine gifts to us. Even as the man was bold enough to think that his neighbor would give him bread at midnight, so we are bold enough to think that God will give us the same gift of the Holy Spirit that empowered Jesus to do his work.

Before you leave this parable, note a couple of things about the story. First, the man is asking for bread not for himself but for his *neighbor*. Any interpretation of this story which sees "ask, and it will be given you" as a license to ask for whatever material things we seek does an injustice to the story. The man is seeking bread for someone else. We seek the Holy Spirit, not for our own selfish needs, but so that we might bless others.

Second, Jesus says that God will "give the Holy Spirit to those who ask

THIRD QUARTER

him" (11:13). This is a parable about praying for the gift of the Spirit, not for material possessions.

The same Spirit which empowered Jesus to fulfill has vocation is available to us so that we might fulfill our vocations. All we have to do is ask.

Let us ask for the Spirit so that God's good work might be done, so that the kingdom might take form even among us, through the empowering work of the Spirit.

Helping Adults Become Involved—Robert G. Rogers

Preparing to Teach

In the past two lessons the emphasis has been on the role of the Holy Spirit in the birth and call of Jesus. Now we have a lesson that explores the Holy Spirit's influence in the public ministry of Jesus. As you prepare, think a bit about how the birth, call to vocation, and public ministry are related. In what ways is the Holy Spirit manifested in all three phases of Jesus' life?

Your specific aim in this lesson is to demonstrate how the Spirit in Jesus' ministry is the power of God "let loose" in the world. In the life of Jesus (and in our lives) this power is a tremendous force for achieving good.

Think of specific evils in the world against which Christians are called to fight. How might the support of God's Spirit help us defeat these sinister forces? Also, note what forces Jesus defeats with the aid of the Spirit.

Introducing the Main Question

In his ministry Jesus confronted evil daily. His enemies, being jealous of him, accused him falsely of being in league with Satan. Yet he continued the fight against the ravages of disease and sin by healing any victims who were brought to him. In these various confrontations, Jesus continually gave credit to God for sustaining him in the attempt to defeat evil.

Are we not in the same position today? Has the world changed all that much since Jesus' day? Men and women still do evil things to other humans, and innocent victims still die from cancer or are crippled by arthritis.

It would be easy to be a pessimist. Will the condition of the world ever get better? What difference does it make whether we personally try to combat evil? Will our modest attempts make any difference? By contrast, dare a Christian be so negative about the world? Do we thereby ignore the advances humanity has made under the guidance of God's Spirit? These and other related questions are useful to consider in beginning the class session.

Developing the Lesson

Your class participants will likely view the presence of evil in the world with mixed feelings. In discussion, they may have indicated that at times they feel overwhelmed by the power of evil. However, probably all can point to situations they know personally in which evil has been stopped or even eliminated entirely. You should acknowledge that the problem is complex and requires discussion, prayer, and action by thoughful Christians.

To facilitate study and discussion, divide your lesson into three parts:

I. Defining the origin of evil
II. Our role in confronting evil
III. Empowered by the Spirit to defeat evil

I. Defining the origin of evil

Begin by asking the class to work with you in determining the different types of evil that exist in the world. For example, you might note such evils as cancer or other diseases, earthquakes or natural disasters, human sins against other humans. Jot these down on the chalkboard or writing pad. Then ask your people to suggest the cause(s) of these various evils, and jot these down as well. Your purpose in conducting this exercise is to encourage individual thinking about the problem.

Next you need to raise directly the question: Is God responsible for evil in the world? Some thinkers have tentatively identified God as causing or at least permitting certain types of evil to exist. Ask class members to respond to Dr. Willimon's statement that "God is not on the side of pain, sickness, and death. Rather, the power of God does battle with these evil forces."

Assuming that most class participants will be reluctant to identify God with evil, ask them what or who is the source of suffering and death. You might suggest that the blame for a fair portion of evil must be assigned to humans. By our indifference and even purposive acts, we often cause others to suffer. However, it is also true that there are evils on earth that are beyond the control of men and women. What causes these?

II. Our role in confronting evil

Discussing the origin of evil is a useful task; it helps pinpoint areas where humans are responsible for inflicting pain and suffering. It is equally necessary that we determine how we might work with God to defeat evil. As Christians, do we have a special calling from God to battle disease, war, and poverty?

Ask the class to examine the assigned scriptures. How does Jesus confront evil? How does he respond to its victims? Does he engage in what for many of us is the usual response—blaming the victim? Or, by contrast, does he seek rather to defeat the evil which created human victims? (Further, by what power does he defeat the "demons"?) Jesus' response to the victims of evil provides a model for all Christian disciples.

Jesus fought evil wherever he found it. Consequently, he was accused of being in league with Satan. Why were some people so threatened by Jesus? Did they fail to see God's Spirit of healing and compassion at work in Jesus? Do class members believe people today are threatened when the church truly confronts evil in the world? For example, what would happen if church members actively sought to eliminate the conditions which foster poverty and discrimination in your hometown? Would they be called "do-gooders" or worse? Would such labeling by scoffers stop the attempt to reform? How did Jesus respond to his many critics?

III. Empowered by the Spirit to defeat evil

In this concluding portion of the lesson, emphasize the role of the Holy Spirit in the struggle to defeat evil. God's Spirit is with us in two ways: as sustainer and comforter in our own individual situations; as source of strength within the fellowship of the church. However, emphasize with your class that in no way is the Holy Spirit merely a confirmer of the status quo. There are those occasions in which the Spirit prods our consciences because we are lax in doing battle against evil.

How do we, who are weak, gain the strength and courage we need? Ask the class members to look at Luke 11:9-10, and remind them of Dr. Willimon's treatment of the passage. The process described is relatively simple. Christians should pray to God, setting before him their needs and seeking his help in the struggle against evil. Jesus assures his disciples (in every age) that God will respond to those who approach him in faith. Prayer will be answered! God's Spirit will be in our midst—guiding, correcting, sustaining—as we seek to end the power of evil.

Helping Class Members Act

Ask class participants to devote specified time to study and prayer in the coming week. The study should focus on identifying a particular sin or evil in the community which needs to be confronted by the Christian gospel. (Perhaps this could be done with your church's Christian action committee.) The prayer should be a form of petition to God, seeking the guidance of his Spirit.

Planning for Next Sunday

For the next session, read Acts 1:4-8, 2:1-21, and 13:1-12. The focus is on the earliest life of the church after the departure of the resurrected Lord. Notice how Luke presents the Holy Spirit's involvement in the life of early Christianity. This guidance extends not only to the fellowship within the church but also to Christian missionary endeavors in the world.

UNIT II: THE HOLY SPIRIT ACTIVE IN THE CHURCH

Horace R. Weaver

THREE LESSONS   **MAY 11–25**

The second unit in our study "The Person and Work of the Holy Spirit" is entitled "The Holy Spirit Active in the Church." In the first lesson; "Promise and Power of the Holy Spirit" (May 11), texts from Acts highlight the empowerment of the early church at Pentecost. The next lesson, "The Gifts of the Holy Spirit" (May 18), focuses on gifts of the Spirit in and for the community of believers, as described in I Corinthians 12–13. A concluding lesson, "The Fruit of the Holy Spirit" (May 25), based on Galatians 5–6, contrasts a life directed by the Spirit with a life directed by the value system of the world.

Promise and Power of the Holy Spirit

Background Scripture: Acts 1:4-8; 2:1-21; 13:1-12

The Main Question—William H. Willimon

Early in my ministry an older pastor gave me some good advice. "Son," he said, "keep praising and encouraging a church rather than criticizing it. That's the way to keep a church moving. Build 'em up rather than tear them down."

I have found his words to be wise counsel. In any congregation, at any time and place, there are usually more reasons for a church to feel discouraged than encouraged. The church is called to be so much for so many people; no wonder we often fall far short of our calling. To us has been entrusted the message of hope and salvation of the world. But we are so weak, so ill-equipped, and the countermessages of the world are so alluring. We can usually tally up more failures than successes.

I suppose that this has always been the difficulty of discipleship. Much more of the New Testament is given to words of hope and encouragement than to those of criticism and judgment.

Consider your own adult class next Sunday. How many will be there? If your class is like most, more people will be absent than present. A change in the weather will affect attendance. Should you hope for rain or sunshine? If it rains, some will not risk getting wet. If the sun shines, others will use the beautiful day to go to the park or the beach. And if they come, will they have studied the lesson? Will they be attentive in class?

No, when you think about it, next Sunday doesn't look too promising, does it? A person could become downright discouraged.

So as you think about your class, your church, your own life, what keeps you going in the midst of discouragement? In what can you take hope?

Today's scripture reminds us that we are not the first disciples to ask these questions. Nor, by God's grace, shall they be the last to have been given the answer to their problems of discoruagement.

As You Read the Scripture—Mike Winters

Acts 1:4-8, 2:1-21, 13:1-12. The day of Pentecost in the New Testament church is the celebration of the Holy Spirit's coming to call out the church and to empower the church to continue the ministry of Jesus in the world. All who have been called to serve God in Jesus have been called out by the working of the Holy Spirit.

Acts 1:4-8. The setting is the imminent ascension of the Lord, forty days after Jesus' resurrection. The faithful disciples are encouraged to wait patiently for the coming kingdom of the Lord. They are also promised the power of the Holy Spirit to witness their faith in ever-widening circles: Jerusalem, Judea, Samaria, and even to the ends of the earth.

Verses 4-5. Whether Jesus was staying with the disciples or eating with them is uncertain. The Greek word translated "staying" can also mean "eating."

307

The promise Jesus is talking about refers to the promised gift of the empowering Holy Spirit (Acts 2:33, Galatians 3:14, and Ephesians 1:13 are verses where the Holy Spirit is promised.) The charge to stay in Jerusalem anticipates the fulfillment of the promise in Acts 2.

Verse 6. The disciples think that the meaning of the promised gift is the restoration of an Israeli kingdom. They do not yet understand the worldwide implications of the kingdom of God.

Verse 7. The Greek word *kairos* here translated "time" means "the crucial moment" or "the right time." It is a word that conveys expectancy.

Verse 8. The pentecostal experience is anticipated.

Verses 2:1-21. The day of Pentecost, fifty days after Passover and the resurrection of Jesus, became the birthday of the church. The church began in the power of the Holy Spirit. Its beginning was epidemic.

Chapter 2:1. Pentecost is also called the Feast of Weeks by the Jews. Tradition holds that the Sinai law was given to the Jews on this day.

Verses 2-3. Here is the description of the phenomenal event of the coming of the Holy Spirit. "Tongues as of fire" signifies baptism with the Holy Spirit and fire anticipated in Luke 3:16. Here the promise (of the Holy Spirit) is fulfilled.

Verse 4. This experience with the Holy Spirit is different from the religious experience that produces ecstatic speech. The Holy Spirit empowered them to speak intelligibly "in other tongues." See I Corinthians 14:1-33, where the gift of tongues is subordinated to other gifts.

Verses 5, 9-11. Jews from the Middle East and Asia and Asia Minor were present for the Feast of Weeks.

Verses 6-8. It was unusual for Galileans to be bilingual.

Verses 12-13. What cannot be understood is and has always been mocked. An experience with the Holy Spirit is an intoxicating type of experience; but it is very different from being drunk with wine. See Ephesians 5:18, which says, "Do not get drunk with wine . . . but be filled with the Spirit."

Verses 14-16. Peter interprets the intoxicating experience of the Holy Spirit in light of the prophet Joel.

Verses 17-21. "The last days" are at hand, because the Spirit has been poured out. See Joel 2:28-32.

Chapter 13:1-3. This is the beginning of Paul's first missionary journey.

Verses 1-3. Prophets and teachers were an important part of the early church. Included in the list of prophets and teachers in the church in Antioch are Barnabas and Saul. Again the Holy Spirit works to call out and "set apart" certain people for special service.

Verses 4-5. The missionary journey begins in the power and the authority of the Holy Spirit.

Verses 6-12. Paphos was the capital of Cyprus. The proconsul, Segius Paulus, was being drawn from the faith by a magician named Bar-Jesus or Elymas. The proconsul had invited Paul to teach at Paphos. When Paul arrived, the Holy Spirit empowered him to defend the faith and disable the magician. As a result, the proconsul believed.

Selected Scripture

King James Version	Revised Standard Version

Acts 1:4-8

4 And, being assembled together with *them,* commanded them that they should not depart from Jerusalem, but wait for the promise of the Father, which, *saith he,* ye have heard of me.

5 For John truly baptized with water; but ye shall be baptized with the Holy Ghost not many days hence.

6 When they therefore were come together, they asked of him, saying, Lord, wilt thou at this time restore again the kingdom to Israel?

7 And he said unto them, It is not for you to know the times or the seasons, which the Father hath put in his own power.

8 But ye shall receive power, after that the Holy Ghost is come upon you: and ye shall be witnesses unto me both in Jerusalem, and in all Judaea, and in Samaria, and unto the uttermost part of the earth.

Acts 2:1-4

1 And when the day of Pentecost was fully come, they were all with one accord in one place.

2 And suddenly there came a sound from heaven as of a rushing mighty wind, and it filled all the house where they were sitting.

3 And there appeared unto them cloven tongues like as of fire, and it sat upon each of them.

4 And they were all filled with the Holy Ghost, and began to speak with other tongues, as the Spirit gave them utterance.

Acts 13:1-5

1 Now there were in the church that was at Ăn´-tĭ-ŏ<u>ch</u> certain prophets and teachers; as Barnabas, and Simeon that was called Niger and Lucius of Cȳ-rē´-nē, and Măn´-ā-ĕn,

Acts 1:4-8

4 And while staying with them he charged them not to depart from Jerusalem, but to wait for the promise of the Father, which, he said, "you heard from me, 5 for John baptized with water, but before many days you shall be baptized with the Holy Spirit."

6 So when they had come together, they asked him, "Lord, will you at this time restore the kingdom of Israel?" 7 He said to them, "It is not for you to know times or seasons which the Father has fixed by his own authority. 8 But you shall receive power when the Holy Spirit has come upon you; and you shall be my witnesses in Jerusalem and in all Judea and Samar´ia and to the end of the earth."

Acts 2:1-4

1 When the day of Pentecost had come, they were all together in one place. 2 And suddenly a sound came from heaven like the rush of a mighty wind, and it filled all the house where they were sitting. 3 And there appeared to them tongues as of fire, distributed and resting on each one of them. 4 And they were all filled with the Holy Spirit and began to speak in other tongues, as the Spirit gave them utterance.

Acts 13:1-5

1 Now in the church at Antioch there were prophets and teachers, Barnabas, Simeon who was called Niger, Lucius of Cyre´ne, Man´a-en a member of the court of Herod the

309

which had been brought up with Herod the tē'-trärch, and Saul.

2 As they ministered to the Lord, and fasted, the Holy Ghost said, Separate me Barnabas and Saul for the work whereunto I have called them.

3 And when they had fasted and prayed, and laid *their* hands on them, they sent *them* away.

4 So they, being sent forth by the Holy Ghost, departed unto Sĕ-leû'-cĭ-ă; and from thence they sailed to Cyprus.

5 And when they were at Săl'-ă-mĭs, they preached the word of God in the synagogues of the Jews: and they had also John to *their* minister.

Key Verse: **Ye shall receive power, after that the Holy Ghost is come upon you: and ye shall be witnesses unto me both in Jerusalem, and in all Judea, and in Samaria, and unto the uttermost part of the earth. (Acts 1:8)**

---

tetrarch, and Saul. 2 While they were worshiping the Lord and fasting, the Holy Spirit said, 'Set apart for me Barnabas and Saul for the work to which I have called them." 3 Then after fasting and praying they laid their hands on them and sent them off.

4 So, being sent out by the Holy Spirit, they went down to Seleu'cia; and from there they sailed to Cyprus. 5 When they arrived at Sal'amis, they proclaimed the word of God in the synagogues of the Jews. And they had John to assist them.

Key Verse: **You shall receive power when the Holy Spirit has come upon you; and you shall be my witnesses in Jerusalem and in all Judea and Samaria and to the end of the earth. (Acts 1:8)**

The Scripture and the Main Question—William H. Willimon

Wait for the Promise

All in all, the disciples were a rather sad bunch after the crucifixion of Christ on "Good Friday." They had been crushed by the events of that week. All hope was gone; Jesus, their master, was dead. So this was the end of the story.

But to their surprise, Easter morning showed that the story was beginning rather than ending. Jesus was raised from the dead, present with them again as a conquering hero. Luke says that Christ now "presented himself alive . . . appearing to them during forty days, and speaking of the kingdom of God" (Acts 1:3).

Those must have been glorious days while he was with them. In our churches today, during these days after Easter until Pentecost, we also celebrate the season of Easter, in which we reflect upon the meaning of the resurrection. It is therefore fitting for us to be studying these passages from the Acts of the Apostles.

It was great to have Jesus present. But now Jesus declares that he is leaving. What about the disciples now? Would they fall back into the same fear and hopelessness that characterized their lives on Good Friday? Were they destined to simply scatter, go their separate ways, and watch as the kingdom which Jesus began crumbled into oblivion?

Jesus tells them to stay in Jerusalem and "wait for the promise of the Father" (1:4). What is that promise? "You shall be baptized with the Holy Spirit" (1:5). The same Spirit which Jesus received when he was baptized by John in the Jordan (Luke 3) shall now be given to the disciples of Jesus.

In previous weeks we have spoken of the call, the power, and the work of the Spirit as it operated in the life of Jesus. Now we focus upon the astounding promise that this same Spirit shall be given to his disciples. "You shall receive power when the Holy Spirit has come upon you," he tells them (1:8).

After receiving that gift, "you shall be my witnesses" (1:8).

Imagine how astounding this promise must have seemed to the disciples. How could these frightened, misunderstanding, poorly equipped men, who had forsaken Jesus and scattered into the night only a short time before, now be the very ones who would boldly testify to the world?

There are times in our lives when we, like the disciples, accomplish deeds which could only be ascribed to the work of some power other than our own. The deeds cannot be explained by reference to human effort or skill, human determination or willpower.

A small group of people meet in a home and decide to form a new church. Three years later three hundred people gather and dedicate a magnificent new building to the glory of God. How could that happen?

A mother of three children becomes a widow. She has few material resources, few marketable skills, and yet twenty years later she sits proudly at her third child's college graduation. How do you account for that?

Could this be concrete evidence that the Spirit once promised has now been given, given to us to enable us to do what God calls us to do?

And They Were Filled with the Holy Spirit

The Spirit that had been promised to the disciples descended on the day of Pentecost—a Jewish festival which celebrates the gift of the Law. The disciples had been told by Christ that they would be his witnesses, "in Jerusalem and in all Judea and in Samaria and to the end of the earth" (1:8).

Now, on Pentecost, they are shocked to find that they "began to speak in other tongues, as the Spirit gave them utterance" (2:4). In other words, Luke is saying that here *the Spirit gave them the equipment they needed to do the Spirit's bidding.*

I suppose that God does not call us to do any work without providing the equipment we need. Like these first disciples, we are given gifts to enable us to fulfill our God-given responsibilities.

Time and again in the church, I have seen people discover gifts and talents in themselves which they never knew they had—when they open themselves up to the call of God.

"I can't speak well in public; I've never made speeches before." Yet when she agreed to serve as lay leader of her church, she was surprised to find that public speaking was not as frightening as she had thought.

It is only with the descent of the Spirit that the church is born. Before the gift of the Spirit, there was no church—just a conglomeration of fearful, confused, bewildered disciples wondering what to do next.

It would be the same for us today. Without the Spirit, how could contemporary disciples possibly keep going? How could you keep preparing to teach your lesson, Sunday after Sunday, even when you may not always see visible results of your labors?

The tasks of discipleship are so demanding, the causes for failure and disappointment so numerous, that without the Spirit it would all be impossible.

Sent Out by the Holy Spirit

So Acts urges us to look again at the earliest disciples. Can it be that these are the same men and women who were once so weak? They and their work became irrefutable proof of the presence of the Spirit.

The Acts of the Apostles takes us to Antioch, an early Christian center. There we see the beginning of Paul's missionary journeys. The church is said to be "worshiping the Lord and fasting" (13:2), that is, fasting in order to be more receptive to the Spirit's leadings. They realized that the Spirit was the source of their power. Fasting helped remind them of their dependence. The Spirit tells them to send out Barnabas and Saul to spread the gospel (13:3). "Sent out by the Holy Spirit," they "proclaimed the Word of God" (13:4-5). The church is doing what Jesus said it would do—serve as his witnesses into all the world.

From the birth of the church at Pentecost, there is a veritable explosion of the church into all the world. These ordinary folk are filled with extraordinary power.

We sometimes focus only upon the Holy Spirit as a comforting, reassuring force in the world. Today's scripture reminds us that this Spirit is also a *prodding* force. Had they been left to their own devices, the disciples might have simply kept this good news to themselves, stayed home, and minded their own business. But the Spirit prodded them out into the whole world. Christianity was a spark which became a conflagration and spread from person to person across the entire world.

We are still those who are called and empowered to spread this flame throughout the world. Here is a faith that demands to be shared with others. It is contagious. How did you become a Christian? Who was filled with the Spirit so much that he or she shared this faith with you? With whom have you shared this good news lately?

"You've got real spirit," we say to someone who has a special enthusiasm, deep dedication, or spirited drive. We see a special glow about the person, a liveliness and bold determination.

Let us pray, as did our brothers and sisters before us, that we might be open to the power and leading of God, so that someone might say of us, "Hey, you've got spirit, *the* Spirit!"

Helping Adults Become Involved—Robert G. Rogers

Preparing to Teach

For three Sundays you and your class have considered the role of the Holy Spirit in the life and ministry of Jesus. For this lesson and the two that follow, the focus shifts from Jesus of Nazareth to his disciples.

As you read in Acts the thrilling accounts of the Spirit's work, try to imagine what it meant for those first Christians to feel comfort and guidance as they began their ministry. They had every reason to feel discouraged, perhaps even abandoned. Their master, Jesus, was no longer available to give direction to their daily lives as he had in Galilee. Then the Holy Spirit descended in their midst as God's gift.

Your aim in this lesson is to focus on God's gift of hope in the midst of difficult human circumstances. Specifically, consider today's reading as the first chapter in God's story for the Christian community, a story which continues in the church today.

Introducing the Main Question

How do we know if our church's work is successful? As Dr. Willimon notes in "The Main Question," our efforts do not always yield the desired results. In commencing the lesson, acknowledge that not all church programs or plans work well. Our best efforts often do not attract the numbers of persons we wish to serve. Encourage class members to share disappointments about church activities or programs they have planned that may not have worked out well. (Be careful that this does not deteriorate into a general criticism of other persons and programs.)

After discussing reasons for being discouraged, ask class members to think of ways in which gains have been made. Remind them of the assigned Bible reading. At first, the early Christians had good reason to be discouraged. Their Lord and master had departed, and they were left to face an indifferent, even hostile world. But then discouragement turned to joy! Use this experience to help persons share what they are grateful for in the church. What has worked out satisfactorily and significantly in your church's program and outreach?

Developing the Lesson

As a means of beginning the lesson, you asked class members to focus briefly on two basic dimensions of Christian life: discouragement in times of difficulty; satisfaction at signs of success. Your task now is to build the lesson on these two dimensions. Specifically, develop three sections:

I. Facing the difficult times
II. Moving from discouragement to hope
III. Identifying our need

I. Facing the difficult times

Begin this section by recounting in detail the situation of the disciples of Jesus just before Pentecost. Granted, the resurrected Lord had promised the gift of the Holy Spirit, but in the period just prior to Pentecost the disciples were on their own. They had to make decisions without the direct guidance of either Jesus or the Holy Spirit. Ask class members in what ways they can identify with those first Christians, who were temporarily without a leader to suggest the right direction. How did those Christians strengthen one another during the days of waiting?

Point out that there are various methods by which we humans deal with difficulties. Sometimes we face them directly; more often, we seek to avoid unpleasant choices. Does the example of the disciples during the "upper room period" suggest a Christian response? Even in the midst of an uncertain time, they faced up to their responsibilities as Christ's witnesses in the world. Let us be specific: How does their example of courage and faith have value for us today? What kind of prayer comforted them in those days?

II. Moving from discouragement to hope

There is no more significant time in the life of the early church than that of Pentecost. In presenting this section, focus on what the Holy Spirit did for the disciples. They became apostles ("those who are sent forth"), and they were given the power and guidance to accomplish the task of preaching the gospel. Ask class members to think along with you about the process of movement in the first chapters of Acts: (1) the disciples are in the upper room, separated from those to whom they will soon preach; (2) the Holy

Spirit comes upon them; and (3) they move freely and confidently into the world, preaching to all.

How can we learn from that exciting time? Is the experience related in Acts 1–2 ours as well? Ask class members to share specific times in their personal lives or in the life of your church when they felt God's Spirit lead them forth out of darkness and uncertainty. As teacher, you might have several examples that are useful illustrations to share. Focus particularly on incidents in the life of your church that would be the common experience of all class participants.

Conclude this section by emphasizing how important our own personal attitude is when seeking the Spirit's aid. Turn again to the disciples in the upper room. They remained open, even expectant, regarding what God had in mind for their future. Not knowing precisely how they would be used by God, they nevertheless prepared themselves in prayer for whatever task would be given. In the church today, is not our hope directly related to how willing we are to let God work in and through us.

III. Identifying our need

What can the Holy Spirit do for us? To begin to answer this question, focus for a few moments on the first Pentecost. Those first Christian witnesses knew they had a truth to proclaim; the Holy Spirit gave them the courage and power to do it! Remind your class that Peter and his fellow Christians were not sophisticated speakers. Rather, they had led rather humble lives in rural Galilee before being called by Jesus. The account in Acts clearly demonstrates that sharing the good news depends more on conviction and enthusiasm than on educational or vocational background.

Now consider together the emphasis in Dr. Willimon's remarks in "The Scripture and the Main Question." What is the power that causes us to exceed our own (and others') expectations? When have we been in positions of helplessness and then felt an unexpected source of strength which helped us complete the task at hand? Ask class members to share specific instances. As Christians, are we recipients of a power that enables us to do more than we could possibly imagine? Discuss.

Does God's Spirit "prod" us (as Dr. Willimon suggests) as well as comfort us? Surely such prodding is a divine gift! Do we humans have more potential to accomplish God's work than we want to admit? Who would have predicted that a Galilean fisherman would become an outstanding leader in Christ's church? Ask members to share ways in which they feel they are being "prodded" by God's Spirit.

Helping Class Members Act

Ask class members to think during the coming week about their own personal lives. In what areas do they already feel the power of God's Spirit leading them? Where do they still need prodding?

You might also suggest that your people reflect on the life of Paul. How did the Spirit prod him to serve God?

Planning for Next Sunday

Next week's assignment is I Corinthians 12–13. Paul's words have served for generations as a blueprint for Christian life. How does his model for discipleship serve us in the present day?

Ask the class to consider your own congregation and note how a "variety of gifts" helps complete the church's ministry.

The Gifts of the Holy Spirit

Background Scripture: I Corinthians 12–13

The Main Question—William H. Willimon

"She is a gifted person." I heard a young teacher say that about one of her students the other day. What a wonderful thing to say about someone, I thought. Of course, it also says something about the teacher herself. She is the sort of teacher who can see and develop the giftedness of her students—which is to say that she is the best kind of teacher.

"Son, you have the gift of gab," a man said to me after I had made a short speech as a teenager. I hope he wasn't just kidding me when he said that, for I've been preaching and speaking ever since.

"Now there are varieties of gifts," Paul says to one of his churches (I Corinthians 12:4). You can look out over your adult class this Sunday and prove the truth of Paul's assertion. Marge Jones is the best cook in town. Sam Reed can make beautiful things out of wood. Sue Latham has taught more children algebra than she can remember. You have the gift for making the Bible come alive for other adults.

But even though we may believe that all of these gifts have come from the same God, not all our gifts are equally valued. A junior high school math teacher may have exactly the same intellectual gifts as a computer programmer, but society must not value them the same—compare their salaries. A pastor may spend as many years in school as a physician, but their material rewards in life will be different. In other words, we see gifts not only as coming from God, but also as causing distinction and division among people. We value some talents; we don't value others. But what about God? Does God make similar distinctions?

Of all the gifts which God gives to people, are some gifts more essential than others? What is the most important gift a Christian can have? These are the questions we will tackle in today's lesson.

As You Read the Scripture—Mike Winters

I Corinthians 12 and 13. The Holy Spirit empowers the church to continue the mission of Jesus Christ in the world. All who believe in Jesus Christ are given gifts which equip them for ministry in the world. This was the apostolic view. It was the view of the Reformation and was at the heart of the Reformers' affirmation, "the priesthood of all believers."

The gifts of the Holy Spirit are many. Christians are given different gifts. This accounts for the great richness and diversity in the church. The most important gift, however, is love. Using imagery from nuclear technology, love is the "strong force" which holds the church together in all its diversity.

Chapter 12:1-3. Here is a reference to the heathen religious ecstasy. Confused ecstasy is not of the Holy Spirit. One thing the Spirit does in all who believe is to inspire the strong affirmation that "Jesus is Lord" (Romans 10:9).

Verses 4-6. All the gifts of the people of God are manifestations of the

Spirit for the common good. Nowhere in Paul's writing is there a systematic view of the Trinity. Nevertheless, we have here a trinitarian prototype: Spirit, Lord, and God. Each one has its own particular function. The "Spirit" gives gifts which empower the church in the mission of Jesus. The "Lord" defines the mission through service. "God" keeps all things operational.

Verse 6. The word for "working" and the word for "inspires" come from the same Greek root which means energy, power, or operation.

Verse 7. The first test of the Spirit is the affirmation of the Lordship of Jesus (12:3). The second test is the upbuilding of the church (12:7). The gifts of the Spirit are meant for the good of all, and not for personal gratification or as proof of one's justification and election by God.

Verses 8-11. Here is a list of nine gifts of the Holy Spirit. Paul's point is made here again and again. In spite of the diversity of gifts, it is the same Holy Spirit who works them all in everyone. In this list of nine gifts, five are related to speaking activities. The importance of words is underscored.

Verse 12. The coordinated functions of the various parts of the body are an illustration of the church's need for both diversity and harmonious operation. This is more than a good illustration. It can truly be said that the church *is* the Body of Christ, and Christ is the head of the body (Colossians 1:18).

Verse 13. The Spirit unifies the whole. Ephesians 4:3, 4, 16 are important verses about the unifying power of the Holy Spirit.

Verses 14-26. Each part of the body provides a particular, useful service.

Verse 27. Each member is vitally important to the whole body.

Verse 28. Paul lists several functions members perform for the body. Perhaps the last listed (speakers in various tongues) is more important to Paul's argument than the first. Those who spoke with ecstatic speech considered themselves to have a more important gift than they really had. Paul implores them to seek a greater gift. He puts these gifts in proper perspective. Love is the greatest gift of all (Romans 5:5). All of the gifts are worthless without love.

Chapter 13:1-7. The King James Version, in an effort to define this love as different from brotherly or erotic love, called it charity. This love includes the qualities of compassion, kindness, faithfulness, and forgiveness.

Verses 1-3. None of the gifts given by the Spirit, even ultimate expressions of faith, amounts to anything if the recipient does not have love. The third test of the Holy Spirit is love.

Verses 4-7. Paul defines this special love in very special and beautiful words and must be read.

Verses 4a, 6b-7. These are the positive aspects of love. There is an endurable optimism to love.

Verses 4b-6a. Love is the opposite of suspicion, pride, and selfishness.

Selected Scripture

King James Version	Revised Standard Version
I Corinthians 12:4-11	*I Corinthians 12:4-11*
4 Now there are diversities of gifts, but the same Spirit.	4 Now there are varieties of gifts, but the same Spirit; 5 and there are
5 And there are differences of administrations, but the same Lord.	varieties of service, but the same Lord; 6 and there are varieties of

6 And there are diversities of operations, but it is the same God which worketh all in all.

7 But the manifestation of the Spirit is given to every man to profit withal.

8 For to one is given by the Spirit the word of wisdom; to another the word of knowledge by the same Spirit;

9 To another faith by the same Spirit; to another the gifts of healing by the same Spirit;

10 To another the working of miracles; to another prophecy; to another discerning of spirits; to another *divers* kinds of tongues; to another the interpretation of tongues:

11 But all these worketh that one and the seflsame Spirit, dividing to every man severally as he will.

working, but it is the same God who inspires them all in every one. 7 To each is given the manifestation of the Spirit for the common good. 8 To one is given through the Spirit the utterance of wisdom, and to another the utterance of knowledge according to the same Spirit, 9 to another faith by the same Spirit, to another gifts of healing by the one Spirit, 10 to another the working of miracles, to another prophecy, to another the ability to distinguish between spirits, to another various kinds of tongues, to another the interpretation of tongues. 11 All these are inspired by one and the same Spirit, who apportions to each one individually as he wills.

I Corinthians 12:28-31

28 And God hath set some in the church, first apostles, secondarily prophets, thirdly teachers, after that miracles, then gifts of healings, helps, governments, diversities of tongues.

29 *Are* all apostles? *are* all prophets? *are* all teachers? *are* all workers of miracles?

30 Have all the gifts of healing? do all speak with tongues? do all interpret?

31 But covet earnestly the best gifts: and yet shew I unto you a more excellent way.

I Corinthians 12:28-31

28 And God has appointed in the church first apostles, second prophets, third teachers, then workers of miracles, then healers, helpers, administrators, speakers in various kinds of tongues. 29 Are all apostles? Are all prophets? Are all teachers? Do all work miracles? 30 Do all possess gifts of healing? Do all speak with tongues? Do all interpret? 31 But earnestly desire the higher gifts.

And I will show you a still more excellent way.

I Corinthians 13:1-7

1 Though I speak with the tongues of men and of angels, and have not charity, I am become *as* sounding brass, or a tinkling cymbal.

2 And though I have *the gift of* prophecy, and understand all mysteries, and all knowledge; and though I have all faith, so that I could remove mountains, and have not charity, I am nothing.

I Corinthians 13:1-7

1 If I speak in the tongues of men and of angels, but have not love, I am a noisy gong or a clanging cymbal. 2 And if I have prophetic powers, and understand all mysteries and all knowledge, and if I have all faith, so as to remove mountains, but have not love, I am nothing. 3 If I give away all I have, and if I deliver my body to be burned, but have not love, I gain nothing.

3 And though I bestow all my goods to feed *the poor*, and though I give my body to be burned, and have not charity, it profiteth me nothing.

4 Charity suffereth long, *and* is kind; charity envieth not; charity vaunteth not itself, is not puffed up,

5 Doth not behave itself unseemly, seeketh not her own, is not easily provoked, thinketh no evil;

6 Rejoiceth not in iniquity, but rejoiceth in the truth;

7 Beareth all things, believeth all things, hopeth all things, endureth all things.

4 Love is patient and kind; love is not jealous or boastful; 5 it is not arrogant or rude. Love does not insist on its own way; it is not irritable or resentful; 6 it does not rejoice at wrong, but rejoices in the right. 7 Love bears all things, believes all things, hopes all things, endures all things.

Key Verse: **But the manifestation of the Spirit is given to every man to profit withal. (I Corinthians 12:7)**

Key Verse: **To each is given the manifestation of the Spirit for the common good. (I Corinthians 12:7)**

The Scripture and the Main Question—William H. Willimon

Now Concerning Spiritual Gifts

Every time I lose heart over the state of the church today, I think of some of the churches Paul served and I feel better. Consider First Church Corinth. Paul had preached the gospel in this cosmopolitan city and a church had been formed. Things went well at first, but then trouble started.

The precise nature of the Corinthians' problems is not known. There are factions among them, Paul says. The church has become splintered into a number of feuding parties. There are arguments over the relationships between the sexes. Worship services have been disruptive. Even the gifts of the Spirit have become a source of division.

"Now concerning spiritual gifts," Paul writes to the feuding Corinthians, "brethren, I do not want you to be uninformed" (I Corinthians 12:1). What was the problem with spiritual gifts at Corinth? We are given a clue in the next verses: "Now there are varieties of spiritual gifts, but the same Spirit, . . . varieties of service, but the same Lord, . . . varieties of working, but it is the same God who inspires them all in every one" (12:4-6).

Evidently someone in Corinth was teaching that there was only one gift of the Spirit, or that one gift was superior to others. Perhaps someone was saying, "Look at me. God has given me the gift of healing, therefore I must be better than you." I am a graduate school Christian—you are only a kindergarten Christian.

Paul counters by saying that all gifts come from one Lord. There can be no division where the one Spirit of the one Lord is present.

More than this, Paul goes on to say, "To each is given the manifestation of the Spirit *for the common good*" (12:7, italics added). These gifts are not bestowed to produce individual joy, personal satisfaction, or smug, self-righteous boasting. These gifts are given for the *church*. They are the skills, talents, insights, and abilities which are required for the church to be the church. Note that all of the gifts which Paul cites are ecclesial, social, group talents which help to build up the Body of Christ (12:8-11).

318

I expect that you have seen this same Spirit at work in your own church. Who is the most important member of your congregation? Whose gifts are so essential that your church would utterly fail if that person were not present?

Your first reaction is probably that there is no *one* person whom you can cite. Many people come to your mind. John Black is the best teacher of adults. Jane Hines has a gift for working with youth. Congregational conflict might become self-destructive were it not for Van Watson's gift of reconciliation. All these talents, working in concert with others, build up the church. It's difficult to imagine a church here without them.

Look at the variety of gifts which Paul lists in I Corinthians 12:4-11. The gifts of knowledge, faith, healing, miracles, prophecy, and the others are the equipment which the church needs to be the church. "All these are inspired by one and the same Spirit" (12:11). Which are most important for a church? That's like asking, "What is the most important part of your body?" There is hardly any organ that we could lose without being at a definite disadvantage. So it is that the church needs diverse, talented people to compose the Body of Christ.

Now You Are the Body of Christ

"Now you are the body of Christ and individually members of it" (12:27). One of the most important committees in a church is the nominations committee. This committee has the holy task of discovering and discerning the gifts which God has given people and then inviting people to exercise these gifts in the church. As a pastor I wish I had more wisdom in this matter of discovering people's talents. So many people are asked to take jobs which they are ill-equipped to handle. Then they feel defeated and frustrated when they fail. When we are able to fit the right person with the right job, the results are beautiful.

"And God has appointed in the church first apostles, second prophets, third teachers, then workers of miracles, then healers, helpers, administrators, speakers in various kinds of tongues" (12:28). What impresses me about Paul's list is its richness and variety. Too often we think of the church as two groups of people—clergy and laity. Ought we not to examine our list of leaders today and ask if we need to claim greater varieties of service in order to enable the church to fulfill its task? Perhaps one reason that today's church has a rather limited idea of leadership is that we have undertaken a limited array of ministry.

Take a moment and ask yourself if these ministries still take place in today's church. Who are today's teachers, prophets, healers, workers of miracles? Together, recognizing and affirming the variety of gifts present in one another, we are the Body of Christ. These are people who are not only gifted by God but also appointed by God (12:28). It is therefore our duty to help these people exercise their divinely appointed tasks.

A More Excellent Way

Paul has expended a great deal of energy in discussing in great detail the nature of spiritual gifts. He has noted that these talents are *gifts*, they are *gifts of God*, they are *diverse*, and they are all given for the *edification* of the church.

As we said in the beginning of the lesson, the main issue in today's scripture is the place of the gifts in the church. Evidently some of the Corinthians valued some gifts more than others. Some Corinthians must have boasted that their gifts were more important, more dramatic, than others. This boasting had led to a division in First Church Corinth. Therefore Paul stresses the variety of gifts and their sources in the one God.

But now, as if Paul's letter reaches a crescendo, as if we have now come to the climax, the heart of it all, Paul says that he will now "show you a still more excellent way" (12:31). He breaks into song, a beautiful hymn to the greatest of all spiritual gifts, *the gift of love.*

This is the gift that enables us to discover and develop the gifts of others, that enables us to respect all gifts. This is the supreme gift which is the test of all others—love.

"If I speak in the tongues of men and of angels, . . . and if I have prophetic powers, and understand all mysteries and all knowledge . . ." (13:1-3). In other words, if I have all the wonderful spiritual gifts that I could hope for, "but have not love" . . . "I gain nothing." This is Paul's laconic verdict on the gifts of the Corinthians. Without love, the gifts of God become perverted into a cause for self-righteous boasting, the antithesis of what God intended, a course for church division and dissension rather than edification. The greatest of all gifts is love (13:13).

What does this say to us today? In what ways have we forgotten that our talents are gifts of the Spirit rather than personal possessions or achievements? Our talents are gifts, given by God for the common good.

Helping Adults Become Involved—Robert G. Rogers

Preparing to Teach

As you prepare for this week's lesson, study I Corinthians 12–13 carefully. What are the different types of spiritual gifts that Paul describes? How do persons possessing these gifts help to complete the ministry of the church? Can you think of corresponding types of gifts that members of your church have?

Your specific aim is to help your class see that all members of the church are of value to God. They are important not because of their wealth or societal status but because they have been touched by God's Holy Spirit. Notice particularly how Paul discusses the attributes of such a person in I Corinthians 13:4-7. You might also read Matthew 6:19-24, where Jesus warns his followers that they must choose carefully the values by which they live.

Reflect for a few moments on the relation between Christian values (such as those affirmed by Paul) and choosing for God. How do the values we hold affect our actions?

Introducing the Main Question

By what means do we value people? Do worldly standards of wealth, social status, education, or vocation provide the "yardstick" for our evaluation? When we think about people in our community, do we tend to identify them by phrases such as the following? "Oh, he's a doctor." "She's a professor." "They live over by the country club." If we are honest with ourselves, most of us do use these and similar ways to describe others. It is easier for us to stick a label on someone than to look more deeply at the personal qualities of that individual before making a judgment.

Now turn to our common life in the church. Do we sometimes use the same worldly standards of success when evaluating the "worth" of various church members? Do certain persons receive undue deference because of their education or occupation or family name?

Ask the class to think briefly about these issues. How can the skills and abilities of different people be used not to confer status but to further the work of the church? How can the contributions of every church member be affirmed and valued?

Developing the Lesson

Your class has spent a few moments focusing on the value of affirming the "gifts" of every person in the congregation. Assuming that they are committed to the principle, you now may develop the lesson specifically in the following ways:

> I. Discerning the gifts of the Holy Spirit
> II. Rejoicing in the variety of gifts
> III. Using God's gifts effectively

I. Discerning the gifts of the Holy Spirit

It is not always easy to discern what God's Spirit is doing in our lives and in the church. Paul suggests various powers or abilities that the Spirit gives—for example, healing or knowledge. Dr. Willimon, in "The Scripture and the Main Question," cites some of the Spirit's gifts to the local church. Ask your class members to think about the gifts visible in your own church. You might list these on a chalkboard or writing pad for easy reference. Encourage them to think widely about the gifts or abilities of individuals. They should not feel limited by those listed by Paul or Dr. Willimon. (In fact, such Pauline gifts as "speaking in tongues" might not be appropriate to your church's experience.) As teacher, you should be prepared to list some gifts that might not be immediately obvious—for example, the person whose gift is the ability to keep the church furnace operating or that member who has the gift of being able to get good music from the nursing home piano.

In the process of describing gifts in the congregation, your class may well identify a number of unsung heroes. What is it that seems to be common to all? Is it the willingness to serve? to give unstintingly? to do so without thought of reward? Does not their giving to the whole church seem strikingly similar to the agape love Paul writes about in I Corinthians 13:4-7?

II. Rejoicing in the variety of gifts

You and the class have identified a variety of gifts and abilities in your church. Now concentrate on specific methods of affirming those ways in which Christians are led by the Spirit. How can all members of the congregation—young and old, skilled and not-so-skilled—be encouraged to view themselves as vital and necessary parts of the Body of Christ? Refer to Paul's imagery in I Corinthians 13:14-26. Emphasize that the church is complete only when all persons feel welcome and accepted. This occurs only when all our individual talents and abilities—diverse though they may be—contribute to the welfare of the whole.

Perhaps your class might think of tangible ways to say "thank you" to various persons who share unstintingly and usually without public acclaim. Not only would such gratitude be affirming the individual persons, but it would be yet another way of praising God for his gift of the Holy Spirit who has shared with us in so many marvelous and diverse ways.

You might conclude this portion of the lesson by reminding the class that unity and diversity have always been key characteristics of the Christian community. The gifts of the Holy Spirit illustrate this beautifully. All Christians are united in the love of God. This love is freely given to all humanity. As individuals, we have unique talents and abilities which are freely given to us by God. When using these diverse gifts in behalf of God's work on earth, we testify to our ultimate unity in him.

III. *Using God's gifts effectively*

Remind class members of Dr. Willimon's statement about the church's nominations committee, in the section "Now You Are the Body of Christ." This group has the task of trying to match people's talents and interests with the tasks to be accomplished. How can we, as church members, help in the effective utilization of God-given talents? You might discuss this question and record class suggestions. (The nominations committee will undoubtedly appreciate helpful suggestions!)

Often there are "blocks" in the minds of Christians regarding their own suitability. Some still believe that if they are not ordained clergy, they can not really minister. Emphasize that from the earliest days to the present, the ministry of the church has been the task of all persons—laity and clergy alike. Still other people are shy, reluctant to volunteer lest they fail at a task. Such persons need reassurance that God's love embraces even the possibility of failure. A key phrase to remember is Paul's statement that "the parts of the body which seem to be weaker are indispensable" (I Corinthians 12:22). Every person's gift from the Holy Spirit is necessary for the Body of Christ to function well.

Helping Class Members Act

You might suggest that some class members accept as their mission a commitment to encourage others to use their talents in the church's ministry.

A further task to suggest is that of self-appraisal. Do individual class members have talents and abilities that are not being used for the common good? Are they willing to venture forth and offer to serve?

Planning for Next Sunday

The assignment for next week is Galatians 5:13–6:10. The topic is the relation between Christian freedom and living by the Spirit. What does it mean to live Christian life responsibly?

Also suggest that class members think back over the entire series on the Holy Spirit. In studying about God's Spirit, has their personal faith grown? Do they sense the presence of the Spirit in a more personal way?

The Fruit of the Holy Spirit

Background Scripture: Galatians 5:13–6:10

The Main Question—William H. Willimon

"By their fruits ye shall know them" a familiar truism goes. The world is correct in assuming that if our faith is genuine, it will be shown forth in our lives. Jesus spoke about the need to bear fruit. Luther notes that you don't expect to pick apples from a thorn bush!

The best testimony to the power of a person's religious conversion is the simple observation that the person looks different, acts differently, and is a person whose life has changed for the better.

"I'd rather *see* a sermon than *hear* one," people sometimes say. If our faith is only a matter of saying certain things without living in a certain way, something is amiss.

In the past lessons in this unit, we have explored the work of the Holy Spirit. Now we study the fruits of the Spirit. When it comes down to it, this is the irrefutable evidence for the presence of the Spirit in our lives—the fruits of the Spirit.

Consider the case of Jane Smith. Jane had lived a rather disordered life. She had grown up in a poor family environment. She failed to receive good parental guidance. By the time she was a young adult, Jane had drifted in and out of relationships with a dozen different men. She had experimented with illegal drugs. Nothing seemed to last for Jane. Nothing took hold for her.

Then, when she was in her late twenties, Jane was invited to attend a young adult discussion group at a neighborhood church. As a result of her participation in that group, Jane's life changed. What is more remarkable is that everyone who knew Jane could see the change. Her life had a new purpose, a new sense of direction.

How do you explain that? How is it possible for us to bear such fruit in our own lives? Let us look at this matter of the fruits of the Spirit more closely.

As You Read the Scripture—Mike Winters

Galatians 5:13–6:10. At the very heart of the argument for Christian liberty is the doctrine of justification by faith. Paul writes, "Did you receive the Spirit by work of the law, or by hearing with faith?" (Galatians 3:2). The law is to no advantage. Salvation is by the grace of God to those who believe in Jesus Christ. The church is freed from bondage to the law. But this new freedom does not justify lawlessness or immorality. Instead, this freedom in Christ works to produce the "fruit of the Spirit." Those who live in the Spirit are intent on "well-doing."

Chapter 5:13. The issue of freedom from the law raises the question, freedom to do what? The freedom "from" quickly becomes a freedom "for." Individually and together, the faithful are called to use their freedom in selfless love for one another. (Matthew 20:26 says, "Whoever would be great among you must be your servant.") More precisely, it is freedom to be a servant/slave to one another.

323

Verse 14. The whole Mosaic and Levitical law had been condensed to two laws. The first was to love God. The second was to love your neighbor as yourself. (Leviticus 19:18 and Mark 12:31 command the love of neighbor. On the question of neighbor, see Luke 10:25-37. The good Samaritan proved neighbor to the one who fell among robbers. See also Romans 13:8, which says, "he who loves his neighbor has fulfilled the law.")

Verse 15. The way of the world is to "do unto your neighbor before your neighbor does unto you." It is a survival-of-the-fittest mentality which contradicts the law of love. This destructive life-style of biting and devouring one another is further elaborated in the list of the works of the flesh (5:19-21).

Verses 16-17. The Spirit fills the body with a desire for love and selflessness, but the flesh fills the body with a desire for selfish gratification and stimulation. Spirit and flesh are opposites. The Spirit is of God. It is the stuff of the new nature of those who believe in Christ and are freed from the law. The flesh is to be understood not in terms of the physical body, but as worldliness, self-centeredness, and preoccupation with the gratification of one's desires which prevent us from doing what we should do. (Romans 7:21 says, "So I find it to be a law that when I want to do right, evil lies close at hand.")

Verse 18. Those who live by the Spirit are freed from the law; but the life lived in the Spirit leads to a morality that far surpasses the morality prescribed in the law.

Verses 19-21. The human sinful tendency is to indulge in the list of "works of the flesh." Those who indulge in these works are not heirs of grace, are not children of God, and thus are not inheritors of God's kingdom.

Verse 22. What is to prevent one from indulging in the works of the flesh if there is no longer any law? It is the Spirit that produces a higher morality than the law demanded.

Verses 22-23. Those who are heirs of God and thus children of God live lives that reflect well their kinship with God.

"Fruit" is the natural produce of the tree or vine that is fertilized, watered, cultivated, and in season. Fruit of the Spirit is the natural response of the heirs of God. Obedience to God is no longer a matter of adherence to a law. Instead, obedience is that natural response of those who are loved by God. Obedience is not a matter of duty, but a response to love—love answering love.

Verses 24-25. Here is a figure suggesting that those who belong to Jesus are crucified with him and also risen with him (2:20). Life in Christ means death to "the works of the flesh" and new life in the Spirit.

Chapter 5:25–6:6. Life in the Spirit is a life-style in obedience to the law of Christ, which is to love one another. It is a life-style of responsibility for one's own appropriate behavior as well as the behavior of others.

Chapter 6:7-8. A popular spiritual song title sums this up, "They'll Know We Are Christians by Our Love."

Verses 9-10. The results and rewards of life in the Spirit may not be immediately apparent, but Christ's people will continue in "well-doing" to all people.

Selected Scripture

King James Version	Revised Standard Version

Galatians 5:13-26

13 For, brethren, ye have been called unto liberty; only *use* not liberty for an occasion to the flesh, but by love serve one another.

14 For all the law is fulfilled in one word, *even* in this; Thou shalt love thy neighbour as thyself.

15 But if ye bite and devour one another, take heed that ye be not consumed one of another.

16 *This* I say then, Walk in the Spirit, and ye shall not fulfil the lust of the flesh.

17 For the flesh lusteth against the Spirit, and the Spirit against the flesh: and these are contrary the one to the other: so that ye cannot do the things that ye would.

18 But if ye be led of the Spirit, ye are not under the law.

19 Now the works of the flesh are manifest, which are *these*, Adultery, fornication, uncleanness, lasciviousness,

20 Idolatry, witchcraft, hatred, variance, emulations, wrath, strife, seditions, heresies,

21 Envyings, murders, drunkenness, revellings, and such like: of the which I tell you before, as I have also told *you* in time past, that they which do such things shall not inherit the kingdom of God.

22 But the fruit of the Spirit is love, joy, peace, longsuffering, gentleness, goodness, faith,

23 Meekness, temperance: against such there is no law.

24 And they that are Christ's have crucified the flesh with the affections and lusts.

25 If we live in the Spirit, let us also walk in the Spirit.

26 Let us not be desirous of vain glory, provoking one another, envying one another.

Galatians 5:13-26

13 For you were called to freedom, brethren; only do not use your freedom as an opportunity for the flesh, but through love be servants of one another. 14 For the whole law is fulfilled in one word, "You shall love your neighbor as yourself." 15 But if you bite and devour one another take heed that you are not consumed by one another.

16 But I say, walk by the Spirit, and do not gratify the desires of the flesh. 17 For the desires of the flesh are against the Spirit, and the desires of the Spirit are against the flesh; for these are opposed to each other, to prevent you from doing what you would. 18 But if you are led by the Spirit you are not under the law. 19 Now the works of the flesh are plain: fornication, impurity, licentiousness, 20 idolatry, sorcery, enmity, strife, jealousy, anger, selfishness, dissension, party spirit, 21 envy, drunkenness, carousing, and the like. I warn you, as I warned you before, that those who do such things shall not inherit the kingdom of God. 22 But the fruit of the Spirit is love, joy, peace, patience, kindness, goodness, faithfulness, 23 gentleness, self-control; against such there is no law. 24 And those who belong to Christ Jesus have crucified the flesh with its passions and desires.

25 If we live by the Spirit, let us also walk by the Spirit. 26 Let us have no self-conceit, no provoking of one another, no envy of one another.

Galatians 6:7-10

7 Be not deceived; God is not mocked: for whatsoever a man soweth, that shall he also reap.

8 For he that soweth to his flesh shall of the flesh reap corruption; but he that soweth to the Spirit shall of the Spirit reap life everlasting.

9 And let us not be weary in well-doing: for in due season we shall reap, if we faint not.

10 As we have therefore opportunity, let us do good unto all *men*, especially unto them who are of the household of faith.

Key Verse: **Walk in the Spirit, and ye shall not fulfil the lust of the flesh. (Galatians 5:16)**

Galatians 6:7-10

7 Do not be deceived; God is not mocked, for whatever a man sows, that he will also reap. 8 For he who sows to his own flesh will from the flesh reap corruption; but he who sows to the Spirit will from the Spirit reap eternal life. 9 And let us not grow weary in well-doing, for in due season we shall reap, if we do not lose heart. 10 So then, as we have opportunity, let us do good to all men, and especially to those who are of the household of faith.

Key Verse: **Walk by the Spirit, and do not gratify the desires of the flesh. (Galatians 5:16)**

The Scripture and the Main Question—William H. Willimon

Servants of One Another

Toward the end of last week's lesson we noted how, in writing to the church at Corinth, Paul said that among all of the gifts of the Holy Spirit, the greatest gift was love (I Corinthians 13).

Paul hits a similar theme in writing to the new Christians in Galatia. The letter to the Galatians has been called "the Magna Charta of Christian liberty." In opposition to all those traditionalists and legalists who would enslave these Christians to their old rules and regulations of Judaism, Paul argues that "for freedom Christ has set us free" (Galatians 5:1).

A Christian is free from legalistic bondage and excessive self-concern. There is only one restraint placed upon this freedom—the law of love. "Through love be servants of one another" (5:13). A Christian is free, but not free to do anything that he or she pleases. A Christian is free to love. This is the fulfillment of all obligation (5:14). Even as the gifts of the Holy Spirit were abused by the Corinthians, so the Galatians must have abused their freedom in the Holy Spirit.

Evidently someone in Galatia had thought, "I am full of the Spirit; therefore, I can behave any way that I please. I am not bound by rules or concern for others."

This same smug attitude was to arise in the church again in the so-called Spiritualists in the years after the Protestant Reformation. Cut loose from the tradition of the medieval Roman Catholic Church, these enthusiasts decided that, since they were filled with the Spirit, they could do as they pleased. They rejected the notion of law, clergy, even rejected the Bible itself since—because they were filled with the Spirit—they received their revelation direct, without the aid of any intermediary.

This Spiritualism was rejected by the church at large. Spiritualist groups eventually fragmented into a dozen bickering factions which gradually died out. But their experience reminds us "to test the spirits" and to evaluate any alleged expression of the Spirit by the test of love. If it is indeed the *Holy*

Spirit, it will unite rather than divide us. It will lead us "through love to be servants of one another" rather than make us smug, self-righteous, arrogant, and conceited.

In our lives, the Spirit is that prodding, freeing, empowering force which motivates us, energizes us, and liberates us. All this energy and vitality has only one qualification—it will all be congruent with the goals and work of love; otherwise, it could not be the same Spirit which infused our Lord himself.

Walk by the Spirit

It is interesting that Paul sees the Spirit as a force, a presence which walks with us in life. "Walk by the Spirit," he tells the Galatians (5:16). The Spirit is not some static possession that we receive, put in our hip pocket, and hold on to. The Spirit is a driving force which is present with us throughout our life pilgrimage.

The Christian life is a movement, a journey. On this journey, the Spirit goes with us. It not only goes with us; it leads us (5:18).

But this is all still a bit vague and ill-defined. What exactly is the Holy Spirit? What is the precise content of this experience? Paul says that the Spirit is best known by its fruits. The only sure-fire way "to test the spirits" is to examine the fruits of the Spirit. Paul gets quite specific in enumerating those fruits—"love, joy, peace, patience, kindness, goodness, faithfulness, gentleness, self-control" (5:22-23).

These fruits are the life qualities which enable us to live together in the church. Once again, they are not simply private and personal attributes, but rather the requisite equipment for our life together.

Take a look at your church. Sometimes, during Sunday worship, I gaze out upon the assembled congregation. I know those people fairly well, so I know their individual backgrounds, their idiosyncrasies, their foibles, strengths, and weaknesses. I can't help thinking as I look at them. There are so many different kinds of people, such diversity, such variety. Some are old, some are young. There are rich and poor, conservative and liberal. My congregation is a rather homogeneous lot; yours may be even more diverse—to say nothing of the worldwide church.

What on earth holds it all together? What mysterious force keeps the church in one piece? I think Paul would tell us that we need look no further than the fruits of the Spirit. The church would be a sad sight were it not for these gift of unity which we have been given. To live by the Spirit is to walk together with these gifts, walking without self-conceit, factionalism, or envy (5:26), because of the Spirit's work in our lives.

The Harvest of the Spirit

"By their fruits ye shall know them." Today's scripture reminds us that it is not enough to simply *talk* about the Spirit. We must also *walk* in the Spirit. If we have the Spirit operative in our lives, others will be able to see its fruits in our lives.

"Whatever a man sows, that he will also reap," says Paul (6:7). The fruits of our lives bear witness to whatever we have given our lives to. If we seek only selfish gain in life, we need not be surprised that we reap only loneliness. If we live for nothing but earthly securities, we shall inherit much boredom. If we seek only momentary pleasures and cheap sensation, one day we shall be impressed at the utter shallowness of it all. We reap whatever we sow.

"You always get what you pay for," one of our local philosophers said. The sad fact of many of our lives is not that we have put too much into life, but rather that we have put too little into life and little shall we receive. We reap whatever we sow.

The promise of the scripture is that if we walk in the Spirit, humbly, expectantly attuning our lives to the Spirits' leadings, we shall receive the fruits of the Spirit. "He who sows to the Spirit will from the Spirit reap eternal life," says Paul (6:8).

Patience is a virtue which all gardeners and farmers need. It takes time for seed to sprout, take root, grow, develop, and finally bear fruit.

Patience is a virtue we Christans need to cultivate too. It takes time for our lives to develop. The promised fruits of "love, joy, peace, patience, kindness, goodness, faithfulness, gentleness, self-control" (5:22-23) are not overnight, instantaneous virtues. Sometimes we must wait for them to grow and mature in us—and you know how we impatient ones hate to wait!

"Let us not grow weary in well-doing, for in due season we shall reap, if we do not lose heart" (6:9).

I wonder, in my own life, how long I'll have to wait before I shall receive the fruit of patience. Well, some fruit takes longer to mature than others! I'll try not to lose heart as I wait for the Spirit to work in me.

In the meantime, we can take Paul's advice. We can keep close to the Spirit, walk in the Spirit, and root our lives in the Spirit rather than in some other, alien, shallow soil. And while we wait, we can do what Paul says: "Let us do good to all men, and especially to those who are of the household of faith" (6:10).

Helping Adults Become Involved—Robert G. Rogers

Preparing to Teach

Since this is the last lesson in the series on the Holy Spirit, spend some time thinking back over the lessons from the previous five weeks. Are there any issues or concerns in the class that need to be addressed again this week? Remember, the class assignment for this week also included a request for members to review the series on their own; therefore, you should be prepared to refer to the previous lessons. Write a short summary of each lesson in your own words. It might prove useful.

The primary purpose of this lesson is to explore in depth what it means to live by the Holy Spirit. In particular, you will seek to show how our freedom as Christians demands responsible living if we have truly been "touched" by God's Spirit. Read Romans 8:1-27 as a supplement to today's required reading in Galatians. Notice especcially the contrast Paul makes between the Spirit and the flesh. What characteristics would you add to each category?

Introducing the Main Question

The work of the Holy Spirit in our lives brings forth good "fruit." Our approach to life is qualitatively better. This is the fundamental truth expressed by Dr. Willimon. Put another way there is a direct relationship between our Christian profession of faith and our Christian action. The Holy Spirit enables our faith to have integrity.

How do others define us as Christians? Do they see in obvious ways that we live by the Spirit in a spirit of agape love? Do we exhibit those "fruits of the Spirit" that Paul defines so succinctly? Or, by contrast, is there a wide gap between what we claim to be and what we really are? Do the so-called works of the flesh dominate our lives?

Before proceeding with the lesson, suggest that class members think for a few moments on what personal characteristics they want to offer the world. Acknowledge that none of us is perfect; we may not always live up to the best of our Christian calling, but we should constantly be open to the guidance of God's Spirit.

Developing the Lesson

In beginning the class, you asked participants to ponder for a few moments those personal characteristics they wished to cultivate in their lives. List some of the suggestions on the chalkboard or writing pad. Build on this time of reflection by emphasizing what authentic Christian traits are. To do this, you will be using and expanding Paul's list of the "fruits of the Spirit."

Divide your work into three sections:

I. Defining Christian freedom
II. Called to Christian responsibility
III. Walking by the Spirit

I. Defining Christian freedom

One of the glories of the Christian life is that it is lived before God in freedom. Our faith is not based on a series of laws, a list of do's and don'ts. Rather, as Dr. Willimon notes, our Christian calling is to live under one restraint: agape love. Remind the class of last week's lesson on I Corinthians 13, where Paul describes the enduring value of love.

On what is this Christian freedom based? Review with your class the traditional Christian belief regarding the meaning of Jesus' crucifixion. Paul expresses it best in his contrast between works and faith (see Galatians 2:15-21). We do not justify ourselves before God by our works; that is, we do not "earn" our salvation. Rather, salvation is God's gift: the death of his Son on the cross as ransom for our sins. In brief, it is Christ's death that reconciles us to God, not our personal works—however worthy they might be.

However, remind the class that belief in the meaning of Christ's death does not exclude our doing good works. God loves us for who we are, not for what we have or have not done. The works that we do are a response to God's love, not an attempt to earn his love. Suggest that this concept is analogous to our human relationships. If others know they are loved by us, they usually want to respond in loving ways.

II. Called to Christian responsibility

What are the implications of a faith freed from religious legalism? Ask the class to consider the phrase "freed to be more responsible." Write it on the chalkboard. In essence, you will be suggesting that they consider what it means to be a mature Christian. Our faith profession does not release us from further obligation—quite the contrary! We become more responsible for our attitudes and behavior, but not because of requirements or rules. Should we not now respond to God and our fellow human beings with acts of love because we want to do so? Indeed, can agape love be legislated in a religious code?

What, then, motivates our Christian life? What gives us the possibility of expressing agape love in our daily lives? This is where you want to emphasize the role of God's Holy Spirit. If we are serious about our Christian commitment, then we should seek continually to improve our character with the help of the Spirit. Remind the class that Christian life is a pilgrimage. Confessing our faith in Jesus Christ is the beginning point of that journey. Our daily struggle to improve, to come closer to God's will for us, is the best sign that we are maturing in our faith pilgrimage.

III. Walking by the Spirit

Christ's death frees us from religious legalism. In response to God's love, we want to live responsibly, not because we are forced, but because we freely choose so to do. In this concluding section, explore with your class how God's Holy Spirit helps us become mature Christians.

Remember the approach of Dr. Willimon: "We reap whatever we sow." Is it not the case that we must first *want* to walk by the Spirit before we can do so? God does not force us into lives of love, joy, peace, and so forth. We ourselves make the decision to let the Spirit work in us. Walking by the Spirit is a commitment to openness and trust. What opportunities for personal growth do we have when we trust God? when we trust one another? How can we work to develop these trust relationships? How can we help our fellow Christians in their commitment to do so?

Reemphasize the fact that life's journeys are not always smooth. No matter how hard we try, some Christian virtues seem to elude us. Even Paul faced the same frustrations. "For I do not do the good I want, but the evil I do not want is what I do" (Romans 7:19). Surely all of us have felt that way on various occasions. Yet, walking by the Spirit means that we try again. By God's grace, our lives eventually begin to take on those Christlike qualities that we seek.

Helping Class Members Act

Ask your class to memorize Galatians 5:25-26. It is a good summary for Christian living—both individually and in the corporate life of the church.

Suggest that they think during the week about those "works of the flesh" they want to eliminate from their lives and the "fruits" they seek to cultivate by the aid of God's Spirit.

Planning for Next Sunday

Ask the class to read Jeremiah 1 in preparation for the beginning of a study of the Old Testament figures Jeremiah, Ezekiel, and Daniel.

FOURTH QUARTER
Jeremiah, Ezekiel, and Daniel

UNIT I: JEREMIAH: GOD'S MESSAGE FOR A TIME OF TURMOIL

Horace R. Weaver

SIX LESSONS   JUNE 1–JULY 6

This course of fourteen lessons continues the survey of the history of Israel that began in the fall quarter of 1982—"Origins of God's Chosen People." This survey has been studied one quarter per year for four years, and now concludes with the review of Jeremiah, Ezekiel, and Daniel.

This course has three units: "Jeremiah: God's Message for a Time of Turmoil"; "Ezekiel: Judgment and Restoration"; "Daniel: Courage and Hope." The unit on Jeremiah has six lessons, the unit on Ezekiel five, and the unit on Daniel three.

Unit 1, "Jeremiah: God's Message for a Time of Turmoil," consists of six lessons drawn from Jeremiah. The book contains a collection of prophecies against Judah and its capital city, Jerusalem, descriptions of events in the life of Jeremiah (who was called to be a prophet in 626 B.C., at the age of nineteen), the confessions of Jeremiah, and prophecies against foreign (pagan) nations.

The titles of these lessons are: "Jeremiah: Called to a Diffcult Task," June 1; "A People Gone Astray," June 8; "False Worship Condemned," June 15; "Overcoming Obstacles to Witness," June 22; "God's Tests of a True Prophet," June 29; "Hope for the Future, July 6."

Contributors for the fourth quarter:

Harrell F. Beck, professor of Old Testament, School of Theology, Boston University, Boston, Massachusetts.

Howard P. Colson, former editorial secretary, Sunday School Board of the Southern Baptist Convention, Nashville, Tennessee.

Lynne M. Deming, editor in the Department of Resource Development—Youth and Adult, Curriculum Resources Committee, Board of Discipleship, The United Methodist Church, Nashville, Tennessee.

Herbert H. Lambert, general editor, Cooperative Uniform Series, Christian Board of Publication, St. Louis, Missouri.

Wilbur C. Lamm, retired coordinating editor, Adult Section, Sunday School Department, Sunday School Board of the Southern Baptist Convention, Nashville, Tennessee.

William H. Willimon.

The Relationship of Grace in the Old Testament and in the New Testament

LYNNE M. DEMING

Many persons speak of a contrast between the wrathful, judging God in the Old Testament and the gracious, loving God in the New Testament. United Methodists often call their church a "New Testament church." Perhaps part of the reason for this label involves these two contrasting concepts of God. However, as we shall see, this contrast between a wrathful God and a loving God does not stand up to scrutiny. Actually, the Old Testament has a clearer concept of God's grace than we find in the New Testament.

Grace in the Old Testament

In the Old Testament, grace is a primary attribute of Israel's God, Yahweh. Through grace, Israel's God loved the Chosen People even when that love was not deserved. The Old Testament narratives portray story after story of God's Chosen People rebelling against God, and God's grace in the face of that rebellion. Exodus 34:6-7 summarizes God's attitude toward the Israelites: "The Lord passed before him, and proclaimed, 'The Lord, the Lord, a God merciful and gracious, slow to anger, and abounding in steadfast love and faithfulness, keeping steadfast love for thousands, forgiving iniquity and transgression and sin, but who will by no means clear the guilty.'"

As we can see from this passage, God's grace in the Old Testament is closely connected to God's sense of fairness and justice. Grace is also connected to the concept of covenant, central to the Old Testament message. Let us look at a few examples of this connection. God's covenant with Noah promised him and all humankind that God would never again destroy the earth. This promise is unconditional. God's covenant with Abraham promised many descendants and a land to settle in. The covenant at Sinai emphasizes that obedience to God's law brings rewards (see Deuteronomy 28).

God's covenant with David is one of the clearest expressions of God's grace in the Old Testament. Second Samuel 7:15-16 states, "But I will not take my steadfast love from him [David], as I took it from Saul, whom I put away from before you. And your house and your kingdom shall be made sure for ever before me; your throne shall be established for ever."

As with the Old Testament narratives, the prophets also contain many allusions to the grace of God. For the prophets, as for the historical writers, grace is related to God's sense of fairness and justice. For example, Jeremiah 31:2-3 states:

> Thus says the Lord:
> "The people who survived the sword
>   found grace in the wilderness:
> when Israel sought for rest,
>   the Lord appeared to him after afar.
> I have loved you with an everlasting love;
>   therefore I have continued my faithfulness to you."

332

Other examples of the prophetic witness to God's grace include Jeremiah 31:31-34; Amos 7:1-6; and Hosea 11:1-9.

In the Old Testament, God's mercy is best signified by the word *hesed,* usually translated "loving kindness" or "steadfast love." God's *hesed* involves not only God's loyalty to covenant obligations, but also the attitude of kindness that is characteristic of God's nature.

Grace in the New Testament

In the New Testament, the idea of God's grace is most prominent in the letters of Paul. Paul's view is concisely stated in Romans 5:1-2: "Therefore, since we are justified by faith, we have peace with God through our Lord Jesus Christ. Through him we have obtained access to this grace in which we stand, and we rejoice in our hope of sharing the glory of God."

In this passage in Romans, Paul relates grace to "peace with God." This grace, or right relationship with God, has been given to all of us through Jesus Christ. Grace is a free gift from God; it is unmerited. It comes to us *from* God, and it comes to us *through* Christ.

Grace from God through Christ is also a theme in Paul's letter to the Galatians. Paul states that God has saved us by grace by making us "alive together with Christ" (Ephesians 2:5). The fact that we have been saved through faith and by God's grace means that God's grace is not something we can achieve through our own means. As Paul states, "By grace you have been saved through faith, and this is not your own doing, it is the gift of God."

The only place in the Gospels where the concept of grace is clearly discussed is in the prologue to the Gospel of John. According to this writer, the "Word," or *logos,* was a source of God's grace. From the fullness of this Word, represented by Jesus Christ, we have "all received, grace upon grace." For the law was given through Moses; grace and truth came through Jesus Christ." In other words, the gospel writer is telling us that we have an inexhaustible supply of God's grace because of the ministry of Jesus Christ. This grace comes to us as a fulfillment of the law of Moses.

Grace in United Methodist Tradition

The Book of Discipline of The United Methodist Church states that the church's tradition has always emphasized the primacy of grace. According to the *Discipline,* grace means "God's loving action in human existence through the ever-present agency of the Holy Spirit." Grace is present in every facet of human living.

One special emphasis in United Methodism is the idea of prevenient grace. Prevenient grace is a kind of "divine love that anticipates all our conscious impulses and that persuades the heart toward faith." We are made new in Christ through the grace of God.

Jeremiah: Called to a Difficult Task

Background Scripture: Jeremiah 1

The Main Question—William H. Willimon

It is a fearful thing to attempt to speak for God. Would you be surprised if I told you that many ministers whom I know report that they never get a good night's sleep on Saturday evening and that they are plagued with chronic stomach problems every Sunday morning before the sermon?

Perhaps, you say, this is the simple nervousness that comes from the anxiety of standing up and speaking before people. But no, it is more than that. I have seen lawyers in my congregation who speak before people nearly every day climb into our pulpit to make an announcement or to read from Scripture. Their knees shake and their hands tremble. It is a fearful thing to speak for God.

Of course, you may now be saying, I am not a preacher. I don't speak for God, so what does this have to do with me?

Who speaks for God? How does God's word get spoken in our world if not through people like you and me who feel that we are called to speak for God, to proclaim the gospel and to say what God desires?

I may be called to stand in a pulpit on Sunday morning and speak for God, but you are no less called to speak for God in your school, your office, your store, your factory on Monday through Saturday mornings. Who speaks for God? You do!

So we should be attentive to how God calls people to speak, how they are given words to say, and what it feels like to be a spokesperson for God. Thus we turn to the call of Jeremiah.

As You Read the Scripture—Howard P. Colson

At the beginning of this study, it is important to realize that a biblical prophet was a spokesman for God. It is also important to realize that the prophets were more than foretellers; they were "forth-tellers." They spoke of the present as well as the future.

Jeremiah's preface (1:1-3) gives us the name of the prophet's hometown, tells us that he came from a family of priests, and states that he had a ministry of some forty years in Judah (627–587 B.C.). During that time the Babylonian Empire was the outstanding foreign power, and it was to Babylon that the Jewish people were later carried captive. But the main function of the preface is to set forth the fact that Jeremiah's message consisted of the word which came to him from the Lord.

Jeremiah 1:4. "The word of the LORD came to me." The Hebrew term translated "word" may be translated either "word" or "deed." The basic reality of Jeremiah's call lies just here. The Lord's word came to him. We might translate as follows: "The word of the Lord happened." It was an event—a most dynamic event—in Jeremiah's life.

Verses 5-6. God told Jeremiah that before he was born he was divinely chosen, set apart, and appointed to be a prophet "to the nations." (His preaching would deal with international affairs.) But Jeremiah was reluctant. He said, "Ah, Lord God! Behold, I do not know how to speak, for I am only a youth." Perhaps he was between eighteen and twenty-five years of age. (Moses, too, was reluctant to accept his call; see Exodus 4:10.)

Verses 7-10. The Lord entreated Jeremiah to accept the call. There were two elements involved: the divinely authoritative command (verse 7) and the assurance of God's presence and care during his ministry (verse 8). (Compare Matthew 28:20.)

Verse 9. God touched Jeremiah's mouth and said, "Behold, I have put my words in your mouth." (Compare Isaiah 6:7; Ezekiel 2:8; 3:1-3; Daniel 10:16.) The touch of God's hand symbolized the bestowal of the gift of prophecy.

Verse 10. Jeremiah's ministry was to be far-reaching. God made him his representative with authority to proclaim principles by which the destinies of nations are determined. In keeping with the fact, God informed Jeremiah that he was to be a prophet of judgment and doom but also a prophet of hope and salvation. Of the six things mentioned in verse 10, the first four are negative; the last two are positive. Jeremiah was to "pluck up," "break down," "destroy," and "overthrow" so as later "to build and to plant." As we shall later note, there are both strongly negative and strongly positive elements in Jeremiah's preaching.

Verses 13-16. These verses tell of Jeremiah's vision of "a boiling pot." This informed him that the nations of the north (mainly Babylon) were going to overpower his people. The people were longing for peace, but the prophet was given a message of doom. Jerusalem would be destroyed because the people had forsaken the Lord and worshiped other gods.

Verses 17-19. The Lord ordered Jeremiah to "gird up your loins" (get ready for strenuous action). He was to "arise" and "say" to the people all that he was commanded. The Lord promised to care for him. He would make him as strong as "a fortified city, an iron pillar, and bronze walls. The prophet's task was an extremely hard one, but God promised to protect him against all opposition.

Selected Scripture

King James Version	Revised Standard Version
Jeremiah 1:4-10, 13-14, 17-19	*Jeremiah 1:4-10, 13-14, 17-19*
4 Then the word of the Lord came unto me, saying,	4 Now the word of the Lord came to me saying,
5 Before I formed thee in the belly, I knew thee; and before thou camest forth out of the womb I sanctified thee, *and* I ordained thee a prophet unto the nations.	5 "Before I formed you in the womb I knew you, and before you were born I consecrated you; I appointed you a prophet to the nations."
6 Then said I, Ah, Lord God! behold, I cannot speak: for I *am* a child.	6 Then I said, "Ah, Lord God! Behold, I do not know how to speak,

7 But the Lord said unto me, Say not, I *am* a child: for thou shalt go to all that I shall send thee, and whatsoever I command thee thou shalt speak.

8 Be not afraid of their faces: for I *am* with thee to deliver thee, saith the Lord.

9 Then the Lord put forth his hand, and touched my mouth. And the Lord said unto me, Behold, I have put my words in thy mouth.

10 See, I have this day set thee over the nations and over the kingdoms, to root out, and to pull down, and to destroy, and to throw down, to build, and to plant.

....

13 And the word of the Lord came unto me the second time, saying, What seest thou? And I said, I see a seething pot; and the face thereof *is* toward the north.

14 Then the Lord said unto me, Out of the north an evil shall break forth upon all the inhabitants of the land.

....

17 Thou therefore gird up thy loins, and arise, and speak unto them all that I command thee: be not dismayed at their faces, lest I confound thee before them.

18 For, behold, I have made thee this day a defenced city, and an iron pillar, and brasen walls against the whole land, against the kings of Judah, against the princes thereof, against the priests thereof, and against the people of the land.

19 And they shall fight against thee; but they shall not prevail against thee; for I *am* with thee, said the Lord, to deliver thee.

Key Verse: The Lord said unto me, Say not, I *am* a child: for thou shalt go to all that I shall send thee, and

for I am only a youth." 7 But the Lord said to me.
"Do not say, "I am only a youth';
for to all to whom I send you you
    shall go.
and whatever I command you you
    shall speak.
8 Be not afraid of them,
for I am with you to deliver you,
                says the Lord."
9 Then the Lord put forth his hand and touched my mouth; and the Lord said to me,
"Behold, I have put my words in
    your mouth.
10 See, I have set you this day over
    nations and over kingdoms,
to pluck up and to break down,
to destroy and to overthrow,
to build and to plant."

....

13 The word of the Lord came to me a second time, saying, "What do you see?" And I said, "I see a boiling pot, facing away from the north." 14 Then the Lord said to me, "Out of the north evil shall break forth upon all the inhabitants of the land."

....

17 But you gird up your loins; arise, and say to them everything that I command you. Do not be dismayed by them, lest I dismay you before them. 18 And I, behold, I make you this day a fortified city, an iron pillar, and bronze walls against the whole land, against the kings of Judah, its princes, its priests, and the people of the land. 19 They will fight against you; but they shall not prevail against you, for I am with you, says the Lord, to deliver you."

Key Verse:
The Lord said to me,
"Do not say, 'I am only a youth';

whatsoever I command thee thou shalt speak. Be not afraid of their faces: for I *am* with thee to deliver thee, said the Lord. (Jeremiah 1:7-8)

for to all to whom I send you you shall go,
and whatever I command you you shall speak.
Be not afraid of them,
for I am with you to deliver you,
says the Lord."

(Jermiah 1:7-8)

The Scripture and the Main Question—William H. Willimon

I Consecrated You

"How did you get here?"

That's the question I always asked seminarians when I met with them on the first day of their field education seminar at the divinity school. You can learn a great deal about someone by finding out how that person began.

The seminarians told stories of influential Sunday school teachers, coaches, parents, about people in the church who looked at them and said, "You ought to be a minister." I never stopped being amazed at all the ways God calls people into the pastoral ministry.

Today's lesson concerns the call of Jeremiah into God's service. In his youth, "the word of the Lord came to me," says Jeremiah (Jeremiah 1:4).

I suppose that, for most of us, there is a sense in which the call of God comes to us when we are still young. A recent study in England, in which hundreds of people were interviewed concerning their religious development, concluded that most people have their most significant religious experiences before age eight. Most of us spend the rest of our lives responding to formative religious experiences that occurred in us while we were still in elementary school.

Think back over your own life. How did you get here—that is, how did you come to where you are today in your relationship with God? More likely than not, you will think of Sunday school teachers, youth retreats, summer camp, and other early experiences which made you who you are.

How early does God's work begin in us? One of the reasons why my church continues the ancient practice of baptizing infants of Christian parents is that we believe God touches our lives from infancy.

In fact, Jeremiah heard God saying that we are being loved, guided, and set apart, even from conception.

Before I formed you in the womb I knew you,
and before you were born I consecrated you;
I appointed you a prophet to the nations. (1:5)

Jeremiah's belief that he was chosen even before birth is confirmed by what we are learning about human development. We do not arrive on the scene of life *de novo*, out of nowhere, a blank slate. We inherit a genetic endowment from our parents. Some physicians believe that our personalities are affected by what influences our mothers while we are in the womb. Erik Erikson says that a child learns trust (and, by implication, religious faith) in the first six months of life, in the little rituals of meeting and love between the child and its parent upon first waking in the morning. Here the child learns that the world is a trustworthy place. The child builds upon these early, basic experiences as the circle of trust grows wider. If for some reason the child is abused or not cared for properly, the child learns not to trust the world and can be damaged for life.

Contemporary child developmentalists say that a child learns half of everything he or she will ever know by the age of three!

Therefore, to ask, "How did you get here?" means to respond, with Jeremiah, that we were formed in infancy, even in the womb.

I Do Not Know How to Speak

Jeremiah's response to his youthful calling is typical of most of us. "Ah, Lord God! Behold, I do not know how to speak, for I am only a youth" (1:6).

Each year, our church nominating committee meets to propose leadership for our church for the coming year. A host of Jeremiahs sometimes thwart our efforts!

—"I lack advanced training and education."
—"I have back problems."
—"I am too old to serve."
—"I am too young to serve."
—"Ask one of the older members."
—"Ask one of the newer members."

Like Moses before the burning bush, Jeremiah pleads that he doesn't know how to speak in front of people. Besides, "I am only a youth." Any of us, if we look over our lives, can find limitations, inadequacies, or lack of experience or training which make us unsuited for God's service.

The fascinating thing is how often God calls people who, on the face of it, appear to be utterly unsuited for difficult work. Moses had a speech impediment. Abraham and Sarah were advanced in years. Mary was young, poor, and unmarried. Peter was impulsive. Jeremiah was inexperienced. And yet, these were the people whom God chose to speak and act in his behalf. What does that tell us about ourselves and our inadequacies?

One thing the Lord told Jeremiah—"I am with you" (1:8). When God calls us for service, we are not on our own.

Sometimes we do church leaders a great disservice by appointing them to tasks and then not giving them the resources and materials they need to do the job. We ask for someone to teach the third grade church school class. When some dedicated soul finally comes forward to volunteer, then we often forget about her. We don't make sure that she is well equipped with teaching materials. We don't see that our children are present every Sunday for the class. Then we wonder why she "burns out" a year later, a victim of defeat and discouragement.

Today's lesson reminds us that, just as it was for Jeremiah, when the Lord calls us, God gives us what we need to do the work. Can you think of instances in your own life when you, like Jeremiah, reluctantly accepted some task, fearing that you would not have the requisite talent and resources to do the job, and were surprised to find God giving you what you needed?

I Am with You

Again and again in the Bible, we see instances of people who are called by God to perform some holy endeavor, people who, on the face of it, have few talents, yet people who somehow get the job done.

One thing we often overlook in assessing our worthiness to do some job for God is that God gives us what we need; God is with us.

Imagine how Jeremiah felt as he, a young, inexperienced man, was sent by God to confront the vast, powerful rulers of his day. Jeremiah may have been young, but he knew enough about human nature to know that people do not gladly hear the words of the true prophet. We do not sit back impassively when one is sent to us, "to pluck up and break down, to destroy and to overthrow, to build and to plant" (1:10). "Do not be dismayed" by the response of your hearers, God tells the young prophet (1:17).

She was only one woman. She had never spoken in public, had never held a paying job. But when the schools integrated in her little southern town, she made it her business to say at school, at church, at the grocery store, wherever she could, "This is a good and right thing to do. My children and I are staying, and we're going to help make this thing work."

He was well over sixty-five, at an age when most men are relaxing and enjoying retirement. But some voice within him, some voice that could not be denied, kept speaking to him about the growing threat of nuclear war.

"What kind of world are we leaving to our grandchildren?" he asked. "Will they have a world at all? Will they still be able to raise children of their own, or will it all be blown to bits?"

He began to study the subject of nuclear armaments. He had a fairly extensive background in the military himself and was good at facts and figures, so he quickly mastered the issues and sorted through all the details.

But he was old, too old, some said. "George must be getting senile," some sneered. "George, stay out of it and let the government worry about it," said some of his friends.

But George didn't stay out of it, so convinced was he that God had called *him* to speak a word against the madness, no matter how people might reject the word.

No one promised us that it would be easy to be called, consecrated, and appointed by God to speak and act in the name of Christ. No one told us that people would always respond positively to what we do and say. All we were told is that, whatever happens, "I will be with you."

Helping Adults Become Involved—Herbert H. Lambert

Preparing to Teach

This session will set the stage for our study of three books: Jeremiah, Ezekiel, and Daniel. We will learn something of the momentous events that took place in Jeremiah's time. We will try to understand this remarkable and tragic figure. We will ask what he can teach us about God's will for us and for our nation.

Here is one way to outline the lesson:

> I. The time of Jeremiah (627–580 B.C.)
> > A. The decline of Assyria
> > B. The threat of Babylon
> > C. Events in Judah
> II. Jeremiah's call in 627 B.C.
> > A. Set apart from birth
> > B. Only a youth!
> > C. Jeremiah's mission
> III. Our call to serve God
> > A. Our fear of involvement
> > B. Dealing with opposition

FOURTH QUARTER

You may need to do more reading for this first session of the quarter than you usually do. The introductory pages of any good commentary on Jeremiah will help. *The Interpreter's Bible*, volume 5, pages 777-87, 794-811, and *The Interpreter's Concise Commentary*, volume 4, pages 124-35 will be helpful.

Introducing the Main Question

Professor James Muilenberg of Union Theological Seminary lectured on the world situation about 640 B.C. He described the decline of Assyrian power after centuries of ruthless oppression. He spoke of unrest as small nations struggled for freedom and evil forces sought to exploit the new situation. As he stroked his chin pensively, he pictured God looking over this scene and saying, "I believe I'll make Jeremiah!"

Jeremiah's life and message were so closely linked to the events of his time that one might conclude he was made to interpret them. Such was the conviction of Jeremiah himself. What were the great events of the late 600s and early 500s? What kind of person did God send to speak about these events?

Developing the Lesson

I. The time of Jeremiah (627–580 B.C.)

A. *The decline of Assyria*

Display a map of the Assyrian Empire in the seventh century B.C., or sketch such a map on the chalkboard. Notice the position of the capital of Assyria, Nineveh. Note Jerusalem and the little nation of Judah. For many years Assyria oppressed the peoples of this area. No wonder the enslaved nations were delighted when they heard of Assyria's weakness, which culminated in the destruction of Nineveh in 612 B.C.

B. *The threat of Babylon*

As the empire crumbled, Babylon sought to enlist Judah and other small nations in a protective alliance. However, Babylon soon became as great a threat as Assyria had been! Long before this happened, Jeremiah warned of a "foe from the north" who would be sent by God to punish Judah. He lived to see the Babylonians besiege Jerusalem twice and destroy its temple. Point to Babylon on your map.

C. *Events in Judah*

As Jeremiah grew up, young Josiah was king. The downfall of Assyria left Judah free to manage its own affairs. This meant an opportunity to return to the Lord and to throw off Assyrian customs and religion. Josiah carried out a moderately successful reform, using part of Deuteronomy as his guide. Josiah was killed by the Egyptians in 609 B.C., and the weak king Jehoiakim took his place. Jeremiah intensified his criticism of Judah after Josiah died.

II. Jeremiah's call in 627 B.C.

A. *Set apart from birth*

Have the class read Jeremiah 1:1-5. The kings under whom Jeremiah preached are named because his message was closely related to their actions and to the events of their time. When God speaks through prophets, the message is not a timeless platitude but specific information about the day's headlines and their significance.

Jeremiah felt that he had been set apart from the day of his birth, and even before. Notice the three verbs in verse 5. God "knew" Jeremiah. This

340

means to have an intimate relation with someone. Jeremiah was "set apart," which can also mean "made holy." Jeremiah was allowed to participate in the awesome holiness of God. And Jeremiah was "anointed" or commissioned to fulfill a great task.

B. *Only a youth!*

Jeremiah protested that he was young and inexperienced. He also had emotional problems which were greatly intensified by his role as a prophet (4:19). In many ways Jeremiah was unqualified for the job, but God was not deterred by this. God chooses strange persons for the work that must be done and the words that must be spoken! It's still true today. Can you think of "unqualified" persons of recent years who managed to serve God in significant ways? Simone Weil was a woman of Jewish ancestry who died of tuberculosis at the age of thirty-four. She left behind a few meditations on God and the Christian faith which have had influence on many millions.

Think of persons in your own congregation who may not be highly trained or specially gifted whom God may be using in a special way.

C. *Jeremiah's mission*

The prophet believed he had a twofold work to do. Have the class members decide what these images suggest: pluck up and break down, build and plant. How would a person do these things today, in a church or in a community?

Jeremiah remained single and set himself against almost everyone. He condemned the priests, the prophets, the kings, the princes, the people of Judah. He warned of impending doom in a time when most people were optimistic. Only in his later years, when his nation lay in ruins, did Jeremiah speak of hope.

Other than his secretary and a few others, Jeremiah had few helpers. He was criticized, ridiculed, jailed, and almost killed by those who hated him and rejected his message.

Helping Class Members Act

III. *Our call to serve God*

A. *Our fear of involvement*

In the summer of 1983, a crowd of people gathered around a park fountain in St. Louis. In the sight of scores of adults, a gang of boys attacked and raped a young girl. Only a nine-year-old boy got on his bike and went for the police. When they arrived, the adults dispersed and refused even to help the police as eyewitnesses. When interviewed by reporters, the lad said, "I did it because I had to. No one else would help."

When there is trouble, no one likes to get involved. Jeremiah didn't want to either. He knew it would mean a lot of trouble for him. Ask the class members to recall problems in their community in which they should have become interested but did not. Why did they avoid involvement?

B. *Dealing with opposition*

Like Jeremiah, we are likely to encounter anger if we stand up for what is right. People will accuse us of being meddlers and hypocrites. Workers who complain about health hazards may be subject to harassment or dismissal. Those who work for change in society are subject to abuse and even physical danger.

Have the class members think of persons who, like Jeremiah, have come under fire while doing what they believed to be right. The list might include politicians, church leaders, and employees. Have any of the class members encountered hostility because of a courageous stand? How did they deal with the situation?

Planning for Next Sunday

Suggest that the class members read Jeremiah 2–6 this week, marking those places about which they have questions and those phrases which stand out. Have them make a list of actions which Jeremiah recommended. Also make a list of striking images, such as the one of the broken cistern (2:13).

LESSON 2   JUNE 8

A People Gone Astray

Background Scripture: Jeremiah 2–6

The Main Question—William H. Willimon

The other day my children and I took a picnic lunch and hiked down to the river where our town was first settled in the late 1700s. We read the marker telling of the first pioneer settlement and imagined what it must have been like to be among the first white settlers of our nation.

You and I can only imagine what the hardships must have been like for the first pioneers in Appalachia, the first immigrants who settled the West, the people who cleared the forests and built the first cabins in the great Northwest. They were hearty, dedicated, resourceful people. It was by the sweat, sacrifice, and prayers of people like these that our nation was born.

As they cleared the forest and built their towns, they also built churches. I am the heir of a host of sturdy Methodist circuit riders who braved the wilderness and its perils to found churches and establish religion in the young nation.

I imagine that those first circuit riders, for all the difficulties they suffered, found receptive ears for their preaching. People who face sickness, perils, death every day, people who know what it is to suffer and sacrifice, are people who seek the consolations and the inspiration of religious faith. The early settlers knew that life can be hard. They also knew what it was to suffer under economic or political or religious persecution back home in the old country. So they must have been a people of deep gratitude for what they had in this new land.

But what about us? Today, with the world of the pioneers centuries behind us, with all of our comforts and conveniences, do we appreciate and feel gratitude for what we have been given? Most of us have never known anything but freedom, comfort, and security. Unfortunately, human nature being what it is, we don't feel the same sense of gratitude, the same sense of dependence upon God that our forebears may have felt. It is so easy to forget.

Yes, it is so easy to forget.

As You Read the Scripture—Howard P. Colson

Jeremiah chapters 2 through 6 give us a summary of what was probably the prophet's teaching during the early years of his ministry. Through Jeremiah, God issued a serious indictment againt his people. Our lesson presents a strong contrast between Judah's former love for the Lord and her later disloyalty. The situation was most pathetic. The people had broken their covenant with God. But in love the Lord issued his complaint. He was greatly disappointed in his people but yearned for them to return to him.

Jeremiah 2:1. This verse repeats Jeremiah 1:4, which marked God's initial call to the prophet.

Verse 2. The Lord's message was to be proclaimed in Jerusalem, which was both the religious and the political capital of the nation. "The devotion of your youth" marked the early days of Israel. Their relationship to the Lord was then like that of a bride to her husband, one of love. "The wilderness" refers to Israel's wanderings as she looked forward to entering the Promised Land. "A land not sown" means the wilderness.

Verse 3. The Israelites had been set apart to the Lord. They were "holy" —set apart—like the "first fruits" of the harvest. According to the law, the first fruits had to be dedicated to the Lord, and only the priest and his family were allowed to eat of them (Leviticus 22:10, 16). If anyone else ate of them, he violated God's holiness and brought divine wrath upon himself. Thus if pagan people interfered with Israel, they would be as guilty as those who ate the first fruits. But Israel herself was guilty because she permitted the pagans to influence her by their false religion.

Verse 7. God brought his people into "a plentiful land," the land of Canaan; but they "defiled" it by their religious apostasy. As a result, they—God's heritage—became "an abomination."

Verse 8. The apostasy of the religious leaders is described here. Even the priests and those who handled the law of God (Levites, the predecessors of the later "scribes," the teachers) "did not know" the Lord and lacked true spiritual concern. The Hebrew word translated "rulers" means "shepherds." These shepherds sinned ("transgressed") against God. And the prophets who should have been speaking for the Lord "prophesied by Baal," the pagan god of fertility, whose worship was grossly immoral. The faithless religious leaders "went after things that do not profit" (a nickname for the gods of the Canaanites).

Verse 11. Verse 11 speaks of the absurdity of turning away from the Lord. The previous verse refers to the island of Cyprus and the land of Arabia (Kedar), representing the West and the East. The point is that even people in those heathen areas were faithful to their gods. Therefore, by contrast, how absurd it was for Israel to change her glory (the presence of the true God and the privilege of serving him) for "that which does not profit"!

Verse 12. In view of Israel's unfaithfulness, the very heavens should be "appalled" and "shocked"!

Verse 13. The results of Israel's apostasy are set forth. The people committed two evils. (1) By turning away from God, they forsook "the fountain of living waters." (Compare John 4:14 and Revelation 22:17.) They forsook the true for the false. They turned to that which never could satisfy the deepest needs of their souls. (2) By turning to false gods they "hewed out for themselves broken cisterns that can hold no water." What a lesson that should be for our day!

FOURTH QUARTER

Selected Scripture

King James Version

Jeremiah 2:1-3, 7-8, 11-13

1 Moreover the word of the LORD came to me, saying,

2 Go and cry in the ears of Jerusalem, saying, Thus saith the LORD; I remember thee, the kindness of thy youth, the love of thine espousals, when thou wentest after me in the wilderness, in a land *that was* not sown.

3 Israel *was* holiness unto the LORD, *and* the firstfruits of his increase: all that devour him shall offend; evil shall come upon them, saith the LORD.

....

7 And I brought you into a plentiful country, to eat the fruit thereof and the goodness thereof; but when ye entered, ye defiled my land, and made mine heritage an abomination.

8 The priests said not, Where *is* the LORD? and they that handle the law knew me not: the pastors also trangressed against me, and the prophets prophesied by Bā´-ăl, and walked after *things that* do not profit.

....

11 Hath a nation changed *their* gods, which *are* yet no gods? but my people have changed their glory for *that which* doth not profit.

12 Be astonished, O ye heavens, at this, and be horribly afraid, be ye very desolate, saith the LORD.

13 For my people have committed two evils; they have forsaken me the fountain of living waters, *and* hewed them out cisterns, broken cisterns, that can hold no water.

Revised Standard Version

Jeremiah 2:1-3, 7-8, 11-13

1 The word of the LORD came to me, saying, 2 "Go and proclaim in the hearing of Jerusalem, Thus says the LORD,
I remember the devotion of your youth,
your love as a bride,
how you followed me in the wilderness, in a land not sown.
3 Israel was holy to the LORD,
the first fruits of his harvest.
All who ate of it became guilty;
evil came upon them,
says the LORD."

....

7 And I brought you into a plentiful land to enjoy its fruits and its good things.
But when you came in you defiled my land.
and made my heritage an abomination.

8 The priests did not say, 'Where is the LORD?
Those who handle the law did not know me;
the rulers transgressed against me;
the prophets prophesied by Ba'al,
and went after things that do not profit.

....

11 Has a nation changed its gods, even though they are no gods?
But my people have changed their glory
for that which does not profit.
12 Be appalled, O heavens, at this, be shocked, be utterly desolate,
says the LORD,
13 for my people have committed two evils:
they have forsaken me,
the fountain of living waters,
and hewed out cisterns for themselves,

broken cisterns,
that can hold no water.

Key Verse: I brought you into a
plentiful country, to eat the fruit
thereof and the goodness thereof;
but when ye entered, ye defiled my
land, and made mine heritage an
abomination. (Jeremiah 2:7)

Key Verse:
I brought you into a plentiful land
to enjoy its fruits and its good
things.
But when you came in you
defiled my land,
and made my heritage an
abomination. (Jeremiah 2:7)

The Scripture and the Main Question—William H. Willimon

I Brought You into a Plentiful Land

Few nations could boast such an inspiring past. They had begun as a tribe
of desert nomads, traveling from place to place, without land, with no real
identity beyond the family. But early on, one of them heard a promise from
God, a promise to make of them "a great nation." Due to a certain set of
circumstances, they found themselves in the land of Egypt. All went well for
a time, then a pharaoh arose "who did not know Joseph," and who put the
Hebrews in slavery.

Yet, even in slavery, they were remembered by their God. In the mighty
deeds and events which became known as the Exodus, they were led out of
slavery and into freedom, out across the desert to what they called the
Promised Land. Here, in this land "flowing with milk and honey," they
made their home. They built cities, erected a temple, planted gardens,
raised flocks of sheep, and founded a nation.

All this occurred, not because of their own strength as a people, not
because they were particularly brave or astute, but because "I brought you
into a plentiful land," says the Lord (Jeremiah 2:7).

The land, the freedom, the prosperity were all gifts, like our own
land.

Of course, we don't usually see it this way. Something about us leads us to
believe that we are in the position we are in today because we earned it,
deserved it, merited it all because of our goodness. How many Americans
assume that we are prosperous and secure because we are especially hard
workers or particularly productive and energetic or morally more righteous
than the rest of the world?

Yet, for all our virtues, we must admit, when we are honest, that most of
what we have has come to us as a gift. What good would our
industriousness do us if we lived in a land with poor, rocky soil, where
droughts were frequent, where natural resources were few? Yet many of
the world's people, in spite of their hard work and goodness, live in such
conditions.

This is to say that when we're honest, we—like Judah—must admit that we
are where we are, to a great extent, as a gift. What did you or I do to be born
in a land rich in resources, rich in freedom and prosperity? For us, as for
those before us in faith, God could say, "I brought you into a plentiful land
to enjoy its fruits and its good things" (2:7).

I Remember the Devotion of Your Youth

Jeremiah hears the Lord say that something is deeply wrong with Judah. The Lord tells Jeremiah the prophet to go tell the people that they have wandered astray from their original purposes. The prophet compares the early love of the people for God to the love of a husband and wife in the marriage vow. "I remember the devotion of your youth, your love as a bride, how you followed me in the wilderness" (2:2).

But that was yesterday. Today, things are quite different between Judah and its God. Now, "when you came in you defiled my land, and made my heritage an abomination" (2:7). The people who were called out from Egypt to be a holy people for the Lord have taken up the false gods of their pagan neighbors, have forgotten their original vision and purpose, and have wandered astray from their early goals.

I suppose this is only human. The most severe crisis to hit the early Pilgrims who settled New England was not the fierce New England winters, the shortages of food and essentials, the bickering and dissension within their own ranks. The thing that caused their early pastors and leaders the most concern, judging from their writings, was the status of the children and grandchildren whom they bore in the new world.

These new ones could not know the original vision which compelled their mothers and fathers to leave the comfort and security of England to come to this wild and forbidding place. They could not appreciate what blessings religious and political freedom were because they had never known anything else.

This was a cause of much grief among the Puritan divines.

We see the same process at work in ourselves and our children. We smile at the grandfather telling the grandchildren how far he had to walk to school in the snow, or the grandmother telling the little ones about having to get up before dawn to feed the cows and do the other backbreaking chores before daylight. Or we try to tell our children about how tough it was during the Great Depression or during the Second World War. But this is a frustrating task. They really don't understand. We can't make them feel grateful because they have never known anything other than prosperity, freedom, and comfort.

How quickly we forget the past sacrifices and past suffering which preceded us into the comfort and wealth we enjoy today! So we erect a statue to the heroes of the past; we engrave a bronze marker telling of the ones who gave their lives for us; we name a building after someone who suffered in our behalf. But how quickly, how easily, we forget and take it all for granted.

Like Judah before us, once we are settled and secure in the Promised Land, once the trials and tribulations are behind us, our dependence upon God seems not so great, our need for divine assistance seems not so essential, and we forget.

So the prophet might cry out to us as Jeremiah cried out to Judah, "My people have changed their glory for that which does not profit" (2:11).

Has a Nation Changed Its Gods?

In a way, this is the question which the troublesome prophet of God is forever asking a people—"Has a nation changed its gods?" (2:11). The prophet Nathan accused the arrogant David of immorality; Amos rebuked the materialistic rich of his day; Jeremiah condemned the priests and leaders of his time for forsaking the loving God who had brought them out of slavery and into this good land for a purpose.

Yet we know this process all too well, for it works in us even as it worked in the people of Judah before us. How easy it is to sell out and exchange our values of freedom, liberty, equality, and national righteousness for crass materialism, profit over people, and raw power. We too bow before the false gods of military might, wealth, security at any price, and sensuality rather than before the true God to whom we owe everything.

Prophets, true prophets, call us back to our roots, our heritage, our originating vision. They remind us of what we so easily forget.

Helping Adults Become Involved—Herbert H. Lambert

Preparing to Teach

In today's lesson we will consider some early sermons of Jeremiah, delivered when he was still a young man. We will try to understand what was wrong in Judah and what Jeremiah said about it. What had the leaders done or failed to do? What did Jeremiah say would happen as a result? What similar problems can we observe in our nation today?

Here is a way to outline the lesson:

I. Judah's sin
    A. Forsaking God
    B. Oppressing the poor
II. The pervasiveness of evil
    A. All classes of people
    B. Refusal to listen
    C. Vain efforts to find salvation
III. The prophet's warning
    A. His own anguish
    B. The woe to come
IV. Implications for today
    A. Our choice
    B. Being open to God

Helpful supplementary reading is found in *The Interpreter's Bible*, volume 5, pages 811-63 (especially 811-23), and in *The Interpreter's Concise Commentary*, volume 4, pages 136-46.

Introducing the Main Question

Today many adults look at young people using harmful drugs, abusing alcohol, and neglecting their education, and say, "If only they would pause and consider the consequences of what they are doing!" In today's lesson we see Jeremiah, a young man touched by God, condemning the sins of the adults of his day and saying, "If only they would pause and consider the consequences of what they are doing!"

One way to begin the lesson is to ask class members to tell what they discovered in reading Jeremiah 2–6, as suggested in the last session. List on the chalkboard the questions they raised while reading. Note chapter and verse of passages they found memorable. With the help of class members, find some of the striking images in these chapters, such as:

347

2:13—broken cisterns
2:20—bowed down as a harlot
2:22—lye and soap won't remove stain
2:32—a bride forget her finery?

Ask what Jeremiah was trying to convey in the use of each of these images.

Developing the Lesson

I. Judah's sin

A. Forsaking God

From the time they entered the land of Canaan, the people of Israel began to adopt the religious practices and even the gods of the nations that were already there. In the spring, religious rites of a sexual nature were performed to ensure fertile fields and vineyards. Idols and other objects of worship were erected. Even children were sacrificed (II Kings 17:7-18).

Although the people of Judah continued to speak of Yahweh, the Lord God, their actions did not indicate loyalty to the Lord. Their God was a special God, with unique characteristics and particular demands. These were made clear in the Ten Commandments and in other laws handed down through the centuries. Jeremiah said that the people could not serve this God and at the same time disregard God's laws.

For a nation to change its gods was unheard of in that time; yet the people of Judah attempted to do just that (Jeremiah 2:11). They had forsaken the God who is an artesian well of fresh water and had made cisterns which will hold only stagnant water or crack and lose the water they had (2:13)! Like a rebellious ox, they had broken the yoke and refused to pull the load. They had committed adultery (covenantal disloyalty) by serving other gods in fertility cults (2:20). Like animals in heat, they had gone recklessly after foreign gods (2:23-24).

B. Oppressing the poor

Amos, Isaiah, and other prophets before Jeremiah had condemned those who robbed or neglected the poor. Jeremiah said, "On your skirts is found the lifeblood of guiltless poor" (2:34). The judges do not protect orphans and needy persons (5:28). Jerusalem will be destroyed because it is full of oppression (6:6-7).

Our relationship to God is determined by our concern for others, especially the unfortunate. Unless we show concern for others, we cannot draw near to God.

II. The pervasiveness of evil

A. All classes of people

The evil of Judah is not confined to the "lower classes" or to laypeople. Jeremiah blames priests, prophets, and rulers for not doing their duty (2:8). "For from the least to the greatest of them, every one is greedy for unjust gain" (6:13).

B. Refusal to listen

Jeremiah may as well have been talking to a stone wall. He was angered by the way in which everyone ignored the word of the Lord. He called them "stupid children" (4:22). Their faces are "harder than rock" (5:3). Their "ears are closed" (6:10), and they refuse to walk in the old, good paths (6:16).

C. Vain efforts to find salvation

Pathetically, the people of Judah realized that they needed something. They hungered and thirsted for what God alone can give. But instead of seeking God, they were satisfied with unsatisfactory substitutes (2:13).

III. The prophet's warning
  A. *His own anguish*
Jeremiah did not deliver God's message like a courier who has no idea what's in his envelope. He took the message into his soul, where it tore him apart!

> My anguish, my anguish! I writhe in pain!
>   Oh, the walls of my heart!
> My heart is beating wildly;
>   I cannot keep silent;
> For I hear the sound of the trumpet,
>   the alarm of war. (4:19)

Jeremiah did not want evil to come upon his people, but he was compelled by God to tell them that, unless they changed their ways, it would.
  B. *The woe to come*
At first Jeremiah proclaimed that a "foe from the north" would besiege and capture Jerusalem. When no foe appeared, Jeremiah was held up to ridicule. He complained to God that he had been deceived (20:7). Notice that religious affairs, social policy, personal matters, and foreign relations are all tied together in the prophet's thinking. A nation that is not concerned about its people and their needs cannot protect itself with chariots—or nuclear bombs! It will crumble from within even if not attacked from without.

Helping Class Members Act

IV. Implications for today
  A. *Our choice*
If Jeremiah is right, it makes a lot of difference whether our justice system penalizes the poor and lets the rich off with probation. It matters whether our worship of God is sincere or only for show. It matters whether we are really concerned for the poor of Central America or are using them as pawns in our search for national security. Our behavior as individuals and as a nation will have lasting consequences on the course of history. By our callousness, neglect, and greed, we sow the wind. No doubt about it—we shall reap the whirlwind!
  B. *Being open to God*
Divide the class into groups of three. Have each group compose a prayer asking for openness to the message of God for our time. May we be sensitive to what God is telling us about the dangers that confront us. Ask God to open our hearts during this study of Jeremiah so that God's word, even if we don't like to hear it, may sound clearly in our ears.

Planning for Next Sunday

Suggest that all class members read Jeremiah 7:1-15 and all of chapter 26 before the next lesson. Note that "Shiloh" refers to an early and most sacred Hebrew sanctuary which was destroyed by the Philistines. Jeremiah says that Jerusalem can likewise be destroyed if the people fail to repent and change their ways.

False Worship Condemned

Background Scripture: Jeremiah 7:1-15; 26

The Main Question—William H. Willimon

As a clergyperson, one of my frequent duties is to appear at important public functions and say a blessing or give an invocation or pronounce a benediction.

I must confess that such duties are not among my most favorite. I have a number of ambivalent feelings when I am called upon to pray or to bless some public functions.

The coach of the high school football team is a religious man and likes to have a devotional for the players before a ball game. I am all for devotionals, but thirty minutes before the big game of the year, with all the players' minds set on nothing but winning the game, is neither the time nor the place for a devotional.

Our city council calls upon local clergy to say a *short* (they always emphasize the "short") prayer before their weekly meetings. I'm all for prayer, but what does one pray for on such occasions? Should one pray that council will at last try to do something about the poor streets and the poor police protection in the poor neighborhoods of the city? I daresay that if I prayed for something *really* important or really controversial, I would not be asked back again.

A friend of mine steadfastly refuses to pray before a football game. "What am I supposed to pray for?" he asks.

Perhaps he should do the usual and pray that everyone will be a good sport and that no one will be hurt. But then, as he notes, the coach tells the team to "get out there and hit hard and tackle hard and win." If someone is injured, is that God's problem? Maybe God doesn't care about football; maybe God doesn't want us to play football in the first place.

What we usually want on such occasions is a little religious veneer to our essentially nonreligious activities, a little pious blessing. We're usually not too interested in what God thinks about such occasions; we just want God's approval and blessing.

Jeremiah is asked to bless a national assembly, a great state occasion. Unfortunately, Jeremiah is a prophet, a true prophet, who says what God wants rather than what the king wants. That's where the trouble starts.

As You Read the Scripture—Howard P. Colson

We have two accounts of Jeremiah's temple sermon. Chapter 7 sets forth the sermon itself; chapter 26 gives a biographical account of the prophet's experience in connection with his sermon.

This was one of the most important events in Jeremiah's life. He was strongly opposed, but he showed unshrinking courage. God needed a man like him for this hour.

The occasion was probably the fall festival of 609 B.C., when great crowds thronged the temple area. It was in the beginning of the reign of Josiah's son Jehoiakim. There was a crisis in the nation's life. Josiah had given royal approval and strong support to the reforms stated in the "Word of God" in 620 B.C. Even Jeremiah had supported this religious form at first, then gradually realized morality and religion cannot be legalized! Good King Josiah had died of wounds received in battle, and his son Jehoahaz, who first succeeded him, had been deported to Egypt by Pharaoh Neco after serving as king only three months (II Kings 23:31-34).

God had commanded Jeremiah to deliver a message in opposition to the current attitude of the religious leaders and the people. In the face of the current crisis, they were placing mistaken reliance on the temple. Their line of reasoning was this: Josiah's reforms had given Solomon's temple the highest priority. All other temples were outlawed, condemned, and demolished! But Solomon's temple had stood through the storms of the years; and since the Lord dwelt in the temple, and since the temple was located in Jerusalem, they concluded that the city was safe. But that was a mistaken conclusion.

Jeremiah preached that going to the place of worship would not in itself bring deliverance; the only thing that would do so was a right relationship with God. The people were trusting in the outward form of religion and paying but little attention to God's demands for ethical living.

Jeremiah 7:1-4. Jeremiah 7:1-2 is introductory. The sermon proper begins with verses 3-4. These verses declare that the priests and prophets who were preaching trust in the temple as the basis of Jerusalem's security were preaching falsehood. They did not trust in God.

Verse 9. Here is a list of the sins of which the people were guilty and which God called on them to abandon. They were breaking the eighth, sixth, seventh, ninth, first, and second commandments (compare Exodus 20:3-17; Deuteronomy 5:7-21). Thus they were breaking practically the entire covenant. How could God bless and spare Jerusalem in view of such unfaithfulness!

Verse 10. It was futile for the people to flock to the place of worship expecting God's help when they were guilty of such gross immoral living and seemed to have no intention of amending their ways.

Chapter 26:8. The leaders stirred up a mob scene. Jeremiah was laid hold of and told, "You shall die!" Behind this outcry was the false idea that Jeremiah could not really be speaking for God. According to the law, such a prophet was to be put to death (Deuteronomy 18:20). The mistaken leaders thought that God would never permit Jerusalem to be destroyed.

Verse 9. For Jeremiah's reference to Shiloh, see verse 6. Shiloh was the area where the sacred ark and the tabernacle had been located in the ancient days of Samuel. The worshipers at Shiloh fell into idolatry. As a result it was overthrown and the ark was captured by the Philistines (I Samuel 4:1-11).

Verse 12. Jeremiah defended his sermon by declaring that the Lord had sent him to deliver it. His message was God's message.

Verse 13. Risking his life, Jeremiah repeated the essence of his message: Only moral living can guarantee protection.

Verse 14. "I am in your hands": Jeremiah was so devoted to God that he was willing to die for him.

Selected Scripture

King James Version

Revised Standard Version

Jeremiah 7:1-4, 8-10

1 The word that came to Jeremiah from the Lord, saying,

2 Stand in the gate of the Lord's house, and proclaim there this word, and say, Hear the word of the Lord, all *ye of* Judah, that enter in at these gates to worship the Lord.

3 Thus saith the Lord of hosts, the God of Israel, Amend your ways and your doings, and I will cause you to dwell in this place.

4 Trust ye not in lying words, saying, The temple of the Lord, The temple of the Lord, The temple of the Lord, *are* these.

....

8 Behold, ye trust in lying words, that cannot profit.

9 Will ye steal, murder, and commit adultery, and swear falsely, and burn incense unto Bā´-ăl, and walk after other gods whom ye know not;

10 And come and stand before me in this house, which is called by my name, and say, We are delivered to do all these abominations?

Jeremiah 26:7-9, 12-14

7 So the priests and the prophets and all the people heard Jeremiah speaking these words in the house of the Lord.

8 Now it came to pass, when Jeremiah had made an end of speaking all that the Lord had commanded *him* to speak unto all the people, that the priests and the prophets and all the people took him, saying, Thou shalt surely die.

9 Why hast thou prophesied in the name of the Lord, saying, This house shall be like Shiloh, and this city shall be desolate without an inhabitant? And all the people were gathered against Jeremiah in the house of the Lord.

Jeremiah 7:1-4, 8-10

1 The word that came to Jeremiah from the Lord: 2 "Stand in the gate of the Lord's house, and proclaim there this word, and say, Hear the word of the Lord, all you men of Judah who enter these gates to worship the Lord. 3 Thus says the Lord of hosts, the God of Israel, Amend your ways and your doings, and I will let you dwell in this place. 4 Do not trust in these deceptive words: 'This is the temple of the Lord, the temple of the Lord, the temple of the Lord.'"

....

8 "Behold, you trust in deceptive words to no avail. 9 Will you steal, murder, commit adultery, swear falsely, burn incense to Ba´al, and go after other gods that you have not known, 10 and then come and stand before me in this house, which is called by my name, and say, 'We are delivered!'—only to go on doing all these abominations?"

Jeremiah 26:7-9, 12-14

7 The priests and the prophets and all the people heard Jeremiah speaking these words in the house of the Lord. 8 And when Jeremiah had finished speaking all that the Lord had commanded him to speak to all the people, then the priests and all the people laid hold of him, saying, "You shall die! 9 Why have you prophesied in the name of the Lord, saying, 'This house shall be like Shiloh, and this city shall be desolate, without inhabitant'?" And all the people gathered about Jeremiah in the house of the Lord.

12 Then spake Jeremiah unto all the princes and to all the people, saying, The Lord sent me to prophesy against this city all the words that ye have heard.

13 Therefore now amend your ways and your doings, and obey the voice of the Lord your God; and the Lord will repent him of the evil that he hath pronounced against you.

14 As for me, behold, I *am* in your hand: do with me as seemeth good and meet unto you.

Key Verse: **Amend your ways and your doings, and obey the voice of the Lord your God. (Jeremiah 26:13)**

12 Then Jeremiah spoke to all the princes and all the people, saying, "The Lord sent me to prophesy against this house and this city all the words you have heard. 13 Now therefore amend your ways and your doings, and obey the voice of the Lord your God, and the Lord will repent of the evil which he has pronounced against you. 14 But as for me, behold, I am in your hands. Do with me as seems good and right to you."

Key Verse: **Amend your ways and your doings, and obey the voice of the Lord your God. (Jeremiah 26:13)**

The Scripture and the Main Question—William H. Willimon

Amend Your Ways and Your Doings

I will never forget the sermon or the setting. A young man from our church had gone off to seminary to study. He was home on his first Christmas vacation from seminary, and our pastor had asked him to preach. Naturally, all were looking forward to hearing him speak.

The choir had planned a special anthem for the day, something on a Christmas theme since this was the first Sunday after Christmas. The minister got up and introduced the young man, glowingly telling about his achievements in high school and his years spent growing up in our church, noting how proud we all were of what he had accomplished and how lucky the church was to have a fine young person like this entering the pastoral ministry.

Then, at last, the young man rose to speak. He thanked the congregation for instilling in him a love of the Scriptures, a loyalty to the church and its values, and a quest for the truth. He noted that this was the season of Christmas, the season when we welcome the advent of the Prince of Peace. This was all well and good. But then, when he began his sermon, the trouble also began.

He told us how, since going to seminary, he had the opportunity to think about many pressing issues of the day in the light of the Scriptures. He had come in contact with many dedicated Christian people. He had gone through a painful process of self-examination and soul searching.

He then told us that he had come to the conclusion that the then-current war in Vietnam was wrong and unchristian. He said that, while he was not telling us what to do, he had decided to use every means at his disposal to speak out against the war and witness to its injustice. I could feel the congregation begin to squirm. This was certainly more than we bargained for on a Christmas Sunday! We had come for a little peace and quite, not for confrontation by this brash young messenger who claimed to speak words from the Prince of Peace.

It was not a pleasant, easy Sunday to be sitting in church. It is never easy to be challenged, to have our cherished assumptions and values held up to the light of the Scriptures, to be forced to step back and examine ourselves and our beliefs.

"Hear the word of the LORD," cries Jeremiah one day in the temple gates, "Amend your ways and your doings, and I will let you dwell in this place" (7:2,3).

Deceptive Words

One of the troubling things about God's prophets, God's real prophets, is that they are forever reminding us that God does not always see things the way we do.

Sometimes our religion—our religious books, our leaders, our churches, our worship—is a clever contrivance to trap God, to tame the Almighty, to domesticate God and cut God down to our size. So there is always the tendency to assume that God looks like us, thinks like us, has our values, our prejudices. We become deceived into thinking that we control God, that we own God for ourselves.

Then along comes a prophet like Jeremiah who reminds us, much to our chagrin, that God is great.

He appears at the temple door and mocks the soothing, pious platitudes of the priests: "Do not trust in these deceptive words: 'This is the temple of the LORD, the temple of the LORD, the temple of the LORD'" (7:4).

Someone evidently has the notion that repeating all the right phrases, all the little slogans of religion, is all that God wants. Then such a person is free to leave the temple, having had a little dose of soothing religion, and be free to go "steal, murder, commit adultery, swear falsely, burn incense to Baal, and go after other gods" (7:9).

How might Jeremiah stand at the door of our church and mock us as we enter in our Sunday best? What might he say in the face of our hymns, sweet words, and soothing services?

Undoubtedly, we would want to go get another preacher, one who would be willing to tell us over and over again that God is here with us, our property, our best friend, our protector of the status quo.

Yet, in our heart of hearts, we know that the words of false prophets are deceptive, that God judges us, not simply for our behavior in church on Sunday, but also for the lives we lead when we leave the pleasant sanctuary. Therefore real prophets and real churches are those who call us to righteousness:

"For if you truly amend your ways and your doings, if you truly execute justice one with another, if you do not oppress the alien, the fatherless or the widow, or shed innocent blood in this place, . . . then I will let you dwell in this place" (7:5-7).

The Bite of Truth

Imagine yourself in church this Sunday with a guest preacher by the name of Jeremiah. What might be your response to his harsh words?

Let us not flatter ourselves. Our response would probably be much like the response of those who heard him so long ago:

"And when Jeremiah had finished speaking all that the LORD had commanded him to speak to all the people, then the priests and the prophets and all the people laid hold of him, saying, "You shall die!" (26:8).

The truth hurts. It is not pleasant to be told that our ways may not be God's ways, in spite of the comforting reassurances from our preachers that they are one.

Do we come to church on Sunday to seek God's way, or do we come to be reassured that we are doing the best we can and that God sees things exactly the way that we see things? Do we want truth or do we simply want reassurance? What is our response when our pastor tries to be faithful to the truth as she or he hears it and takes an unpopular position in a sermon?

So here we are in church, having come here on this pleasant Sunday in June for a little religion, a little reassurance. But unfortunately for us, the guest Bible teacher is a young man by the name of Jeremiah. He opens the Scriptures, begins to speak to us, begins to point to the connections between our lives and the word of God . . . and then the trouble starts.

Helping Adults Become Involved—Herbert H. Lambert

Preparing to Teach

It may seem strange to us that the people whom Jeremiah condemned were very religious. They often had God's name on their lips and frequently gathered in the temple. Why, then, did the prophet condemn them? Their daily lives did not conform to the faith they professed in worship. They claimed God's power to protect them, but they did not obey God's law or help God's other children.

The lesson today will lead us to examine our Christian commitment. We attend church, but do we know what the church demands of us? We claim to be followers of Christ, but do we walk in his pathways? Is our Christianity a sham, a hollow pretense, like the piety of those whom Jeremiah condemned?

Here is a way to outline this lesson:

    I. Jeremiah's indictment of the people
        A. Misguided trust
        B. Sin against people
        C. Sin against God
    II. Prophecy of destruction
        A. Jerusalem like Shiloh
        B. Possibility of repentance
    III. Response to Jeremiah's sermon
        A. Anger and condemnation
        B. Jeremiah's defense
        C. Second thoughts about killing Jeremiah
    IV. A look at our own religion
        A. Why are we religious?
        B. Is our faith a sham?

In preparation for this session, read the background scriptures and commentaries on them. *The Interpreter's Bible*, volume 5, pages 867-73, 1005-9, and *The Interpreter's Concise Commentary*, volume 4, pages 146-48, 178-80 will be helpful.

Introducing the Main Question

I was working on a sermon in my study, while outside in the hall two painters were working. I gathered from their conversation that they were Roman Catholic and that the daughter of one was about to marry a Protestant.

"My wife is very upset," the painter said, "but I told her not to worry about it. The way I look at it, what has religion got to do with love?"

I stopped typing and started a new sheet. I had my sermon title: "What Has Religion Got to Do with Love?" Can't a person be religious without loving people? Can't we serve God without doing anything except attending our church and paying our pledge? Why should religion interfere with our personal lives, our business deals, our political views?

I understood what the painter outside my door was saying, and I partly agreed with him. But I rejected the idea that religion could be neatly separated from everything else we do. So did Jeremiah!

Developing the Lesson

I. Jeremiah's indictment of the people

A. Misguided trust

In his famous temple sermon, Jeremiah did not accuse the people of lacking religion. He condemned them for trusting in God without showing any real interest in keeping God's laws. They had grown accustomed to worshiping in the Jerusalem temple. It gave them a good feeling, an assurance that in spite of world turmoil they would be all right. This was partly because Judah had been invaded by the Assyrians a hundred years earlier, and the temple had not fallen. The people had come to believe that God would protect the temple and its worshipers, no matter what they did or failed to do. Jeremiah emphatically denied that this was so.

B. Sin against people

The people of Judah had turned the holy temple into a hideout for a gang of outlaws! They lied, stole, committed adultery, burned incense to false gods, then ran into the temple and gasped, "We are saved! We escaped again!" (see 7:8-10). Jeremiah warned that God would not allow the temple to be desecrated in this way. Those who seek refuge in God's temple must live by God's laws when they are outside God's temple. Otherwise, neither God nor the temple will protect them.

C. Sin against God

Apparently the people worshiped Baal as well as Yahweh, the Lord God. They worshiped, not because they were grateful for God's help and desirous of God's guidance, but as a kind of insurance against the evils they feared. Such a relationship to God is wrong because it is an attempt to use God for our own purposes.

II. Prophecy of destruction

A. Jerusalem like Shiloh

Just as the early sanctuary at Shiloh had fallen to the Philistines, Jerusalem would fall to the Babylonians unless the worshipers changed their ways. What had happened before could happen again!

B. Possibility of repentance

Both versions of Jeremiah's sermon indicate that he held out the possibility of averting destruction if the people of Jerusalem heeded his warning and changed their ways.

III. Response to Jeremiah's sermon

A. Anger and condemnation

Ask class members to imagine some of the feelings they might have had if they had been present when Jeremiah spoke. List these reactions on the chalkboard. The text indicates that the people and leaders were angry with Jeremiah. This was partly because they believed that Jeremiah's harsh words would help to bring about the terrible events he predicted. They could not ignore him as we sometimes ignore persons today whom we regard as mistaken or deluded.

B. *Jeremiah's defense*

Like Amos, Jeremiah said he was only speaking what God had commanded him to say. He offered to surrender to the people and to let them kill him if they chose. He was not defending himself or promoting himself but only speaking God's truth.

C. *Second thoughts about killing Jeremiah*

We read an account of an interesting discussion about what to do with Jeremiah. The leaders remembered Micah, another prophet who had said Jerusalem would fall. The king in Micah's time had not killed him but had listened to his warning. Another prophet of doom, Uriah, had been put to death. While they deliberated about what to do with Jeremiah, one of his few friends saw that he was protected from harm.

Helping Class Members Act

IV. *A look at our own religion*

A. *Why are we religious?*

Write this question on the chalkboard. With the help of class members list some reasons why we go to church: to meet friends, to set an example, to find inner peace, etc. After you have listed about ten reasons, go back and decide on two or three that you think are the best ones. Decide which are not good reasons for going to church. Why did the people of Jerusalem go to the temple? In what ways are we like them?

B. *Is our faith a sham?*

List the following on the chalkboard and ask each person to decide privately whether or not his or her religion plays a part in these matters: choice of friends, the way we vote, relations with fellow employees, our intimate family encounters, concern about suffering persons in our neighborhood, concern about world hunger and oppression. If religion plays no part in some areas of our lives, could it mean that we have a false and ineffective faith like the people of Judah?

Planning for Next Sunday

Can we imagine a time when we as Christians might feel compelled to oppose our government? That is one question posed by the next lesson. Write it on the chalkboard and have class members think about it during the coming week.

Overcoming Obstacles to Witness

Background Scripture: Jeremiah 36

The Main Question—William H. Willimon

"Mankind cannot stand too much reality," wrote the poet T. S. Eliot. In Eliot's day, our day, or Jeremiah's day reality is in short supply because it's something that few of us go looking for. Sometimes, in spite of our attempts to evade it, reality comes looking for us. So it was for Jehoiakim, king of Judah, when reality came looking for him in the form of this young prophet named Jeremiah.

Like Jehoiakim, we don't mind a little preaching—as long as it doesn't really hit home, as long as it doesn't really tell it like it is. But when the preacher starts to meddle in political or economic or military affairs, then we get angry.

Name one popular, successful television preacher today who has made a national reputation on his or her ability to speak about us or our world as we really are. Most popular preachers are popular because they do not rock the boat. They are filled with soothing words and assuring platitudes. No Jeremiahs on television on Sunday morning!

Some time ago, I wrote a book which was critical of some aspects of our denominational life and raised some hard questions about the way business was being done in our church. Among the letters I received in response to the book was a long one from a national church administrator. After chiding me for "meddling" in other people's affairs, he wrote, "I disagree with what you said and do not think that you are right. Even if you were right, I don't think you should have said it."

His words stuck in my mind. Even if something is the truth, if it hurts or challenges our way of doing things, then we don't want to hear it and despise anyone for daring to say it. Even if Jesus was right in declaring that "the truth shall make you free," we also know that the truth has a way of making us very uncomfortable.

How dare some meddling Jeremiah disturb our comfortable arrangements with reality?

As You Read the Scripture—Howard P. Colson

Jeremiah 36 is unique in being the only detailed account we have of the production of a prophetical book. The situation was critical. The Babylonian army under Nebuchadnezzar had just defeated the Egyptians at Carchemish and was moving southward in Palestine. This was in December, 604 B.C. For twenty-three years Jeremiah had warned that God's judgment would come upon the people if they did not repent.

Jeremiah 36:1-5. It was time for Jeremiah to plead again. However, he was "debarred" from going to the temple. So he called his secretary and friend Baruch to act for him. He dictated to Baruch "all the words of the LORD which he had spoken to him." Then Baruch read those words to the assembled crowd. The reason Jeremiah was kept from the temple area

358

was probably because of the reaction of the temple leaders to his temple sermon.

Verse 6. It seems that fasts could be called whenever there was a crisis. The event occurred long before the development of the codex (similar to books as we know them). To make a scroll, many sheets of papyrus were pasted together to form a long strip. This was then attached to a roller of wood. In fact, there could be a roller at each end of the long strip. The writing was done in columns parallel to the rollers so that as the scroll was gradually unrolled the successive columns could be read.

Verse 8. There were three readings of Jeremiah's scroll. The one recorded in this verse was to the people. The second was to the princes (verses 14-15). The third was to King Jehoiakim (verses 21-23).

The princes were not members of the king's family but were administrative officers. When they had heard the reading of the scroll, they decided that it ought to be read to the king as well, and they made arrangements for this to be done. It is noteworthy that these men had respect for Baruch and took careful thought for him and Jeremiah when they realized the danger they were in (verse 19).

Verses 20-26. Wicked King Jehoiakim was so incensed by Jeremiah's message that as the reading proceeded he cut the scroll to pieces and burned it. He and his ministers were so calloused that they showed no sign of sorrow or fear while the dreadful message of God's word was being read (verse 24). The princes urged him not to burn the scroll, but to no avail (verse 25). Jehoiakim had contempt for the words read. Someone has said that he "rent the roll his father [Josiah] would have reverenced."

Verse 27. If Jehoiakim thought that his burning of the scroll was the end of the matter, he was badly mistaken.

Verse 28. The words inscribed on the second scroll were all the words that were on the first scroll, and more (see verse 32).

Verse 29. Jehoiakim refused to believe that the king of Babylon would destroy Judah. How pitifully mistaken he was!

Verses 30-31. God predicted disaster for Jehoiakim. He would be severely punished for his malicious action.

Verse 32. The purpose of the second scroll was not to call the people to repent but to preserve the revelation for future readings.

A mighty lesson from Jeremiah 36 is that though it is possible to destroy the words of Scripture, it is not possible to destroy God's word. See Isaiah 40:8.

Selected Scripture

King James Version

Jeremiah 36:4-8, 27-31

4 Then Jeremiah called Bâr'-ŭch the son of Nē-rī'-ăh: and Baruch wrote from the mouth of Jeremiah all the words of the Lord, which he had spoken unto him upon a roll of a book.

5 And Jeremiah commanded Bâr'-ŭch, saying, I *am* shut up; I

Revised Standard Version

Jeremiah 36:4-8, 27-31

4 Then Jeremiah called Baruch the son of Neri'ah, and Baruch wrote upon a scroll at the dictation of Jeremiah all the words of the Lord which he had spoken to him. 5 And Jeremiah ordered Baruch, saying, "I am debarred from going to the house of the Lord; 6 so you are to go,

cannot go into the house of the Lord:

6 Therefore go thou, and read in the roll, which thou hast written from my mouth, the words of the Lord in the ears of the people in the Lord's house upon the fasting day: and also thou shalt read them in the ears of all Judah that come out of their cities.

7 It may be they will present their supplication before the Lord, and will return every one from his evil way: for great is the anger and the fury that the Lord hath pronounced against this people.

8 And Bâr´-ŭ<u>ch</u> the son of Nē-rī´-ăh did according to all that Jeremiah the prophet commanded him, reading in the book the words of the Lord in the Lord's house.

....

27 Then the word of the Lord came to Jeremiah, after that the king had burned the roll, and the words which Bâr´-ŭ<u>ch</u> wrote at the mouth of Jeremiah, saying.

28 Take thee again another roll, and write in it all the former words that were in the first roll, which Jĕ-hoî´-ă-kĭm the king of Judah hath burned.

29 And thou shalt say to Jĕ-hoî´-ă-kĭm king of Judah, Thus saith the Lord; Thou hast burned this roll, saying, Why hast thou written therein, saying, The king of Babylon shall certainly come and destroy this land, and shall cause to cease from thence man and beast?

30 Therefore thus saith the Lord of Jĕ-hoî´-ă-kĭm king of Judah; He shall have none to sit upon the throne of David: and his dead body shall be cast out in the day to the heat, and in the night to the frost.

31 And I will punish him and his seed and his servants for their iniquity; and I will bring upon them, and upon the inhabitants of Jerusalem, and upon the men of Judah, all

and on a fast day in the hearing of all the people in the Lord's house you shall read the words of the Lord from the scroll which you have written at my dictation. You shall read them also in the hearing of all the men of Judah who come out of their cities. 7 It may be that their supplication will come before the Lord, and that every one will turn from his evil way, for great is the anger and wrath that the Lord has pronounced against this people."

8 And Baruch the son of Neri´ah did all that Jeremiah the prophet ordered him about reading from the scroll the words of the Lord in the Lord's house.

....

27 Now, after the king had burned the scroll with the words which Baruch wrote at Jeremiah's dictation, the word of the Lord came to Jeremiah: 28 "Take another scroll and write on it all the former words that were in the first scroll, which Jehoi´akim the king of Judah has burned. 29 And concerning Jehoi´akim king of Judah you shall say, 'Thus says the Lord, You have burned this scroll, saying, "Why have you written in it that the king of Babylon will certainly come and destroy this land, and will cut off from it man and beast?" 30 Therefore thus says the Lord concerning Jehoi´-akim king of Judah, He shall have none to sit upon the throne of David, and his dead body shall be cast out to the heat by day and the frost by night. 31 And I will punish him and his offspring and his servants for their iniquity; I will bring upon them, and upon the inhabitants of Jerusalem, and upon the men of Judah, all the evil that I have pronounced against them, but they would not hear."

the evil that I have pronounced against them; but they hearkened not.

Key Verse: **They shall fight against thee; but they shall not prevail against thee; for I *am* with thee, saith the Lord, to deliver thee. (Jeremiah 1:19)**

Key Verse: **They will fight against you; but they shall not prevail against you, for I am with you, says the Lord, to deliver you. (Jeremiah 1:19)**

The Scripture and the Main Question—William H. Willimon

So That They May Turn from Evil

It was the reign of Jehoiakim the son of Josiah. Jeremiah, the meddlesome prophet of doom, was barred from speaking in the temple, from even appearing in the temple. With Jeremiah's preaching, and with his tendency to speak the truth no matter whom it offends, we are not surprised to learn that the temple is declared off limits for him.

But Jeremiah is not silenced. He is not put off by Jehoiakim's ban against him. He sends Baruch to read his scroll in his stead. How difficult it is to silence the true prophet of God!

A couple of things strike us when we read Jeremiah 36:1-8. First, while the judgment against Judah is severe, the Lord has not yet given up on the people. Jeremiah is sent to warn them one more time in the hope that "it may be that the house of Judah will hear all the evil which I intend to do to them, so that every one may turn from his evil way, and that I may forgive their iniquity and their sin" (36:3).

Here is a God who is persistent, who does not simply leave the beloved Chosen People in silence but continually sends the prophets to speak to them, even when they stubbornly refuse to listen. Every means is tried to get them to listen.

It reminds one of some of the parables Jesus told—about the shepherd who searches for the lost sheep in the wilderness, about the woman who turns her house upside down to find the one lost coin. Here is divine persistence, a love which does not let us go in our iniquity.

Jeremiah couldn't get to the pillars of the temple, but he could send his words through Baruch so that "the words of the Lord in the Lord's house" could be spoken (36:8).

So often we think of the prophets as people who pronounced God's wrath and judgment. Of course, Jeremiah does preach wrath and judgment upon an unfaithful nation and an arrogant king.

But it is unfair to separate God's judgment from God's love and grace. Without the prophetic judgment, the country is headed toward disaster. Thus, the prophetic judgment is an aspect of divine love and grace. The alternative would be for God to wash his hands of the whole matter, walk off, and leave Judah to its own devices. But persistent, patient divine love keeps reaching out to a wayward people through courageous, determined prophets like Jeremiah.

Jeremiah sends Baruch because, "It may be that the house of Judah will hear all the evil which I intend to do to them, so that every one may turn from his evil way, and that I may forgive their iniquity and their sin" (36:3).

361

FOURTH QUARTER

I Will Punish Him and His Offspring

We live in a permissive age. Punishment is not a popular concept in our day. Parents are urged to be patient with children, to lovingly correct them, not to punish them. We think of our penal justice system as the department of corrections, not as a system of punishment.

Of course, this is all as it should be, for punishment is usually a poor teacher. But today's text from Jeremiah does raise the issue of divine punishment. Jeremiah is sent to tell Jehoiakim that either things shall be set right by the wicked king, or there shall be divine retribution.

Upon hearing this, perhaps we wonder how this view of God as a divine executioner squares with Jesus' emphasis upon the love and forbearance of God.

There are a couple of ways to look at this, ways you may wish to discuss in your adult class today.

We must note that our ideas about God change. God may not change, but our perceptions of God do. When the armies of Babylon knock at the gates of Judah and the king of that hostile country "will certainly come and destroy this land, and will cut off from it man and beast" (36:29), is this the result of God's anger or of human sin and injustice?

A person spends twenty years smoking tobacco. Then he is diagnosed as having lung cancer. "Why is God punishing me like this?" he may ask. But where is the source of this evil—God or our own folly? We are putting the blame upon God that should rightly fall upon us.

When a nation like Judah forgets its past, forsakes its unique vocation and identity, behaves in an immoral and godless manner, then collapses (as Judah would) from internal decay, is this the punishment of God or the result of human sin (or, perhaps, both)?

When Jeremiah speaks of the wrath of God upon Judah, is he simply noting the expected result of Judah's behavior? God's anger in this matter is related to God's great love for this Chosen People. God is angry that they have finally brought their doom upon themselves.

G. K. Chesterton once noted that if a person comes to the edge of a cliff and keeps on walking, that person will not break the law of gravity, he will prove it! Jehoiakim perhaps thought that he could break the laws of God, but eventually, the truth broke him. It all caught up with him in the person of the invading king of Babylon.

But They Would Not Hear

When the prophet announces this truth, it is a hard truth for Jehoiakim and the people of Judah to hear. Thus, the king and the people do everything possible to try to avoid the truth. Yet whether they hear or refuse to hear, as Jeremiah was told at the beginning of his ministry, the truth of the matter still stands.

So, whether we like judgment or not, whether we believe it or not, judgment is still a part of life. We look in the mirror at ourselves, we look into the face of our children, we slump forward in the easy chair one night, the bleeper on the heart scanner falls silent and it is judgment day for us, a day of accounting and reckoning, even as it was for Jehoiakim.

We can silence and ignore our prophets, but we can't stop the judgment.

Who are the prophets of our day who stand against us and our leaders and pronouce judgment against us and our ways? Do we hear and heed them, or do we respond as Jehoiakim and Judah responded? Do we hear or refuse to hear?

Alas, our leaders are often an extension of ourselves and our own avoidance of reality. We elect people to office who too often resemble Jehoiakim in their arrogance and in their refusal to hear and to face facts, leaders who will lead us only where we want to go, who lead by the latest public opinion poll, who look upon God's prophets much as Jehoiakim looked upon Jeremiah. What shall be the future for us if we do not hear?

Helping Adults Become Involved—Herbert H. Lambert

Preparing to Teach

Today's lesson is interesting for several reasons. It shows a courageous prophet warning his nation and even daring to oppose the king. It shows how some prophetic sermons, originally oral, came to be written and preserved, eventually to become part of our Bible. It raises the question whether we as Christians ought to oppose our government under some circumstances and asks how that opposition may be expressed.

Here is a way to outline this lesson:

     I. The prophet and the word
       A. Compelled to speak
       B. Reasons for writing
       C. Seriousness of the word
    II. Reaction to Jeremiah's message
       A. The princes were concerned.
       B. The king rejected the message.
   III. The result of disobedience
       A. For King Jehoiakim
       B. For the nation of Judah
       C. For our own nation
   IV. Our need to speak and to hear God's word today
       A. What is God's word for our day?
       B. How shall we make it known?
       C. What will be the result?

In preparation for the session, read Jeremiah 36 and helpful aids such as *The Interpreter's Concise Commentary*, volume 4, pages 191-93, or *The Interpreter's Bible*, volume 5, pages 1063-69.

Introducing the Main Question

Retell the incident described by Dr. Willimon under "The Main Question" in which a national church executive wrote him, "Even if you were right, I do not think you should have said it."

What would cause a church leader to write such a letter? Are these times when the truth is too painful to deal with honestly and openly? Are we ever justified in suppressing the truth about church affairs? about wrongdoing of national leaders? about individual sins and failures? There are times when it is inappropriate to condemn persons and institutions—when there is insufficient evidence, for example. On the other hand, to avoid all suggestion of error is to invite greater evil.

FOURTH QUARTER

Developing the Lesson

I. The prophet and the word

A. Compelled to speak

Jeremiah 36 deals with an event in 605 B.C., more than twenty years after Jeremiah began to speak. Jeremiah had long condemned the nation and was forbidden to come to the temple. He had apparently not committed his sermons to scrolls. They had been directed to a particular people at special times. The idea that later generations might want to read them and would regard them as holy scripture had not occurred to the prophet. All of the early prophets were basically speakers, not writers.

B. Reasons for writing

Because he was forbidden to come to the temple and address the leaders there, Jeremiah dictated his sermons to Baruch, who copied them on a scroll and read them from the pillars of the temple. This shows one of the reasons the books of the prophets came to be written. Why were the letters of Paul written? Why were the Gospels recorded? In each case it was because oral communication was not possible, and writing was at first a substitute for speaking.

C. Seriousness of the word

When the princes heard the words of Baruch, they were afraid (36:16). They understood this as a momentous event, not to be taken lightly. The spoken and written word were regarded with much more seriousness in Bible times than today. People believed that predictions had a way of bringing about what was predicted. That is why Jeremiah was banned and then arrested for speaking words of warning about Judah.

Even in democratic countries it is difficult to raise objections during wartime because such objections may weaken the resolve of those who are fighting and their supporters at home. But what if the war policy is wrong and needs to be reexamined? There are serious consequences of speaking out and also of keeping silent—both for the speaker and for those who hear. Jeremiah carefully weighed these consequences before he spoke about the wrongs of his nation.

II. Reaction to Jeremiah's word

A. The princes were concerned.

The relatives of the king had positions of leadership. They were alarmed by the words of Jeremiah which Baruch read. They sent the scroll to the king, thinking he needed to do something to avert the terrible evil Jeremiah predicted.

B. The king rejected the message.

In a dramatic gesture, the king cut pieces of the scroll as they were read and burned them in an open fire. It was his way of showing contempt for what Jeremiah had written. He ordered the arrest of Jeremiah and Baruch. Some political leaders do not like advice, even when it is good advice. List some examples of such leaders in recent times.

III. The result of disobedience

A. For King Jehoiakim

Jeremiah predicted that the king would die a shameful death and leave no descendants. His son ruled only three months before being taken to Babylon in chains (II Kings 24:6-15). King Jehoiakim was remembered as one who failed in a time of crisis.

B. For the nation

Both the king and the nation were corrupt, unresponsive, and blameworthy. The nation suffered terrible losses because of what was done during Jehoiakim's reign. The prophets warned not only individuals but the whole people about the terrible results of their bad actions and neglect of duty.

C. *For our own nation*

Several critical decisions are before our nation today. How shall we care for the poor? How can medical care be made affordable? How shall we deal with factions in other nations which are struggling to be free of the dictatorial governments we support? How shall we protect our national interests without stifling small nations and their citizens? How shall we get along with the Russians in a world threatened by our continuing quarrels? What we decide and do about these will have consequences for our nation and for the world.

Helping Class Members Act

IV. *Our need to speak and to hear God's word today*

A. *What is God's word for our day?*

What is God saying to us about the issues raised in the previous section and about other such issues? Does God want us to destroy our nuclear weapons? Does God want us to seek peace in other ways? Does God want us to help persons in need? How? What is God telling us about the way we are using the created world? Is it possible to have two or more opinions about what God is saying to us? If so, should we keep silent?

B. *How shall we make it known?*

Have the group members think of some appropriate ways to make God's word known today. Jeremiah used oral speech and a written scroll. What ways of communicating are open to us today? What are some nonverbal ways of witnessing for God?

C. *What will be the result?*

Some persons listened to Jeremiah, and some refused to listen. His life and freedom were jeopardized, but he was protected by a few friends. What is likely to happen to us if we fearlessly say what God speaks to us? How will we be treated by our families? By fellow church members? By the community at large? Will this keep us from speaking?

Planning for Next Sunday

Next Sunday we will learn about an encounter between Jeremiah and a "false prophet." In Bible times, there were many more false prophets than true ones. How can we tell a false prophet from a true one? Assign Jeremiah 23:9-40; 27-28 for the next session, and have the class members ponder this question during the coming week.

God's Tests of a True Prophet

Background Scripture: Jeremiah 23:9-40; 27–28

The Main Question—William H. Willimon

One of the frustrating things about being a minister is that it is hard to know how well you are doing your job. The ordained ministry is one of those jobs where it is very difficult to get good evaluation. It is hard to know, at the end of the day, if you have really done much for the advancement of the kingdom of God. Certainly, I often feel a great sense of accomplishment and satisfaction, but how can I be sure that the accomplishments in which I am taking so much satisfaction are those which God wants?

I come home exhausted from a daily round of pastoral activities, but were they really important activities? "Well, you never really know how much good you're doing," some may say. But you never really know how much harm you are doing either!

Even if many people hold diverse views about what a "good" pastor looks like, how can they be sure that their views are really what God wants the clergy to be and to do?

Does being a man or woman of God simply mean that one is likeable, popular, kind, or some other human attribute? Or are there higher, more significant, more biblical tests for the person who serves God and God's people?

If you were making an evaluation form for a prophet, what attributes would you include for people to rate on a scale from one to five?

Today's lesson from the book of Jeremiah raises some of these questions and then offers some guidelines for judgment of God's prophets.

As You Read the Scripture—Howard P. Colson

The subject of Jeremiah 23:9-40 is the false prophets who were condemned. Chapters 27 and 28 record some of Jeremiah's activities during the early years of the reign of Zedekiah, the final king of Judah. A false prophet named Hananiah figures prominently in chapter 28.

Jeremiah 23:16. Jeremiah advised the people not to listen to the false prophets who were filling them with vain hopes. The messages of such prophets came not from the Lord but from their own imaginings.

Verse 17. Those prophets were saying to the people, "It shall be well with you" and "No evil shall come upon you." In other words, they were actually optimistic at a time when certain disaster was on its way.

Verse 18. Why were those prophets preaching falsehood? They had not "stood in the council of the Lord." God is here portrayed as a great king, surrounded by his court. The members of his court are his servants, who are in communion with him. In some remarkable way a true prophet is privileged to be included in such a council, and there he receives the word of the Lord. Jeremiah said that if the prophets he was condemning had stood in the Lord's council, they would have spoken the Lord's word.

Verses 21-22. God is the speaker. He wants the people to realize that

366

those prophets were not his representatives. If they had stood in his council, they would have proclaimed his words to the people. Then the people would have been warned and would have turned "from the evil of their doings."

Chapter 28:1-4. Hananiah, one of the false (though doubtless sincere) prophets, spoke to Jeremiah in the temple, disagreeing with the idea that Judah should be subject to Babylonia. Hananiah had predicted that within two years the temple vessels which Nebuchadnezzar had taken to Babylon would be returned. He predicted also that the deposed young king Jehoiachin (Jeconiah), who had been taken to Babylon as an exile, would be brought back to Jerusalem along with all the other exiles from Judah who had been carried to Babylon first in 597 B.C.

Verse 6. Jeremiah would have liked to agree with Hananiah's optimistic prophecy, but he knew there was something more to be considered.

Verse 8. Jeremiah warned that true prophets usually brought messages of judgment.

Verse 9. Any prediction of peace, before it was judged to be true, should wait for its fulfillment. (Compare Deuteronomy 18:20-22.)

Verses 8 and 9 should not be interpreted to mean that previous prophecy had been entirely a message of judgment. There were indeed hopeful passages in early prophets, but the usual message included threats of doom. Jeremiah's message was more in line with earlier prophecy than Hananiah's was.

Verse 12. Jeremiah did not immediately contradict Hananiah's prophecy. He waited before responding.

Verses 13-17. God's plan was that Judah and the surrounding nations should be subject to Babylon. On the basis of that divine plan, Jeremiah made his reply to Hananiah. He plainly told Hananiah that the Lord had not sent him and that he had made the people trust in a lie. Then he predicted Hananiah's death would occur that same year. His prediction came true.

In 587 B.C., Jerusalem was captured and the temple burned by the Babylonians. Zedekiah and most of the people remaining in Judah were carried captive to Babylon. Jeremiah's prediction came true.

Selected Scripture

King James Version

Revised Standard Version

Jeremiah 23:16-18, 21-22

16 Thus saith the Lord of hosts, Hearken not unto the words of the prophets that prophesy unto you: they make you vain: they speak a vision of their own heart, *and* not out of the mouth of the Lord.

17 They say still unto them that despise me, The Lord hath said, Ye shall have peace; and they say unto every one that walketh after the imagination of his own heart, No evil shall come upon you.

Jeremiah 23:16-18, 21-22

16 Thus says the Lord of hosts: "Do not listen to the words of the prophets who prophesy to you, filling you with vain hopes; they speak visions of their own minds, not from the mouth of the Lord. 17 They say continually to those who despise the word of the Lord, 'It shall be well with you'; and to every one who stubbornly follows his own heart, they say, "No evil shall come upon you."'

18 For who hath stood in he counsel of the Lord, and hath perceived and heard his word? who hath marked his word, and heard *it?*

....

21 I have not sent these prophets, yet they ran: I have not spoken to them, yet they prophesied.

22 But if they had stood in my counsel, and had caused my people to hear my words, then they should have turned them from their evil way, and from the evil of their doings.

Jeremiah 28:5-9, 15-16b
5 Then the prophet Jeremiah said unto the prophet Hananiah in the presence of the priests, and in the presence of all the people that stood in the house of the Lord,
6 Even the prophet Jeremiah said, Amen: the Lord do so: the Lord perform thy words which thou hast prophesied, to bring again the vessels of the Lord's house, and all that is carried away captive, from Babylon into this place.
7 Nevertheless hear thou now this word that I speak in thine ears, and in the ears of all the people;
8 The prophets that have been before me and before thee of old prophesied both against many countries, and against great kingdoms, of war, and of evil, and of pestilence.
9 The prophet which prophesieth of peace, when the word of the prophet shall come to pass, *then* shall the prophet be known, that the Lord hath truly sent him.

....

15 Then said the prophet Jeremiah unto Hananiah the prophet,

18 For who among them has stood
    in the council of the Lord
  to perceive and to hear his
    word,
  or who has given heed to his
    word, and listened?

....

21 "I did not send the prophets,
    yet they ran;
  I did not speak to them,
    yet they prophesied.
22 But if they had stood in my
    council,
    then they would have pro-
      claimed my words to my
      people,
  and they would have turned them
    from their evil way,
    and from the evil of their
      doings."

Jeremiah 28:5-9, 15-16b
5 Then the prophet Jeremiah spoke to Hanani´ah the prophet in the presence of the priests and all the people who were standing in the house of the Lord; 6 and the prophet Jeremiah said, "Amen! May the Lord do so; may the Lord make the words which you have prophesied come true, and bring back to this place from Babylon the vessels of the house of the Lord, and all the exiles. 7 Yet hear now this word which I speak in your hearing and in the hearing of all the people. 8 the prophets who preceded you and me from ancient times prophesied war, famine, and pestilence against many countries and great kingdoms. 9 As for the prophet who prophesies peace, when the word of that prophet comes to pass, then it will be known that the Lord has truly sent the prophet."

....

15 And Jeremiah the prophet asid to the prophet Hanani´ah, "Listen,

Hear now, Hananiah; The LORD hath not sent thee; but thou makest this people to trust in a lie.

16 Therefore thus saith the LORD; Behold, I will cast thee from off the face of the earth: this year thou shalt die.

Key Verse: **Thus saith the LORD of hosts, Hearken not unto the words of the prophets that prophesy unto you: they make you vain: they speak a vision of their own heart,** *and* **not out of the mouth of the LORD. (Jeremiah 23:16)**

Hanani´ah, the LORD has not sent you, and you have made this people trust in a lie. 16 Therefore thus says the LORD: 'Behold, I will remove you from the face of the earth. This very year you shall die.'"

Key Verse: **Thus says the LORD of hosts: "Do not listen to the words of the prophets who prophesy to you, filling you with vain hopes; they speak visions of their own minds, not from the mouth of the LORD." (Jeremiah 23:16)**

The Scripture and the Main Question—William H. Willimon

Prophets of Vain Hopes

Again and again the prophets seem to be reminding us of a truth we so easily forget: God looks at things differently from the way we look at things.

Certainly this is a continuous thread running throughout Jeremiah's message. Today we consider the differences in the ways we often evaluate religious leaders and the ways that God may evaluate them. "Thus says the LORD of hosts: 'Do not listen to the words of the prophets who prophesy to you, filling you with vain hopes; they speak visions of their own minds, not from the mouth of the LORD'" (Jeremiah 23:16).

Sometimes when someone purports to speak for God, we may suspect that he or she is only speaking the thoughts of his or her own mind. But how do we know?

One test, according to today's scripture, seems to be whether or not the prophet is willing to speak the truth, come what may.

A true prophet, as the old saying goes, "comforts the afflicted and afflicts the comfortable." Our image of the Old Testament prophet is usually that of an abrasive, confrontative, controversial figure who is forever in hot water because of something he said to the king or to the religious leaders. Certainly Jeremiah fits that image. Last Sunday's lesson dealt with Jeremiah's harsh words to the king. Today's lesson concerns itself with Jeremiah's tough thoughts about the religious leaders of his day.

Jeremiah says that the false prophets don't speak the truth. Judah is in a desperate situation. Only the most extreme and radical measures can save her from total destruction at the hands of the invading Babylonians.

But what do the false prophets say? "It shall be well with you," they reassure the wrongdoers. "No evil shall come upon you" (23:17).

Think positively, relax, be comforted, don't worry, you're doing the best that you can. It isn't so much what you do or don't do as long as you are sincere. These are the cheap comforts and reassuring platitudes of false prophets who tell us what we want to hear rather than what God speaks to us.

So I am watching my local Christian television talk show where a smiling host is interviewing some famous guest. "Fred," he says, "tell us what happened when God came into your life."

Fred tells of how his family is happy, his business is more lucrative and profitable than ever, and he is always smiling and happy. All these positive aspects are a result of God's coming into Fred's life. God has made Fred healthy, wealthy, and happy, or so we are told.

No doubt, God does good things for us. But is this always the case? Imagine that same host with Jeremiah for a Christian talk-show visitor one day. "Jeremiah, tell us what happened when God came into your life."

I was ostracized from my own people, barred from attending the temple, threatened by the king with capital punishment. All this happened to me when God came into my life and I tried to bring God into the life of Judah.

Wouldn't Jeremiah's response make an interesting testimony!

Who Has Given Heed and Listened?

Concerning the false prophets, Jeremiah asks, "Who among them has stood in the council of the Lord to perceive and to hear his word, or who has given heed to his word and listened?" (23:18).

The implication is that they have done more talking than listening. They have spoken what *they* think, what *they* believe the people want to hear, rather than listening and worrying about what God wants to say.

This arrogance on the part of the false prophets, this lack of humility before the word of the Lord, has angered God (23:19-20).

Of course, it isn't easy to listen—really listen—for the word of God, particularly when that word cuts through our cherished assumptions and preconceived notions of what God ought to be saying.

One of the reasons why a preacher must spend many hours in Bible study is that she or he is attempting to listen to the text, to cut through preconceptions and prior assumptions about what the Bible is supposed to be saying, and to listen to what it is actually saying.

Have you ever come to this class or prepared to teach this class, having read some familiar passage or biblical story and said to yourself, "Yes, I already know what this says, what this means"? Then, after you study, were you surprised that a commentator heard something quite different from what you heard? Therefore, it is always important to stand in the council of the Lord and listen (23:18).

We can sympathize with the divine wrath which is kindled against Judah. Even now, Jeremiah speaks of "the storm of the Lord" (23:19), which is poised to break over Judah. One of the most frustrating things in life is to be speaking to someone who seems to be listening, but doesn't really hear us. When has this last happened to you? You try to make a point; the other person appears to be paying attention, but for some reason doesn't get your point.

When I preach, this happens to me all the time! I never cease to be amazed how people will listen to a sermon of mine, but when I ask them what they heard, will relate something totally different from what I had intended to say.

Some of this has to do with my inadequacy as a speaker. But it also has to do with the way we don't listen to people. We listen with all sorts of preconceptions, filters, and blocks to real communication.

Undoubtedly, God has the same problem with us in his attempts to communicate with us. God sends the prophets, but we ignore their challenging words because we can't stand the truth. We find false prophets of our own speak a more soothing message. God's frustration rises; God's anger is kindled because we are not hearing.

Visions of Their Own Minds

Unfortunately for the truth, we usually judge a religious speaker by certain criteria: Do I agree with this person? Is this what I have always thought about this subject? How does this square with what I have always believed? Does this anger or upset me?

I suppose that Judah was unprepared for the words of Jeremiah because Judah assumed that her being a part of the Chosen People meant that nothing the nation could do would be able to anger God or provoke divine wrath.

If we are the chosen ones, then our God is our property. Our God affirms us, blesses us, and confirms us in all that we do. Our God is the God who pats us on the head and says, "There, there now, everything will work out all right," like an indulgent parent to a spoiled child.

Who shall be asked to address the mayor's prayer breakfast, to have the devotional at the political banquet, to say a prayer before the local football game, a Jeremiah? No. More than likely it will be some popular speaker, someone who is able to speak what we like to hear.

Next week is July 4, the day when we celebrate our national independence. Does our independence now mean that we have declared our independence from the word and will of God?

Are there still true prophets like Jeremiah among us? And when they speak words of truth against us as a people, can we hear?

Helping Adults Become Involved—Herbert H. Lambert

Preparing to Teach

As Jeremiah had predicted, Judah was conquered by the Babylonians in 597 B.C., and the nation's leaders were taken into exile with their king. For a time there was talk of rebelling against Babylon, restoring the nation to freedom, and bringing back the exiled leaders. The prophet Hananiah favored this course, and he predicted success. Jeremiah warned against it, wearing an ox-yoke to symbolize the submission to Babylon which he believed to be the only wise course.

Today we honor Jeremiah and regard his words as scripture. But in his day there was no sure way to distinguish his message from that of false prophets like Hananiah. Indeed, what Hananiah said seemed more appealing and patriotic. It offered hope. If we had lived in that day, we would probably have agreed with the many who heeded Hananiah. How can we know when we are being duped by someone who does not speak the truth, does not speak for God?

Here is a way to outline this lesson:

    I. Jeremiah's yoke
        A. Prophetic symbolism
        B. Why Jeremiah wore a yoke
    II. Hananiah's message
        A. Breaking the yoke
        B. All will be well—or will it?
    III. The nature of false prophecy
        A. Self-serving
        B. A cover-up

IV. The nature of true prophecy
   A. Sensitive to God's guidance
   B. Open to truth, even when painful
   C. Stresses our responsibility
V. Hearing God's message today
   A. Some false prophecies today
   B. Some true prophecies today

Reading for today's lesson could include Jeremiah 27–28, *The Interpreter's Concise Commentary*, volume 4, pages 170-72, and *The Interpreter's Bible*, volume 5, pages 990-96, 1009-16.

Introducing the Main Question

Write on the chalkboard the following messages. As a group, decide which are false prophecies. Give reasons for each decision.

—Put your hand on the television, and pray with me, and you will be healed.
—God will not let human beings destroy the world.
—You can do anything if you believe that you can.
—You must reap what you have sown.
—A good Christian will not criticize his country and its policies.
—The world will come to an end next Tuesday.
—All of us must make sacrifices to preserve our fragile environment.

After considering these and deciding which may be false, ask: What are some consequences of believing false prophecies? Can you think of some examples, such as the Jonestown disaster?

Developing the Lesson

I. *Jeremiah's yoke*
   A. *Prophetic symbolism*
Jeremiah wore a yoke made of wood with leather straps. A yoke like this was worn by an ox when plowing or pulling. This was more than just a dramatic way of getting attention. Some of the prophets performed such symbolic acts, often at the command of God, in order to help bring about the events predicted. Thus Ezekiel erected a model of Jerusalem and attacked it with toy troops (Ezekiel 4:1-3). This was to predict and bring about the fall of that city.
   B. *Why Jeremiah wore a yoke*
The prophet believed it was God's will for Judah to be subjected to the Babylonians as a punishment for its sins. To try to throw off the yoke would be to invite destruction. He told the people to accept their misery and not to hope for deliverance. He wore a yoke to show what he meant and to confirm its reality.
II. *Hananiah's message*
   A. *Breaking the yoke*
Hananiah took the wooden yoke from Jeremiah's shoulders and broke it. This was his way of proclaiming and seeking to bring liberation. But Jeremiah was told by God to go back wearing a yoke of iron that could not be broken. Thus the two prophets struggled to make their differing messages prevail.

B. All will be well—or will it?

Jeremiah said that he wished the soothing message of Hananiah were true (28:6). His private prayers indicate he really wanted peace (17:16). Jeremiah had to speak the truth, even though it was not what he wanted to happen. One mark of a true prophet is the willingness to face the hard facts and to help others do so.

III. *The nature of false prophesy*

A. *Self-serving*

We cannot always tell when a prophet is false, but there are clues. A second-century guide for Christians says, "Welcome every apostle on arriving, as if he were the Lord. But he must not stay beyond one day. In case of necessity, however, the next day too. If he stays three days, he is a false prophet" (Didache 11:4-5). Today, the equivalent of this might be asking for a generous "love-gift." A true prophet is not interested in personal gain.

B. *A cover-up*

A false prophet helps us conceal something we do not want to face. This is why false prophets are popular. Jeremiah noted that real prophets usually warn of trouble. He conceded that some may speak of peace, but that is the exception and should be treated with suspicion (28:8-9). We usually don't need a prophet to make us optimistic and complacent. We need a prophet to force us to admit our sin and failure and to be prepared for the consequences.

IV. *The nature of true prophecy*

A. *Sensitive to God's guidance*

Jeremiah spoke what God commanded, even thought he did not want to do it. How can we know what God is speaking in our time? The Old and New Testaments serve as a kind of standard by which to measure what we hear. If it is not consistent with the Bible as a whole, it probably is not from God.

B. *Open to truth, even when painful*

Sometimes the government tries to prevent certain facts from getting out. This may be an effort to protect vital secrets, but it may also conceal ineptitude or wrongdoing. We as individuals tend to block out bad news, especially if it is about our failures or is something that may cause us anguish. If we seek truth, we have to face the painful facts.

C. *Stresses our responsibility*

True prophets do not make life easy for people, even when they bring good news. They tell us what we must do: repent, change our ways, or go forth to accept God's new blessing! False prophets tell us God will take care of us without our doing anything.

Helping Class Members Act

V. *Hearing God's message today*

A. *Some false prophecies today*

List some false prophecies often heard today. Use some of those listed under "Introducing the Main Question," and add others. These could deal with national policies, the work of the church, or personal well-being.

B. *Some true prophecies today*

True prophets tell us something we need to know but may not want to hear! What would true prophets tell us about the possibility of nuclear war, dangers to the environment, possible results of neglecting or abusing minorities, possible results of our growing ignorance of the Bible? True prophets give us a task to do. List on the chalkboard some tasks that true prophets would give us along with their message.

Planning for Next Sunday

Assign Jeremiah 31 to be read before next Sunday. Ask the class members to decide how a prophet who warned of so much evil could also offer hope of good things. What did the prophet foresee? Has it come to pass, or is it still to be realized?

LESSON 6   JULY 6

Hope for the Future

Background Scripture: Jeremiah 31

The Main Question—William H. Willimon

Some time ago, we, along with millions of other Americans, watched the television drama *The Day After*. We watched as nuclear holocaust struck a typical American city. The suffering, the social collapse, and the disappearance of everything that we hold dear and live for are not pleasant thoughts. It was not an easy two hours that we spent before the television. Undoubtedly, while many watched the show, many chose not to watch, too frightened, too horrified by the thoughts of a nuclear disaster.

In the discussion that followed the television show, someone noted that a recent poll indicated that 80 percent of today's college students believe that we shall have a nuclear war within their lifetime.

What does it do to young people to believe that the future is so bleak and the prospects for human survival so unpromising? Yet, when we face facts, when we honestly look at the prospects for our future, who cannot feel anxiety and apprehension at what tomorrow may bring?

Is there any hope? If there is no hope for the future, then what is there worth living for today?

Hope is not a luxury; it is essential for human survival. What you think will happen tomorrow determines, to a great extent, how you act today. So we look toward the future, the future with all its uncertainty, fears, and alarming possibilities, and we ask, "Is there any hope?"

Today's scripture speaks to this pressing question. In reading the words of the prophet Jeremiah, we learn that we are not the first generation of believers to feel anxiety and fear about tomorrow. Fortunately, we may also learn that Jeremiah's people were not the last to be comforted and reassured by God's word of eternal faithfulness.

As You Read the Scripture—Howard P. Colson

Not all of Jeremiah's prophecies dealt with judgment; he also spoke marvelous words of hope and joy for God's people. This lesson from Jeremiah 31 contains two great promises: the promise of return from captivity (verses 2-6) and the promise of a new covenant (verses 31-34).

Jeremiah 31:2. "The people who survived the sword" are those in captivity. The word *wilderness* represents their period of trial and tribulation. The verbs, which are in the perfect tense, speak of the future as though it were already past, for with God even the future is already a reality.

Verse 3. This verse contains one of the most beautiful sentences in the Bible. It tells us that God's love underlies the troubles of life; his love underlies even his judgments. The word translated "faithfulness" is often rendered in the Revised Standard Version by the words *steadfast love*. Here God's faithfulness is paralleled with his never-failing love.

Verse 4-6. A great homecoming is pictured. Israel is spoken of as a virgin, suggesting that, renewed, she is the object of God's continuing love. (Compare Jeremiah 2:2-3.) These verses assure the captives that their former blessings will be restored. Ruined cities will be rebuilt. There will be joyous celebrating. Farming will be revived and its products enjoyed. The supreme joy will be that of worship in Zion (Jerusalem). (Compare Jeremiah 33:7-9.)

Verses 31-34. Jeremiah's prophecies reach their climax. The passage has rightly been called "the Gospel before the Gospel." Of all Old Testament passages it comes the closest to the Christian faith. It is quoted in full in Hebrews 8:8-12 and in part in Hebrews 10:16-17. Jesus referred to it at the Last Supper (see Luke 22:20 and I Corinthians 11:25).

Jeremiah's prediction of a new covenant is important to the Christian church. *New Testament* is just another term for *New Covenant*. What Jeremiah predicted came true in Jesus Christ.

Verses 31-32. A covenant is a solemn agreement between two or more parties. The old covenant was the agreement between the Lord and the people of Israel which was made just before Moses went up on Mount Sinai to receive the Ten Commandments (Exodus 19:19).

"My covenant which they broke" refers to the failure of the old covenant because the people constantly broke it. "I was their husband" means that God loved them and sought to lead them, even though they rejected him.

Verse 33. "I will put my law within them" is a contrast to the old covenant, where the law was external, written on tablets of stone; under the new covenant it is internal. "I will write it upon their hearts" suggests the Holy Spirit, who teaches the believer what God's will is, and then gives him or her the power to obey it. This calls for personal fellowship with God. It is not the result of creed or ceremony. "I will be their God, and they shall be my people" is the divine purpose under both the old covenant and the new. See Jeremiah 24:7.

Verse 34. "They shall all know me" compares with Isaiah 11:9*b*. This knowledge is the result of personal experience. Personal faith in the Lord is at the heart of the new covenant. "I will forgive their iniquity" reminds us that the promise is not of sinlessness but rather of the forgiveness of sin. In this way broken fellowship with God is restored. Divine forgiveness moves the sinner to love the Forgiver and leads to obedience. God not only forgives; he forgets. "I will remember their sin no more." Our forgiven sin is the only thing God ever forgets!

FOURTH QUARTER

Selected Scripture

King James Version	Revised Standard Version

Jeremiah 31:2-6, 31-34

2 Thus saith the LORD, The people *which were* left of the sword found grace in the wilderness; *even* Israel, when I went to cause him to rest.

3 The LORD hath appeared of old unto me, *saying*, Yea, I have loved thee with an everlasting love: therefore with loving-kindness have I drawn thee.

4 Again I will build thee, and thou shalt be built, O virgin of Israel: thou shalt again be adorned with thy tabrets, and shalt go forth in the dances of them that make merry.

5 Thou shalt yet plant vines upon the mountains of Samaria: the planters shall plant, and shall eat *them* as common things.

6 For there shall be a day, *that* the watchmen upon the mount É'-phră-ĭm shall cry, Arise ye, and let us go up to Zion unto the LORD our God.

....

31 Behold, the days come, saith the LORD, that I will make a new covenant with the house of Israel, and with the house of Judah:

32 Not according to the covenant that I made with their fathers in the day *that* I took them by the hand to bring them out of the land of Egypt; which my covenant they brake, although I was an husband unto them, saith the LORD.

33 But this *shall be* the covenant that I will make with the house of Israel; After those days, saith the LORD, I will put my law in their inward parts, and write it in their hearts; and will be their God, and they shall be my people.

Jeremiah 31:2-6, 31-34

2 Thus says the LORD:
"The people who survived the sword found grace in the wilderness;
when Israel sought for rest,
3 the LORD appeared to him from afar.
I have loved you with an everlasting love;
therefore I have continued my faithfulness to you.
4 Again I will build you, and you shall be built,
O virgin Israel!
Again you shall adorn yourself with timbrels.
and shall go forth in the dance of the merrymakers.
5 Again you shall plant vineyards upon the mountains of Samar'ia;
the planters shall plant,
and shall enjoy the fruit.
6 For there shall be a day when watchmen will call
in the hill country of E'phraim:
'Arise, and let us go up to Zion, to the LORD our God.'"

....

31"Behold, the days are coming, says the LORD, when I will make a new covenant with the house of Israel and the house of Judah, 32 not like the covenant which I made with their fathers when I took them by the hand to bring them out of the land of Egypt, my covenant which they broke, though I was their husband, says the LORD. 33 But this is the covenant which I will make with the house of Israel after those days, says the LORD: I will put my law within them, and I will write it upon their hearts; and I will be their God, and they shall be my people. 34 And no longer shall each man teach his neighbor and each his brother,

34 And they shall teach no more every man his neighbour, and every man his brother, saying, Know the Lord: for they shall all know me, from the least of them unto the greatest, saith the Lord: for I will forgive their iniquity, and I will remember their sin no more.

saying, 'Know the Lord,' for they shall all know me, from the least of them to the greatest, says the Lord; for I will forgive their iniquity, and I will remember their sin no more."

Key Verse: **I have loved thee with an everlasting love: therefore with loving-kindness have I drawn thee.** (Jeremiah 31:3)

Key Verse:
I have loved you with an everlasting love:
therefore I have continued my faithfulness to you.
(Jeremiah 31:3)

The Scripture and the Main Question—William H. Willimon

The People Found Grace

Never one to mince words with people, Jeremiah has told Judah of its future fate. Aliens shall overcome the weakened and demoralized nation and shall bring chaos and destruction to the Chosen People. Jeremiah never pulled any punches about Judah's situation. Even today, the word *jeremiad* is used to describe a scathing, rebuking tirade against someone or something, a fitting tribute to the harsh, critical words of Jeremiah.

Judah has no one but itself to blame for the predicament it now faces. It was a hopeless, fearful situation.

Yet, here, in the midst of all this hopelessness and confusion, Jeremiah now sounds a word of hope.

> The people who survived the sword
> found grace in the wilderness;
> when Israel sought for rest,
> the Lord appeared to him from afar. (31:2-3)

Jeremiah recalls an image from the Exodus. During that long, forty-year trek through the wilderness, God did not abandon the chosen ones. Even when they disobeyed and angered God, as they often did, still God preserved them. Will God now desert the people who have been the beneficiaries of God's gracious love and care all these years?

By no means! says Jeremiah. They shall be preserved because God, even though God may be angered by their faithlessness and immorality, is still their God and they are still God's people. "I have loved you with an everlasting love" (31:3).

In fact, as we have noted in earlier lessons, God's anger, God's judgments against Judah are an aspect of God's steadfast love. God will not simply let Judah go without an argument, without using every means possible to win Judah back.

When does God give up on a nation or when does God walk out on a relationship with a person? Is there one unforgivable, irretrievable, unredeemable sin? When does God turn his back on us and leave us entirely to our own devices? Can you think of many good examples from the Scriptures where God gives up on us?

I doubt that you can. It is hard to think of God completely calling it quits on the human race because we have given God so many good opportunities to do so, and yet God has always reached out to us and tried to win us back. We are loved by an eternal, resourceful, everlasting love which does not easily give up on us. "Therefore I have continued in my faithfulness to you" (31:3).

Like the prodigal son, we have time and again turned back to God, fully deserving all of God's wrath and fearful judgment, only to find, to our surprise, all of God's grace.

I Have Continued My Faithfulness to You

Jeremiah found Judah in a hopeless situation. He faced that situation honestly and urged his fellow citizens to do the same.

When we find ourselves in similar circumstances, there is always the temptation to delude ourselves—to look at our situation through rose-colored glasses, think positively, and hope for the best. We thus avoid the situation by deceiving ourselves about the gravity of our plight.

One reason we may do this is that we are afraid to be honest. After all, if things are as bleak as they seem, if it is all up to us, if in the final analysis we are on our own, then who can bear to be truthful? Such is the source of human delusion.

But if there is a love which upholds us and which transcends even the worst of circumstances, then we, like Jeremiah, can dare to look the situation in the face and be honest.

Jeremiah was so convinced that the purposes of God would not be defeated, he was so sure that God would preserve the Chosen People, that he could dare to be accurate and honest about their present plight

I have notice a similar dynamic at work in people who have serious illness. It seems to me that seriously ill people often have two choices: either to accept their condition and try to make the best of it, or to deny their situation and spend the rest of their days lying to themselves and others in a kind of make-believe game.

"I know that I am dying of cancer," a woman told me. I was somewhat startled by her forthright manner. "But it's OK because, whatever happens to me in the midst of all this, I know that the Lord will be with me."

This person had hope—maybe not hope that she would be cured, but hope that, whatever happened, she would be loved.

There are many varieties of hope. There is the false hope that comes from deluding ourselves and avoiding the facts. There is the superficial hope that comes from a kind of Pollyanna attitude that somehow everything will turn out all right if we just wish that it will be all right. Then there is the hopefulness that comes from an abiding trust that, come what may, we shall be loved by God.

> I have loved you with an everlasting love;
> therefore I have continued my faithfulness to you. (Jeremiah 31:3)

There Shall Be a Day

Wherein is our hope? How is it possible for anyone to be honest and hopeful at the same time? In the midst of a national calamity such as the one which Jeremiah faced, how could any sober person be hopeful?

The question hits us where we live today. How can we be hopeful as we go about our lives under the shadow of the nuclear mushroom cloud? In the face of ecological problems, shortages of natural resources, unrest at home and abroad, to say nothing of our own personal dilemmas of sickness, aging, and family troubles—wherein is there hope?

Jeremiah is able to speak a word of hope, hope based not upon faith in the essential goodness of the people of Judah or their leaders, not upon some mushy-headed notion that everything will eventually turn out OK just because we want it to, but hope based upon remembrance of God's faithfulness in the past.

God has delivered the people from great tribulation before, God has preserved the people so that the promises of God might be fulfilled, and God will continue to be faithful.

Here is hope based upon past experience with God. So, the woman who found herself sick with terminal cancer could feel hope because she knew enough about God's faithfulness in the past to be confident of faithfulness in the future, in spite of her dismal prognosis.

Israel shall have hardship. There will be great trials and tribulation, but God's will shall not be completely defeated. A remnant shall remain to tell the story and live out the promise: "Behold, the days are coming, says the LORD, when I will make a new covenant with the house of Israel and the house of Judah, not like the covenant which I made with their fathers when I took them by the hand to bring them out of the land of Egypt, . . . I will put my law within them, and I will write it upon their hearts; and I will be their God, and they shall be my people" (31:31-32a, 33b).

Helping Adults Become Involved—Herbert H. Lambert

Preparing to Teach

We close our study of Jeremiah with a message of hope, so different from the rest of the book that many believe it was written after the time of Jeremiah. But Jeremiah was called to build and to plant as well as to pluck up and to destroy (1:10).

What hope did the prophet hold out to the people of Israel and Judah, who had been carried into exile, their cities destroyed, their worship disrupted? What would God do for these people? What signs of hope are there in our own time, and what do we need to do in order to participate in these new blessings?

Here is a way to outline the lesson:

     I. Restoration of Ephraim
        A. Return from foreign lands
        B. Penitence
        C. Joy and renewal
    II. The new covenant
        A. Within the heart
        B. Closeness to God
        C. No need to teach
        D. Sin to be forgiven
   III. The new covenant in Christ
        A. Centered on Jesus Christ
        B. Creates a new people of God
        C. Transmitted to each new generation
        D. Means forgiveness and renewal

IV. Our participation in the new covenant in Christ
    A. Admitting sin and accepting forgiveness
    B. Knowing God and serving God

Read Jeremiah 31 and *The Interpreter's Concise Commentary*, volume 4, pages 184-86, and *The Interpreter's Bible*, volume 5, pages 1028-42.

Introducing the Main Question

During the Korean conflict, a tide of Chinese soldiers swept the United Nations forces back with great loss of life. It looked for a time as though the U.N. forces would be swept into the sea. One who had predicted just such a result was theologian Reinhold Niebuhr. But at this critical point he began to express hope. He said, "I can be hopeful because I never expected very much good to come of this from the beginning."

Sometimes a "prophet of doom" is the very person who can help us pick up the pieces after a terrible loss. He or she has been facing reality while we have been hiding behind smokescreens. The prophet has our best interests at heart and has been trying to get us to wake up. Now that we know how bad things are, the prophet is ready to assure us of God's continuing love and to guide us to a better, more honest way of life.

Developing the Lesson

I. Restoration of Ephraim

  A. Return from foreign lands

The fall of Samaria to the Assyrians in 722 B.C., a hundred thirty years before the time of Jeremiah and the captivity, left a scar on the memory of God's people. To disrupt the nation and its traditions, the leaders were moved to distant places and other people were brought into Israel. In this section the prophet foretells a time when the people and their nation will be restored.

  B. Penitence

The return must be accompanied by recognition that the suffering endured was brought on by Israel's sin. God's mercy comes to those who recognize the need for it.

  C. Joy and renewal

The joy of returning to the lost homeland is graphically described. It will be "like a watered garden." Although the prophecy of Israel's restoration did not come true as predicted here, we know that individuals and nations experience the grace and power of God in unexpected ways. During the United States bicentennial celebration in 1976, the tall ships sailed into New York harbor to the music of "Amazing Grace." It was a reminder that all of the nation's greatness would not have been possible without God's gifts.

II. The new covenant

  A. Within the heart

Jeremiah was dismayed by the way in which the people of Judah ignored and rejected the requirements of their covenant with God. When he dreamed of a new covenant, he saw it as something written indelibly upon the heart so that it could not be forgotten. It will not be something people hear about and accept but something which is an essential part of their whole existence!

B. *Closeness to God*

"I will be their God, and they shall be my people." Under the new covenant, God would be able to guide persons like a hand causing a glove to move. People will know what God wants and will do it without objection or question. This will not seem burdensome but will be the fulfillment of true freedom.

C. *No need to teach*

All through Jewish and Christian history the traditions have been one generation from extinction. This is because each generation must pass on, through teaching, the values and beliefs received from the past. Jeremiah foresaw a time when this would not be necessary because persons would be born with the knowledge and love of God. Has this dream of Jeremiah come true, or is it still unrealized?

D. *Sin to be forgiven*

Jeremiah never passed over lightly the terrible wrongs of which he spoke in earlier chapters. "I will remember their sin no more" is an acknowledgment that there has been sin and that forgiveness is essential. Often it is hard to admit this. Some have said that the hardest part of the Apostles' Creed to say is "I believe in the forgiveness of sins." It is hard to believe we have committed sin and, once we have recognized the truth, it is hard to believe sin can be taken away.

III. *The new covenant in Christ*

A. *Centered on Jesus Christ*

Whether Jeremiah foresaw the coming of Jesus or not, Christians have taken his words and applied them to Jesus. The new relationship made possible in Christ is much like the one described in Jeremiah 31:31-34. It is a new covenant, one made possible only in intimate communion with Jesus.

B. *Creates a new people of God*

Both the old and new covenants were communal rather than individual. One participates in the covenant only by participating in the church, the people of God.

C. *Transmitted to each new generation*

Jeremiah's dream of a law written upon the heart is not yet a reality. Until it is, we must carefully nurture growing persons in the meaning of the new covenant.

D. *Means forgiveness and renewal*

At the heart of the new covenant in Christ is the hope of beginning anew and putting behind us all the past failures. That is as exciting today as it must have been in Jeremiah's day, when the people realized their folly and its awful results.

Helping Class Members Act

IV. *Our participation in the new covenant*

A. *Admitting sin and accepting forgiveness*

Have each person write on a piece of paper some ways in which we, like the people of Judah, have sinned or failed to do God's will. Point out that if we acknowledge our sins, God forgives them (I John 1:9). We are forgiven!

B. *Knowing and serving God*

Remember that the word *know* in the Bible often means intimate personal closeness (Genesis 4:1). To know God means more than just having information. It means transformation. Have we been transformed by our acquaintance (fellowship) with God?

Preparing for Next Sunday

Before we begin our study of Ezekiel, let us look over the past six lessons and review the different messages of Jeremiah. Note any remaining questions we still have about Jeremiah. What aspect of this prophet do we most admire?

UNIT II: EZEKIEL: JUDGMENT AND RESTORATION

Horace R. Weaver

FIVE LESSONS   **JULY 13–AUGUST 10**

This unit consists of five lessons from Ezekiel. In addition to introducing the prophet, the lessons focus on the important themes of personal responsibility for one's actions and their consequences, God's charges against a corrupt society, and the hope of restoration of the homeland and temple by a just and holy God.

The titles of these five lessons from Ezekiel are: "Ezekiel: Messenger to a Rebellious People," July 13; "Personal Responsibility," July 20; "God's Charges Against a Corrupt Society," July 27; "God's Promises of Renewal," August 3; "A Vision of God's Glory," August 10.

LESSON 7   JULY 13

Ezekiel: Messenger to a Rebellious People

Background Scripture: Ezekiel 1–3

The Main Question—William H. Willimon

As part of my ecclesiastical duties, I sit on the district Board of Ordained Ministry for our denomination. It is our task to interview and then to approve or to disapprove candidates for the ordained ministry in our church.

I'm always interested to hear the candidates describe how they feel they have been called into the ministry. Of course, each one is different and each call into the pastoral ministry is different, but a common thread runs through nearly all of their testimonies—nearly every one of them reports a long process of struggle, resistance, and doubt, finally culminating in their saying yes.

We tell them that their reluctance and struggle are good signs—anyone would be out of touch with reality not to resist the call of God into the pastoral ministry. It is not an easy vocation; the demands are great; the material rewards are few. Then there are the people—people who are hurting, sometimes difficult to live with in the church, sometimes resistant to the gospel message. So one ought to avoid getting involved if one can.

In fact, that's what we often tell them—"If there is any way to stay out of this, you ought to do it." We mean this advice half in seriousness, half in jest. We want to tell them that the job is too tough unless they are truly called to do it.

Those who speak for God need all the divine equipping that they can get. For those of us who hear the words of God's messengers do not always receive the message gladly, do we?

As You Read the Scripture—Howard P. Colson

The prophet Ezekiel, who had been a priest in Jerusalem, was an exile in Babylonia. He was taken there in 597 B.C. when many leading men of Jerusalem were carried captive. (The larger captivity began ten years later when Jerusalem was captured and the temple burned.)

Ezekiel's call to the prophetic office came in the fifth year of his exile. He prophesied to the Jewish captives by the river Chebar in lower Babylonia for some twenty-two or twenty-three years. This was one of the most critical periods in Israel's history. Ezekiel was the prophet-pastor to the Jewish exiles. Before the fall of Jerusalem he kept combatting the false hopes of a speedy restoration. After the city fell, his message changed and he spoke more and more of the coming restoration.

His book is in three parts. Chapters 1–24 deal with events up to the fall of Jerusalem; chapters 25–32 contain messages (diatribes) against foreign nations; and chapters 33–48 consist of prophecies of the restored Jerusalem. The book is full of parables, allegories, visions, and symbolic acts.

The chapters in our lesson record the prophet's vision of God's majesty and splendor (Ezekiel 1) and his call and initiation into his ministry (Ezekiel 2:1–3:3). Overpowered by the vision of God's glory, Ezekiel was prepared for the call to be a prophet. Ezekiel 2:1-7 is a warning that his message would meet with opposition. Ezekiel 2:8–3:3 is a symbolic presentation of the fact that the prophet is to communicate God's words.

Ezekiel 2:1. The expression "son of man" is used about ninety times in the book. It has no messianic connotation, nor is it a title of honor; it emphasizes the fact that the prophet is merely human in contrast to God's majesty. Ezekiel's vision of the enthroned Lord had caused him to fall upon his face (see 1:28). He is now told, "Stand upon your feet."

Verses 2-7. Those to whom God would send Ezekiel were in extremely bad spiritual condition.

Verse 5. "A rebellious house" is a straightforward and striking description of the Jewish community. When Ezekiel's prediction of the destruction of Jerusalem has been fulfilled, the people will recognize that he is a God-sent prophet. The fact that Jerusalem's destruction had been clearly foretold came to be a powerful factor in preserving the true religion of the Jews. The only conception of God on which Israel's future could be built was one which would lead the people to genuine repentance.

Verse 6. "Briers and thorns" and "scorpions" are symbols of the opposition Ezekiel would face from the Jews before Jerusalem was destroyed. (Some students of the Bible think the apostle Paul was referring to such a "thorn in the flesh.")

Verse 9. The "written scroll" represented the message he was to deliver.

FOURTH QUARTER

The divine message was a stern one—"words of lamentation and mourning and woe"—a message of coming calamity.

Chapter 3:1. "Eat this scroll" is the instruction to Ezekiel to make God's words his own by "digesting" them. Of course, this was a figurative experience. But he was to make the message so much a part of himself that it would permeate his entire being.

Verse 3. The message itself was a sad one, but the sweetness—"as sweet as honey"—came from the fact Ezekiel was now aware of being God's fellow worker. That brought him joy and satisfaction. Compare Jeremiah 15:16. Jesus had to endure terrible suffering, but he found great joy in doing the Father's will.

Selected Scripture

King James Version	Revised Standard Version

Ezekiel 1:1

1 Now it came to pass in the thirtieth year, in the fourth *month*, in the fifth *day* of the month, as I *was* among the captives by the river of Chē´-bär, *that* the heavens were opened, and I saw visions of God.

Ezekiel 2:1-10

1 And he said unto me, Son of man, stand upon thy feet, and I will speak unto thee.

2 And the spirit entered into me when he spake unto me, and set me upon my feet that I heard him that spake unto me.

3 And he said unto me, Son of man, I send thee to the children of Israel, to a rebellious nation that hath rebelled against me: they and their fathers have transgressed against me, *even* unto this very day.

4 For *they are* impudent children and stiffhearted. I do send thee unto them; and thou shalt say unto them, Thus saith the Lord God.

5 And they, whether they will hear, or whether they will forbear, (for they *are* a rebellious house,) yet shall know that there hath been a prophet among them.

6 And thou, son of man, be not afraid of them, neither be afraid of their words, though briers and thorns *be* with thee, and thou dost

Ezekiel 1:1

1 In the thirtieth year, in the fourth month, on the fifth day of the month, as I was among the exiles by the river Chebar, the heavens were opened, and I saw visions of God.

Ezekiel 2:1-10

1 And he said to me, "Son of man, stand upon your feet, and I will speak with you." 2 And when he spoke to me, the Spirit entered into me and set me upon my feet; and I heard him speaking to me. 3 And he said to me, "Son of man, I send you to the people of Israel, to a nation of rebels, who have rebelled against me; they and their fathers have transgressed against me to this very day. 4 The people also are impudent and stubborn: I send you to them; and you shall say to them, 'Thus says the Lord God.' 5 And whether they hear or refuse to hear (for they are a rebellious house) they will know that there has been a prophet among them. 6 And you, son of man, be not afraid of them, nor be afraid of their words, though briers and thorns are with you and you sit upon scorpions; be not afraid of their words, nor be dismayed at their looks, for they are a rebellious house. 7 And you shall speak my words to them, whether

dwell among scorpions: be not afraid of their words, nor be dismayed at their looks, though they *be* a rebellious house.

7 And thou shalt speak my words unto them, whether they will hear, or whether they will forbear: for they *are* most rebellious.

8 But thou, son of man, hear what I say unto thee; Be not thou rebellious like that rebellious house: open thy mouth, and eat that I give thee.

9 And when I looked, behold, an hand *was* sent unto me; and, lo, a roll of a book *was* therein;

10 And he spread it before me; and it *was* written within and without: and *there was* written therein lamentations, and mourning, and woe.

Ezekiel 3:1-3

1 Moreover he said unto me, Son of man, eat that thou findest; eat this roll, and go speak unto the house of Israel.

2 So I opened my mouth, and he caused me to eat that roll.

3 And he said unto me, Son of man, cause thy belly to eat, and fill thy bowels with this roll that I give thee. Then did I eat *it;* and it was in my mouth as honey for sweetness.

Key Verse: Thou shalt speak my words unto them, whether they will hear, or whether they will forbear. (Ezekiel 2:7)

they hear or refuse to hear; for they are a rebellious house.

8 "But you, son of man, hear what I say to you; be not rebellious like that rebellious house; open your mouth, and eat what I give you." 9 And when I looked, behold, a hand was stretched out to me, and lo, a written scroll was in it; 10 and he spread it before me; and it had writing on the front and on the back, and there were written on it words of lamentation and mourning and woe.

Ezekiel 3:1-3

1 And he said to me, "Son of man, eat what is offered to you; eat this scroll, and go, speak to the house of Israel." 2 So I opened my mouth, and he gave me the scroll to eat. 3 And he said to me, "Son of man, eat this scroll that I give you and fill your stomach with it." Then I ate it; and it was in my mouth as sweet as honey.

Key Verse: You shall speak my words to them, whether they hear or refuse to hear. (Ezekiel 2:7)

The Scripture and the Main Question—William H. Willimon

I Send You to Them

In a way the call of Ezekiel, as it is recorded in the first chapter of this book, is a model, a standard for the divine call of the prophet. Ezekiel is depicted as a person who is swept up into divine purposes, perhaps swept up against his own will.

I have always been delighted by the description of the people whom Ezekiel is called to serve as it is given in the second chapter of the book. The Lord has no illusions about the difficulty of the task which Ezekiel is being called to fulfill. After all, the Lord ought to know better than anyone else what a difficult, rebellious people these are! "I send you to the people of

Israel, to a nation of rebels, who have rebelled against me; they and their fathers have transgressed against me to this very day. The people also are impudent and stubborn: I send you to them" (Ezekiel 2:3).

In fact, one could say the Bible itself, Old and New Testaments, is the long record of how God's people are also "a nation of rebels, who have rebelled against me." From Adam and Eve, from Cain and Abel, down through the people dancing before the golden idol in the wilderness even while Moses was on the mountain receiving the commandments, this is truly a "nation of rebels."

One could also say that this morning's newspaper is a record of how our rebellion continues today. We continue to want to do things our way rather than God's way, and our way brings us to grief.

Some years ago I served a church that had been served by a prophet. Like Ezekiel, this man spoke the truth, come what may. He was active in the civil rights movement, an outspoken critic of the then-current Vietnam War. His conservative, Southern congregation greeted his prophetic sermons, not with gratitude that there was indeed a courageous prophet among them, but with silence followed by active resistance. In one year, two hundred people responded to his prophetic ministry by leaving the church. They decided to go to a church that was a "nonprophet" institution!

Whether They Hear or Refuse to Hear

I think one of the most difficult things for a pastor to learn is his or her own limitations. Of course, none of us easily learns to accept and live with our limitations, but pastors, from what I have observed, may find this aspect of life particularly difficult.

Pastors may enter the ministry hoping to "help people," which they often think means to *change* people. There is the subtle temptation to think of ourselves as being in the business of fixing people's marriages, leading them to fulfillment in their jobs, helping them to have obedient children.

Early in their ministry, most pastors learn that the task is not so simple. People are trapped in a tangled web of self-delusion, fear, anxiety, and a host of other forces which may severely limit their ability to change their lives for the better, even though they may earnestly want to change.

Jesus spoke of the need for his disciples to preach the good news—then, if the town refused to receive it, to shake the dust off their feet and move to another place where the audience might be more receptive.

But part of me wants to believe that I am so intelligent, so persuasive, so endearing, that I can win over the most hardhearted person. If I can just preach the right sermon, lift up the right scripture verse, use a particularly apt illustration, I can convert others at will.

But God has created us as free creatures, free to turn to the truth or free to turn away. I am not as powerful and persuasive as I like to think. I do not control other people's lives. They are free to say yes or no.

Do you have trouble accepting this fact of life, as I do? I think one of my most frequent tasks as a counselor who talks to people with problems is helping them to define those areas of life that they have some control over and those areas of life that they have no control over.

A woman sits in my office complaining about her husband's problem with alcohol. I don't blame her for being worried and upset about his problem, but we both need to remind ourselves that it is *his* problem. More often than not, he is not in my office and he will probably never consent to talk with me about the problem, so we must acknowledge our limitation in changing him. What we do have power over is ourselves—our attitudes and behavior. We may be able to change ourselves and the way we respond to his problem, but we may not be able to change him.

It takes a lot of faith to admit that there are some things in life, some people we meet, that we may not be able to change. We have our limits. In a way, it is arrogant and prideful of us to think that we have power over everything and everyone. We are not God. We can accept responsibility for some things, but not all things. There comes a time when we must admit that, try though we may, we cannot do all things.

So Ezekiel, right at the start of his ministry, is urged to be bold and speak the truth. But then he is told (and, as a pastor, I should read this text over after nearly every pastoral counseling session) that "whether they hear or refuse to hear," Ezekiel is to speak nonetheless (2:5, 7).

Whether they hear or refuse to hear (for ultimately, that choice is up to them and you cannot manipulate or force them to hear), you must do the will of God for your life and let God work in their lives as God wills and let them respond to God as they will.

I wish I could have the freedom to really believe and do that in my relations with other people—to simply do the best I can and then let them be free to do the best they can—without manipulation or scolding because they do not do what I want them to do!

When I counsel a couple on the eve of their marriage, I ask each person to write down three things that he or she really loves about the other person. Then I have each write down three things that he or she just can't stand about the other person. I tell them, "Now look at your list. Can you live with those three unpleasant things for the rest of your life? That's what marriage is all about—learning to change the things you can and learning to accept the things in the other person which you cannot change."

Of course, we all know that in a relationship like marriage, sometimes the other person does change in ways that we want them to change—but the best climate for change is that one in which the other person feels free to respond in his or her own free way, without fear of coercion of manipulation.

Perhaps that is why the new prophet is told, "And you shall speak my words to them, whether they hear or refuse to hear; for they are a rebellious house" (2:7).

Helping Adults Become Involved—Herbert H. Lambert

Preparing to Teach

The work of Ezekiel began about thirty years after the call of Jeremiah. When Ezekiel began to preach among the exiles in Babylon, some of Jeremiah's dire predictions had come true. Like Jeremiah, Ezekiel warned of God's continuing punishment and called the people of Judah to repent. In spite of their reverses, however, the people refused to listen to Ezekiel.

Ezekiel strikes us as an odd character. He sees strange visions that are difficult for us to imagine. Unlike Jeremiah, he seems to be a passive, mechanical figure, controlled by the Spirit within him. He not only sees visions but also performs symbolic actions as a part of his task. This session is an introduction to Ezekiel and his work.

Here is a way to outline the lesson:

387

FOURTH QUARTER

I. Historical background
   A. Why some people were in exile in 593 B.C.
   B. Two disasters (597 and 587 B.C.)
   C. False hopes of the exiles
II. Ezekiel the prophet
   A. Like and unlike other prophets
   B. The strange visions of Ezekiel
   C. Ezekiel's call and his task
III. The message of Ezekiel
   A. The fall of Jerusalem
   B. God's presence and power
   C. Our responsibility to God
IV. The message for today
   A. God is everywhere.
   B. God requires obedience.
   C. God calls us to speak.

Helpful reading for this lesson is in *The Interpreter's Concise Commentary,* volume 4, pages 233-48 and *The Interpreter's Bible,* volume 6, pages 56-62 and 67-85. Also look for "Ezekiel" in any good Bible dictionary.

Introducing the Main Question

Turn to the end of the last lesson and note the suggestions about reviewing Jeremiah. You might briefly summarize impressions of your class members as they surveyed the last six lessons.

In "The Main Question," Dr. Willimon tells about persons who receive a call to ministry. Why does he try to discourage persons from accepting such a call? Why do persons still respond to the call in spite of the difficulties involved? Discuss these questions as an introduction to Ezekiel.

Developing the Lesson

I. Historical background

   A. Why some people were in exile in 593 B.C.

Display or draw a map showing Jerusalem and Babylon. As Jeremiah had predicted, the Babylonians besieged Jerusalem and took its leaders into exile. The prophet said this was a punishment for the people's basic disloyalties (sin) and that even worse would follow if they did not repent and seek God's way.

   B. Two disasters (597 and 587 B.C.)

Between the two sieges of Jerusalem, Ezekiel spoke among the exiles in Babylon while Jeremiah preached in Jerusalem. Both warned against trusting in God to save Judah. God, they said, had turned against the people because they had broken the covenant. Few were willing to listen to either prophet.

   C. False hope of the exiles

Encouraged by deceivers like Hananiah, the people dreamed of an immediate return to Jerusalem and a restoration of its former glory. Instead, the city was besieged again and in 587 B.C. was virtually destroyed. A large number were killed and many others were taken to Babylon. This tragedy may have been averted if the people had taken a more realistic and humble attitude toward their predicament, if they had listened to Ezekiel and Jeremiah.

388

II. Ezekiel the prophet
  A. Like and unlike other prophets
  In many respects Ezekiel was like other prophets. He warned of catastrophe but also offered hope. He received a call to speak an unpopular message. His book is different from other prophetic books in its strange visions and the bizarre behavior the prophet is ordered to perform. It is harder for us to identify with this man than with Isaiah or Jeremiah.
  B. The strange visions of Ezekiel
  Recount briefly the visions described in Ezekiel 1. "Such was the appearance of the likeness of the glory of the Lord" (1:28). While it is difficult to explain all the details, Ezekiel seems to emphasize the mobility of God and the fact that God can go with the people even to Babylon. The strange living creatures, wheels, and other images point to the mystery and majesty of God. Here is one who is beyond human comprehension and control, the prophet says.
  C. Ezekiel's call and his task
  Unlike Moses, Isaiah, and Jeremiah, Ezekiel offers no objection to the call he receives. We sense that he has no choice and hardly any control over his thoughts and feelings. He is warned that the people will not listen to his words. He is told to speak, nevertheless, and the people will know that a prophet has been among them. Ezekiel was called to be faithful, not to be successful; to do his duty, not to compel others to do theirs.
III. The message of Ezekiel
  A. The fall of Jerusalem
  Chapters 4–7 dramatically portray the agony yet to come upon the people of Judah. The prophet lay on his side and carried out a "toy siege" to demonstrate and bring about God's punishment of Jerusalem. For that day it was the equivalent of the television movie *The Day After,* a preview of a time when everything of value would be destroyed. To understand the fall of Jerusalem, read together Lamentations 5.
  B. God's presence and power
  One thing will not perish—the presence and power of God. Many people saw in these evils a sign that God was powerless. Far from it! The destruction was willed by God as a punishment, said Ezekiel. Any hope that remained must be based on the power and faithfulness of that same God. We must turn to God to be renewed.
  C. Our responsibility to God
  Like all the prophets, Ezekiel made clear that personal and community sins would not go unpunished. Tragic events were seen as a result of centuries of disobedience and neglect of God's laws.

Helping Class Members Act
IV. The message for today
  A. God is everywhere
  We may think we have progressed since the time of Ezekiel, when people assumed that God lived in the temple at Jerusalem and could only be worshiped there (Psalm 137:4). The fact is, however, that we regularly exclude God from political affairs, from business decisions, and from our personal lives. How can we show greater awareness of God's involvement in all of life? List some answers on the chalkboard.

B. *God requires obedience.*

Like the people to whom Ezekiel preached, we assume that God will take care of us, and we pay too little attention to the ways in which our actions cut us off from God. Are we doing what God requires of us?

C. *God calls us to speak.*

We cannot evade our responsibility to speak for God by saying it will be ineffective. Even if no one listens, we must still say and do what we know is right. This is one case where we are not to calculate results before springing into action. What are some matters about which God wants us to speak today, whether others listen to us or not? Make a list of these.

Planning for Next Sunday

What are the limits of our responsibility? Are we responsible for what our children do? for what our parents do? for what we cannot control? Have class members write down these questions and ponder them in preparation for the next lesson.

LESSON 8 JULY 20

Personal Responsibility

Background Scripture: Ezekiel 18

The Main Question—William H. Willimon

One of the unhappy characteristics of our age is our tendency to blame our situation on external factors. In this century we have discovered how important environment is in human development. Child psychologists have documented how influential parental guidance and love are in the life of the developing child. Social and economic conditions, other people's treatment of us, our neighborhood—all these external factors are influential over us. All this is true and few of us will deny it.

But also true is the observation that external factors may not be as influential over us as we like to believe. When we are faced with our shortcomings and failures, it is easy for us to lay the blame at the feet of others.

"If only I had more attentive parents," we may say. "If only the schools were better when I was growing up."

"If someone had given me a break when I was coming along," we complain.

In other words, it is all their fault, not ours. We are the hapless victims of circumstances and irresistible forces which are beyond our control, mere cogs in the grinding wheels of fate, we say.

Mommy, Daddy, God, the schools, the government—we have dozens of scapegoats upon whom we heap the blame for our condition.

"Why did this happen to me?" we sometimes cry out when misfortune hits us. Why did someone or something do this to me?

Sometimes—not always, but sometimes—we have no one to blame but ourselves. We attempt to shift the responsibility for our situation onto someone else's shoulders, only to find it coming back to rest upon our own.

Personal responsibility—standing up and facing the facts about our own responsibility for who we are and where we are—is the major concern of today's lesson. Ezekiel reminds us that, while we do not control everything in our lives and in our future, we often have more control over things than we like to admit.

As You Read the Scripture—Howard P. Colson

The theme of Ezekiel 18 is the personal responsibility of the individual before God. This means that each person is rewarded according to his own doings. The righteous person lives; the unrighteous person dies.

There was a popular proverb which held that Israel's hardships were the punishment of the sins of former generations (see Ezekiel 18:2, compare Exodus 20:5, 34:7, Numbers 14:18, Deuteronomy 5:9). There was some truth in this, but the idea led the members of the present generation to ignore their own sin.

Ezekiel's doctrine of individual responsibility is one of the more advanced in the Old Testament. With Jeremiah 31:29-30, it marks a new understanding of personal responsibility.

The chapter presents two basic facts about personal religion: (1) God is absolutely righteous in his dealings with the individual, and (2) he is ever ready to forgive the penitent.

In presenting personal responsibility Ezekiel used three illustrations: that of a righteous man (verses 5-9), that of the sinful son of a righteous man (verses 10-13), and that of the righteous son of a wicked father (verses 14-18).

Ezekiel 18:2. Ezekiel's hearers felt that their exile was due to their forefathers' sins, not their own. Their forebears had "eaten sour grapes" (that is, had sinned) and they, the exiles, were paying the penalty (their teeth were "set on edge"). The exile was the punishment for sins of the past, but also for sins of the present. When God brought about the exile, he was dealing with the nation as a whole, but that did not excuse individuals from personal responsibility for their sins.

Verse 3. The proverb was being misapplied. A new day had come, the day of personal religion.

Verse 4. Here and elsewhere in the Old Testament, soul means a person. In view of God's ownership of every person, each is directly responsible to him and must answer for his own sin. Therefore, it is "the soul that sins" that "shall die."

Verses 6-9. In this list of virtues characteristic of a righteous person, some are stated negatively and some positively. They may be classified under three heads: devotion to God, sexual purity, and charity.

Verse 6. To "eat upon the mountains" means to share in an idolatrous meal at a high place (see I Kings 11:7, 14:23; II Kings 17:9-12).

Verse 7. On restoring "to the debtor his pledge," see Exodus 22:26-27 and Deuteronomy 24:12-13.

Verse 8. The Israelites were forbidden to charge interest for any loan to a poor fellow Israelite (see Exodus 22:25 and Leviticus 25:35-37).

Verse 9. The righteous person reaps the result of his righteousness.

FOURTH QUARTER

Righteousness includes the two ideas of a right character and a right relationship to God.

Verses 10-13. These verses present a case opposite to the one in verses 5-9.

Verse 13. The unrighteous person reaps the result of his unrighteousness. "He shall surely die."

Verse 25. God's ways are just; Israel's ways are unjust. Ezekiel insisted on action as a test of character.

Verse 30. Each person is to be judged on the basis of his or her individual religious and moral condition.

Verses 31-32. If a wicked person repents, he or she will live. On the basis of this fact, everyone is called on to repent, for God has no pleasure in the death of anyone. Thus there is the possibility of a change in any and every person's destiny, for God is a God of love.

Selected Scripture

King James Version

Ezekiel 18:1-13, 25, 30

1 The word of the LORD came unto me again, saying,

2 What mean ye, that ye use this proverb concerning the land of Israel, saying, The fathers have eaten sour grapes, and the children's teeth are set on edge?

3 *As* I live, saith the Lord GOD, ye shall not have *occasion* any more to use this proverb in Israel.

4 Behold, all souls are mine; as the soul of the father, so also the soul of the son is mine: the soul that sinneth, it shall die.

5 But if a man be just, and do that which is lawful and right,

6 *And* hath not eaten upon the mountains, neither hath lifted up his eyes to the idols of the house of Israel, neither hath defiled his neighbour's wife, neither hath come near to a menstruous woman,

7 And hath not oppressed any, *but* hath restored to the debtor his pledge, hath spoiled none by violence, hath given his bread to the hungry, and hath covered the naked with a garment;

8 He *that* hath not given forth upon usury, neither hath taken any increase, *that* hath withdrawn his

Revised Standard Version

Ezekiel 18:1-13, 25, 30

1 The word of the LORD came to me again: 2 "What do you mean by repeating this proverb concerning the land of Israel, 'The fathers have eaten sour grapes, and the children's teeth are set on edge'? 3 As I live, says the Lord GOD, this proverb shall no more be used by you in Israel. 4 Behold, all souls are mine; the soul of the father as well as the soul of the son is mine: the soul that sins shall die.

5 "If a man is righteous and does what is lawful and right—6 if he does not eat upon the mountains or lift up his eyes to the idols of the house of Israel, does not defile his neighbor's wife or approach a woman in her time of impurity, 7 does not oppress any one, but restores to the debtor his pledge, commits no robbery, gives his bread to the hungry and covers the naked with a garment, 8 does not lend at interest or take any increase, withholds his hand from iniquity, executes true justice between man and man, 9 walks in my statutes, and is careful to observe my ordinances—

hand from iniquity, hath executed true judgment between man and man,

9 Hath walked in my statutes, and hath kept my judgments, to deal truly; he *is* just, he shall surely live, saith the Lord GOD.

10 If he beget a son *that* is a robber, a shedder of blood, and *that* doeth the like to *any* one of these *things,*

11 And that doeth not any of those *duties,* but even hath eaten upon the mountains, and defiled his neighbour's wife,

12 Hath oppressed the poor and needy, hath spoiled by violence, hath not restored the pledge, and hath lifted up his eyes to the idols, hath committed abomination,

13 Hath given forth upon usury, and hath taken increase: shall he then live? he shall not live: he hath done all these abominations; he shall surely die; his blood shall be upon him.

. . . .

25 Yet ye say, The way of the Lord is not equal. Hear now, O house of Israel; Is not my way equal? are not your ways unequal?

. . . .

30 Therefore I will judge you, O house of Israel, every one according to his ways, saith the Lord GOD. Repent, and turn *yourselves* from all your transgressions; so iniquity shall not be your ruin.

Key Verse: **I have no pleasure in the death of him that dieth, saith the Lord GOD: Wherefore turn *yourselves,* and live ye. (Ezekiel 18:32)**

he is righteous, he shall surely live, says the Lord GOD.

10 "If he begets a son who is a robber, a shedder of blood, 11 who does none of these duties, but eats upon the mountains, defiles his neighbor's wife, 12 oppresses the poor and needy, commits robbery, does not restore the pledge, lifts up his eyes to the idols, commits abomination, 13 lends at interest, and takes increase; shall he then live? He shall not live. He has done all these abominable things; he shall surely die; his blood shall be upon himself."

. . . .

25 "Yet you say, 'The way of the Lord is not just.' Hear now, O house of Israel: Is my way not just? Is it not your ways that are not just?"

. . . .

30 "Therefore I will judge you, O house of Israel, every one according to his ways, says the Lord GOD. Repent and turn from all your transgressions, lest iniquity be your ruin."

Key Verse: **I have no pleasure in the death of any one, says the Lord GOD; so turn, and live. (Ezekiel 18:32)**

The Scripture and the Main Question—William H. Willimon

The Sins of the Parents

It is an awesome task to be a parent, frightening too. It is frightening to realize how influential parents can be over the development of their children. So we parents must do the best we can to make wise decisions and to set the best example we can for our children.

Yet there comes that time in our children's lives when we must say, in effect, "You're on your own now. We have given you what we could. We have done our best, but we have made many mistakes and, looking back, we might have done many things differently, but that's all behind us now. Now you must stand on your own two feet and take responsibility for your own life."

At the bar mitzvah ceremony when a Jewish boy reaches adolescence, the parents present their son to the community with the statement that they have done their best to educate their child into the Jewish way of life. Then the parents give their child to God as an adult. The child is given responsibilities to perform in the family and in the synagogue, then the parents offer a prayer which says, in so many words, "God, we thank you for relieving us of the responsibility of this child."

Some have said that we Christians need something similar to the bar mitzvah, some way of telling our children that they have now become adults and are now to assume responsibility for their own faith development.

This might be a good idea because it seems to be taking people longer and longer to grow up. Only a few generations ago, people became adults in their early teen years. Parents were forced, due to economic circumstances, to push their children into an apprenticeship or some other job at an early age. The child was forced to go out and earn a living.

Today this process can be postponed indefinitely. Children are free to live at home longer; parents seem to assume economic and personal responsibility for their children longer and longer.

In my own congregation I have noted the tendency—evidently it is a national trend—for young adults to go off to college and then to return home to live with their parents. Some of this has to do with economic uncertainty and problems in finding a good job. But some of it also has to do with a greater sense of dependence which adult children seem to feel on their parents. I suspect that some of these adult children are uncertain about their ability to cope with the world completely on their own, or that they realize that they will not be able to duplicate the comforts of their parents' home. So they stay at home for a longer period of time.

We used to think of adolescence as ending when a person was eighteen years old. Now, we are still able to speak of a person as being an adolescent and displaying adolescent tendencies well into the twenties.

Isn't part of this the unhappy tendency of our society to avoid personal responsibility?

Most of us have given our children so many things. We have given them everything that we did not have while we were growing up—everything but responsibility.

In another time and place, children had more responsibilities for the support and care of the family. On the farm, there were always chores to be done. Today, even in farming, there are fewer things for children to do, fewer meaningful tasks to assign them, so that few children think of themselves as contributing to the well-being of the family. They have no responsibility for the day-to-day life of the family. They are not really responsible to anyone.

Unfortunately, the same sense of irresponsibility is carried over into the society at large.

What can we do to help our young people feel more responsibility for caring for their world and taking charge of their future?

The Righteousness of the Righteous

Ezekiel says, "The son shall not suffer for the iniquity of the father, nor the father suffer for the iniquity of the son; the righteousness of the righteous shall be upon himself, and the wickedness of the wicked shall be upon himself" (18:20).

Elsewhere in Scripture, it is noted that the sins of the parents often influence the lives of the children. We all have seen examples of how parental irresponsibility leads to problems in the lives of the children, problems which may not surface for many years in the life of the child.

But here the case is different. Here Ezekiel notes that God does judge people and hold them accountable for their actions, but that God also begins anew with each generation and lets each generation make its own way. There is a word of freedom here. Future generations are not utterly enslaved to our mistakes. God gives each generation the possibility of new life and fresh options.

As a parent, I am glad to hear this, because I would hate to think that my children's future is completely determined by all my mistakes and all the mistakes of my generation as a whole.

In Israel's situation in Ezekiel's day, one can imagine how comforting his words would be. The present generation had made a mess of the nation. Now they were in exile in a foreign land, wondering if they would ever again see their beloved country. Would their children never know the joys of their own land?

While Ezekiel tells of the tragedies which have come and are yet to come to Israel, he also speaks this word of hope. The children's future shall not be utterly determined by the parents' past.

This seems to me to be an important word to say to our children. We need to convince them that they can learn from our mistakes, that they don't have to simply accept the world as we leave it to them. They have the gifts, the divine help, and the knowledge to do better than we have with the world we received.

Youthful confidence and enthusiasm are a blessed gift to the future. Each new generation is confident that it has what it takes to work with God in making a better world.

So in a sense we are the first generation to struggle with the age-old problems of hunger, war, poverty, racial injustice, and political despotism. We need not believe that any human problem is without a possible solution. Nor need we despair at the state of the world as we inherited it.

The Child Shall Not Suffer for the Iniquity of the Parent

After a couple of decades of experience in counseling troubled people, one gift that I wish I had was the ability to help people grow up and assume their God-given responsibility for their lives. How many times have I heard the cop-out, "If only my mother had let me . . ." or "If someone had just told me to . . ."

True, many of us have come from parents and home situations that were less than ideal. But at some point in our lives, we must put that behind us and begin anew, even as Israel was called to put its tragic past behind it and launch forth into a brighter future—a future that was bright because it was upheld and guided by a loving God.

Helping Adults Become Involved—Herbert H. Lambert

Preparing To Teach

Who is responsible for wrongdoing? Only the person directly involved? What about the person's family and friends, who may have influenced the behavior of the guilty one? What about society as a whole, which contributed to the crime by helping to shape the criminal's character? These questions are as pertinent as the day's news and are often asked today.

All the prophets thundered against the sins of Israel and Judah. The disastrous end of those two nations was blamed on the sins of their peoples. The purpose of Ezekiel 18 was to offer hope that the sins of the past could be forgiven. Each person is responsible only for what he or she does, not for the actions of others or for the sins of former generations. This was a breath of fresh air in a time of despair!

Here is a way to outline this lesson:

I. Belief in inherited guilt
  A. Scriptures supporting this view
  B. Resulting hopelessness
II. Ezekiel's new teaching
  A. Each generation begins anew.
  B. A person can change either way.
  C. Individuals have responsibility.
III. What this means for us
  A. It matters what we decide and do.
  B. God is just and merciful.
  C. We need not be burdened with guilt.
  D. We are held responsible for what we ourselves do.
IV. An appeal to us
  A. What we must avoid
  B. What we must do
  C. A call to responsible action

Suggested readings for this lesson are Ezekiel 18 and *The Interpreter's Concise Commentary*, volume 4, pages 226-67, and *The Interpreter's Bible*, volume 6, pages 157-63.

Introducing the Main Question

In his novel *Armageddon*, Leon Uris tells about life in Germany after World War II. Some Germans who had known about the atrocities under Hitler felt no sense of remorse because, they said, they could not have prevented what happened to the Jews and to others. Some sensitive Germans were so overwhelmed with remorse, even though they were not personally involved, that they became despondent and even suicidal. Others accepted blame and then tried to pull the nation and its people out of the quagmire of guilt. Such different reactions happened among members of the same family. A problem similar to this confronted the people of Judah in Ezekiel's time.

Developing the Lesson

I. Belief in inherited guilt

  A. Scriptures supporting this view

"I the LORD your God am a jealous God, visiting the iniquity of the fathers upon the children to the third and fourth generation (Deuteronomy 5:9). This idea of inherited guilt was common in Old Testament times. Sin has a way of contaminating everyone with whom it is associated. Thus the sinner Achan was destroyed along with his family and even his cattle and his tent (Joshua 7:24).

  B. Resulting hopelessness

Many of those to whom Ezekiel spoke had been mere children when carried into exile in Babylon. Yet they were so overwhelmed by what their parents had done that they saw no way to change themselves or the terrible situation.

II. Ezekiel's new teaching

  A. Each generation begins anew.

What is the meaning of the proverb in Ezekiel 18:2? Have the class read 18:1-18. Note especially verses 14-18. A son cannot be held responsible for what his father has done. How did this truth offer hope to Ezekiel's hearers?

  B. A person can change either way.

Not only can we separate ourselves from our erring parents, but we can also cast off our own unfortunate past through God's forgiveness (18:21-24). Here Ezekiel proclaims the radical freedom of persons to determine their own destiny by obeying God's commands.

  C. Individuals have responsibility.

"The soul [or person] that sins shall die" (18:4). Write this on the chalkboard and discuss it. It sounds scary, but for Ezekiel's time it was a message of hope. It meant: *Only* the person who sins, not his or her children, will suffer.

III. What this means for us

  A. It matters what we decide and do.

Ezekiel believed that we are free to decide our behavior and must therefore accept responsibility for the results. We cannot blame anyone or anything else!

  B. God is just and merciful.

God does not want to trap people in wrongdoing in order to punish them. God wants to guide people into the only behavior that promises life. Note 18:23, 25-29.

  C. We need not be burdened with guilt.

We do not need to brood over the mistakes of the past or to assume we never can change. The future can be different, and we can be different persons, with God's help.

  D. We are held responsible for what we ourselves do.

God is still concerned about our basic loyalties. It still matters whether we abuse and neglect other persons. If we fail to do God's will, we cut ourselves off from God and from life.

Ezekiel's message is both hopeful and demanding. He made it clear that God still cares what we do. He said we must accept responsibility for our own lives and stop worrying about what others have done or failed to do.

Helping Class Members Act

IV. *An appeal to us*

A. *What we must avoid*

Ezekiel would tell us to lift up our heads and stop feeling bad because of our parents' mistakes or the unfortunate childhood we had or our own past sins. Stop feeling sorry for yourselves, the prophet warns.

B. *What we must do*

The prophet gives clear details about what he considers necessary for persons to live in God's kingdom. We must not rob or kill. We must not exploit the poor. We must serve God alone, not idols. We must feed the hungry and clothe the naked. Read Ezekiel 18:14-17, and make a list of acts we could do today to fulfill Ezekiel's command. This might include visiting the sick, respecting marriage commitments, driving with care to avoid injuring persons, etc.

C. *A call to responsible action*

If we fail to live up to the demands set forth by Ezekiel, it will be because we do not think they are important or because we think we cannot carry them out. Either we fail to take them seriously or we regard them as so difficult that we can never measure up. Ezekiel wants us to recognize that God has given us the power to do right and that we need not give up—either on ourselves or on God! God will forgive and help us if we make a sincere effort to do what is right.

On the chalkboard, list some responsible actions we can take in the light of what we have learned in this lesson (1) in the place where we work, (2) in relation to other members of our family, and (3) in our church life. By "responsible actions" we mean acts that show we are concerned and believe something can be done to make things better. We reject both the attitude of unconcern on the one hand, and despair on the other hand. These are the two mistaken ideas Ezekiel emphasized in chapter 18 of his book.

Planning for Next Sunday

Have the class members read Ezekiel 22 during the following week. Ask them to write out a few things Ezekiel would probably say about the wrongs in our own nation today if he were to return and speak to us.

LESSON 9   JULY 27

God's Charges Against a Corrupt Society

Background Scripture: Ezekiel 22

The Main Question—William H. Willimon

I wonder what our forebears would think of our country if they could somehow return and walk modern American streets. I wonder what those who sacrificed and worked to found a new nation where "liberty and justice for all" were to be a reality would conclude. Undoubtedly, they would be impressed by the technological and material progress we have made—skyscrapers and jetports, computers and superhighways are all a far cry from their log cabins, one-acre farms, and rustic villages.

Yet, though we have learned to fly like birds, to float through the water better than fish; to build and travel better than any of the animals, we have not yet learned to live like human beings. The threats of war, the acts of violence and oppression which caused our great-grandparents to flee their native lands and come to America have intensified rather than lessened.

The founding dream of a land of "liberty and justice for all" is still just that—a dream. The poor we still have with us; racial prejudice and violence exist in our streets; vast amounts of our national resources still go for the making of war rather than for the building of peace.

So what would our pioneering fathers and mothers think of us today? In what ways would they think that we had fulfilled their dreams? In what ways would they think that we had betrayed their sacrifices and struggles with our present American society?

The pilgrims came to these shores to, in their words, found a "light to the nations, a beacon in the wilderness." They believed that they were instituting something new and inspiring, a nation that would be an example to others. They also thought that they were recovering the ancient vision of a just and God-fearing people.

When the yardstick of God's justice and righteousness is set next to our land, what is the verdict concerning us?

As You Read the Scripture—Howard P. Colson

Ezekiel's most detailed indictment of Jerusalem and Judah is found in chapter 22. Verses 1-16 tell of Jerusalem's crimes; verses 17-22 describe the Lord's smelting furnace and predict the coming punishment; verses 23-31 set forth the sins of Israel's leaders and people. Much of the material in verses 1-16 is very similar to what we found in last Sunday's lesson.

Ezekiel 22:3. The wicked rulers were guilty of unjustly putting people to death. Compare Ezekiel 11:6. The sins of murder and idolatry are here grouped together. This could mean that human sacrifices were offered to foreign gods. It was as if Jerusalem were sinning for the purpose of hastening the time of her punishment. The situation was desperate.

Verse 4. Here again murder and idolatry are grouped together. The people should have repented, but they did not. They seemed bent on bringing about the city's destruction. Surrounding countries would look with scorn on Israel.

Verses 23-29. This is an orderly indictment of four groups: princes, priests, prophets, and people. The princes were the governing officials. Instead of governing justly, protecting their subjects and promoting their welfare, they were destroying them (verses 25 and 27). The priests had the duty of teaching the people God's law (see Leviticus 10:10-11), but instead they perverted and profaned it (verse 26). The prophets were supposed to proclaim God's message, but they were prophesying falsehoods (verse 28). The people of the land, instead of living righteously, were guilty of extortion, robbery, and oppression of the poor and the strangers within their midst (verse 29).

Verse 24. Ezekiel here speaks to the entire country. "Not cleansed" refers to the bad moral conditions. There were no refreshing showers. This is a figurative way of saying that the springs of spiritual devotion and social concern had dried up.

Verse 25. The officials were fierce in committing judicial murders. They were dishonest, misusing their offices for the sake of making personal gain.

Verse 26. In perverting and profaning God's law the "priests made no distinction between the unclean and the clean." They also disregarded the sabbath.

Verse 28. The false prophets covered over the sins of the priests instead of exposing them.

Verse 29. "The people of the land" were not the poor peasants. "The people of the land" oppressed the poor and the stranger "without redress" and denied them justice.

Verse 30. God wanted a man to stand against the tide of evil, for he longed to spare the nation. But he found no such man. What about Jeremiah? To be sure, Jeremiah might have seemed the most likely one, but even he was despised and rejected. The sins and the rebellion of the nation were so great that Jeremiah's brave warnings were of no avail.

Verse 31. What could the Lord do? There was nothing left for him to do except to visit Jerusalem with destruction. "I have consumed them with the fire of my wrath." God speaks here as if his judgment were already accomplished. It was really that certain.

Selected Scripture

King James Version	Revised Standard Version
Ezekiel 22:3-4, 23-31	*Ezekiel 22:3-4, 23-31*
3 Then say thou, Thus saith the Lord GOD, The city sheddeth blood in the midst of it, that her time may come, and maketh idols against herself to defile herself.	3 "You shall say, Thus says the Lord GOD: A city that sheds blood in the midst of her, that her time may come, and that makes idols to defile herself! 4 You have become guilty by the blood which you have shed, and defiled by the idols which you have made; and you have brought your day near, the appointed time of your years has come. Therefore I have made you a reproach to the nations, and a mocking to all countries."
4 Thou art become guilty in thy blood that thou hast shed; and hast defiled thyself in thine idols which thou hast made; and thou hast caused thy days to draw near, and art come *even* unto thy years: therefore have I made thee a reproach unto the heathen, and a mocking to all countries.	
....	....
23 And the word of the LORD came unto me, saying,	23 And the word of the LORD came to me: 24 "Son of man, say to her, You are a land that is not cleansed, or rained upon in the day of indignation. 25 Her princes in the midst of her are like a roaring lion tearing the prey; they have devoured human lives; they have taken treasure and precious things; they have made many widows in the midst of her. 26 Her priests have
24 Son of man, say unto her, Thou *art* the land that is not cleansed, nor rained upon in the day of indignation.	
25 *There is* a conspiracy of her prophets in the midst thereof, like a roaring lion ravening the prey; they have devoured souls; they have taken the treasure and precious	

things; they have made her many widows in the midst thereof.

26 Her priests have violated my law, and have profaned mine holy things: they have put no difference between the holy and profane, neither have they shewed *difference* between the unclean and the clean, and have hid their eyes from my sabbaths, and I am profaned among them.

27 Her princes in the midst thereof *are* like wolves ravening the prey, to shed blood, *and* to destroy souls, to get dishonest gain.

28 And her prophets have daubed them with untempered *mortar,* seeing vanity, and divining lies unto them, saying, Thus saith the Lord God, when the Lord hath not spoken.

29 The people of the land have used oppression, and exercised robbery, and have vexed the poor and needy: yea, they have oppressed the stranger wrongfully.

30 And I sought for a man among them, that should make up the hedge, and stand in the gap before me for the land, that I should not destroy it: but I found none.

31 Therefore have I poured out mine indignation upon them; I have consumed them with the fire of my wrath: their own way have I recompensed upon their heads, saith the Lord God.

done violence to my law and have profaned my holy things; they have made no distinction between the holy and the common, neither have they taught the difference between the unclean and the clean, and they have disregarded my sabbaths, so that I am profaned among them. 27 Her princes in the midst of her are like wolves tearing the prey, shedding blood, destroying lives to get dishonest gain. 28 And her prophets have daubed for them with whitewash, seeing false visions and divining lies for them, saying, 'Thus says the Lord God,' when the Lord has not spoken. 29 The people of the land have practiced extortion and committed robbery; they have oppressed the poor and needy, and have extorted from the sojourner without redress. 30 And I sought for a man among them who should build up the wall and stand in the breach before me for the land, that I should not destroy it; but I found none. 31 Therefore I have poured out my indignation upon them; I have consumed them with the fire of my wrath; their way have I requited upon their heads, says the Lord God."

Key Verse: I sought for a man among them, that should make up the hedge, and stand in the gap before me for the land, that I should not destroy it: but I found none. (Ezekiel 22:30)

Key Verse: I sought for a man among them who should build up the wall and stand in the breach before me for the land, that I should not destroy it; but I found none. (Ezekiel 22:30)

The Scripture and the Main Question—William H. Willimon

A Reproach to the Nations

In some ways it might have been easier for Israel if it had not been chosen by God for deliverance from Egyptian slavery. For the Israelites quickly found that God chooses not only for blessings but also for responsibilities. Israel had been brought out of slavery so that it could be a "light to the nations."

Now, a few centuries later, it is all different. The people who were to have been a light to guide others have become "a reproach to the nations" (22:4), a warning to other peoples of what happens when a nation forgets its destiny and its purpose.

Ezekiel's words indict Israel for a whole list of transgressions: idolatry, abuse of aliens, profanation of the sabbath, violence, lewdness, immorality, extortion, mistreatment of the poor.

We know too well, in our individual lives, how it is possible for us as individuals to forget our purpose in life, to get off track in our direction. Youthful dreams and ideals are so easily corrupted. We lose sight of our goals and allow the unimportant things to crowd out the important things.

She went to college to become a doctor. The study was difficult and demanding, but she worked hard and did well. She not only did her academic work but also worked part time in a nearby laboratory to earn funds for her education since she had come from a family of very limited means.

When people asked her what she planned to do with her education and her medical degree once she finished, she said that she wanted to treat the poor, the people whom she had learned to feel pity for when her church youth group went on a mission trip one summer. She saw her life as a life of mission and helping the sick who were so often forgotten by the medical establishment.

But then, when she finally completed her work, she thought about how hard she had worked for her degree. She remembered all the long hours, burning the midnight oil, the sacrifices, and the cost. "Maybe I might go into private practice for just a few years," she thought to herself, "until I pay back the money I borrowed, then I will go out to help the poor."

But the years went by. Then she had car payments, a mortgage, other responsibilities, and besides, the well-to-do need help too, don't they? So she never did go out to help the poor. She had good intentions, really and sincerely wanted to help, but you know how it goes.

Yes, we do know how it goes because it has happened to nearly all of us. We set out with a dream, with some purpose in life, some calling, and then we lose sight of where we are going, we compromise our ideals, we give in to other competing visions.

What happened in the national life of Israel in Ezekiel's day is acted out in our own individual lives in our day.

A Mocking to All the Countries

It also happens to our nation, this process of compromising our original visions.

When we look back at our glorious past, the pilgrim forebears, the signers of the Declaration of Independence, the revolutionaries, those who risked everything in the cause of freedom and justice, we cannot help raising questions about our present national situation.

The people that once fought power and tyrannical oppression now finds itself in the position of being the most powerful nation on earth. With that power sometimes come belligerence and oppression of others who are weaker.

Alas, many other nations look upon us not as a bastion of democracy and justice, but as an international bully which manipulates other countries for our own economic and military gain. Our multinational corporations are often looked upon as agencies of economic tyranny, victimizing the poor of other countries in order to enrich ourselves at home.

Of course, we feel that many of these charges are unfair to us and our nation. But surely, if we are honest, we can understand why other nations might think these things about us. Sometimes we know that they are justified in looking at us as international bullies. We say that we are defending them and their interests when in reality we are looking after ourselves. We see ourselves as a democratic, free people and yet we support and aid despotic dictatorships elsewhere because it suits our self-interest to do so.

Thus, to many other countries, we are looked upon not as a friend and an ally of freedom, but as a nation that offers slogans and hypocrisy instead of true good will. We thus mock the very principles which we thought we were defending.

Because we are free, because we have a democratic form of government, do we not have a solemn obligation to witness to truth, to resist every form of political and governmental oppression, and to model those structures of justice in our own country which shall be a light to the rest of the nations?

A black pastor whom I know recalled how strange it felt to come back home after World War II, having risked his life to fight for freedom against Nazi tyranny, to get off the troop ship and see "Whites Only" signs in the first American city he visited and to be discriminated against by many people. This discrimination and racial prejudice mocked our pretensions of justice.

Israel thought itself to be a holy nation, but its immorality, idolatry, and sin had made it a nation which was mocked and ridiculed by its neighbors.

I Have Poured Out My Indignation

The Lord looks upon the Chosen People and is angry. The people who have been given so much have betrayed God's gifts. They have proved unworthy of divine trust. Therefore divine wrath and indignation are kindled against them.

If the Lord looked upon the United States, what would the Lord's prophets say to us? Of course, there would be many things which the Lord might take pleasure in. But there would also be many things that would anger a just and righteous God. How is it that the richest nation in the world still has problems with poverty among some of its citizens?

Helping Adults Become Involved—Herbert H. Lambert
Preparing to Teach

Ezekiel 22 is a detailed account of the sins of the people and leaders of Judah. It tells of the coming destruction of Jerusalem. As a priest, Ezekiel was more concerned about purity than were most of the other prophets. We will see why he criticized the prophets, priests, princes, and people of Jerusalem. We will ask what his message might be to us in our time.

Here is a way to outline this lesson:

> I. Detailed list of wrongs
> A. Sins of the princes
> B. Sins of the priests
> C. Sins of the prophets
> D. Sins of the people

II. Consequences of sin
   A. Destruction of Jerusalem
   B. Scattering of the people
   C. "You shall know that I am the Lord"
III. What are our wrongdoings?
   A. Of political leaders?
   B. Of religious leaders?
   C. Of church members?
IV. Someone to stand in the breach
   A. The concept explained
   B. Standing in the breach today

An explanation of Ezekiel 22 may be found in *The Interpreter's Concise Commentary,* volume 4, pages 275-76, and in *The Interpreter's Bible,* volume 6, pages 182-89.

Introducing the Main Question

A minister was invited to speak at a college which was known for its stringent rules. He began by saying: "Being against dancing, drinking, smoking, and card-playing is a monumental waste of time!" A ripple of applause from the students and frowns from the faculty followed. The minister then explained that the time we waste in concern about these matters might better be spent opposing the evils that really harm us and in doing the things that really fulfill God's purposes. He was not inviting the students to do whatever they wished, but was calling them to what he believed to be a higher purpose.

What are the evils that really matter in our world today? What is destructive about the policies of government and the attitudes of citizens? What would Ezekiel condemn if he spent some time with us in 1986?

Developing the Lesson

I. Detailed list of wrongs
(Put this list on the chalkboard and discuss each item.)

A. Sins of the princes
Ezekiel gives a detailed description of the sins of various groups in Judah. The princes, members of the royal family, "are like wolves tearing the prey" (verse 27). They use their position to enrich themselves and to steal from those who have less power. We are reminded of Queen Jezebel and King Ahab, who arranged for the killing of Naboth in order to take his vineyard (I Kings 21). Like the other prophets, Ezekiel held rulers responsible for their use of power. God demands that they use it for the good of persons and not for their own purposes.

B. Sins of the priests
Being a priest himself, Ezekiel knew about the wrongs of this group. The priests were careless about purity and about separating the holy from the profane. As a student I visited a church and asked to see the minister after worship. He sat in a pew, lit a cigarette, and began dropping his ashes in the communion cup. Maybe it was a small thing, but it made me wonder if anything was sacred for this man.

C. Sins of the prophets
"Her prophets have daubed for them with whitewash" (verse 28). Whitewash provides a temporary cover for dirt and deterioration. It is a way

to put off dealing with real problems. The prophets of Judah told the people nothing was seriously wrong with them and that God would take care of them. This made the prophets popular, but it did not lead to reform.

D. *Sins of the people*

The people of Judah had committed robbery, especially against the poor and alien (verse 29). It is interesting that aliens were protected by God's law, even though they were not strictly a part of the people of Israel. This shows God's concern for the well-being of all peoples.

II. *Consequences of sin*

A. *Destruction of Jerusalem*

Although Ezekiel was in Babylon, he was concerned about Jerusalem because both he and his hearers hoped to return to it. The prophet said that God would melt the city like metal in a very hot furnace. He referred to the destruction of Jerusalem and its temple in 587 B.C.

B. *Scattering of the people*

Still more of Judah's leading citizens were taken to Babylon in 587 B.C. Others, including Jeremiah, went to Egypt and elsewhere. The dispersion of the Jews had begun before this, but the destruction of their chief city accelerated the trend. Some Christians wrongly regard the scattering of Jews as a punishment for their rejecting Jesus, but it began long before the birth of Jesus.

C. *"You shall know that I am the Lord"*

This means to recognize the power of God. When the Egyptians were defeated and the Israelites escaped into the desert, the Egyptians knew God's power (Exodus 14:18). The Israelites also knew God's power when they saw the signs God performed (Exodus 10:2). Both those who receive God's blessing and those who defy God's will must learn to respect God's rule.

III. *What are our wrongdoings?*

(Enlist the help of class members in deciding what these are.)

A. *Of political leaders?*

Taking bribes and using drugs occasionally earn headlines for political leaders. There are wrongs that do not get publicity but may be worse, such as defaming an opponent with malicious falsehood or ignoring the needs and rights of citizens. How do national and state leaders harm persons by the laws they support or refuse to support?

B. *Of religious leaders?*

Ezekiel warned against prophets who try to put a good face on bad circumstances. Do some religious leaders overlook wrong in order to be popular? Do our religious leaders mix the sacred and the secular in a way that harms the holiness of their work? Give examples.

C. *Of church members?*

A reporter put on the garb of a vagrant. He went into some churches and was snubbed. Some church people gave him food but also a big hassle. He said the only people who treated him like a human being were other vagrants. How do church people treat outsiders, especially those who are in need? How do church members treat one another?

Helping Class Members Act

IV. *Someone to stand in the breach*

A. *The concept explained*

God planned an invasion and looked for someone to oppose it! God wanted someone to protect the people and to intercede for them. But no one appeared, either because no one took the danger seriously or because there was no one righteous enough to stand before God, as Abraham did when he pleaded for the people of Sodom (Genesis 18:22-33).

B. *Standing in the breach today?*

How can we prevent evil from coming upon our nation and its people? What can an individual do to work for justice and peace? to prevent the destruction of our environment? List some examples.

Planning for Next Sunday

Have class members read Ezekiel 36, written after Jerusalem was destroyed. How does Ezekiel's message here differ from the ones already studied? How is it similar to the earlier ones?

LESSON 10   AUGUST 3

God's Promises of Renewal

Background Scripture: Ezekiel 36

The Main Question—William H. Willimon

"God has been testing me through the time of my illness. It has been a tough, difficult time for me, but now that it's all over, I feel that I am a better person because of it. I have a new outlook on life and I feel a lot closer to God."

This is what a person said to me the other day, at the end of a long and difficult illness. She was saying that her illness, her time of struggle and difficulty, had actually helped her and had made her a better person.

While I may not believe that God sends sickness and problems to us in order to teach us a lesson or to make us better people, I do believe that God is able to use even the worst of circumstances to bring about some good. I feel that this is what this woman was talking about. God had used even her time of illness to make her a better person with a new outlook on life.

Isn't it interesting that some of our worst times can lead to goodness? Sometimes a severe crisis in life turns us around, sets us back in the right direction, puts things into focus, and helps us see life differently than we would have without the crisis.

When this happens, we can say that this is the work of God—not necessarily that God sent the crisis to us, but rather that God used even the worst of circumstances to bring about good results.

We have noted this dynamic at work in our own individual lives. In today's lesson, we shall see it at work in the life of Israel as Israel is promised renewal after its national downfall.

As You Read the Scripture—Howard P. Colson

This lesson is from the final section of Ezekiel, which deals with the return of Israel to Palestine (chapters 33–48).

In order to gain the best understanding of the lesson, it is important to know that in the Old Testament the Hebrew name which is rendered "the Lord" is *Yahweh*. It is from the verb meaning "to be" and is the name of the God of Israel. As used, it means "he causes to be" or "he is" or "he will be." (The editor, Horace R. Weaver, follows Gerhard von Rad's interpretation of the verb as "I [Yahweh] am/have been/will be with you" as needed.)

The lesson passage predicts that Yahweh will bring about the return of Israel to its homeland. He will give the people a new heart and a new spirit, and the land will produce abundantly. Yahweh will bring this about not for Israel's sake but for his own sake.

At that time each nation had its own god or gods. Yahweh was the God of the Hebrews in Palestine. He had sent Israel into exile because of their sins, but the neighboring nations did not realize that this was the case. Israel's exile was regarded by those nations as evidence that Yahweh was not able to save his people. Thus the exiles had brought about the desecration of Yahweh. In order to demonstrate his sovereign power and holiness, it as necessary for him to restore them to their homeland. Their return would prove to the nations that he was not the powerless God they thought him to be.

The passage predicts that Israel will remember her evil ways and loathe herself. Yahweh pleads with Israel to recognize her shameful ways.

Ezekiel 36:22. "For the sake of my holy name" is the key phrase of the passage. Israel will not be restored because she deserves to be; rather, she will be Yahweh's instrument to teach the nations the great truth that he is sovereign and powerful.

Verse 23. Israel's restoration and renewal will prove that Yahweh is a holy God. Only Yahweh could accomplish such a result.

Verse 24. The outward proof of Israel's salvation would be the return to Palestine, but the inward change of Israel's character was the basic goal God had in mind.

Verses 25-27. The experience by which the people would be spiritually renewed is predicted. They would be cleansed of the impurities they had contracted by past sins (verse 25). This, of course, implies forgiveness. And they would be regenerated by being given a new heart and a new spirit (verse 26). (Note: the heart, in Hebrew, means the seat of volition, conscious, attitudes, motives.) God would put his own Spirit within them with the result that they would then keep the requirements of his law (verse 27). When these conditions became a reality, Israel would be completely restored to Yahweh. They would be his people, and he would be their God (verse 28).

Verses 29-30. These verses speak of the blessings of nature that the returned exiles would experience in their homeland.

Verse 31. The Lord says, "You will loathe yourselves." The people's experience of God's goodness in restoring them would make them ashamed of the way they had treated him. His forgiveness would create in them regret and repentance. They would remember their past history and contrast it with their present blessings. This would keep them from repeating their disloyalty to Yahweh.

Verse 32. "Not for your sake" repeats and emphasizes the thought of verse 22. However, we should not fail to realize that Yahweh loved his people. "Be ashamed and confounded" is Yahweh's plea that Israel should recognize that his restoration of them was the result not of their merit but of his grace.

Selected Scripture

King James Version

Revised Standard Version

Ezekiel 36:22-32

22 Therefore say unto the house of Israel, Thus saith the Lord God; I do not *this* for your sakes, O house of Israel, but for mine holy name's sake, which ye have profaned among the heathen, whither ye went.

23 And I will sanctify my great name, which was profaned among the heathen, which ye have profaned in the midst of them; and the heathen shall know that I *am* the Lord, saith the Lord God, when I shall be sanctified in you before their eyes.

24 For I will take you from among the heathen, and gather you out of all countries, and will bring you into your own land.

25 Then will I sprinkle clean water upon you, and ye shall be clean: from all your filthiness, and from all your idols, will I cleanse you.

26 A new heart also will I give you, and a new spirit will I put within you: and I will take away the stony heart out of your flesh, and I will give you an heart of flesh.

27 And I will put my spirit within you, and cause you to walk in my statutes, and ye shall keep my judgments, and do *them.*

28 And ye shall dwell in the land that I gave to your fathers; and ye shall be my people, and I will be your God.

29 I will also save you from all your uncleannesses: and I will call for the corn, and will increase it, and lay no famine upon you.

30 And I will multiply the fruit of the tree, and the increase of the field, that ye shall receive no more reproach of famine among the heathen.

31 Then shall ye remember your

Ezekiel 36:22-32

22 "Therefore say to the house of Israel, Thus says the Lord God: It is not for your sake, O house of Israel, that I am about to act, but for the sake of my holy name, which you have profaned among the nations to which you came. 23 And I will vindicate the holiness of my great name, which has been profaned among the nations, and which you have profaned among them; and the nations will know that I am the Lord, says the Lord God, when through you I vindicate my holiness before their eyes. 24 For I will take you from the nations, and gather you from all the countries, and will bring you into your own land. 25 I will sprinkle clean water upon you, and you shall be clean from all your uncleannesses, and from all your idols I will cleanse you. 26 A new heart I will give you, and a new spirit I will put within you and I will take out of your flesh the heart of stone and give you a heart of flesh. 27 And I will put my spirit within you, and cause you to walk in my statutes and be careful to observe my ordinances. 28 You shall dwell in the land which I gave to your fathers; and you shall be my people, and I will be your God. 29 And I will deliver you from all your uncleannesses; and I will summon the grain and make it abundant and lay no famine upon you. 30 I will make the fruit of the tree and the increase of the field abundant, that you may never again suffer the disgrace of famine among the nations. 31 Then you will remember your evil ways, and your deeds that were not good; and you will loathe yourselves for your iniquities and your abominable deeds. 32 It is not for your sake that I will act, says the Lord God; let that be

own evil ways, and your doings that *were* not good, and shall loathe yourselves in your own sight for your iniquities and for your abominations.

32 Not for your sakes do I *this*, saith the Lord God, be it known unto you: be ashamed and confounded for your own ways, O house of Israel.

known to you. Be ashamed and confounded for your ways, O house of Israel."

Key Verse: **A new heart also will I give you, and a new spirit will I put within you: and I will take away the stony heart out of your flesh, and I will give you an heart of flesh. (Ezekiel 36:26)**

Key Verse: **A new heart I will give you, and a new spirit I will put within you; and I will take out of your flesh the heart of stone and give you a heart of flesh. (Ezekiel 36:26)**

The Scripture and the Main Question—William H. Willimon

I Will Vindicate My Holiness

Through many angry chapters of the book of Ezekiel, we read of the judgment of God against an unfaithful nation, a nation which had been given so much by God but had responded with such ingratitude.

The mood shifts here in chapter 36 of Ezekiel. "I am about to act," says God, "but not for your sake."

God is still angry with the nation. God does not want the nation to believe that it is out of pity or lack of standards or any other reason that action is coming. Rather, "I will vindicate the holiness of my great name, which has been profaned among the nations, and which you have profaned among them; and the nations will know that I am the Lord" (Ezekiel 36:23).

One might expect that the Lord's holiness would be vindicated by some searing act of wrath and condemnation. But that is not the case. God's holiness is to be vindicated by compassion.

Israel, fully deserving wrath and condemnation from its God, receives, as was so often the case in its long history, the love and salvation of its God.

The people whom God has continued to love with an everlasting love shall be scattered, but not forever. "For I will take you from the nations, and gather you from all the countries, and bring you into your own land. I will sprinkle clean water upon you, and you shall be clean from all your uncleannesses" (36:24-25). The image is tender, maternal, and compassionate.

I think that when most of us hear the phrase "the holiness of God," we tend to think in terms of aloofness, power, justice, judgment, and distance. But here the stress is different. Divine holiness, the otherness of God, is precisely in the way that God forgives and loves—quite in contrast to the way that you and I usually respond when someone has wronged us.

The Chosen People do not cease being the chosen ones. The same divine love which brought them out of bondage in Egypt shall continue to preserve them because God's only desire is that "you shall be my people, and I will be your God" (36:28).

Let this be the sign of God's holiness to all the peoples of the world. Let this be the certain proof that God is great, good, and righteous—God forgives and preserves even in the midst of our wrongs, or sin, and our infidelity.

With what images do you see the holiness of God in your own life? Do you see the aloof and uncaring judge who sits on a throne looking down upon wayward humanity? Or do you see the shepherd who searches until the one lost sheep is found, the waiting father who waits until the one lost son has returned, the mother hen who gathers her brood beneath her wings, the wronged friend who forgives seven times only to forgive seven times seven?

What might it then mean for you and me to image the holiness of God in our lives? We are called to be a holy people, a righteous people. What does this mean, then, when we are wronged? What might this say about the way we conduct our criminal justice system, our international affairs, and other activities of state?

The holiness of God may be a much more dynamic, much more compassionate matter than we at first imagine.

A New Heart I Will Give You

And so we find Israel, in the midst of a gloomy and desperate situation, looking to its God and taking heart. The nation shall come forth from this crisis strengthened, sadder perhaps, but much wiser.

I have seen it happen in much the same way in people's lives. Someone goes through a painful breakup of a marriage. He or she had not wished for something like this to happen. It may take its toll on the person's emotional and physical strength. But, looking back from the vantage point of the years, that person sees that he or she grew in the process. Lessons were learned that might have been impossible to learn any other way. Maturity was achieved, though the way to it was most painful.

"I'm not the same person I was when I flunked out of college two years ago," she said to me. Now I could see that she was more mature, that at last she seemed to have some much-needed direction in her life.

The 1960s were rough, trying times for many of us in our nation. The Vietnam War, the civil rights movement. During the course of those years, we learned some painful things about our shortcomings as a nation. There were many incidents of unrest and violence. Undoubtedly many people would have liked to avoid the whole decade. Many more were moved to despair over the future, to cynicism about their nation. Yet I like to think that we emerged from this difficult period as a better people. Our laws are now more just; our grasp of the international situation is more mature. We have grown in spite of the pain. Maybe there's never much growth without the pain.

Of course, one person goes through a difficult time—say a painful illness—and grows to be a better person; another person experiences the same illness but is defeated by it and is left cynical and bitter. What is the difference?

I think the difference is often our relationship with God. If we really believe that God is good and wills the best for us, if we believe that God never gives up on us and is always working in our lives to bring us closer to himself, then even the worst crises and calamities can be redeemed. We can come through them with a sense of victory because God comes through them with us.

It truly is as if we have a new heart in us, given to us by the love of the God who stands beside us in our difficult days.

I Will Be Your God

Being the people of God does not guarantee that life will always be good to us. All of us know that. To say that I am a Christian does not mean that I am immune to the tragedies, heartaches, and difficulties which beset those who are not Christians. What it does mean is that I go through those tragedies and heartaches with a sense that I am loved by a love that does not let me go, a love that wants to work with me to wrest goodness out of evil, light out of darkness.

"You shall be my people, and I will be your God," the Lord promises us (36:28). That is the promise which leads to renewal, even in the midst of defeat.

Helping Adults Become Involved—Herbert H. Lambert

Preparing to Teach

Both Jeremiah and Ezekiel began their work with proclamations of doom. After Jerusalem fell and the people were dispersed, both prophets expressed hope of restoration. The hopeful words of Ezekiel are found chiefly in chapters 33–48.

Ezekiel 36 foresees a time when the people will be restored to their homeland and renewed by the Spirit of God. It is important for us to note the motivation for God's action. It is not because the people have changed and have paid for their misdeeds. It is to protect the reputation of God among the nations. God acts to redeem Israel for the sake of God's name and to protect God's holiness. What does this tell us about God's faithfulness and mercy toward persons today?

Here is a way to outline the lesson:

I. Situation reversals promised
  A. Punish enemies
  B. Bring the people home
  C. Renew the people
II. Purpose of God's action
  A. For the sake of God's name
  B. An example of God's grace
III. A new heart and a new spirit
IV. Grounds for our hope today
  A. Not in ourselves
  B. Hope based on God

Suggested additional readings are found in *The Interpreter's Concise Commentary*, volume 4, pages 291-92, and *The Interpreter's Bible*, volume 6, pages 260-66.

Introducing the Main Question

On the chalkboard write the statement made by Dr. Willimon near the beginning of this lesson: "I believe that God is able to use even the worst of circumstances to bring about some good." Under this rubric list some circumstances that could have adverse results: illness, accident, death, divorce, etc. Have the class members help you extend this list.

Dr. Willimon does not say that God causes these evils. He writes that God can sometimes use them for good. Look at each of the circumstances you have listed and decide how God might use each for good. Perhaps some of the class members can relate experiences in their own lives when an apparent calamity opened some door of opportunity.

Developing the Lesson

I. Situation reversals promised

   A. *Punish enemies*

The destruction of Jerusalem and the exile of its citizens was a shameful defeat. The traditional enemies of Judah, especially Edom to the south, held God's people up to ridicule. Even harder than the physical hardship was Judah's loss of dignity in the presence of other nations. In Ezekiel 36:1-7, the prophet promises that this will be reversed. The nations who reproached and ridiculed Judah will themselves be crushed and humiliated. This is not one of the best hopes expressed in the Bible, since it is based on vengeance. But in the light of Israel's suffering, it is understandable.

   B. *Bring the people home*

God will cause the exiled and wandering people to return to Jerusalem and to the hills of Judah (36:8-15). Waste places will be planted. Cities will flourish. The population will grow. Instead of a land that kills its people, it will be a land that gives life. Instead of causing disgrace, the land will be a place of joy and hope. This would be a complete reversal of what had happened in the lifetime of Jeremiah and Ezekiel. What would cause Ezekiel to predict such a radical change? How do you think his hearers received it?

   C. *Renew the people*

Have the class members read Ezekiel 36:24-31. Here is something more than simply a return to the land of Judah, something more than national prosperity. What changes within the people did Ezekiel foresee? What did he mean by a "heart of stone" and "heart of flesh" in verse 26? Recall that Ezekiel was a priest and was therefore concerned about cleanliness. What kind of uncleanness did he want to remove from Judah? What kinds of uncleanness would Ezekiel find among us?

II. Purpose of God's action

   A. *For the sake of God's name*

God's reputation had suffered because of what had happened to Israel. The Lord will restore Israel in order to protect and restore God's reputation, not because Israel has done anything to deserve help. God's mighty acts reveal who God is—a Lord of power and of mercy. Because Israel had suffered and had been scattered, people said their God was helpless. But it was not true, and God would act to reveal the real situation. Can people look at our lives and say, "What a wonderful God works through that person!"? How does God reveal power and mercy through our lives?

   B. *An example of God's grace*

All through this chapter Ezekiel makes clear that God has not forgotten and does not treat lightly the people's sins. This may sound discouraging, but it isn't. God will bless this people because of who God is, not because of what they have done or said. Our best hope is in God's grace, not in our own ability to reform and to remain faithful.

What God does for Christians today is also undeserved. God gives a gift in order to reveal God's name and character. It is not something we can claim because we have been good. We can only receive it gratefully and live by its promise. We sometimes hear the Old Testament disparaged as a "book of law," but here in Ezekiel we find the same basic concept of grace that Jesus and Paul taught.

III. A new heart and a new spirit

Ezekiel hoped for a complete transformation of the people so that they could serve God faithfully. Like Jeremiah, he dreamed of a complete change of heart. Instead of being rebellious as in the past, the people would be faithful to God. Instead of being defiled by idols, they would be pure in thought and deed. Ezekiel 36:28-30 emphasizes the transformation of the people as well as the increase in prosperity. One without the other is not enough, wrote Oliver Goldsmith in "The Deserted Village":

> Ill fares the land, to hastening ills a prey,
> Where wealth accumulates, and men decay.

Helping Class Members Act

IV. Grounds for our hope today

A. Not in ourselves

There are many reasons for discouragement in 1986: the arms race, small wars that could quickly escalate into big wars, pollution of our streams and air, worldwide hunger, increase of crime, and the breakdown of traditional values. There is little evidence that we can cope with these problems or even agree on how serious they are! If the future is up to us, it isn't very promising!

Paul Scherer told of a man who scanned the day's papers and exclaimed, "It's almost enough to make me lose my faith in humanity!" Scherer said that faith in humanity wouldn't be a great loss. It's faith in God that really matters. Of course, God does not work by rescuing a few people from disaster and letting the rest stew. God works though people, ordinary people, even through persons who do not acknowledge God. In quiet ways the purposes of God are carried out and God's great name is glorified.

B. Hope based on God

Like Ezekiel, we need not base our hope on human goodness. We can base it on God's love and God's power working through people. God will find a way to use us to create a better world. List some ways in which God is at work in persons to make a better world. Choose two or three of the following questions for class discussion. How is God using news reporters, medical workers, government leaders, homemakers, business leaders, farmers, factory laborers, scientists, space explorers, and others to make a better world? How is God working through Christians? through persons who have other religious views? through persons who have no religious allegiance? How is God working through our nation and its people? through other nations, even those who oppose us as enemies?

Planning for Next Sunday

Have class members read Ezekiel 43:1-12 before the next session. It tells of the prophet's vision of a restored temple. We do not worship God with animal sacrifice in a temple like the one Ezekiel described. How do we worship God? What meaning can this passage have for us?

The next lesson completes our study of the prophet Ezekiel. Suggest that some class members summarize their impressions of this prophet and what message he has for us today.

A Vision of God's Glory

Background Scripture: Ezekiel 43:1-13; 47:1-12

The Main Question—William H. Willimon

When is the occasion when you have felt closest to God? Did it occur when you were sitting on a mountaintop one afternoon at sunset, watching the sun turn ancient hills many colors of red, blue, and gold? Or was it when you walked in a brilliant spring garden, amidst flowering blossoms, radiant trees, and the wonders of nature in bloom? Or was it as you stood beside the raging sea, sensing its power and glory, the foam, the waves, the dark and awesome beauty of the sea in a storm?

The wonders of nature do seem to bring us close to the presence of God. Yet, as Christians, perhaps we most often think of the grandeur of God in times of public worship, when we are gathered with those whom we love in our church and the organ is playing and Sunday morning light is streaming in through stained-glass windows and we are singing one of the great hymns of the church. Perhaps your times of closeness to God are here, in church.

These are the moments—alas, they are too few—when life seems right and it all fits together and we feel that inner peace, that sense of well-being that makes life worth living. For God is the source of life, and to live through such moments is to be in touch with the very source and meaning of life.

Yet moments of closeness to God are not always pleasant. Sometimes it is a fearful thing to fall into the hands of the living God. Sometimes it hurts to be too near the God of Abraham, Isaac, and Jacob.

Moses before the burning bush, Isaiah in the temple at prayer, Ezekiel in the temple as the Lord's glory finally returns to Israel—these are moments full of majesty but also of fear and trembling, containing much glory but also much apprehension. These moments are at the heart of what we call "worship" and are the source of our faith and life.

As You Read the Scripture—Wilbur Lamm

About twenty years after receiving his call by the River Chebar, Ezekiel was ready to bring his final messages of redemption and restoration. The date was probably 573 B.C. Only his faith in God had maintained the prophet.

The main truth in this focal passage, Ezekiel 43:2-12, is that God dwells forever with persons who commit themselves to him.

In vision, Ezekiel was in Jerusalem. A heavenly guide had conducted him around the temple area. At the eastern gate he caught a glimpse of God's glory.

Ezekiel 43:1-3. Ezekiel previously had seen a vision of God's glory departing from the city (10:1-19). Here he witnessed God's return. God's glory was his manifest presence with his people. When God's glory had departed, its course was through the eastern gate. It will return by the same route to bring hope to a despairing and disillusioned people whom God had abandoned because of their sins and corruption (Ezekiel 8:1–11:24).

God's voice sounded familiar to Ezekiel. This sound was like that of

414

"many waters" he had heard by the River Chebar. As God spoke, the earth shone with the effulgence of its Creator.

This vision reminded Ezekiel of two earlier visions of God's presence. One was when God took him to Jerusalem to pronounce judgment on it (Ezekiel 8). The other was God's initial appearance to him by Chebar (Ezekiel 1). Then Ezekiel learned that God was not limited geographically but was indeed present with the captives in Babylon.

In response, Ezekiel fell on his face because one dares not stare at the glory of God. Furthermore, he must be humble in God's presence and recognize his own inferiority. Indeed, he must profess his willingness to hear and obey.

Verses 4-6. The glory of God came from the east to the temple and took residence in the holy of holies. God was not finished with his people or with the temple. God's Spirit brought Ezekiel into the inner court where selected priests served. Ezekiel could see God's glory fill the house, while Ezekiel himself did not infringe on this most sacred place.

Verses 7-9. God addressed Ezekiel as "son of man," which means that the priest was only human, a servant called of God to a special task. God told him three things about the temple. It was the place of God's throne, the place for God's feet, and God's dwelling place. God, who resided in heaven and on earth, would inhabit his temple forever.

God's holy name represented the very being of God. When his people misrepresented him by sinful living, his name was defiled. Specifically, his name had been defiled by sexual immoralities and by burying kings too near the temple precincts. The temple and the palace complex shared a common wall on the south side. Kings lived there who were not faithful to God. Their bodies were buried there, and the area became defiled. Such practices would no longer be allowed.

Verses 10-12. Ezekiel was instructed to tell the people of the plans for the new temple and the laws and ordinances related to it. The reason was to make the people ashamed of their perverseness, sin, and guilt. Ezekiel was to give in full the details of the building and the people were to respond by trust and obedience. They must consider the entire temple complex holy because of the abiding presence of God. Evidently, he saw no need for the ark of the covenant. (The ark and its contents had been taken to Babylon and desecrated there. Its location was later unknown ["lost"].) God would fill the whole area in all his holiness.

Chapter 47:1-12. This allegory of the sacred river flowing out of the temple into the Dead Sea and Arabah teaches how God's presence and his worship will bring blessings to all the land and to the world. God's glory in the temple will renew the whole nation. His glory will renew, restore, and vitalize both land and people. According to Ezekiel, faithfulness to God will be rewarded by material prosperity.

Can we testify about what God's eternal presence means to us?

Selected Scripture

King James Version	Revised Standard Version
Ezekiel 43:2-12	*Ezekiel 43:2-12*
2 And, behold, the glory of the God of Israel came from the way of	2 And behold the glory of the God of Israel came from the east; and the

the east: and his voice *was* like a noise of many waters: and the earth shined with his glory.

3 And *it was* according to the appearance of the vision which I saw, *even* according to the vision that I saw when I came to destroy the city: and the visions *were* like the vision that I saw by the river Chē'-bär; and I fell upon my face.

4 And the glory of the LORD came into the house by the way of the gate whose prospect *is* toward the east.

5 So the spirit took me up, and brought me into the inner court; and, behold, the glory of the LORD filled the house.

6 And I heard *him* speaking unto me out of the house; and the man stood by me.

7 And he said unto me, Son of man, the place of my throne, and the place of the soles of my feet, where I will dwell in the midst of the children of Israel for ever, and my holy name, shall the house of Israel no more defile, *neither* they, nor their kings, by their whoredom, nor by the carcasses of their kings in their high places.

8 In their setting of their threshold by my thresholds, and their post by my posts, and the wall between me and them, they have even defiled my holy name by their abominations that they have committed: wherefore I have consumed them in mine anger.

9 Now let them put away their whoredom, and the carcasses of their kings, far from me, and I will dwell in the midst of them for ever.

10 Thou son of man, show the house to the house of Israel, that they may be ashamed of their iniquities: and let them measure the pattern.

11 And if they be ashamed of all that they have done, show them the form of the house, and the fashion thereof, and the goings out thereof, and the comings in thereof, and all

sound of his coming was like the sound of many waters; and the earth shone with his glory. 3 And the vision I saw was like the vision which I had seen when he came to destroy the city, and like the vision which I had seen by the river Chebar; and I fell upon my face. 4 As the glory of the LORD entered the temple by the gate facing east, 5 the Spirit lifted me up, and brought me into the inner court; and behold, the glory of the LORD filled the temple.

6 While the man was standing beside me, I heard one speaking to me out of the temple; 7 and he said to me, "Son of man, this is the place of my throne and the place of the soles of my feet, where I will dwell in the midst of the people of Israel for ever. And the house of Israel shall no more defile my holy name, neither they, nor their kings, by their harlotry, and by the dead bodies of their kings, 8 by setting their threshold by my threshold and their doorposts beside my doorpost, with only a wall between me and them. They have defiled my holy name by their abominations which they have committed, so I have consumed them in my anger. 9 Now let them put away their idolatry and the dead bodies of their kings far from me, and I will dwell in their midst for ever.

10 "And you, son of man, describe to the house of Israel the temple and its appearance and plan, that they may be ashamed of their iniquities. 11 And if they are ashamed of all that they have done, portray the temple, its arrangement, its exits and its entrances, and its whole form; and make known to them all its ordinances and all its laws; and

the forms thereof, and all the ordinances thereof, and all the forms thereof, and all the laws thereof: and write *it* in their sight, that they may keep the whole form thereof, and all the ordinances thereof, and do them.

12 This *is* the law of the house; Upon the top of the mountain the whole limit thereof round about *shall be* most holy. Behold, this *is* the law of the house.

Key Verse: I will dwell in the midst of them for ever. (Ezekiel 43:9)

write it down in their sight, so that they may observe and perform all its laws and all its ordinances. 12 This is the law of the temple: the whole territory round about upon the top of the mountain shall be most holy. Behold, this is the law of the temple."

Key Verse: I will dwell in their midst for ever. (Ezekiel 43:9)

The Scripture and the Main Question—William H. Willimon

The Glory of the God of Israel

It was a time of despair, a time when the glory seemed to have departed from Israel. Desolate, under the domination of foreign powers, Israel was in a sad state.

But here, expressed in the forty-third chapter of the book of Ezekiel, the prophet sees the glory returning. The Lord, who had forsaken the temple because the people had forsaken the Lord, now returns and dwells in the midst of Israel. The glory has come back.

Ezekiel, in the temple, has a stirring vision, a vision which compares in power and glory to his earlier visions: "The Spirit lifted me up, and brought me into the inner court; and behold, the glory of the LORD filled the temple" (Ezekiel 43:5).

What we have reported here is a classic theophany—that is, a classic account of a vision of God. In most of our lives, God seems vague, distant, far from us. But in certain moments we are brought very close to the divine presence; we know that God is very real. When have you experienced such times in your own life?

We have a word for it: *ecstasy.* The word *ecstasy* comes from two Greek words meaning literally "to stand outside oneself." In ecstatic moments we are swept up in some presence greater than our own; it is as if time stops, the heavens open, and we stand outside ourselves and the humdrum daily round of activity.

Have you ever come to church on a Sunday morning, not really wanting to be there, not really in the mood to worship or to praise God? Perhaps you went out of a sense of duty. You just didn't feel like worship today. But then, for some reason, you were caught off guard by the service. Some hymn, some word spoken by the preacher, something got hold of you and you were caught up, "lost in wonder, love and praise" as the hymn says. You were literally ecstatic. In spite of yourself, you worshiped.

The Lord Entered the Temple

These moments are at the very heart of our faith. We are seeking them when we come to worship each week. Of course, we can't program such times of worship and ecstasy. As Ezekiel knew, such moments are the work of the Spirit, a gift.

But we can put ourselves in the context where they can happen. We can open ourselves up to the gift of the presence. This is why it is important to go to worship at the church even when we don't feel like it, maybe especially when we don't feel like it.

Perhaps many modern people don't feel close to God, not because God is absent from our world, but because they have not put themselves in places where they can receive the gift of the Spirit and worship. A married couple who never sit down and talk with each other will eventually come to feel quite distant from each other. Their marriage will be in trouble before long. It is therefore important for the couple to set aside times to be together—even when they may not feel a special need to be together.

This is true for our relationship with God. It is important for us to set aside times to be with God. Of course, we can be with God anywhere at anytime, but how often do we feel close to God when we are working or when we are preoccupied with other day-to-day activities? We need times apart, times when we settle down, when we focus our thoughts on what is important in life, when we are quiet long enough to hear God speaking to us over the roar of the ordinary.

So today's text reminds us that Ezekiel was in the temple. He was surprised by the presence of God's glory, but he was there seeking that glory. We are to do the same.

"Can't I feel just as close to God out on the golf course as here in church?"

Yes, we all know moments outside of church when we have felt very near to the Spirit of God, when we have truly worshiped. But how often have these moments come on the golf course? And how can we be sure that the presence we are feeling is the presence of the one true God of Abraham, Isaac, and Jacob and not merely our own inner feelings or vague religious thoughts?

It is in the church—in the presence of fellow believers who have come together to focus their thoughts and lives, to stand before God's word, to listen to the interpretation and study of that word, to be challenged by others who share our commitments—that we grow in our faith and deepen our relationship with God.

There is a lot to be said for communing with God in nature or alone in our home, but there is also much to be said—perhaps much more than we have said here—about the need to come together in a communal, corporate place of worship in order to focus our thoughts and test our visions with other believers.

It was a dark time in the national life of Israel. As so often happens in times of national distress, people were gathered in the temple to pray. This was where Ezekiel was and this was where the vision came to him. Should we expect it to be any different for us?

I Heard One Speaking to Me

Martin Luther said that we come together on Sunday to listen to God so that we might then speak to God. If you look at the Sunday order of worship in your church, you will find this dynamic still at work in our worship.

Some acts of worship give us the opportunity to listen—the anthems by the choir, hymns sung by the congregation, the scripture readings, the sermon. Then other acts of worship enable us to speak to God—the prayers, the offering when we respond to God with ourselves and our gifts, our hymns, baptism, the Lord's Supper.

Ezekiel was told to listen that he might speak and tell his fellow citizens what he had heard.

In a way, that is the way we are on Sunday morning. We come to this place where we are apt to meet the glory of God. Then, having done our best to humbly, openly listen to what God has to say to us in this hour of worship, we go forth to tell our brothers and sisters in the world what we have heard. This is the interplay between worship and life, the dynamic which keeps us going in the midst of our times of difficulty, the very heart of our faith.

"Son of man, this is the place of my throne and the place of the soles of my feet, where I will dwell in the midst of the people of Israel for ever" (43:7).

Helping Adults Become Involved—Herbert H. Lambert

Preparing to Teach

This lesson is about something that is difficult for modern persons to grasp—what is meant by the presence of "the holy." We may have no faith in God, or we may believe that God dwells in the distant heavens and has no concern for us. Or we may piously say that "God is everywhere" and may thereby miss the significance of special times and places when God is disclosed to persons.

In order for God to speak to us, we must try to understand Ezekiel's teaching about holiness. We must open ourselves to God's presence by setting aside special times and by hallowing sacred places.

Here is a way to outline the lesson:

    I. The return of God to Jerusalem
    II. Ezekiel's concern for purity
       A. Ritual purity
       B. Moral purity
    III. A place for God
       A. The temple in Jerusalem
       B. Where God is today
    IV. The river of life
    V. Our hope for renewal
       A. A sense of God's presence
       B. Concern for what is sacred
       C. Reflecting God's holiness

Additional information about today's lesson may be found in *The Interpreter's Concise Commentary,* volume 4, pages 299-300, 304, and in *The Interpreter's Bible,* volume 6, pages 300-303, 325-28.

Introducing the Main Question

My most impressionable years were turbulent ones. Our large family moved thirteen times during my preschool years. I don't remember much about home, but I do remember the church. It was a safe haven for me!

I felt tranquility and strength in the sanctuary. I vowed I would never be far from its doors and that the meaning I had found there would guide my life. I have often had to rethink my beliefs, but I have never lost my respect and love for God's house. It was there I found peace and wholeness, and I still find it there today.

Have class members tell what the church as a place has meant to them.

Developing the Lesson

I. The return of God to Jerusalem

Other prophets foresaw a time when God's people would return to their land, but only Ezekiel longed for a restoration of the temple. This was the center of Ezekiel's faith. He had foretold the destruction of the temple as a punishment for the people's sin. Now he had a vision of the new temple in a renewed land, where God would come and live with the people. "The glory of the LORD entered the temple by the gate facing east" (Ezekiel 43:4). For Ezekiel this great event would be the fulfillment of his fondest hope—the restoration of worship and of the life-giving relationship between God and God's people.

II. Ezekiel's concern for purity

A. Ritual purity

Ezekiel described the new temple in great detail. It would be different from the old temple, which had allowed the walls of secular buildings and the dead bodies of buried kings to encroach on God's house. To us that may sound like nitpicking, but Ezekiel felt that those who are careless about God's special place easily lose respect and reverence for God altogether.

B. Moral purity

Ezekiel was more concerned than other prophets about purity. Like the other prophets, however, he wanted God's people to be pure and holy in their daily lives. If we really sense God's presence and recall what God requires of us, our lives will be transformed. We cannot be cruel, unjust, or unfaithful if we take God seriously, as Ezekiel wanted his hearers to do.

III. A place for God

A. The temple in Jerusalem

Jeremiah had denounced the people for using the temple as a place of escape after committing robbery. The book of Revelation, long after Ezekiel, tells of a new Jerusalem in which there will be no temple, "for its temple is the Lord God the Almighty and the Lamb" (21:22). But for Ezekiel, the building and its courts were very important. He recognized that people need a special place in which to meet God.

B. Where God is today

God is everywhere. We can pray to God in our homes, in a hospital, or on a woodland trail. But throughout history people have set aside special places where God may be worshiped. Have the class members tell about places that have had special spiritual significance for them. Why did they sense God's presence in these places? Is it a mistake to think of God's being closer to us in some places?

IV. The river of life

Allow time for class members to read Ezekiel 47:1-12. Ezekiel beheld in a vision a river flowing from the temple down to the arid valley south of the Dead Sea, a region which is dry, salty, and forbidding. The river in Ezekiel's vision was full of fish, and the trees that grew on its banks were lush and fruitful. Now read Revelation 22:1-5. Compare Ezekiel 47:12 with Revelation 22:2. What is meant by this symbol of a river flowing from God's temple bringing life and healing? What meaning can it have for us in 1986? Remember that in the Bible symbols like this one of the "river of life" are

constantly recycled, adapted, and reinterpreted to express new meanings—new ways to say what cannot be said in ordinary words.

Helping Class Members Act

V. *Our hope for renewal*

  A. *A sense of God's presence*

We may learn something from Ezekiel to help us have a richer experience
of God in our time. A priest who had been taken away from his beloved
temple, Ezekiel appreciated the importance of this holy place.
Make a list of suggestions for improving your own congregation's
sanctuary. What is needed to make it more worshipful? How can children,
youth, and adults be trained to enter the sanctuary in reverence? What steps
should be taken to improve the place and manner of worship, and how can
your class help in this? What symbols will help to foster a sense of God's
presence—crosses, candles, banners, pictures, windows? What uses of music
and silence do you suggest? Should the sanctuary be open for worship
when individuals may come and silently pray? If so, how can the presence of
God be expressed?

  B. *Concern for what is sacred*

During the 1960s a young city minister found that his church was not
reaching many persons. He took out the pews and installed a cafeteria in the
sanctuary. Every noon, business people and students flocked into this
building to eat and converse where generations had knelt in prayer. I went
to this "church" several times but never heard or felt anything specifically
religious. It reached a lot of people but didn't give them anything except an
inexpensive lunch. Have we sometimes lost a sense of "the sacred"? Are
there sacred times and places for our congregation, and for us as
individuals?
George Arthur Buttrick, noted minister and writer, was scheduled to
speak in several cities in Texas. His hosts showed him a schedule of places
and times. "But you haven't put in time for my prayers!" Buttrick exlaimed.
They had forgotten something that for Buttrick was essential. Do we have a
time each day that is set apart for God? Do we observe it faithfully? How
strong is our sense of the sacred, the holy?

  C. *Reflecting God's holiness*

If we open ourselves to God's presence in a special place at designated
times, God will be able to transform our lives. We will be loving, forgiving,
hopeful, and strong. Other persons will sense the presence of God in us. Are
there persons in whom your class members have found the presence of
God? Did such persons have regular habits of prayer? Discuss how such
persons affected you.

Planning for Next Sunday

Have the class members read the first chapter of Daniel during the
coming week. One member may be asked to report on an article on "Daniel"
in a Bible dictionary. Try to find out when the book was written. How is it
different from other books of the Old Testament? What was its purpose?

The Relationship of Daniel's Visions and Apocalyptic Literature

HARRELL BECK

The book of Daniel as we have it in the Hebrew Bible is made up of two parts. Chapters 1–6 include six stories about Daniel and his friends who remain faithful to God despite trial and persecution. In chapters 7–12, we have an account of four visions. In these visions the author describes four kingdoms, beginning with Babylon, which persecute God's people. The writer also envisions God's establishment of his own kingdom for the faithful Jews.

Daniel is our first great apocalyptic work. Most apocalypses were written in a time of foreign occupation and severe persecution. There were to be many similar apocalypses in late Old Testament times and in early Christianity, including the New Testament book of Revelation. These apocalypses were usually attributed to some ancient hero of the faith such as Adam, Enoch, Noah, Abraham, or Ezra.

This apocalypse is named after Daniel, its chief character. (The name Daniel means "God is my judge.") The name is referred to by Ezekiel (14:14, 20; see also 28:3) as an ancient contemporary of Noah and Job. The unknown author was a devout Jew who live in the time of intense persecution of Jerusalem by Antiochus IV Epiphanes (167–164 B.C.). This Antiochus was a Seleucid, successors in Syria of Alexander the Great. Antiochus's persecution of the Jews, his desecration of the temple, and his demand that the Jews practice the pagan religion of his empire led to the Maccabean revolt in 167–166 B.C.

Under such circumstances many faithful Jews were tempted to forsake their historic faith in favor of Hellenistic culture and pagan religious practices. Such a change, it was promised, would bring an end to suffering and persecution.

In these four visions the author celebrates the superior wisdom and power of the God of Israel over pagan wisdom (which at best is human) and over earthly tyrants. Here the plan and promise of God are revealed: destruction of the oppressors is imminent (present woes and conflict are parts of a climactic but passing age); the son of man will rule victoriously (the term in 7:13 probably refers to the faithful of Israel); a great judgment and a reign of peace are promised. The message of the author to his contemporaries is clear: God will rescue the faithful from their persecutors. The enduring faith of this apocalypse is central in later apocalypses: the God of Israel is the Lord of history; the rise and decline of empires is only a prelude to the establishment of God's righteous rule over all the earth. Plainly, apocalypse is a vital and specialized form of prophecy.

Since the visions of Daniel influenced many later apocalypses, we ought to consider each of them briefly.

The vision of the four beasts (Daniel 7). The four beasts of this striking vision represent the successive pagan empires which ruled over the Jews after the exile in 586: Babylonians (winged lion); Medes (the bear); Persians (leopard with wings); and the Greek empire (a beast like a dragon). The ten horns stand for the ten rulers who succeeded Alexander the Great. The last and most terrible tyrant, the little horn, was Antiochus IV Epiphanes, who gained the throne by violence and ruled with unrelenting brutality. But the judgment of God (the Ancient of Days, 7:9) is about to befall Antiochus. One like a "son of man" (7:13), probably a reference to the faithful Jews, will be given universal and everlasting dominion. The promise has been made to the saints of the Most High (7:27).

The ram and the he-goat (chapter 8). This vision, dated two years later than the preceding one (7:1), came to the author at Susa, a Persian capital. The symbolism of the vision is explained to Daniel by Gabriel, the angelic messenger. The two-horned ram represents the kings of Media and Persia; the he-goat symbolizes Alexander the Great (the great horn) who came from the west, "across the face of the whole earth, without touching the ground" (8:5)! The he-goat trampled the ram, gained a vast empire and power, but was broken at the zenith of his reign (the death of Alexander at an early age). There arose four "conspicuous horns," successors of Alexander (among them Seleucus in Syria and Ptolemy in Egypt). From the former arose a little horn (Antiochus IV), who expanded his kingdom and in 167 conquered Jerusalem. He desecrated the temple, trampled the truth, and affronted God (the Prince of Peace) by banning worship. The climactic promise of the vision is heartening: in due course (after 1150 complete days or about three and a half years, i.e., "time, times, and half a time") God will destroy this tyrant and restore the Jerusalem sanctuary. But the vision must be kept secret.

The prophecy of the seventy weeks (chapter 9). This chapter is not a symbolic vision but a revelation to Daniel by the angel Gabriel. It is set in the first year of Darius the Mede (538 B.C.). The chapter includes (1) Daniel's reflection on Jeremiah's word from the Lord that seventy years must pass (from 586) before the restoration of Jerusalem (Jeremiah 25:11, 12, 29:10); (2) Daniel's prayer of confession for his own sins and those of his people and his supplications; and (3) Gabriel's explanation of seventy weeks of years (meaning seventy times seven, or 490 years) which must pass following the destruction of Jerusalem (9:2) before Jerusalem is restored. (References to numbers of weeks and years, an anointed one, etc., raise questions which cannot be pursued here.) Most interpreters hold that the 490-year period will end when Antiochus's abominable rule ends. And that end has been decreed (9:27).

The succession of empires (chapters 10–12). This lengthy apocalypse differs in style from the first three, suggesting the possibility of different authors for these visions. The focal point of the vision is a lengthy account of Seleucid rule (kings of the north), especially in their relationships with the Ptolemies of Egypt (the kings of the south) and with Asia Minor. Antiochus IV's reign is described in detail (11:21-45).

The vision ends with an important description of the end of the age (12:1-4). After Antiochus will come unprecedented trouble, but Daniel's people (whose names are written in a book) will be delivered. A general resurrection will follow (our clearest Old Testament reference to physical resurrection, 12:2). The revelation is to be kept a secret. The closing verses are calculations about the time of the end. Whenever it occurs, Daniel will have a place at the final consummation.

All these apocalypses have a common purpose: affirming the ultimate salvation of the people by interpreting as prophecies what are actually historical events.

UNIT III: DANIEL: COURAGE AND HOPE
Horace R. Weaver

THREE LESSONS   AUGUST 17–31

"Daniel—Courage and Hope," consists of three lessons from Daniel. The book was written about 175 B.C. in the times of the persecution of Antiochus Epiphanes against loyal Jews. The book is composed of six stories and four visions designed to encourage suffering believers. The three lessons in the unit focus on God's sustaining power and presence with the faithful and on the ultimate triumph of God's people.

The titles of the three lessons are: "Daniel: A Man of Courageous Convictions," August 17; "God's Presence with the Faithful," August 24; and "God's Rule Will Come," August 31.

LESSON 12   AUGUST 17

Daniel: A Man of Courageous Conviction

Background Scripture: Daniel 1

The Main Question—William H. Willimon

As a teenager, I read John F. Kennedy's *Profiles in Courage*. I remember being deeply moved by these stories of courageous men and women who, in a time of crisis, faced life's challenge with unusual courage.

Biographies of great men and women are appropriate reading for youth. Young people are looking for role models, heroes to emulate, sure paths to follow. Of course, courageous lives make for interesting reading at any age because, in any age, courage is in short supply.

We are animals who are born seeking pleasure and avoiding pain. We instinctively flee from danger and distress. Thus it is natural for us to feel fear in a time of crisis; it is natural for us to look for the easy way out; it is only natural for us to go along with the crowd, try to fit in, avoid rocking the boat. We are anxiety-ridden creatures who live more by fear than by courage.

Fear is instinctual, natural, but courage is not. Courage arises out of some source other than our natural inclinations. Perhaps that's why truly courageous people—people who can brave public disapproval in order to stand up for what is right—are few. We love stories of human courage, not only because courage is so rare but also because we know that courage is a good example of humanity.

Courage is the stubborn human refusal to crouch in fear or flee in terror. It is the determined human will to trust the power of the truth rather than the strength of brute force; it is the soaring human desire to be obedient to one's convictions, come what may.

Let us listen to an ancient profile in courage, the story of Daniel, in hopes of receiving contemporary encouragement.

424

As You Read the Scripture—Wilbur Lamm

Who was Daniel? All we know we learn from the book itself. He was a young Jew, perhaps akin to King Zedekiah, taken captive to Babylon by Nebuchadnezzar in 605 B.C. He soon rose to prominence and served as a government official under Babylonian rulers until 538 B.C.

Daniel 1–6 chronologically is set in the Babylonian and Persian periods. The rest of the book is set after Alexander the Great with specific emphasis on the period of Jewish persecution by Antiochus IV Epiphanes, who ruled from 175 to 164 B.C.

Daniel 1:1-2. Verse 1 has its setting immediately after the battle of Carchemish (605 B.C.), in which Nebuchadnezzar defeated Neco of Egypt. This was the third year of the reign of Jehoiakim in Judah. Judah became subject to Babylon and made lavish gifts and tribute to Babylon. Vessels from the temple were taken and placed in the treasury of the Babylonian pagan gods. Such an act attributed victory to the god so honored, and, at the same time, preserved the holy vessels which later would be returned.

Verses 3-5. Nebuchadnezzar sought to strengthen his nation by developing the human potential to the fullest. His chief court official, Ashpenaz, was assigned the task of selecting and training high-ranking (kings' seed and princes) Jews for official service for the ruler. He was to select youths, perhaps still in their teens, who possessed physical perfection, good appearance, and intelligence.

These youths were to serve the king while pursuing a strict regimen of study. They must learn the Babylonian literature and language. Thus they had to imbibe many pagan concepts and polytheistic myths that would challenge their faith in God.

Their food consisted of delicacies from the king's table (*patbag*, or delicacies of royalty). One of the benefits of royal service was eating from the king's menu. Their food included a generous ration of the best wine. For three years they were to receive rigorous academic training designed to produce strong bodies and keen minds.

Verses 6-7. Four young men chosen were from the tribe of Judah. Their names, including Daniel, indicated they possessed a strong religious heritage. Believing that a change in name meant a change in life and purpose, the youth were given names containing titles of Babylonian deities. So the elements in Hebrew worship were replaced by Babylonian pagan concepts.

Verses 8-14. The king's food, though most desirable, would not have been prepared and served according to Jewish priestly rules and would include some unclean animals according to Hebrew laws. Furthermore, the food was not prepared by ritual regulations. On moral and religious grounds, Daniel refused to take the king's food and drink. He dared to be different.

Daniel's determination upset Ashpenaz, who could be held liable for Daniel's treason. He contended that the food was specified by the king and was the best available. He feared that Daniel and his friends might prove lacking in health.

Daniel proposed a test to last ten days: that they eat vegetables (something sown) and drink water. By this request, made through Ashpenaz's steward, Daniel risked his life. He had only his faith to support him. The request was granted, and the test was on.

Verses 15-17. God honored the faith of Daniel and his friends. They attained a healthier physical appearance than did those not in the test. They gained weight and had a fairer countenance. Their food and drink proved agreeable and profitable to them. Now they were free to abstain from food and drink that violated their dietary rules and religious convictions.

This material may have been written during a time when Jews were forbidden to observe their ceremonial and dietary laws. One such time was during the persecution by Antiochus IV Epiphanes when many Jews "chose to die rather than to be defiled by food or to profane the holy covenant" (I Maccabees 1:62-63).

When the testing period was over, the Hebrew youths excelled in learning, wisdom, and various skills. Daniel especially stood out in his understanding of visions and dreams. The four youths demonstrated their newly acquired abilities before the king, who found them ten times more competent than all the rest of the king's servants. Daniel's position was secure and he continued to serve until the time of Cyrus the Persian (538 B.C.).

God honors persons who obey and serve him faithfully. Faithfulness to God is to be valued above all worldly considerations.

Selected Scripture

King James Version

Daniel 1:3-5, 8-12, 15-17

3 And the king spake unto Ashpenaz the master of his eunuchs, that he should bring *certain* of the children of Israel, and of the king's seed, and of the princes;

4 Children in whom *was* no blemish, but well favoured, and skilful in all wisdom, and cunning in knowledge, and understanding science, and such as *had* ability in them to stand in the king's palace, and whom they might teach the learning and the tongue of the Chăl-dē´-ăns.

5 And the king appointed them a daily provision of the king's meat, and of the wine which he drank: so nourishing them three years, that at the end thereof they might stand before the king.

....

8 But Daniel purposed in his heart that he would not defile himself with the portion of the king's meat, nor with the wine which he drank: therefore he requested of the prince of the eunuchs that he might not defile himself.

9 Now God had brought Daniel

Revised Standard Version

Daniel 1:3-5, 8-12, 15-17

3 Then the king commanded Ash´penaz, his chief eunuch, to bring some of the people of Israel, both of the royal family and of the nobility, 4 youths without blemish, handsome and skilful in all wisdom, endowed with knowledge, understanding learning, and competent to serve in the king's palace, and to teach them the letters and language of the Chalde´ans. 5 The king assigned them a daily portion of the rich food which the king ate, and of the wine which he drank. They were to be educated for three years, and at the end of that time they were to stand before the king.

....

8 But Daniel resolved that he would not defile himself with the king's rich food, or with the wine which he drank; therefore he asked the chief of the eunuchs to allow him not to defile himself. 9 And God gave Daniel favor and compassion in the sight of the chief of the

into favour and tender love with the prince of the eunuchs.

10 And the prince of the eunuchs said unto Daniel, I fear my lord the king, who hath appointed your meat and your drink: for why should he see your faces worse liking than the children which *are* of your sort? then shall ye make *me* endanger my head to the king.

11 Then said Daniel to Melzar whom the prince of the eunuchs had set over Daniel, Hananiah, Mī-shā-ĕl, and Ăz-ă-rī′-ăh,

12 Prove thy servants, I beseech thee, ten days; and let them give us pulse to eat, and water to drink.

....

15 And at the end of ten days their countenances appeared fairer and fatter in flesh than all the children which did eat the portion of the king's meat.

16 Thus Melzar took away the portion of their meat, and the wine that they should drink; and gave them pulse.

17 As for these four children, God gave them knowledge and skill in all learning and wisdom: and Daniel had understanding in all visions and dreams.

Key Verse: As for these four children, God gave them knowledge and skill in all learning and wisdom. (Daniel 1:17)

eunuchs; 10 and the chief of the eunuchs said to Daniel, "I fear lest my lord the king, who appointed your food and your drink, should see that you were in poorer condition than the youths who are of your own age. So you would endanger my head with the king." 11 Then Daniel said to the steward whom the chief of the eunuchs had appointed over Daniel, Hanani′ah, Mish′a-el, and Azari′ah, 12 "Test your servants for ten days; let us be given vegetables to eat and water to drink."

....

15 At the end of ten days it was seen that they were better in appearance and fatter in flesh than all the youths who ate the king's rich food. 16 So the steward took away their rich food and the wine they were to drink, and gave them vegetables.

17 As for these four youths, God gave them learning and skill in all letters and wisdom; and Daniel had understanding in all visions and dreams.

Key Verse: As for these four youths, God gave them learning and skill in all letters and wisdom. (Daniel 1:17)

The Scripture and the Main Question—William H. Willimon

The Times That Try Men's Souls

"Once to every man and nation comes the moment to decide," writes the poet. In every age, there are times of crisis, times when people are presented with the choice of whether to stand or flee. These are the times that try our souls, that test what we are made of and measure the strength of our character. Some meet the test, responding with courage and conviction. Some slink away into cowardly obscurity. What makes the difference? That is today's question.

To answer that question, we turn to the story of Daniel. Daniel lived during one of those "times that try men's souls." We believe that the author of the book of Daniel wrote sometime around 168–165 B.C., during a time of national peril for the people of God. The Jewish people were suffering under the heavy hand of Antiochus, a Seleucid (Syrian) strongman who ruled Judah with an iron fist and set up his own puppet government in Jerusalem.

The Jewish people resisted this external domination, particularly when Antiochus began to meddle in their religious affairs. From time to time, there was armed resistance to the Seleucid rule. Finally, Antiochus had had enough. He decided that the people's Jewish religion was a major source of their resistance, so he determined to put an end to Judaism. He plundered the temple in Jerusalem and made it a capital crime to worship as Jews, to own a copy of the Torah, or to circumcise one's male children. A statue of the Greek god Zeus was erected in the temple, and a pig was sacrificed on the altar there—just to prove to the people that Judaism was finished.

But the Jews resisted. Maccabeus waged guerrilla warfare in the mountains, finally defeating the Syrians in a battle, a victory that won them freedom from the proscription against Judaism. Some of the fighters continued to battle for political independence for the next twenty or thirty years.

This was the setting for the book of Daniel. Those people who attempted to keep the Jewish law and to remain faithful to it were forbidden to do so under pain of death. In the midst of this terrible oppression, the author of Daniel writes to encourage the suffering people to keep the faith through this time of soul testing.

Undefiled

Today's scripture comes from the section of the book of Daniel that tells the story of certain Jewish youths who found themselves in exile in Babylon years before the current (165 B.C.) crisis. Their stories of courage are meant to strengthen people in the present persecution of Antiochus.

Daniel is a youth who was singled out by King Nebuchadnezzar for special service. With other Jewish youths—Hananiah, Mishael, and Azariah—Daniel was to be trained for three years to serve the king. The youths were to be fattened up in order that they would be healthy servants for Nebuchadnezzar.

Now for these exiles to receive the rich food of the king's table would be considered by most people to be a great good fortune. But this food, delightful though it may have been to the stomach, was not kosher; it violated Jewish food laws.

"But Daniel resolved that he would not defile himself with the king's rich food, or with the wine which he drank" (Daniel 1:8). Daniel's objection to the food is based not on concern over health but on concern over religious conviction. The food issue was important to these Jews because it signified for them the need to keep their religion pure, even in the midst of political pressure to blend in with other faiths.

Daniel stood his ground and refused to be tempted by the thought of this rich food. He thus becomes a symbol for the Jewish resistance to all the forces that try to corrupt and compromise the faith.

In the middle of the Yale University campus is a statue of Nathan Hale, the young Yale graduate who was hanged by the British for spying in the American Revolution. "I regret that I have only one life to give for my country," said Hale as the noose was fitted around his neck. His statue stands today as a reminder to present Yale students of youthful courage.

Daniel is another example. We could think of others: David before Goliath, Isaiah and Stephen before their executors. Whom would you put on a pedestal if you were erecting a monument to courage? Perhaps you would depict Martin Luther nailing his theses on the Wittenberg Door, Wycliffe perishing in the flames, Wesley facing an angry mob, Martin Luther King in the Birmingham jail.

Or perhaps you would place some lesser-known hero on your pedestal of courage—the woman who stood up in the church board meeting and spoke against the attempt of the church trustees to close the church's day care center for the needy, the man who chose not to register for the military draft and suffer the legal consequences because he was a pacifist, the teenager who suffers ostracism from the "in group" at school because she refused to take an illegal narcotic at a party.

Heroism comes in many forms—sometimes in courageous, public, visible instances; sometimes in quiet, everyday, anonymous circumstances which are not recorded in the history books.

How much would you or I be willing to suffer for our faith? Across our world, Christians are suffering for what they believe. In many countries in our world, it costs something to be a Christian. What if we lived there? Would we be able to pay the cost of discipleship?

In today's world, it is difficult to keep ourselves pure and aloof from any contact with non-Christian influences. We live in a pluralistic society where there are many varieties of life-style and many approaches to the truth.

Furthermore, it isn't always easy to know what a defiling influence might be. My grandfather thought that tobacco was one of the most corrupting influences on people. I'm sure that he would believe it is most important for a Christian not to smoke. While there is little good to be gained from the use of tobacco, could it be said that tobacco in itself is the most defiling influence upon a Christian?

Reading the story of Daniel and his determination to remain undefiled by not eating the king's food from our contemporary perspective may make us wonder why Daniel made such a big fuss over such a small matter. What harm could there be in eating a bit or two of nonkosher viands?

But isn't that the way we succumb to temptation, sell out to the mob, and give in to the status quo—bit by bit, in those small, insignificant matters, until we realize too late that nothing is worth holding onto anymore?

"There is nothing worth dying for," declared a Princeton student when asked if she would be willing to fight to aid a country that had been invaded by another—which means that one day she shall die for nothing.

The story of Joesph's being tempted by Potophar's seductive wife strikes us as strange—"Go ahead! Don't be a stuffed shirt, Joseph. What harm can there be in a little sex, so long as no one gets hurt?"

What we eat "doesn't make any difference." How we live our personal lives is "a private matter." "It doesn't matter what you believe as long as you're sincere." "Don't rock the boat." "Be a good team player." These are all slogans of cowardly conformity.

But discipleship means *discipline*, the willingness to conform our lives, not to the status quo, not to conventional standards of right and wrong, but to God's will. Our courage may bring us good health, as it did Daniel, or it may not. The main thing is to be true to our convictions.

What we eat, what we drink—these are small matters. And yet in such small, everyday ways, the battle is lost or won, and we demonstrate our fidelity or our cowardice. How we talk, how we spend our money, the work we do, the friends we choose, the way we use our leisure time, what we do with our bodies and our minds—these are all small matters.

Yet such "small matters" add up to the sum of our character. They testify to what we value, the principles by which we live, the God whom we worship.

The small, everyday heroics of everyday people like you and me become the proving ground for our faith, the test of our commitment to God.

Helping Adults Become Involved—Herbert H. Lambert

Preparing to Teach

This lesson is about standing up for what one believes in spite of opposition, temptation, and danger. It is a story which was first told to encourage Jews in a time of persecution, when many abandoned their traditions in order to avoid trouble. The story of Daniel and his companions reminds us of times when we need to stand firm for what is right and what is good.

Here is a way to outline the lesson:

     I. The origin and purpose of the book of Daniel
       A. The situation in the second century B.C.
       B. A story from the time of the exile
       C. The message of the book of Daniel
    II. The character of Daniel
       A. Daniel's wisdom
       B. Refusal to comply
       C. Strength of character
   III. When we need to stand firm
       A. Civil disobedience
       B. At our place of work
       C. Resisting our friends
   IV. Ways to follow Daniel
       A. Deciding what is important
       B. Being ready to explain your view
       C. Standing firm against opposition

Additional information may be found in *The Interpreter's Concise Commentary*, volume 4, pages 307-16, and in *The Interpreter's Bible*, volume 6, pages 341-44, 355-72.

Introducing the Main Question

I once knew a capable executive who came to me with a dilemma. After months of observation, she knew that officials of her company were manipulating records to conceal profits and to avoid taxes. She listed four options she had to choose from: (1) do nothing: she preferred this because she was afraid the other options would mean trouble for her, but this would give her an uneasy conscience; (2) make copies of important documents and turn them over to authorities: this would appear to be betrayal of her friends; (3) confront her superiors with what she had discovered: this could lead to dismissal; (4) resign and say nothing about what she knew: this would be costly and would not ease her conscience.

There was no easy way to solve her dilemma. If she had had no concern for honesty and fairness there would have been no choice to make. It was because she had convictions that she was forced to deal with the matter. Today's lesson on Daniel deals with such choices and ways to cope with them.

Developing the Lesson

I. The origin and purpose of the book of Daniel

A. *The situation in the second century* B.C.

If you asked someone to prepare a report on Daniel as suggested at the end of the last lesson, now would be a good time to have it. You may find that reference books differ about the date and origin of the book of Daniel. This resource agrees with those who date it in the second century B.C., when the Jews were persecuted by the Seleucid monarch Antiochus IV. Use Dr. Willimon's information given above under the heading "The Times That Try Men's Souls."

B. *A story from the time of the exile*

Daniel is in part a historical novel based on events and characters dated four centuries earlier, at the time of the Jews' exile in Babylon. Report on I Maccabees 1 about specific acts of persecution. (New RSV Bibles include this reference.)

In Babylon, Daniel and his young companions found both opportunity for advancement and danger of losing their ancestral religious traditions and moral values.

Have the class read the printed scripture and discuss these questions: Was Daniel's place in the royal court a good thing for him? What opportunities did it hold? What dangers were present? Why did Daniel reject the king's rich food? What was the result?

C. *The message of the book of Daniel*

Many Jews in the second century B.C. adopted Greek ways in order to avoid a clash with the powerful ruler Antiochus. This meant giving up sabbath observance, prayers, rituals, and even circumcision. It meant giving up concerns about cleanliness and kosher food which characterized strict Jews. How could a story like Daniel's influence such Jews to remain firm in their traditional beliefs and practices?

II. The character of Daniel

A. *Daniel's wisdom*

Today's lesson tells us that Daniel received from God "learning and skill in all letters and wisdom; and Daniel had understanding in all visions and dreams" (verse 17). In chapter 2, Daniel was able to interpret King Nebuchadnezzar's dream. Clearly, this young man had God-given talent that made him stand out from others. For this reason he was chosen to serve the king.

B. *Refusal to comply*

Daniel refused to "defile himself" with the rich food and wine of the king's table. He was not on a diet to lose weight but was concerned about the ritual purity of gentile food. Pork and other unclean foods were probably offered. Daniel refused the king's food because of loyalty to the religious law of his people. He showed courage because such behavior could cost him his favored position and possibly his life.

C. *Strength of character*

Not many young persons, especially when far from home, can retain their treasured ways in the face of pressure to change. Daniel's refusal and his explanation show remarkable maturity and inner strength.

FOURTH QUARTER

III. When we need to stand firm

A. Civil disobedience

Henry Thoreau was jailed for refusing to pay a small tax to support the Mexican War. When Ralph Waldo Emerson visited him, he asked, "What are you doing in there, Henry?" Thoreau replied: "What are you doing out there?" There may come times when we have to explain our giving in to pressure from government, not our refusal to do so!

There is such a thing as responsible disobedience of law. Those who choose it do so not on some whim but because they believe deeply that a specific law is immoral. They are willing to accept the consequences of their actions. Often the law is changed as a result of their defiance, and later generations regard these persons as revered prophets. Susan B. Anthony was arrested in 1872 for voting. Today her face is on the U.S. silver dollar.

B. At our place of work

I have known many persons who found it difficult to maintain high personal standards at work. They are tempted to conceal wrongdoing, to share in gossip about other employees, to compete unfairly for favors. The person who resists these temptations may at last win respect and honor, but he or she may also suffer great loss.

C. Resisting our friends

Standing firm against the urging of friends is most difficult. We do not want to lose friends or to look ridiculous in their eyes. When the state wanted to locate a home for mental patients in his neighborhood, Ben saw a chance to help the patients. He opposed a campaign to stop the program, even though his neighbors were angry with him.

Helping Class Members Act

IV. Ways to follow Daniel

List on the chalkboard some ways to follow Daniel. Discuss.

A. Deciding what is important

Most issues are not clearly right or wrong. Be sure you have the facts and know the probable consequences of various options. Decide what is necessary for you to do or refuse to do.

B. Being ready to explain your view

Think about the reasons you feel as you do, and try to explain them calmly. Recognize that others have a right to their opinion and that they may have good reasons for it. Don't belittle or blame those who differ from you.

C. Standing firm against opposition

Do what you need to do as a result of your prayerful study of the situation. Ask God's help as you resist those who try to persuade you or threaten you. Don't be surprised if you have to suffer for your convictions. Think of examples of persons who stood firm in the face of heavy pressure to conform. Remember the courage of Daniel and his companions.

Planning for Next Sunday

Stay tuned for another episode in the adventures of Daniel and his friends! Have the class members read Daniel 3 for the next lesson, keeping in mind the temptations and threats by those who first read Daniel in the time of Antiochus IV.

God's Presence with the Faithful

Background Scripture: Daniel 3

The Main Question—William H. Willimon

You and I are fortunate to live in a country where we are afforded freedom of religion. Not all people are so fortunate. In many countries of the world, many countries which we consider to be our nation's allies and friends, religion is under the control of the state.

In fact, the state itself has become a religion for many. Totalitarian regimes of the left and the right present the state in godlike dimensions. The government is depicted as the beneficent deity whose weapons and armaments are to protect us and watch over us from the cradle to the grave. If we just put our trust in this god, it will care for us in our youth and in our old age. It will give us something eternal and immortal to identify with, something all-powerful and all-embracing.

Despotic rulers from Nebuchadnezzar to Hitler, from Stalin to Mao, have understood that religion can be a dangerous adversary of the state. Religious belief tends to relativize and judge the godlike claims of governments and to call into question the divine aspirations of rulers. Therefore most despots have chosen to fight the influence of religion, not by eradicating it, but by offering a substitute faith—faith in the state. Give the people a flag, a song, great temples of government, rites and ceremonies of nationhood and patriotism; offer them an inspiring slogan and a lofty ideal, and they will fall into ranks and march by the millions into the chains of servitude.

Here is a pattern as old as Nebuchadnezzar, as new as today's youngest nations, as close to home as our own struggles to keep our patriotism and our faith in proper relationship.

As You Read the Scripture—Wilbur Lamm

During the persecution of Jews by Antiochus IV Epiphanes of Syria (174–165 B.C.), the Jews were reminded of how Nebuchadnezzar had done essentially the same thing to their forefathers in Babylon. This chapter relates that story. Daniel's three friends were officials in Babylon (Daniel 2:49) at Daniel's suggestion but got in trouble when they refused to worship Nebuchadnezzar's golden image.

This image was ninety feet high and nine feet wide, an immense and grand figure. The god possibly represented Marduk or Nebuchadnezzar himself. All the officials in the government except the Hebrew youths came to the mount of Dura to dedicate and worship the image. The penalty for failure to worship at the king's command was death in a burning fiery furnace—a "beehive kiln" fed from the top with a side opening near the bottom.

The king assembled an orchestra of brass, wind, stringed, and horn instruments. As the music began, all persons were to bow before the golden image. Three Hebrew youths did not bow. Jealous men reported them to Nebuchadnezzar.

Daniel 3:14-18. The king reacted to this news with furious rage. How could any of his honored servants refuse to give total allegiance to him? He gave the three young men another chance to obey his command. To serve his god was to serve him.

Fire was a strong force that people feared. Often, pagan worship was accompanied by fire (cf. Molech). Nebuchadnezzar asked the youths, "Who is the god that will deliver you?" To give total loyalty to Jehovah meant death. The king demanded compromise.

The Hebrews acted in vitality of faith as they insisted they did not need to answer. They regarded the king's question as an affront to God but responded positively and courteously. They said that their God was able and would deliver them, for God was stronger than the pagan king. If they were not delivered they would rather die as martyrs than to live in luxury as political leaders who compromised their faith.

Verses 19-22. In fury the king had the furnace heated to its capacity. His mighty men threw the youths into the furnace fully clothed in their official robes. This fact may have meant that the three could not hide behind their official status. The fire was so fierce that the flames burned the mighty men to death, a noted characteristic of such martyr stories.

Some ancient versions have sixty-eight additional verses that relate a prayer of Abednego, details about the furnace, the fuel, the angel of the Lord, and a song by the three young men in praise to God. The versions say, for example, that the flames reached seventy-three and a half feet above the rim of the furnace.

Verses 23-26. Nebuchadnezzar was astonished and came in haste to the furnace. Greater astonishment was caused by five facts. First, he saw four men in the fire. Second, the men were loose and not bound. Third, they were walking in the fire unhurt. Fourth, they were not suffering any pain. Fifth, the fourth person was of unusual appearance—"like a son of the gods."

This unusual "son" may have been the angel of the Lord who had revealed himself to Hagar, Abraham, Jacob, and Moses. He at least was a godly being, unique from man. Nebuchadnezzar was not knowledgeable enough to understand anything concerning the power and resources of the true and living God. We can be certain that this figure's presence meant that God was taking care of his faithful servants and comforting them in the midst of affliction.

The king came as near the door of the furnace as he could. He called for the young men to come out, addressing them as "servants of the Most High God." Such address does not mean that he regarded their God as the only God. He did acknowledge that theirs was a true God who is to be reckoned with and is possibly greater than any of the gods he worshiped.

The three young men walked out of the fire unhurt and approached the king without fear. All the government officials saw that the fire of the king had no power over the bodies of these men. God proved his ability to deliver his faithful servants. The king acknowledged God's existence and permitted worship of him within his kingdom (verses 28-29). And, the three youths received promotions (material reward) in the realm!

This story, told and retold, would encourage the sufferers under Antiochus IV Epiphanes as well as others who would experience persecution. We can count on God's presence and power when we are faithful despite opposition. The main point is to be faithful to God under all circumstances.

Selected Scripture

King James Version	Revised Standard Version

Daniel 3:14-18, 23-26

14 Nĕb-ū-chăd-nĕz´-zär spake and said unto them, *Is it* true, O Shā´-drăch, Mē´-shăch, and A-bed-nego, do not ye serve my gods, nor worship the golden image which I have set up?

15 Now if ye be ready that at what time ye hear the sound of the cornet, flute, harp, sackbut, psaltery, and dulcimer, and all kinds of music, ye fall down and worship the image which I have made; *well:* but if ye worship not, ye shall be cast the same hour into the midst of a burning fiery furnace; and who *is* that God that shall deliver you out of my hands?

16 Shā´-drăch, Mē´-shăch, and Abed-nego, answered and said to the king, O Nĕb-ū-chăd-nĕz´-zär, we *are* not careful to answer thee in this matter.

17 If it be *so,* our God whom we serve is able to deliver us from the burning fiery furnace, and he will deliver *us* out of thine hand, O king.

18 But if not, be it known unto thee, O king, that we will not serve thy gods, nor worship the golden image which thou hast set up.

....

23 And these three men, Shā´-drăch, Mē´-shăch, and Abed-nego, fell down bound into the midst of the burning fiery furnace.

24 Then Nĕb-ū-chăd-nĕz´-zär the king was astonished, and rose up in haste, *and* spake, and said unto his counsellors, Did not we cast three men bound into the midst of the fire? They answered and said unto the king, True, O king.

25 He answered and said, Lo, I see four men loose, walking in the midst of the fire, and they have no hurt; and the form of the fourth is like the Son of God.

Daniel 3:14-18, 23-26

14 Nebuchadnez´zar said to them, "Is it true, O Shadrach, Meshach, and Abed´nego, that you do not serve my gods or worship the golden image which I have set up? 15 Now if you are ready when you hear the sound of the horn, pipe, lyre, trigon, harp, bagpipe, and every kind of music, to fall down and worship the image which I have made, well and good; but if you do not worship, you shall immediately be cast into a burning fiery furnace; and who is the god that will deliver you out of my hands?"

16 Shadrach, Meshach, and Abed´nego answered the king, "O Nebuchadnez´zar, we have no need to answer you in this matter. 17 If it be so, our God whom we serve is able to deliver us from the burning fiery furnace; and he will deliver us out of your hand, O king. 18 But if not, be it known to you, O king, that we will not serve your gods or worship the golden image which you have set up."

....

23 And these three men, Shadrach, Meshach, and Abed´nego, fell bound into the burning fiery furnace.

24 Then King Nebuchadnez´zar was astonished and rose up in haste. He said to his counselors, "Did we not cast three men bound into the fire?" They answered the king, "True, O king." 25 He answered, "But I see four men loose, walking in the midst of the fire, and they are not hurt; and the appearance of the fourth is like a son of the gods."

26 Then Nĕb-ū-<u>ch</u>ăd-nĕz´-zär came near to the mouth of the burning fiery furnace, *and* spake, and said, Shā´-dră<u>ch</u>, Mĕ´-shă<u>ch</u>, and Abed-nego, ye servants of the most high God, come forth, and come *hither.* Then Shadrach, Meshach, and Abed-nego, came forth of the midst of the fire.

Key Verse: Then **Nebuchadnezzar spake, and said, Blessed *be* the God of Shadrach, Meshach, and Abednego, who hath sent his angel, and delivered his servants that trusted in him, and have changed the king's word, and yielded their bodies, that they might not serve nor worship any God, except their own God. (Daniel 3:28)**

26 Then Nebuchadnez´zar came near to the door of the burning fiery furnace and said, "Shadrach, Meshach, and Abed´nego, servants of the Most High God, come forth, and come here!" Then Shadrach, Meshach, and Abed´nego came out from the fire.

Key Verse: **Nebuchadnezzar said, "Blessed be the God of Shadrach, Meshach, and Abednego, who sent his angel and delivered his servants, who trusted in him . . . and yielded up their bodies rather than serve and worship any god except their own God." (Daniel 3:28)**

The Scripture and the Main Question—William H. Willimon

Fall Down and Worship the Golden Image

"The human mind is a perpetual factory of idols," said John Calvin. Something within us is always leading us to fashion a golden calf of one form or another. "Whatever you would die for, whatever means the most to you, that is thy God," said Luther.

What would we die for? Our family's protection? our flag? our faith? If we were forced to set down a list of all of our cherished values, in order, what would be at the top of our list? That list and its order of priorities would be a good clue to our gods. It would tell us a good deal about whom we *really* worship.

Nebuchadnezzar, no fool about human nature, has an idea. He makes a giant image of gold and orders all the people to bow down before the image. With so many captured, alien peoples in his land, including the captured Jews, uniformity of religion would be a good way to ensure uniformity in the kingdom.

But Nebuchadnezzar underestimated the strength of conviction to be found in three young Jewish men—Shadrach, Meshach, and Abednego. In spite of his law that anyone who refused to bow down to the golden image should be thrown into the furnace of fire, three young Jews refuse to bend.

Perhaps this is an early instance of the suffering which has afflicted God's Chosen People time and again through their painful history. Time and again the Jews have suffered because of their chosenness—they refused to bow to alien gods, to blend into the crowd, to go along with the program. And they have suffered greatly for their courage.

So some malicious Chaldeans come to the king saying, "There are certain Jews whom you have appointed over the affairs of the province of Babylon: Shadrach, Meshach, and Abednego. These men, O king, pay no heed to you; they do not serve your gods or worship the golden image which you have set up" (3:12).

"Certain Jews," they say. Perhaps these Chaldeans were jealous or resentful of the progress which these aliens had made in their country. Down through the ages, the Jews have been used as scapegoats by many countries. National problems have been blamed on them. Hitler told the German people the lie that their troubles were due to Jewish bankers, Jewish Communists, Jewish aliens who were not patriotic.

While all Hitler's charges against the Jews were lies—a scurrilous attempt to foster national unity by blaming national problems on these people—Hitler perhaps did have the sense to see that the Jews were a problem for his mad delusions of totalitarian domination. Hitler, like Nebuchadnezzar, knew that the Jews, who see themselves as God's people wherever they find themselves, have known persecution since ancient times, have kept the faith in the face of the cruelties of a score of tryants, and "do not serve your gods or worship the golden image you have set up" (3:12).

Who Is the God That Will Deliver You?

Nebuchadnezzar did not take this challenge lightly. He was "in furious rage" (3:13). Calling the offenders before him, he said to Shadrach, Meshach, and Abednego, "You shall immediately be cast into a burning fiery furnace" (3:15).

Hitler murdered dissenting pastors who would not sign his loyalty oath. Mao executed Catholic nuns whom he knew to be critical of his revolution. Stalin sent many Orthodox priests to their death. The Central African emperor Bokassa ordered school children shot who refused to wear his state school uniforms. Archbishop Romero was gunned down while leading worship because his advocacy of the poor was an embarrassment to his government. So Shadrach, Meshach, and Abednego were perhaps the earliest in a long line of political martyrs.

What happened to them? "The church is nourished by the blood of martyrs," wrote one of the early fathers of the church. In times of persecution and peril, faith seems to thrive. In their time of testing the three young men reached out for strength and found it. Little wonder then that, in the early Christian catacomb paintings, the story of three young men in the fiery furnace was a popular theme. Persecuted early Christians must have seen them as an encouraging example of fortitude in the midst of persecution.

A typical story of a martyr usually emphasizes one of two patterns. Either the persecuted ones are delivered or they are not. In either case, they do not compromise their beliefs. The three young men were given an opportunity to recant. Instead of compromise, they use the occasion to make a public declaration of their faith in their God.

We Will Not Serve Your Gods

The speech of the three young men is interesting. They had faith that their God could deliver them from this grave danger; nevertheless, they were wise enough to know that God does not always operate this way.

"Our god whom we serve is able to deliver us from the burning fiery furnace; . . . *but if not,* be it known to you, O king, that we will not serve your gods" (3:17-18, italics added). In the story that follows, the deliverance of the three young men is important, but it is not the heart of the matter. The faithfulness of the three young men, their courage even in the face of so horrible an ordeal, is what impresses the writer of Daniel.

We have no more guarantees that our faithfulness will lead to dramatic deliverance than the three young men could be sure that they would be rescued. For these three who were saved from the ordeal, countless others paid for their faith with their lives. This story of Shadrach, Meshach, and Abednego does not include the promise that deliverance always comes to the steadfast and the faithful. It does affirm that God knows our fidelity and supports us whether we are forced to suffer for our faith or whether we escape the persecution. God is with us in the furnace of persecution—as God was with Christ on the cross!

A few years ago, when Pope John Paul II visited Poland while it lay in the grip of martial law, a cartoon in one of our papers showed the military overlords crouching in a fox hole, behind sandbags and fortifications, peering out in terror as a man in a white robe bore a cross. How odd, the cartoonist seemed to say, that these people, thinking their brute force to be so powerful, found themselves put in rout by one who comes in the name of the Prince of Peace.

Let us pray that, when testing and ordeal come to us, we, like these three courageous young men, may be able to summon forth the faith to meet the test, to refuse to bow before the golden idols of success or money or nationalism or whatever false gods would lure us from worship and service of the one-time God.

Helping Adults Become Involved—Herbert H. Lambert

Preparing to Teach

Today's lesson deals with a story that has had great meaning for Jews and Christians, especially in times of great stress and danger of defection from the faith. Be faithful to God,. the story says, like these young men who refused to bow down to the pagan idol. God rescued them from the fiery furnace, and God will provide some kind of help for those who remain faithful today.

Here is a way to outline the lesson:

I. When Daniel was written
   A. Persecution by Antiochus IV
   B. Resistance and its consequences
II. A helpful story—Daniel 3
   A. Command to worship
   B. Reply of the youths
   C. Outcome of the story
III. Message for today
   A. Times when we are tested
   B. Reasons for being faithful
   C. Results of our faithfulness

Helpful additional comments may be found in *The Interpreter's Concise Commentary*, volume 4, pages 320-22, and *The Interpreter's Bible*, volume 6, pages 394-405.

Introducing the Main Question

This lesson is about faithfulness to God. It is expected of us today, just as it was in the days of Daniel. The introductory remarks by Dr. Willimon clearly show that Christians are still forced to choose between arrogant powers that demand loyalty and the true God who requires single-minded obedience. Ask the class members what this means in (1) countries like Poland, where the government seeks to discourage religion and abolish freedom; (2) countries like El Salvador, where many Christians have been killed by death squads because of their outspoken advocacy of the rights of the poor; (3) countries like our own, where Christians who work for peace are often accused of disloyalty and cowardice; (4) a world in which nations seem willing to break every international law and to risk any loss in order to protect their "national security." Those who raise questions of morality and concern for innocent civilians are shouted down. Christians ask, "Do our nation and its security deserve our highest loyalty, or is there something else more important?"

Developing the Lesson

I. *When Daniel was written*

   A. *Persecution by Antiochus IV*

Remind the class of the situation which caused the book of Daniel to be written. In the second century B.C., an evil foreign king sought to make the Jews forsake their traditions and adopt Greek customs. Antiochus seemed mentally deranged in his determination to eradicate Judaism. He robbed the temple and desecrated its altar. He forced Jews within his empire to worship Zeus or face death.

   B. *Resistance and its consequences*

Many Jews surrendered to the king's demands, but others refused to do so. Some of the latter were killed by the king's agents, and others fled to the desert for refuge. In the town of Modein, a compliant Jew began to offer sacrifice on a pagan altar. A Jewish priest named Mattathias killed this traitor as well as the king's officer who stood by. Mattathias and his sons led a revolt against Antiochus which eventually led to the restoration of temple worship (with its Feast of Lights) and a measure of independence for the Jews for the first time in four centuries.

II. *A helpful story—Daniel 3*

   A. *Command to worship*

Help the class members see how this story from Daniel 3 helped the Jews when they were persecuted by Antiochus. In a similar situation, the three young Jews in the story remained faithful. The plot of the story begins when King Nebuchadnezzar orders everyone to fall down before the golden image. Anyone could easily do this except the Jews, whose religion did not allow them to worship idols or foreign gods.

   B. *Reply of the youths*

The three Jewish youths refused to worship the idol, even if it meant death in the fiery furnace. They expressed confidence that God could deliver them, but even if God did not do so, they would not obey the king. Read Daniel 3:17-18. The reply of the youths seems to show that they recognized the danger. God does not always rescue those who remain faithful. List some persons in the Bible and in recent history who were faithful to God but did not escape suffering and even violent death.

   C. *Outcome of the story*

The disobedient youths were bound and cast into the great furnace. Inside the furnace they were seen to be unhurt, and a mysterious fourth figure was with them. The king called them to come out and acknowledged their God, commanding everyone to respect the God of these faithful youths.

What message did this story convey to the Jews who were persecuted under Antiochus IV? What message did it convey to Jews and Christians through the centuries when they were tempted or commanded to renounce their faith in God? List some answers on the chalkboard.

Helping Class Members Act

III. Message for today

A. Times when we are tested

Few of us experience anything like a demand to fall down and worship an idol on pain of death. However, we are subjected to more subtle pressures, and because they are subtle they may be even more dangerous. Here are a few examples. Discuss these and try to think of others.

In times of crisis, such as national conflict or war, citizens are expected to endorse government policy without raising questions about its purpose, its effectiveness, or its morality.

Many people speak of "God and country" as though the two belong together and God is always on our side. That these might sometimes be in conflict is unthinkable for some persons.

We live in a consumer society, one in which spending and self-indulgence are constantly held up as ideals. The person who prefers to live a simple life and to help others is regarded as out of step.

B. Reasons for being faithful

The three youths in Daniel 3 believed that God would deliver them from the furnace, but they refused to obey the king, even if it meant death. What motivates persons to be so faithful? Here are some possible answers:

—If I lose my self-respect by disobeying God's will, of what value is anything else I may gain?

—I love my country and want it to be safe and prosperous. I also want the peoples of the world to look to my country with hope and gratitude, not with anger.

—Because God has touched my life, there are some things more important to me than an expensive home and material well-being.

—I believe the very survival of our world depends on our willingness to live together peacefully, in spite of our differences, in a worldwide family of nations and peoples.

—I am convinced that those who serve God faithfully, in spite of opposition, will be proved right in the end.

Assign each of the above to one or more class members for discussion and explanation.

C. Results of our faithfulness

We cannot know or predict what the result of our faithfulness will be. Many of those who opposed Hitler in the name of God were imprisoned or executed. Persons who follow their conscience, in our own country or elsewhere, do not always receive honor and understanding. But sometimes events prove them right. One community was threatened by racial strife, decay of buildings, and neglect of human needs. Many moved away to escape the problems. One Christian layman mobilized concerned persons and worked patiently for decades to solve the difficulties. At last his labors were recognized. "Others cursed the darkness," a minister said, "but you lit a candle."

Planning for Next Sunday
Have the class members read chapter 8 of Daniel. Here we find symbols which are difficult for most readers to understand. Have the class members make a list of the symbols Daniel saw, such as the ram and the he-goat. Ask them to list questions they have about what they are reading. You may ask someone to report on "Apocalyptic Literature" during the next class meeting.

LESSON 14   AUGUST 31

God's Rule Will Come

Background Scripture: Daniel 7–8

The Main Question—William H. Willimon

I was talking with a young couple the other day about the possibility of their getting married. They had been dating for some time but seemed hesitant to finally take the step into marriage. I asked why.

"With the world in the shape it's in today," he said, "with the threat of nuclear war, the unrest and tensions around the globe, economic and political uncertainty at home, we're just not sure what the future holds. We don't know whether or not to commit ourselves to each other in a world where none of us may even be here tomorrow."

It grieved me to hear this in those who are young. Here, at the time in their lives when they should be joyfully making plans for their future, entering into careers, starting a home, they are paralyzed by fear and uncertainty.

What do you think about when you ponder the future? Do you see darkness or light? Do you feel hope and expectation or fear and despair?

Today's lesson reflects upon the question of what the future holds for us. Where are we headed? it asks. What about tomorrow?

As You Read the Scripture—Wilbur Lamm

Daniel 7 and 8 describe visions by Daniel. They consist of movements in the history that we call Interbiblical. Persons familiar with that history of the successive empires of Babylon, Medo-Persia, and Greece, with the conquests of Alexander the Great and the various rival divisions left by Alexander, have little difficulty interpreting the basic chronology of Daniel's visions.

Daniel 7:1-8. The Jews had been in Babylonian exile nearly fifty years. Daniel related a significant dream. He saw, in turn, four beasts come up from the sea. The first was like a lion with eagle's wings (Babylonian Empire). The second was like a bear with three ribs in its mouth (Medo-Persian Empire). The third was like a leopard with four heads and four wings (Greece: Alexander the Great and the four rulers of his divided empire). The fourth was a beast with ten horns. This beast "devoured and

441

broke in pieces." This beast may have been the Roman Empire. However, it probably was the Seleucid Empire with ten divisions of territory and rulers following Alexander. If so, the little horn (verse 8) would be Antiochus Epiphanes. His character and actions are spelled out in Daniel 7–8. During his years of Jewish persecution (175–164 B.C.), the Jews needed much encouragement and hope.

Verses 9-20. Then God's kingdom came into view while the other empires vanished. God, the "ancient of days," sat on his throne. Advanced age meant honor, wisdom, and respect. The scene was the court of judgment. "The books were opened." In symbolic language Daniel told of a son of man who would be presented by God. To him God would give dominion over "all peoples, nations, and languages." His kingdom would be eternal.

Verses 21-28. Daniel saw prolonged warfare between the saints of the Most High and the fourth beast with the ferocious little horn. For a while the beast would win, but victory would come to the saints at last. Daniel expressed the end of the matter, the cessation of struggle, and the ultimate victory in verse 27.

Chapter 8:5-14. Then a he-goat charged from the west with a single horn. He broke the horns of the ram and trampled him. With a little horn, he (Antiochus Epiphanes) advanced in several directions, including toward Israel. In the holy city he desecrated the house of worship and destroyed sacred books. This was a time of suffering and testing for God's people. But hope prevailed. The sanctuary would be restored (verse 14). God would intervene.

Verses 15-19. Daniel wanted an interpretation of his vision. A man addressed Gabriel and told him to interpret for Daniel. (Angels are named in the Old Testament only in Daniel, and Michael is the other named.) In fear and humility Daniel fell on his face. Gabriel told him that God's judgment (indignation) would come to the enemy as it had come to Israel. There would soon be an end to God's wrath on Israel and to persecution by Antiochus.

Verses 20-22. Gabriel gave further interpretation of Daniel's vision of the opposing nations. The ram with two horns was indeed Medo-Persia. The kings were probably Cyrus and Cambyses, the first two rulers. The he-goat was Greece, and the great horn was Alexander (336–323 B.C.). Alexander extended Greek culture throughout the eastern world but did not fully succeed because of his premature death (verse 22). At his death, four of his followers divided his realm. Cassandra took Macedonia and Greece; Lysimachus had Asia Minor and Thrace; Ptolemy headed Egypt and Palestine; Seleucus took Syria and Babylonia. None of these possessed the power or genius of Alexander. The Jews in Palestine (who had returned under Cyrus, 538 B.C.) were subject to Egypt, then Syria, then were independent, then were under Rome.

Verses 8:23-26. Gabriel continued his explanation. Rather than trace history in detail from the four kingdoms that succeeded Alexander, he moved quickly to "a king of bold countenance," Antiochus IV Epiphanes of the Seleucid (Syrian) dynasty. He was a proud, crafty, and cruel ruler whom many interpreters view as a type of Antichrist. His power was great. He wrought great destruction on Jerusalem and the region round about. His intelligence was misused by his arrogant schemes. He magnified himself against God. This act assured his destruction by divine intervention. Polybius reported that Antiochus died suddenly of madness.

This vision spoke to God's people of Daniel's day and also to later generations. Daniel was told to seal up the vision because it would speak to days yet to come. The vision gave assurance that God's victory for his people would surely come.

Selected Scripture

King James Version	Revised Standard Version

Daniel 8:1, 15-26

1 In the third year of the reign of king Bĕl-shăz′-zär a vision appeared unto me, *even unto* me Daniel, after that which appeared unto me at the first.

....

15 And it came to pass, when I, *even* I Daniel, had seen the vision, and sought for the meaning, then, behold, there stood before me as the appearance of a man.

16 And I heard a man's voice between *the banks* of Ū′-lâi, which called, and said, Gā′-brĭ-ĕl, make this *man* to understand the vision.

17 So he came near where I stood: and when he came, I was afraid, and fell upon my face: but he said unto me, Understand, O son of man: for at the time of the end *shall be* the vision.

18 Now as he was speaking with me, I was in a deep sleep on my face toward the ground: but he touched me, and set me upright.

19 And he said, Behold, I will make thee know what shall be in the last end of the indignation: for at the time appointed the end *shall be.*

20 The ram which thou sawest having *two* horns *are* the kings of Mē′-dĭ-ă and Persia.

21 And the rough goat *is* the king of Grē′-çī-ă: and the great horn that *is* between his eyes *is* the first king.

22 Now that being broken, whereas four stood up for it, four kingdoms shall stand up out of the nation, but not in his power.

23 And in the latter time of their kingdom, when the transgressors are come to the full, a king of fierce

Daniel 8:1, 15-26

1 In the third year of the reign of King Belshaz′zar a vision appeared to me, Daniel, after that which appeared to me at the first.

....

15 When I, Daniel, had seen the vision, I sought to understand it; and behold, there stood before me one having the appearance of a man. 16 And I heard a man's voice between the banks of the U′lai, and it called, "Gabriel, make this man understand the vision." 17 So he came near where I stood; and when he came, I was frightened and fell upon my face. But he said to me, "Understand, O son of man, that the vision is for the time of the end."

18 As he was speaking to me, I fell into a deep sleep with my face to the ground; but he touched me and set me on my feet. 19 He said, "Behold, I will make known to you what shall be at the later end of the indignation; for it pertains to the appointed time of the end. 20 As for the ram which you saw with the two horns, these are the kings of Media and Persia. 21 And the he-goat is the king of Greece; and the great horn between his eyes is the first king. 22 As for the horn that was broken, in place of which four others arose, four kingdoms shall arise from his nation, but not with his power. 23 And at the latter end of their rule, when the transgressors have reached their full measure, a king of bold countenance, one who under-

countenance, and understanding dark sentences, shall stand up.

24 And his power shall be mighty, but not by his own power: and he shall destroy wonderfully, and shall prosper, and practise, and shall destroy the mighty and the holy people.

25 And through his policy also he shall cause craft to prosper in his hand; and he shall magnify *himself* in his heart, and by peace shall destroy many: he shall also stand up against the Prince of princes; but he shall be broken without hand.

26 And the vision of the evening and the morning which was told *is* true: wherefore shut thou up the vision; for it *shall be* for many days.

stands riddles shall arise. 24 His power shall be great, and he shall cause fearful destruction, and shall succeed in what he does, and destroy mighty men and the people of the saints. 25 By his cunning he shall make deceit prosper under his hand, and in his own mind he shall magnify himself. Without warning he shall destroy many; and he shall even rise up against the Prince of princes; but, by no human hand, he shall be broken. 26 The vision of the evenings and the mornings which has been told is true; but seal up the vision, for it pertains to many days hence."

Key Verse: His dominion *is* an everlasting dominion, which shall not pass away, and his kingdom *that* which shall not be destroyed. (Daniel 7:14)

Key Verse:
**His dominion is an everlasting dominion,
which shall not pass away,
and his kingdom one
that shall not be destroyed.
(Daniel 7:14)**

The Scripture and the Main Question—William H. Willimon

A Vision Appeared

"Where there is no vision, the people perish," cries the prophet. Human beings live, not only upon the stuff of past experiences, but also by whatever vision we hold for our future. Our vision of tomorrow determines how we act today.

What is your vision of tomorrow? "Eat, drink, and be merry, for tomorrow we die" is the grim vision of the self-indulgent hedonist. We're all headed toward death and oblivion, so grab what little happiness you can, "eat, drink, and be merry," for this is as good as life gets. You might as well have a good time since it doesn't matter what you do or don't do when you're on your way to the gallows.

Our vision of the future determines the present in all sorts of ways. Some Christians' vision of heaven, a blissful place of afterlife, keeps them from being too concerned about present problems. Why work to eliminate war, poverty, racism, and other causes of pain and injustice since one day all this shall come to an end and we shall be in heaven? This has led some to characterize Christianity as promoting a "pie in the sky, by and by" outlook toward the world. "Religion is the opiate of the people" charged Karl Marx. He felt that the hope of a better afterlife was used by the rich to keep the poor sedated, content with their present lot, and in bondage.

Daniel has a vision, a strange dream of a two-horned ram beside a river. This two-horned ram (the Medo-Persian Empire) is vanquished by a great he-goat (Alexander the Great). At his death, the goat's large horn is supplanted by four smaller ones (the four kingdoms which were carved up by Alexander's generals after his death). A little horn (Antiochus IV) emerges, but it is to survive only about three and one half years. Then the temple would be restored to its rightful state (Daniel 8:14).

Daniel is confused by this strange vision. An interpreter, Gabriel, explains it to him as events which all relate to "the time of the end" (8:17). All of this is called "apocalyptic" writing, that is, writing which uses symbols and signs to reveal or uncover the meaning of past, present, or future events. Apocalyptic writing takes world events and uncovers their significance for people of faith.

Obviously we are dealing with events which relate to a troubled, violent, chaotic time in history. Out of this seething cauldron of political intrigue, oppression, and the rise and fall of great kings and petty tryants, the writer of Daniel sees a message for the people of his own day.

What is the message of this vision for our day?

I Will Make Known to You What Shall Be

The Maccabean era was a time of great turmoil and unrest for the Jewish people. The old empire of Hellenistic Greece had broken apart. Political instability and economic chaos followed. What was to come of the people of God in the midst of this struggle? Would the God of Israel, who had preserved the Chosen People during their Egyptian bondage, in the wilderness of the Exodus, in Babylonian exile, now desert them?

How many people today are wondering much the same thing? With energy shortages, economic crises, the breakup of old political alliances and the formation of new ones, and the threat of the great, dark mushroom cloud of nuclear holocaust hovering over all, who can blame people for their fear and uncertainty?

Perhaps this uncertainty about the future accounts for the rise in popularity of apocalyptic literature in our own day. Take a trip to your local bookstore and you will see successful books on science fiction, interpretation of your horoscope, and an assortment of strange literature which uses all sorts of devices—some even purporting to use the Bible itself—to tell people what the future holds. Popular books of the early 1980s were books by people who were called "futurists"—books with titles like *The Third Wave* and *Megatrends*. Wouldn't it be good if we had some reliable crystal ball in which to gaze and see a sure vision of the future?

Many of these books attempt to be crystal balls and to make minute, specific predictions about the future. Most of them will be wrong because the future is unknown. Too many factors influence the final result.

Biblical visions—the vision of Daniel, for instance—are not so concerned to make minute, detailed predictions about the future but rather to affirm that the future, whatever it holds, is held in the hands of God. This was the basic message of Daniel's vision: the rulers of this world may strut upon the stage of history for a time; there will be dark and difficult days for God's people; but in the end God shall triumph.

"Behold, I will make known to you what shall be," says Gabriel. What shall be is that God still rules the rulers. God shall not forsake the Chosen People. They shall be preserved in whatever events shall follow. Though the evil one's "power shall be great, and he shall cause fearful destruction. . . . and destroy mighty men and the people of the saints," he shall neither utterly destroy the Chosen nor utterly thwart the purposes of God.

445

The Vision Is True

To those who are of a fearful heart, to those who wonder who is in control and what the future holds, today's vision from the book of Daniel offers a ringing affirmation.

"His dominion is an everlasting dominion, which shall not pass away, and his kingdom one that shall not be destroyed" (Daniel 7:14).

What do you think? Does this speak to your own feelings about the future? Would it give you something to say to the anxious young person, the troubled soul who feels that everything is in tumult and that nothing is holding firm?

In reading a book like Alvin Toffler's *The Third Wave,* one finds good news and bad news. The first wave was the agricultural revolution, when humanity changed from a nomadic, hunting-oriented existence to a settled, agricultural way of life. The second wave occurred when we moved from agriculture into the industrial revolution. Now, says Toffler, we are entering the third wave in which we move from a world of smokestacks and foundries to a world of computers, high technology, rapid communication, and rapid transit. We will live, he says, in an "electronic cottage," where we will be limited to the rest of the world through our computer, our video screen, and other electronic marvels.

In this progress is peril. Thousands of jobs will be lost as the new technology replaces the old, and robots do work formerly done by people. We will make advances over disease and save lives, but we shall also, alas, make even more deadly weapons to destroy lives. So, as always, the present wave of progress will mix new evils with whatever good may come.

Whatever happens, whatever good or ill comes tomorrow, we rest in the sure hope that God shall reign tomorrow even as today, that God's love and care for us "shall not pass away."

Helping Adults Become Involved—Herbert H. Lambert

Preparing to Teach

This lesson is important for two reasons. First, we need to know the nature of apocalyptic literature so that we will not misunderstand it. Many persons are led astray by untrained preachers and writers who use Daniel and Revelation to predict in detail what will happen soon. This lesson will contend that this is an abuse of scripture.

Second, it is important to study Daniel because this book carries a timeless message. When events seem to be out of control and God's people seem helpless to change the situation, we must remember that God has a plan for the world and will act to bring good out of evil. We must never despair or quit trying.

Here is a way to outline the lesson:

    I. The nature of apocalyptic literature
        A. The use of symbols
        B. Everything determined in advance
        C. A call for faithfulness
    II. Daniel's visions and their meaning
    III. Daniel's visions speaking to our time
        A. Not in specific detail
        B. God in control of history
        C. "Little people" emerging victorious
        D. Hope beyond the present darkness

Additional information may be found in *the Interpreter's Concise Commentary*, volume 4, pages 332-39, and *The Interpreter's Bible*, volume 6, pages 450-83.

Introducing the Main Question

Dr. Willimon begins this lesson with an account of a young couple reluctant to get married because of world turmoil today. Read this account and ask the class members if they understand this attitude. How would they respond to the couple? Can we as Christians offer any hope that the world will continue or conditions improve? What does the future hold? What can we do about it?

Apocalyptic literature appeared in order to answer just such questions as these. You or the class member assigned to report on apocalyptic writing might briefly explain it. Dr. Willimon defines it as "writing which uses symbols and signs to reveal or uncover the meaning of past, present, and future events."

Developing the Lesson

I. The nature of apocalyptic literature

A. The use of symbols

Have the class members turn to Daniel 8 and see how many symbols they can identify in this vision of Daniel. The list would include a ram, a he-goat, a "conspicuous horn," a "little horn." Each of these stands for something—an empire, a ruler, etc. Some of the symbols are explained in Daniel 8:19-21.

Why were such strange symbols used in this type of literature? While these names and events are strange to most of us, they were quite familiar to the readers of Daniel. By telling of a vision seen "long ago" in which events were correctly predicted, the writer gains credibility for a new revelation about what will happen next. We can be sure the first readers of Daniel were eager to hear about these visions.

B. Everything determined in advance

Apocalyptic literature is fatalistic. God has determined almost everything that happens. Even evil kings are allowed to prevail for a time in order to test the saints. Most of the Bible rejects the idea that everything is fated. The classic prophets pleaded with people to act because they believed events could be caused or averted. Only a few chapters of apocalyptic writing were allowed in the Bible.

C. A call for faithfulness

About all we can do is "hang in there" until the troubles are over and God comes to rescue and reward those who stand firm. This view is quite different from that of Jeremiah and Isaiah, who taught that people could change history by their sinfulness or their repentance.

II. Daniel's visions and their meaning

This presentation can be more effective if you can find or improvise maps. Here is a chart that may also help.

Symbol and Scripture	Meaning	Dates
two-horned ram (8:3-4)	Medo-Persian Empire	538–334 B.C.
he-goat (8:5-8)	Greek Empire	336–323 B.C.
four horns (8:8)	Four divisions after Alexander	323 B.C.
little horn (8:9-12)	Antiochus IV	175–164 B.C.

Notice what Antiochus did, according to 8:9-12 and 23-26. Living as they did in the time of this cruel Antiochus, the readers of Daniel took comfort in the fact that his rule would soon come to an end. They just had to hold out a little longer!

Helping Class Members Act

III. Daniel's vision speaking to our time

A. Not in specific detail

Many Christians think of the Bible as a message from God directly to us, not to the persons who wrote it and read it long ago. If this is true, Daniel 8 must mean something about events in 1986, and there are many who will gladly explain it. Scholars of the Bible cite Daniel 8:20-21 as evidence that this chapter, and others like it, really refer to ancient events. If we want to understand it, we must put ourselves in the situation of its first readers.

B. God in control of history

The visions of Daniel describe the turmoil of shifting power and the oppression of God's people by cruel rulers. The effect of such writing on the readers was to assure them that all had been foreseen and planned by God. History was not meaningless and chaotic, as one might easily assume. God is in control. They naturally asked, "What happens next?"

How do we look at the momentous events of our time—wars and danger of war, famine, pollution, the struggle for justice, rapid technological change, and dislocation? Does the world seem out of control, or is God guiding it toward some goal? Discuss this.

C. "Little people" emerging victorious

The people who read Daniel felt helpless to control the powers of evil. Nevertheless, they took heart because they believed God would reward their faithfulness at last. This will come only after great suffering and temptation, but it will come!

Read Daniel 8:23-26. Choose several of the following questions for discussion. What in these verses would make the first readers fearful? What would make them take heart? Do we in our time sometimes feel that our world is getting worse instead of better? Is this feeling justified? Is it harder to be a loyal Christian today than it was a generation ago? What do Christians have to look forward to in this life? in the life beyond?

D. Hope beyond the present darkness

Many Christians feel that this world is evil and beyond hope. They say we can only try to keep ourselves from evil and then escape to a better world where we can be with God. Books like Daniel and Revelation are used to support this view.

But other people, guided by the great Old Testament prophets and by the teachings of Jesus, believe that we have a mission to change the world, to work for peace and justice among all peoples. Christ came not to rescue a few saints from a perishing world but to commission many to proclaim God's love for all humankind. This is why it is a mistake to put too much emphasis on Daniel to the exclusion of other parts of the Scriptures. Read Matthew 28:16-20, and ask how it differs from Daniel 8. One valuable aspect of the Bible is that it balances different experiences of God, different ways of responding to God's truth, within the same holy book. We err if we try to force the Bible to say only one thing or if we overemphasize some parts and neglect others.